Fod
Flo

Fodor's Travel Publications, Inc.
New York & London

Grateful acknowledgment is made to Alfred A. Knopf, Inc. for permission to reprint excerpts from TROPICAL SPLENDOR: AN ARCHITECTURAL HISTORY OF FLORIDA by Hap Hatton. Copyright © 1987 by Hap Hatton. Reprinted by permission of Alfred A. Knopf, Inc.

ISBN 0-679-01623-6

Fodor's Florida

Editor: Andrew E. Beresky
Editorial Contributors: April Athey, Al Burt, Kathryn Kilgore, George Leposky, Rosalie Leposky, Honey Naylor, Karen Smith, Joice Veselka, David Wilkening, Fred Wright
Cartographer: David Lindroth
Illustrator: Karl Tanner
Cover Photograph: Krist/Leo de Wys

Cover Design: Vignelli Associates

Special Sales

Fodor's Travel Publications are available at special discounts for bulk purchases (100 copies or more) for sales promotions or premiums. Special editions, including personalized covers, excerpts of existing guides, and corporate imprints, can be created in large quantities for special needs. For more information write to Special Marketing, Fodor's Travel Publications, 201 East 50th St., New York, NY 10022. Inquiries from the United Kingdom should be sent to Merchandise Division, Random House U.K., 30–32 Bedford Square, London WC1B 3SG.

MANUFACTURED IN THE UNITED STATES OF AMERICA
10 9 8 7 6 5 4 3 2 1

Contents

Maps

Foreword

Florida is one of the world's most popular tourist destinations. Visitors from far and near are attracted to the state's sandy beaches, warm and sunny climate, and theme parks such as Disney World. Travelers find Florida rich in historic sites, vast stretches of wildlife preserves, fine restaurants and accommodations to suit every budget. Our Florida writers have put together information on the widest possible range of activities, and within that range present you with selections of events and places that will be safe, worthwhile, and of good value. The descriptions we provide are just enough for you to make your own informed choices from among our selections.

This is an exciting time for Fodor's, as it begins a three-year program to rewrite, reformat, and redesign all 140 of its guides. Here are just a few of the exciting new features:

★ Brand-new computer-generated maps locating all the top attractions, hotels, restaurants, and shops

★ A unique system of numbers and legends to help readers move effortlessly between text and maps

★ A new star rating system for hotels and restaurants

★ Restaurant reviews by major food critics around the world

★ Stamped, self-addressed postcards, bound into every guide, give readers an opportunity to help evaluate hotels and restaurants

★ Complete page redesign for instant retrieval of information

★ FODOR'S CHOICE—Our favorite museums, beaches, cafes, romantic hideaways, festivals, and more

★ HIGHLIGHTS '89—An insider's look at the most important developments in tourism during the past year

★ TIME OUT—The best and most convenient lunch stops along the shopping and exploring routes

★ Exclusive background essays create a powerful portrait of each destination

★ A mini-journal for travelers to keep track of their own itineraries and addresses

While every care has been taken to assure the accuracy of the information in this guide, the passage of time will always bring change, and, consequently, the publisher cannot accept responsibility for errors that may occur.

All prices and opening times quoted here are based on information available to us at press time. Hours and admission fees may change, however, and the prudent traveler will avoid inconvenience by calling ahead.

Fodor's wants to hear about your travel experiences, both pleasant and unpleasant. When a hotel or restaurant fails to live up to its billing, let us know, and we will investigate the complaint and revise our entries where the facts warrant it.

Send your letters to the editors of Fodor's Travel Publications, 201 E. 50th Street, New York, NY 10022, or 30–32 Bedford Square, London WC1B 3SG, England.

Highlights '89 and Fodor's Choice

Highlights '89

Upscale is the word for hotels throughout Florida. New hotels are being built, and old standbys are being renovated to make them more enjoyable for all-season visitors, not only for "snowbirds" during the winter. In the Florida Keys, the landmark **Cheeca Lodge** at Islamorada reopened and retains its prominent status. In Walt Disney World, the new 900-room **Grand Floridian Beach Resort,** featuring architecture reminiscent of turn-of-the-century Florida, was slated to open at press time. Under renovation at press time and scheduled for completion in late 1988 were **Biscayne Bay Marriott Hotel and Marina,** the **Miami International Airport Hotel,** and the **Hotel Regency Miami.** Among recently restored hotels are three in the **Art Deco District** of Miami Beach: Hotel Cardozo, Hotel Carlyle, and Hotel Leslie.

Other developments include the **Bayside Project,** by the Rouse Corporation, along the waterfront in Miami. Included in the complex is the newly opened Bayside Marketplace, a $93-million cluster of boutiques, restaurants, and pavilions; a 28-acre park with a 4,500-seat amphitheater; and Baywalk, a landscaped promenade.

Most of the entertainment developments are in **Walt Disney World** or **Epcot Center.** The new Walt Disney/MGM Studio will open for scheduled tours in the spring of 1989. Typhoon Lagoon, the world's largest water-thrill park, is slated to open in early 1989, as is Pleasure Island, a nighttime entertainment complex. The Dream Flight attraction in Tomorrowland, within the Magic Kingdom, is scheduled for a December 1988 opening, and Epcot's Wonders of Life pavilion will open a year later. Nearing completion at press time were two new rides at **Wet 'n Wild** in Orlando: Blue Niagara, looping tubes that descend 57 feet, and Bubble Up, a giant inflated bubble 90 feet in diameter. At **Kennedy Space Center,** the new Satellites and You exhibit allows visitors to experience conditions that astronauts working on a space station might encounter. The new **Tampa Bay Performing Arts Center,** a $57 million, three-theater complex, is mounting Broadway productions and performances by American Ballet Theatre, the New York City Opera, and the Leningrad State Symphony, among others.

On the east coast's Hutchinson Island, Indian River Plantation Resort & Marina has become home port to the ***Island Princess,*** a 75-foot cruiser available for private charter for up to 150 people. On Captiva Island, near Fort Myers on the west coast, guests at the South Seas Plantation Resort & Yacht Harbour can now enjoy a new adventure—a Back Bay Photo Safari on the Captiva and nearby Sanibel islands.

On the sports scene, the 1989 **Super Bowl** football game is to be played at the new Joe Robbie Stadium in Miami. A new $89 million, 16,600-seat arena in downtown Orlando was slated to open at the end of 1988. Starting in 1989, it will be home to the city's new National Basketball Association franchise, the **Orlando Magic.**

Fodor's Choice

No two people will agree on what makes a perfect vacation, but it's fun and helpful to know what others think. We hope you'll have a chance to experience some of Fodor's Choices yourself while visiting Florida. For detailed information about each entry, refer to the appropriate chapter in this guidebook.

Sights

The Gulf of Mexico at sunset, particularly at Mallory Square in Key West, where sunset watching is an evening ritual

The boardwalk at Royal Palm Hammock in the Everglades

Art Deco District in Miami Beach

The main span of Sunshine Skyway Bridge, St. Petersburg

The eight-mile Palm Beach Bicycle Trail along Lake Worth

Gulf of Mexico beaches seen from a fixed-wing glider at Clearwater

White tigers at Busch Gardens, Tampa

Singing Apes of Borneo, Central Florida Zoo, Sanford

The view from the battlements at the Castillo de San Marcos, St. Augustine

Edison's Home, with adjoining museum displaying many of his inventions, Fort Myers

San Agustin Antiguo, a restored Spanish colonial village in St. Augustine

Hotels

Boca Raton Hotel and Club, Boca Raton *(Very Expensive)*

The Breakers, Palm Beach *(Very Expensive)*

Grand Bay Hotel, Coconut Grove *(Very Expensive)*

South Seas Plantation, Captiva Island *(Very Expensive)*

Amelia Island Plantation, Amelia Island *(Expensive–Very Expensive)*

Jacksonville Omni Hotel, Jacksonville *(Expensive–Very Expensive)*

Sandestin Beach Resort, Destin *(Expensive–Very Expensive)*

Bahia Mar Quality Royale Hotel and Yacht Center, Fort Lauderdale *(Expensive)*

Disney Inn, Walt Disney World *(Expensive)*

Grand Floridian Hotel, Walt Disney World *(Expensive)*

Don CeSar Hotel, St. Petersburg Beach *(Moderate)*

Knights Inn Orlando Maingaite East, Walt Disney World *(Inexpensive)*

Snug Harbor, Amelia Island *(Inexpensive)*

Restaurants

Grand Cafe, Coconut Grove *(Very Expensive)*

Arthur's 27, atop Buena Vista Palace, Walt Disney World *(Expensive)*

Bernie's Steak House, Tampa *(Expensive)*

Savannah Moon, Kendall suburb of Miami *(Expensive)*

The Yearling Inn, Cross Creek, near Gainesville *(Expensive)*

Hy-Vong Vietnamese Cuisine, Little Havana section of Miami *(Moderate)*

Jamie's, Pensacola *(Moderate)*

Joe's Stone Crab House, Miami Beach *(Moderate)*

Harbor Docks, Destin *(Inexpensive–Moderate)*

Seagull, Fort Walton Beach *(Inexpensive–Moderate)*

Christini's Ristorante Italiano, Orlando *(Inexpensive)*

Homestead, Jacksonville *(Inexpensive)*

Numero Uno, Orlando *(Inexpensive)*

Oviedo Inn, Orlando *(Inexpensive)*

Wekiva Marina Restaurant, Longwood *(Inexpensive)*

Beaches

Crystal Beach Wayside Park

The Fort Pickens area of Gulf Islands National Seashore

John U. Lloyd Beach State Recreation Area, Dania

Pier Park, at the southern tip of Miami Beach and Lummus Park

Events

The ground shaking underfoot as a rocket soars spaceward from Cape Canaveral

King Orange Jamboree Parade preceding the Orange Bowl football game, Miami

Village Wine Festival, each February, Walt Disney World

Carnaval Miami, including the *Calle Oche* Open House, in the Little Havana district of Miami

Coconut Grove and Winter Park arts festivals

Sports

Fishing from the Redington Long Pier, or game fishing for the big ones off the Florida Keys

A jai-alai game at any of the many frontons throughout the state

Horse racing at Hialeah

Greyhound dog racing at Biscayne Kennel Club

The Orange Bowl Classic football game and its two attendant tennis tournaments, Miami

A round of golf at Key Biscayne Golf Course, which *Golf Digest* calls one of the best in the nation

Canoeing through a pristine forest at Wekiva Springs State Park, north of Orlando

After Hours

Disco at the art deco–style Club 1235, Miami Beach

For local color, a drink at Captain Tony's, the original Sloppy Joe's, Hemingway's favorite bar in Key West

Comedy Corner, Palm Beach

Ragtime Tavern for Dixieland and classic jazz, Atlantic Beach

Cabaret shows, casino gambling, and dancing aboard the *Viking Princess*, off the Port of Palm Beach

Florida

Gulf of Mexico

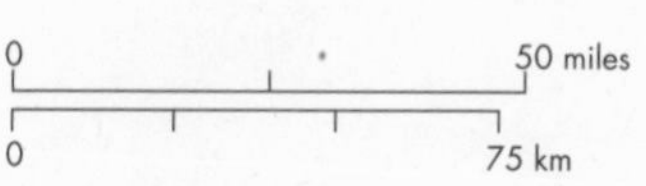

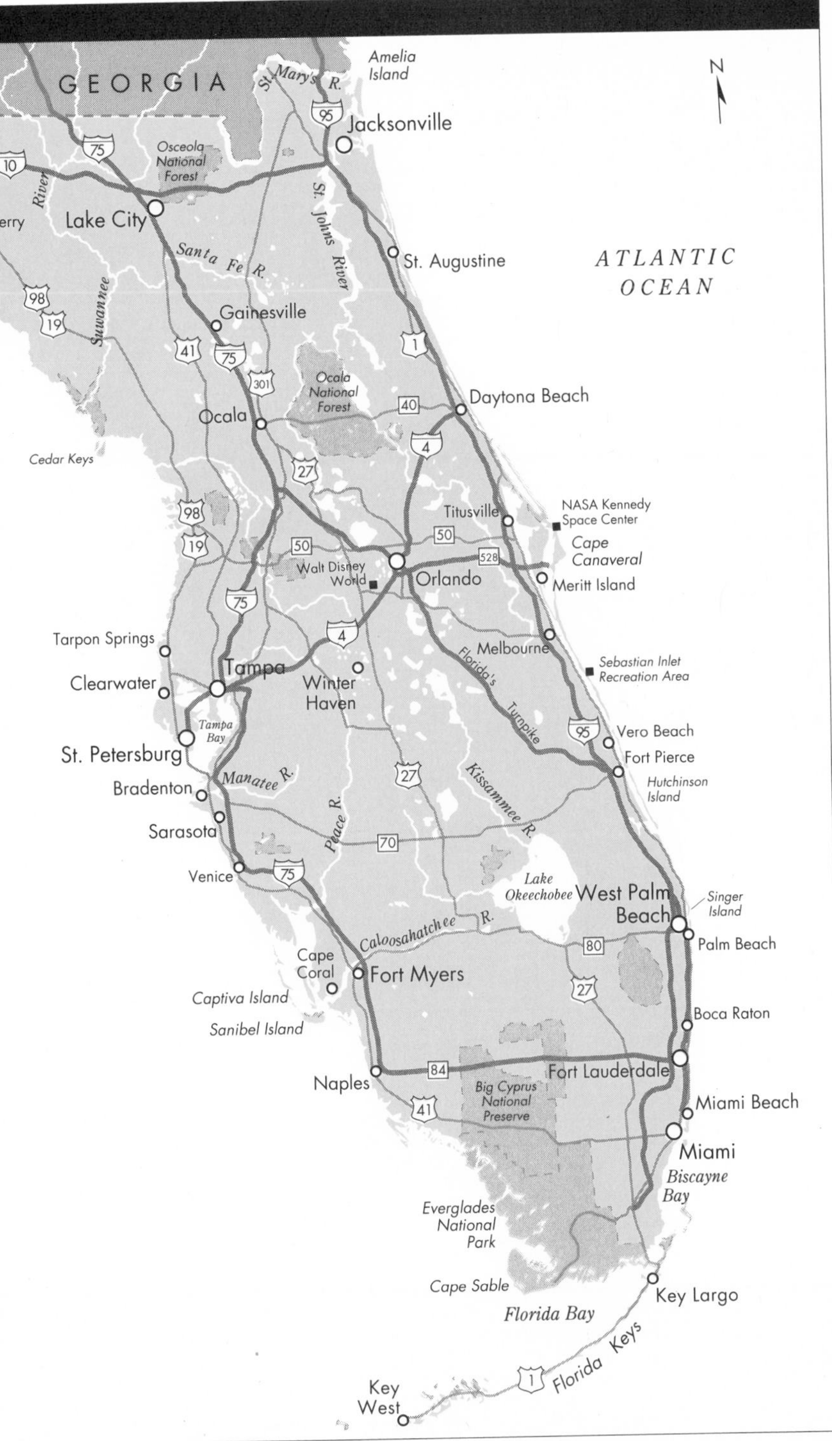
GEORGIA
Amelia Island
St. Mary's R.
Jacksonville
Osceola National Forest
Perry
Lake City
River
Suwannee
Santa Fe R.
St. Johns River
St. Augustine
ATLANTIC OCEAN
Gainesville
Ocala National Forest
Ocala
Daytona Beach
Cedar Keys
Titusville
NASA Kennedy Space Center
Cape Canaveral
Walt Disney World
Orlando
Meritt Island
Tarpon Springs
Melbourne
Sebastian Inlet Recreation Area
Clearwater
Tampa
Winter Haven
Florida's Turnpike
Tampa Bay
St. Petersburg
Vero Beach
Fort Pierce
Hutchinson Island
Bradenton
Manatee R.
Peace R.
Kissammee R.
Sarasota
Venice
Lake Okeechobee
West Palm Beach
Singer Island
Caloosahatchee R.
Palm Beach
Cape Coral
Fort Myers
Captiva Island
Sanibel Island
Boca Raton
Naples
Big Cyprus National Preserve
Fort Lauderdale
Miami Beach
Miami
Biscayne Bay
Everglades National Park
Cape Sable
Florida Bay
Key Largo
Florida Keys
Key West

World Time Zones

+11 +12 - -11 -10 -9 -8 -7 -6 -5 -4 -3 -2

Numbers below vertical bands relate each zone to Greenwich Mean Time (0 hrs.). Local times frequently differ from these general indications, as indicated by light-face numbers on map.

Auckland, **1**
Honolulu, **2**
Anchorage, **3**
Vancouver, **4**
San Francisco, **5**
Los Angeles, **6**
Edmonton, **7**
Denver, **8**
Chicago, **9**
Dallas, **10**
New Orleans, **11**
Mexico City, **12**
Toronto, **13**
Ottawa, **14**
Montreal, **15**
New York City, **16**
Washington, DC, **17**
Miami, **18**
Bogotá, **19**
Lima, **20**
Santiago, **21**
Caracas, **22**
Rio de Janeiro, **23**
Buenos Aires, **24**
Reykjavik, **25**
Dublin, **26**
London (Greenwich), **27**
Lisbon, **28**
Algiers, **29**
Paris, **30**
Zürich, **31**

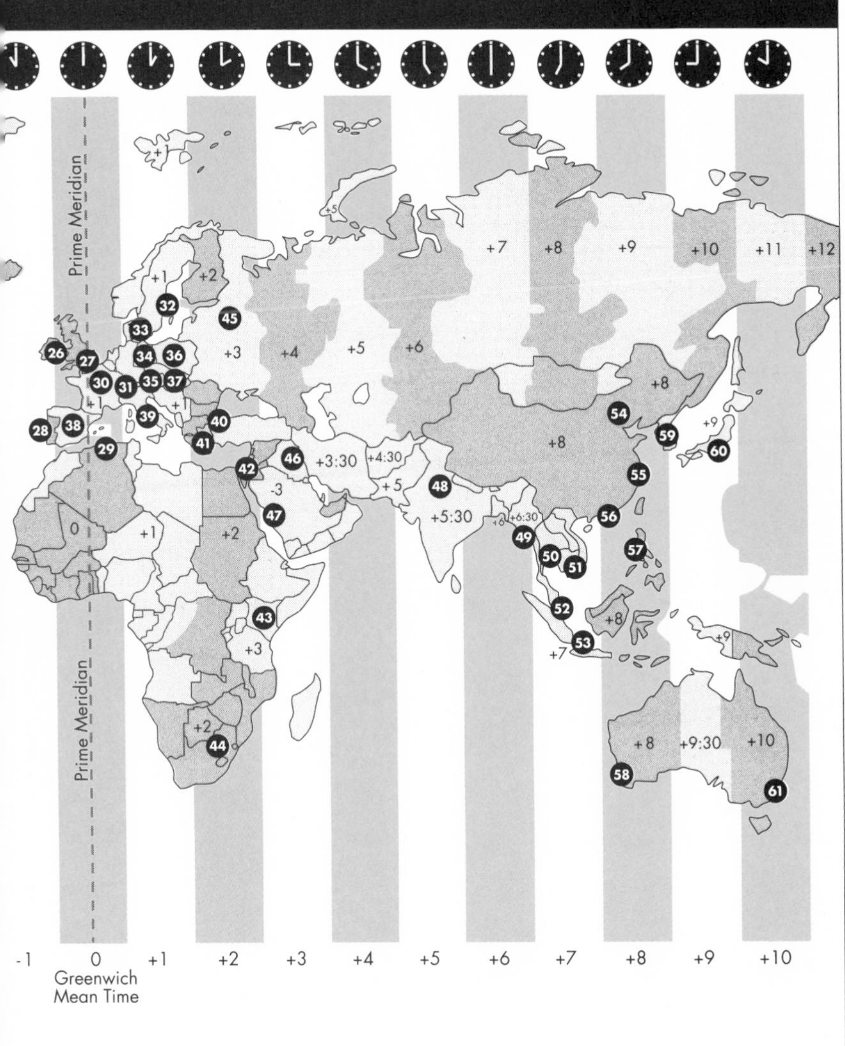

Stockholm, **32**
Copenhagen, **33**
Berlin, **34**
Vienna, **35**
Warsaw, **36**
Budapest, **37**
Madrid, **38**
Rome, **39**
Istanbul, **40**
Athens, **41**
Jerusalem, **42**
Nairobi, **43**
Johannesburg, **44**
Moscow, **45**
Baghdad, **46**
Mecca, **47**
Delhi, **48**
Rangoon, **49**
Bangkok, **50**
Saigon, **51**
Singapore, **52**
Djakarta, **53**
Beijing, **54**
Shanghai, **55**
Hong Kong, **56**
Manila, **57**
Perth, **58**
Seoul, **59**
Tokyo, **60**
Sydney, **61**

Introduction

by Kathryn Kilgore

A freelance journalist, Kathryn Kilgore has worked for The Village Voice *(New York City), and the* Montreal Gazette. *She recently completed her second novel. She has a house in Key West, where she lives and writes for part of each year.*

Florida casts no shadow. A snowbird (part-time resident) in jogging clothes makes this remark to me, the sunburned traveler, while I'm standing on the sunny steps of a small Florida library, holding 10 books on the history of Florida.

I study the snowbird's pale northern profile. He adjusts his sunglasses and continues: Cedar Key is nice; there are still Greek sponge divers at Tarpon Springs; the south edge of the Okefenokee Swamp is certainly worth a trip; don't forget all those empty county roads; and be sure to visit the Everglades. But it's not New England—he shakes his head. You can't feel the past, and you can't see it. The snowbird puts on his Walkman headphones and jogs away.

This traveler plans to drive all around the state, and she isn't ready to agree with this guy. Florida, after all, is bigger than New York State and New Jersey put together. She has just read that the "discovery" of Florida by Ponce de León in 1513 preceded the landing of the Mayflower by 107 years. St. Augustine is the oldest city in the United States. The Seminole Indians, whose ancestors refused to sign any treaty with the white man, still live as they wish in the Everglades and the Big Cypress Swamp. Miami is a glittering Spanish-speaking metropolis, a wide-open door to the Caribbean, Central America, and South America.

It is true, however, that hurricanes, mold, rot, ants, termites, floods, fires, and droughts have made a mess out of the monuments. The earliest architecture in North America has long since rotted away; the Indians left only shell mounds and pottery, and the Spanish left the mere foundations of forts. Although there were homesteads, of course, none has survived the intervening four centuries. As John Rothschild put it in his book *Up for Grabs*, "Historic St. Augustine inadvertently teaches Florida history: 450 years and no proof of occupancy." Still, there's got to be a shadow.

This traveler went to St. Augustine when she was young—in the back seat of her parents' station wagon. She remembers the narrow, peaceful streets of the little town, so different from industrial Jacksonville to its north. She climbed around the Spanish fort, the San Marcos, last rebuilt in 1672: the oldest building in America. She also saw Henry Flagler's fantastic hotels, built in the late 19th century for wealthy northern vacationers, which are among the oldest existing buildings in the state.

Yet in a way, that old snowbird had a point. Florida does feel as though it exists for a different, less serious purpose than does the rest of the country. It always has been a refuge for adventurers, entrepreneurs, and outcasts: conquistadores, both missionaries and gold hunters; escaped slaves and pirates; Seminoles from Georgia; cigar makers from Cuba, sponge divers from Greece; settlers from Minorca and Scandinavia; migrant laborers, refugees from Vietnam: *Marielitos*, who departed from Mariel, Cuba, in 1980, boat-people from Haiti, retirees, the rich, eccentrics from everywhere, Mickey Mouse from Hollywood—and tourists.

It is also beautiful—a vast, wet, prickly state, empty of people in the center, with hundreds of lakes and huge cattle ranches and horse farms; with red-soil hills to the north, rockets to the east, castles at Orlando, and Confederate town squares near the Georgia border. Fantasy and fish, herons and gators thrive here; panthers still eke it out. The miles of swamps and plains, forests, and lakes outnumber the miles of crowded beaches. Often, even now, only the landscape survives for long, and that, too, floats, blows, or is dredged through changes, making it hard to place the past. The newspapers, even *The New York Times*, run their annual stories on how a hurricane could destroy Florida's high-rise-lined coast. The traveler already knows that this is a land that is still in control of those who live here.

A good way to begin to understand this land is to visit the Citrus Tower, "Florida's showplace for citrus," in Clermont. This traveler rode the elevator to the top of Citrus Tower, where she was supposed to "thrill to the panorama of 17 million citrus trees." What she actually saw were many, many acres of dead twisted branches, trunks, and empty fields, not a living orange tree in sight. This, Florida's finest citrus-growing country, was wiped out by the freeze of 1985 and then by citrus canker. This traveler was surprised, but the natives were sanguine: a killing freeze will occasionally happen. The last one was in 1895, and it resulted in the founding of that frost-free city, Miami. Every hundred years, someone informed the traveler, it's time to move the trees.

Florida is mutable, whimsical, and at odds with itself, the traveler sees. As she begins to read.

On one side of Florida's history are the Indians and the Spanish, and later the Cubans and the Crackers (white farmers). The Spanish-Catholic and Cuban settlers looked to Havana and South America for support; they would have nothing to do with the northern colonies (Cuba is only 90 miles from Florida). The Indians and Crackers stuck to themselves.

On the other side of Florida's history are the slave owners, the hotel builders and land sellers, and the vacationers, all of whom came down from the North and divided the state between them: conquerers who fell for Florida's appeal as a fountain of youth—or at least as a place to begin again.

The poles of Florida now got switched; the northern part became "southern" as it filled with slave-operated plantations and joined the Confederate South. The swampy southern part of Florida gradually became "northern" (as well as Spanish and Caribbean), when pleasure-seeking invaders from the cold, northern states arrived, following the developers' dredges.

The glorification of Florida as the "Sunshine State," friend of the ill and the feeble—and the tourist—has been going on for a long while."

The early Cracker settlers found their country beautiful just as it was: a land of custard apple, moonvine, catfish, and moonshine. These Floridians developed their own attitude toward all the northern invaders. It was spread across the first state flag, which stated, "Let Us Alone."

The Sunshine State has 1,350 miles of coastline, on which the tourist loves to bake whenever possible. It has 10,000 miles of rivers and streams and 7,000 springs and lakes, including the 730-square-mile Lake Okeechobee. It has 12,000,000 residents, making it the fourth largest state in population. It has more than 40,000,000 tourists a year, and the recovering citrus industry produced, in 1988, 130 million boxes of oranges, 51 million boxes of grapefruit, and 799 million gallons of orange juice.

This traveler took off for a trip in her rental car. She explored the city of Miami, ate Cuban food on Calle Ocho, strolled down man-made Miami Beach, looking at the Art Deco hotels. She rode through the Everglades in an airboat driven by a Seminole. She went searching for bears and panthers in Big Cypress Swamp. She drove north through the sugarcane, past the migrant labor camps, the vast Lake Okeechobee. She fished and ate frog legs and then catfish. She drove past miles of cattle on the 35,000-acre Brighton Seminole Reservation. She then went to the west coast, to Sanibel and Captiva islands, walked the beaches, and picked her way among millions of shells. She cruised down to condominium-lined Marco Island, which had changed horribly since the days when her father had brought her there to fish. She struggled back up the coast, caught in a Winnebago spring-flow, and finally got to Sarasota. She visited Ringling's house and museum of Baroque art. She went on to Tampa and stopped among the old Ybor City cigar factories. She drove up to the sponging port in Tarpon Springs and walked through neighborhoods settled by Greeks.

She finally headed toward the quiet country of northern Florida. She went to tiny Cedar Key, with its wooden fishermen's cottages, and slept in a room right over the gulf. She went further off the track, driving small roads out along the bayous, finding fishing villages, where she ate delicious shrimp. She entered the Spanish-moss-covered woods and the empty pinelands. She drove on fine county roads, far from the highways, all the way up to pretty Tallahassee.

Then she started back, following the Suwannee River. She meandered into the center of the state and cut through Marjorie Rawlings's rustic Cross Creek. She stopped at Ocala National Forest to swim in a spring and to camp. She dropped over to Lakeland to see all the buildings designed by Frank Lloyd Wright at Florida Southern College, then headed up across the state back to St. Augustine to see Ripley's Believe It or Not Museum. She dawdled down the east coast along the long white shore, passing John D. Rockefeller's last home at Ormond Beach. She studied the massive old rockets parked along Cape Canaveral. She saw fabulous Addison Mizner houses in Palm Beach. She cut back inland through the orange groves, up to Disney World and Epcot Center, which dip into the collective dream. She went back down the coast again and ambled along the boardwalk at Hollywood. She mailed postcards and set off for the Keys. She went deep-sea fishing and caught a tarpon. As she drove back up to Miami, she began to think about Florida's shadow.

Florida raised itself slightly out of the ocean some 20 million years ago, a swampy newcomer to the continent. It never experienced an ice age, but during the last one it became a popular migrating place, in spite of its rain. It did not take its final shape until 10,000 years ago.

Since the time it was first glimpsed by John Cabot, Florida has always been the object of some sort of land-claim frenzy.

In 1498, the mapmaker Cabot, out exploring for British King Henry VII, sailed down the coast from Labrador and discovered Florida, although it had already been claimed, unseen, by Christopher Columbus for Spain.

Ponce de León, representing Spain, got there second. He first saw La Florida on April 2, 1513, and landed a few days later at what is now St. Augustine. He was looking not for the fountain of youth but for the missing Bimini, where he was supposed to become governor. Finding nothing, he headed down the coast, past Los Martires (as he called the Florida Keys, which looked to him like kneeling martyrs), and up the west coast, stopping at present-day Fort Myers, where he encountered hostile Indians who shouted at him in Spanish. At this, he returned to Puerto Rico. He came back to conquer La Florida in 1521, bringing 200 settlers, including the first Catholic priests, who were supposed to reason with the heathens. The settlement near Charlotte Harbor was soon attacked by Apalachee or Calusa Indians. Ponce de León was wounded by an arrow, and the entire crew removed to Cuba, where he died.

Continuing the Spanish conquest, Pánfilo de Narváez arrived and landed in Tampa Bay in 1528. He immediately headed north, looking for the source of the Indian's gold, little suspecting that the gold he saw the Indians wearing around their necks was actually Spanish gold collected from shipwrecks.

Hernando de Soto came next. He landed at Tampa Bay in 1539 and quickly headed off in search of the same source of gold jewelry, going as far as North Carolina. He died after three years, still looking.

But then the Indians began to lose.

The Spaniard Pedro Menéndez de Aviles founded St. Augustine at long last in 1565. However, Jean Ribaut had established a French settlement at nearby Fort Caroline on the St. Johns River, and the Spanish knew this wouldn't do. Menéndez did not like those card-playing "Lutheran" French, whom he also considered pirates. Therefore, during a hurricane, he and his forces slaughtered them. All that survives of the French settlement are the journals and beautiful drawings of Native Americans done by Ribaut's mapmaker, Jacques le Moyne, who said of the Indians' costumes: "It is wonderful that men so savage should be capable of such tasteful inventions."

In a somewhat serendipitous revenge, England's Sir Francis Drake leveled St. Augustine in 1585. However, St. Augustine was rebuilt and survived (to become the town that Ralph Waldo Emerson, visiting in 1826, found to be full of "lazy desperadoes and land speculators" and that John J. Audubon called "the poorest hole in creation" in 1831).

Meanwhile, by 1560, the Indian population had withered away, as the native people were taken into slavery or died of smallpox, colds, diphtheria, or syphilis. In the 17th century, the total Indian population of 25,000, reduced by more than three-quarters, was tended to by Jesuits and Franciscans at some 50 monasteries.

The Spanish Cubans established "fishing ranchos" south in Calusa territory, and disease killed every Calusa. New British settlers arrived in the 17th century, seized native land, and drove the Timucuans and Apalachees south to their deaths.

By 1763 (when the British first took Florida from Spain in trade for Havana), the native Indians had all vanished. However, Creek Indians and Seminoles (a Creek name for wanderers or renegades), who had been crowded out of Georgia and the Carolinas, came down to replace the native Indians. They made their own land claims, which were soon challenged by the arriviste British/American settlers. Those competing claims eventually resulted in the first, second, and third Seminole wars, during the last of which Andrew Jackson crossed the border into Florida to (among other intentions) "punish" the Indians for living on land that was also claimed by white settlers.

Long before the wars, Florida's genetic pool began growing fast. The Creeks bred with Scots settlers to produce blue-eyed Creeks; the Seminoles kept black slaves and bred with them to produce black Seminoles. The result is that today you can't always guess the background of those you're talking to. In 1764, Londoner Denys Rolle started a colony near Palatka by importing vagrants, beggars, and debtors, who all abandoned him. A Scotsman named Dr. Andrew Turnbull started a colony at New Smyrna in 1768 by importing 1,255 starving Minorcans (and Greeks and Italians), all of whom fled to St. Augustine. The territory was a sort of renegade melting pot.

After Americans won its revolutionary war, Britain no longer wanted to bother with Florida and traded it back to Spain in 1783.

In 1821, Spain accepted the United States's offer to cancel a $5-million (somewhat bogus) debt in exchange for Florida, and Andrew Jackson again entered Pensacola, this time as governor. His stay was brief. In three months, he left what his wife Rachel called the "vast howling wilderness" and returned to Washington.

In 1830, Congress passed the Removal Law, which required all Indians in the East to be sent west to the Arkansas Territory. A delegation of Seminoles was tricked into signing this white man's treaty, which enraged the Indian Osceola, who pledged, "I will make the white man red with blood." This pledge was the beginning of the Second Seminole War, an affair that cost the white man $40,000 and some 1,500 lives. Osceola was defeated by an U.S. commander's treachery. He was captured during a false truce, and he died of malaria and grief in prison in Charleston, SC, an event that caused the white man to get much bad press in America.

Osceola's successor, Coacoochee, and his people, ragged and starving, soon requested a meeting with the white man. The Seminoles arrived at the parlay dressed in clothes they had stolen, which turned out to be an entire wardrobe of Shakespearean theater costumes. The American military negotiated with Hamlet, Richard III, Horatio, King Lear, and Caliban. Coacoochee said, "The red man's heart will always be free."

In 1842, 3,000 Seminoles were shipped along the "Trail of Tears," across the Mississippi. However, the fighting continued after 1855, when the last Seminole renegade leader, Billy Bowlegs, was caught and sent west. Three hundred of his Seminoles remained forever at large in the Florida swamps. Today their descendants raise cattle and fish, run bingo parlors, and sell trinkets and beads in south-central Florida. In 1976, the Seminoles accepted $16 million (or about 55 cents an acre) for their original 29 million acres of Florida.

Slaveholding Florida became a state in 1845, and five years later the population reached 87,445, of which 39,000 were black slaves who belonged to only 3,000 slave owners. The plantations produced cotton, turpentine, and lumber. The state's first senator, slave owner David Levy Yulee, whose grandfather was the grand vizier to the sultan of Morocco, built Florida's first cross-state railroad in the 1850s, from Fernandina to Cedar Key laying the tracks for the subsequent land boom.

Florida seceded from the Union in 1861 and became the third state to join the Confederacy. The Civil War cost Florida $20 million and 5,000 lives, and, worse, recovery took a century. The Ku Klux Klan emerged with a vengeance and became a powerful force. Blacks still drank at separate fountains, as they did elsewhere in the South, until the Civil Rights Act of 1964.

Events that tilted Florida toward the tourist market started quietly in the 19th century. In 1844, John Gorrie of Apalachicola invented an ice-making machine and the air conditioner, but nobody paid any attention to him, and his patents ran out. In 1873, Dr. John Wall discovered that mosquitoes carry yellow fever, but nobody paid any attention to him, either. In the 1880s, when the population of Florida reached 270,000, Hamilton Disston came down from Philadelphia, PA, bought four million acres, and began to drain the Caloosahatchee and Kissimmee valleys to make (and sell) a settlers' empire. A Chinese immigrant at Deland, named Lue Gim Gong, invented the frost-proof orange, which prospered along the Indian River. In 1871, Gen. Henry Sanford, Lincoln's former ambassador to Belgium, started a citrus plantation and began to import and experiment with every kind of citrus then known. He also brought in an entire colony of Swedes to work the land.

Perhaps the biggest boost to Florida's image came in 1885, when the American Medical Association endorsed Pinellas Point at St. Petersburg as the healthiest spot in the United States. After that, the land race was on. The land boom that began at the turn of the century became madness by the mid-1920s, ebbed through the Great Depression and World War II, then took off again in the 1950s and 1960s. People were—and are—irrationally attracted to the sun.

Ailing 38-year-old Thomas Edison moved from Menlo Park, NJ, to Fort Myers in 1885. There, he built the first modern swimming pool in America, and his incandescent lights lit his estate and workshop 30 miles from the Seminoles who were hiding in Big Cypress Swamp.

The year 1885 also saw the influx of Cuban cigar makers into Tampa, attracted from Cuba and the Keys when Vincent Ybor, followed by others, built his Ybor cigar plant. Ybor spirited his workers away from the labor problems of Key West to this new tax haven after his Key West factory burned. Not much later, sponge divers also deserted Key West for the deep-water sponge beds off Tarpon Springs, in a move initiated by a Greek who recruited deep-water divers from his homeland until there was (and still is) a sizable Greek colony in that city.

After the cigar makers decided to come to Ybor City, the success of their business was guaranteed by Henry Plant, who constructed the Atlantic Coastline Railroad from Richmond, Virginia, to Tampa. Starting in 1884, Plant built the enormous Tampa Bay Hotel, which is modeled on the Alhambra in Grenada, Spain, and has 13 silver Moorish minarets. The guests traveled the long corridors of this hotel by riding in rickshas. The hotel, worth seeing, now houses a college.

Ybor City became deeply involved in Cuba's effort to free itself from Spain. Money and guns were run, and José Martí came from Cuba to Tampa to raise funds. In 1898, after the U.S.S. *Maine* was blown apart in Havana harbor and the United States entered the Spanish-American War, Plant arranged for Tampa to be the port of embarkation for the 30,000 American troops. The porch of the Tampa Bay Hotel was filled with reporters filing stories on their "rocking-chair war." Winston Churchill was there reporting, and Clara Barton came to set up a Red Cross hospital. Stephen Crane, Frederic Remington, and Richard Harding Davis spent time on this porch. Theodore Roosevelt and his Rough Riders shipped out of Tampa. The end of Spain in the New World was orchestrated from the very shore where Hernando de Soto, conquistador, first landed.

Meanwhile, Henry Morrison Flagler came to visit St. Augustine in income-tax-free Florida. Flagler, a retired Standard Oil baron, was annoyed with St. Augustine's reputation as a place for the sickly and bored by its lack of a decent hotel. In 1885, he started to build. He began with the immense and opulent poured-concrete Ponce de León Hotel, a Moorish-Renaissance monument for the very rich that is still in existence (though no longer a hotel), and followed up with the slightly more frugal Alcazar across the street. Flagler, of course, provided the transportation to his hotels, in the form of the Florida East Coast Railroad, which had an enormous impact on the state. He then continued down the coast, seeking warmth and constructing a series of fantastic hotels to popularize his railroad. Flagler set the tone for the "bastard-Spanish-Moorish-Romanesque-Gothic-Renaissance-bull-market-damn-the-expense" building style, which lasted through the land boom of the 1920s and peaked most elaborately in Addison Mizner's Palm Beach mansions, to which those with the socially necessary private railroad cars traveled. The St. Augustine hotels all closed after half a century when the tourists moved south. But Flagler was south before them, having bought the Ormond Hotel in Ormond Beach in 1890. He built the Royal Poinciana Hotel at Palm Beach in 1893, the largest wooden hotel ever constructed, where Afromobiles (white wicker carts pulled by blacks—competition for Plant's rickshas) carried the guests about. Palm Beach wasn't even a town when the railroad came through, just a land spit covered by 20,000 coconut palms from a shipwreck.

At the persuasion of Julia Tuttle, who supposedly sent him an orange blossom during the freezing winter of 1894–95 (which had discouraged too many a fragile tourist), Flagler laid his railroad tracks down to the tiny settlement of Miami and incorporated it as a city. By 1896, he had built and opened the Royal

Palm Hotel. From Miami, "America's sun porch," Flagler pushed on to Homestead and built the Overseas Railroad to Key West by 1912. (The Overseas Railroad blew away in the hurricane of 1935.) Flagler died in 1913, having been granted a free 2.4 million acres of Florida for his efforts.

In 1912, when millionaire Carl Fisher of Indianapolis came to Miami, all the hotels were on the Miami mainland. Because there was still not much to do, Fisher poked around Biscayne Bay and discovered a mangrove-covered barrier sandbar, where he soon bought land from Quaker avocado farmer John Collins. Fisher applied a dredge to it and came up with the tabula rasa that became Miami Beach, which he began to fill with imported birds, plants, polo fields, golf courses, tennis courts, grandstands, elephants, and picturesque architecture, including the Flamingo Hotel (Spanish-Moorish-Venetian-Arab style) and the Lincoln, Nautilus, King Cole, and Boulevard hotels.

"Carl discovered that sand could hold up a real estate sign, and that was all he wanted it for," said humorist Will Rogers. "Had there been no Carl Fisher, Florida would be known today as the Turpentine State."

In 1925 alone, 481 hotels and apartment buildings rose on Miami Beach. Fisher even built the Dixie Highway from Miami to Michigan. But his flashy bootleg resort was less stable than the competition at Palm Beach; after the land bust and the 1929 stock market crash, Al Capone and others of his ilk moved in. Fisher died broke and an alcoholic.

In 1916, John Deering's architect, the wacky Paul Chalfin, began work on the monstrously imposing Villa Vizcaya in Miami—a kind of Venetian palace with gardens and waterways and a village, furnished in the Medieval-Renaissance-Baroque-Rococo-Neoclassical style. After it was finished, Deering rattled around in Vizcaya alone or with his mother for 10 years until his death. The house and gardens, now restored, are open to the public, for whom there is ample room.

Addison Mizner came to Palm Beach in 1918 to rest his 300-pound frame. The flamboyant self-proclaimed architect, who frequently forgot to include a kitchen or stairs in his plans, soon began his first Palm Beach project, the Everglades Club, which the newspapers called "a little of Seville and the Alhambra, Madeira and Algiers, with Italian lagoon and terrace and garden."

In 1925, right in the middle of the land-sales boom (by which time 2.5 million suckers had rushed to buy their lots), Addison Mizner and his brother Wilson bought 17,500 acres of scrub, which they called Boca Raton. Addison built the Cloister Club and, with Wilson, went into the "surreal" real estate business, immediately selling $26 million of lots.

The scrupulous George Merrick created his beautifully designed Coral Gables (now part of Miami) out of his father's farm. In 1921, he began to sell lots in this, the country's first fully planned, city (with stucco gates and Chinese-and-French-style houses along Venetian canals in the Italian style, with roof tiles removed from houses in Cuba, imported, and reused). Merrick soon hired ex-Secretary of State William Jennings Bryan at $100,000 a year (along with 3,000 other salesmen) to stand by the Venetian pool and sell $150 million worth of property. Before the bust, Merrick had completed the Miami

Biltmore Hotel and five international villages, each with houses in a different style: Dutch South African, Chinese, French City, French Country, and French Provincial. He had also established the University of Miami. (The Miami Biltmore reopened in 1987; this ghost-rich towering structure is well worth a visit.)

In the meantime, Florida natives—the white Crackers—farmed, fished, and harvested pines and turpentine to the north and inland. "Conchs" down in the Keys salvaged, caught turtles, rolled cigars, and went broke. Blacks worked at their tenant farms and went to juke joints to listen to music. Marjorie Kinnan Rawlings wrote *The Yearling* on her orange farm at Cross Creek (still there and still mysterious). Zora Neale Hurston of Eatonville, the first all-black community in the United States, wrote *Their Eyes Were Watching God*, about the 1928 hurricane that killed 2,000 people near Lake Okeechobee (there's a handsome WPA-built hurricane monument in Belle Glade). John Ringling, the circus king, set himself up at Sarasota, where he collected fine Baroque art and eventually built his Venetian ducal palazzo, Ca' d'Zan, and his art museum (well worth visiting) and where, in 1927, he first brought the "Greatest Show on Earth" to its new winter quarters.

The "Tin Can Tourists," back from World War I, arrived from the north in the early 1920s and hit the coasts in their new Fords. At first, they set up tent cities and ate out of cans, but before long they grew interested in owning a piece of the pie. Real estate scam artists, called "binder boys," flooded the state, buying up options on lots that they then resold over and over for a spiraling profit.

Things had gotten out of hand, but they didn't stop. The freeze of 1926 caused a temporary slowdown in the Florida land boom. The cold weather put a lot of people off, as did the crash of 1929, which wiped out the "paper" millionaires. The common people abandoned the small hurricane-swept lot that they'd been ill advised to buy in some impenetrable swamp and went back home. Ernest Hemingway, however, continued to fish off his royalties, down in Key West.

The WPA came to Florida and helped rescue the state from stagnation. Miami Beach's beautiful Streamline, Depression, and Tropical Deco hotels were built during the 1930s and managed to thrive. A steady migration of retirees to Florida also continued through the decade, because land was now cheap and the state still had no state income tax or inheritance tax. Later, many of the elderly ended up living in these same now-downgraded and run-down Art Deco hotels, only to be thrown out in the 1980s when some of the hotels were rescued but the tenants were not.

After World War II, business picked up a bit. By the 1950s, Florida was being redivided again, this time into lots with the kind of tract housing that had been tried successfully by visionaries such as William Levitt of Long Island, who came to Florida and started to build suburbs.

The subdividing continued briskly, and, by the 1960s, it was booming again, led by companies like the giant General Development Corporation, which offered roadless, serviceless land for $50 down, $10 a month, and by the treacherous Gulf American Corporation, which utilized the hard sell to force swamps on customers.

Now we're into visible history. This traveler believes she has glimpsed, but hasn't yet caught, the shadow. So what was she going to tell the snowbird?

She is on her way to meet the snowbird for cocktails. She crosses the bridge to Miami Beach and drives through the dusk down Collins Avenue, toward the Fontainebleau Hotel. That is the Fontainebleau ahead, isn't it? Yes, it is. No, it isn't!

It's even more startling and grandiose than the Fontainebleau she remembers. And it seems they've somehow slightly moved the Fontainebleau. Or else that gateway has distorted the view of the Fontainebleau? From this distance the tourist sees a beautiful Deco arch, beyond which is her destination. But as soon as she decides to drive through this gate, she sees she will crash right into . . . a solid wall. It's the Fontainebleau itself! And this thing before her, it's some sort of mural; it's a fake, a trompe l'oeil of the Fontainebleau Hotel! Painted by some type of trickster.

The traveler slows down. In her mind's eye, Florida's shadow rises over the flimsy suburbs of the 1950s and 1960s and the cement-slab condominiums of the 1970s, which now block the view of Florida's beaches, and farther over the alarm-controlled time-shares of the 1980s, where often nobody's home; and on again across those beautiful condominiums on wealthy Brickell Avenue in Miami—the colorful 21-story Atlantis, for instance, the one in the TV series "Miami Vice," the one with the hole in it, the one you can see best from the highway at high speeds. It's like Disney World escaped from Orlando and mutated. Like everything else here, it has the irresistibly playful spirit of a state that won't conform; it's fantastic. And, finally, she understands: that hole, that trompe l'oeil, this is the heart of Florida. Florida plays with shadows.

Conservationist Marjorie Stoneman Douglas wrote that she first saw Florida in 1915 as "lost in the light, as I was, streets, roofs, fringing round-leaved trees over wharves and houseboats, all silent, all asleep. Sea gulls floated in it, white shadows. It caught the pale breasts of pelicans on pilings in dancing nets. Bay or sky, it was all dazzling, diamond-edged."

Catch it if you can.

1 Planning Your Trip

Before You Go

Visitor Information

Contact the Florida Division of Tourism (126 Van Buren St., Tallahassee 32301, tel. 904/487–1462). For additional information, ask for the local chambers of commerce in the areas you wish to visit. *See* also Useful Addresses and Numbers under each city/area section of this guide.

In the United Kingdom contact the U.S. Travel and Tourism Administration (22 Sackville St., London W1X 2EA, England, tel. 01/439–7433).

Tour Groups

If you prefer to leave the driving to someone else, consider a package tour. Although you will have to march to the beat of a tour guide's drum rather than your own, you are likely to save money on airfare, hotels, and ground transportation. For the more experienced or adventurous traveler, a variety of special-interest and independent packages are available. Listed below is a sampling of available options. Check with your travel agent or the Florida Division of Tourism (tel. 904/488–4952) for additional resources.

When considering a tour, be sure to find out exactly what expenses are included (particularly tips, taxes, side trips, additional meals, and entertainment); ratings of all hotels on the itinerary and the facilities they offer; cancellation policies for you and for the tour operator; and, if you are traveling alone, the cost for a single supplement. Most tour operators request that bookings be made through a travel agent; there is no additional charge for doing so.

General-Interest Tours

Cosmos/Globus Gateway (150 S. Los Robles Ave., Suite 860, Pasadena, CA 91101, tel. 818/449–0919 or 800/556–5454) offers a comprehensive eight-day tour that includes entry to Disney World and Epcot Center. **American Express Vacations** (Box 5014, Atlanta, GA 30302, tel. 800/241–1700 or in GA 800/282–0800) heads down the coast from New York to Miami in its "Southern Highlights" program. "Sunshine State" is a ramble through much of Florida. **Maupintour** (Box 807, Lawrence, KA 66044, tel. 913/843–1211 or 800/255–4266) sells sunny Florida packages during the winter months. **Domenico Tours** (751 Broadway, Bayonne, NJ 07002, tel. 800/554–TOUR) offers packages to Orlando, Miami Beach, Palm Beach, St. Petersburg, and Miami Beach/Bahamas/Walt Disney World.

Special-Interest Tours

Adventure

Sobek's International Explorers Society (Box 1089, Angels Camp, CA 95222, tel. 209/736–4524) will take you canoeing through the Florida Everglades or island-hopping by sailboat off the gulf coast of Florida. **Wilderness Southeast** (711 Sandtown Rd., Savannah, GA 31410, tel. 912/897–5108) runs rugged trips through the Everglades and places like the Okefenokee Swamp in Georgia.

Nature

Visit the loggerhead turtle on Sanibel Island, off Florida's gulf coast, with conservationists in an outing arranged by **Smithsonian Associates Travel Program** (1100 Jefferson Dr. SW, Washington, DC 20560, tel. 202/357–4700). You must pay a $20 fee to become a member of the Smithsonian to take any of the trips offered in the program. "Everglades, Dry Tortugas, and Southwest Florida," from **Questers Tour & Travel** (257 Park Ave. S, New York, NY 10010, tel. 212/673–3120), unveils a vast array of birds, plants, and other wildlife.

Package Deals for Independent Travelers

American Fly AAway Vacations (tel. 800/433–7300 or 817/355–1234) offers city packages with discounts on hotels and car rentals. The airline's "Vacation Enchantment" package to Florida includes admission to Disney World and Epcot Center. Also check with **Delta Air Lines** (tel. 800/241–6108 or 404/765–2952) and **Eastern Airlines** (tel. 305/873–3000) for packages. **American Express** has similar city packages, with half-day sightseeing tours, available from any American Express office.

Tips for British Travelers

Government Tourist Offices The **United States Travel and Tourism Administration** (22 Sackville St., London W1X 2EA, tel. 01/439–7433) will send brochures and give you advice on your trip to Florida.

Passports and Visas You will need a valid passport (cost: £15) and a U.S. Visitor's Visa that you can get either through your travel agent or by post from the **United States Embassy** (Visa and Immigration Dept., 5 Upper Grosvenor St., London W1A 2JB, tel. 01/499–3443). The embassy no longer accepts visa applications made by personal callers. No vaccinations are required.

Customs Visitors of 21 or over can take in 200 cigarettes or 50 cigars or three pounds of tobacco; one U.S. quart of alcohol; and duty-free gifts to a value of $100. Be careful not to try to take in meat or meat products, seeds, plants, fruits, etc. Avoid illegal drugs like the plague.

Returning to Britain you may bring home: (1) 200 cigarettes or 100 cigarillos or 50 cigars or 250 grams of tobacco; (2) two liters of table wine with additional allowances for (a) one liter of alcohol over 22% by volume (38.8° proof, most spirits), (b) two liters of alcohol under 22% by volume (fortified or sparkling wine), or (c) two more liters of table wine; and (3) 50 grams of perfume and ¼ liter of toilet water; and (4) other goods up to a value of £32.

Insurance We recommend that you insure yourself to cover health and motoring mishaps through **Europ Assistance** (252 High St., Croydon, Surrey CRO 1NF, tel. 01/680–1234).

It is also wise to take out insurance to cover loss of luggage (though check that this isn't already covered in any existing home-owner's policy). Trip-cancellation insurance is another wise buy. **The Association of British Insurers** (Aldermary House, Queen St., London EC4N 1TT, tel. 01/248–4477) will give comprehensive advice on all aspects of vacation insurance.

Tour Operators Numerous tour operators offer packages to Florida. Here we list just a few; contact your travel agent to find companies best suited to your needs and pocketbook.

Albany Travel (Manchester) Ltd. (190 Deansgate, Manchester M3 3WD, tel. 061/833–0202) offers an eight-day tour of the

Florida resorts featuring southern Florida and the Florida Keys. Prices start from £645 per person.

Jetlife Holidays (169–171 High St., Orpington, Kent BR6 OLW, tel. 0689/77061) has a wide range of vacations to various destinations in Florida.

Jetways (93 Newman St., London W1P 3LE, tel. 01/637–5444) offers seven nights in a Gulf coast resort from £545 per person. A two-destination, two-week vacation, for example, at Miami and Orlando, costs from £589 to £655 per person, depending on the hotel and season.

Poundstretcher (Airlink House, Hazelwick Ave., Three Bridges, Sussex RH10 1YS, tel. 0293/548241) offers seven nights in Clearwater from £475 per person; seven nights in Fort Lauderdale from £549; and seven nights in Miami from £539. It also offers a wide range of fly-drive vacations, golf and tennis vacations, and cruises.

Speedbird (Alta House, 152 King St., London W6 0QU, tel. 01/741–8041) has excellent fly-drive offers and motor-camper vacations that are particularly flexible. Ask for the brochure.

Airfares If you want to make your own way to Florida and need a reasonably priced ticket, try the small ads in the daily or Sunday newspapers or in magazines such as *Time Out*. You should be able to pick up something at rock-bottom prices. You should be prepared to be flexible about your dates of travel, and you should book as early as possible.

Also check out the APEX tickets offered by the major airlines, which are another good option. As we went to press, round-trip tickets to Orlando offered in the small ads cost about £290; to Miami, £255. Be sure to ask if there are any hidden extras, since airport taxes and supplements can increase the price dramatically.

Car Rental There are offices of the major car rental companies in most large towns, and you can either make your arrangements before you leave or when you get to your destination.

Avis (Hayes Gate House, Uxbridge Rd., Hayes, Middlesex UB4 0JN, tel. 01/848–8733) offers seven days' rental of, say, a Chevette for £52; extra days at £13 per day. Its Driveaway checks are also worth considering. Available for £15, £23, or £31, each covers the cost of one day's car rental (depending on the country and type of car). Buy your checks before you leave and then rent your car on arrival.

Hertz (Radnor House, 1272 London Rd., London SW16 4XW, tel. 01/950–5050) offers seven days' rental of, say, a Ford Escort for about £51. Most rental offers include unlimited mileage, but don't forget to budget for the price of gas, local taxes, and collision insurance. Also check out the fly-drive offers from tour operators and airlines; some good bargains are usually available.

When to Go

Florida is a state for all seasons, although most visitors prefer October–April, particularly in southern Florida.

Winter is the height of the tourist season, when southern Florida is crowded with "snowbirds" fleeing the cold weather in the

North. Hotels, bars, discos, restaurants, shops, and attractions are all crowded. Hollywood and Broadway celebrities appear in sophisticated supper clubs, and other performing artists hold the stage at ballets, operas, concerts, and theaters.

During the winter season, the Magic Kingdom at Disney World is more magical than ever, especially from mid-December through January 2, with daily parades and other extravaganzas. The crowds are overwhelming then, too. Winter fairs and festivals, art shows, parades, and fiestas take place in other parts of the state as well. In Tarpon Springs, the Diving of the Golden Cross festivals on Epiphany (Jan. 6) are among the top events in the United States. And in Tampa, the swashbuckling Gasparilla Pirate Days attract enormous crowds in mid-February.

Summer in Florida, as smart budget-minded visitors have discovered, is often hot and very humid, but the season is made bearable along the coast by ocean breezes. Besides, many hotels lower their prices considerably during summer. Alas, some of the attractions are closed from April to October.

Families who want to explore Disney World–Epcot, Sea World, Busch Gardens, and other outstanding attractions will find some crowds in summer—but fewer when children return to school in September.

For the college crowd, **spring** vacation is still the time to congregate in Florida, though students are now branching out from the hectic Fort Lauderdale and Daytona Beach areas.

For senior citizens, September–December are months for discounts to many attractions and hotels in Orlando and along the Pinellas Suncoast in the Tampa Bay area.

Climate

What follows are average daily maximum and minimum temperatures for major cities in Florida.

Key West (The Keys)

Jan.	76F	24C	**May**	85F	29C	**Sept.**	90F	32C
	65	18		74	23		77	25
Feb.	76F	24C	**June**	88F	31C	**Oct.**	83F	28C
	67	19		77	25		76	24
Mar.	79F	26C	**July**	90F	32C	**Nov.**	79F	26C
	68	20		79	26		70	21
Apr.	81F	27C	**Aug.**	90F	32C	**Dec.**	76F	24C
	72	22		79	26		67	19

Miami

Jan.	74F	23C	**May**	83F	28C	**Sept.**	86F	30C
	63	17		72	22		76	24
Feb.	76F	24C	**June**	85F	29C	**Oct.**	83F	28C
	63	17		76	24		72	22
Mar.	77F	25C	**July**	88F	31C	**Nov.**	79F	26C
	65	18		76	24		67	19
Apr.	79F	26C	**Aug.**	88F	31C	**Dec.**	76F	24C
	68	20		77	25		63	17

Orlando	**Jan.**	70F	21C	**May**	88F	31C	**Sept.**	88F	31C
		49	9		67	19		74	23
	Feb.	72F	22C	**June**	90F	32C	**Oct.**	83F	28C
		54	12		72	22		67	19
	Mar.	76F	24C	**July**	90F	32C	**Nov.**	76F	24C
		56	13		74	23		58	14
	Apr.	81F	27C	**Aug.**	90F	32C	**Dec.**	70F	21C
		63	17		74	23		52	11

Updated hourly weather information in 235 cities around the world—180 of them in the U.S.—is only a phone call away. Telephone numbers for WeatherTrak in the 12 cities where the service is available may be obtained by calling 800/247–3282. A taped message will tell you to dial the three-digit access code to any of the 235 destinations. The code is either the area code (in the USA) or the first three letters of the foreign city. For a list of all access codes, send a stamped, self-addressed envelope to Cities, Box 7000, Dallas, TX 75209. For further information, phone 214/869–3035 or 800/247–3282.

Festivals and Seasonal Events

Top seasonal events in Florida include Speed Weeks auto racing celebration in Daytona Beach in February; Miami Film Festival in February; Florida Derby Festival from February through April; Sunfest in Palm Beach in May; and Key West's celebration of Hemingway Days in July. For exact dates and details about the following events, contact the Florida Department of Commerce, Division of Tourism (107 W. Gaines St., Tallahassee 32399, tel. 904/488–8230).

Early Jan.: Polo Season opens at the Palm Beach Polo and Country Club (13198 Forest Hill Blvd., West Palm Beach 33414, tel. 304/798–7040).
Early Jan.: Winter Regatta Sailing Event takes place on the Caloosahatchee River, Fort Myers (tel. 813/334–1133).
Jan. 6: Greek Epiphany Day includes religious celebrations, parades, music, dancing, and feasting at the St. Nicholas Greek Orthodox Cathedral (Box 248, Tarpon Springs 33589, tel. 813/937–3540).
Mid Jan.: Art Deco Weekend spotlights Miami Beach's historic district with an Art Deco street fair, a 1930s-style Moon over Miami Ball, and live entertainment (tel. 305/599–5225).
Mid-Jan.: Taste of the Grove Food and Music Festival is a popular fund-raiser put on in Coconut Grove's Peacock Park by area restaurants (tel. 305/962–4117).
Late Jan.: South Florida Fair and Exposition takes place in West Palm Beach (tel. 305/969–2888).
Late Jan to mid-Feb.: Speed Weeks is a three-week celebration of auto racing that culminates in the famous Daytona 500 in Daytona Beach (Daytona International Speedway, Drawer S, Daytona Beach 32015, tel. 904/253–6711).
Late Jan. or early Feb.: Key Biscayne Art Festival is an annual juried show of 150 talented artists at the entrance to Cape Florida State Park (tel. 305/361–1922).
Feb.–Apr.: Winter Equestrian Festival includes more than 1,000 horses and three grand-prix equestrian events at the Palm Beach Polo and Country Club in West Palm Beach (tel. 305/798–7000).
First weekend in Feb.: Sarasota Classic is a major event on the

LPGA tour (Classic, Box 2199, Sarasota 33578, tel. 813/366–7113).

Early Feb.: Scottish Festival and Games features a variety of events in Key Biscayne (tel. 305/757–6730).

Mid-Feb.: Florida State Fair includes carnival rides and 4-H competitions in Tampa (tel. 813/621–7821).

Mid-Feb.: Miami Film Festival is 10 days of international, domestic, and local films sponsored by the Film Society of America (7600 Red Rd., Penthouse Suite, Miami 33157, tel. 305/444–FILM).

Mid-Feb.: Florida Citrus Festival and Polk County Fair in Winter Haven showcases the citrus harvest with displays and entertainment (tel. 813/293–3175).

Mid-Feb.: Islamorada Sportfishing Festival features a weekend of fishing, arts and crafts, races, and prizes (tel. 305/664–4503).

Mid-Feb.: Coconut Grove Art Festival is the state's largest (tel. 305/447–0401).

Late Feb.–early Apr.: Florida Derby Festival is a series of cultural, social, artistic, and athletic events in Broward, Dade, and Palm Beach counties (Festival, Box 705, Hallandale 33009, tel. 305/454–8544).

Last full weekend in Feb.: Labelle Swamp Cabbage Festival is a salute to the state tree, the cabbage palm (tel. 813/675–0697).

Early Mar.: Florida International Air Show at the Charlotte County Airport features the U.S. Navy's Blue Angels (tel. 813/639–2788).

First weekend in Mar.: Sanibel Shell Fair is the largest event of the year on Sanibel Island (tel. 813/472–2684).

Early Mar.: Carnival Miami is a carnival celebration staged by the Little Havana Tourist Authority (900 S.W. First St., Miami 33130, tel. 305/324–7349).

Early Mar.: Cycle Week is a major motorcycle racing event at Daytona International Speedway that always takes place three weeks after the Daytona 500 (tel. 904/253–6711).

Mid-Mar. and early July: Arcadia All-Florida Championship Rodeo is professional rodeo at its best (Rodeo, Box 1266, Arcadia 33821, tel. 813/494–2014).

Mid-Mar.–Mid-Apr.: Springtime Tallahassee is a major cultural, sporting, and culinary event in the state capital (tel. 904/224–5012).

Late Mar.: Azalea Festival is a beauty pageant, arts and crafts show, and parade held in downtown Palatka and Riverfront Park (tel. 904/325–3815).

Late Mar.: Festival of Flowers blooms in Boca Raton (tel. 305/393–7700).

Late Mar.: Port Canaveral Seafood Festival requires hearty appetites at Cape Canaveral (tel. 305/783–7831).

Early Apr.: Spring Arts Festival attracts more than 300 artists and craftspeople from across the country to Gainesville (tel. 904/377–0046).

Early Apr.: Bounty of the Sea Seafood Festival in Miami includes a limbo contest, a chowder competition, an Underwater Film Festival, and more (International Oceanographic Foundation/Planet Ocean, 3979 Rickenbacker Causeway, Miami 33149, tel. 305/361–5786).

Early Apr.–late May: Addison Mizner Festival in Boca Raton celebrates the 1920s in Palm Beach County (tel. 305/368–7509).

Palm Sunday: Blessing of the Fleet is held on the bay front in St. Augustine (tel. 904/829–5681).

Mid-Apr.–mid-May: Water Weeks in Panama City Beach is a spring festival of fishing tournaments, scuba treasure hunts, and sailing regattas (tel. 904/234–6575).

Easter Sunday: Easter Sunrise Service in Orlando is held at Sea World (tel. 305/345–4385).

Late Apr.: River Cities Festival is a three-day event in Miami Springs and Hialeah that focuses attention on the Miami River and the need to keep it clean (tel. 305/887–1515).

Late Apr.–early May: Sun 'n' Fun Festival includes a bathtub regatta, golf tournament, and nighttime parade in Clearwater (tel. 813/461–0011).

Late Apr.–early May: Conch Republic Celebration in Key West honors the founding fathers of the Conch Republic, "the small island nation of Key West" (tel. 305/294–4440).

Early May: Artfest in Orlando is a showcase for Central Florida's arts community (tel. 305/THE–ARTS).

First weekend in May: Sunfest includes a wide variety of cultural and sporting events in West Palm Beach (tel. 305/659–5980).

Mid-May: Arabian Nights Festival in Opa-locka is a mix of contemporary and fantasy-inspired entertainment (tel. 305/686–4611).

Mid-May: Pompano Seafood Festival includes one of the nation's premier billfish tournaments, plus area restaurants that showcase their offerings (tel. 305/941–2940).

Late May: Aqua Fest in Clearwater is a weekend of water-related activities (tel. 813/461–0011).

Early–mid-June: Billy Bowlegs Festival in Fort Walton Beach is a week of entertaining activities in memory of a pirate who ruled the area in the late 1700s (tel. 904/244–8191).

July 4: Firecracker Festival in Melbourne is one of the state's most colorful Independence Day celebrations (tel. 305/254–2491).

Mid-July: Hemingway Days Festival in Key West includes plays, short-story competitions, and a Hemingway look-alike contest (tel. 305/294–4440).

Mid-July: The Greater Jacksonville King Fish Tournament offers a number of cash prizes (tel. 904/241–7127).

Month of Aug.: Boca Festival Days includes many educational, cultural, and recreational activities in Boca Raton (tel. 305/395–4433).

Mid-Aug.: Shark Tournament at Port of the Islands on Marco Islands awards prizes for the largest shark in three categories; at Port of the Islands Resort and Marina (Rte. 41, Marco 33937, tel. 800/237–4173 or in FL 800/282–3011).

Late Aug.: Worm Fiddler's Day is the biggest day of the year in Caryville (tel. 904/548–5116).

Labor Day Weekend: Florida Pro Surfing Event is held in Sebastian (tel. 305/727–1752).

Early Sept.: Anniversary of the Founding of St. Augustine is held on the grounds of the Mission of Nombre de Dios (tel. 904/829–5681).

Mid- to late Sept.: Festival Miami is three weeks of performing and visual arts sponsored by the University of Miami. (University Office of Public Affairs, Box 248105, Coral Gables 33124, tel. 305/284–5500).

Late Sept.: Pensacola Seafood Festival means food and entertainment in Pensacola (tel. 904/438–4081).

Early Oct.: Miami Boat Show in the Grove draws up to 200,000 people to Coconut Grove in Miami (tel. 305/442–2001).

Mid-Oct.: Florida State Chili Cookoff Championship at Port of the Islands Resort on Marco Island means all the chili you can eat (tel. 800/237-4173 or in FL 800/282-3011).
Mid-Oct.: Paul Revere 250 Motorcycle Race is at Daytona International Speedway (tel. 904/253-6711).
Late Oct.: Fantasy Fest in Key West is an unrestrained Halloween costume party, parade, and town fair (tel. 305/294-4440).
Early Nov.: Hollywood Sun 'n' Fun Festival includes celebrity entertainment and top-notch food (tel. 305/920-33330).
Mid-Nov.: Banyan Art Festival attracts craftspeople and artists to Coconut Grove (tel. 305/444-7270).
Late Nov.: River Manatee Festival in Crystal River focuses on both the river and the endangered manatee (tel. 904/795-3149).
Early-late Dec.: Winterfest and Boat Show in Fort Lauderdale has a rodeo, shoreline competitions, and cultural events (tel. 305/462-6000).
Mid-Dec.: Walt Disney World's Very Merry Christmas Parade in the Magic Kingdom is a seasonal festival in Orlando (Walt Disney World, Box 10000, Lake Buena Vista 32830-1000).
Mid-Dec.: Christmas Regatta of Lights is a colorful display in St. Augustine (tel. 904/829-5681).
Late Dec.: Coconut Grove King Mango Strut is an unusual parade through Coconut Grove (tel. 305/441-0944).

What to Pack

Pack light, because porters and luggage trolleys are hard to find. Luggage allowances on domestic flights vary slightly from airline to airline. Most allow three checked pieces and one carry-on. In all cases, check-in luggage cannot weigh more than 70 pounds each or be larger than 62 inches (length + width + height) and must fit under the seat or in the overhead luggage compartment.

The northern part of the state is much cooler in the winter than is the southern part. Winters are mild in the Orlando area, with daytime temperatures in the 70s and low 80s. But the temperature can dip to the 60s, so take a sweater or jacket, just in case. Farther north, in the Panhandle area, winters are cool and there's often frost at night.

The Miami area and the Tampa/St. Petersburg area are warm year-round and often extremely humid during the summer months. Be prepared for sudden summer storms, but leave the plastic raincoats at home because they're uncomfortable in the high humidity.

Dress is casual throughout the state, with sundresses, jeans, or walking shorts appropriate during the day. A pair of comfortable walking shoes or sneakers is a must for Disney World. A few of the better restaurants request that men wear jackets and ties, but most do not. Be prepared for air-conditioning bordering on the glacial, especially in the Miami/Fort Lauderdale areas.

You can swim in Florida year-round. Be sure to take a sun hat and a good sunscreen because the sun can be fierce, even in the winter.

Cash Machines

Virtually all U.S. banks belong to a network of ATMs (automatic teller machines), which gobble up bank cards and spit out cash 24 hours a day in cities throughout the country. There are some eight major networks in the United States, the largest of which are **Cirrus,** owned by MasterCard, and **Plus,** affiliated with Visa. Some banks belong to more than one network. These cards are not automatically issued; you have to ask for them. Cards issued by Visa and MasterCard may also be used in the ATMs, but the fees are usually higher than the fees on bank cards, and there is a daily interest charge on the "loan," even if monthly bills are paid on time. Each network has a toll-free number you can call to locate machines in a given city. The Cirrus number is 800/4–CIRRUS; the Plus number is 800/THE–PLUS. Check with your bank for fees and for the amount of cash you can withdraw per day.

Traveling with Film

Film doesn't like hot weather. If you're driving in summer, don't store film in the glove compartment or on the shelf under the rear window. Put it behind the front seat on the floor, on the side opposite the exhaust pipe.

On a plane trip, never pack unprocessed film in check-in luggage; if your bags get X-rayed, say goodbye to your pictures. Always carry undeveloped film with you through security and ask to have it inspected by hand. (It helps to isolate your film in a plastic bag, ready for quick inspection.) Inspectors at American airports are required by law to honor requests for hand inspection.

The newer airport scanning machines used in all U.S. airports are safe for anything from five to 500 scans, depending on the speed of your film. The effects are cumulative; you can put the same roll of film through several scans without worry. After five scans, though, you're asking for trouble.

If your film gets fogged and you want an explanation, send it to the National Association of Photographic Manufacturers (600 Mamaroneck Ave., Harrison, NY 10528). It will try to determine what went wrong. The service is free.

Car Rentals

Florida is a car renter's bazaar, with more discount companies offering more bargains—and more fine print—than anywhere else in the nation. If you're planning to rent a car in Florida, shop around for the best combination rate for car and airfare. Jacksonville, for example, is often somewhat cheaper to fly into than Miami, but Miami's car-rental rates are usually lower than Jacksonville's. In major Florida cities, peak-season rates for a subcompact average around $110 a week, often with unlimited mileage. Some companies advertise peak-season promotional rates as low as $59 a week with unlimited mileage, but only a few cars are available at this rate, and you may have to pay twice as much if you keep the car less than seven days! Some of these companies require you to keep the car in the state and are quick to charge for an extra day when you return a vehicle late.

Avis (800/331–1212), **Budget** (tel. 800/527–0700), **Dollar** (tel. 800/421–6868), **Hertz** (tel. 800/654–3131), **National** (tel.

800/328–4567), **Sears** (tel. 800/527–0770), and **Thrifty** (tel. 800/367–2277) maintain airport and city locations throughout Florida. So do **Alamo** (tel. 800/327–9633) and **General** (tel. 800/327–7607), which offer some of the state's lowest rates. **Rent-A-Wreck** (tel. 800/221–8282) and **Ugly Duckling** (800/231–5508) rent used cars throughout the state, usually with more stringent mileage restrictions.

Besides the national rental companies, several regional and local firms offer good deals in major Florida cities. These include **Ajax** (tel. 800/331–1212), **Auto Host** (tel. 800/237–2991), **Holiday Payless** (tel. 800/282–4682), **Lindo's** (tel. 800/237–8396), **USA** (tel. 800/872–2277), and **Value** (tel. 800/327–2501). Ajax is a major budget renter in Jacksonville, with three beach offices. In Fort Lauderdale, local companies include **Aapex Thompson** (tel. 305/566–8663), **Air and Sea** (tel. 305/764–1008), and **Atlantic** (tel. 305/760–4119). In Orlando, try **Buck An Hour** (tel. 305/237–4000) and **Wheels** (tel. 305/291–9843). Tampa–St. Petersburg companies include **A-Florida Rent-a-Heap** (tel. 813/581–4805), **American** (tel. 813/527–7999), **Central Van Rentals** (tel. 813/327–3453), and **Phoenix** (tel. 813/360–6941). In Miami, **A-OK** (tel. 305/633–3313) and **Dolphin** (tel. 305/871–3440) are local budget companies, while **AutoExotica** (tel. 305/871–3686) and **Cars of the Rich and Famous** (tel. 305/945–2737) rent cars fit for a "Miami Vice" set. Down in Key West, try **Tropical Rent-a-Car** (tel. 305/294–8136).

It's always best to know a few essentials *before* you arrive at the car-rental counter. Find out what the collision damage waiver (CDW), usually an $8–$12 daily surcharge, covers and whether your corporate or personal insurance already covers damage to a rental car (if so, bring a photocopy of the benefits section along). More and more companies are now holding renters responsible for theft and vandalism damages if they don't buy the CDW; in response, some credit card and insurance companies are extending *their* coverage to rental cars. These include **Access America** (tel. 800/851–2800), **Chase Manhattan Bank Visa Cards** (tel. 800/645–7352), and **Dreyfus Consumer Bank Gold and Silver MasterCards** (tel. 800/847–9700). Find out, too, if you must pay for a full tank of gas whether you use it or not, and make sure you get a reservation number.

Traveling with Children

Publications ***Family Travel Times,*** an 8- to 12-page newsletter published 10 times a year by Travel with Your Children (80 Eighth Ave., New York, NY 10011, tel. 212/206–0688). Subscription includes access to back issues and twice-weekly opportunities to call in for specific advice.

Great Vacations with Your Kids: The Complete Guide to Family Vacations in the U.S. by Dorothy Ann Jordon and Marjorie Adoff Cohen (E. P. Dutton, 2 Park Ave., New York, NY 10016; $9.95) details everything from city vacations to adventure vacations to child-care resources.

Bimonthly publications for parents that are filled with listings of events, resources, and advice are available free at such places as libraries, supermarkets, and museums: ***Florida Parent*** (4331 N. Federal Hwy., Ft. Lauderdale 33060, tel. 305/776–3305) covers Palm Beach, Broward, and Dade counties; ***Tampa Bay Family Times*** (Box 17481, Tampa 33682, tel. 813/877–0217) covers Hillsborough County. For a small fee, you can usually have an issue sent to you before your trip.

Hotels Florida may have the highest concentration of hotels with organized children's programs in the United States. **Club Med** (40 W. 57th St., New York, NY 10019, tel. 800/CLUB–MED) opened its new Sandpiper resort village in Port St. Lucie, including a "Baby Club" (4–23 months), "Mini Club" (2 years and up), and "Kids Club" (8 years and up). **Guest Quarters Suite Hotels** (Ft. Lauderdale and Tampa locations, tel. 800/424–2900) offers the luxury of two-room suites with kitchen facilities and children's menus in the restaurant. It also allows children under 18 to stay free in the same suite with their parents. Two **Sonesta International Hotels** (tel. 800/343–7170) have children's programs: Sonesta VillHotel Orlando and Sonesta Beach Hotel Key Biscayne. The **Hyatt Regency Grand Cypress** at Orlando (1 Grand Cypress Blvd., Orlando 32819, tel. 407/239–1234 or 800/228–9000) staffs a year-round child-care center for kids 3–12 and organizes summer activities for toddlers through teens. There's a Children's Creative Center at the **Delta Court of Flags** (5715 Major Blvd., Orlando 32819, tel. 305/351–3340). Also look for children's programs at **Marriott's Harbor Beach Resort** (3030 Holiday Dr., Ft. Lauderdale 33316, tel. 305/525–4000 or 800/228–9290); The **Stouffer Orlando Resort** (6677 Sea Harbor Dr., Orlando 32821, tel. 407/351– 5555 or 800/468–3571); **Amelia Island Plantation Resort** (Rte. A1A, Amelia Island 32034, tel. 904/261–6161); **Holiday Inn Main Gate East** at Disney World (5678 Space Coast Hwy., Kissimmee 32741, tel. 407/396–4488 or 800/465–4329); and **Marriott's Marco Island Resort** (400 S. Collier Blvd., Marco Island 33937, tel. 813/394–2511 or 800/228– 9290). Most **Days Inn** hotels (tel. 800/325–2525) charge only a nominal fee for children under 18 and allow kids 12 and under to eat free (many offer efficiency-type apartments, too).

Condo Rentals See ***The Condo Lux Vacationer's Guide to Condominium Rentals in the Southeast*** by Jill Little (Vintage Books/Random House, New York; $9.95).

Home Exchange See ***Home Exchanging: A Complete Sourcebook for Travelers at Home or Abroad*** by James Dearing (Globe Pequot Press, Box Q, Chester, CT 06412, tel. 800/243–0495 or in CT 800/962–0973; $9.95).

Getting There On domestic flights, children under 2 who do not occupy a seat travel free. Various discounts apply to children 2–12. Reserve a seat behind the bulkhead of the plane, which offers more legroom and can usually fit a bassinet (supplied by the airline). At the same time, inquire about special children's meals or snacks, offered by most airlines. (See "TWYCH's Airline Guide," in the Feb. 1988 issue of ***Family Travel Times,*** for a rundown on the services offered by 46 airlines.) Ask the airline in advance if you can bring aboard your child's car seat. (For the booklet "Child/Infant Safety Seats Acceptable for Use in Aircraft," write Community and Consumer Liaison Division, APA-400 Federal Aviation Administration, Washington, DC 20591, tel. 202/267–3479.)

Baby-sitting Services First check with the hotel concierge about child-care arrangements. **Sitters Unlimited** (tel. 305/595–1885) has a franchise in the Miami area.

Hints for Disabled Travelers

The Information Center for Individuals with Disabilities (20 Park Plaza, Room 330, Boston, MA 02116, tel. 617/727–5540) offers useful problem-solving assistance, including lists of travel agents that specialize in tours for the disabled.
Moss Rehabilitation Hospital Travel Information Service (12th St. and Taber Rd., Philadelphia, PA 19141, tel. 215/329–5715) provides information on tourist sights, transportation, and accommodations in destinations around the world. The fee is $5 for each destination. Allow one month for delivery.
Mobility International (Box 3551, Eugene, OR 97403, tel. 503/343–1284) has information on accommodations, organized study, and so forth.
The Society for the Advancement of Travel for the Handicapped (26 Court St., Penthouse Suites, Brooklyn, NY 11242, tel. 718/858–5483) offers access information. Annual membership costs $40, or $25 for senior travelers and students. Send $1 and a stamped, self-addressed envelope.
The Itinerary (Box 1084, Bayonne, NJ 07002, tel. 201/858–3400) is a bimonthly travel magazine for the disabled.
Access to the World: A Travel Guide for the Handicapped, by Louise Weiss, is useful but out of date. Available from Facts on File (460 Park Ave. S, New York, NY 10016, tel. 212/683–2244).
Frommer's Guide for Disabled Travelers is also useful but dated.
"Information/Referral Numbers for Physically Challenged Visitors" is a useful booklet available without charge from the Florida Bureau of Visitor Services (101 E. Gaines St., Fletcher Bldg., Room 422, Tallahassee 32399, tel. 904/488–7300).
Greyhound/Trailways (tel. 800/531–5332) will carry a disabled person and companion for the price of a single fare. Amtrak (tel. 800/USA–RAIL) requests 24-hour notice to provide redcap service, special seats, and a 25% discount.

Hints for Older Travelers

The **American Association of Retired Persons** (AARP, 1909 K St. NW, Washington, DC 20049, tel. 202/662–4850) has two programs for independent travelers: (1) The Purchase Privilege Program, which offers discounts on hotels, airfare, car rentals, and sightseeing, and (2) the AARP Motoring Plan, which offers emergency aid and trip-routing information for an annual fee of $29.95 per couple. The AARP also arranges group tours, including apartment living in Europe, through two companies: Olson-Travelworld (5855 Green Valley Circle, Culver City, CA 90230, tel. 800/227–7737) and RFD, Inc. (4401 West 110th St., Overland Park, KS 66211, tel. 800/448–7010). AARP members must be 50 or older. Annual dues are $5 per person or per couple.

When using an AARP or other identification card, ask for a reduced hotel rate at the time you make your reservation, not when you check out. At restaurants, show your card to the maître d' before you're seated, because discounts may be limited to certain set menus, days, or hours. When renting a car, remember that economy cars, priced at promotional rates, may cost less than cars that are available with your ID card.

Travel Industry and Disabled Exchange (TIDE, 5435 Donna Ave., Tarzana, CA 91356, tel. 818/343–6339) is an industry-based organization with a $15-per-person annual membership fee. Members receive a quarterly newsletter and information on travel agencies and tours.

National Council of Senior Citizens (925 15th St. NW, Washington, DC 20005, tel. 202/347–8800) is a nonprofit advocacy group with some 4,000 local clubs across the country. Annual membership is $10 per person or $14 per couple. Members receive a monthly newspaper with travel information and an ID card for reduced-rate hotels and car rentals.

Mature Outlook (Box 1205, Glenview, IL 60025, tel. 800/336–6330), a subsidiary of Sears Roebuck & Co., is a travel club for people over 50, with hotel and motel discounts and a bimonthly newsletter. Annual membership is $7.50 per couple. Instant membership is available at participating Holiday Inns.

"Travel Tips for Senior Citizens" (U.S. Dept. of State Publication 8970, revised Sept. 1987) is available for $1 from the Superintendent of Documents (U.S. Government Printing Office, Washington, DC 20402).

Golden Age Passport is a free lifetime pass to all parks, monuments, and recreation areas run by the federal government. People over 62 should pick one up in person at any national park that charges admission. A driver's license or other proof of age is required.

Although Florida probably attracts more elderly people than any other state, the state publishes no booklet addressed directly to senior citizens.

Senior-citizen discounts are common throughout Florida, but there are no set standards. Some discounts, like those for prescriptions at the Eckerd Drug chain, require that you fill out a card and register. The best bet is simply to ask whether there is a senior-citizen discount available on your purchase, meal, or hotel stay.

Further Reading

Suspense novels that are rich in details about Florida include Elmore Leonard's *La Brava*, John D. MacDonald's *The Empty Copper Sea*, and Joan Higgins's *A Little Death Music*. Pat Frank's *Alas Babylon* describes a fictional nuclear disaster in Florida.

Marjorie K. Rawlings's classic, *The Yearling*, poignantly portrays life in the brush country, and her *Cross Creek* re-creates the memorable people the author knew from 13 years of living at Cross Creek.

Look for *Snow White and Rose Red* and *Jack and the Beanstalk*, Ed McBain's novels about Matthew Hope, an attorney who practices law in a Florida gulf city. Pat Booth's novel *Palm Beach* describes the glittering Palm Beach scene of sun and sex.

Other recommended novels include Evelyn Mayerson's *No Enemy But Time; To Have and Have Not*, by Ernest Hemingway; *The Day of the Dolphin*, by Robert Merle; and *Their Eyes Were Watching God*, by Zora Neale Hurston, a tale of life in a black town in northern Florida.

Among the recommended nonfiction books are *Key West Writers and Their Homes,* Lynn Kaufelt's tour of homes of Hemingway, Wallace Stevens, Tennessee Williams, and others; *The Everglades: River of Grass,* by Marjory S. Douglas; *Florida,* by Gloria Jahoda, published as part of the Bicentennial observance; *Miami Alive,* by Ethel Blum; and *Florida's Sandy Beaches,* University Press of Florida.

Getting to Florida

By Plane

Most major U.S. airlines schedule regular flights into Florida, and some, such as Delta, serve the Florida airports extensively.

Delta, Eastern, and Piedmont all have regular service into Jacksonville, Daytona Beach, Orlando, Melborne, West Palm Beach, Fort Lauderdale, Miami, Fort Meyers, Tampa, Tallahassee, Gainesville, and Key West. Delta also flies into Sarasota, Naples, Pensacola, and Fort Pierce.

Other major airlines that serve the Florida airports include Continental, American, USAir, American Trans Air, Northwest, Pan Am, United, and TWA. Many foreign airlines also fly into some of the major airports in Florida; the smaller, out-of-the-way airports are usually accessible through the commuter flights of major domestic carriers.

Packages that combine airfare and vacation activities at special rates are often available through the airlines. For example, Delta (tel. 800/872–7786) and Pan Am (tel. 800/221–1111) both offer travel packages to Disney World in Orlando (*see* Package Deals for Independent Travelers).

When booking reservations, keep in mind the distinction between nonstop flights (no stops and no changes), direct flights (no changes of aircraft, but one or more stops), and connecting flights (one or more changes of planes at one or more stops). Connecting flights are often the least expensive, but they are the most time-consuming, and the biggest nuisance.

Smoking If cigarette smoke bothers you, request a seat *far away from* the smoking section. Remember, FAA regulations require airlines to find seats for all nonsmokers.

Carry-on Luggage Under new rules in effect since January 1988, passengers are usually limited to two carry-on bags. For bags stored under your seat, the maximum dimensions are 9″ × 14″ × 22″, a total of 45″. For bags that can be hung in a closet, the maximum dimensions are 4″ × 23″ × 45″, a total of 72″. For bags stored in an overhead bin, the maximum dimensions are 10″ × 14″ × 36″, a total of 60″. Any item that exceeds the specified dimensions will generally be rejected as a carry-on and handled as checked baggage. Keep in mind that an airline can adapt these rules to circumstances; on an especially crowded flight, don't be surprised if you are allowed only one carry-on bag.

In addition to the two bags, passengers may also carry aboard: a handbag (pocketbook or purse), an overcoat or wrap, an umbrella, a camera, a reasonable amount of reading material, an infant bag, crutches, cane, braces, or other prosthetic device upon which the passenger is dependent, and an infant/child safety seat.

Note that these regulations are for U.S. airlines only. Foreign airlines generally allow one piece of carry-on luggage in tourist class, in addition to handbags and bags filled with duty-free goods. Passengers in first and business class are also allowed to carry on one garment bag. It is best to check with your airline ahead of time to find out what their exact rules are regarding carry-on luggage.

Checked Luggage U.S. airlines allow passengers to check in two suitcases whose total dimensions (length + width + height) do not exceed 60″. There are no weight restrictions on these bags.

Rules governing foreign airlines vary from airline to airline, so check with your travel agent or the airline itself before you go. All the airlines allow passengers to check in two bags. In general, expect the weight restriction on the two bags to be not more than 70 pounds each, the size restriction on the first bag to be 62″ total dimensions, and that on the second bag to be 55″ total dimensions.

Lost Luggage On domestic flights, airlines are responsible for lost or damaged property only up to $1,250 per passenger. If you're carrying valuables, either take them with you on the airplane or purchase additional insurance for lost luggage. Some airlines will issue additional luggage insurance when you check in, but many do not. Insurance for lost, damaged, or stolen luggage is available through travel agents or directly through various insurance companies. Two that issue luggage insurance are **Tele-Trip** (tel. 800/228–9792), a subsidiary of Mutual of Omaha, and **The Travelers Insurance Co.** (Ticket and Travel Dept., 1 Tower Sq., Hartford, CT 06183, tel. 800/243–0191). Tele-Trip operates sales booths at airports, and it also issues insurance through travel agents. Tele-Trip will insure checked luggage for up to 180 days at $500–$3,000 valuation. For 1–3 days, the rate for a $500 valuation is $8.25; for 180 days, $100. The Travelers Insurance Co. will insure checked or hand luggage at $500–$2,000 valuation per person, also for a maximum of 180 days. Rates for 1–5 days for $500 valuation are $10; for 180 days, $85.

Other companies with comprehensive policies include **Access America Inc.**, a subsidiary of Blue Cross-Blue Shield (Box 807, New York, NY 10163, tel. 800/851–2800); **Near, Inc.** (1900 N. MacArthur Blvd., Suite 210, Oklahoma City, OK 73127, tel. 800/654–6700); and **Travel Guard International** (*see* Health and Accident Insurance).

Before you go, itemize the contents of each bag in case you need to file an insurance claim. Be certain to put your home address on each piece of luggage, including carry-on bags. If your luggage is stolen and later recovered, the airline must deliver the luggage to your home free of charge.

By Car

Three major interstates lead to Florida from various parts of the country. I–95 begins in Maine, runs south through New England and the Mid-Atlantic states, and enters Florida just north of Jacksonville. It continues south through Daytona

Beach, Vero Beach, Palm Beach, and Fort Lauderdale, eventually ending in Miami.

I–75 begins at the Canadian border in Michigan and runs south through Ohio, Kentucky, Tennessee, and Georgia before entering Florida. The interstate moves through the center of the state before veering west into Tampa. It follows the west coast for a time before turning inland and ending in Miami.

California and all the most southern states are connected to Florida by I–10. This interstate originates in Los Angeles and moves east through Arizona, New Mexico, Texas, Louisiana, Mississippi, and Alabama before entering Florida at Pensacola on the west coast. I–10 continues straight across the northern half of the state until it terminates in Jacksonville.

Speed Limits In Florida the speed limits are 55 mph on the state highways, 30 mph within city limits and residential areas, 55–65 mph on the interstates. These limits may vary, so be sure to watch road signs for any changes.

By Train

Amtrak (tel. 800/USA–RAIL) provides service to Orlando, Tampa, Miami, Tallahassee, Jacksonville, and several other major cities in Florida.

By Bus

Greyhound–Trailways passes through practically every major city in Florida, including Jacksonville, Daytona, Orlando, West Palm Beach, Fort Lauderdale, Miami, Sarasota, Tampa, Tallahassee, and Key West. For information about bus schedules and fares, contact your local Greyhound Information Center.

Staying in Florida

Shopping

For the souvenir seeker or the serious shopper, Florida has something for practically everyone. Following is a list of some of the items most sought after by visitors.

Indian Artifacts Indian crafts are abundant and often low priced, particularly in the southern part of the state, where you'll find billowing dresses, hand-sewn in striking colors and designs. At the Miccosukee Indian Village, 25 miles west of Miami on the Tamiami Trail (U.S. 41), as well as at the Seminole and Miccosukee reservations in the Everglades, you can also find handcrafted dolls, wall hangings, and beaded belts and shirts.

Seashells Seashells and the shops that sell them are seemingly everywhere in Florida. At most of the shops the art objects made from the shells are largely kitsch. The serious collector, however, can make some real finds at Sanibel Island, off Fort Myers.

The Shell Factory and Malacological Museum near Fort Myers, on North Tamiami Trail (U.S. 41), claims to be the largest shop in the world.

Citrus Fruits Wherever you travel in Florida, you are sure to see sacks of oranges and grapefruits to buy or ship to friends and relatives.

Most of these roadside places offer free, freshly squeezed orange juice while you are selecting your purchase—even if you end up buying nothing. From winter to late spring is the best time to buy; most of the shippers are closed for the summer.

The fruit is less expensive around the Orlando area, where the roads are lined with citrus groves. If you're sending fruit to friends, the shipping cost is figured into the total price. At some places, you can also handpick the fruit, and the grove will ship it for you. If you are flying home and want to take sacks of fruit with you, check them in with your luggage. Just make sure your name tag is on each sack, for many passengers will be carrying fruit of their own.

Malls and Boutiques The Greater Miami area has shops ranging from designer boutiques to discount houses. Many of the boutiques are located at luxurious specialty malls like Mayfair, Bal Harbour Shops, and the Falls. Discount Shops on Flagler Street in downtown Miami are crowded with international visitors in search of bargains in cameras, electronics, and jewelry.

Designer shops along Fort Lauderdale's fashionable Las Olas Boulevard are helping that city to change its image from home base for raucous college students on spring break to a more sophisticated urban center. To the north is Palm Beach and its renowned Worth Avenue, still one of the finest shopping streets in the world. Here, you'll find designer names, such as Gucci and Ralph Lauren, tucked alongside galleries selling ancient Chinese art or Oriental rugs, gourmet restaurants, one-of-a-kind jewelry stores, and chocolatiers.

On the west coast, Tampa Bay and environs can boast of specialty shops along St. Armand's Circle in Sarasota and fine clothing and boating shops along Beach Drive in St. Petersburg. Nautical and Greek souvenirs and art can be found at the fishing village of nearby Tarpon Springs.

North, along the Panhandle, Pensacola's Quayside Thieves Market offers fine antiques as well as a flea market. Seville Square, in Pensacola, is also a good place to shop for crafts, fine gifts, and specialty foods.

Antiques and Souvenirs Some of the best—and certainly most interesting—antique shopping is found in old St. Augustine, whose streets and alleys still look a bit as they did when it became Florida's first permanent settlement. There's the fine Antiques Mall in the Lightner Museum, as well as many craft shops in the city's Historic District.

In the center of the state, most good buys are found in the Orlando area. At Disney World, you can find everything from souvenirs to fine gifts. Orlando's North Orange Avenue has been transformed into Antique Row by the growth of shops along that thoroughfare.

Other interesting shops? Satisfy your sweet tooth with candy made from pure citrus juice at Davidson of Dundee (near Orlando) or with honey from Honey Bee Observatory in Fort Meyers. Check out the Key West Fragrance/Cosmetic Factory; buy sponges in Tarpon Springs or cigars hand-rolled by Cubans at factories in Tampa or Miami; or go to Fowlers in Coral Gables and have them pack stone crabs in ice for the flight home.

Beaches

Beaches are synonymous with Florida. In a state with an 8,000-mile coastline and a peninsula that's seldom wider than 150 miles, you're never far away from a beach. Even in the largest cities—except for inland Orlando—you're usually only a 15- or 20-minute drive from white sands and blue waters.

One beach in particular—Miami Beach—is what made Florida famous as a tourist destination. Developers discovered that attraction shortly after Miami Beach, a man-made island, was dredged out of the Atlantic in the 1920s. Miami Beach has 10 miles of beach, all replenished and broadened in the past few years under a multimillion-dollar beach-nourishment project.

However, Miami Beach is no longer the only beach that visitors frequent. Just a bit up the Atlantic coast, for instance, are the beaches of Fort Lauderdale's "Strips," made famous (or infamous?) by the *Where the Boys Are* movie and sequels of the 1960s. Many of the boys—and girls—have since gone to other Florida beach towns, especially Daytona Beach, to enjoy their spring break from college studies.

About 100 miles north along the Atlantic coast is quiet Marin County, home of the Hutchinson Island beaches. Here, white-sand oases backed by tall Florida pines make these beaches favorites for families as well as for young singles.

On the Gulf coast, Pinellas County boasts the most beaches in the state, with 28 miles of soft white sand and 128 miles of shoreline. Particularly popular, too, are the white beaches of Sanibel and Captiva islands, two thin islands off the Fort Myers coast, that offer the best shelling in the state.

In the Panhandle, you'll find another kind of beach—the dune beach created by crisp Gulf breezes that occasionally blow the sand into dunes. Here, the beach may be more suitable to beachcombing than to bathing. The Florida Keys, too, disappoint many visitors with their lack of great beaches. The Keys are more conducive to sailing and game-fishing.

Most of the state's beaches are public. Access to some, however —particularly those fronting on hotels—is private. But if your hotel doesn't front on a beach and you don't mind a bit of a walk, you have the same right of space as the person next to you, who may be paying twice as much for an oceanfront hotel room.

Participant Sports

Bicycling Despite the flatness of most of the state (or because of it), cycling is enormously popular here. Although there are not as yet a large number of cycling trails, cyclists can wind along public roads or parks, and there are an increasing number of cycling events. Call a special number set up by the State Division of Tourism (tel. 904/488–4640) to request a list of biking trails.

Fishing People visit Florida from all over the world to try for the big ones off the coast. Stuart, about 120 miles north of Miami, bills itself as the "Sailfish Capital of the World," although you might find some argument about that from boosters of the central Keys. Dolphin, shark, wahoo, snapper, and pompano are just a few of the prizes found off the coast. Inland lakes, such as Lake Okeechobee, are dotted with a number of good fishing camps.

It's easy to find a boat-charter service that will take you out into deep water. Some of the best are found in the Panhandle, where small towns like Destin and Fort Walton Beach have huge fleets. The Keys, too, are dotted with charter services, and Key West has a sportfishing and shrimping fleet that you would expect to find in large cities. Depending on your taste, budget, and needs, you can charter anything from an old wooden craft to a luxurious, waterborne palace with state-of-the-art amenities.

Florida also has a number of public fishing piers that jut into the ocean; one of the most popular is Miami's Haulover Park Pier. The causeways and bridges leading into downtown Miami are also dotted with fishermen almost all day and long into the night.

Saltwater fishing anywhere in the state is free. A 10-day non-resident license for freshwater fishing costs $10, a year's license costs $25. The Florida Game and Freshwater Fish Commission (620 S. Meridian, Tallahassee 32399–1600, tel. 904/488–1960) will send you a list of regulations and a sportfishing guide.

Golf Wherever you choose to vacation in Florida, you'll never be very far from a golf course. The state is liberally sprinkled with public courses, and all the top resorts have either their own courses or access to neighboring ones. Among the most prominent private courses are those found in the popular tourist areas of Miami and Palm Beach on the east coast, between Sarasota and the area north of Tampa on the west coast, and in the Jacksonville area in the north.

Hunting Florida is not known as a hunting mecca, partially because a number of its wild animals, such as the Florida panther, are on the Endangered Species List and are therefore protected. The Florida Game and Freshwater Fish Commission (620 S. Meridian, Tallahassee 32399, tel. 904/488–1960) will send you the *Florida Hunting Handbook* and a list of regulations.

Tennis This is an immensely popular sport throughout Florida. All the top resorts and many other hotels have their own courts or guest privileges at nearby clubs. There are many public courts, along with schoolyards and public parks (*see* individual chapters for details).

Jogging Most large cities or counties have parks or running courses, but Floridians themselves aren't choosy. You'll see them jogging in the big-city streets as well as in the most bucolic parks (for jogging trails, see individual chapters).

State and National Parks

Fittingly for such a large state, Florida has 105 state parks, ranging from bucolic green forests to white-sand seashores. Admission is $1 for the driver, and 50 cents per passenger. For information, write for the *State Parks Brochure*, Department of Commerce, Florida Division of Tourism (101 E. Gaines St., Fletcher Bldg., Room 404, Tallahassee 32399, tel. 904/487–1462).

There are four national parks, three national seashores, and three national forests, each with different admission prices. Information booklets are available from the National Park

Service, S.E. Archaeological Center (Box 2416, Tallahassee 32316, tel. 904/222–1167).

Among the most popular of the state parks are those in the Keys, particularly **John Pennekamp State Park** on Key Largo and **Bahia Honda State Park** on Bahia Honda Key. The former has some of the best diving conditions around, along with a living coral reef, and the latter offers picnic areas and every conceivable kind of water sport. There are two good parks in the Panhandle, **Big Lagoon** and **Torreya.** Northern Florida residents and visitors enjoy **Ichetucknee State Park** near Gainesville and **Fort Clinch State Park** in the Fernandina Beach area. Well known in Central Florida is **Blue Springs State Park.**

The biggest in the state is **Everglades National Park,** hundreds of square miles of some of the most fascinating and primeval wilderness in the United States. **Biscayne National Park** is another south Florida attraction, while **Canaveral National Seashore,** south of Jacksonville, features the Cape Canaveral Space Center nearby. **Gulf Islands National Seashore,** near Pensacola in the Panhandle, offers visitors picturesque serenity.

Dining

Besides the Continental, ethnic, and American cuisines found here and in practically every other state, Florida has its own three distinctive cuisines—Cracker, Cuban/Spanish, and, simply, Floridian.

The Cracker influence is prevalent in the north and in the Panhandle, where you'll find fried catfish and frogs' legs on many menus. Cracker cookin' is inexpensive, plentiful, and down-home good eatin'.

Cuban/Spanish restaurants number in the hundreds in the Miami area, and they are also found in the Ybor City section of Tampa. They feature a long list of wonderful specialties—plantains, black beans and rice, *arroz con pollo* (chicken with rice), pork dishes, and the legendary paella, a mixture of meats, poultry, fish, and vegetables atop a mound of yellow rice, which generally takes 45 minutes to prepare.

Floridian food can best be described as those subtropical specialties that most people identify with the state: stone crabs (Joe's Stone Crab Restaurant in Miami Beach is the world's most famous place for this dish), conch (pronounced "konk") chowder, fritters, or salad, made from a large shellfish with a unique flavor, and Key-lime pie.

Each south Florida restaurant claims to make the best Key-lime pie. Pastry chefs and restaurant managers take their Key-lime pie seriously; they discuss the problems of getting good lime juice and maintaining top quality every day. Traditional Key-lime pie is yellow, not green, and has an old-fashioned graham cracker crust. The pie should be tart, and should be chilled but not frozen. In some parts of Florida, Key-lime pie is served with a meringue; elsewhere, eggs are beaten into the pie. Each will be a little different. Make your own choice.

Fresh seafood, of course, can be found throughout the state.

Ratings

Category	Cost*: Major City	Cost*: Other Areas
Very Expensive	over $50	over $40
Expensive	$30–$50	$25–$40
Moderate	$15–$30	$10–$25
Inexpensive	under $15	under $10

**per person, without wine, 6% state sales taxes, or tip*

Lodging

Hotels All the major chains—Sheraton, Hilton, Holiday Inn, Marriott, Ramada, Hyatt—are represented in Florida, especially in major cities and in tourist areas like Disney World. The state also has numerous luxurious resort properties, which are not part of chains and offer just about the best of everything, from cuisine to recreation. Many of the finer resorts offer suites or cottages.

Motels All the major motel chains are represented in the state, from strict-budget places like Motel 6 to the ever-present Days Inn, many of which have the amenities of some hotels. For a comprehensive listing of the major motels and hotels throughout the state, contact the Florida Department of Commerce, Division of Tourism (101 E. Gaines St., Fletcher Bldg., Room 104, Tallahassee 32399–2000, tel. 904/487–1462).

Camping and RV Facilities For a description of state park facilities (electrical and water hookups, etc.), request a free copy of the *State Parks Brochure* from the Florida Department of Commerce, Division of Tourism (101 E. Gaines St., Fletcher Bldg., Room 104, Tallahassee 32399, tel. 904/487–1462).

Ratings

Category	Cost*: Major City	Cost*: Other Areas
Very Expensive	$150 peak season $100 off-peak	$100
Expensive	$120–$150 peak season $80–$100 off-peak	$70–$100
Moderate	$80–$120 peak season $50–$80 off-peak	$40–$70
Inexpensive	under $80 peak season under $50 off-peak	under $40

**per room, double occupancy, without 6% sales tax and nominal (1%–3%) tourist tax*

Interval Ownership Vacation "Interval ownership vacation" means investing a few thousand dollars, paid in monthly installments, for a resort condominium apartment or hotel room for a specified period of vacation time—anything from one week to one month every year. Florida is the worldwide leader of the interval ownership condominium phenomenon. The two specialists are Interval International of Miami (7000 S.W. 62nd Ave., Miami 33143, tel. 305/666–1861) and Resort Condominiums International (4901 N.W. 17th Way, Ft. Lauderdale 33309, tel. 305/491–1342). Among the resort hotels and condominiums that offer this vacation concept are the Longboat Bay Club and White Sands, Longboat Key; Vistana and Resort World, Orlando; Eagles Nest, Marco Island; Plantation Beach Club, Hutchinson Island; Tierre Verde Resort (near St. Petersburg); Bayshore Yacht and Tennis Club, Indian Shores (near St. Petersburg Beach); Penthouse Beach Club, Treasure Island; and Sanibel Beach Club I and II, Lighthouse Resort, Tortuga Beach Club, Casa Ybel, and Kahlua Beach Club, all on Sanibel Island, off Fort Myers.

2 Portraits of Florida

In Search of the Real Florida

by April Athey

A freelance writer based in Tallahassee, April Athey has been writing about her home state for magazines and newspapers since 1977. Her work has appeared in many publications, including the New York Times, Chicago Tribune, Christian Science Monitor, Frequent Flyer, *and* Gulfshore Life.

It's hard to imagine a Florida without a magic kingdom, a spaceport to the stars, interstate highways, or high-rise beachfront hotels. But such a Florida exists, and today the state's natural and historical treasures are being imitated, refurbished, restored, and recognized for their lasting appeal.

Even the state's leader in family entertainment—Walt Disney World—is imitating and popularizing Old Florida with its new Grand Floridian Beach Resort, featuring gabled roofs and Victorian balustrades that were typical of Florida's turn-of-the-century beach resorts. Disney officials say the resort recalls the days when John D. Rockefeller, Thomas Edison, and even President Theodore Roosevelt led the annual winter pilgrimage to Florida's warm shores.

There are those who recall the day when Walt Disney World's fantasy lands and futuristic hotels opened in 1971, setting a technological standard in entertainment that may still be unrivaled. The owners of natural attractions like Silver Springs, Weeki Wachee, and Homosassa Springs struggled to keep the attention of technology-hungry Americans. The lush jungle-lined rivers, exotic wildlife, and crystal-clear spring waters somehow paled in contrast to the make-believe, never-a-dull-moment amusements for which the Disney corporation had become famous. The convenience of a one-stop, no-surprise vacation apparently made real wilderness cruises, beaches, wildlife, and historical attractions passé.

To see and appreciate the real thing, one had to leave the interstate highways and brave a few side roads. Because not many tourists cared to take the road less traveled, many owners of natural attractions were forced to expand their offerings with man-made amusements. If budgets weren't sweet enough to permit this sort of commercialization, the attractions (usually the lesser-known botanical gardens, great homes, and wildlife reserves) saw lean years.

Fortunately, the cycle is coming full circle. Technology-harassed Americans are now looking for the good old days, and Florida is obliging them.

Today, developers of new resorts are focusing attention on the Florida of the 19th century. New resorts not only imitate Old Florida architecture but also, through their landscaping, recall when the only silhouettes scraping Florida's sky were of stout cabbage palms, mossy oaks, towering cypress, and hardy evergreens.

Maintaining the ecological integrity of the land and its often-endangered inhabitants has become an increasing concern of developers. The Grand Cypress Resort in Orlando was designed to be complemented by a stand of native cypress, and the Registry Resort in Naples nestles at the edge of a 1,000-acre nature preserve, through which a $1-million boardwalk was built to provide access to the beach and protection for the delicate sand dunes.

St. Augustine is the oldest permanent European settlement in the United States—with an extensive historic district to prove it—and was the first Florida resort popularized by Henry Flagler when he brought his Florida East Coast Railroad and friends south for the winter. Key West was the last resort Flagler helped build. His Casa Marina hotel still stands, having been restored and expanded under management by Marriott. The island's "conch houses" also are being restored, and many have been converted into guest houses and restaurants. Flagler also put Palm Beach and its sister, West Palm Beach, on the map. Though his original wooden hotels burned to the ground, his private estate is now the Flagler Museum.

Sharing space with the glinting glass of skyscrapers are the castlelike villas and Old Florida-style homes of former Florida residents. You can tour Ca'd'Zan, the bayside villa that John Ringling and his wife Mable built, which now is part of the Ringling Museums Complex in Sarasota. Like an oasis in the middle of Miami's asphalt-and-concrete desert, the palatial bay-front estate of John Deering, with its formal gardens and surrounding natural jungles (Vizcaya Museum and Gardens), may be toured daily. Visit Thomas Edison's Winter Home in Fort Myers, and dine out on Cabbage Key, the tiny island accessible by boat (offshore from Captiva)—the retreat of mystery writer Mary Roberts Rinehart. Ormond Beach has reminders of its heyday, when John D. Rockefeller and friends made the riverfront Ormond Hotel a world-renowned wintering spot. Rockefeller eventually built his winter home, The Casements, across the street from the hotel, and both still stand proudly by the shores of the Halifax River, just north of Daytona Beach. The Casements is now an art museum and site of an annual antique-auto show.

Fort Jefferson, the Civil War island fortress on which Samuel Mudd—the physician who treated Lincoln's assassin—was imprisoned, is only a seaplane flight away from tropical Key West. On Key West are the 19th-century fortifications—East and West Martello Towers—one now home to the city's historical museum, and the other the setting of the garden club. Recently excavated and open to the public on Key West is Fort Zachary Taylor. Living-history interpretations are conducted daily at Fort Clinch, a Civil War fortress in Fernandina Beach, and at Fort Foster in Hillsborough State Park, just west of Tampa. Speaking of Tampa, the next time you order a rum and Coke, remember that the concoction was invented there by Teddy Roosevelt's Rough Riders.

In addition to the monuments of recent history, there are the archaeological reminders of Florida's first residents, the aboriginal Indians who greeted European explorers and expatriates. Several state parks preserve treasured archaeological sites, like Hontoon Island on the St. Johns River, Tomoka River State Park, near Daytona Beach (both sites of Timucuan Indian settlements), and Jonathan Dickinson State Park, near the Palm Beaches (site of a Quaker shipwreck and their subsequent imprisonment by Jaega Indians).

These and later Indians left their place names as a lasting legacy—names like Ichetucknee (now a tubing river north of Gainesville), Pensacola, Apalachicola, Tequesta, Kissimmee, Chassahowitzka (a national wildlife refuge near Homosassa Springs), Okeechobee (a 590-square-mile inland lake), Ocala, and Tallahassee (the state capital).

Victorian homes with gingerbread-trimmed wrap-around verandas, shaded by sloping tin roofs, are being restored and operated as bed-and-breakfast inns or chic restaurants. Check out K. C. Crump on the River in Homosassa Springs, near Ocala in Central Florida, a posh new restaurant in a restored, turn-of-the-century homestead. In Ocala, the newest B&B is the Seven Sisters Inn, which serves gourmet fare. Florida's B&Bs have increased from an estimated five in 1980 to more than 50 in 1988.

Main Street programs are flourishing throughout the state, revitalizing the business/entertainment districts of towns like Winter Park, Orlando, DeLand, and Quincy (in northwest Florida).

Historic hotels and inns, once threatened by wrecking crews, are living new lives. Check out the Heritage in St. Petersburg, a restored, 60-year-old hotel (the original Florida "cracker" home in the backyard now serves as an atrium-greenhouse bar); or book a weekend at Apalachicola's 100-year-old Gibson Inn.

Waterfront redevelopment projects like Miami's Bayside and Jacksonville Landing (Rouse Marketplace developments) are focusing fresh attention on the inlets and bays that once harbored renegade pirates and adventurous pioneers.

Quiet waterfront hamlets, built during the boom in steamboat travel—Sanford and Crescent City are good examples—are beginning to blossom again with the reemergence of riverboat cruising.

Wildlife and wilderness, once overlooked in favor of make-believe amusements, are once again attracting awed attention. In response, Silver Springs turned back the clock with a complete Victorian redesign.

Oddly enough, it may be easier to find an Old Florida vacation experience now than it was 20 years ago.

Though serving to popularize Old Florida, newcomers and their artful imitations are no substitutes for the real thing. The wilderness, wildlife, and historic homes and resorts are already here to enjoy.

Washed by both the Gulf of Mexico and the Atlantic Ocean, Florida seems to be more water than land. Underground freshwater rivers course through the limestone bedrock of its north and central highlands, often boiling to the surface and flowing overland to the sea. A bird's-eye view reveals a peninsula whose upper reaches are dotted and crisscrossed by hundreds of lakes and streams and whose ragged southern borders are home to a vast, shallow river of grass called the Everglades and a maze of mangrove clumps called the Ten Thousand Islands. From the town of Everglades City, on Florida's southwest tip, sightseeing boats meander through the maze of islands, and just off the Tamiami Trail (U.S. 41), on the north-central boundary of Everglades National Park, you can climb the observation deck at Shark Valley Overlook for a good look at the river of grass.

This view, perhaps more than anything, helps to remind people of what Floridians are trying to recapture.

The Florida Scrub

by Al Burt

A roving writer-columnist for The Miami Herald *for the past 15 years, Al Burt specializes in Florida's history, natural habitat, and future. He has written two books on the state—* Becalmed in the Mullet Latitudes *and* Florida: A Place in the Sun. *In 1974, Burt left Miami's city life to make his base in his beloved Scrub Country, near Melrose in north Florida.*

Understanding Florida requires at least some knowledge of the historic Scrub Country, the oldest, the driest, the harshest, and, in some ways, the most delicate part of the state. In water-loving Florida, the Scrub struggles to remain a desert outlaw.

If you have ever walked a beach and observed how the tides and the wind have rolled the sterile sands into a long, graceful dune on which grow a few scraggly, scratchy plants, you may have gotten some idea about Florida's unique Scrub Country and its peculiar beauty.

The Scrub, which once covered most of Florida with bone-dry sandhills, is the legitimate kin to a desert, and it's full of puzzles. The life forms there are persistent, thrifty, and fragile. Once, you could look across the low profile of its vegetation and see odd "islands" of fertility, little oases of tall trees and green life, while all around was the stunted, prickly, vulnerable Scrub growth. They were like oddly matched siblings of nature, growing up side by side, but, by freakish accident, one had been denied its vitamins.

The name came from an early and natural lack of appreciation. It was scrubby country, not like the scenic Florida of the travel books. Except in those "islands," it lacked the towering slash pines and the comfortable shade of large-crowned live oaks and the open landscapes beneath. The Scrub was a place unto itself, with few easy pleasures, and it was not good for conventional farming.

Loving the Scrub came easiest if you grew up with it, if it came naturally to you. Sometimes it became a fierce, protective thing, like a stubbornly loyal Cracker Mama who adored the scrawniest of her children most because it was the misfit.

Flooding rains leached quickly through Scrub sands and left them dry as ever. Rosemary bushes, prickly pears, saw palmettos, sand pines, sandburs, gnarled dwarf oaks, and other scraggly little trees commonly grew there.

The deep sand made it difficult to walk with shoes on. The sands in summer burned the soles of bare feet with temperatures of 135–140 degrees. Everything in the Scrub seemed to scratch and claw at you, fighting for life.

Rattlesnakes loved it. Exotic little creatures (in addition to raccoons, bobcats, and deer), some of them now rare and endangered, made it home—scrub jays, lizards, skinks, gopher frogs and gopher tortoises, exotic mice, red widow spiders, and such.

For years, big patches of the Scrub Country, especially if they were inland and off the main tracks, lay abandoned. If they attracted anyone, it was likely to be the young, who sometimes found the sandhills great places for exploring or play, sliding down them, burrowing into them, and holding beer parties and buggy chases on the tricky sand.

The Scrub did not rebound easily from such use, but nobody cared. The track of a jeep across virgin scrub vegetation might take unaided nature years to erase. That was minor compared with what else happened in the history of the Scrub.

It began when Florida began. The Scrub probably was the first part of Florida to emerge from the ocean, geologists say. Its dunes or sandhills formed under pressures of wind and tides as the ocean levels rose and fell during the ice ages. Great, irregular ridges took shape, almost like terraces. Time altered them into graceful sandhills.

The original Scrub Country became the Central Highlands of Florida, which stretches from east of Gainesville in the north-central part of the state south for some 200 miles and flatten out into the prairies of Lake Okeechobee. In places, the elevation reaches 300 feet.

For Florida, those great sandhills became Sierra Citrus, center of one of its greatest trademark industries. The well-drained Scrub lands were easily cleared and were perfect for oranges—once the growers added fertilizers and artificial irrigation.

You can ride that ridge today in one of the state's most scenic inland drives and imagine the beginning. U.S. 27, a fine highway, rolls up and down those great sandhills, past a series of lakes, along the fringes of Disney World country, and through miles and miles of green and seasonally fragrant citrus groves. (Even though the freezes of recent winters blighted many of them, the scene remains impressive.)

Like smaller versions of the Central Highlands, lesser dunes trailed away to the ocean. All had similar characteristics, but closer to the coast there were subtle changes, particularly if they were close enough to get the windblown ocean spray.

The dunes and the life on them also differed in their northern stretches, where the climate was temperate and subject to more seasonal changes than in southern Florida. In the south, the influence of the Gulf Stream and the more prominent crosswinds from the gulf and the ocean produced an exotic subtropical climate.

Scrub Country was high ground. Water did not collect there, but in strategic or special places development did, especially along the coast. Around the turn of the century, Henry Flagler built his pioneering railroad partially on a high dune ridge running down the east coast. Then he opened up cities like Palm Beach, Miami and eventually Key West to tourists and development.

For the most part, the Scrub Country was an ugly duckling among Florida real estate developers. Many wanted to use it as raw material or take advantage of its special location, but few perceived it as anything that was uniquely beautiful or valuable in itself. As a result, 90% or more of this original Florida scene no longer exists.

The sand, some of it as fine as sugar, was mined for construction materials. Great areas were leveled for shopping centers and other development. Subdivisions turned dune ripples into square blocks of cottages. Water was piped in, and developers covered these desert sands with St. Augustine grass.

Except for exploiters, the Scrub Country had few advocates. The most notable of them was the writer, Marjorie Kinnan

Rawlings, an easterner. Rawlings's work elevated one area of the Scrub into legend.

In 1928, Rawlings fled the rigors of newspaper life in Rochester, NY, and settled in an old Cracker house by an orange grove in an unlikely little village oasis called Cross Creek. She sought inspiration in isolation and frontier surroundings. The creek (between Ocala and Gainesville) was a lane of water connecting two large lakes in north-central Florida.

Her love of the creek and its people expanded to the areas nearby, which included a significant piece of Scrub Country known locally as the Big Scrub. To enrich her knowledge of it, she lived for a while with a family in the Scrub, hunted there, and befriended the Crackers who chose it as a place to live.

Rawlings's novels, particularly *The Yearling,* which won the Pulitzer Prize and then was made into a popular movie, realistically acknowledged but nevertheless romanticized the Big Scrub. She depicted the impoverished Crackers as primitives who lived by their own code—a code that she clearly thought had a noble base.

Rawlings gave the Big Scrub and Florida's Scrub Country a national identity. Within the past few years, her book of essays on Cross Creek and a short story entitled "Gal Young 'Un" also were made into well-received movies. Those films renewed and enlarged Rawlings's loving images of the Cross Creek area and the Big Scrub. Since then, the importance of the Scrub as a unique plant and animal habitat has been recognized. Many scientists and conservationists have dedicated themselves to its study and preservation.

Rawlings's books became especially significant because the largest remaining area of Scrub left in Florida, modified though it may be, is the one she idealized. It lies in the central and western portions of the 380,000-acre Ocala National Forest (a multiple-use forest that permits hunting and camping) and still is called the Big Scrub.

The Big Scrub contains the world's largest stand of sand pines. Many of them occur naturally, but, because in some areas the pines were planted in rows so neat that the natural poetry of the forest is altered, some have criticized it as a sand-pine plantation. In either case, both the pines and the patches of dunes, as close as the road shoulders, are visible from the car during a drive through the forest. The area illustrates how sand pines and other scrub vegetation, over time, tend to close and fill in an area, giving it a canopy above and a soil below slowly being altered by collections of natural forest debris, especially leaves, fallen limbs, and root systems. This cycle can change the natural characteristics of the Scrubs, unless fire (the sand pine is highly flammable) or timbering activities interfere. Even so, the Scrub retains its mysteries. Even the foresters cannot always predict with certainty that the Scrub cycle will begin again after a fire.

Most of Florida's Scrub Country is now scattered in bits and pieces around the state. You have to search and guess and inquire locally. Aside from the Ocala forest, a visitor can see examples of it in the Jonathan Dickinson State Park, 13 miles south of Stuart on U.S. 1.

In that same area, you may see from the highway a typical patch of surviving Scrub—a high roadside dune topped by a windswept sand pine, so stressed that it seems picturesquely oriental. The same sand pine, seen in the Ocala Forest, may grow bushy and erect and look like an ideal Christmas tree.

Finding examples of the Scrub elsewhere becomes a matter of travel and identification, of looking for inland dunes left untouched by development. Where there is a low, sandy hill there could be scrub. You can find areas of it down the east coast, from St. Augustine to West Palm Beach, in northeast Florida near the coast and along Rte. AIA, and there are some that sweep back off the Panhandle beaches in northwest Florida. Little of the scrub, however—except that in public parks—has tourist convenience for study and enjoyment. Even in the state and national forests, the sandy footing, the heat, and the numerous insects discourage all but the most hardy explorers.

At least two large tracts are being maintained for scientific research. The University of Florida owns several thousand acres of Scrub east of Gainesville, and the Archbold Biological Station (established in 1941) has 3,800 acres of distinctive Scrub near Lake Placid on the southern slope of the Central Highlands. These are not open for public roaming, however.

One good thing to remember is that, globally, Florida lies in the zone of the great deserts, including the Sahara, so the Scrub is not out of character. Florida began with those ocean sands that bleached into dunes and sandhills and then into the variety that visitors enjoy today.

Remembering the past explains a lot about the true nature of Florida, no matter how wet it looks right now. The Scrub Country reminds us that the makings of a desert are still there, waiting.

Miami Beach Art Deco

by Hap Hatton

Born and raised in Florida, Hap Hatton now lives in New York City, where he is in charge of still photography for PBS station WNET 13. His previous books include The Tent Book *and* The Virgin Homeowner's Handbook.

By 1910 Miami Beach had failed first as a coconut plantation, then as an avocado farm. Now it was being tried as a residential development. It took 10 years to create the present landmass. Carl Fisher, the Hoosier millionaire who financed much of the dredging and land-clearing, envisioned the area as a playground for the wealthy. Interspersed between his opulent hotels were huge estates on lots running 400 feet in from Biscayne Bay. Meanwhile, the southern portion of the barrier island was developed by the Lummus brothers, who plotted smaller lots for a middle-class resort. Scarcely had the dredging begun than the Lummus brothers in 1912 opened the Ocean Beach Realty Company, the first real estate office on the beach. Steady growth was interrupted by World War I, but then Miami Beach took off—until the collapse of the Florida real estate boom and the ensuing Depression.

By 1936, assisted by an expanding tourist industry, south Florida had emerged from the Depression. Hundreds of small hotels and apartment buildings were constructed on the small Lummus lots at the rate of 100 a year until 1941, making Miami Beach one of the few cities in the United States to have a building boom during the Depression. Ernest Hemingway's brother Leicester, also a writer, explains the phenomenon:

During the Depression, people needed to let go. . . . They became wild on Miami Beach. . . . They didn't watch their nickels. . . . [Architects] were determined not to use any older styles like the Spanish. . . . They wanted something modern, so they smoothed out all the Spanish things. They smoothed everything until you got the feeling that life was smooth. The buildings made you feel all clean and new and excited and happy to be there.

The style that prevailed in South Miami Beach was a zesty, crowd-pleasing Art Deco built by a handful of architects and contractors. Many of the architects were not formally trained but freely adapted national design trends to this tropical setting, creating a uniformity in style and scale rarely found in an urban setting. Called Miami Beach Art Deco (the name Tropical Deco has also been applied to the style), this brand of Art Deco was both relatively inexpensive to construct and offered a slick, dramatic, fashionable appearance, while its strong visual tropical symbols—"Floridiana"—impressed upon visitors the unique charms of the area.

Florida didn't invent the decorative vegetative and animal motifs that dominated the more ornate Miami Beach Art Deco buildings, but it raised them to new stylistic heights with facade bas-reliefs of cast or dyed stone, etched windows, and decorative metalwork on doors and porches. Flowers, especially voluptuous gladiolas, alluded to the fecund floral paradise. Nymphs and nudes hedonistically stressed sensuous youth and romance. Fountains as well as sunbursts and symbolic zigzag equivalents of rays conjured up the life-renewing natural properties of the climate. Animals such as peacocks, flamingos, greyhounds, herons, and pelicans were chosen for their romantic associations, arabesque shapes, and exaggerated proportions. Originally, most of the buildings were stark white, with trims of azure blue, ocean turquoise, blazing yellow, palm tree green, erotic pink, or purples and mauves that evoked tropical sunsets, bougainvillea, and feelings both sensuous and exotic. The sense of place is strong among these Deco buildings, leaving no doubt that this is the tropics, far from the cold, gray, sooty, industrial North.

The variances in Miami Beach Art Deco reflected what was occurring economically and architecturally on the national scene. Among others, four prevalent Deco styles comprising Miami Beach Art Deco.

Art Deco. The earliest buildings adapted the original Art Deco style's sharply angular massing with shallow stepped-back facades. Ornate bas-relief panels often framed large central openings. The French love of luxurious, sensuous textures such as crystal, mother-of-pearl, and unusual woods translated into indigenous Florida oolitic limestone, etched glass, stucco, and terrazzo (a cast agglomerate of marble or granite particles in colored and polished cement).

Depression Moderne. By 1937 the mode had shifted to a deco with the more austere look of the reigning International Style. Art Moderne's vertical stucco bands, flat roof with stepped parapet, and facade symmetry were still there, but with an increased horizontal emphasis that would later become dominant in streamlining. Depression Moderne was also readapted for government buildings such as the Miami Beach Post Office, and called PWA Moderne for the Public Works Administration.

Streamlined Moderne. By 1939, a full-blown aerodynamic Moderne featured curved forms, applied racing stripes that accentuated horizontal emphasis, and "eyebrow" shading of the windows with cantilevered slabs to reduce the angle of penetration of the sun. The continuously wrapped stucco surfaces expressed concepts associated with travel and speed. Here the angularity of the originally imported Art Moderne was entirely replaced by soft flowing masses accented with horizontal lines and rows of windows. This phase combined smooth, sweeping curves with straight lines of the machine age in simple, definite, contrasting shapes. Combinations of Cubism's suggestion of dimensionality, Futurism's romance with speed, and Surrealist fantasy are cited as sources of inspiration. This streamlining restored the fun and humor drained by Depression Moderne.

Mannerism. A final development of Miami Beach streamlining was called Resort Mannerism or Mannerist Moderne (from Mannerism, a late 16th-century reaction against the High Renaissance characterized by a deliberate distortion of the existing artistic and architectural repertoire; it gave way to the Baroque, and today the term is associated with the exaggeration and/or distortion of existing themes). Resort Mannerism included Nautical Moderne, with its exaggerated and literal invocations of ships at sea with porthole windows, decklike balconies, and flagstaffs. This mature Moderne emphasized sinuous curves, stylized directional ornament, and bold projections, marking a conscious search by architects both here and in Europe for a unique form to express contemporary modernity. Never a pure style, it even incorporated highlights from the Spanish Mediterranean, such as sloping tile roofs or colored ceramic tiles. The late 1930s film influence brought soaring "trylons" or space-age needles to roofs and facades. This Flash Gordon touch turned the buildings visually into spaceships with Hollywood stage-set lobbies that were also referred to as Cinema Style and Hollywood Style.

Larger Deco hotels did make their appearance, but, by and large, the area known as Old Miami Beach consists of two- and three-story hostelries small in scale and rich in expression. Deco architecture prevailed here later than anywhere else in the country, until World War II abruptly terminated construction. By 1941, most hotels were occupied by the military in training for the war effort. After the war, the area began to decline as Miami Beach continued its development northward.

In 1979, one square mile of Miami Beach became this country's first 20th-century national historic district. It reflects a trend in architecture that took place between the two world wars, when more than 500 Art Deco structures went up in one small area. It is not only the largest and most cohesive concentration of Art Deco buildings in the world but the first historic district that has registered buildings less than 50 years old. It sits on one of the best pieces of real estate in Florida, perhaps on the entire East Coast.

The fight for preservation of these landmarks has raged for years between developers who want to erect more profitable high-rise condominiums and the local Miami Design Preservation League, founded by Barbara Baer Capitman. A former art historian and now president of the Art Deco Society of Miami, she held her first organizational meeting in 1976 with six people and spoke of the area's potential as "capital of the Art Deco world." Capitman attracted 100 volunteers to survey and research the locality. Then the battle was launched that resulted in tax and zoning incentives for the owners of Deco buildings who preserve their original structures.

Developers fought back and, to block the legislation, lobbied successfully for an ordinance that required 100% owner approval for historic district designations (51% is standard). This ordinance was later struck down when, to avoid costly litigation, Miami Beach changed its ordinance to 51% approval. Some local businessmen see the preservation issue as one of property rights versus government coercion. A few, however, realize that the Art Deco district will yield them long-term beneficial results: It will create a desirable cultural center and provide a sense of identity vital to establishing Miami Beach as a unique city rather than a second-rate Las Vegas.

Because no corresponding local legislation had been passed to protect the district, its designation on the National Register of Historic Places did not prevent demolition of several landmark Art Deco hotels. The turning point came in July of 1986, when Richard Hoberman, president of the Miami Design Preservation League, orchestrated a campaign to secure designation of two key areas: a quarter-mile district covering Ocean Drive/Collins Avenue (from Fifth to Sixteenth streets) as well as

Espanola Way, a six-block street that includes a 1920s Spanish theme village. Hoberman packed the city commission chambers with supporters wearing "Deco-pink" ribbons to witness the decisive 6–1 vote. Local designation means that a design review board must approve all renovation work for appropriateness, all new construction must be compatible with surrounding buildings, and—most important—there will be a six-month moratorium on demolition to allow time for other investors to step in. Now prospective developers need not fear that their preservation efforts will be invalidated by high rises, and successful rehabilitation within these two districts should help in the essential designation of additional areas. Things are looking good: Already one developer has turned a million-dollar profit in 10 months by restoring and reselling one of the district's Art Deco hotels. Seven years after federal recognition, the city fathers have finally understood the economic benefits of preservation.

The preservation movement on Miami Beach has generated admiration for Art Deco, and south Florida developers have invested millions of dollars building imitation Deco residential communities for those who want the look of Deco but wish to live outside the troubled inner-city area. These new homes have much of the generic look of huge housing developments, despite their attempt to blend International Style and Deco. They feature stepped walls and entrances, porthole windows, geometric shapes, and two-tone pastel colors. Builders toned down the bright Deco colors to Necco wafer hues of quiet pastels when a local homeowners' association complained of the bright aqua, peach, and intense pinks. This "switch rather than fight" approach is an attempt to sidestep the complex problems of gentrification. The buildings themselves mark a rejection of International Style anonymity, a recognition of the value of Art Deco, and a positive trend in Miami's search for its own architectural identity.

Meanwhile, in the Deco District the tax credits to be obtained by rehabilitating these architectural treasures have brought developers into the area, and dozens of hotels and apartment houses are being refurbished. The small hotels average 60 to 120 rooms, many having been converted to "pullmanettes" (rooms with kitchenettes). For the past quarter-century these have been popular with mostly Jewish and Eastern European retirees, and a decade ago more than half of the south Beach population was 65 or older. With retirement communities now proliferating in south Florida, for about a decade Miami Beach has ceased to be a destination point for the elderly, and now the percentage is less than one-quarter.

By its nature, rehabilitation means modernization and deviation from original design schemes, and nowhere is this more apparent than in color restoration. The original white with vivid color accents has been rejected in favor of a palette of Post-Modern cake-icing pastels now associated with the television series "Miami Vice." Leonard Horowitz, the designer who introduced these colors, rationalized that because the neighborhood had deteriorated and much of the original vegetation had died, there was justification for using a plethora of color. Finally, white is being reintroduced.

The buildings of the Miami Beach Historical District chronicle more than a decade of historic cultural change and served the emotional needs of the public in a time of national crisis. No orthodox academic style has accomplished this. Whatever their historical significance or their eventual evaluation as art, these Miami Art Deco habitations are built to the human scale where the desires of the people are met rather than dictated to by sociological or aesthetic theory. Such a value in buildings has generally been condescended to or given mere lip service by respected architects who consider the tastes of the public beneath contempt. Yet the art of living cannot be measured by formal architectural standards of purity or style, only by the pleasure of the time and place. Miami Beach Art Deco created this quality of life with consummate success.

Today, the buildings still hold magic for visitors and inhabitants. Although the romance is slightly tarnished by peeling facades, and idealistic dreams have succumbed to more jaded views, there is still a sense of desire and expectation in the air. There is a glamour about these buildings that invites thoughts of moonlit walks on sparkling beaches, movie-screen romances, dancing under starry skies. There is a sadness, too, of once-vital dreams lost, either demolished or covered over with gaudy wallpaper and wall-to-wall carpeting. But this special fantasy of Florida still twinkles seductively among the vast pile of urban mediocrity that threatens to engulf the Miami Beach Deco District.

3 Miami

Introduction

by George and Rosalie Leposky

A husband-wife team, George and Rosalie Leposky are veteran Florida travel writers. Their articles have appeared in some 100 newspapers and consumer magazines throughout North America. They also write for trade publications in the travel and hospitality field, including Hotel & Resort Industry *and* Lodging. *The Leposkys live in the Coconut Grove section of Miami.*

What they say about Miami is true. The city *is* different. Miami is different from what it once was and it's different from other cities.

Once a sleepy southern resort town, Miami today is a burgeoning giant of international commerce and finance as well as a place to find pleasure and relaxation. Like all big cities, Miami inspires the first-time visitor with hopes and dreams. Also as in other cities, many of these hopes and dreams can be sidetracked by crime and violence.

Miami's natural difference can be detected when you fly into the city. Clinging to a thin ribbon of dry land between the marshy Everglades and the Atlantic Ocean, Miami remains vulnerable to its perennial mosquitoes, periodic flooding, and potential devastation by hurricanes. These perils give life in Miami a flavor of urgency, a compulsion to prosper and party before the dream ends.

Miami may be the wrong place for a city, but it's the right place for a crossroads. Long before Spain's gold-laden treasure ships passed offshore in the Gulf Stream, the Calusa Indians who lived here had begun to trade with their mainland neighbors to the north and their island brethren to the south. Repeating this prehistoric pattern, many U.S. and multinational companies now locate their Latin American headquarters in Greater Miami because no other city can match its airline connections to the Western Hemisphere.

That same ease of access, coupled with a congenial climate, attracts hordes of Latin tourists—especially in Miami's steamy summer months (South America's winter), when domestic visitors from the northern United States are less in evidence.

Access and climate also explain why Miami has become what *Newsweek* calls "America's Casablanca." Whenever a Latin American or Caribbean government erupts in revolution and economic chaos, the inevitable refugees flock inexorably to Miami (and open restaurants). Even without a revolution, Miami's cosmopolitan character and entrepreneurial spirit attract other immigrants from all over the world.

Today, more than 40% of Greater Miami's population is Hispanic—the majority from Cuba, with significant populations from Colombia, El Salvador, Nicaragua, and Panama. About 150,000 French- and Creole-speaking Haitians also live in Greater Miami, as do Brazilians, Germans, Greeks, Iranians, Israelis, Italians, Jamaicans, Lebanese, Malaysians, Russian Jews, Swedes, and more—a veritable Babel of tongues. Most either know or are trying to learn English. You can help them by speaking slowly and distinctly.

Try not to think of Miami as a "melting pot." Where ethnic and cultural diversity are the norm, there's less pressure to conform. Miamians practice matter-of-factly the customs they brought here—much to the consternation of other Miamians whose customs differ. The community wrestles constantly with these tensions and sensitivities.

As a big city, Miami has its share of crime, violence, and drug trafficking—but not the pervasive lawlessness portrayed on the "Miami Vice" TV show. You probably won't find the city's seamy underside unless you go looking for it.

What you will find just by coming to Miami is a multicultural metropolis that works and plays with vigor and that welcomes you to share its celebration of diversity.

Arriving and Departing

By Plane

Commercial Flights. Miami International Airport (MIA), six miles west of downtown Miami, is Greater Miami's only commercial airport. MIA has the nation's second-largest volume of international passenger and cargo traffic. MIA's busiest hours, when flight delays may occur, are 11 AM–8 PM.

MIA contains 100 aircraft gates along seven concourses. During 1989, expect to encounter renovation on concourses D, F, and H.

When you fly out of MIA, plan to check in 55 minutes before departure for a domestic flight and 90 minutes before departure for an international flight. Services for international travelers include 24-hour multilingual information and paging and foreign currency conversion, both on Concourse E.

Between the Airport and City Center

Metrobus. The county's Metrobus system has one benefit—its modest cost—if you're willing to put up with the inconveniences of infrequent service, scruffy equipment, and the circuitous path that many routes follow. *Fare $1 (exact change), transfers 25 cents.*

Greyhound. You can take a Greyhound bus from the Metrobus depot at MIA to Homestead and the Florida Keys or to other Greyhound stations in Greater Miami (*see* By Bus).

Taxicabs. For trips originating at MIA or the Port of Miami, a $1 toll is added to the meter fare—except for the flat-fare trips described below:

You'll pay a $12 flat fare between MIA and the Port of Miami, in either direction.

For taxi service from the airport to destinations in the immediate vicinity, ask a uniformed county taxi dispatcher to call an ARTS (Airport Region Taxi Service) cab for you. These special blue cabs will offer you a short-haul flat fare.

Red Top Sedan, Inc. Express van service from MIA directly to the Port of Miami and to hotels east of I–95 on Key Biscayne (two-passenger minimum), in Miami Beach, and in downtown Miami. Look for Red Top supervisors in kiosks just outside the airport's baggage claim area. Phone for return reservations. *Tel. 305/871–3167. Price based on distance. No credit cards.*

Limousines. Red Top has chauffeur-driven four-door town cars and stretch limousines available on demand at MIA or through the 24-hour reservation service. *4300 N.W. 14th St., Miami, tel. 305/871–3167. AE, DC (for Town Cars and stretch limousines only).*

By Bus

Greyhound/Trailways buses (tel. 305/374–7222 or 305/373–6561) stop at seven bus stations in Greater Miami. No reservations.

By Car

The main highways into Greater Miami from the north are Florida's Turnpike (toll) and I–95. In Broward County (the next county north), you'll encounter major delays throughout 1989 from construction to widen the highway.

Delays on roads into Miami from other directions are most likely on weekends, when recreational traffic is the heaviest. From the northwest, take I–75 or U.S. 27 into town. From the Everglades to the west, use the Tamiami Trail (U.S. 41). From the south, use U.S. 1 and the Homestead Extension of Florida's Turnpike.

Rental Cars Six rental-car firms—**Avis Rent-a-Car, Budget Rent-a-Car, Dollar Rent-a-Car, Hertz Rent-a-Car, National Rent-a-Car,** and **Value Rent-a-Car**—have booths near the baggage claim area on MIA's lower level—a convenience when you arrive.

By Train Amtrak's two trains between Miami and New York City, the Silver Meteor and Silver Star, make different stops along the way. Each has a daily Miami arrival and departure.

Amtrak's "All Aboard" fare is the most economical way to travel to Florida, if you have time to meet the length-of-stay requirements. Trains run full all year, except in October and May. For the best fare, contact Amtrak as soon as you decide to take a trip. Ask for Amtrak's 1989 travel planner. *Amtrak Station, 8303 N.W. 37th Ave., Miami 33147. General office tel. 305/835–1200, passenger service tel. 305/835–1225. Advance reservations required. Reservations: Amtrak Customer Relations, 400 N. Capitol St., NW, Washington, DC 20001, tel. U.S. 800/USA–RAIL, Canada 800/4AM TRAK.*

Getting Around

Greater Miami resembles Los Angeles in its urban sprawl and traffic congestion. You'll need a car to visit many of the attractions and points of interest listed in this book. Some are accessible via public transportation.

A department of county government, the Metro-Dade Transit Agency, runs the public transportation system. It consists of 450 Metrobuses on 61 routes, the 21-mile Metrorail elevated rapid transit system, and the 1.9-mile Metromover in downtown Miami. Free maps, schedules, and a First-Time Rider's Kit are available. *111 N.W. 1st St., Miami 33128. Maps by Mail, tel. 305/638–6137. Route information tel. 305/638–6700 daily 6 AM–11 PM. Fare $1, transfers 25 cents, exact change only.*

By Train Metrorail runs from downtown Miami north to Hialeah and south along U.S. 1 to Dadeland. *Service every 7 minutes in peak hours, 15–30 minutes other times. Weekdays 6 AM–9 PM, weekends 6:30 AM–6:30 PM. Runs until midnight for special events such as the Orange Bowl Parade.*

Metromover's two loops circle downtown Miami, linking major hotels, office buildings, and shopping areas (*see* Exploring Downtown Miami). *Service every 90 seconds. Weekdays 6:30 AM–9 PM, Sat. 8:30 AM–11 PM, Sun. 8:30 AM–6:30 PM. Later for special events. Fare 25 cents.*

By Bus Metrobus stops are marked by blue-and-green signs with a bus logo and route information. The frequency of service varies widely. Obtain specific schedule information in advance for the routes you want to ride.

South Florida Trolley Co. A San Francisco–style trolley on a bus chassis carries 40 passengers hourly to Bayside Marketplace from Coconut Grove; from Miami Beach south of the Carriage Club, 5025 Collins Avenue; and from Omni International. Trolleys travel every half-hour between the Port of Miami and Bayside Marketplace. In North Miami, they go every half hour from North Miami to Aventura Mall. The trolleys stop at major hotels and restaurants. You can also flag a trolley at any Metrobus stop along its route and ask to be dropped off at any Metrobus stop. *For detailed route and schedule information, write 998 S. Military Trail, Deerfield Beach 33442. Miami, tel. 305/948–8823. Route hours: Coconut Grove daily 3–11. Miami Beach Mon.–Sat. noon–8, Sun. noon–6. Omni International Mon.–Sat. 10–10, Sun. noon–6. Port of Miami daily 10:30–2:55. Fare $1 for Coconut Grove and Miami Beach; 25 cents for Omni and Port of Miami; 50 cents seniors, 75 cents others for Aventura. No credit cards.*

By Taxicab There are 1,509 taxicabs in Dade County. Fares are $1 for the first ⅓ mile, 20 cents for each additional 1/6 mile; waiting time 20 cents for the first 1 3/5 minutes, 20 cents for each additional 4/5 minute. No additional charge for extra passengers, luggage, or road and bridge tolls. Taxi companies with dispatch service are **Central Taxicab Service** (tel. 305/534–0694), **Diamond Cab Company** (tel. 305/545–7575), **Magic City Cab Company** (tel. 305/757–5523), **Metro Taxicab Company** (tel. 305/888–8888), **Society Cab Company (tel. 305/757–5523), Super Yellow Cab Company** (tel. 305/885–5555), **Tropical Taxicab Company** (tel. 305/945–1025), and **Yellow Cab Company** (tel. 305/444–4444).

By Car Finding your way around Greater Miami is easy if you know how the numbering system works. Miami is laid out on a grid with four quadrants—northeast, northwest, southeast, and southwest—which meet at Miami Avenue and Flagler Street. Miami Avenue separates east from west and Flagler Street separates north from south. *Avenues* and *courts* run north–south; *streets*, *terraces*, and *ways* run east–west. *Roads* run diagonally, northwest–southeast.

Many named streets also bear numbers. For example, Unity Boulevard is N.W. and S.W. 27th Avenue, LeJeune Road is N.W. and S.W. 42nd Avenue. However, named streets that depart markedly from the grid, such as Biscayne Boulevard and Brickell Avenue, have no corresponding numerical designations. Dade County and most other municipalities follow the Miami numbering system.

In Miami Beach, *avenues* run north–south; *streets*, east–west. Numbers rise along the beach from south to north and from the Atlantic Ocean in the east to Biscayne Bay in the west.

In Coral Gables, all streets bear names. Coral Gables uses the Miami numbering system for north–south addresses but begins counting east–west addresses westward from Douglas Road (S.W. 37th Ave.).

Hialeah has its own grid. Palm Avenue separates east from west; Hialeah Drive separates north from south. *Avenues* run north–south and *streets* east–west. Numbered streets and avenues are designated west, east, or southeast.

Important Addresses and Numbers

Information Centers The Greater Miami Convention and Visitors Bureau plans to open tourist information centers in downtown Miami, Miami Beach, Homestead–Florida City, Miami International Airport, and the Port of Miami. Contact the bureau for locations and hours or to request information by mail.

Visitor Services, Greater Miami Convention and Visitors Bureau (4770 Biscayne Blvd., Miami 33137, tel. 305/573–4300).

Chambers of Commerce Greater Miami has more than 20 local chambers of commerce, each promoting its individual community. Most maintain racks of brochures on tourist information in their offices and will send you information about their community. Local chambers of commerce serving the main tourist areas are

Coconut Grove Chamber of Commerce (2820 McFarland Rd., Coconut Grove 33133, tel. 305/444–7270).
Coral Gables Chamber of Commerce (50 Aragon Ave., Coral Gables 33134, tel. 305/446–1657).
Gold Coast Chamber of Commerce (1100 Kane Concourse, Suite 210, Bay Harbor Islands 33154, tel. 305/866–6020). Serves the beach communities of Bal Harbour, Bay Harbor Islands, Golden Beach, North Bay Village, Sunny Isles, and Surfside.
Key Biscayne Chamber of Commerce (Key Biscayne Bank Bldg., 95 W. McIntyre St., Key Biscayne 33149, tel. 305/361–5207).
Miami Beach Chamber of Commerce (1920 Meridian Ave., Miami Beach 33139, tel. 305/672–1270).
South Miami Chamber of Commerce (6410 S.W. 80th St., South Miami 33143, tel. 305/661–1621).

Emergencies Dial 911 for **police** and **ambulance.** You can dial free from pay phones.

Telecommunication lines for the hearing impaired are used by hearing-impaired travelers with telecommunication devices (TDD) to reach TDD-equipped public services:

Fire/Police/Medical/Rescue (tel. 305/595–4749 TDD)
Operator and Directory Assistance (tel. 800/855–1155 TDD)
Deaf Services of Miami (4800 W. Flagler St., Room 213, Miami, tel. 305/444–2211 TDD or voice 305/444–2266). Operates daily 6 AM–midnight. Relays calls to help the hearing-impaired contact people who hear and speak normally.

Ambulance **Randle Eastern Ambulance Service Inc.** Serves all of Greater Miami. Meets air ambulances and takes patients to hospitals. Services include advanced life-support systems. *35 S.W. 27th Ave., Miami 33135, tel. 305/642–6400. Open 24 hrs. AE, MC, V.*

Hospitals The following hospitals have 24-hour emergency rooms:

Miami Beach: *Mt. Sinai Medical Center* (4300 Alton Rd., Miami Beach, tel. 305/674–2121; physician referral, tel. 674–2273). Just off Julia Tuttle Causeway (I–195).
St. Francis Hospital (250 W. 63rd St., Miami Beach, tel. 305/868–5000; physician referral, tel. 305/868–2728). Near Collins Ave. and north end of Alton Rd.

Central: *University of Miami/Jackson Memorial Medical Center.* Includes Jackson Memorial Hospital, a county hospital with Greater Miami's only trauma center. Near Dolphin Expressway. Metrorail stops a block away. *1611 N.W. 12th Ave., Miami, tel. 305/325–7429. Emergency room, tel. 305/549–6901. Interpreter service, tel. 305/549–6316. Patient relations, tel. 305/549–7341. Physician referral, tel. 305/547–5757.*
Mercy Hospital (3663 S. Miami Ave., Coconut Grove, tel. 305/854–4400; physician referral, tel. 305/285–2929). Greater Miami's only hospital, with an emergency boat dock.
Miami Children's Hospital (6125 S.W. 31st St., tel. 305/666–6511; physician referral, ext. 2563).

South: *Baptist Hospital of Miami* (8900 N. Kendall Dr., Miami, tel. 305/596–1960; physician referral, tel. 305/596–6557).

24-Hour Pharmacies

Of the 287 pharmacies in Greater Miami, only two are open 24 hours a day. Most pharmacies open at 8 or 9 AM and close between 9 PM and midnight. Many pharmacies offer local delivery service.

Eckerd Drugs. 1825 N.E. Miami Gardens Dr. (185th St.), North Miami Beach, tel. 305/932–5740 and 9031 S.W. 107th Ave., Miami, tel. 305/274–6776.

Physician Referral Services

24-Hour Doctors House Calls. Many Greater Miami hotels use this referral service, which will send a physician to you. Medical services available include general medicine, pediatrics, and geriatrics. In-office dental referrals. Translators available. *3801 N. University Dr., Suite 507, Sunrise, tel. 305/945–6325.*

East Coast District Dental Society. Office open weekdays 9 AM–4:30 PM for dental referral. Services include general dentistry, endodontics, periodontics, and oral surgery. *420 S. Dixie Hwy., Coral Gables, tel. 305/667–3647.*

Guided Tours

Orientation Tours

Miami Vision. (2699 Collins Ave., Suite 113, Miami Beach, tel. 305/532–0040). Several packages combine city tours with attractions. Prices include admission to attractions. Mini-van and private car tours. Well-informed, congenial guides speak English, French, German, Italian, Portuguese, and Spanish. Phone for hotel pickup time or ask your concierge.

Special-Interest Tours

Boat Tours

Dixie Belle Cruises. Sightseeing in Biscayne Bay on a 350-passenger paddlewheeler, past Miami Beach hotels, Millionaires' Row, and the Miami skyline. *6500 Indian Creek Dr., Miami Beach, tel. 305/861–1234. Cruises daily all year.*
Haulover Park Dinner Boats. 399-passenger boats cruise to the Port of Miami and back through Indian Creek and Millionaires' Row. *10880 Collins Ave., Miami Beach, tel. 305/947–6105. Oct. 15–May 15.*
Heritage of Miami. Miami's official tall ship, a gaff-rigged 70-ft. wooden schooner, built in the Bahamas in 1963, has participated in all tall-ship events since 1976, including the Statue of Liberty 100th-birthday party. Docks at Crandon Marina. Carries up to 39 passengers for day sailing, sleeps 11; children and cameras welcome. Ice and ice chest on board, soft drinks for sale; bring your own food. Standard Biscayne Bay day trip lasts two hours. Reservations recommended. *Dinner Key Marina, Miami, tel. 305/858–6264. Sails daily, weather permitting.*

Cost: $20 adults, $15 seniors, $10 armed forces personnel and children under 12.

Island Queen. 90-passenger tour boat docks at the Hyatt Regency Hotel's patio dock, 400 S.E. 2nd Ave., Miami. Two-hour narrated tours of Port of Miami and Millionaires' Row. Transportation to and from Island Queen available from Miami Vision. *17443 S.W. 85th Ave., Miami, tel. 305/379–5119. Tours daily. Cost: $9 adults, $4 children.*

Nikko Gold Coast Cruises. Three 150-passenger boats based at Haulover Park Marina specialize in water tours to major Greater Miami attractions. *10800 Collins Ave., Miami Beach, tel. 305/945–5461. Tours daily. Bayside Marketplace, $8 adults, $4.50 children under 12.*

History Tours

Art Deco District Tour. Meet guide at 10:30 AM Sat. at 12th St. entrance to Miami Design Preservation League's welcome center, 1201 Washington Ave., Miami Beach, for 90-minute tour. Wear comfortable shoes and bring a hat. Also available is the League's *Art Deco District Guide*, a book with 6 detailed walking or driving tours of the square-mile Art Deco District on Miami Beach. *1236 Ocean Dr., Miami Beach, tel. 305/672–2014. Cost: $5. Reservations required.*

Historical Museum of Southern Florida. Guided tours available in English or Spanish. **Museum Tour** covers the exhibits, which survey 10,000 years of Miami-area history; includes 15-minute slide show. The **Curator's Cabinet Tour** combines the Museum Tour with a look behind the scenes at departments that visitors seldom see, including a research center with 500,000 photos and the cataloging and conservation departments. The museum also conducts tours throughout the Greater Miami area. *101 W. Flagler St., Miami, tel. 305/375–1492*

Prof. Paul George. Explore Miami's history with a professional historian on a four-hour walking tour of downtown. Paul George is a history professor at Florida International University and president of the Florida Historical Society. Tour begins on the north bank of Miami River behind the Hyatt Regency Hotel, 400 S.E. 2nd Ave. Wear comfortable walking shoes and a hat. Sat. 9 AM–1 PM by appointment. *1345 S.W. 14th St., Miami, tel. 305/858–6021. Cost $7 adults, $5 children 7–14, under 7 free.*

Rickshaw Tours

Royal Rickshaw. Look for rickshas along Main Highway in Coconut Grove's Village Center, and at Metrozoo (Box 331671, Coconut Grove, tel. 305/447–0545). Nightly 8 PM–2 AM in Coconut Grove, fall and spring weekends at Metrozoo. Rickshaw holds two adults. $3 per person for 10-minute ride through Coconut Grove, $6 per person for 20-minute lovers' moonlight ride down to Biscayne Bay, $5 per person for 10-minute Metrozoo ride. No credit cards.

Exploring Downtown Miami

Orientation

From a distance, you see downtown Miami's future—a 21st-century skyline already stroking the clouds with sleek fingers of steel and glass. By day, this icon of commerce and technology sparkles in the strong subtropical sun; at night, it basks in the man-made glow of floodlights.

On the streets downtown, you encounter a polyglot present. Staid-suited lawyers and bankers share the sidewalks with Hispanic merchants wearing open-neck, intricately embroidered shirts called *guayaberas*. Fruit merchants sell their wares from pushcarts. European youths with backpacks stroll the streets. Foreign businessmen haggle over prices in import-export shops. You hear Arabic, Chinese, Creole, French, German, Hebrew, Hindi, Japanese, Portuguese, Spanish, Swedish, Yiddish, and even a little English now and then.

With effort, you can find remnants of downtown Miami's past. Most of the city's "old" downtown buildings date from only the 1920s and 1930s—an incongruity if you're from someplace that counts its past in centuries. Remember that Miami is a young city, incorporated in 1896 with just 3,000 residents. A Junior League book, *Historic Downtown Miami*, locates and describes 27 elderly structures in and near downtown, including 21 you can see in a two-hour self-guided walking tour of slightly more than a mile.

Parking downtown is inconvenient and expensive. If you're staying elsewhere in the area, leave your car at an outlying Metrorail station and take the train downtown. Metromover, a separate light-rail mass-transit system, circles the heart of the city on twin elevated loops.

No part of downtown is more than two blocks from one of Metromover's nine stations. We've organized the downtown Miami tour around those stations, so you can ride Metromover directly to the attractions downtown that interest you most.

Touring Downtown Miami

Numbers in the margin correspond with points of interest on the Downtown Miami map.

1 When you get off the Metrorail train at **Government Center Sta-**
2 **tion**, notice the **Dade County Courthouse** (73 W. Flagler St.). It's the building to the east with a pyramid at its peak, where turkey vultures roost in winter. Built in 1928, it was once the tallest building south of Washington, DC.

3 As you leave the Metrorail station, you'll enter **Metro-Dade Center,** the county government's 30-story office building. Designed by architect Hugh Stubbins, it opened in 1985.

Across N.W. 1st Street from Metro-Dade Center stands the
4 **Metro-Dade Cultural Center** (101 W. Flagler St.), opened in 1983. The 3.3-acre complex is a Mediterranean expression of architect Philip Johnson's postmodern style. An elevated plaza provides a serene haven from the city's pulsations and a superb setting for festivals and outdoor performances.

Center for the Fine Arts is an art museum in the tradition of the European *kunsthalle* (exhibition gallery). With no permanent collection, it organizes and borrows temporary exhibitions on many artistic themes. Shows scheduled for 1989 include Greek icons and frescoes and the works of architect Frank Lloyd Wright. *Tel. 305/375-1700. Open Tues.-Sat. 10-5 except Thurs. 10-9, Sun. noon-5. Admission: $3 adults, $2.50 senior citizens, $2 children 6-12, under 6 free. Donations Tues.*

Historical Museum of Southern Florida is a regional museum that interprets the human experience in southern Florida from prehistory to the present. Artifacts on permanent display include Tequesta and Seminole Indian ceramics, clothing, and tools; a 1920 streetcar; and an original edition of Audubon's *Birds of America*. Special exhibitions planned for 1989 include dirigibles and south Florida folk arts. *Tel. 305/375-1492. Open*

Mon.–Sat. 10–5 except Thurs. 10–9, Sun. noon–5. Admission: $3 adults, $2 children 6–12, under 6 free. Donations Mon.

Main Public Library, with 700,000 volumes and a computerized card catalog. Inside the entrance, look up at the rotunda mural, where artist Edward Ruscha interpreted a quotation from Shakespeare: "Words without thought never to heaven go." You'll find art exhibits in the auditorium and second-floor lobby. *Tel. 305/375–BOOK. Open Mon.–Sat. 10–5 except Thurs. 10–9, Sun. noon–5. Closed Sun. May–Sept.*

At Government Center Station, you can also transfer to Metromover's inner and outer loops through downtown. We've listed the stations and their attractions in sequence along the outer loop.

5 The first stop is **Ft. Dallas Park Station.** If you disembark here,
6 you're a block from the **Miami Ave. Bridge,** one of 11 bridges on the river that open to let ships pass. From the bridge approach, watch freighters, tugboats, research vessels, and luxury yachts ply this busy waterway.

Time Out Stroll across the bridge to **Tobacco Road** for some liquid refreshment and a sandwich or snack. Built in 1912, this friendly neighborhood pub was a speakeasy during Prohibition. *626 S. Miami Ave., tel. 305/374–1198. Open weekdays 11:30 AM–5AM, weekends 1 PM–5 AM. Lunch 11:30–2:30 Mon.–Fri. Dinner served Sun.–Thurs. AE, DC.*

---

7 The next Metromover stop, **World Trade Center Station,** nestles
8 in a niche inside the **CenTrust Tower** (100 S.E. 1st St.), a wedge-
shape 47-story skyscraper designed by I. M. Pei & Partners.
The building is brilliantly illuminated at night. Inside the
9 CenTrust Tower, follow signs to the **James L. Knight International Center** (400 S.E. 2nd Ave., tel. 305/372–0929), a convention and concert hall adjoining the Hyatt Regency Hotel.

At the World Trade Center Station, you can transfer to the in-
10 ner loop and ride one stop to the **Miami Avenue Station,** a block south of **Flagler Street,** downtown Miami's commercial spine. Like most such thoroughfares, Flagler Street lost business in recent years to suburban malls—but unlike most, it found a new lease on life. Today, the half-mile of Flagler Street from Biscayne Boulevard to the Dade County Courthouse is the most important import-export center in the United States. Its stores and arcades supply much of the world with automotive parts, audio and video equipment, medical equipment and supplies, photographic equipment, clothing, and jewelry.

11 If you stay on the outer loop, you'll come next to **Bayfront Park**
12 **Station,** opposite **Bayfront Park,** which extends from Biscayne
Boulevard east to the edge of the bay. Japanese sculptor
Isamu Noguchi recently redesigned the park, which now includes a memorial to the *Challenger* astronauts, an amphitheater, and a fountain honoring veteran Florida Congressman
Claude Pepper and his wife. Just south of Bayfront Park,
13 the lobby of the **Hotel Inter-Continental Miami** (100 Chopin Plaza) contains *The Spindle,* a huge sculpture by Henry Moore.

West of Bayfront Park Station stands the tallest building in
14 Florida, the 55-story **Southeast Financial Center** (200 S. Bis-

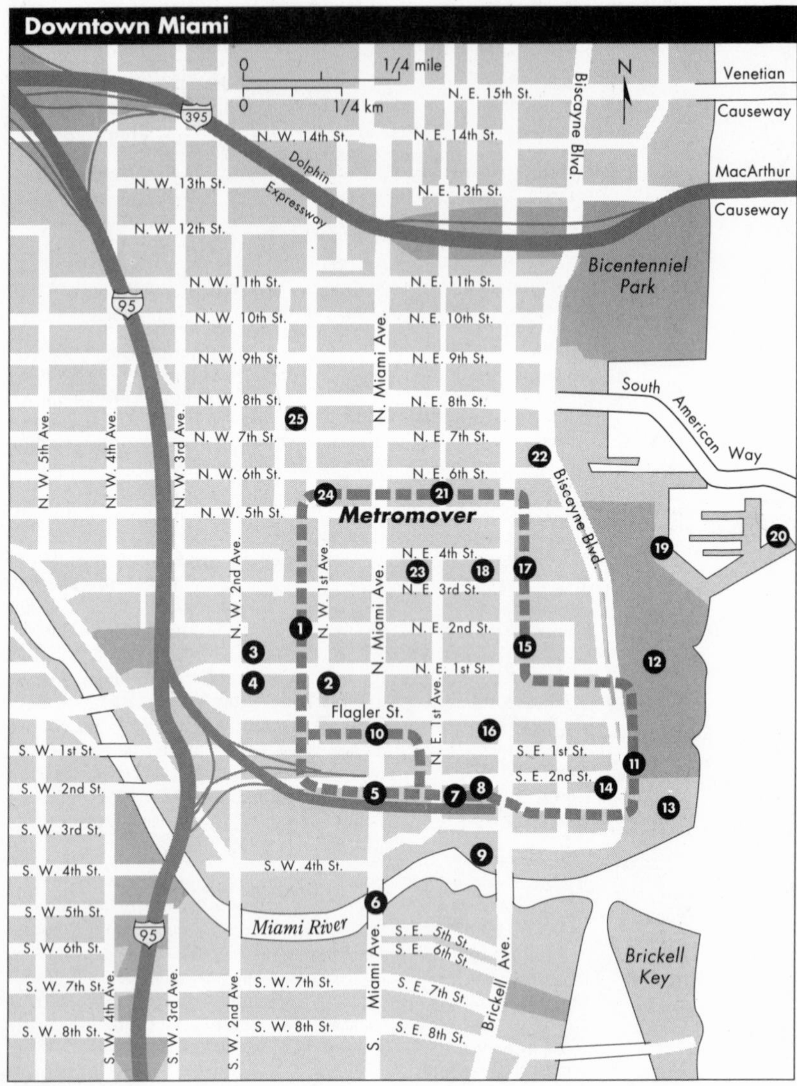

Bayfront Park, **12**
Bayfront Park Station, **11**
Bayside Marketplace, **19**
CenTrust Tower, **8**
College Station, **17**
Dade County Courthouse, **2**
Edcom Station, **21**
First St. Station, **15**
Ft. Dallas Park Station, **5**
Freedom Tower, **22**
Government Center Station, **1**
Gusman Center, **16**
HMS *Bounty*, **20**
Hotel Inter-Continental Miami, **13**
James Knight Center, **9**
Metro-Dade Center, **3**
Metro-Dade Cultural Center, **4**
Miami Arena, **25**
Miami Ave. Bridge, **6**
Miami Ave. Station, **10**
Miami-Dade Community College, **18**
Plaza Station, **24**
Southeast Financial Center, **14**
U.S. Courthouse, **23**
World Trade Center Station, **7**

cayne Blvd.), with towering royal palms in its one-acre Palm Court plaza beneath a steel-and-glass space frame.

15 The next Metromover stop, **First Street Station,** places you a
16 block north of Flagler Street and the **Gusman Center for the Performing Arts,** an ornate former movie palace restored as a concert hall. Gusman Center resembles a Moorish courtyard with twinkling stars in the sky. Performances there include the Miami City Ballet, under the direction of Edward Villella, and the New World Symphony, a unique, advanced-training orchestra led by Michael Tilson Thomas. *Gusman Center: 174 E. Flagler St., Miami 33131. Box office tel. 305/372–0925; Ballet: 905 Lincoln Rd., Miami Beach, 33139, tel. 305/532-4880; Symphony: Box 110809, Miami 33111, tel. 305/371–3005.*

17 The **College Station** Metromover stop serves the downtown
18 campus of **Miami-Dade Community College,** where you'll enjoy browsing through two fine galleries. The Francis Wolfson Art Gallery on the fifth floor houses traveling exhibitions of contemporary art. *300 N.E. 2nd Ave., tel. 305/347–3278. Weekdays 9–5:30. Free.* The Mitchell Wolfson, Jr., Collection of Decorative and Propaganda Arts on the third floor displays works from Mr. Wolfson's personal holdings. *Tel. 305/347–3429. Weekdays 10–5. Admission free.*

College Station is also the most convenient Metromover stop
19 for **Bayside Marketplace,** a waterside mall built by The Rouse Company, between Bayfront Park and the entrance to the Port of Miami. Bayside's 235,000 square feet of retail space include 81 specialty shops, pushcarts in the mall's Pier 5 area, conventional restaurants, and a fast-food court with some 30 vendors. The mall adjoins the 208-slip Miamarina, where you can see luxurious yachts moored and ride in an authentic 36-foot-long Venetian gondola. *401 Biscayne Blvd., tel. 305/577–3344, for gondola rides 305/529–7178. Open Mon.–Sat. 10–10, Sun. noon–8.*

20 While you're at Bayside, tour the **H.M.S. *Bounty*,** a fully rigged reproduction of an 18th-century armed merchant ship. Built in Nova Scotia for the 1962 MGM film *Mutiny on the Bounty*, the ship has since participated in the Bicentennial tall-ships parade and Statue of Liberty celebration in New York Harbor. *Tel. 305/375–0486. Open Sun.–Thurs. noon–8, Fri. noon–10, Sat. 10–10. Admission: $3.50 adults, $2 seniors, $1.50 children 4–12, under 4 free.*

As Metromover rounds the curve between College Station and
21 22 **Edcom Station,** look northeast to see **Freedom Tower** (600 Biscayne Blvd.), where the Cuban Refugee Center processed more than 500,000 Cubans who entered the United States to flee Fidel Castro's regime in the 1960s. Built in 1925 for the *Miami Daily News*, this imposing Spanish-baroque structure was inspired by the Giralda, an 800-year-old bell tower in Seville, Spain. After years as a derelict, Freedom Tower was renovated in 1988. To see it up close, walk north from Edcom Station to N.E. 6th Street, then two blocks east to Biscayne Boulevard.

A two-block walk south from Edcom Station will bring you to
23 the **U.S. Courthouse,** a handsome keystone building erected in 1931 as Miami's main post office. Go to the second-floor central courtroom to see *Law Guides Florida Progress*, a huge depression-era mural by artist Denman Fink. *300 N.E. 1st*

Ave. Building open weekdays 8:30–5; during those hours, security guards will open courtroom on request. No cameras or tape recorders allowed in building.

24 From **State Plaza Station,** walk two blocks north on N.W. 1st
25 Avenue to the new **Miami Arena** (721 N.W. 1st Ave., tel. 305/374–6877), home of the Miami Heat, a National Basketball Association team. Other sports and entertainment events also take place there.

Just across the Miami River from downtown, a canyon of tall buildings lines **Brickell Avenue,** a southward extension of S.E. 2nd Avenue that begins in front of the Hyatt Regency Hotel (400 S.E. 2nd Ave.). For the best views, drive Brickell Avenue from north to south. You'll pass the largest concentration of international banking offices in the United States.

South of S.E. 15th Street, several architecturally interesting condominiums rise between Brickell Avenue and Biscayne Bay. Israeli artist Yacov Agam painted the rainbow-hued exterior of **Villa Regina** (1581 Brickell Ave.). Arquitectonica, a nationally prominent architectural firm based in Miami, designed three of these buildings: **The Palace** (1541 Brickell Ave.), **The Imperial** (1617 Brickell Ave.), and **The Atlantis** (2025 Brickell Ave.). The 20-story Atlantis, where a palm tree grows in a hole in the building between the 12th and 16th floors, forms a backdrop for the opening credits of the television show "Miami Vice."

At S.E. 25th Road, turn right, follow signs to **I–95,** and return to downtown Miami on one of the world's most scenic urban highways. I–95 parallels Brickell Avenue and soars 75 feet above the Miami River, offering a superb view of the downtown skyline. At night, the CenTrust Tower is awash with light, and, on the adjoining Metrorail bridge, a neon rainbow glows—Rockne Krebs's 3,600-foot-long light sculpture, *The Miami Line.* Just beyond the river, take the Biscayne Boulevard exit back to S.E. 2nd Avenue in front of the Hyatt Regency Hotel.

Exploring Miami Beach

Orientation

Most visitors to the Greater Miami area don't realize that Miami and Miami Beach are separate cities. Miami, on the mainland, is south Florida's commercial hub. Miami Beach, on 17 islands offshore in Biscayne Bay, is sometimes considered America's Riviera, luring refugees from winter to its warm sunshine, sandy beaches, and graceful palms.

In 1912, what would become Miami Beach was little more than a sandspit in the bay. Then Carl Graham Fisher, a millionaire promoter who built the Indianapolis Speedway, began to pour much of his fortune into developing the island city.

Ever since, Miami Beach has experienced successive waves of boom and bust—thriving in the early 1920s and the years just after World War II, but also enduring the devastating 1926 hurricane, the Great Depression, travel restrictions during World War II, and an invasion of criminals released from Cuba during the 1980 Mariel boatlift.

Today, a renaissance is under way as Miami Beach revels in the architectural heritage of its mile-square Art Deco District. About 650 significant buildings in the district are listed on the National Register of Historic Places.

The term "Art Deco" describes the modern architecture that emerged in the 1920s and 1930s. Its forms are eclectic, drawn from nature (including birds, butterflies, and flowers); from ancient Aztec, Mayan, Babylonian, Chaldean, Egyptian, and Hebrew designs; and from the streamlined, aerodynamic shapes of modern transportation and industrial machinery. For detailed information on touring the Art Deco District, contact the Miami Design Preservation League (*see* Guided Tours).

In our exploration, we direct you from the mainland to Miami Beach and through a cross section of the Art Deco District, and the elegant residential neighborhood surrounding the La Gorce Country Club.

Driving Tour of Miami Beach

From the mainland, cross the **MacArthur Causeway** to Miami Beach. To reach the causeway from downtown Miami, turn east off Biscayne Boulevard north of N.E. 11th Street. From I–95, turn east onto I–395. The eastbound Dolphin Expressway (Rte. 836) becomes I–395 east of the I–95 interchange. As you approach the MacArthur Causeway bridge across the Intracoastal Waterway, *The Miami Herald* building looms above Biscayne Bay on your left.

1 Cross the bridge to **Watson Island,** created by dredging in 1931. Make the first left turn to the **Japanese Garden,** which has stone lanterns, a rock garden, and an eight-ton, eight-foot-tall statue of Hotei, Japanese god of prosperity. Industrialist Kiyoshi Ichimura gave the one-acre garden to the City of Miami in 1961 as an expression of friendship. It was restored in 1988.

East of Watson Island, the causeway leaves Miami and enters
2 Miami Beach. On the left, you'll pass the bridge to **Palm and**
3 **Hibiscus islands** and then the bridge to **Star Island.** Past and present celebrities who have lived on these islands include Al Capone (93 Palm Ave., Palm Island), author Damon Runyon (271 Hibiscus Island), and TV star Don Johnson (8 Star Island).

East of Star Island, the causeway mounts a high bridge. Look
4 left to see an island with an obelisk, the **Flagler Memorial Monument.** The memorial honors Henry M. Flagler, who built the Florida East Coast Railroad to Miami, opening south Florida to tourism and commerce.

Just beyond the bridge, turn right onto Alton Road past the **Mi-**
5 **ami Beach Marina** (300 Alton Rd., tel. 305/673–6000), where dive boats depart for artificial reefs offshore in the Atlantic Ocean.

Continue to the foot of Alton Road, turn left on Biscayne Street, then go right at Washington Avenue to enter **South**
6 **Pointe Park** (1 Washington Ave.). From the 50-yard Sunshine Pier, which adjoins the mile-long jetty at the mouth of Government Cut, you can fish while watching huge ships pass. No bait or tackle is available in the park. Other facilities include two observation towers, and volleyball courts.

When you leave the park, take Washington Avenue north. On the northwest corner of Washington Avenue and 5th Street, Cassius Clay (now Muhammad Ali) prepared for his champion-
7 ship bouts in the **Fifth Street Gym.** You can visit to watch young boxers train. *501 Washington Ave., tel. 674–8481. Open Mon.–Sat. 8–7, Sun. 8–2. Admission: $1.*

Art Deco District, **8**
Bass Museum of Art, **15**
Espanola Way, **9**
Fifth Street Gym, **7**
Flagler Memorial, **4**
Fontainebleau Hilton, **16**
La Gorce Country Club, **17**
Hibiscus Island, **3**
Hotel National, **14**
Jackie Gleason Theater, **13**
Lincoln Rd. Arts District, **10**
Miami Beach City Hall, **11**
Miami Beach Marina, **5**
Palm Island, **2**
South Pointe Park, **6**
Stephen Muss Convention Center, **12**
Watson Island, **1**

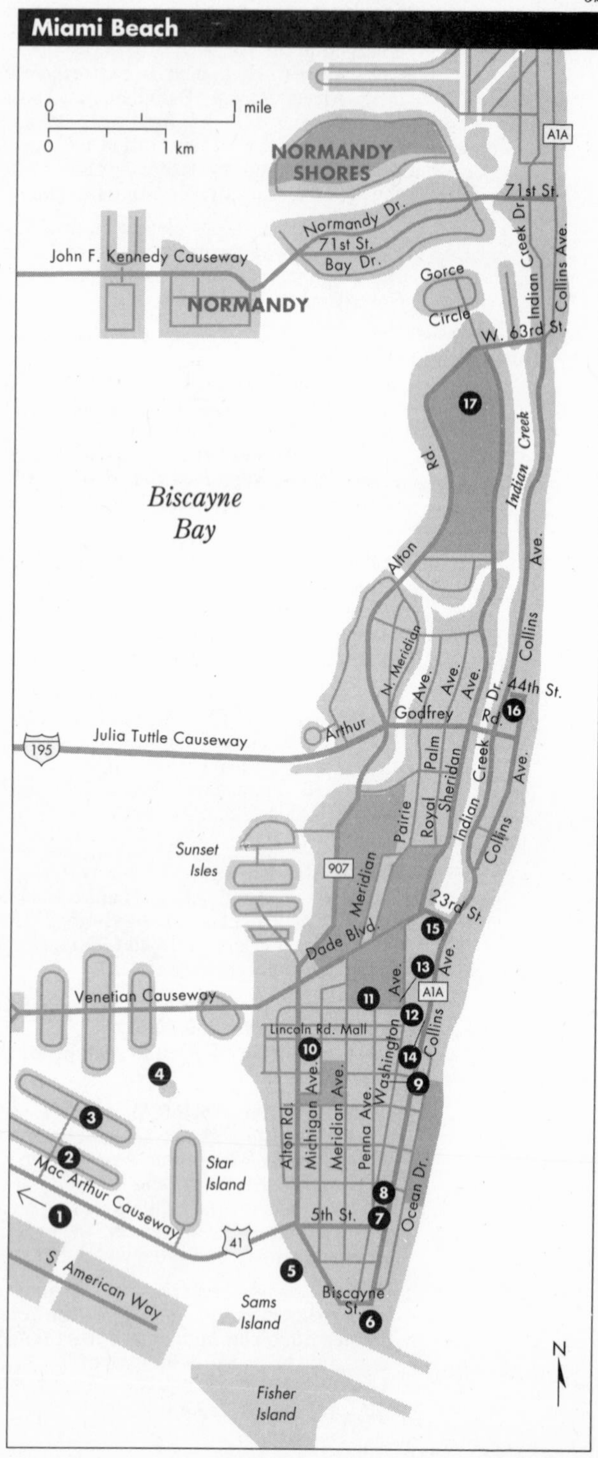

Time Out A block east on 5th Street and a block north on Collins Avenue, Albert Starr's **Nature's Garden Bakery** makes delicious kosher special-diet breads and cakes. Try the millet cookies and the apple strudel without salt, sweetener, eggs, or yeast. *600 Collins Ave., tel. 305/534–1877. Closed Fri. afternoon and Sat.*

Return to 5th Street, go a block east to Ocean Drive, and turn
8 left. A block north at 6th Street, the **Art Deco District** begins. Take Ocean Drive north past a line of pastel-hued Art-Deco hotels on your left and palm-fringed Lummus Park and the beach on your right. Turn left on 15th Street, and left again at the next corner onto Collins Avenue.

Now drive along the Art Deco District's two main commercial streets. Take Collins Avenue south, turn right at 5th Street, and right again at the next corner onto **Washington Avenue,** an intriguing mixture of delicatessens, produce markets, and stores selling Jewish religious books and artifacts.

9 Go north on Washington Avenue past 14th Street to **Espanola Way,** a narrow street of Mediterranean-revival buildings constructed in 1925 and frequented through the years by artists and writers. In the 1930s, Cuban bandleader Desi Arnaz performed in the Village Tavern, now part of the **Clay Hotel & International Youth Hostel** (406 Espanola Way, tel. 305/534–2988). The hostel caters to young visitors from all over the world who seek secure, inexpensive lodgings within walking distance of the beach.

Turn left onto Espanola Way, go five blocks to Jefferson Avenue, and turn right. Three blocks north of Espanola Way is **Lincoln Road Mall,** a landscaped shopping thoroughfare known during its heyday in the 1950s as "Fifth Avenue of the South." Trams shuttle shoppers along the mall, which is closed to all other vehicular traffic between Washington Avenue and Alton Road.

Park in the municipal lot a half-block north of the mall to stroll
10 through the **Lincoln Road Arts District,** where three blocks of storefronts on Lincoln Road from Meridian Avenue to Lenox Avenue have been transformed into galleries, studios, classrooms, and art-related boutiques and cafes.

The arts district also includes the 500-seat **Colony Theater** (1040 Lincoln Rd., tel. 305/673–7486), a former movie house. Now it's a city-owned performing arts center featuring dance, drama, music, and experimental cinema.

From the parking lot, go to the first main street north of Lincoln Road Mall and turn right. You're on 17th Street, recently renamed **Hank Meyer Boulevard** for the local publicist who encouraged comedian Jackie Gleason to broadcast his TV show from Miami Beach in the 1950s. Two blocks east on your left,
11 beside the entrance to **Miami Beach City Hall** (1700 Convention Center Dr., tel. 305/673–7030), stands *Red Sea Road,* a huge red sculpture by Barbara Neijna.

12 Also to your left is the **Stephen Muss Convention Center** (1901 Convention Center Dr., tel. 305/673–7311), doubled in size in 1988 to 1.1 million square feet of exhibit space.

Continuing two more blocks east, admire another large sculpture, *Mermaid,* by Roy Lichtenstein, in front of **Jackie Gleason**
13 **Theater of the Performing Arts** (1700 Washington Ave., tel.

305/673–8300), where Gleason's TV show once originated. Now the 3,000-seat theater hosts touring Broadway shows and classical concert performers. Near the sculpture, stars appearing in the theater since 1984 have left their footprints and signatures in concrete. This **Walk of the Stars** includes George Abbott, Julie Andrews, Leslie Caron, Carol Channing, and Edward Villella.

Go two more blocks east on Hank Meyer Boulevard to Collins Avenue, toward three of the largest Art Deco hotels, built in the 1940s with streamlined tower forms reflecting the 20th century's transportation revolution:

14 The round dome atop the tower of the 11-story **Hotel National** (1677 Collins Ave., tel. 305/532–2311) resembles a balloon. The tower at the 12-story **Delano Hotel** (1685 Collins Ave., tel. 305/538–7881) sports fins suggesting the wings of an airplane or a Buck Rogers spaceship. The 11-story **Ritz Plaza** (1701 Collins Ave., tel. 305/531–6881) rises to a cylindrical tower resembling a submarine periscope.

Turn left on Collins Avenue. At 21st Street, turn left beside the Miami Beach Public Library in Collins Park, go two blocks to
15 Park Avenue, and turn right. You're approaching the **Bass Museum of Art,** with a diverse collection of European art, including *The Holy Family,* a painting by Peter Paul Rubens; *The Tournament,* a 16th-century Flemish tapestry; and works by Albrecht Dürer and Henri de Toulouse-Lautrec. Park behind the museum and walk around to the entrance past massive tropical baobab trees. *2121 Park Ave., tel. 305/673–7530. Open Tues.–Sat. 10–5, Sun. 1–5. Admission: $2 adult, $1 students with ID, children 16 and under free. Donations Tues.*

Return on 21st Street or 22nd Street to Collins Avenue and turn left. As you drive north, a triumphal archway looms ahead, framing a majestic white building set in lush vegetation beside a waterfall and tropical lagoon. This vista is an illusion—a 13,000-square-foot outdoor mural on an exterior
16 wall of the **Fontainebleau Hilton Resort and Spa** (4441 Collins Ave., tel. 305/538–2000). Artist Richard Haas designed the mural to illustrate how the hotel and its rock-grotto swimming pool would look behind the wall. Locals call the 1,206-room hotel "Big Blue." It's the giant of Miami Beach, with 190,000 square feet of meeting and exhibit space.

Go left on 65th Street, turn left again at the next corner onto Indian Creek Drive, and right at 63rd Street, which leads into Alton Road, a winding, landscaped boulevard of gracious
17 homes styled along Art Deco lines. You'll pass the **La Gorce Country Club** (5685 Alton Rd. tel. 305/866–4421), which developer Carl Fisher built and named for his friend Oliver La Gorce, then president of the National Geographic Society.

To return to the mainland on the MacArthur Causeway, stay on Alton Road south to 5th Street, then turn right.

Exploring Little Havana

Orientation Thirty years ago, the tidal wave of Cubans fleeing the Castro regime flooded an elderly neighborhood just west of downtown Miami with refugees. This area became known as Little Havana. Today, with a half-million Cubans widely dispersed throughout Greater Miami, Little Havana remains a magnet for Cubans and Anglos alike. They come to experience the flavor of traditional Cuban culture.

That culture, of course, functions in Spanish. Many Little Havana residents and shopkeepers speak almost no English. If you don't speak Spanish, point and smile to communicate.

Touring Little Havana

Begin this tour in downtown Miami, westbound on Flagler Street. Cross the Miami River to Little Havana, and park near Flagler Street and Ronald Reagan Avenue (S.W. 12th Ave.) to explore a thriving commercial district.

1 Continue west on Flagler Street to Teddy Roosevelt Avenue (S.W. 17th Ave.) and pause at **Plaza de la Cubanidad,** on the southwest corner. Red-brick sidewalks surround a fountain and monument with a quotation from José Martí, a leader in Cuba's struggle for independence from Spain: "*Las palmas son novias que esperan.*" (The palm trees are girlfriends who will wait.)

2 Turn left at Douglas Road (S.W. 37th Ave.), drive south to **Calle Ocho** (S.W. 8th St.), and turn left again. You are now on the main commercial thoroughfare of Little Havana.

Time Out

For a total sensory experience, have a snack or meal at **Versailles,** a popular Cuban restaurant. Etched-glass mirrors lining its walls amplify bright lights and the roar of rapid-fire Spanish. Most of the servers don't speak English; you order by pointing to a number on the menu (choice of English or Spanish menus). Specialties include *palomilla*, a flat beefsteak; *vieja ropa* (literally, old clothes), a shredded-beef dish in tomato sauce; and *arroz con pollo*, chicken and yellow rice. *3555 S.W. 8th St., tel. 305/445–7614. Open Sun.–Thurs. 8 AM–2 AM, Fri. 8 AM–3:30 AM, Sat. 8 AM–4:30 AM.* AE, CB, DC, MC, V.

East of Unity Boulevard (S.W. 27th Ave.), Calle Ocho becomes a one-way street eastbound through the heart of Little Havana, where every block deserves exploration. If your time is limited, we suggest the three-block stretch from S.W. 14th Avenue to S.W. 11th Avenue. Parking is more ample west of Ronald Reagan Avenue (S.W. 12th Ave.).

3 At Calle Ocho and Memorial Boulevard (S.W. 13th Ave.) stands the **Brigade 2506 Memorial,** commemorating the victims of the unsuccessful 1961 Bay of Pigs invasion of Cuba by an exile force. An eternal flame burns atop a simple stone monument with the inscription: "*Cuba—A Los Martires de La Brigada de Asalto Abril 17 de 1961.*" The monument also bears a shield with the Brigade 2506 emblem, a Cuban flag superimposed on a cross. Walk a block south on Memorial Boulevard from the Brigade 2506 Memorial to see other monuments relevant to Cuban history, including a statue of José Martí.

4 When you return to your car, drive five blocks south on Ronald Reagan Avenue to the **Cuban Museum of Art and Culture.** Created by Cuban exiles to preserve and interpret the cultural heritage of their homeland, the museum has expanded its focus to embrace the entire Hispanic art community. It has a small permanent collection and mounts temporary exhibitions. On its schedule for early 1989 are black culture in Cuba from the 16th century to the present and a retrospective display of works by Mario Carreno, a Cuban painter now living in Chile. *1300 S.W.*

Miami, Coral Gables and Key Biscayne

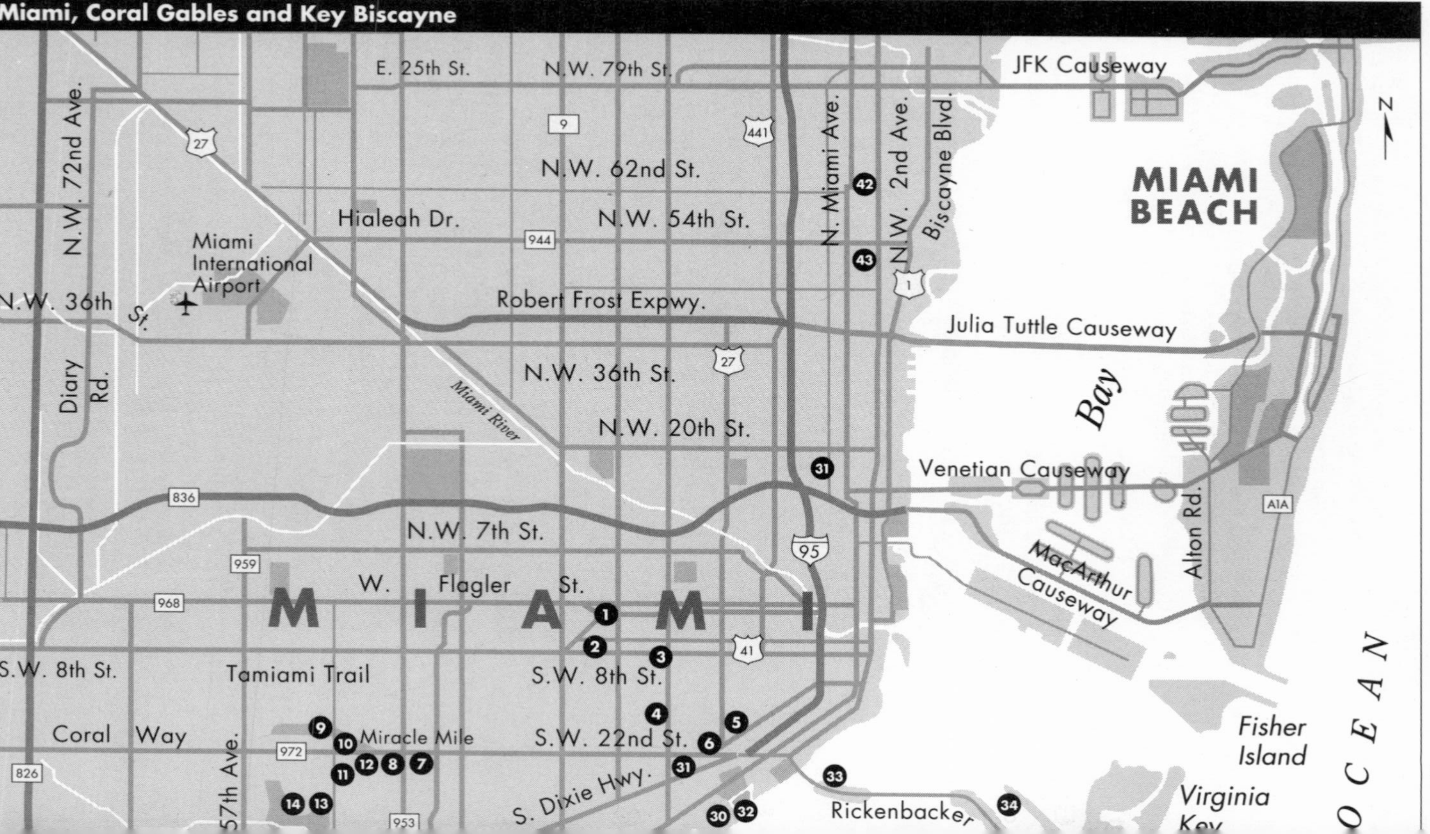

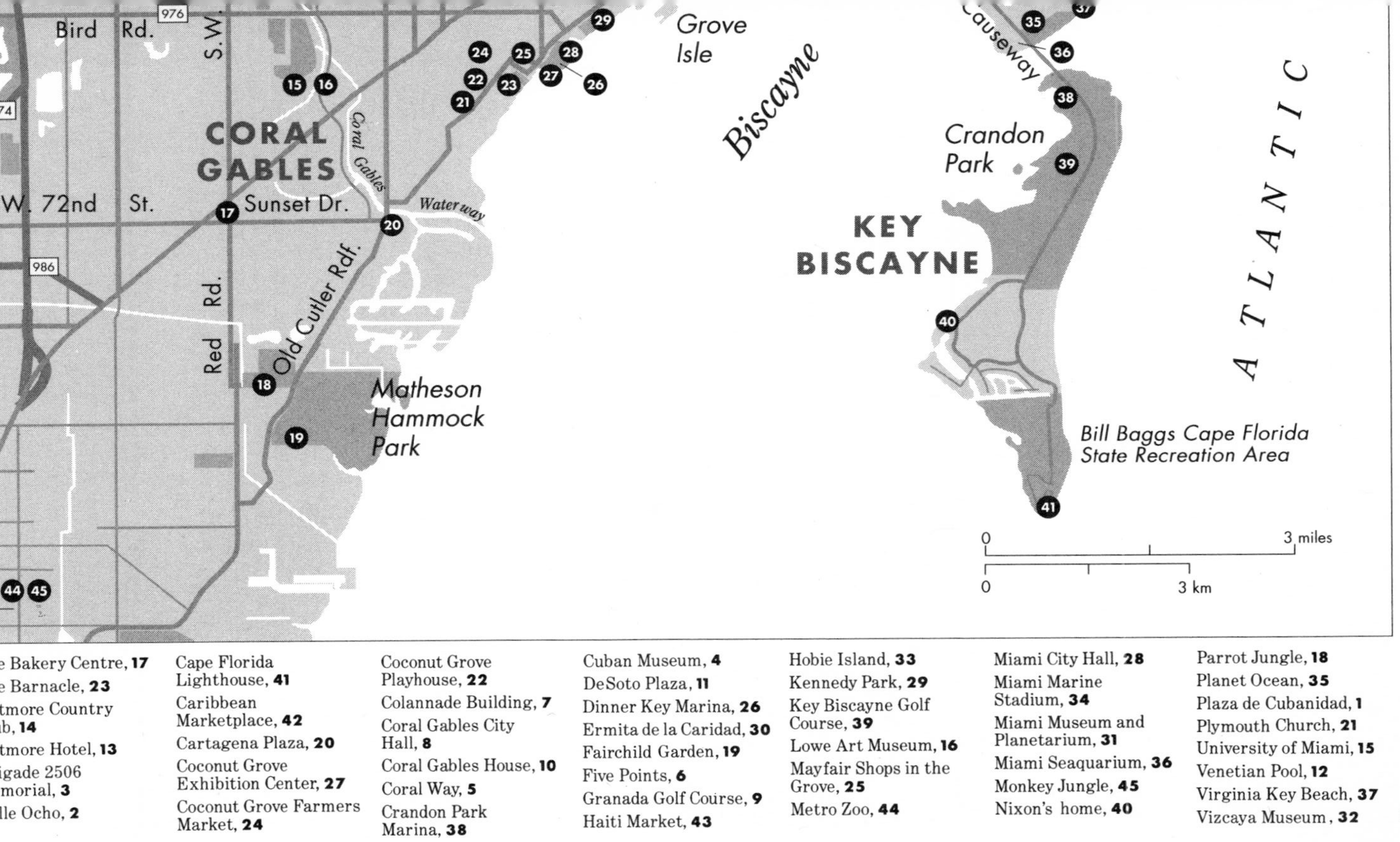

The Bakery Centre, **17**
The Barnacle, **23**
Biltmore Country Club, **14**
Biltmore Hotel, **13**
Brigade 2506 Memorial, **3**
Calle Ocho, **2**
Cape Florida Lighthouse, **41**
Caribbean Marketplace, **42**
Cartagena Plaza, **20**
Coconut Grove Exhibition Center, **27**
Coconut Grove Farmers Market, **24**
Coconut Grove Playhouse, **22**
Colannade Building, **7**
Coral Gables City Hall, **8**
Coral Gables House, **10**
Coral Way, **5**
Crandon Park Marina, **38**
Cuban Museum, **4**
DeSoto Plaza, **11**
Dinner Key Marina, **26**
Ermita de la Caridad, **30**
Fairchild Garden, **19**
Five Points, **6**
Granada Golf Course, **9**
Haiti Market, **43**
Hobie Island, **33**
Kennedy Park, **29**
Key Biscayne Golf Course, **39**
Lowe Art Museum, **16**
Mayfair Shops in the Grove, **25**
Metro Zoo, **44**
Miami City Hall, **28**
Miami Marine Stadium, **34**
Miami Museum and Planetarium, **31**
Miami Seaquarium, **36**
Monkey Jungle, **45**
Nixon's home, **40**
Parrot Jungle, **18**
Planet Ocean, **35**
Plaza de Cubanidad, **1**
Plymouth Church, **21**
University of Miami, **15**
Venetian Pool, **12**
Virginia Key Beach, **37**
Vizcaya Museum, **32**

12th Ave., tel. 305/858–8006. Open weekdays 10–5, weekends 1–5. Admission: donation requested.

To return to downtown Miami, take Ronald Reagan Avenue back north to S.W. 8th Street, turn right, go east to Miami Avenue or Brickell Avenue, turn left, and go north across the Miami River.

Exploring Coral Gables/Coconut Grove/ South Miami

Orientation This tour directs you through three separate communities, each unique in character. Two of them, Coral Gables and South Miami, are independent suburbs. The third, Coconut Grove, was annexed to the City of Miami in 1925 but still retains a distinctive personality.

Coral Gables, a planned community of broad boulevards and Spanish Mediterranean architecture, justifiably calls itself "The City Beautiful." Developer George E. Merrick began selling Coral Gables lots in 1921 and incorporated the city in 1925. He named most of the streets for Spanish explorers, cities, and provinces. Street names are at ground level beside each intersection on whitewashed concrete cornerstones.

The 1926 hurricane and the Great Depression prevented Merrick from fulfilling many aspects of his plan. The city languished until after World War II but then grew rapidly. Today, Coral Gables has a population of about 43,000. In its bustling downtown, many multinational companies maintain headquarters or regional offices.

A pioneer farming community that grew into a suburb, South Miami today retains small-town charm. Its main attraction for visitors is an artsy new mall, The Bakery Centre, with galleries, specialty shops, movie theaters, and restaurants on the former site of Holsum Bakery. Samples of the old bakery's architectural ornamentation are on display in The Bakery Centre.

Coconut Grove is south Florida's oldest settlement, inhabited as early as 1834 and established by 1873, two decades before Miami. Its early settlers included Bahamian blacks, "conchs" from Key West, and New England intellectuals. They built a community that attracted artists, writers, and scientists to establish winter homes. By the end of World War I, more people listed in *Who's Who* gave addresses in Coconut Grove than anyplace else.

To this day, Coconut Grove reflects the pioneers' eclectic origins. Posh estates mingle with rustic cottages, modest frame homes, and starkly modern dwellings—often on the same block. To keep Coconut Grove a village in a jungle, residents lavish affection on exotic plantings while battling to protect remaining native vegetation.

The historic center of the Village of Coconut Grove went through a hippy period in the 1960s, laid-back funkiness in the 1970s, and a teenybopper invasion in the early 1980s. Today, the tone is increasingly upscale, mellow, and sophisticated—a congenial mix of art-cinema and legitimate theaters, galleries, boutiques, elegant restaurants, and bars and sidewalk cafes where the literati hang out.

Two Junior League books, *Historic Coral Gables* and *Historic Coconut Grove*, give directions for self-guided walking tours.

Driving Tour of Coral Gables/Coconut Grove/South Miami

This tour begins in downtown Miami. Go south on S.E. 2nd Avenue, which becomes Brickell Avenue and crosses the Miami River. Half a mile south of the river, turn right onto **Coral Way,** which at this point is S.W. 13th Street. Within half a mile, Cor-
5 al Way doglegs left under I–95 and becomes S.W. 3rd Avenue.
6 It continues another mile to a complex intersection, **Five Points,** and doglegs right to become S.W. 22nd Avenue.

Along the S.W. 3rd Avenue and S.W. 22nd Avenue segments of Coral Way, banyan trees planted in the median strip in 1929 arch over the roadway. The banyans end at the Miami/Coral Gables boundary, where **Miracle Mile** begins. This four-block stretch of Coral Way, from Douglas Road (37th Ave.) to Le Jeune Road (42nd Ave.) in the heart of downtown Coral Gables, is really a half-mile long. To stroll the full mile, walk up one side and down the other. Miracle Mile's 160 shops range from chain restaurants and shoe stores to posh boutiques and beauty salons. The stores are numbered from 1 to 399. As you go west, numbers and quality both increase. Request a complete directory from the Miracle Mile Merchants' Association (220 Miracle Mile, Suite 218, Coral Gables, tel. 305/445–0591).

7 **The Colonnade Building** (133–169 Miracle Mile, Coral Gables) on Miracle Mile once housed George Merrick's sales office. Its rotunda bears an ornamental frieze and a Spanish-tile roof 75 feet above street level. The Colonnade Building has been restored and connected to an adjacent new high-rise hotel and office building that echoes the rotunda's roofline.

The ornate Spanish Renaissance structure facing Miracle Mile
8 just west of Le Jeune Road is **Coral Gables City Hall,** opened in 1928. It has a three-tier tower topped with a clock and a 500-pound bell. Inside the bell tower, a mural by artist Denman Fink depicts the four seasons. *405 Biltmore Way, Coral Gables, tel. 305/442–6400. Open weekdays 8–5.*

Follow Coral Way west of Le Jeune Road to the right of City
9 Hall. You'll pass the **Granada Golf Course** (2001 Granada Blvd., Coral Gables, tel. 305/442–6484), one of two public courses in Coral Gables.

One block west of the golf course, turn right on Toledo Street to
10 park behind **Coral Gables House,** George Merrick's boyhood home. The city acquired the dwelling in 1976 and restored its 1920s appearance. It contains many Merrick family furnishings and artifacts. *907 Coral Way, Coral Gables, tel. 305/442–6593. Open Sun. and Wed. 1–4. Admission: $1 adults, 50 cents children.*

Return to Coral Way, turn right, then left at the first stoplight. Now you're southbound on Granada Boulevard, approaching
11 **De Soto Plaza and Fountain,** a classical column on a pedestal with water flowing from the mouths of four sculptured faces. The closed eyes of the face looking west symbolize the day's end. Denman Fink designed the fountain in the early 1920s.

Follow the traffic circle almost completely around the fountain to northeast-bound De Soto Boulevard. On your right in the
12 next block is **Venetian Pool,** a unique municipal swimming pool

transformed from a rock quarry. *2701 De Soto Blvd., Coral Gables, tel. 305/442–6483. Summer hours: weekdays 11–7:30, weekends 10–4:30; winter hours: Tues.–Fri. 11–4, weekends 10–4:30. Admission (nonresident): $2.85 adults, $1.14 children under 13. Free parking across De Soto Blvd.*

From the pool, go around the block with right turns onto Almeria Avenue, Toledo Street, and Sevilla Avenue. You'll return to the De Soto Fountain and take De Soto Boulevard southeast to
13 emerge in front of **The Biltmore Hotel** (1200 Anastasia Ave., Coral Gables, tel. 305/445–1926). Like the Freedom Tower in downtown Miami, the Biltmore's 26-story tower is a replica of the Giralda Tower in Seville, Spain.

The opulent Biltmore opened in January 1926 as the centerpiece of George Merrick's planned city. It suffered financially during the Great Depression, became a veterans' hospital during World War II, and stood vacant from 1968 to 1986. After extensive restoration and renovation, it has reopened as a 279-unit hotel.

Go inside the Biltmore to admire the lobby's vaulted ceiling and gargoyles, the two ballrooms' impressive chandeliers and intricately painted ceilings, and the open courtyard's fountain and gracious proportions. A second-floor promenade overlooks the 18-hole Biltmore Golf Course, now a public course known for its scenic and competitive layout, and the largest hotel pool in the United States, with a capacity of 1.25 million gallons.

Just west of The Biltmore Hotel stands a separate building,
14 **The Biltmore Country Club,** which the city restored in the late 1970s. It's a richly ornamented beaux arts–style structure with a superb colonnade and courtyard. On its ground floor are facilities for golfers. In the former club lounge, Le Biltmore Restaurant occupies a lofty room paneled with veneer from 60 species of trees. The first-floor wings and entire second floor house the **Metropolitan Museum and Art Center,** with a permanent collection of contemporary graphics, pre-Columbian artifacts, and historic costumes. *Our Tree of Life,* a Jacques Lipchitz sculpture in front of the building, depicts muscular, foreshortened figures straining to reach the twin tablets of the Ten Commandments. *1212 Anastasia Ave., Coral Gables, tel. 305/442–1448. Open Tues.–Sat. 10–5, Sun. noon–5. Admission: $2 adults, $1 children 12–18 and senior citizens, children under 12 free. Donations Wed.*

From the museum, turn right on Anastasia Avenue, go east to Granada Boulevard, and turn right. Continue south on Granada Boulevard over a bridge across the **Coral Gables Waterway,** which connects the grounds of The Biltmore Hotel with Biscayne Bay. In the hotel's heyday, Venetian gondolas plied the waterway, bringing guests to a bayside beach.

At Ponce de León Boulevard, turn right. On your left is Metrorail's Stonehenge-like concrete structure, and on your
15 right, the **University of Miami**'s 260-acre main campus. With nearly 20,000 students, UM is the largest southeast private university.

Turn right at the first stoplight to enter the campus and park in
16 the lot on your right designated for visitors to UM's **Lowe Art Museum.** The Lowe's permanent collection of 8,000 works includes Renaissance and Baroque art, American paintings,

Latin American art, and Navajo and Pueblo Indian textiles and baskets. The museum also hosts traveling exhibitions. *1301 Stanford Dr., Coral Gables, tel. 305/284–3535 for recorded information, 305/284–3536 for museum office. Open all year Sun. and Tues.–Fri. noon–5, Sat. 10–5. Admission: $2 adults, $1 students and seniors, children under 16 free.*

Now exit the UM campus on Stanford Drive, pass under Metrorail, and cross Dixie Highway. Just beyond the Burger King on your right, bear right onto Maynada Street. Turn right at the next stoplight onto **Sunset Drive.** Fine old homes and mature trees line this officially designated "historic and scenic road" that leads to and through downtown South Miami.

On the northwest corner of Sunset Drive and Red Road (57th Ave.), note the pink building with a mural on which an alligator seems ready to devour a horrified man. This trompe l'oeil fantasy, *South Florida Cascade,* by illusionary artist Richard Haas,
17 highlights the main entrance to **The Bakery Centre.** To park, turn right on Red Road, go two blocks, and turn left into the mall's lot. Merchants will validate your ticket for two hours of free parking. *5701 Sunset Dr., South Miami, tel. 305/662–4155. Open daily 10–9, except Sun. noon–5.*

On the third level of The Bakery Centre, the **Miami Youth Museum** features cultural arts exhibits, hands-on displays, and activities to enhance a child's creativity and inspire interest in artistic careers. *5701 Sunset Dr., South Miami, tel. 305/661–ARTS. Open Tues.–Fri. 10–5, weekends noon–5. Admission: $2, children under 2 free.*

Go south on Red Road, turn right onto Killian Drive (S.W.
18 112th St.), and right again into the grounds of **Parrot Jungle,** where more than 1,100 exotic birds are on display. Many of the parrots, macaws, and cockatoos fly free, but they'll come to you for seeds that you can purchase from old-fashioned gumball machines. Attend a trained-bird show, watch baby birds in training, and pose for photos with colorful macaws perched on your arms. The "jungle" is a natural hammock surrounding a sinkhole. Stroll among orchids and other flowering plants nestled among ferns, bald-cypress trees, and massive live oaks. Also see the cactus garden and Flamingo Lake, with a breeding population of 75 Caribbean flamingos. Opened in 1936, Parrot Jungle is one of Greater Miami's oldest and most popular commercial tourist attractions. *11000 S.W. 57th Ave., Miami, tel. 305/666–7834. Open daily 9:30–5. Admission: $8.50 adults, $4 children 6–12.*

From Parrot Jungle, take Red Road ⅓ mile south and turn left at Old Cutler Road, which curves north along the uplands of
19 South Florida's coastal ridge. Visit 83-acre **Fairchild Tropical Garden,** the largest tropical plant research institution in the United States. *10901 Old Cutler Rd., Coral Gables, tel. 305/667–1651. Open daily except Christmas 9:30–4:30. Admission: $4 adults, children 12 under free with parents. Hourly tram rides, $1 adults, 50 cents children.*

North of the garden, Old Cutler Road traverses Dade County's oldest and most scenic park, **Matheson Hammock Park.** The Civilian Conservation Corps developed the 100-acre tracts of upland and mangrove swamp in the 1930s on land donated by a local pioneer, Commodore J. W. Matheson. The park's most popular feature is a bathing beach, where the tide flushes a saltwater "atoll" pool through four gates. *9601 Old Cutler Rd., Coral Gables, tel. 305/666-6979. Park open 6 AM–sundown. Pool lifeguards on duty winter 7:30 AM–6 PM, summer 7:30 AM–7 PM. Parking fee for beach and marina $2 per car, $5 per car with trailer. Limited upland parking free.*

20 Continue north on Old Cutler Road to **Cartagena Plaza,** cross the Le Jeune Road bridge over the waterway, and turn right at the first stoplight onto Ingraham Highway. Four blocks later, you're back in the City of Miami, at the south end of Coconut Grove. Follow Ingraham Highway to Douglas Road and turn right at the next stoplight onto Main Highway. You're following old pioneer trails that today remain narrow roads shaded by a canopy of towering trees.

One block past the stoplight at Royal Palm Avenue, turn left
21 onto Devon Road in front of **Plymouth Congregational Church.** Opened in 1917, this handsome coral-rock structure resembles a Mexican city mission church. The front door, of hand-carved walnut and oak with original wrought-iron fittings, came from an early 17th-century monastery in the Pyrenees. A hole in the lower right side of the door gives cats access to the church mice. *3429 Devon Rd., Coconut Grove, tel. 305/444-6521. Ask at the office to go inside the church, weekdays 9–4:30. Services Sun. 8:30 and 10 AM.*

When you leave the church, go around the block opposite the church. Turn left from Devon Road onto Hibiscus Street, left again onto Royal Palm Avenue, and left at the stoplight onto Main Highway.

You're now headed for the historic **Village of Coconut Grove,** a trendy commercial district with red-brick sidewalks and more than 300 restaurants, stores, and art galleries.

Parking can be a problem in the village—especially on weekend evenings, when police direct traffic and prohibit turns at some intersections to prevent gridlock. Be prepared to walk several blocks from the periphery into the heart of the Grove.

As you enter the village center, note the apricot-hued Spanish
22 rococo **Coconut Grove Playhouse** to your left. Built in 1926 as a movie theater, it became a legitimate theater in 1956 and is now owned by the State of Florida. The playhouse presents current and vintage Broadway plays, musical reviews, and experimental productions in its 1,100-seat main theater and 100-seat cabaret-style Encore Room. *3500 Main Hwy., Coconut Grove, tel. 305/442-4000 to box office; tel. 305/442-2662 to administrative office. Parking lot $2 weekdays, $3 weekends.*

Benches and a shelter opposite the playhouse mark the en-
23 trance to **The Barnacle,** a pioneer residence that is now a state historic site. Commodore Ralph Munroe built The Barnacle in 1891. Its broad, sloping roof and deeply recessed verandas channel sea breezes into the house. A central stairwell and rooftop vent allow hot air to escape. Many furnishings are original. While living at The Barnacle, Munroe built shallow-draft sailboats. One such craft, the ketch *Micco*, is on display. *3485 Main Hwy., Coconut Grove, tel. 305/448-9445. Open for tours only Thurs.–Mon. 9, 10:30, 1, and 2:30; closed Tues.–Wed. Admission: $1, children under 6 free. Reservations for groups of 8 or more; others meet ranger at entrance gate.*

Time Out Turn left at the next street, Commodore Plaza, and pause. **To Market/To Market,** a French gourmet cafe, features 16 kinds of muffins and a superb Greek-style salad bulging with brine-soaked olives and feta cheese. Other fare includes quiches, pates, sandwiches, cheeses, French pastries, wine, beer, and soft drinks. On weekend mornings, locals bicycle in for a croissant-and-eggs brunch and a chat with the neighbors. *3195 Commodore Plaza, Coconut Grove, tel. 305/446-6090. Open Sun.–Thurs. 7:30* AM*–10* PM*, Fri.–Sat. 7:30* AM*–midnight. Inside and outdoors service and carryouts available. AE, CB, DC, V.*

---

24 If your timing is right, visit the **Coconut Grove Farmers Market,** a laid-back, Brigadoon-like happening that appears as if by magic each Saturday on a vacant lot. To get there from Commodore Plaza, go north to Grand Ave., cross McDonald Ave. (S.W. 32nd Ave.), and go a block west to Margaret Street. Vendors set up outdoor stands to offer home-grown tropical fruits and vegetables (including organic produce), honey, seafoods, macrobiotic foods, and ethnic fare from the Caribbean, the Middle East, and Southeast Asia. Nonfood items for sale include plants, handicrafts, candles, jewelry, and homemade clothing. A masseur plies his trade, musicians play, and the Hare Krishnas come to chant. People-watching is half the fun. Open Saturday 8–3.

Now return to the heart of the village center. Then take Grand
25 Avenue a block east to Virginia Street and enter **Mayfair Shops in the Grove,** an exclusive open-air mall with a small branch of high-fashion Burdines department store and 74 other upscale shops. The 181 rooms of Mayfair House, a luxury hotel, surround the mall's southern section. As you stroll through Mayfair, admire its fountains, copper sculptures, and lavish Romanesque ornamentation formed in concrete. The design recalls a classic building in Chicago, The Rookery—with good reason. Frank Lloyd Wright, who remodeled The Rookery in 1905, taught Mayfair's architect, Kenneth Treister. *2911 Grand Ave., Coconut Grove, tel. 305/448–1700. Open Mon., Thurs., and Fri. 10–9; Tues., Wed., and Sat. 10–7; Sun. noon–5:30.*

Leaving the village center, take McFarlane Road east from its intersection with Grand Avenue and Main Highway. Peacock Park, site of the first hotel in Coconut Grove, is on your right.
26 Ahead, seabirds soar and sailboats ride at anchor in **Dinner Key Marina** (3400 Pan American Dr., Coconut Grove, tel. 305/579–6980), named for a small island where early settlers held picnics. With 374 moorings, it's one of Greater Miami's largest anchorages.

McFarlane Road turns left onto South Bayshore Drive. Turn right at the first stoplight onto Unity Boulevard (S.W. 27th Ave.), and go east into a parking lot that serves the marina and
27 the 105,000-square-foot **Coconut Grove Exhibition Center** (3360 Pan American Dr., Coconut Grove, tel. 305/579–3310), where antique, boat, and home-furnishings shows are held.

28 At the northeast corner of the lot is **Miami City Hall,** which was the terminal for the Pan American Airways's seaplane base at Dinner Key, 1934–35. The building retains its nautical-style art-deco trim. *3500 Pan American Dr., Coconut Grove, tel. 305/579–6666. Open Mon.–Fri. 8–5.*

From City Hall, drive west on Pan American Drive toward South Bayshore Drive, with its pyramidlike Grand Bay Hotel.
29 Turn right on South Bayshore Drive, and go north past **Kennedy Park.** Leave your car in the park's lot north of Kirk Street and walk toward the water. From a footbridge over the mouth of a small tidal creek, you'll enjoy an unobstructed view across Biscayne Bay to Key Biscayne. Film crews use the park often to make commercials and Italian westerns.

Continue north on South Bayshore Drive to Fair Isle Street and turn right. You're approaching **Grove Isle,** a 26-acre island with a 49-room hotel, high-rise apartments, and a private club. Developer Martin C. Margulies displays selections from his extensive private art collection in the lobbies. Along a walk beside the bay stand massive sculptures by modern luminaries, including Alexander Calder, Jean Dubuffet, Willem de Kooning, Alexander Liberman, and Isamu Noguchi. *4 Grove Isle Dr., Coconut Grove, tel. 305/250-4000. Phone the club's membership office, Mon.–Fri. 9–5, and mention* Fodor's Florida 1989 *to obtain a free guest pass. For a guided tour for a group of six or more, write two weeks in advance to Katherine Hinds, art curator.*

Return to South Bayshore Drive, turn right, and go north past the entrance to Mercy Hospital, where South Bayshore Drive becomes South Miami Avenue. At the next stoplight beyond the hospital, turn right on a private road that goes past St.
30 Kieran's Church to **Ermita de La Caridad**—Our Lady of Charity Shrine—a conical building 90 feet high and 80 feet wide overlooking the bay so worshipers face toward Cuba. A mural above the shrine's altar depicts the history of Cuba. *3609 S. Miami Ave., Coconut Grove, tel. 305/854-2404. Open daily 9–9.*

Return to South Miami Avenue, turn right, go about three-
31 tenths of a mile, and turn left to the **Miami Museum of Science and Space Transit Planetarium.** This is a participatory museum, chock-full of sound, gravity, and electricity displays for children and adults alike to manipulate and marvel at. A wildlife center behind the museum houses native Florida snakes, turtles and tortoises, birds of prey, and large wading birds. *3280 S. Miami Ave., Miami, tel. 305/854-4247; 24-hour Cosmic Hotline for planetarium show times and prices, 305/854-2222. Open daily 10–6. Admission to museum: $4 adults, $2.50 children; to planetarium shows $5 adults, $2.50 children and seniors; to laser light shows $6 adults, $3 children and seniors.*

32 South Miami Avenue, is the entrance to **Vizcaya Museum and Gardens,** an estate with an Italian Renaissance–style villa built in 1912–16 as the winter residence of Chicago industrialist James Deering.

The house and gardens overlook Biscayne Bay, east of South Miami Avenue, on a 30-acre tract that includes a native hammock and more than 10 acres of formal gardens and fountains. You can leave your car in the Museum of Science lot and walk across the street or drive across and park in Vizcaya's own lot.

The house contains 34 rooms of antique furniture, plus paintings, sculpture, and other decorative arts. These objects date from the 15th through the 19th centuries, representing the

Renaissance, Baroque, Rococo, and Neoclassic styles. *3251 S. Miami Ave., Miami, tel. 305/579–2813 (recording) or 305/579–2808. House open 9:30–4:30; ticket booth open to 5, gardens to 5:30. Admission $6 adults; $4 children 6 and over, students with ID, and seniors. Guided tours available, group tours by appointment.*

As you leave Vizcaya, turn north (left from the Museum of Science lot, right from the Vizcaya lot).

This short section of Brickell Avenue dead-ends at the north end of Alice Wainright Park. Retrace your path south to S.W. 32nd Road, and return to Miami Avenue, where our tour ends.

Turn right onto South Miami Avenue. You may follow South Miami Avenue all the way downtown or turn right at the first stoplight onto Federal Highway, which runs into Brickell Avenue one long block north, in front of the entrance to the Rickenbacker Causeway to Key Biscayne.

Exploring Virginia Key and Key Biscayne

Orientation

Government Cut and the Port of Miami separate the dense urban fabric of Miami Beach from Greater Miami's playground islands, Virginia Key and Key Biscayne. Parks occupy much of both keys, providing congenial upland with facilities for basking on the beach, golf, tennis, softball, and picnicking—plus uninviting but ecologically valuable stretches of dense mangrove swamp. Also on the keys are several marinas, an assortment of water-oriented tourist attractions, and the laid-back village where Richard Nixon set up his presidential vacation compound.

Driving Tour of Virginia Key and Key Biscayne

To reach Virginia Key and Key Biscayne, take the **Rickenbacker Causeway** across Biscayne Bay from the mainland at Brickell Avenue and S.W. 26th Road, about two miles south of downtown Miami. A fitness pathway for biking and jogging parallels the causeway. *Toll: $1 per car, bicycles and pedestrians free.*

33 About 200 feet east of the toll gate (just across the first low bridge), you can rent windsurfing equipment on **Hobie Island.** *Sailboards Miami, Box 16, Key Biscayne, tel. 305/361–SAIL, 305/441–2232, or 800/545–SAIL, windsurfing weather report at 305/361–WAVE. Daily 9:30–dusk. Cost: $12/hour.*

The **Old Rickenbacker Causeway Bridge,** built in 1947, is now a fishing pier. The west stub begins about a mile from the toll gate. Park near its entrance and walk past fishermen tending their lines to the gap where the center draw span across the Intracoastal Waterway was removed. There you can watch boat traffic pass through the channel, pelicans and other seabirds soar and dive, and porpoises cavort in the bay.

The new high-level **William M. Powell Bridge** rises 75 feet above the water to eliminate the need for a draw span. The panoramic view from the top encompasses the bay, keys, port, and downtown skyscrapers, with Miami Beach and the Atlantic Ocean in the distance. The speed limit is 45 mph, and you can't stop on the bridge, so park in the fishing pier lot and walk up.

34 Next along the causeway stands the 6,538-seat **Miami Marine Stadium** (3601 Rickenbacker Causeway, Miami, tel. 305/361–6732), where summer pops concerts take place and name entertainers perform throughout the year. You can join the audi-

ence on land in the stadium or on a boat anchored just offshore. Fourth of July concertgoers enjoy a spectacular fireworks display that is visible for miles up and down the bay. The grand prix of boat racing, the Miss Budweiser Unlimited Hydroplane Regatta, roars past the Marine Stadium for two weekends each June. The world's fastest boats compete for a $120,000 prize over a 1⅔-mile course at speeds up to 140 mph.

35 Adjoining the stadium is **Planet Ocean,** the world's largest marine science museum. Most of its displays invite your participation. Touch an iceberg; walk through the eye of a hurricane; and measure yourself against the smallest sailing vessel ever to cross the Atlantic, *April Fool*—an inch under six feet long. *3979 Rickenbacker Causeway, Miami, tel. 305/361–5786; recorded program information, 305/361–9455. Open daily 10–6. Admission: $6.50 adults, $5 seniors, $3 children 6–12.*

36 Down the causeway from Planet Ocean at the **Miami Seaquarium,** Lolita, a killer whale, cavorts in a huge tank. She performs three times a day, as do sea lions and dolphins in separate shows. Exhibits include a shark pool, 250,000-gallon tropical reef aquarium, and manatees. *4400 Rickenbacker Causeway, Miami, tel. 305/361–5705; recorded program information, 305/361–5703. Open daily 9:30–6:30. Admission: $12.95 adults, $11 seniors, $8.95 children.*

Opposite the causeway from the Seaquarium, a road leads
37 north to **Virginia Key Beach,** a City of Miami park, with a two-
mile stretch of ocean frontage, shelters, barbecue grills, ball
fields, nature trails, and a fishing area. Ask for directions at
the entrance gate. Cost is $2 per car.

From Virginia Key, the causeway crosses **Bear Cut** to the north
end of Key Biscayne, where it becomes Crandon Boulevard.
38 The **Crandon Park Marina,** behind Sundays on the Bay Restaurant, sells bait and tackle. *4000 Crandon Blvd., Key Biscayne,
tel. 361–1161. Open 7–6.*

Beyond the marina, Crandon Blvd. bisects 1,211-acre **Crandon Park.** Turnouts on your left lead to four parking lots, adjacent picnic areas, ball fields, and 3.3 miles of beach. *Open all year 8 AM—sunset. Parking: $2 per car.*

39 On your right are entrances to the **Key Biscayne Golf Course,** and the **International Tennis Center.**

From the traffic circle at the south end of Crandon Park,
Crandon Boulevard continues for two miles through the developed portion of Key Biscayne. You'll come back that way,
40 but first detour to the site of **President Nixon's home** (485 W.
Matheson Dr.). Turn right at the first stoplight onto Harbor
Drive, go about a mile, and turn right at Matheson Drive. A later owner enlarged and totally changed Nixon's home, which
was on the market at press time for $5.3 million.

Emerging from West Matheson Drive, turn right onto Harbor Drive and go about a mile south to Mashta Drive, and follow Mashta Drive east past Harbor Drive to Crandon Boulevard, and turn right.

You are approaching the entrance to **Bill Baggs Cape Florida State Recreation Area,** named for a crusading newspaper editor whose efforts prompted the state to create this 406-acre park. The park includes 1¼ miles of beach and a seawall along Biscayne Bay where fishermen catch bonefish, grouper, jack, snapper, and snook. There is a nature trail with native plants now rare on Key Biscayne.

Also in the park is the oldest structure in south Florida, the
41 **Cape Florida Lighthouse,** erected in 1825 to help ships avoid the shallows and reefs offshore. In 1836, a band of Seminole Indians attacked the lighthouse and killed the keeper's helper. You can climb the 122 steps to the top of the 95-foot-tall lighthouse and visit a keeper's dwelling reconstructed and furnished as it might have appeared in the early 1900s, when Key Biscayne was a coconut plantation with just a handful of residents. *1200 S. Crandon Blvd., Key Biscayne, tel. 305/361–5811. Park open all year 8–sunset. Lighthouse tours daily except Tues. at 10:30, 1, 2:30, and 3:30. Admission to park: $1 per vehicle with driver, 50 cents per passenger, children under 6 free; to lighthouse and keeper's residence: $1 per person.*

When you leave Cape Florida, follow Crandon Boulevard back to Crandon Park through Key Biscayne's commercial center, a mixture of posh shops and stores catering to the needs of the neighborhood. On your way back to the mainland, pause as you approach the Powell Bridge to admire the downtown Miami skyline. At night, the brightly lit Centrust Building looks from this angle like a clipper ship running under full sail before the breeze.

Exploring Little Haiti

Of the nearly 150,000 Haitians who have settled in Greater Miami, some 60,000 live in Little Haiti, a 200-block area on Miami's north side. More than 350 small Haitian businesses operate in Little Haiti.

For many Haitians, English is a third language. French is Haiti's official language, but much day-to-day conversation takes place in Creole, a French-based patois. Smiling and pointing will bridge any language barriers you may encounter.

This tour takes you through the Miami Design District on the margin of Little Haiti, then along two main thoroughfares which form the spine of the Haitian community. The tour begins in downtown Miami. Take Biscayne Boulevard north to N.E. 36th Street, turn left, go about four-tenths of a mile west to North Miami Avenue. Turn right, and go north through the **Miami Design District,** where about 225 wholesale stores, showrooms, and galleries feature interior furnishings and decorative arts.

Little Haiti begins immediately north of the Design District in an area with some of Miami's oldest dwellings, dating from the dawn of the 20th Century through the 1920s land-boom era. Drive the side streets to see elegant Mediterranean-style homes, and bungalows with distinctive coral rock trim.

Return to North Miami Avenue and go north. A half-block east on 54th Street is the tiny storefront office of the **Haitian Refugee Center,** a focal point of political activity in the Haitian community. *32 N.E. 54th St., tel. 305/757–8538.*

Continue north on North Miami Avenue past the former Cuban consulate, a pretentious Caribbean-Colonial mansion which is now a Haitian physician's clinic.

North of 85th Street, cross the Little River Canal into **El Portal**, a tiny suburban village of modest homes where more than a quarter of the property is now Haitian-owned. Turn right on N.E. 87th Street and right again on N.E. 2nd Avenue. You are now southbound on Little Haiti's main commercial thoroughfare.

Time Out Stop for Haitian breads and cakes made with coconut and other tropical ingredients at **Baptiste Bakery.** *7488 N.E. 2nd Ave., tel. 756–1119. Open 8–8.*

Along N.E. 2nd Avenue between 79th Street and 45th Street, a riot of color assails your eyes. Merchants have painted their buildings in vivid yellows, greens, reds, pinks, purples, and blues that Haitians find congenial and mellow.

42 Look for the **Caribbean Marketplace** which the Haitian Task Force (an economic development organization) plans to open early in 1989. Its merchants will sell tropical fruits and vegetables, handmade baskets, and Haitian art and craft items. *5927 N.E. 2nd Ave., Miami, tel. Haitian Task Force, 305/751–9783, for marketplace phone number.*

43 Continue south on N.E. 2nd Avenue to **Haiti Market,** a typical Little Haiti grocery store. It sells tropical fruits and vegetables, *morue* (dried codfish), dry beans to make *akara* (bean cakes), and other Caribbean fare. *5060 N.E. 2nd Ave., tel. 305/758–8980. Open Mon–Sat. 9–9, Sun. 9–6:30. No credit cards.*

This concludes the Little Haiti tour. To return to downtown Miami, take N.E. 2nd Avenue south to N.E. 35th Street, turn left, go east one block to Biscayne Boulevard, and turn right to go south.

Exploring South Dade

This tour directs you to attractions in the suburbs southwest of Dade County's urban core.

From downtown Miami, take the Dolphin Expressway (Rte. 836) west to the Palmetto Expressway (Rte. 826) southbound. Bear left south of Bird Road (S.W. 40th St.) onto the Don Shula Expressway (Rte. 874). Exit westbound onto Killian Drive (S.W. 104th St.) and go west of Lindgren Road (S.W. 137th Ave.). Turn left and go south to S.W. 128th Street, the entrance to the Tamiami Airport and **Weeks Air Museum,** where aircraft on display include a World War I-vintage Sopwith Camel (of Snoopy fame), and a B–17 Flying Fortress bomber and P–51 Mustang from World War II. *14710 S.W. 128th St., tel. 305/233–5197. Open: Wed.–Sun. 10–5. Admission: $4 adults, $2 children 12 and under and seniors.*

Continue south on Lindgren Road to Coral Reef Drive (S.W.
44 152nd St.). Turn left and go east to **Metro Zoo** and the **Gold Coast Railroad Museum.**

Metro Zoo covers 280 acres and is cageless; animals roam free on islands surrounded by moats. In "Wings of Asia," a 1.5-acre aviary, hundreds of exotic birds from southeast Asia fly through a rainforest beneath a protective net enclosure. The zoo has 3 miles of walkways, a monorail with 4 stations, and an open-air amphitheater for concerts. *12400 Coral Reef Dr. (S.W. 152nd St), tel. 305/251–0400 for recorded information.*

Gates open daily 10–4. Park closes at 5:30. Admission $6 adults, $3 children 3–12, under 3 free. Monorail tickets (unlimited use on day of purchase) $2.90 adults, $1.90 children. AE, MC; no credit cards at monorail and snack bar.

The railroad museum's collection includes a 1941 Silver Crescent dome car; and the *Ferdinand Magellan*, the only Pullman car ever constructed specifically for U.S. presidents, used by Roosevelt, Truman, Eisenhower, and Reagan. *12450 Coral Reef Dr. (S.W. 152nd St.), tel. 305/253–0063. Open Mon.–Fri. 10–3, Sat.–Sun. 10–5. Train rides Sat.–Sun., holidays. Phone for details. No credit.*

Return to Coral Reef Drive, turn right (east) to the Homestead Extension of Florida's Turnpike, take the turnpike south, exit at Hainlin Mill Drive (S.W. 216th St.), and turn right. Cross South Dixie Hwy. (U.S. 1), go three miles west, and turn right
45 into **Monkey Jungle,** home to more than 4,000 monkeys representing 50 species—including orangutans from Borneo and Sumatra, golden lion tamarins from Brazil, and brown lemurs from Madagascar. Performing monkey shows begin at 10 AM and run continuously at 45-minute intervals. The walkways of this 30-acre attraction are caged; the monkeys roam free. *14805 Hainlin Mill Dr., tel. 305/235–1611. Open daily 9:30–5. Admission $7.50 adults, $6.50 seniors, $4 children 5–12, under 5 free. AE, MC.*

Continue west on Hainlin Mill Drive to Newton Road (S.W. 157th Ave.), turn left and go south to **Orchid Jungle,** where you can stroll under live-oak trees to see orchids, ferns, bromeliads, and anthuriums, and peer through the windows of an orchid-cloning laboratory. *26715 SW 157th Ave., Homestead, tel. 305/247–4824 or US 800–327–2832. Open daily 8:30–5:30. Admission $5 adults, $4 seniors, $4 children 13–17, $1.50 children 6–12, under 6 free.*

Continue south on Newton Road to South Dixie Hwy. (U.S. 1), and turn left. Almost immediately, you'll find **Coral Castel of Florida** on your right. It was built by Edward Leedskalnin, a Latvian immigrant, between 1920 and 1940. The 3-acre castle has a 9-ton gate a child can open, an accurate working sundial, and a telescope of coral rock aimed at the north star, Polaris. *28655 South Dixie Hwy., Homestead, tel. 305/248–6344. Open daily 9–9. Admission $6.75 adults, $4.50 children 7–14, under 7 free. MC, Visa.*

Leaving Coral Castle, take South Dixie Hwy. onto Biscayne Drive (S.W. 288th St.) and go east to the turnpike. Take the turnpike back to the Don Shula Expressway (Rte. 874), which leads to the Palmetto Expressway (Rte. 826), which leads in turn to the Dolphin Expressway (Rte. 836).

Miami for Free

Concerts **PACE** (Performing Arts for Community and Education) (tel. 305/681–1470) supports free concerts in parks and cultural and religious institutions throughout the Greater Miami Area.

University of Miami School of Music (tel. 305/284–6477) offers many free concerts on the Coral Gables campus.

Museums Some museums are free all the time. Others have donation days, when you may pay as much or as little as you wish. (*See*

Exploring and Historical Buildings and Sites for free-admission policies at major museums.)

Views Ride an elevator to the 18th floor of the new Metro-Dade Center to enjoy spectacular views east to Miami Beach and Biscayne Bay and west to the Orange Bowl and Miami International Airport. Open Mon.–Fri. 8–5 (*see* Exploring Downtown Miami).

What to See and Do with Children

Greater Miami is a family-oriented vacation destination. Most of the major hotels can provide access to baby-sitting for young children. Although the area lacks major theme parks, families stay occupied with visits to the beach, zoo, and museums. Activities for teenagers are most prevalent on the beaches during spring break but occur throughout the year.

Family Activities **Dade County Youth Fair.** For 18 days at the end of March each year, Greater Miami's only amusement park comes to life at the Dade County Youth Fair in 260-acre Tamiami Park. The fairgrounds features a mile-long midway with over 80 amusement and thrill rides. The world's largest youth fair displays 50,000 student exhibits in 30 categories, including science projects and farm animals and equipment. Professional entertainers perform daily on seven stages. If you buy something at a local Publix supermarket, you'll get a gate pass good for free admission on Thursdays. *10901 Coral Way, Miami, tel. 305/223–7060. Open weekdays 4–11, weekends, 10 AM–11 PM. Admission: $4 adults, $2 children 6–12, under 6 free.*

Shopping

Except in the heart of the Everglades, visitors to the Greater Miami area are never more than 15 minutes away from a major shopping area. Downtown Miami long ago ceased to be the community's central shopping hub. Today Dade County has more than a dozen major malls, an international free zone, and hundreds of miles of commercial streets lined with storefronts and small neighborhood shopping centers. Many of these local shopping areas have an ethnic flavor, catering primarily to one of Greater Miami's immigrant cultures.

In the Latin neighborhoods, children's stores sell *vestidos* (party dresses) made of organza and lace. Men's stores sell the *guayabera*, a pleated, embroidered shirt that replaces the tie and jacket in much of the tropics. Traditional bridal shops display formal dresses that Latin families buy or rent for a daughter's *quince*, a lavish 15th-birthday celebration.

No standard store hours exist in Greater Miami. Phone ahead. When you shop, expect to pay Florida's 6% sales tax unless you have the store ship your goods out of Florida.

Shopping Districts
Coconut Grove Fashion District

Greater Miami is the fashion marketplace for the southeastern United States, the Caribbean, and Latin America. Many of the 500 garment manufacturers in Miami and Hialeah sell their clothing locally, in more than 30 factory outlets and discount fashion stores in the Miami Fashion District, east of I-95 along 5th Avenue from 29th Street to 25th Street. Most stores in the district are open 9–5 Monday–Saturday and accept credit cards.

Miami Free Zone The Miami Free Zone (MFZ) is an international wholesale trade center where the U.S. Customs Service supervises the exhibition and sales space. You can buy goods duty-free for export or pay duty on goods released for domestic use. More than 140 companies sell products from 75 countries, including aviation equipment, chemicals, clothing, computers, cosmetics, electronics, liquor, and perfumes. The 54-acre MFZ is five minutes west of Miami International Airport off the Dolphin Expressway (Rte. 836), and about 20 minutes from the Port of Miami. *Miami Free Zone, 2305 N.W. 107th Ave., tel. 305/591–4300. Open 9–5 Mon.–Fri.*

Cauley Square A tearoom and craft, antique, and clothing shops now occupy this complex of clapboard, coral-rock, and stucco buildings erected 1907–20 for railroad workers who built and maintained the line to Key West. Turn right off U.S. 1 at S.W. 224th Street. *22400 Old Dixie Hwy., Goulds, tel. 305/258–3543. Open Mon.–Sat. 10–4:30.*

Books Greater Miami's best English-language bookstore, **Books & Books, Inc.,** specializes in books on the arts, architecture, Floridiana, and contemporary and classical literature. Collectors enjoy browsing through the rare book room upstairs, which doubles as a photography gallery. Frequent poetry readings and book signings. *296 Aragon Ave., Coral Gables, tel. 305/442-4408. Open Mon.–Fri. 10–8, Sat. 10–7, Sun. noon–5.*

Children's Books and Toys The friendly staff at **A Likely Story** will help you choose books and educational toys that are appropriate to your child's interests and stage of development. *5740 Sunset Dr., South Miami, tel. 305/667–3730. Open Mon.–Sat. 10–5.*

Beaches

Miami Beach From Haulover Cut to Government Cut, a broad sandy beach extends for 10 continuous miles. Amazingly, it's a man-made beach—a marvel of modern engineering to repair the ravages of nature.

Along this stretch, erosion had all but eliminated the beach by the mid-1970s. Waves threatened to undermine the seawalls of hotels and apartment towers. From 1977 to 1981, the U.S. Army Corps of Engineers spent $51.5 million to pump tons of sand from offshore, restoring the beach to a 300-foot width. Between 21st and 46th streets, Miami Beach built a boardwalk atop a protective dune landscaped with sea oats, sea grape, and other native plants whose roots keep the sand from blowing away.

The new beach lures residents and visitors alike to swim and stroll. More than 7 million people visit the 7.1 miles of beaches within the Miami Beach city limits annually. The other 2.9 miles are in Surfside and Bal Harbour. Here's a guide to where kindred spirits gather:

The best windsurfing on Miami Beach occurs at First Street, just north of the Government Cut jetty, and at 21st Street. You can also windsurf at Penrod's windsurfing area in Lummus Park at 10th Street and in the vicinity of 3rd, 14th, and 21st streets. Lifeguards discourage windsurfing from 79th Street to 87th Street.

From 1st Street to 14th Street, senior citizens predominate early in the day. Later, a younger crowd appears, including family groups who flock to the new children's play areas in Lummus Park, between Ocean Drive and the beach at 5th and 14th streets.

The beaches opposite the Art Deco District, between 6th Street and 21st Street, attract a diverse clientele of locals and tourists from Europe and Asia. In this area, in an effort to satisfy foreign visitors, city officials don't enforce the law against female bathers going topless as long as everyone on the beach behaves with decorum. Topless bathing also occurs from 35th to 42nd streets. Gays tend to gather at 21st Street.

University of Miami students like the stretch of beach along Millionaires' Row (*see* Exploring), around 46th Street, where the big hotels have outdoor concession stands on the beach.

If you like a quiet beach experience, go to 35th, 53rd, or 64th streets. Tired young professionals there seek solitude to read a book. Paradoxically, young mothers like to bring their children to these beaches. The two groups coexist nicely.

French-Canadians frequent the 72nd Street beach.

High-schools groups gather at 85th Street for pickup games of volleyball and football.

During the winter, the wealthy condominium crowd clusters on the beach from 96th Street to 103rd Street in Bal Harbour.

City of Miami Beach beaches open daily with lifeguards, winter 8:30–5, summer 8–6. Bal Harbour and Surfside have no lifeguards, beaches open daily 24 hours. Beaches free in all three communities; metered parking nearby.

County Park Beaches

Metropolitan Dade County operates beaches at several of its major parks. Each county park operates on its own schedule that varies from day to day and season to season. Phone the park you want to visit for current hours and information on special events.

Crandon Park. Atlantic Ocean beach, popular with young Hispanics and with family groups of all ethnic backgrounds. *4000 Crandon Park Blvd., Key Biscayne, tel. 305/361–5421. Open daily winter 9–5, summer 9–7. Admission: $2 per car.*
Haulover Beach Park. Atlantic Ocean beach. A good place to be alone. Lightly used compared to other public beaches, except on weekends and in the peak tourist season, when it attracts a diverse crowd. *10800 Collins Ave., Miami, tel. 305/947–3525. Open daily winter 9–5, summer 9–7. Admission: $2 per car.*

Cape Florida

Bill Baggs Cape Florida State Recreation Area (*see* Exploring).

Participant Sports

Miami's subtropical climate is paradise for active people, a place where refugees from the frozen north can enjoy warm-weather outdoor sports, such as boating, swimming, and golf, all year long. During Miami's hot, humid summers, people avoid the sun's strongest rays by playing early or late in the day. We've listed below some of the most popular individual and group sports activities.

Water Sports
Marinas

Listed below are the major marinas in Greater Miami. The dock masters at these marinas can provide information on other marine services you may need. Also ask the dockmasters for *Teall's Tides and Guides, Miami-Dade County*, and other local nautical publications.

The U.S. Customs Service requires boats of less than five tons that enter the country along Florida's Atlantic Coast south of

Sebastian Inlet to report to designated marinas and call U.S. Customs on a direct phone line. The phones, located outside marina buildings, are accessible 24 hours a day. U.S. Customs phones in Greater Miami are at Haulover Marina and Watson Island Marina (both listed below).

Dinner Key Marina. Operated by City of Miami. Facilities include dockage with space for transients and a boat ramp. *3400 Pan American Dr., Coconut Grove, tel. 305/579–6980. Open daily 7 AM–11 PM.*

Haulover Park Marina. Operated by county lessee. Facilities include a bait-and-tackle shop, marine gas station, and boat launch. *10800 Collins Ave., Miami Beach, tel. 305/944–9647. Open daily 7–5.*

Watson Island Marina. City of Miami marina. Facilities include bait and tackle, boat ramp, and fuel. When the marina is busy, it stays open until all boaters are helped. *1050 MacArthur Causeway, Miami, tel. 305/371–2378. Open Mon.–Thurs. 7 AM–7:30 PM, Fri.–Sun. 7 AM–11 PM.*

Sailing

Dinner Key and the Coconut Grove waterfront remain the center of sailing in Greater Miami, although sailboat moorings and rentals are located along other parts of the bay and up the Miami River.

Windsurfing and Jet Skis

Penrod's. Rents jet skis, Hobie Cats, Windsurfers, and surfboards. *1001 Ocean Dr., Miami Beach, tel. 305/534–0687 or 305/534–0689. Open daily 10–sunset.*

Sailboards Miami. (*See* Exploring Virginia Key and Key Biscayne.)

Diving

Summer diving conditions in greater Miami equal or exceed the best of those in the Caribbean. Winter diving can be adversely affected when cold fronts come through. Dive-boat schedules vary with the season and with local weather conditions.

Fowey, Triumph, Long, and Emerald Reefs all are shallow 10–15-foot dives that are good for snorkelers and beginning divers. These reefs are on the edge of the continental shelf, a quarter of a mile from depths greater than 100 feet. You can also paddle around the tangled prop roots of the mangrove trees that line Florida's coastline, peering at the fish, crabs, and other onshore creatures that hide there.

Dive Boats and Instruction. Look for instructors who are affiliated with PADI (Professional Association of Dive Instructors) or NAUI (National Association of Underwater Instructors).

Divers Paradise Corp (4000 Crandon Blvd., Key Biscayne, tel. 305/361–DIVE). Complete dive shop and diving charter service, including equipment rental and scuba instruction. PADI affiliation.

Omega Diving International. Private instruction throughout Greater Miami. Equipment consultation and specialty courses, including instructor training and underwater photography. PADI affiliation. *8420 S.W. 133 Ave., Miami, tel. 305/385–0779 or 800/255–1966. Open daily 8–6.*

Pisces Divers Inc. (1290 5th St., Miami Beach, tel. 305/534–7710). Rents diving equipment and boats with captains at Miami Beach Marina. NAUI affiliation.

Underwater Art: Dive or snorkel to sculptor Lluis Dalmau's **ARTificial Reef,** 17 surrealistically painted culvert pipes and five reinforced-concrete ballerinas. *In 10 feet of water, north of Newport Fishing Pier, 16701 Collins Ave., Sunny Isles.*

Tennis Greater Miami has more than 60 private and public tennis centers, of which 11 are open to the public. All public tennis courts charge nonresidents an hourly fee.

Florida Tennis Association (9620 N.E. 2nd Ave., Miami Shores, tel. 305/757–8568). Contact for amateur tournament information.

Coral Gables **Biltmore Tennis Center.** Ten well-maintained hard courts. Site of annual Orange Bowl Junior International Tennis Tournament for children 18 and under in December. *1210 Anastasia Ave., tel. 305/442–6565. Open weekdays 8 AM–10PM, weekends 8–8. Nonresident day rate $3.04, night rate $4.33.*

Miami Beach **Flamingo Tennis Center.** Has 20 well-maintained clay courts. Site of the Rolex–Orange Bowl Junior International Tennis Tournament for teenagers 18 and under. *1000 12th St., tel. 305/673–7761. Open weekdays 8 AM–9 PM, weekends 8–6. Cost: day $2.12, night $2.65.*

Metropolitan Dade County **International Tennis Center.** Has 17 Laykold Cushion Plus hard courts, four lighted. Reservations necessary for night play. Closed to public play for about two weeks before and after the annual Lipton International Players Championships in March *7200 Crandon Blvd., Key Biscayne, tel. 305/361–8633. Open daily 8 AM–10 PM. Cost: weekdays $3, weeknights $4, weekend days $4, weekend nights $5.*

Spectator Sports

Greater Miami offers a broad variety of spectator sports events, including such popular pastimes as football and baseball, and more specialized events, such as boat racing and rugby. However, the community lacks a central clearinghouse for sports information and ticket sales.

You can find daily listings of local sports events on page 3 of *The Miami Herald* sports section, and in *The Miami News*. Both papers publish weekend sections on Friday with more detailed schedules and coverage of spectator sports. The *Herald* has a larger weekend section than The *News*, and it provides a recorded "sports line" message with a brief selection of major sports scores (tel. 305/376–3505).

Orange Bowl Festival. The activities of the annual Orange Bowl and Junior Orange Festival take place early November–late February. Best-known for its *King Orange Jamboree Parade* and *Orange Bowl Football Classic*, the festival also includes two tennis tournaments: the *Rolex/Orange Bowl International Tennis Championships* for top amateur national and international tennis players 16 and under, and an international tennis tournament for players 14 and under.

Other Orange Bowl sports events include a regatta series for university and professional sailors, a 5-km run in Coral Gables, the *Orange Bowl 10-km Race* on the 6.2-mile Grand Prix course, the annual *American Savings/Orange Bowl Marathon*, which draws over 2,500 runners, soccer games, bowling events, and a sports competition for physically disabled athletes. For tickets and a calendar of events: **Tickets, Orange Bowl Committee** (Box 350748, Miami 33135, tel. 305/642–5211).

Auto Racing **Hialeah Speedway.** The Greater Miami area's only independent raceway holds stock-car races on a ⅓-mile asphalt speedway in a 5,000-seat stadium. Four divisions of stock cars run weekly.

The Marion Edwards, Jr., Memorial Race for late-model stock cars is in November. Located on U.S. 27, ¼ mile east of Palmetto Expressway. (Rte. 826). *3300 W. Okeechobee Rd., Hialeah, tel. 305/821-6644. Open every Sat. late Jan.–early Dec. Gates open 6 PM, racing 7:45–11. Admission: $7 adults, $1 children 6–12.*

Grand Prix of Miami. Held in February for the Camel GT Championship on a 1.9-mile, E-shape track in downtown Miami, south of MacArthur Causeway and east of Biscayne Boulevard. Drivers race three hours; the winner completes the most laps. Sanctioned by International Motor Sports Association (IMSA). *Miami Motor Sports, Inc., 7254 S.W. 48th St., Miami 33155, tel. 305/662-5660. Tickets available from all Bass outlets, tel. 305/633-BASS or 800/221-2277.*

Nissan Indy Challenge. Held each November at Tamiami Park. Final event in annual CART/PPG Indy Car World Series races to determine the championship. Attracts famous Indy 500 drivers, such as Mario and Michael Andretti; Al Unser, Sr., and Jr.; and Danny Sullivan. *Miami Motor Sports, Inc., 7254 S.W. 48th St., Miami 33155, tel. 305/662-5660. Tickets available from all Bass outlets.*

Baseball

University of Miami Hurricanes. The baseball Hurricanes play home games in the 5,000-seat Mark Light Stadium, at 1 Hurricane Drive on UM's Coral Gables campus. The Hurricanes were the 1982 and 1985 NCAA baseball champions. *University of Miami Athletic Department, Box 248167, Coral Gables 33124, tel. 305/284-2655 or 800/GO-CANES. Open weekdays 8–6. Season: 48 home games Feb.–May, day games 2 PM, night games 7:30. AE, CB, DC, MC, V.*

Basketball

Miami Heat. In the 1988–89 National Basketball Association, Miami's new professional basketball team is playing its inaugural season. Team offices: *100 Chopin Plaza, Suite 200, Miami 33131, tel. 305/577-4328. Season: 41 home games, Nov.–May.*

University of Miami Hurricanes. Fledgling basketball team plays in the Miami arena. *University of Miami Athletic Department, Box 248167, Coral Gables 33124, tel. 305/284-2655, 800/GO-CANES. Open weekdays 8–6. Game time 7:30. AE, CB, DC, MC, V.*

Dog Racing

Biscayne Kennel Club. Greyhounds chase a mechanical rabbit around illuminated fountains in the track's infield. Near I–95 at N.W. 115th Street. Call for race time and starting dates. *320 N.W. 115th St., Miami Shores, tel. 305/754-3484. Season: Nov.–Dec. and May–June. Admission: reserved seats $1, grandstand $1, clubhouse $2. Parking 50 cents–$2.*

Flagler Dog Track. Inner-city track in the middle of Little Havana, five minutes east of Miami International Airport off Dolphin Expressway (Rte. 836) and Douglas Road (N.W. 37th Ave.). *401 N.W. 38th Ct., Miami, tel. 305/649-3000. Open Sept. 5–Oct. 30. General admission $1, clubhouse $2, parking 50 cents–$2.*

Football

Miami Dolphins. Owner Joe Robbie enjoys a reputation for doing things his own way. In 1987, he moved the Dolphins from the Orange Bowl near downtown Miami into his own privately financed $100-million Joe Robbie Stadium. *Super Bowl XXIII* will be played there January 22, 1989. Robbie also intends to use the stadium for baseball.

The new 74,914-seat stadium has a grass playing-field surface, with built-in drainage under the sod to carry off rainwater quickly. Stadium tours include the field, team locker rooms, sky boxes, executive suites, and baseball and football press boxes. *Tel. 305/623–6183. Tours daily, except event days, 11 AM, 1 PM, and 3 PM. Admission: $3.*

Joe Robbie Stadium is on a 160-acre site, 16 miles northwest of downtown Miami, one mile south of the Dade-Broward County line, accessible from I–95 and Florida's Turnpike. On game days, the Metro-Dade Transit Authority runs buses to the stadium. Bus information, tel. 305/638–6700; other Dolphins information, tel. 305/576–1000.

Dolphins tickets: *Miami Dolphins, Joe Robbie Stadium, 2269 N.W. 199th St., Miami 33056, tel. 305/620–2578. Open Mon.–Fri. 10–6.*

University of Miami Hurricanes. The Hurricanes, winners of the 1987 national college football championship, play home games in the Orange Bowl, near the Dolphin Expressway (Rte. 836) just west of downtown Miami. *1400 N.W. 4th St., tel. 305/579–6971. Game time 7:30 PM (unless changed for the convenience of the TV networks). Schedule and tickets: University of Miami Athletic Department, Box 248167, Coral Gables 33124, tel. 305/284–2655 or 800/GO–CANES. Open Mon.–Fri. 8–6.*

Horse Racing

Calder Race Course. Opened in 1971, Calder is Florida's largest glass-enclosed, air-conditioned sports facility. This means that Calder actually has two racing seasons, one in fall or winter, another in spring or summer. Contact the track for this year's dates. In April, Calder holds the Tropical Park Derby for three-year-olds, the last major race in Florida before the Kentucky Derby. On the Dade-Broward County line near I–95 and the Hallandale Beach Boulevard exit., ¾ mile from Joe Robbie Stadium. *21001 N.W. 27th Ave., Miami, tel. 305/625–1311. Gates open 11 AM, post time 1 PM, races end about 5 PM. General admission $2, clubhouse $4, programs 50 cents, parking $1–$3.*

Hialeah Park. A superb setting for Thoroughbred racing, Hialeah's 228 acres of meticulously landscaped grounds surround paddocks and a clubhouse built in a classic French Mediterranean style. Since it opened in 1925, Hialeah Park has survived hurricanes, economic reverses, and changing trends in racing without losing its air of elegant informality.

During the racing season, the gates open early Sunday mornings for breakfast at Hialeah Park. Admission is free. You can watch the horses work out, explore Hialeah's gardens, munch on breakfast fare of tolerable palatability, and admire the park's breeding flock of 600 Cuban flamingos.

When racing is not in session, Hialeah Park opens daily for free tours 10–4:30. Metrorail's Hialeah Station is on the grounds of Hialeah Park. *105 E. 21st St., Hialeah, tel. 305/885–8000. Admission: grandstand $2, clubhouse $4, parking $1.50–$4 during racing season.*

Jai Alai

Miami Jai-Alai Fronton. This game, invented in the Basque region of northern Spain, is the world's fastest. Jai-alai balls, called *pelotas*, have been clocked at speeds exceeding 170 mph. The game is played in a 176-foot-long court called a *fronton.* Players climb the walls to catch the ball in a *cesta*—a woven basket—with an attached glove. You bet on a team to win or on the order in which teams will finish. Built in 1926, Miami Jai-Alai is the oldest fronton in America. Each evening, it presents 13 games—some singles, some doubles. Located a mile east of Miami International Airport. *3500 N.W. 37th Ave., Miami, tel. 305/633-6400. Open nightly late Nov.–early Sept. except Sun., 7:15 –midnight. Matinees Mon., Wed., and Sat. noon–5. Admission: $1, clubhouse $5, free parking. Dinner available.*

Rugby Without a large corporate organization, a regular office staff, or even a permanent home field, local rugby players have organized themselves into two regular teams. Although one team is called the *University of Miami Rugby Team*, it is not part of the university. The other is the *Miami Tridents*. Weekly throughout the year, a local rugby team plays a visiting team from a 16-team Florida league, from the Caribbean, or from a foreign ship in port. Both local teams participate each August in an annual tournament. Games Saturday 2 PM. *7900 Bird Rd. (S.W. 40th St.). Spectators welcome. Free. Schedule information: 750 N.E. 64th St., Miami, tel. 305/758–2635 for recorded message. Schedule also posted at Churchill's Hideaway, 5501 N.E. 2nd Ave., Miami, tel. 305/757–1807.*

Soccer **Miami Sharks.** This American Soccer League team played its first season in spring 1988. The Sharks' 1989 season includes at least 10 regular-season home games and five international exhibition games, all in the stadium at Tamiami Park (11201 Coral Way [S.W. 24th St.], Miami). *Tickets: 8021 N.W. 14th St., Miami 33126, tel. 305/477–2050. Tickets available from all Bass outlets, tel. 305/633–BASS or 800/221–2277.*

Tennis **Lipton International Players Championship (LIPC).** Shearson Lehman Brothers sponsors this two-week spring tournament at the 64-acre International Tennis Center of Key Biscayne. The tournament follows the Grand Slam format of the Australian, United States and French Opens and Wimbledon. The two main professional tennis organizations—Association of Tennis Professionals and Women's International Tennis Association—helped create this tournament and own part of it. *7300 Crandon Blvd., Key Biscayne, tel. for tickets 305/361–5252. Tickets available from all Bass outlets, tel. 305/633–BASS or 800/221–2277.*

Triathlon **Bud Light U.S. Triathlon Series.** Opens the triathlon season in May in Miami, with 1,500 participants in a 1.5-km swim, a 40-km bicycle ride, and a 10-km run. Swimmers swim .9 miles in 75-degree water in Biscayne Bay near Bicentennial Park. The 24.8-mile bike course goes from the Grand Prix course in downtown Miami to Key Biscayne and back. The 6.2-mile run loops around the Japanese Garden on Watson Island along the MacArthur Causeway. Contact CAT Sports, Inc. (2235 Encinitas Blvd., Suite 210, Encinitas, CA 92024, tel. 619/436–5050), producer of the event.

Dining

by Rosalie Leposky

You can eat your way around the world in Greater Miami, enjoying just about any kind of cuisine imaginable in every price category. The rich mix of nationalities here encourages individual restaurateurs and chefs to retain their culinary roots. Thus,

Miami offers not just Latin fare but dishes distinctive to Spain, Cuba, Nicaragua, and other Hispanic countries; not just Oriental fare but specialties of China, India, Thailand, Vietnam, and other Asian cultures.

And don't neglect American fare just because it's not "foreign." Miami today is a center for innovation in regional cuisine and in combinations reflecting the diversity of domestic climates and cultures.

The most highly recommended restaurants in each price category are indicated by a star ★.

Category	Cost*
Very Expensive	over $55
Expensive	$35–$55
Moderate	$15–$35
Inexpensive	under $15

**per person without sales tax (6% in Florida), service, or drinks*

The following credit card abbreviations are used: AE, American Express; CB, Carte Blanche; DC, Diners Club; MC, MasterCard; V, Visa.

American
Downtown Miami
★

The Pavillon Grill. By day a private club, the Pavillon Grill becomes a gourmet restaurant at night. The mahogany, jade marble, and leather appointments of its salon and dining room exude the conservative classiness of an English private club. A harpist plays. The attentive staff serves regional American fare, including items that are low in calories, cholesterol, and sodium for diners who are on restricted diets. Specialties include corn-and-crabmeat chowder; mesquite-grilled soup (a lobster broth with Maine lobster, clams, and fresh baby vegetables); and mesquite-grilled Florida pompano. *100 Chopin Plaza, tel. 305/577–1000, ext. 4494 or 4490. Jacket and tie. Reservations required. AE, CB, DC, MC, V. Closed Sun. Very Expensive.*

Kendall (S.W. Suburb)

Savannah Moon. Though you drive up to a typical shopping center, Savannah Moon's door leads to the foyer of a Southern mansion, complete with formal staircase. In the second-floor dining room, bentwood chairs, hanging plants, shuttered windows, sheer curtains, and original Audubon engravings suggest a tidewater inn. Evening and late-night entertainment —mellow blues, conservative jazz—makes the place popular with suburban professionals. Chef Bernard Simon gives a nouvelle-cuisine twist to traditional Low Country coastal fare. Specialties include jambalaya (red rice with Creole sauce, chicken, shrimp, escargot, and Texas sausage); lamb with Southern Comfort sauce; and a dessert cart groaning with delights such as Kirsch-toasted almond cake, and southern bread pudding with nuts and raisins. *13505 South Dixie Hwy., tel. 305/238–8868. Jacket and tie. Reservations required on weekends, advised other times. AE, CB, DC, MC, V. Dinner only weekends. Expensive.*

Shorty's Bar-B-Q. Shorty Allen opened his barbecue restaurant in 1951 in a log cabin. Parents bring their teenage children to show them where mom and dad ate on their honeymoon.

Huge fans circulate fresh air through the single screened dining room, where you dine family style at long picnic tables. The walls display an assortment of cowboy hats, horns, saddles, an ox yoke, and heads of boar and caribou. Specialties include barbecued pork ribs, chicken, and pork steak slow cooked over hickory logs and drenched in Shorty's own warm, spicy sauce, and side orders of tangy baked beans with big chunks of pork, corn on the cob, and coleslaw. *9200 South Dixie Hwy., tel. 305/665–5732. Dress: informal. Reservations not accepted. No credit cards. Closed Thanksgiving and Christmas. Inexpensive.*

North Miami Beach
★

Chef Allen's. In an art-deco world of glass block, neon trim, and silk flowers, your gaze nonetheless remains riveted on the kitchen. Chef Allen Susser designed it with a picture window, 25 feet wide, so you can watch him create new American masterpieces almost too pretty to eat. Specialties include mesquite-grilled rare tuna with glazed onions and cranberry chutney; and lamb medallions with pine nuts, baby squash, and wilted spinach garnished with goat cheese. Desserts include white-chocolate mousse, chocolate pizza, and a sugar junkie's delight—scoops of vanilla, caramel, and pistachio ice cream floating in caramel sauce. Fine wines by the glass from a wine bar. Chef Allen's free monthly newsletter includes recipes and announcements of special regional menus on Thurs. *19088 N.E. 29th Ave., tel. 305/935–2900. Dress: informal weekdays, tie and jacket weekends. Reservations accepted. AE, MC, V. Closed for lunch weekends. Expensive.*

Chinese
Key Biscayne

Two Dragons. Robert Chow and his staff run this place like a small family restaurant, serving a Chinese cuisine with all ingredients fresh and prepared to order. Specialties include a Cantonese seafood nest (shrimp, scallops, and crabmeat with Chinese vegetables in a nest of crisp noodles), an orange beef Mandarin, and Szechuan eggplant with a spicy garlic-mustard sauce guaranteed to clear the sinuses. Dine in an intimate pagodalike booth behind hanging curtains of wooden beads or at an open table overlooking an outdoor Oriental garden. A Japanese steak house—the "second dragon"—serves Teppanyaki-style cuisine at six cooking tables in a separate room. *Sonesta Beach Hotel, 350 Ocean Dr., tel. 305/361–2021. Dress: semiformal. Dinner only. Reservations advised. AE, CB, DC, MC, V. Closed 2 weeks in Aug. or Sept. Moderate.*

South Miami

Tiger Tiger Teahouse. Design awards have been bestowed on Tiger Tiger's contemporary Chinese decor, with its embroidered silk panels depicting fierce tigers and its elegant rosewood chairs with jade cushions. Specialties include Peking duck (available without advance notice), lean and succulent beneath crisp orange-glazed skin, wrapped with plum sauce in wheat pancakes; hot, spicy Szechuan beef, marinated in sherry and spices, then stir-fried with Chinese vegetables; honey-garlic chicken; and creamy-smooth litchi ice cream. *The Bakery Center, 5785 Sunset Dr., tel. 305/665–5660. Dress: casual. Closed for lunch Sun. Reservations accepted. AE, CB, DC, MC, V. Closed Thanksgiving. Moderate.*

Continental
Coconut Grove
★

Grand Cafe. Understated elegance at all hours is the Grand Cafe's hallmark—a bilevel room with pink tablecloths and floral bouquets, sunbathed by day, dim and intimate after dark. Japanese-born, French-trained executive chef Katsuo Sugiura creates "international" cuisine, combining ingredients from all

Dining in the Miami Area

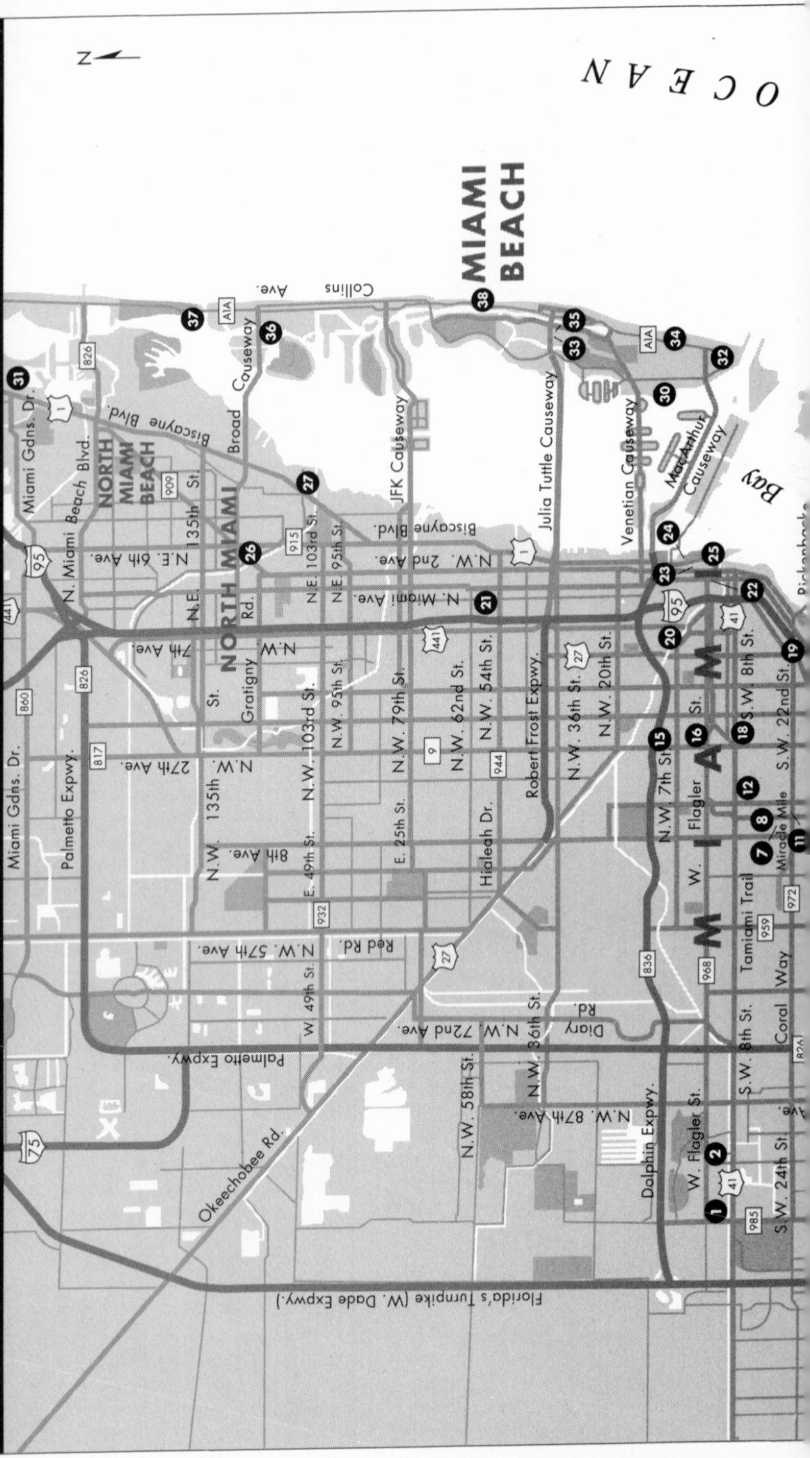

MIAMI BEACH
NORTH MIAMI BEACH
NORTH MIAMI
MIAMI
OCEAN
Bay
Miami Gdns. Dr.
Palmetto Expwy.
N. Miami Beach Blvd.
Biscayne Blvd.
Broad Causeway
Collins Ave.
JFK Causeway
Julia Tuttle Causeway
Venetian Causeway
MacArthur Causeway
Okeechobee Rd.
Florida's Turnpike (W. Dade Expwy.)
Dolphin Expwy.
Robert Frost Expwy.
Tamiami Trail
Coral Way
Miracle Mile
W. Flagler St.
S.W. 8th St.
S.W. 22nd St.
S.W. 24th St.
N.W. 7th St.
N.W. 20th St.
N.W. 36th St.
N.W. 54th St.
N.W. 58th St.
N.W. 62nd St.
N.W. 79th St.
N.W. 95th St.
N.W. 103rd St.
N.W. 135th St.
N.E. 135th St.
N.E. 103rd St.
N.E. 95th St.
W. 49th St.
E. 49th St.
E. 25th St.
Hialeah Dr.
Gratigny Rd.
Red Rd.
Diary Rd.
N.W. 87th Ave.
N.W. 72nd Ave.
N.W. 57th Ave.
8th Ave.
N.W. 27th Ave.
N.W. 7th Ave.
N. Miami Ave.
N.W. 2nd Ave.
N.E. 6th Ave.

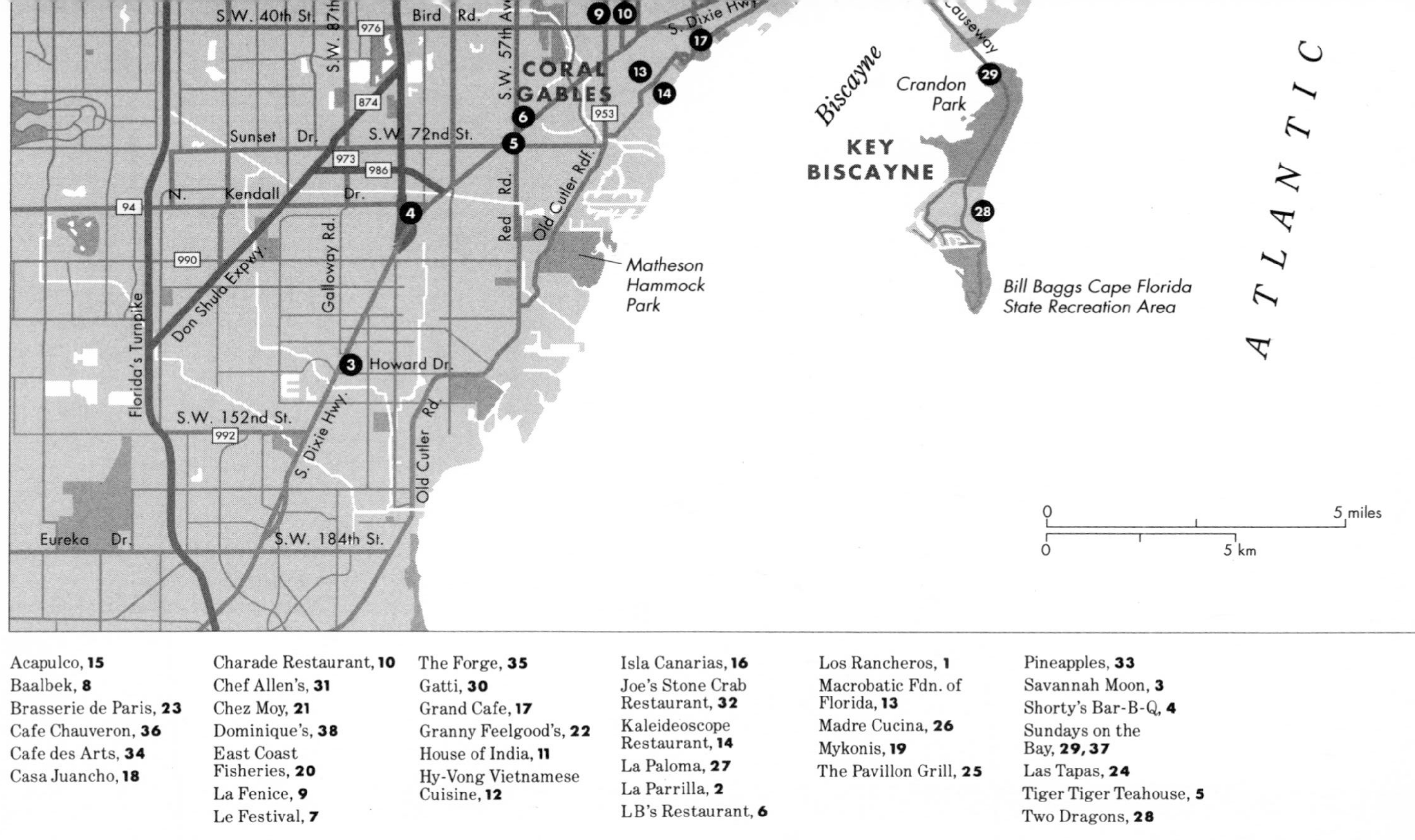

Acapulco, **15**
Baalbek, **8**
Brasserie de Paris, **23**
Cafe Chauveron, **36**
Cafe des Arts, **34**
Casa Juancho, **18**
Charade Restaurant, **10**
Chef Allen's, **31**
Chez Moy, **21**
Dominique's, **38**
East Coast Fisheries, **20**
La Fenice, **9**
Le Festival, **7**
The Forge, **35**
Gatti, **30**
Grand Cafe, **17**
Granny Feelgood's, **22**
House of India, **11**
Hy-Vong Vietnamese Cuisine, **12**
Isla Canarias, **16**
Joe's Stone Crab Restaurant, **32**
Kaleideoscope Restaurant, **14**
La Paloma, **27**
La Parrilla, **2**
LB's Restaurant, **6**
Los Rancheros, **1**
Macrobatic Fdn. of Florida, **13**
Madre Cucina, **26**
Mykonis, **19**
The Pavillon Grill, **25**
Pineapples, **33**
Savannah Moon, **3**
Shorty's Bar-B-Q, **4**
Sundays on the Bay, **29, 37**
Las Tapas, **24**
Tiger Tiger Teahouse, **5**
Two Dragons, **28**

over the world in pleasing presentations that intrigue the palate. Specialties include black linguini (colored with squid ink) and calamari dressed in virgin olive oil and lime; truffle pasta and Oregon porcini mushrooms sautéed with slicked smoked duckling breast; a superbly rich she-crab soup with roe, sherry, and cayenne pepper; "boned" Maine lobster presented in the shape of a lobster, with artichokes and a cream sauce of vermouth and saffron; herb-roasted rack of lamb au jus with an herb and wild rice flan; and veal in lime sauce. Dessert specialties include a white-chocolate and pistachio mousse, with blackberry sauce and Beaujolais essence. *2669 S. Bayshore Dr., tel. 305/858–9600. Jacket preferred. Reservations advised. AE, CB, DC, MC, V. Very Expensive.*

Kaleidoscope Restaurant. The tropical ambience here extends to a choice of indoor or outdoor seating—all in air-conditioned comfort, because fans blow cold air around a glass-roofed terrace overlooking a landscaped courtyard. Specialties include veal Oscar, lobster thermidor, and the chef's own fresh apple strudel. *3112 Commodore Plaza, tel. 305/446–5010. Dress: casual. Reservations advised. AE, CB, DC, MC, V. Moderate.*

Coral Gables **Charade Restaurant.** Spanish and Italian craftsmen toiled in the 1920s in this former furniture factory. Now it's a fern-filled room surrounded by portraits of unknown dignitaries. The menu changes daily. Specialties include deboned frogs' legs with angel-hair pasta; medallions of venison grilled and served with cranberry sauce; braised rabbit in Burgundy sauce with julienne vegetables and wild rice; and duckling charade, roast duck breast served with mango chutney and fresh green pepper sauce. *2900 Ponce de León Blvd., tel. 305/448–6077. Jacket required. Reservations advised. Closed for lunch Sat. AE, CB, DC, MC, V. Expensive.*

Miami Beach **The Forge.** After closing for the summer of 1988 for a $2 million renovation (its first in 20 years), The Forge reopened early in October. Seating has expanded to 325, and spectacular new displays of antiques and art objects amplify the opulence of this incredible restaurant. Additions include a sports room where attention centers on six semicircular stained-glass windows of 19th-century sports figures, and on a room where carved-glass Erte figures grace cabinets from an 1813 English pharmacy. The new menu acknowledges California and northern Italian influences, cutting back on steak, prime rib, and lamb chop entrees in favor of lighter fare. Specialties include creative preparations of chicken and veal served with a bouquet of fresh vegetables, and a wide variety of salads and pasta dishes. *432 Arthur Godfrey Rd. tel.305/538–8533. Dress: Jacket required. Entertainment in the lounge. Reservations advised. AE, CB, DC, MC, V. Expensive.*

Gatti. Owner Michael Gatti's Italian grandfather opened Gatti in 1925 as an Italian restaurant. Now preparations and flavors now reflect the Franco-Rhenish ambiguities of chef Alfred Herzog's Alsatian origins. The decor is simple—art-deco apricot, gray, and white—with fluted moldings and pilasters. Specialties include Florida stone crabs with a sweet, delicate mustard sauce; veal chops seasoned with tarragon and sage, in a light butter-cream glaze; and broiled pompano amandine. *1427 West Ave., tel. 305/673–1717. Dress: semiformal. Reservations advised. AE, CB, DC, MC, V. Closed Mother's Day–early Nov.; closed Mon. Expensive.*

North Miami **La Paloma.** This fine Swiss Continental restaurant offers a total sensory experience: fine food, impeccable service, and the ambience of an art museum. In sideboards and cases throughout, owners Werner and Maria Staub display ornate European antiques that they have spent decades collecting. The treasures include Bacarrat crystal, Limoges china, Meissen porcelains, and Sevres clocks. The staff speak Spanish, French, German, Portuguese, or Arabic. Specialties include fresh local fish and seafood; Norwegian salmon Caroline (poached, served on a bed of spinach with hollandaise sauce); Wiener schnitzel; lamb chops à la *diable* (coated with bread crumbs, mustard, garlic, and herbs) passion-fruit sorbet; and kiwi soufflé with raspberry sauce. *10999 Biscayne Blvd., tel. 305/891–0505. Jackets requested. Reservations advised. AE, MC, V. Closed Mon. and July and part of Aug. Expensive.*

Cuban
Little Havana **Islas Canarias.** A gathering place for Cuban poets, pop music stars, and media personalities. Wall murals depict a Canary Islands street scene and an indigenous dragon tree *(Dracaena draco)*. The menu includes such Canary Islands dishes as baked lamb, ham hocks with boiled potatoes, and *tortilla Española* (a Spanish omelet with onions and chorizo sausage), as well as Cuban standards, including palomilla steak, and fried kingfish. Don't miss the three superb varieties of homemade chips—potato, malanga, and plantain. Islas Canarias has another location in Westchester. *285 N.W. Unity Blvd. (N.W. 27th Ave.), tel. 305/649–0440. Dress: informal. Reservations not accepted. No credit cards. Inexpensive.*

Family Style
Coral Gables **LB's Restaurant.** Town and gown meet at this sprout-laden haven a half-block from the University of Miami's baseball stadium. Kitschy food-related posters plaster the walls. Relaxed atmosphere, low prices, no waiters. You order at the counter and pick up your food when called. Vegetarians thrive on LB's salads and daily meatless entrees, such as lasagna and moussaka. Famous for Saturday night lobster. (If you plan to come after 8, call ahead to reserve a lobster.) Other specialties include barbecued baby-back ribs, lime chicken, croissant sandwiches, and carrot cake. *5813 Ponce de León Blvd., tel. 305/661–7091. Dress: informal. Reservations not accepted. No credit cards. Closed Sun. Inexpensive.*

French
Coral Gables **Le Festival.** The modest canopied entrance to this classical French restaurant understates the elegance within. Decor includes etched-glass filigree mirrors and delicate floral wallpaper. Specialties include appetizers of salmon mousse, baked oysters with garlic butter, and lobster in champagne sauce en croute; rack of lamb (for two), and medallions of veal with two sauces—a pungent, creamy lime sauce and a dark port-wine sauce with mushrooms. Entrees come with real french-fried potatoes. Don't pass up dessert here; the mousses and soufflés are positively decadent. *2120 Salzedo St., tel. 305/442–8545. Jacket and tie. Reservations required for dinner, and for lunch parties of 5 or more. AE, MC, V. Closed Sat. noon, all day Sun., and Sept.–Oct. Expensive.*

Downtown Miami **Brasserie de Paris.** Miami's legal and financial elite adjourn for lunch to this rosewood-paneled retreat; at night, it's popular with late-dining Latins. Classical French specialties include Marseille-style bouillabaisse, lobster thermidor, and Grand Marnier cake. *Everglades Hotel, 244 Biscayne Blvd., tel. 379–5461. Jacket and tie. Reservations advised, but not re-*

quired. AE, CB, DC, MC, V. Closed Sat. noon and Sun. Expensive.

Miami Beach ★ **Cafe Chauveron.** André Chauveron traces his cafe's roots to Cafe Chambord, which his father began in New York in 1935 on the block where the Citicorp Building now stands. A Florida institution since 1972, Cafe Chauveron serves classical French cuisine in rooms decorated with original paintings and wood paneling. The atmosphere is hushed, the service superb. Mounted pheasants guard the wine cabinet. Specialties include wild duck and pheasant pâté, filet of sole *bonne femme,* frogs' legs Provençale, sautéed veal chop Bercy (white wine and shallots) with braised endive, and dessert soufflés flambéed at tableside. *9561 E. Bay Harbor Dr., tel. 305/866–8779. Jacket and tie. Reservations required. AE, CB, DC, MC, V. Closed Aug.–Sept. Very Expensive.*

Cafe des Arts. Enjoy French-provincial cuisine in an art-deco setting amid tropical plants, antiques, and an art gallery that changes every six to eight weeks. Indoor and outdoor seating. Specialties include smoked-salmon pasta with artichokes, mushrooms, and brie sauce; roast duck in grape sauce; and quail salad. *918 Ocean Dr., tel. 305/534–6267. Dress: casual. Reservations advised. AE, MC, V. Closed 2 weeks in Aug. Moderate.*

★ **Dominique's.** Woodwork and mirrors from a Vanderbilt home and other demolished New York mansions create an intimate setting for a unique nouvelle-cuisine dining experience. Specialties include exotic appetizers, such as buffalo sausage, sautéed alligator tail, and rattlesnake-meat salad; rack of lamb (which accounts for 35% of the restaurant's total sales) and fresh seafood; and an extensive wine list. The restaurant also serves brunch on Sunday. *Alexander Hotel, 5225 Collins Ave., tel. 305/865–6500. Jacket required. Reservations advised. AE, CB, DC, MC, V. Very Expensive.*

Greek
Southwest Miami

Mykonos. A family restaurant serving typical Greek fare in a Spartan setting—a single 74-seat room adorned with Greek travel posters. Specialties include gyro; moussaka; marinated lamb and chicken; kalamari (squid) and octopus sautéed in wine and onions; and sumptuous Greek salads thick with feta cheese and briny olives. *1201 Coral Way, tel. 305/856–3140. Dress: informal. Reservations accepted for dinner. AE. Closed Sun. at noon, Christmas, and New Year's Day. Inexpensive.*

Haitian
Little Haiti

Chez Moy. Seating is outside on a shaded patio or in a pleasant room with oak tables and high-backed chairs. Chef Bettsy Maurice, who speaks excellent English. Specialties include *grillot* (pork boiled, then fried with spices); fried or boiled fish; stewed goat; and conch with garlic and hot pepper. Try a tropical fruit drink, such as sweet sop (also called *anon* or *cachiman)* or sour sop (also called *guanabana* or *corrosol)* blended with milk and sugar, and sweet potato pie for dessert. *1 N.W. 54th St., tel. 305/756–7540. Dress: informal. No reservations. No smoking allowed inside. MC, V. Moderate.*

Indian
Coral Gables

★ **House of India.** Dine to the haunting strains of sitar music, reclining on cushions in an Indian-style gazebo booth. (Tables and chairs are also available.) Specialties include hot coconut soup with coconut, cardamon, milk, rose water, and sugar; curried goat; and authentic chicken tandoori, cooked in a clay oven. *22 Merrick Way, tel. 305/444–2348. Dress: casual. Weekend reservations accepted. AE, MC, V. Closed for Sun. lunch, Labor Day, Christmas. Moderate.*

Italian
Coral Gables

La Fenice. The restaurant is named for the Venice opera house that rose, phoenixlike, from the ashes of an earlier structure after an 1831 fire; and it is decorated with paintings of St. Mark's Square in Venice, ornate mahogany chairs from Padua, a four-tier fountain, and stained-glass windows. Specialties include rigatoni in creamy vodka sauce topped with caviar; veal scallopini sautéed with Gorgonzola cheese, cream sauce, and mushrooms; and poached salmon with a sauce of sweet red peppers pureed with lemon juice. *2728 Ponce de León Blvd., tel. 305/445–6603. Jacket and tie. Reservations advised. AE, MC, V. Closed Sat.– Sun. noon. Moderate.*

North Miami

Madre Cucina. Old friends have followed chef Raimondo Laudisio from Miami's Little River area south to Coral Gables, and now back north to Madre Cucina. The decor is simple "so you can concentrate on the food." With a theatrical flourish, the waiters warm all hot dishes on a burner at tableside. Specialties include veal Loren (after Sophia), a voluptuous presentation of a thin veal cutlet stuffed with sweet peas, wild mushrooms, and imported Fontina cheese with pesto sauce; creation Raimondo—shrimp with shallots in a sauce of cream and white wine; and, for dessert, a Grand Marnier soufflé with brandied fruit. *12350 N.E. 6th Ave., tel. 305/893–6071. Dress: informal. Reservations advised. AE, MC, V. Closed Mon. Moderate.*

Lebanese
Coral Gables

Baalbek. Named after a Lebanese city near Beirut, this 74-seat restaurant creates a Middle Eastern mood with tapes by Fairuz (a popular chanteuse) and vivid Lebanese-style paintings. Many diners at Baalbek choose the traditional Lebanese fare on the "Royal Plate"—*tabbouleh* (crushed wheat salad), *falafel* (fried chick-pea croquette), *kibbeh nayyeh* (raw minced beef with crushed wheat and spices), *kibbeh aras* (ground beef cooked in a crushed-wheat coating with onions and spices), *labneh* (yogurt), *homos bi tahineh* (chick pees pureed with lemon and sesame oil), and *warak inab bizeit* (grape leaves stuffed with rice and vegetables). For the more adventurous, Baalbek also offers uncommon specialties, such as lamb-brain salad, grilled quail, and *mloukhieh* (a spinachlike green vegetable from Lebanon shunned by devout Moslems, who believe it's an aphrodisiac). *1930 Ponce de León Blvd., tel. 305/447–3886. Jacket preferred. Reservations advised. AE, MC, V. Closed Sat. noon and Sun. Moderate.*

Mexican
Little Havana

Acapulco. Authentic Mexican cuisine in an intimate 70-seat room with adobe walls, wooden beams, tabletops of Mexican tiles, and sombreros and serapes on the walls. As soon as you sit down, a waiter descends on you with a free, ample supply of *totopos*, homemade corn chips served hot and crunchy, salt free, with a fiery *pico de gallo* sauce. Specialties include a rich, chunky guacamole; *carnitas asadas* (marinated pork chunks in lemon and butter sauce); *mole poblano* (chicken in chocolate sauce); shrimp and rice in a cherry wine sauce; and combination platters of tacos, burritos, and enchiladas. *727 N.W. Unity Blvd. (N.W. 27th Ave.), tel. 305/642–6961. Dress: informal. Weekend reservations required. AE, CB, DC, MC, V. Inexpensive.*

Natural
Coconut Grove

Macrobiotic Foundation of Florida. All-natural meals are prepared fresh daily with organic vegetables, seeds, grains, and fruits to balance acid and alkaline, Yin and Yang. Even if you don't share this philosophy, the people are nice and the food is tasty. Meals are served boardinghouse style at long tables in a former church parish house. Specialties include miso soup, whole grains, pasta primavera and *arame* (an edible seaweed). International Night, on Friday, features cuisine of a different country each week. *3291 Franklin Ave., tel. 305/448–6625. Dress: informal. Reservations required. No smoking allowed. MC, V. Closed for lunch Sat.; dinner Mon., Wed., and Sun. Moderate.*

Downtown Miami **Granny Feelgood's.** "Granny" is a shrewd gentleman named Irving Field, who caters to health-conscious lawyers, office workers, and cruise-ship crews at six locations. Specialties include chicken salad with raisins, apples, and cinnamon; spinach fettuccine with pine nuts; grilled tofu; apple crumb cake; and carrot cake. *190 S.E. 1st Ave., tel. 305/358–6233. Dress: casual. No reservations. No smoking in restaurant. AE, MC, V. Closed Sun. Inexpensive.*

Miami Beach **Pineapples.** Art-deco pink pervades this health-food store and restaurant. Specialties include Chinese egg rolls; lasagna filled with tofu and mushrooms; spinach fettuccine with feta cheese, fresh garlic, walnuts, and cream sauce; and salads with a full-flavored Italian-style dressing. *530 Arthur Godfrey Rd., tel. 305/538–0350. Dress: casual. No reservations. No smoking in restaurant. AE, MC, V. Moderate.*

Nicaraguan
Little Managua **La Parrilla.** Ten miles west of downtown Miami, about 50,000 Nicaraguans have moved into the Fontainebleau Park subdivision and the tiny suburban town of Sweetwater. Typical of their fare are the beef and fish at La Parilla (Spanish for "the grille"), where hanging plants and sloping barrel-tile roofs above the booths create a rural ambience. An adjoining bar that is popular with Nicaraguan *contras*. Specialties include *gallos pintos* (red beans and rice); *chicharron* (fried pork with yucca); and *pargo a la Tipitapa*, baby red snapper fried and served whole in Creole sauce with onions and peppers. *9611 W. Flagler St., tel. 305/553–4419. Dress: informal. Reservations accepted. AE, CB, DC, MC, V. Moderate.*

Los Ranchos. Julio Somoza, owner of Los Ranchos and nephew of Nicaragua's late president, Anastasio Somoza, fled to south Florida in 1979. Somoza sustains a tradition begun 30 years ago in Managua, when the original Los Ranchos instilled in Nicaraguan palates a love of Argentine-style beef—lean, grass-fed tenderloin with *chimichurri*, a green sauce of chopped parsley, garlic, oil, vinegar, and other spices. Nicaragua's own sauces are a tomato-based marinara and the fiery *cebollitas encurtidas*, with slices of jalapeño pepper and onion pickled in vinegar. Specialties include *chorizo* (sausage); *cuajada con maduro* (skim cheese with fried bananas); and shrimp sautéed in butter and topped with a creamy jalapeño sauce. *125 S.W. 107th Ave., tel. 305/221–9367. Dress: informal. Reservations advised, especially on weekends. AE, CB, DC, MC, V. Closed Good Friday, Christmas, New Year's Day. Moderate.*

Seafood
Downtown Miami **East Coast Fisheries.** This family-owned restaurant and retail fish market on the Miami River features fresh Florida seafood from its own 38-boat fleet in the Keys. From tables along the second-floor balcony railing, watch the cooks prepare your dinner in the open kitchen below. Specialties include a complimentary fish-pâté appetizer, blackened pompano with owner David Swartz's personal herb-and-spice recipe, lightly breaded fried grouper, and a homemade Key-lime pie so rich it tastes like ice cream. *360 W. Flagler St., tel. 305/373–5515. Dress: informal. Beer and wine only. MC, V. Inexpensive.*

Key Biscayne **Sundays on the Bay.** Two locations overlook the water—the Crandon Park Marina at Key Biscayne and the Intracoastal Waterway at Haulover. Both have inside dining and outdoor decks, bars, live bands nightly playing reggae and top 40 hits, and an energetic young serving staff. Specialties from an extensive seafood menu include conch fritters, conch chowder (tomato-based, served with sherry and Tabasco sauce), frogs' legs lightly breaded and fried, and baked grouper topped with crabmeat and shrimp scampi. *Key Biscayne: 5420 Crandon Blvd., tel. 305/361–6777; Haulover Beach Park: 10880 Collins Ave., tel. 305/945–6065. Dress: informal. Reservations accepted; advised for Sun. brunch. AE, CB, DC, MC, V. Moderate.*

Miami Beach ★ **Joe's Stone Crab Restaurant.** A south Florida tradition since 1913, Joe's is a family restaurant in its fourth generation. You go to wait, people watch, and finally settle down to an ample à la carte menu. Joe's serves about a ton of stone crab claws a day, with drawn butter, lemon wedges, and a piquant mustard sauce (recipe available). Popular side orders include a vinegary coleslaw, salad with a brisk house vinaigrette dressing, creamed garlic spinach, french-fried onion rings and eggplant, and hash brown potatoes. Save room for dessert—a slice of Key-lime pie with graham cracker crust and real whipped cream or apple pie with a crumb-pecan topping. *227 Biscayne St., tel. 305/673–0365. Dress: informal, but no T-shirts, tank tops, or shorts. No reservations; to minimize the wait, come for lunch before 11:30, for dinner before 5 or after 9. AE, CB, DC, MC, V. Closed May 15–Oct. 15. Moderate.*

Spanish
Downtown Miami **Las Tapas.** *Tapas*—"little dishes"—come in appetizer-size portions to give you a variety of tastes during a single meal. Specialties include *la tostada* (smoked salmon on melba toast, topped with a dollop of sour cream, across which are laid baby eels, black caviar, capers, and chopped onion) and *samfaina con lomo* (eggplant, zucchini, green pepper, onions, tomato, and garlic sautéed with two thin, delicately flavored slices of fresh boneless pork loin). Also available are soups, salads, sandwiches, and standard dinners. *Bayside Marketplace, 401 Biscayne Blvd., tel. 305/372–2737. Dress: casual. Reservations for large parties only. AE, CB, DC, MC, V. Moderate.*

Little Havana ★ **Casa Juancho.** A meeting place for the movers and shakers of Miami's Cuban community, Casa Juancho serves a cross section of Spanish regional cuisines. The interior recalls old Castile: brown brick, rough-hewn dark timbers, and walls adorned with colorful Talavera platters. Strolling Spanish balladeers will serenade you. Specialties include *cochinillo Segoviano* (roast suckling pig), and *parrillada de mariscos* (fish, shrimps, squid, and scallops grilled in a light garlic sauce) from the Pontevedra region of northwest Spain. For dessert, the *crema Catalana* has a delectable crust of burnt caramel atop a rich pastry custard. The wine list includes fine labels from Spain's Rioja region. *2436 S.W. 8th St., tel. 305/642–2452. Dress: semiformal. Reservations advised; not accepted after 8 PM Fri. and Sat. AE, CB, DC, MC, V. Closed Christmas Eve. Expensive.*

Vietnamese
Little Havana ★ **Hy-Vong Vietnamese Cuisine.** Chef and part owner Tung Nguyen's magic has poured forth from the tiny kitchen of this 36-seat restaurant since 1980. Now the word is out, so come before 7 PM to avoid a long wait. Specialties include spring rolls, a Vietnamese version of an egg roll, with ground pork, cellophane noodles, and black mushrooms wrapped in homemade

rice paper; a whole fish panfried with *nuoc man* (a garlic-lime fish sauce); and thinly sliced pork, barbecued with sesame seeds and fish sauce, served with bean sprouts, rice noodles, and slivers of carrots, almonds, and peanuts. *3458 S.W. 8th St., tel. 305/446–3674. Dress casual. Reservations accepted for 5 or more. No smoking. No credit cards. Closed Mon., American and Vietnamese/Chinese New Years, and 2 weeks in Aug. Moderate.*

Lodging

Few urban areas can match Greater Miami's diversity of hotel accommodations. The area has hundreds of hotels and motels with lodgings in all price categories, from $8 for a night in a dormitory-style hostel bed to $2,000 for a night in the luxurious presidential suite atop a posh downtown hotel.

As recently as the 1960s, many hotels in Greater Miami opened only in the winter to accommodate Yankee "snowbirds." Now most stay open all year. In summer, they cater to business travelers and to vacationers from the South and South America who find Miami quite congenial despite the heat, humidity, and intense thunderstorms almost every afternoon.

Although some hotels (especially on the mainland) have adopted year-round rates, many still adjust their rates to reflect the ebb and flow of seasonal demand. The peak occurs in winter, with only a slight dip in summer when families with schoolchildren take vacations. You'll find the best values between Easter and Memorial Day (a delightful time in Miami but a difficult time for many people to travel), and in September and October (the height of hurricane season).

The list that follows is a representative selection of the best hotels and motels, organized geographically.

The rate categories in the list are based on the all-year or peak-season price; off-peak rates may be a category or two lower.

The most highly recommended places in each price category are indicated by a star ★.

Category	Cost*
Very Expensive	over $120
Expensive	$90–$120
Moderate	$50–$90
Inexpensive	under $50

**per person without the 6% state sales tax and nominal tourist tax*

The following credit card abbreviations are used: AE, American Express; CB, Carte Blanche; DC, Diners Club; MC, MasterCard; V, Visa.

Coconut Grove

Doubletree Hotel at Coconut Grove. This high rise with a bay view was built in 1970 and renovated in 1988. Rooms are large, most with balcony, comfortable chairs, armoires, original artwork. Choice of a salmon or turquoise color scheme. Best rooms are on upper floors with bay views. Homemade chocolate-chip cookies are offered to arriving guests. *2649 S. Bayshore Dr.,*

Coconut Grove, 33133, tel. 305/858-2500 or 800/327-8771, in FL 800/432-6155. 190 rooms with bath, including 32 nonsmoker rooms, and 3 rooms for handicapped guests. Facilities: outdoor freshwater pool, 2 tennis courts, restaurant, bar. Guests have access to Casablanca, a private club on the top floor. AE, CB, DC, MC, V. Expensive.

★ **Grand Bay Hotel.** This modern high rise overlooks Biscayne Bay; rooms have traditional furnishings and original art. The building's stairstep facade, like a Mayan pyramid, gives each room facing the bay a private terrace. Best views, at the northeast corner, include downtown Miami. The staff pays meticulous attention to guests' desires. Only slightly more special than most rooms is 814, Luciano Pavarotti's two-level suite with a baby-grand piano, circular staircase, and canopied king-size bed. You can rent it when he's not there. *2669 S. Bayshore Dr., Coconut Grove 33133, tel. 305/858-9600. 181 rooms with bath, including 48 suites, 20 nonsmoker rooms. Facilities: outdoor pool, hot tub, health club, saunas, masseur, afternoon tea in lobby, gourmet restaurant and lounge, poolside bar. AE, CB, DC, MC, V. Very Expensive.*

★ **Grove Isle.** This luxurious mid-rise urban resort sits on 26-acre island and adjoins the equally posh condominium apartment towers and private club. Developer Martin Margulies displays selections from his extensive private art collection on the premises (*see* Exploring). The oversized rooms have patios, bay views, ceiling fans, and tropical decor with area rugs and Spanish tiles. The rooms with the most light and best bay view are 201-205. *4 Grove Isle Dr., Coconut Grove 33133, tel. 305/858-8300 or 800/858-8300. 49 rooms with bath, including 9 suites. Facilities: outdoor freshwater swimming pool and whirlpool; 12 tennis courts; 85-slip marina; 40-ft. sailboat that guests can charter; health spa with saunas and steam rooms, Nautilus equipment, masseur and masseuse, running track around the island; in-room refreshment bar and coffee maker; free cable TV; free movies in room; complimentary Continental breakfast; restaurant with indoor and outdoor seating. AE, CB, DC, MC, V. Very Expensive.*

Mayfair House. This European-style luxury hotel sits within an exclusive open-air shopping mall (*see* Exploring). Public areas have Tiffany windows, polished mahogany, marble walls and floors, and imported ceramics and crystal. A glassed-in elevator whisks you to the corridor on your floor—a balcony overlooking the mall's central fountains and walkways. In all suites, outdoor terraces face the street, screened from view by vegetation and wood latticework. Each has a Japanese hot tub on the balcony or a Roman tub in the bathroom. Otherwise, each suite is unique in size and furnishings. Sunset (Room 505) is one of 48 suites with antique pianos. Some aspects of the building's design are quirky; you can get lost looking for the ballroom or restaurant, and, in many rooms, you must stand in the bathtub to turn on the water. The worst suite for sleeping is Featherfern (Room 356), from which you can hear the band one floor below in the club. *3000 Florida Ave., Coconut Grove 33133, tel. 305/441-0000 or 800/433-4555. 181 suites, including 22 nonsmoker suites. Facilities: rooftop recreation area with sauna in a barrel, small outdoor freshwater swimming pool, and snack bar; preferred shopper card for discounts in mall shops; complimentary airport limousine service. AE, CB, DC, MC, V. Very Expensive.*

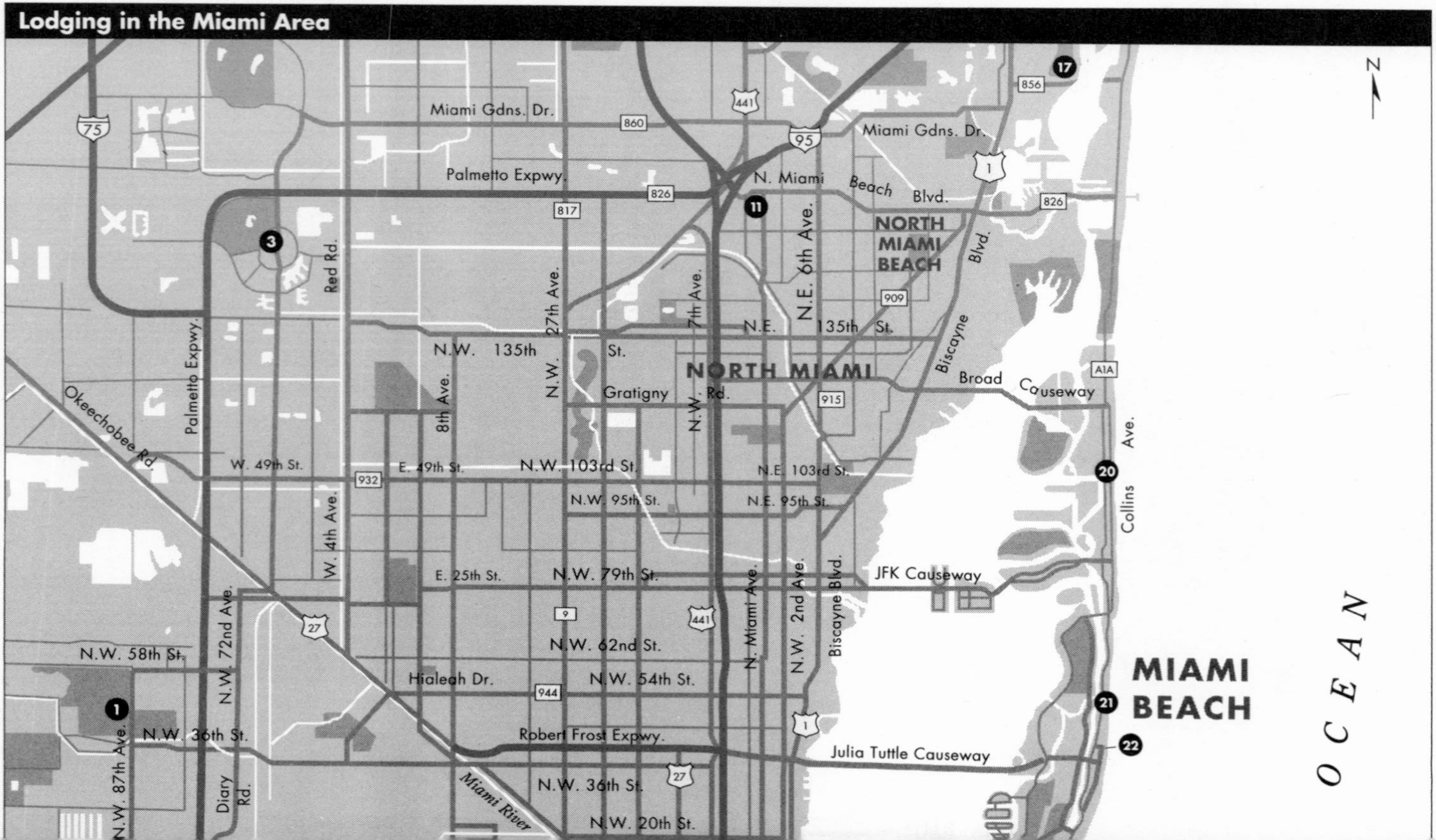
Lodging in the Miami Area
N
Miami Gdns. Dr.
860
441
95
Miami Gdns. Dr.
75
Palmetto Expwy.
826
N. Miami Beach Blvd.
1
826
817
11
3
NORTH MIAMI BEACH
Red Rd.
27th Ave.
7th Ave.
N.E. 6th Ave.
Blvd.
909
N.E. 135th St.
Biscayne
N.W. 135th St.
NORTH MIAMI
A1A
Broad Causeway
Okeechobee Rd.
Palmetto Expwy.
8th Ave.
N.W.
Gratigny Rd.
N.W.
915
Ave.
W. 49th St.
932
E. 49th St.
N.W. 103rd St.
N.E. 103rd St.
20
N.W. 95th St.
N.E. 95th St.
Collins
W. 4th Ave.
E. 25th St.
N.W. 79th St.
JFK Causeway
Biscayne Blvd.
N.W. 72nd Ave.
9
441
27
N. Miami Ave.
N.W. 2nd Ave.
N.W. 58th St.
N.W. 62nd St.
MIAMI BEACH
Hialeah Dr.
944
N.W. 54th St.
1
21
N.W. 36th St.
Robert Frost Expwy.
1
22
N.W. 87th Ave.
Julia Tuttle Causeway
Diary Rd.
27
Miami River
N.W. 36th St.
N.W. 20th St.
OCEAN

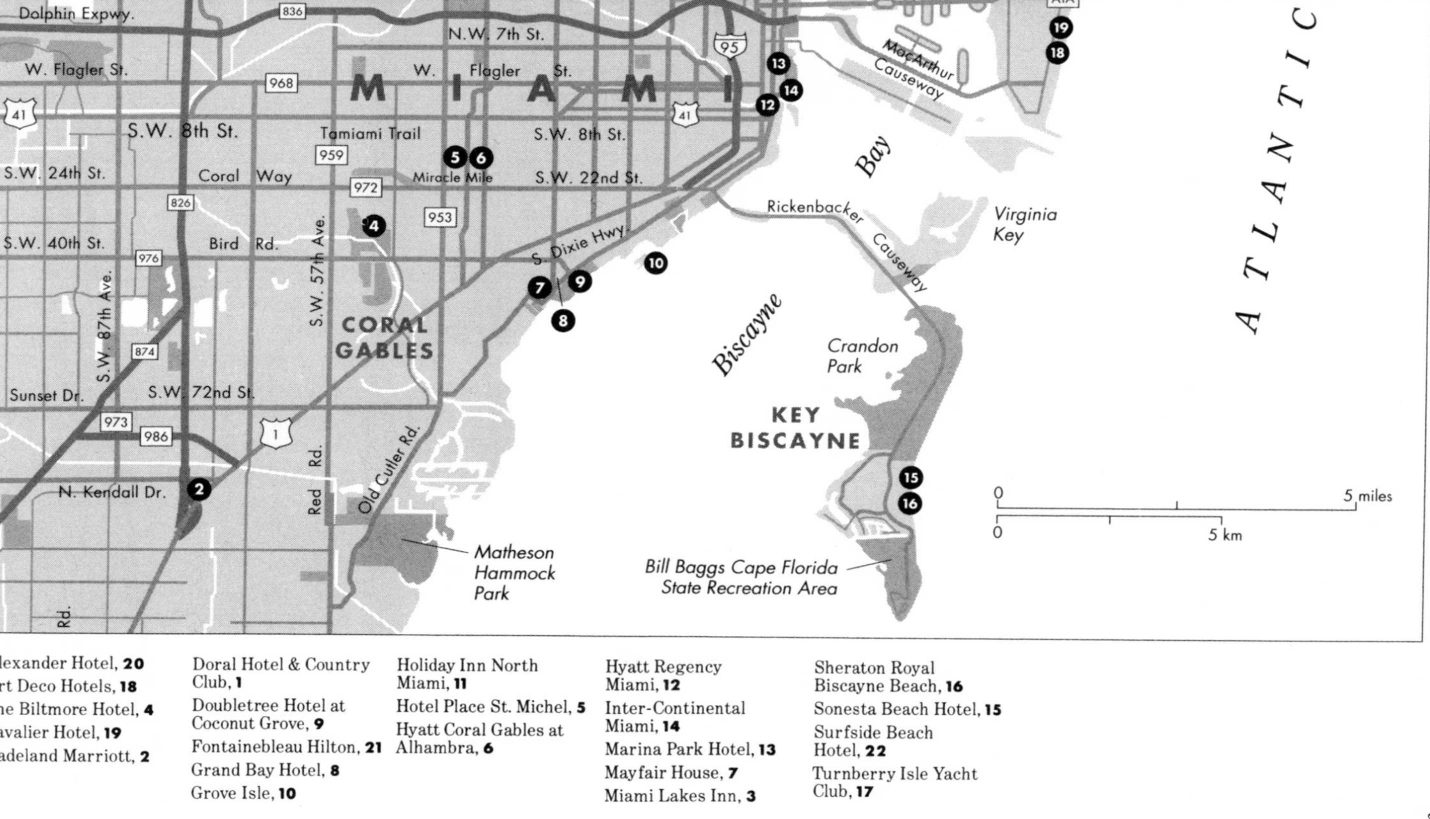

Alexander Hotel, **20**
Art Deco Hotels, **18**
The Biltmore Hotel, **4**
Cavalier Hotel, **19**
Dadeland Marriott, **2**
Doral Hotel & Country Club, **1**
Doubletree Hotel at Coconut Grove, **9**
Fontainebleau Hilton, **21**
Grand Bay Hotel, **8**
Grove Isle, **10**
Holiday Inn North Miami, **11**
Hotel Place St. Michel, **5**
Hyatt Coral Gables at Alhambra, **6**
Hyatt Regency Miami, **12**
Inter-Continental Miami, **14**
Marina Park Hotel, **13**
Mayfair House, **7**
Miami Lakes Inn, **3**
Sheraton Royal Biscayne Beach, **16**
Sonesta Beach Hotel, **15**
Surfside Beach Hotel, **22**
Turnberry Isle Yacht Club, **17**

Coral Gables **The Biltmore Hotel.** A historic high rise built in 1926, the Biltmore was restored and renovated in 1986 and reopened as a luxury hotel, but the luxury exists primarily in the historic, restored public spaces *(see* Exploring). The rooms have high-quality furnishings befitting their price tag, but they are nondescript, lacking the boom-time ambience you might expect from such a legendary property. The service can be uneven. Without telling guests in the tower suites, the management often turns off the tower elevators to discourage sightseers from going up there. Upper-floor rooms facing north and east toward the airport, downtown Miami, and Biscayne Bay have the most spectacular views but more airplane noise. *1200 Anastasia Ave., Coral Gables 33134, tel. 305/445–1926 or 800/445–2586. 279 rooms with bath, including 45 suites. Facilities: 18-hole championship golf course, 10 lighted tennis courts, health spa with sauna, swimming pool, restaurant, coffee shop, and lounge. AE, CB, DC, MC, V. Very Expensive.*

★ **Hotel Place St. Michel.** Historic low-rise urban hotel built in 1926 and restored 1981–86. Art-nouveau chandeliers suspended from vaulted ceilings grace the public areas of this intimate jewel in the heart of downtown Coral Gables. Paddle fans circulate the air, filled with the scent of fresh flowers. Each room has its own dimension, personality, and imported antiques from England, Scotland, and France. *162 Alcazar Ave., Coral Gables 33134, tel. 305/444–1666. 28 rooms with bath, including 3 suites. Facilities: welcome basket of fruit and cheese in every room, Continental breakfast, restaurant, lounge, French snack shop. AE, CB, DC, MC, V. Moderate.*

★ **Hyatt Coral Gables at the Alhambra.** This urban high rise caters to business travelers. Opened in 1987, the hotel is part of a megastructure that includes two office towers. The entire structure follows the area tradition of Spanish Mediterranean architecture, with tile roofs, white-frame casement windows, and pink-stucco exterior. The hotel's interior decor of pastel hues and antique-style furnishings gives a comfortable, residential feel to the rooms and public areas. The best rooms face the pool; the worst face north toward the airport. *50 Alhambra Plaza, Coral Gables 33134, tel. 305/441–1234. 242 rooms with bath, including 50 suites, 45 nonsmoker rooms. Facilities: 2,900-sq.-ft. ballroom, restaurant, lounge, rooftop swimming pool, outdoor whirlpool, health club with Nautilus equipment and Life Cycles, and sauna and steam rooms. AE, CB, DC, MC, V. Very Expensive.*

Downtown Miami ★ **Hotel Inter-Continental Miami.** Stand on the fifth-floor recreation plaza and gaze up at this granite 34-story monolith that appears to be arching over you. This optical illusion aside, the Inter-Continental deals in congenial realities. The grain in the lobby's marble floor match that in *The Spindle*, a massive centerpiece sculpture by Henry Moore. With all that marble, the lobby could easily look like a mausoleum—and did before the addition of palm trees, colorful umbrellas, and wicker chairs and tables. Atop a five-story atrium, a skylight lets the afternoon sun pour in. The triangular hotel tower offers bay, port, and city views that improve with height. *100 Chopin Plaza, Miami 33131, tel. 305/577–1000 or 800/327–0200. 645 rooms with bath, including 34 suites, 48 nonsmoker rooms; corner rooms have extra-wide doors for handicapped guests. Facilities: outdoor heated freshwater swimming pool beside the bay, 2 lighted clay tennis courts, 2 indoor racquetball courts, ¼-mile jogging* *track with rubber surface, in-room minibar, restaurants, and lounge. AE, CB, DC, MC, V. Very Expensive.*

Hyatt Regency Miami. This centrally located, 24-story convention hotel adjoins the James L. Knight International Center (*see* Exploring). It nestles beside the Brickell Avenue Bridge on the north bank of the Miami River. From its lower lobby, you can watch tugboats, freighters, and pleasure craft ply the river. The best rooms are on the upper floors, facing east toward Biscayne Bay. A $7-million renovation of the hotel's public area was was scheduled for completion in late 1988. *400 S.E. 2nd Ave., Miami 33131, tel. 305/358–1234 or 800/228–9000. 615 rooms with bath, 25 suites, 43 nonsmoker rooms, 19 rooms for handicapped guests. Facilities: outdoor freshwater swimming pool; health club with sauna, steam rooms, and Jacuzzis; in-room safe; in-house pay-TV movies, 2 restaurants and a lounge. AE, CB, DC, MC, V. Very Expensive.*

Marina Park Hotel. Centrally located mid rise owned by a French chain. A stark exterior hides the hotel's warm Gallic personality. Rooms have an attractive pastel color scheme with rattan and wicker furnishings, soft mattresses, and trilingual TV. The best views are from east rooms that overlook Bayside and the Port of Miami. *340 Biscayne Blvd., Miami 33132, tel. 305/371–4400 or 800/327–6565. 200 rooms with bath, including 25 suites, 55 newly remodeled. Facilities: pool, restaurant, bar. AE, CB, DC, MC, V. Moderate.*

Kendall

Dadeland Marriott. Catering to business travelers, this 24-story hotel is part of a megastructure that includes the Datran Center office building and the southernmost Metrorail station, Dadeland South. Within walking distance of Dadeland Mall, the hotel has a four-story atrium overlooking the Datran Center's lobby and its extensive sculpture collection. The hotel's contemporary decor, in corals and light greens, incorporates Asian accents. All rooms have desks and good reading lights. The best rooms face the city on the upper floors; 717 and 719 have glass doors opening to the pool. The worst room, 805, overlooks the roof of the exercise room. *9090 Dadeland Blvd., Miami 33156, tel. 305/663–1035 or 800/228–9290. 303 rooms with bath, including 2 suites, nonsmoker floor with 15 rooms, 4 rooms for handicapped guests. Facilities: outdoor heated freshwater swimming pool, Jacuzzi, whirlpool, sauna, exercise room, restaurant, lounge, complimentary airport transportation. AE, MC, V. Expensive.*

Key Biscayne

Sheraton Royal Biscayne Beach Resort and Racquet Club. Art-deco pinks, wicker furniture, and chattering macaws and cockatoos in the lobby set the tone for this three-story beachfront resort set amid the waving fronds of coconut palms. Built in 1952 and restored in 1985, this laid-back place has managed to keep its casual demeanor even after starring as a "Miami Vice" set. All rooms have garden and bay views; most have terraces. *555 Ocean Dr., Key Biscayne 33149, tel. 305/361–5775. 192 rooms with bath, including 4 suites with ocean view, 15 suites with kitchenette, 15 nonsmoker rooms. Facilities: a ¼-mile of ocean beachfront; 2 outdoor freshwater heated swimming pools; children's wading pool and playground; 10 tennis courts (4 lighted); sailboats, Windsurfers, Hobie Cats, aquabikes, snorkeling kits, and bicycles for rent; pay-TV movies; unisex beauty salon; restaurants and lounge. AE, CB, DC, MC, V. Expensive.*

★ **Sonesta Beach Hotel & Tennis Club.** Built in 1969, this eight-story beachfront resort underwent a $5-million renovation in 1985. Tropical hues focus attention on museum-quality modern art by prominent painters and sculptors. Don't miss Andy Warhol's five drawings of rock star Mick Jagger in the hotel's disco bar, Desires. The best rooms face the ocean on the eighth floor, a "club floor" with a small lobby and bar where breakfast is served. *350 Ocean Dr., Key Biscayne 33149, tel. 305/361–2021 or 800/343–7170. 315 rooms with bath, including 12 suites and 15 villas (3-, 4-, and 5-bedroom homes with full kitchens and screened-in swimming pools). Facilities: 750 feet of ocean-front beach; outdoor freshwater heated Olympic-size swimming pool and whirlpool; 10 tennis courts (3 lighted); health center with Jacuzzi, dry and hot steam rooms, aerobic dance floor, weight room, massage room, and tanning room; gift shops; restaurants, snack bar, deli, disco lounge. AE, CB, DC, MC, V. Very Expensive.*

Miami Beach

★ **Alexander Hotel.** Newly remodeled throughout, with antique furnishings and original art in every suite, this 16-story hotel offers ocean and bay views from every room. Rooms facing south have the best views. A computer keeps track of the mattresses, so you can request the degree of firmness you prefer. *5225 Collins Ave., Miami Beach 33140, tel. 305/865–6500. 211 suites, each with two baths. Facilities: ocean beach, 2 outdoor heated freshwater pools, 4 poolside Jacuzzis, cabanas, Sunfishes and catamarans for rent, Dominique's gourmet restaurant, and coffee shop. AE, DC, MC, V. Expensive.*

Art Deco Hotels. A trio of restored three-story hotels facing the beach are under common ownership and management. The **Hotel Cardozo** dates from 1939, the **Hotel Carlyle** from 1941, and the **Hotel Leslie** from 1937. All three are attractively decorated in art-deco pinks, whites, and grays. Many contain original walnut furniture, restored and refinished. Rooms are comfortable but small; inspect your room before registering to assure that it meets your needs. Air-conditioning has been installed, but most of the time you won't need it—especially in rooms facing the water, where a sea breeze usually blows. *1244 Ocean Dr., Miami Beach 33139, tel. 305/534–2135 or 800/327–6306, in Canada 800/327–3435. 168 rooms with bath, including 15 suites. Facilities: restaurants and bars with live entertainment in the Carlyle and Cardozo. AE, CB, DC, MC, V. Moderate.*

Fontainebleau Hilton Resort and Spa. The Miami area's foremost convention hotel boasts an opulent lobby with massive chandeliers and a sweeping staircase and new meeting rooms in art-deco hues. However, many guest rooms need refurbishing. Upper-floor rooms in the Chateau Building have the best views. *4441 Collins Ave., Miami Beach 33140, tel. 305/538–2000. 1,206 rooms with bath, including 60 suites, 55 nonsmoker rooms. Facilities: ocean beach with 30 cabanas, windsurfing, parasailing, Hobie Cats, volleyball, basketball, 2 outdoor pools (one fresh, one salt), 3 whirlpool baths, 7 lighted tennis courts, health club with exercise classes, saunas, marina, free children's activities, 12 restaurants and lounges, Tropigala night club. AE, CB, DC, MC, V. Expensive.*

★ **Hotel Cavalier.** Rooms in this three-story beachfront hotel have period marble furnishings, new baths, and air-conditioning. The Cavalier is popular with the film and fashion industry; many guests are artists, models, photographers, and writers. The best rooms face the ocean; the worst are on the ground floor, rear south, where the garbage truck goes by in the morning. *1320 Ocean Dr., Miami Beach 33139, tel. 305/531-6424 or 800/338-9076. 44 rooms with bath, including 2 suites. Facilities: bottled water and flowers in all rooms, Continental breakfast in lobby each morning, airport pickup available. AE, CB, DC, MC, V. Expensive.*

Surfside Beach Hotel. If you like classic American cars of the 1950s, you'll love this 10-story Quality Inn franchise. Built in 1951, it was restored in 1986 and transformed into a museum for owner Michael Dezer's collection of cars and automotive memorabilia. The lobby display includes a turquoise 1955 Ford Thunderbird hardtop, a 1957 Studebaker Golden Hawk, a red 1950 Willys Jeepster, and their ancestor—a 1931 Ford Model A roadster. Every room is named after a car. *8701 Collins Ave., Miami Beach 33154, tel. 305/865-6661 or 800/228-5151. 220 rooms with bath, including 36 nonsmoker rooms. Facilities: 300 feet of ocean beach frontage, outdoor freshwater swimming pool with mosaic of pink 1959 Cadillac El Dorado convertible on the bottom, American Classics restaurant, Chevy's dance club, lobby bar, gift shop. AE, CB, DC, MC, V. Moderate.*

North Dade

Holiday Inn North Miami–Golden Glades. Mid-rise suburban hotel at major highway interchange; two miles from the beach, from Calder Race Course, and from Joe Robbie Stadium (where the Miami Dolphins football team plays home games). A 1987 renovation gave public areas modern furnishings and mauve, peach, and purple wallpaper. Rooms have a green-and-white color scheme with oak furniture. Local police patrol the premises nightly. Restaurant offers Weight Watchers menu. *148 N.W. 167th St., Miami 33169, tel. 305/949-1441 or 800/HOLIDAY. 163 rooms with bath, including 18 nonsmoker rooms, 12 lady executive rooms, 1 room for handicapped guests. Facilities: outdoor freshwater swimming pool, children's pool, outdoor exercise area for aerobics, in-room refreshment center, restaurant, and lounge. AE, CB, DC, MC, V. Moderate.*

Miami Lakes Inn, Athletic Club and Golf Resort. This low-rise suburban resort is part of a planned town being developed by Florida Senator Bob Graham's family about 35 miles northwest of downtown Miami. The golf resort opened in 1962 and added two wings in 1978. Its decor is English-traditional throughout, rich in leather and wood. All rooms have balconies. The inn opened in 1983 with a typically Florida-tropic look—light pastel hues and furniture of wicker and light wood. In both locations, the best rooms are near the lobby for convenient access; the worst are near the elevators. *Main St., Miami Lakes 33014, tel. 305/821-1150. 303 rooms with bath, including 21 suites. Facilities: 2 outdoor freshwater swimming pools; 10 lighted tennis courts; golf (18-hole par-72 course, lighted 18-hole par-54 executive course, golf school); saunas, steamrooms, and whirlpool baths; 9 indoor racquetball courts; Nautilus fitness center; full-size gym for volleyball and basketball; aerobics classes; restaurants and lounges; shopping discount at Main St. shops. AE, CB, DC, MC, V. Very Expensive.*

★ **Turnberry Isle Yacht and Country Club.** Part of an upscale condominium community on a 300-acre bayfront site 12 miles north of downtown Miami. Celebrities who live here include tennis stars Jimmy Connors, Vitas Gerulitis, and John McEnroe. Choose from the European-style Marina Hotel or the Country

Club Inn beside the golf course. Rooms are oversize, with light woods and earth-tone colors at the inn, a nautical-blue motif at the hotel, large curving terraces, Jacuzzis, honor bar, and in-room safes. *19735 Turnberry Way, North Miami Beach 33163, tel. 305/932–6200. 111 rooms with bath, including 23 suites. Facilities: Ocean Club with 250 feet of private beach frontage, diving gear, Windsurfers and Hobie Cats for rent, and complimentary shuttle service to the hotel; 2 outdoor freshwater swimming pools; 24 tennis courts, 18 with lights; 2 18-hole golf courses; helipad; marina with moorings for 125 boats up to 150 ft.; full-service spa with physician, nutritionist, saunas, steamrooms, whirlpools, facials, herbal wraps, Nautilus exercise equipment, indoor racquetball courts, and jogging course; 5 private restaurants, lounge, nightly entertainment. AE, CB, DC, MC, V. Very Expensive.*

West Dade **Doral Hotel & Country Club.** Millions of airline passengers annually peer down upon this 2,400-acre jewel of an inland golf and tennis resort while fastening their seat belts. It's seven miles west of Miami International Airport and consists of eight separate three- and four-story lodges nestled beside the golf links. A renovation completed in 1988 gave the resort a tropical theme, with light pastels, wicker, and teak furniture. All guest rooms have minibars; most have private balconies or terraces with views of the golf courses or tennis courts. *4400 N.W. 87th Ave., Miami 33178, tel. 305/592–2000. 650 rooms with bath, including 56 suites. Facilities: 5 18-hole golf courses, and a 9-hole, par-3 executive course; pro shop and boutique; 15 tennis courts; Olympic-size heated outdoor freshwater swimming pool; 24-stall equestrian center, offers riding instruction; 3-mi jogging and bike path; bicycle rentals; lake fishing; restaurant and lounge; transportation to beach. AE, CB, DC, MC, V. Very Expensive.*

The Arts

Performing arts aficionados in Greater Miami will tell you they survive quite nicely despite the area's historic inability to support a professional symphony orchestra. In recent years, this community has begun to write a new chapter in its performing arts history.

The New World Symphony, a unique advanced-training orchestra, marks its second season in 1989. The fledgling Miami City Ballet has risen rapidly to international prominence in its three-year existence. The opera company ranks with the nation's best, and a venerable chamber music series brings renowned ensembles to perform here. Several churches and synagogues also run classical music series with international performers.

In theater, Miami offers English-speaking audiences an assortment of professional, collegiate, and amateur productions of musicals, comedy, and drama. Spanish theater also is active.

In the cinema world, the Miami Film Festival attracts more than 45,000 people annually to screenings of new films from all over the world—including some made here.

Arts Information: Greater Miami's two English-language daily newspapers, *The Miami Herald* and *The Miami News*, publish information on the performing arts in their weekend editions—The *Herald* in the Weekend Section on Friday and the Lively

Arts Section on Sunday; The *News*, on Saturday. The *Herald* is notorious for its inaccurate listings of the location and time of arts events. Phone ahead to confirm details before you go.

If you read Spanish, check *El Nuevo Herald* (a Spanish version of *The Miami Herald)* or *Diario Las Americas* (the area's largest independent Spanish-language paper) for information on the Spanish theater and a smattering of general performing arts news.

Other good sources of information on the performing arts are the calendar in *Miami Today*, a free weekly newspaper available each Thursday in downtown Miami, Coconut Grove, and Coral Gables; and *New Times*, a free weekly distributed throughout Dade County each Wednesday.

Miami's Guide to the Arts. A monthly guide covering music of all kinds, from the classics to rock and art gallery openings, theater, and major cultural events. Editor Margo Morrison tries to be encylopedic and does a good job. Sold at newsstands all over Greater Miami. *Tel. 305/854–1790. 9–5. Annual subscription $12, individual copy $2. No credit cards.*

Tickets: If possible, obtain tickets for concerts, plays, and other performing arts events through your travel agent when you book a trip to Miami. However, that's not always possible, because many cultural events in Miami aren't publicized far in advance. When you arrive, quickly learn what will be available during your stay and scurry to buy tickets.

You can order tickets for many performances by telephone, for the price of the event plus a service fee. **Caution:** Neither of the telephone ticket-sales organizations will sell you tickets where you may want to sit; you get whatever is available. *Tix-By-Phone* (tel. 305/633–BASS or 800/221–BASS), *Select-A-Seat* (800-323–SEAT). *AE, CB, DC, MC, V.*

Ballet **Miami City Ballet.** The Cubans brought to Miami their love of classic ballet. The result: many small ballet schools and a wellspring of support for the Miami City Ballet, Florida's first major fully professional resident ballet company. Edward Villella, the artistic director, was principal dancer of the New York City Ballet under George Balanchine. Now the Miami City Ballet re-creates the Balanchine repertoire and has begun to introduce new works of its own. All Greater Miami performances are at Gusman Center for the Performing Arts. Demonstrations of works in progress are at the 450-seat Colony Theater on Miami Beach. Villella narrates the children's and works-in-progress programs. *905 Lincoln Rd., Miami Beach 33139, tel. 305/532–7713. Season: Oct.–May. AE, MC, V. Tix-By-Phone until 2 weeks before a performance, tel. 305/633–BASS or 800/221–BASS. AE, CB, DC, MC, V.*

Cinema **The Miami Film Festival.** During eight days in February, new films from all over the world are screened in the Gusman Center for the Performing Arts. Tickets and schedule: *444 Brickell Ave., Miami 33131, tel. 305/377–3456. AE, MC, V. Tix-By-Phone, tel. 305/633–BASS or 800/221–BASS. AE, CB, DC, MC, V.*

Concerts **Concert Association of Greater Miami.** A not-for-profit organization, directed by Drucker, plans two seven-concert series annually: the Great Artists Series at the Jackie Gleason Theater and the Prestige Series at Dade County Auditorium. Guest artists include world-renowned orchestras, conductors, and soloists. Ticket and program information: *555 Hank Meyer Blvd. (17th St.), Miami Beach 33139, tel. 305/532–3491. AE, CB, DC, MC, V.*

Friends of Chamber Music (44 W. Flagler St., Miami 33130, tel. 305/372–2975) presents an annual series of chamber concerts by internationally known guest ensembles, such as the Beaux Arts Trio, I Musici, and the Juilliard String Quartet.

Drama Check *Miami's Guide to the Arts* for a complete English-language theater schedule. Traveling companies come and go; amateur groups form, perform, and disband. Listed below are the more enduring groups of Greater Miami's drama scene.

Coconut Grove Playhouse. Arnold Mittelman, artistic director, stages current and vintage Broadway plays, musical reviews, and experimental productions. *3500 Main Hwy., Coconut Grove 33133, tel. 305/442–4000. AE, MC, V.*

Ruth Forman Theater. Six Actors Equity productions in her 315-seat theater on Florida International University's North Miami campus. Each production lasts five weeks. *N.E. 151 St. and Biscayne Blvd., North Miami 33181, tel. 305/940–5903. Season: Oct.–May. Wed.–Sun. 8 PM, matinees Wed., Thurs., Sat., and Sun. 2 PM. No credit cards.*

Ring Theater. The University of Miami's Department of Theatre Arts presents four complete plays a year in this 311-seat hall. *University of Miami, 1312 Miller Dr., Coral Gables 33124, tel. 305/284–3355. No credit cards.*

Opera **Greater Miami Opera Association.** Miami's resident opera company has the seventh-largest operating budget of any American opera organization. It presents two complete casts of each opera in the Dade County Auditorium. The International Series brings such luminaries as Placido Domingo and Luciano Pavarotti; the National Series features rising young singers in the principal roles, with the same sets and chorus, but with more modest ticket prices. All operas are sung in their original language, with superscripts in English projected onto a screen above the stage. *1200 Coral Way, Miami 33145, tel. 305/854–7890. AE, MC, V. Tix-By-Phone, tel. 305/633–BASS or 800/221–BASS. AE, CB, DC, MC, V.*

Symphony **New World Symphony.** Although Greater Miami still has no resident symphony orchestra, the New World Symphony, conducted by Michael Tilson Thomas, helps to fill the void. It's a unique phenomenon, a national advanced training orchestra for musicians aged 21–30 who have finished their academic studies and need performing experience in a professional setting before moving on to a permanent job. *Box 110809, Miami 33111–0809, tel. 305/371–3005. Tix-By-Phone, tel. 305/633–BASS or 800/221–BASS. AE, CB, DC, MC, V. Season: Oct.–Apr.*

Theaters Greater Miami lacks a modern performing arts center. Every auditorium and theater in town suffers from a shortage of space on and off the stage, and some have acoustical problems.

Dade County Auditorium (2901 W. Flagler St., Miami 33135, tel. 305/545–3395) satisfies patrons with 2,497 comfortable seats, good sight lines, and acceptable acoustics. Performers grumble at its shortcomings. The lack of a proper orchestra pit frustrates the Greater Miami Opera Association, and storage space is so minimal that the opera company must keep its paraphernalia outside the hall in trailers between performances.

Jackie Gleason Theater of the Performing Arts (1700 Washington Ave., Miami Beach 33119, tel. 305/673–8300), with 3,000 seats, has visibility and acoustics problems. Many top performers reportedly won't play there; many patrons are outspoken about not attending.

Gusman Center for the Performing Arts (174 E. Flagler St., Miami 33131, tel. 305/372–0925). In downtown Miami, the center has 1,700 seats made for sardines—and the best acoustics in town. An ornate former movie palace, the hall resembles a Moorish courtyard. Lights twinkle, starlike, from the ceiling. Musicians dread Gusman because they must carry everything they need in and out for each performance.

Gusman Concert Hall (1314 Miller Dr., Coral Gables 33124, tel. 305/284–2438). This 600-seat hall on the University of Miami's Coral Gables campus has good acoustics, an orange and purple color scheme, and plenty of room for UM's basketball players to stretch their legs. Parking is a problem when school is in session.

Legitimate Theater

Zev Bufman, associated with the best Broadway theater in Miami for over 25 years, is bringing six subscription shows plus specials to the *Jackie Gleason Theater* for the 1988–89 season, including *Me and My Girl* and *Les Misérables*. Tickets: *Jackie Gleason Theater of the Performing Arts, Box 190240, Miami Beach 33119, tel. 305/673–8300. Season: Sept.–May. AE, MC, V. Tix-By-Phone, tel. 305/633–BASS or 800/221–BASS. AE, CB, DC, MC, V.*

Spanish Theater

Spanish theater prospers, although many companies have short lives. About 20 Spanish companies perform light comedy, puppetry, vaudeville, and political satire. To locate them, read the Spanish newspapers. When you phone, be prepared for a conversation in Spanish. Most of the box-office personnel don't speak English.

Coconut Grove Playhouse Hispanic Theater Project (3500 Main Hwy., Coconut Grove, tel. 305/442–2662). Faces severe budget problems but may have more staying power than other Spanish groups because of its association with an English-language theater.

Prometo. Has produced three to four bilingual Spanish-English plays a year for 15 years. *Miami-Dade Community College, New World Center Campus, 300 N.E. 2nd Ave., Miami, tel. 305/347–3263.*

Teatro de Bellas Artes. A 255-seat theater on Calle Ocho, Little Havana's main commercial street, presents eight Spanish plays and musicals a year. *Dramas Fri.–Sat. 9 PM and Sun. 3 PM. Musical comedy Sat. midnight and Sun. 9 PM. Recitals Sun. 6 PM. 2173 S.W. 8th St., Miami, tel. 305/325–0515. No credit cards.*

Nightlife

Greater Miami has no concentration of night spots like Bourbon Street in New Orleans or Rush Street in Chicago, but nightlife thrives throughout the Miami area in scattered locations, including Miami Beach, Little Haiti, Little Havana, Coconut Grove, the fringes of downtown Miami, and south-suburban Kendall. Individual clubs offer jazz, various forms of rock-and-roll, and top 40 sounds on different nights of the week. Some clubs refuse entrance to anyone under 21; others set the age limit at 25.

For current information, see the Weekend Section each Friday in *The Miami Herald;* the calendar in *Miami Today,* a free weekly newspaper available each Thursday in downtown Miami, Coconut Grove, and Coral Gables; and *New Times,* a free weekly distributed throughout Dade County each Wednesday.

Bass Tickets and Love 94 (WLVE, 93.9 FM) sponsor a concert line with information on touring groups of all kinds, except classical (tel. 305/654–9436). Blues Hot Line lists local blues clubs and bars (tel. 305/666–6656). Jazz Hot Line lists local jazz programs (tel. 305/382–3938).

On Miami Beach, where the sounds of jazz and reggae spill into the streets, fashion models and photographers frequent the lobby bars of small art-deco hotels.

Throughout the Greater Miami area, bars and cocktail lounges in larger hotels operate discos nightly, with live entertainment on weekends. Many hotels extend their bars into open-air courtyards, where patrons dine and dance under the stars throughout the year.

Bars

Churchill's Hideaway. This enclave of Anglicism in Little Haiti is popular with cruise-line employees and international sports fans. Its satellite dish picks up BBC news programs, and a Sharp Six System VHS plays foreign-format tapes of international soccer and rugby games. Four English beers on tap, 40 kinds of imported bottled beers. Four dart boards. The outdoor bar in back came from an old Playboy Club on Biscayne Boulevard. Entertainment on weekends. *5501 N.E. 2nd Ave., Miami, tel. 305/757–1807. Open 10 AM–2 AM Mon.–Thurs. and Sun., to 3 AM Fri.–Sat. No credit cards.*

Hungry Sailor. This small English-style pub is decorated with nautical charts, marine flags, and flotsam and jetsam. Five English ales and beers are on tap. There's traditional English food, and live entertainment nightly: folk, jazz, or reggae. *3064½ Grand Ave., Coconut Grove, tel. 305/444–9359. Open 11:30 AM–2:30 AM. AE, MC, V.*

Stuart's Bar-Lounge. Named for its owner and located in the Hotel Place St. Michel, Stuart's is an original Coral Gables hostelry built in 1926. *Esquire* called Stuart's one of the best new bars of 1987. It is decorated with beveled mirrors, mahogany paneling, French posters, pictures of old Coral Gables, and art-nouveau lighting. Live jazz on weekends. *162 Alcazar Ave., Coral Gables, tel. 305/444–1666. Open 5 PM–12:30 AM Mon.–Sat., 6 PM–12:30 AM Sun. AE, CB, DC, MC, V.*

Taurus Steak House. The bar, built in 1922 of native cypress, nightly draws an over-30 singles crowd that drifts outside to a patio. A band plays on weekends. Lunch and dinner. *3540 Main Hwy., Coconut Grove, tel. 305/448–0633. Open daily 5 PM–midnight. All major credit cards.*

Tobacco Road. This bar, opened in 1912, holds Miami's oldest liquor license. Upstairs, in space occupied by a speakeasy during Prohibition, local and national blues bands perform Friday and Saturday and in scheduled weeknight concerts. The bar draws a diverse clientele from all over south Florida. *626 S. Miami Ave., Miami, tel. 305/374–1198. Open weekdays 11:30 AM–5 AM, weekends 1 PM–5 AM. Lunch served Mon.–Fri. Dinner served Sun.–Thurs. AE, DC.*

Tropics International Restaurant. Reggae is featured in art deco surroundings in the lobby of the Edison Hotel, built in

1936. Dinner. *960 Ocean Dr., Miami Beach, tel. 305/531–5335. Open daily 5 PM–3 AM. AE, MC, V.*

Comedy Clubs

Coconuts Comedy Clubs. This 1980s version of vaudeville comedy thrives with humor that's adult, but not obscene. Two acts per show; new performers each week. *Dadeland Marriott Hotel, 9090 S. Dadeland Blvd., Kendall, tel. 305/670–2022. Wed.–Sat. 9PM, 2nd show Fri. and Sat. 11 PM. Also at Howard Johnson, 16500 N.W. 2nd Ave., North Miami Beach, tel. 305/948–6887. Thurs. and Sun. 9 PM, Fri. 9 and 11 PM, Sat. 9:30 and 11:30 PM. Both suggest reservation. Cover and drink minimum AE, MC, V.*

Disco/Rock Clubs

Biscayne Baby. Upstairs, above offices and shops in a rustic wood building, this club's dining area has a 1950s soda-parlor motif, two bars, and a separate champagne room. Biscayne Baby draws an under-30 crowd for serious dancing. D.J. plays '50s–'80s rock. Wood dance floor. *3336 Virginia St., Coconut Grove, tel. 305/445–3751. Open 8 PM–5 AM Tues.–Sat. MC and V in restaurant and boutique only.*

China Club. A 1940 art-deco building with glass block, turrets, and flagstaffs outside, Chinese-style interior, and wood dance floor, this club serves excellent Chinese dinners. Live entertainment Thursday–Sunday, disco Wednesday. Attracts significant rock stars as performers and patrons. *1450 Collins Ave., Miami Beach, tel. 305/534–7001. Open 10 PM–5 AM Wed.–Sun. AE, MC, V.*

Club Oz. This is a haven for south-suburban yuppies. The theme changes nightly, with many special events. Wood dance floor. *19995 S. Dixie Hwy., Miami, tel. 305/238–3700. Open Wed.–Sat. 9 PM–5 AM. AE, MC, V.*

Stefano's of Key Biscayne. Live band performs nightly, 7–11 PM. Then this northern Italian restaurant becomes a disco. Wood dance floor. *24 Crandon Blvd., Key Biscayne, tel. 305/361–7007. Open 5 PM–5 AM nightly. AE, CB, DC, MC, V.*

Folk Music

Our Place Natural Foods Eatery. On weekends, this small South Beach vegetarian restaurant becomes Greater Miami's only smoke-free live folk music club. Features local and national artists. Last Saturday of each month is "open mike" night. Full menu all night. *830 Washington Ave., Miami Beach, tel. 305/674–1322. Open 9 PM Fri.–Sat. till the musicians quit. No credit cards.*

Nightclubs

Les Violins Supper Club. This standby has been owned for 25 years by the Cachaidora-Currais family, who ran a club and restaurant in Havana. The club's ceiling rises 10 feet during two nightly Las Vegas–style reviews, reminiscent of old Busby Berkeley movies. Live dance band. Wood dance floor. Dinner. *1751 Biscayne Blvd., Miami, tel. 305/371–8668. Open 7 PM. Closes Tues.–Thurs. and Sun. 1 AM, Fri. 2 AM, Sat. 3 AM. Closed Mon. Reservations suggested. AE, CB, DC, MC, V.*

Club Tropigala at La Ronde in the Fontainebleau Hilton Hotel. A seven-level round room decorated with orchids, banana leaves, and philodendrons to resemble a tropical jungle, this club is operated by owners of Les Violins. Two bands play Latin music for dancing on wood floor. Two live costumed shows nightly. Dinner. Long wait for valet parking. *4441 Collins Ave., Miami Beach, tel. 305/672–7469. Open Wed.–Sun. 7 PM–4 AM. Reservations advised. AE, CB, DC, MC, V.*

4 The Everglades

Introduction

by George and Rosalie Leposky

Greater Miami is the only metropolitan area in the United States with two national parks in its backyard: Everglades and Biscayne. Both have image problems.

Because Everglades is famous, people come expecting a spectacle like the mountainous western parks. What they see is a wide expanse of saw grass that at first glance looks frustratingly like a midwestern wheat field. In sea-girded Biscayne, you need a boat and snorkel or scuba gear.

At least these parks are easy to reach. You can drive to either one from downtown Miami in an hour, and their main entrances are just 21 miles apart. Between them sits Homestead, a bustling agricultural city of 25,000.

The creation of Everglades National Park in 1947 made many people in Homestead unhappy. The farmers wanted to plow much of the land that came under the park service's protection.

Today, Homestead is beginning to view the park with a less-jaundiced eye and transforming itself into a tourist center. New motels, shopping centers, and restaurants have opened; old ones are sprucing up. City officials have created a historic district downtown to promote restoration of Homestead's commercial heart. It's all an effort to house, feed, and amuse many of the million visitors who will explore the Everglades in 1989—and the 30,000 hardy souls who will discover Biscayne.

If you intend to spend just one day at Everglades National Park, take the 38-mile main park road from the Main Visitor Center to Flamingo to see a cross section of the park's ecosystems: hardwood hammock (tree islands), freshwater prairie, pineland, freshwater slough, cypress, coastal prairie, mangrove, and marine/estuarine.

At Shark Valley, on the park's northern edge, a 14-mile tram ride takes you to an observation tower overlooking the "river of grass" (*see* Guided Tours).

The Gulf Coast and Key Largo ranger stations and the Flamingo Visitor Center offer access to the mangroves and marine habitats—Gulf Coast in the Ten Thousand Islands region along the Gulf of Mexico near Everglades City; Flamingo and Key Largo in Florida Bay. You can take tour boat rides from Everglades City and Flamingo through this ecosystem (*see* Guided Tours) and hire a fishing guide to show you where the big ones bite (*see* Participant Sports).

Biscayne National Park encompasses almost 274 square miles, of which 96% are under water. Biscayne includes 18 miles of inhospitable mangrove shoreline on the mainland and 45 mangrove-fringed barrier islands seven miles to the east across Biscayne Bay. The bay is a lobster sanctuary and a nursery for fish, sponges, and crabs. Manatees and sea turtles also frequent its warm, shallow waters.

The islands (called keys) are fossilized coral reefs that emerged from the sea when glaciers trapped much of the world's water supply during the Ice Age. Today, a tropical hardwood forest grows in the crevices of these rocky keys.

East of the keys, coral reefs three miles seaward attract divers and snorkelers. (*See* Participant Sports). Biscayne is the only national park in the continental United States with living coral reefs and is the nation's largest marine park.

The park boundary encompasses the continental shelf to a depth of 60 feet. East of that boundary, the shelf falls rapidly away to a depth of 400 feet at the edge of the Gulf Stream.

Getting Around

By Plane *Commercial Flights.* **Miami International Airport** (MIA) is the closest commercial airport to Everglades National Park and Biscayne National Park. It's 34 miles from Homestead and 83 miles from the Flamingo resort in Everglades National Park.

By Car From the north, the main highways to Homestead–Florida City are U.S. 1, the Homestead Extension of the Florida Turnpike, and Krome Avenue (Rte. 997).

From Miami to Biscayne National Park, take the turnpike extension to the Tallahassee Road (S.W. 137th Ave.) exit, turn left, and go south. Turn left at North Canal Drive (S.W. 328th St.), go east, and follow signs to park headquarters at Convoy Point. The park is about 30 miles from downtown Miami.

From Homestead to Biscayne National Park, take U.S. 1 or Krome Avenue (Rte. 997) to Lucy Street (S.E. 8th St.). Turn east. Lucy Street becomes North Canal Drive (S.W. 328th St.). Follow signs about eight miles to the park headquarters.

From Homestead to Everglades National Park's Main Visitor Center and Flamingo, take U.S. 1 or Krome Avenue (Rte. 997) south to Florida City. Turn right (west) onto Rte. 9336. Follow signs to the park entrance. The Main Visitor Center is 11 miles from Homestead; Flamingo is 49 miles from Homestead.

To reach the north end of Everglades National Park, take U.S. 41 (the Tamiami Trail) west from Miami. It's 40 miles to the Shark Valley Information Center and 83 miles to the Gulf Coast Ranger Station at Everglades City.

To reach the south end of Everglades National Park in the Florida Keys, take U.S. 1 south from Homestead. It's 27 miles to the Key Largo Ranger Station (between Mile Markers 98 and 99 on the Overseas Hwy.).

Rental Cars **Homestead Freedom Rent-a-Car.** Tel. 305/248–8352 or 305/257–2525. Rental cars also available at MIA (*see* Miami Arriving and Departing).

By Bus **Metrobus** Route 1A runs from Homestead to MIA only during peak weekday hours: 6:30–9 AM and 4–6:30 PM.
Greyhound/Trailways operates two trips daily north and south from MIA (*see* Miami Arriving and Departing).

By Taxi **Homestead Cab Company.** Service in Homestead–Florida City area. Full service to and from Flamingo and the tour boats in Biscayne National Park. Service from Homestead to MIA; *416 N.E. 1st Rd., Homestead, tel. 305/247–7777. Open 24 hours daily except 6 AM Sun.–5 AM Mon. No credit cards.*

By Boat **U.S. Customs.** The nearest U.S. Customs phones to the two national parks are at **Watson Island Marina** (1050 MacArthur Causeway, Miami, tel. 305/371–2378), about 25 nautical miles to Biscayne National Park headquarters, 50 nautical miles to Flamingo; and **Tavernier Creek Marina** (Mile Marker 90-½, U.S. 1, Tavernier, tel. 305/252–0194 from Miami, 305/852–5854 from the Keys), about 48 nautical miles to Biscayne National Park headquarters, 25 nautical miles to Flamingo.

Scenic Drives

Main road to Flamingo in Everglades National Park. It's 38 road miles from the Main Visitor Center to Flamingo, across six distinct ecosystems (with access from the road to two others). Highlights of the trip include a dwarf cypress forest, the ecotone (transition zone) between saw grass and mangrove forest, and a wealth of wading birds at Mrazek and Coot Bay Ponds. Boardwalks and trails along the main road and several short spurs allow you to see the Everglades without getting your feet wet. Well-written interpretive signs en route will help you understand this diverse wilderness.

Tamiami Trail. U.S. 41 from Miami to the Gulf Coast crosses the Everglades and the Big Cypress Swamp. Highlights of the trip include sweeping views across the saw grass to the Shark River Slough, a visit to the Miccosukee Indian Reservation, and the Big Cypress Swamp's variegated pattern of wet prairies, ponds, marshes, sloughs, and strands. It's 83 miles to the Gulf Coast Ranger Station at Everglades City.

Guided Tours

Tours of Everglades National Park and Biscayne National Park typically focus on native wildlife, plants, and park history. Concessionaires operate the Everglades tram tours and the boat cruises in both parks.

In addition, the National Park Service organizes a variety of free programs at Everglades National Park. Ask a ranger for the daily schedule.

Orientation Tours

All Florida Adventure Tours. All-day narrated 250-mile tour of south Florida wetlands, through the Big Cypress Swamp to Everglades City and Chokoloskee Island, and Corkscrew. *11137 North Kendall Dr., D105, Miami 33176, tel. 305/270–0219. Tours Tues. and Sat. Cost: $69.50 adults, $49.50 children. No credit cards.*

Miami Vision. Miccosukee Indian Village, lunch, and airboat ride. Minivan and private car tours. Well-informed, congenial guides speak English, Spanish, French, German, Italian, and Portuguese. *2699 Collins Ave., Suite 113, Miami Beach, tel. 305/532–0040. Cost: $49 adults, $39 children. MC, V.*

Safari Sightseeing Tours. Everglades tour includes airboat ride, indian village, Shark Valley, and lunch. *6547 S.W. 116th Pl., Miami, tel. 305/226–6923 (day) or 305/223–3804 (night). Tours Wed., Sat., Sun. 8:30–5. Cost: $29.50 adults, $14.75 children under 12, includes transportation and admissions (but not lunch). No credit cards.*

Special-Interest Tours

Airboat Rides

Buffalo Tiger's Florida Everglades Airboat Ride. The former chairman of the Miccosukee tribe will take you on a 30-minute airboat ride through the Everglades, with a stop at an old Indian camp. Opportunities to watch birds, turtles, and alligators. *Tour location: 29701 S.W. 8th St., 12 mi west of Krome Ave., 20 mi west of the Miami city limits (Rte. 997), tel. 305/559–5250. Open daily 9–6. Cost: $6 adults, $4 children under 10. No credit cards.*

Coopertown Airboat Ride. Chuck Norris filmed *Invasion U.S.A.* here. A 30-minute airboat ride through the Everglades saw grass to visit two hammocks (subtropical hardwood forests) and alligator holes. Bird-watching opportunities. *Tour location: S.W. 8th St., 5 mi west of Krome Ave., 15 mi west of Miami city limits, tel. 305/226-6048. Open daily 8:30–dusk. Cost: $6 per person. No credit cards.*

Everglades Air Boat Tours. A four-mile, 30-minute tour of the River of Grass leaves every half hour. *Tour location: 40351 S.W. 192nd Ave., tel. 305/AIRBOAT. Open daily 9–5. Cost: $7.50 adults, $6.50 senior citizens, $3.50 children 4–12, under 4 free. No credit cards.*

Boat Tours

Biscayne Aqua-Center, Inc. You'll ride to Biscayne National Park's living coral reefs 10 miles offshore on a 53-foot glass-bottom boat. A separate tour to Elliott Key visitor center, on a barrier island seven miles offshore across Biscayne Bay, is conducted only in winter when mosquitoes are less active. *Tour location: East end of North Canal Dr. (S.W. 328th St.), Homestead, tel. 305/247–2400. Office open daily 8:30–5:30. Phone for schedule. Reservations required. AE, MC, V.*

Back Country Tour. A two-hour cruise from Flamingo Lodge Marina & Outpost Resort aboard a 40-passenger pontoon boat covers 12–15 miles through tropical estuaries fringed with impenetrable mangrove forests. You may see manatees, dolphins, sharks, alligators, and many species of bird life, including bald eagles. *Tour location: Flamingo Marina, Flamingo, tel. 305/253–2241 or 813/695–3101. Cruises daily. Phone for schedule. Reservations accepted. AE, DC, MC, V.*

Everglades National Park Boat Tours. Sammy Hamilton operates three separate 12-mile tours through the Ten Thousand Islands region along the Gulf of Mexico on the western margin of the park. *Tour location: A half mile south of Everglades National Park's Gulf Coast Ranger Station on Rte. 29, about 3 mi south of U.S. 41 (Tamiami Trail), tel. 813/695–2591 or in FL 800/445–7724. Office open daily 8:30–4:30. Phone for schedule. No credit cards.*

Florida Bay Cruise. A 90-minute tour of Florida Bay from Flamingo Lodge Marina & Outpost Resort aboard *Bald Eagle*, a 90-passenger pontoon boat. The tour offers a close look at bird life on rookery islands in the bay and on sandbars during low tide. In winter, you're likely to see white pelicans; in summer, magnificent frigate birds. *Tour location: Flamingo Marina, Flamingo, tel. 305/253–2241 or 813/695–3101. Cruises daily. Phone for schedule. Reservations accepted. AE, DC, MC, V.*

Florida Boat Tours. Back-country tours outside Everglades National Park in Everglades City area. Runs three 24-passenger airboats for 30-minute rides, 48-passenger pontoon boat for one-hour cruise. Boats are Coast Guard approved. *Tel. 813/695–4400 or in FL 800/282–9194. Phone for schedule. MC, V.*

Tram Tours

Wilderness Tram Tour. Snake Bight is an indentation in the Florida Bay shoreline near Flamingo. You can go there aboard a 48-passenger screened tram on this two-hour tour through a mangrove forest and a coastal prairie to a 100-yard boardwalk over the mud flats at the edge of the bight. It's a good birding spot. Tram operates subject to mosquito, weather, and trail conditions. Driver has insect repellent on board. *Departs from*

Flamingo Lodge, tel. 305/253–2241 or 813/695–3101. Phone for schedule. Reservations accepted. AE, CB, DC, MC, V.

Shark Valley Tram Tours. The trams began running again early in 1988 after a 20-month hiatus to rebuild the 15-mile loop road. Now the road is two feet higher, with 200 culverts, and considerably less flood prone when the summer rains come. Propane-powered trams travel into the interior, stopping at a 50-foot observation tower on the site of an oil well drilled in the 1940s. From atop the tower, you'll view the Everglades' vast "river of grass" sweeping south toward the Gulf of Mexico. The trams are covered but have open sides, so carry rain gear. *Tour location: Shark Valley entrance to Everglades National Park, 40 mi west of Miami off U.S. 41 (Tamiami Trail), tel. 305/221–8455. Open daily all year 9–4. Cost: $5 adults, $2.47 children, $4.50 senior citizens. Reservations recommended Dec.–Mar. No credit cards.*

Personal Guides **Flamingo Lodge Marina & Outpost Resort.** Six captains of charter fishing boats are available to give individual tours out of Flamingo. Make reservations several weeks in advance through Gary Sabbag, the resort's general manager. *TW Services Inc., Everglades National Park, Box 428, Flamingo 33030, tel. 305/253–2241 or 813/695–3101. Nov. 1–Apr. 30 (except Christmas week). Cost: $100 a day, $75 a half day per person. AE, CB, DC, MC, V (see* Miami Guided Tours).

Important Addresses and Numbers

Tourist Information **South Dade Visitors Information Center.** The Greater Miami Convention and Visitors Bureau plans to open this new center in late 1988. *100 U.S. 1, Florida City 33034, tel. 305/245–9180. Open daily 8–6.*

Greater Homestead–Florida City Chamber of Commerce (650 U.S. 1, Homestead 33030, tel. 305/247–2332).

Emergencies Homestead, Florida City, and unincorporated Dade County use the same emergency number, 911. You can dial free from pay phones.

In the national parks, the rangers perform police, fire, and medical-emergency functions. Look for the rangers at park visitor centers and information stations, or phone the park switchboards: *Biscayne* (tel. 305/247–2400); *Everglades* (tel. 305/624–6211).

Hospitals **James Archer Smith Hospital.** 24-hour emergency room. *160 N.W. 13th St., Homestead, tel. 305/248–3232. Physician referral service, tel. 305/248–DOCS.*

Marine Phone Numbers **Biscayne National Park** (tel. 305/247–2044). Rangers staff Elliott Key Visitor Center and Adams Key Information Center around the clock and can call the mainland on ship-to-shore radio. Park headquarters on Convoy Point open daily 8–5.

Florida Marine Patrol. Law-enforcement arm of the Florida Department of Natural Resources. Boating emergencies: *24-hour tel. 305/325–3346.* Natural resource violations, including marine fishery laws, mangrove cuttings, manatee reports, filling of wetlands. 24-hour Resource Alert Hot Line: *tel. 800/342–1821.*

National Weather Service. National Hurricane Center office in Coral Gables supplies local forecasts. *Open Mon.–Fri.*

7:30–5, tel. 305/665-0429. For 24-hr phone weather recording, tel. 305/661–5065.

U.S. Coast Guard **Miami Beach Coast Guard Base** (tel. 305/535–4314 or 305/535–4315, VHF-FM Channel 16). Local marine emergencies, search-and-rescue, and reporting of navigation hazards.

Exploring Biscayne National Park

Because 96% of Biscayne National Park's acreage is under water, you must take a boat ride to visit most of it and snorkel or scuba dive to appreciate it fully. If you don't have your own boat, a concessionaire will take you to the coral reefs 10 miles offshore. These dome-shape patch reefs—some the size of a student's desk, others as broad as a large parking lot—rely on the delicate balance of temperature, depth, light, and water quality that the park was created to maintain.

A diverse population of colorful fish flits through the reefs: angelfish, gobies, grunts, parrot fish, pork fish, wrasses, and many more.

From December through April, when the mosquito population is relatively quiescent, you can comfortably explore several of the mangrove-fringed barrier islands seven miles offshore. Tropical hardwood forests cloak the upper reaches of these fossilized coral reefs.

The list below describes the facilities at each of Biscayne National Park's visitor service areas, and also at the Metro-Dade County parks within the national park's boundaries.

Numbers in the margin correspond with points of interest on the Everglades National Park map.

1 **Adams Key Information Station.** Boat dock, picnic area, rest rooms, short nature trail. Ranger station has ship-to-shore radio contact with mainland. Day use only.

2 **Boca Chita Key.** Mark C. Honeywell, former president of Minneapolis's Honeywell Co., bought this island in 1937 and built the ornamental lighthouse, rainwater catchment cisterns, a wall, and other buildings of coral rock. A boat dock, picnic area, rest rooms. Lighthouse open on occasion; ask rangers.

3 **Convoy Point Information Station.** Park headquarters. Small visitor center and outdoor kiosk with bulletin boards. Launching ramp for canoes and small boats. Boardwalk over shallow water near shore to jetty and path along jetty. Picnic area. Dock where you board tour boats to reefs and Elliott Key. *At east end of North Canal Dr. (S.W. 328th St.), Homestead, tel. 305/247–2044. Open Dec.–Apr. Mon.–Fri. 8–5, Sat.–Sun. 9–5:30; May–Nov. Mon.–Fri. 10–4, Sat.–Sun. 10–6. Admission free.*

4 **Elliott Key Visitor Center.** Indoor exhibit area on second floor displays coral, sponges, and sea-turtle shells on a "touching table" that children especially enjoy. A screened enclosure under the exhibit area houses picnic tables, bulletin boards, slide show. *Open Sat.–Sun. and holidays only 10–4.*

Sands Key. Back-country camping allowed; no facilities.

Exploring the Everglades

Winter is the best time to visit Everglades National Park. Temperatures and mosquito activity are moderate. Low water

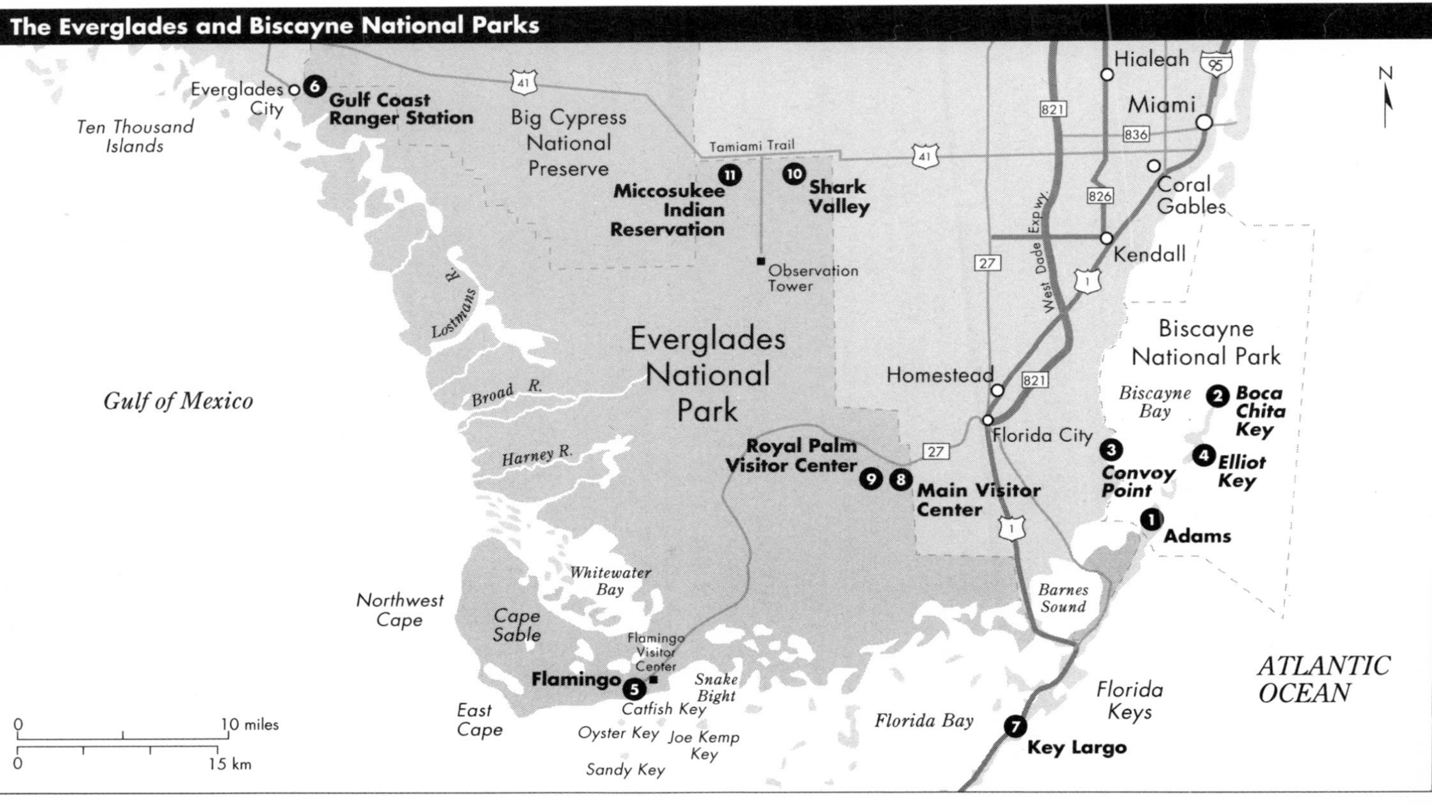
The Everglades and Biscayne National Parks
Everglades City
6 Gulf Coast Ranger Station
Ten Thousand Islands
41
Big Cypress National Preserve
Tamiami Trail
11 Miccosukee Indian Reservation
10 Shark Valley
Observation Tower
Lostmans R.
Gulf of Mexico
Broad R.
Harney R.
Everglades National Park
Royal Palm Visitor Center
9 8 Main Visitor Center
Whitewater Bay
Northwest Cape
Cape Sable
Flamingo Visitor Center
Flamingo 5
Snake Bight
East Cape
Catfish Key
Oyster Key
Joe Kemp Key
Sandy Key
0 10 miles
0 15 km
Hialeah
95
Miami
821
836
Coral Gables
826
Kendall
27
West Dade Expwy.
1
Homestead
Biscayne National Park
Biscayne Bay
2 Boca Chita Key
Florida City
3 Convoy Point
4 Elliot Key
1 Adams
Barnes Sound
Florida Bay
7 Key Largo
Florida Keys
ATLANTIC OCEAN
N

levels concentrate the resident wildlife around sloughs that retain water all year. Migratory birds swell the avian population.

Winter is also the busiest time in the park. Make reservations and expect crowds at Flamingo, the Main Visitor Center, and Royal Palm—the most popular visitor service areas.

In spring the weather turns increasingly hot and dry. After Easter, fewer visitors come, and tours and facilities are less crowded. Migratory birds depart, and you must look harder to see wildlife. Be especially careful with campfires and matches; this is when the wildfire-prone saw-grass prairies and pinelands are most vulnerable.

Summer brings intense sun and billowing clouds that unleash torrents of rain on the Everglades. Thunderstorms roll in almost every afternoon, bringing the park 90% of its annual 60-inch rainfall from June through October. Water levels rise. Wildlife disperses. Mosquitoes hatch, swarm, and descend on you in voracious clouds. It's a good time to stay away, although some brave souls do come to explore. Europeans constitute 80% of the summer visitors.

Summer in south Florida lingers until mid-October, when the first cold front sweeps through. The rains cease, water levels start to fall, and the ground begins to dry out. Wildlife moves toward the sloughs. Flocks of migratory birds and tourists swoop in, as the cycle of seasons builds once more to the winter peak activity.

Whenever you come, we urge you to experience the real Everglades by getting your feet wet—but most people who visit the park won't do that. Boat tours at Everglades City and Flamingo, a tram ride at Shark Valley, and boardwalks at several locations along the main park road allow you to see the Everglades with dry feet.

The list below describes the facilities at each of the park's visitor service areas.

5 **Flamingo.** Museum, lodge, restaurant, lounge, gift shop, marina, and campground. *Mailing address: Box 279, Homestead 33030, tel. 305/247–6211. Visitor center open daily 8–5.*

6 **Gulf Coast Ranger Station.** Visitor center, where back-country campers pick up free permits, exhibits, gift shop. *Follow Everglades National Park signs from Tamiami Trail (U.S. 41) south on Rte. 29, tel. 813/695–3311. Open daily winter 8–5, reduced hours in summer. Admission free.*

7 **Key Largo Ranger Station.** No exhibits. *98710 Overseas Hwy., Key Largo, tel. 305/852–5119. Not always staffed; phone ahead. Admission free.*

8 **Main Visitor Center.** Exhibits, film, bookstore, park headquarters. *11 mi west of Homestead on Rte. 9336, tel. 305/247–6211. Open 24 hrs. Admission: $5 per car (good for 7 days); $3 per person on foot, bicycle, or motorcycle; senior citizens over 62 free.*

9 **Royal Palm Visitor Center.** Anhinga Trail boardwalk, Gumbo Limbo Trail through hammock, museum, bookstore, vending machines. *Tel. 305/247–6211. Open 8–4:30, with a half hour off for lunch.*

10 **Shark Valley.** Tram tour, boardwalk, hiking trails, rotating exhibits, bookstore. *Box 42, Ochopee 33943, tel. 305/221–8776.*

Open daily 8:30–6. Admission: $3 per car, $1 per person on foot, bicycle, or motorcycle (good for 7 days); senior citizens over 62 free. Show Shark Valley admission receipt at Main Visitor Center and pay only the difference there.

Miccosukee Indian Village 11

A mile from the Shark Valley entrance to Everglades National Park, the Miccosukee tribe operates an Indian village as a tourist attraction. You can watch Indian families cooking and making clothes, dolls, beadwork, and baskets. You'll also see an alligator-wrestling demonstration. The village has a boardwalk and a museum. *On Tamiami Trail (U.S. 41) 40 mi west of Miami. Mailing address: Box 440021, Miami 33144, tel. 305/223–8380. Open daily 9–5. Admission: $5 adults, $3.50 children and seniors. Airboat rides $6 for 30-min trip to another Indian camp on an island in the heart of the Everglades.*

Shopping

Biscayne National Park

Biscayne Aqua-Center. T-shirts, snorkeling and diving gear, snacks, and information on Biscayne National Park are available in a trailer near park headquarters north of the canal. A dive shop van with air compressor is parked south of the canal at Homestead Bayfront Park. *Tel. 305/247–2400. Open daily. Office open 8:30–5:30. AE, MC, V.*

Everglades National Park

Flamingo Lodge Marina & Outpost Resort. The gift shop sells mosquito repellent, Everglades guides, popular novels, T-shirts, souvenirs, and artwork (*see* Participant Sports). *Tel. 305/253–2241 or 813/695–3101. Open daily Nov.–Apr. 8–5. AE, CB, DC, MC, V.*

Florida City

Robert Is Here. A remarkable fruit stand. Robert grows and sells (in season) any tropical fruit that will grow near Everglades National Park. *19200 Palm Dr. (S.W. 344th St.), tel. 305/246–1592. Open daily 8–7. No credit cards.*

Homestead

Homestead's main shopping streets are Homestead Boulevard (U.S. 1), Krome Avenue (Rte. 997), and Campbell Drive (S.W. 312th St., N.E. 8th St.). Shopping centers with major department stores are 10–20 miles north of Homestead along South Dixie Highway (U.S. 1).

Participant Sports

Most of the sports and recreational opportunities in Everglades National Park and Biscayne National Park are related in some way to water or nature study, or both. Even on land, be prepared to get your feet wet on the region's marshy hiking trails. In summer, save your outdoor activities for early or late in the day to avoid the sun's strongest rays and use a sunscreen. Carry mosquito repellent at any time of year.

Water Sports
Boating

Carry aboard the proper *NOAA Nautical Charts* before you cast off to explore the waters of the parks. The charts cost $12.25 each. They are sold at many marine stores in south Florida, at the Convoy Point Visitor Center in Biscayne National Park, and in Flamingo Marina. The charts cost $12.25 each.

Waterway Guide (southern regional edition) is an annual publication of *Boating Industry Magazine*, which many boaters use as a guide to these waters. Bookstores all over south Florida sell it, or you can order it directly from the publisher. *Circulation Department,* Waterway Guide, *850 Third Ave., New York,*

NY 10022, tel. 800/233–3359 or 212/715–2600 in NY. Cost: $18.95 plus $3 shipping and handling.

Canoeing The subtropical wilderness of southern Florida is a mecca for flat-water paddlers. In winter, you'll find the best canoeing that the two parks can offer. Temperatures are moderate, rainfall is minimal, and the mosquitoes are tolerable.

Before you paddle into the back country and camp overnight, get a free permit from the rangers in the park where you plan to canoe (at Convoy Point, Elliott Key, and Adams Key for Biscayne; at Everglades City or Flamingo for Everglades. The Biscayne permit isn't valid for Everglades, and vice versa.

You don't need a permit for day-trips, but tell someone where you're going and when you expect to return. Getting lost out there is easy, and spending the night without proper gear can be unpleasant, if not dangerous.

At Biscayne, you can explore five creeks through the mangrove wilderness within 1½ miles of park headquarters at Convoy Point.

Everglades has six well-marked canoe trails in the Flamingo area, including the southern end of the 100-mile Wilderness Waterway from Flamingo to Everglades City. The two canoe-rental firms in Everglades City run a seven-hour shuttle service to haul people, cars, and canoes 151 road-miles between Everglades City and Flamingo.

The vendors listed below all rent aluminum canoes. Most have 17-foot Grummans. Bring your own cushions.

Biscayne Aqua-Center, Inc. At Convoy Point in Biscayne National Park. *Tel. 305/247–2400. Office open daily 8:30–5:30. Cost: $5 per hr, $17.50 for 4 hrs, $22.50 per day. No launch fee. AE, MC, V.*

Everglades National Park Boat Tours. A half mile south of the Gulf Coast Ranger Station in Everglades City. *Tel. 813/695–2591, in FL 800/445–7724. Open daily 8:30–4:30. Cost: $10 per half day, $15 per day; Flamingo-Everglades City shuttle: $100. No credit cards.*

North America Canoe Tours at Glades Haven. This outfitter rents canoes and runs guided Everglades trips approved by the National Park Service. *800 S.E. Copeland Ave., Box 443, Everglades City 33929, tel. 813/695–2746. Open daily 7 AM–9 PM; guided trips Nov. 1–Mar. 31. Canoes $18 the first day, $15 per day thereafter. No children under age 8 on guided tours. No pets in park campsites. Reservations required. MC, V.*

Marinas Listed below are the major marinas serving the two parks. The dock masters at these marinas can provide information on other marine services you may need.

Black Point Marina. A new 155-acre Metro-Dade County Park with a hurricane-safe harbor basin, five miles north of Homestead Bayfront Park. Facilities include 65 dry and 178 wet slips, 10 ramps, fuel, a bait-and-tackle shop, canoe-launching ramp, power-boat rentals, and police station. Shrimp fleet docks at the park. At east end of Coconut Palm Drive (S.W. 248th St.). From Florida's Turnpike, exit at S.W. 112th Avenue, go two blocks north, and turn east on Coconut Palm Drive. *24775 S.W. 87th Ave., Naranja, tel. 305/258–4092. Open daily 6 AM–9 PM. AE, MC, V.*

Club Biscayne Boat Rentals, Inc. At Black Point Marina. The club rents fully equipped 16-foot runabouts, 18-foot open fisherman boats, and canoes. *Tel. 305/258–1477. Open daily Oct.–Mar. 8–5, Apr.–Sept. daily except Tues. MC, V.*

Pirate's Spa Marina. Just west of Black Point Park entrance. Shrimp boats dock along canal. Facilities include boat hoist, wet and dry storage, fuel, bait and tackle, and boat rental. *8701 Coconut Palm Dr. (S.W. 248th St.), Naranja, tel. 305/257–5100. Open Mon.–Fri. 7 AM–sundown, Sat.–Sun. open 6 AM. No credit cards.*

Flamingo Lodge Marina & Outpost Resort. Fifty-slip marina rents 40 canoes, 10 power skiffs, 5 houseboats, and several private boats available for charter. There are two ramps, one for Florida Bay, the other for Whitewater Bay and the back country. The hoist across the plug dam separating Florida Bay from the Buttonwood Canal can take boats up to 26 feet long. A small marina store sells food, camping supplies, bait and tackle, and automobile and boat fuel. *Tel. 305/253–2241 from Miami, 813/695–3101 from Gulf Coast. Open winter 6 AM–7 PM, summer 7–6. AE, DC, MC, V.*

Homestead Bait and Tackle. Facilities include dock and wet slips, fuel, bait and tackle, ice, boat hoist, and ramp. The marina is near Homestead Bayfront Park's tidal swimming area and concessions. *North Canal Dr., Homestead, tel. 305/245–2273. Open daily Mon.–Fri. 7–5, Sat. and Sun. 7–6. MC, V.*

Diving

Dive Boats and Instruction

Biscayne Aqua-Center, Inc. This is the official concessionaire for Biscayne National Park. The center provides equipment on dive trips and sells equipment. Snorkeling and scuba trips include about 2½ hours on the reefs. *Reef Rover III*, an aluminum dive boat, carries up to 49 passengers. The resort course and private instruction lead to full certification. *Office and dive boat at Convoy Point. Mailing address: Box 1270, Homestead 33030, tel. 305/247–2400. Open daily 8:30–5:30. Snorkeling and scuba trips Tues. and Sat. 1–5; group charters any day. Cost: $19.52 snorkeling, $24.50 scuba. Reservation required. AE, MC, V.*

Pirate's Cove Dive Center. This is the last dive store north of the Keys, and it rents, sells, and repairs diving equipment. Staff teaches all sport-diving classes, including resort course, deep diver, and underwater photography. The center does not have a boat; instead they use dive boats at Homestead Bayfront Park. PADI affiliation. *116 N. Homestead Blvd., Homestead 33030, tel. 305/248–1808. Open all year Mon.–Fri. 9–6:30, Sat. 8–6, Sun. 8–4. Open to 7:30 May.–Sept., around the clock during annual 4-day sport divers' lobster season (in July or Aug.). AE, DC, MC, V.*

Fishing

The rangers in the two parks enforce all state fishing laws and a few of their own. Ask at each park's visitor centers for that park's specific regulations.

Swimming

Homestead Bayfront Park. This saltwater atoll pool, adjacent to Biscayne Bay, which is flushed by tidal action, is popular with local family groups and teenagers. *N. Canal Dr., Homestead, tel. 305/247–1543. Open daily, winter 7:30–6, summer 7:30–7. Admission: $2 per car.*

Elliott Key. Boaters like to anchor off Elliott Key's 30-foot-wide sandy beach, the only beach in Biscayne National Park. It's about a mile north of the harbor on the west (bay) side of the key.

Bicycling and Hiking

Biscayne National Park. Elliott Key's resident rangers lead informal nature walks on a 1½-mile nature trail.

You can also walk the length of the seven-mile key along a rough path that developers bulldozed before the park was created.

Everglades National Park. Shark Valley's concessionaire has rental bicycles. You may ride or hike along the Loop Road, a 14-mile round-trip. Yield right of way to trams. *Shark Valley Tram Tours, Miami 33144, tel. 305/221–8455. Rentals daily 8:30–3, return bicycles by 4. Cost: $1.50 per hr. No reservations. No credit cards.*

Ask the rangers for *Foot and Canoe Trails of the Flamingo Area*, a leaflet that also lists bike trails. Inquire about water levels and insect conditions before you go. Get a free backcountry permit if you plan to camp overnight.

Dining

Although the two parks are wilderness areas, there are restaurants within a short drive of all park entrances: between Miami and Shark Valley along the Tamiami Trail (U.S. 41), in the Homestead–Florida City area, in Everglades City, and in the Keys along the Overseas Highway (U.S. 1). The only food service in either park is at Flamingo in the Everglades.

The list below is a selection of independent restaurants on the Tamiami Trail, in the Homestead–Florida City area, and at Flamingo. Many of these establishments will pack picnic fare that you can take to the parks. (You can also find fast-food establishments with carryout service on the Tamiami Trail and in Homestead–Florida City.) The most highly recommended restaurants are indicated with a star ★.

Category	Cost*
Very Expensive	over $60
Expensive	$40–$60
Moderate	$20–$40
Inexpensive	under $20

**per person without sales tax (6% in Florida), service, or drinks*

The following credit card abbreviations are used: AE, American Express; CB, Carte Blanche; DC, Diners Club; MC, MasterCard; V, Visa.

Flamingo
American

Flamingo Restaurant. The view from this three-tier dining room on the second floor of the Flamingo Visitor Center will knock your socks off. Picture windows overlook Florida Bay, giving you a bird's-eye view (almost) of soaring eagles, gulls, pelicans, terns, and vultures. Try to dine at low tide when flocks of birds gather on a sandbar just offshore. Specialties include a flavorful, mildly spiced conch chowder; teriyaki chicken breast; and pork loin roasted Cuban-style with garlic and lime. The tastiest choices, however, are the seafood. If marlin is on the dinner menu, order it fried so that the moisture and flavor of the dark, chewy meat are retained. *Picnic baskets available. Will cook fish you catch if you clean it at the marina. At Fla-*

mingo Visitor Center in Everglades National Park, Flamingo, tel. 305/253–2241 from Miami, 813/695–3101 from Gulf Coast. Dress: informal. Reservations required for dinner. AE, MC, V. Closed early May–mid-Oct. (The snack bar at the marina store stays open all year.) Moderate.

Florida City
Mixed Menu
★

Richard Accursio's Capri Restaurant and **King Richard's Room.** This is where locals dine out—business groups at lunch, the Rotary Club each Wednesday at noon, and families at night. Specialties include pizza with light, crunchy crusts and ample toppings; mild, meaty conch chowder; mussels in garlic-cream or marinara sauce; Caesar salad with lots of cheese and anchovies; antipasto with a homemade, vinegary Italian dressing; pasta shells stuffed with rigatoni cheese, in tomato sauce; yellowtail snapper Française; and Key-lime pie with plenty of real Key lime juice. *935 N. Krome Ave., Florida City, tel. 305/247–1542. Dress: Capri informal, jacket and tie in King Richard's. Reservations advised. AE, MC, V. Closed Sun. except Mother's Day, Christmas. Inexpensive.*

Seafood
★

Captain Bob's. The Greek family who owns this restaurant has a list of more than 800 ways to prepare seafood. Specialties include snapper wrapped in phyllo dough in dill volute sauce; sea trout senator, with sliced almonds, mushrooms, scallions, and sherry-lemon butter sauce; and blackened wahoo. Save room for the Key-lime pie. *326 S.E. 1st Ave., Florida City, tel. 305/247–8988. Dress: informal. Reservations accepted. AE, CB, DC, MC, V. Inexpensive.*

Homestead
American

Downtown Bar and Outdoor Cafe. A south Florida interpretation of a New Orleans courtyard restaurant, complete with a wrought-iron gate and live entertainment. Specialties include Buffalo chicken wings (hot or mild) with celery and bleu-cheese dip; blackened or grilled dolphin or grouper from the Keys; raspberry nut cake; and refreshingly tart lemonade. *28 S. Krome Ave., Homestead, tel. 305/245–8266. Dress: informal. Reservations accepted. AE, MC, V. Closed Easter, Thanksgiving, Christmas. Inexpensive.*

Potlikker's. This southern country-style restaurant takes its name from the broth—*pot liquor*—left over from the boiling of greens. Live plants dangle from open rafters in his lofty pine-lined dining room. Specialties include fried Okeechobee catfish (all you can eat on Mondays), with Cajun spicing in a cornmeal–matzo-meal breading; roast turkey with homemade dressing, and at least 11 different vegetables to serve with lunch and dinner entrees. For dessert, try sweet potato pie. The Key-lime pie here is four inches tall and frozen; it tastes great if you dawdle over dessert while it thaws. *591 Washington Ave., Homestead, tel. 305/248–0835. Dress: informal. No reservations. MC, V. Inexpensive.*

Mexican

El Toro Taco. The Hernandez family came to the United States from San Luis Potosí, Mexico, to pick crops. They opened this Homestead-area institution in 1971. They make salt-free tortillas and nacho chips with corn from Texas that they cook and grind themselves. The cilantro-dominated salsa is mild for American tastes; if you like more fire on your tongue, ask for a side dish of minced jalapeño peppers to mix in. Specialties include chile rellenos (green peppers stuffed with meaty chunks of ground beef and topped with three kinds of cheese), and chicken *fajitas* (chunks of chicken marinated in vinegar and spices, charbroiled with onions and peppers, and served with tortillas and salsa). Bring your own beer and wine; the staff will keep it cold for you and supply lemon for your Corona beer. *1 S. Krome Ave., Homestead, tel. 305/245–5576. Dress: informal. No reservations. No credit cards. Closed Christmas Day and Dec. 26. Inexpensive.*

Seafood **The Seafood Feast Restaurant.** Bob and Julie Cisco gave up a steak-house franchise to open this all-you-can-eat seafood buffet. It features shrimp, crabs' legs, frogs' legs, several choices of fish, salads, breads, and desserts. Specialties include cheese bread, Cajun-style crawfish from Louisiana, garlic crabs, steamed mussels, and oysters on the half shell (on request). *27835 S. Dixie Hwy., Naranja (3½ mi northeast of downtown Homestead), tel. 305/246–1445. Dress: informal. Reservations not accepted. No alcohol on premises. AE, MC, V. Moderate.*

Tamiami Trail
American **The Pit Bar-B-Q.** This place will overwork your salivary glands with its intense aroma of barbecue and blackjack oak smoke. You order at the counter, then come when called to pick up your food. Specialties include barbecued chicken and ribs with a tangy sauce, french fries, coleslaw, and fried biscuit, and catfish, frogs' legs, and shrimp breaded and deep-fried in vegetable oil. *16400 S.W. 8th St., Miami, tel. 305/226–2272. Dress: informal. No reservations. MC, V. Closed Christmas Day. Inexpensive.*

American Indian **Miccosukee Restaurant.** Murals with Indian themes depict women cooking and men engaged in a powwow. Specialties include catfish and frogs' legs breaded and deep-fried in peanut oil, Indian fry bread (a flour-and-water dough deep-fried in peanut oil), pumpkin bread, Indian burger (ground beef browned, rolled in fry bread dough, and deep-fried), and Indian taco (fry bread with chili, lettuce, tomato, and shredded cheedar cheese on top). *On Tamiami Trail, near the Shark Valley entrance to Everglades National Park, tel. 305/223–8380, ext. 332. Dress: informal. No reservations. AE, CB, DC, MC, V. Inexpensive.*

Floridian **Coopertown Restaurant.** A rustic 30-seat restaurant full of Floridiana, including alligator skulls, stuffed alligator heads, alligator accessories (belts, key chains, and the like). Specialties include alligator and frogs' legs, breaded and deep-fried in vegetable oil, available for breakfast, lunch, or dinner. *22700 S.W. 8th St., Miami, tel. 305/226–6048. Dress: informal. No reservations. No credit cards. Inexpensive.*

Lodging

Many visitors to the two parks stay in the big-city portion of Greater Miami and spend a day visiting one or both of the parks. For serious outdoors people, such a schedule consumes too much time in traffic and leaves too little time for nature-study and recreation.

At Shark Valley, due west of Miami, you have no choice. Only the Miccosukee Indians live there; there is no motel.

Southwest of Miami, Homestead has become a bedroom community for both parks. You'll find well-kept older properties and shiny new ones, chain motels, and independents. Prices tend to be somewhat lower than in the Miami area.

Hotel and motel accommodations are available on the Gulf coast at Everglades City and Naples.

The list below is a representative selection of hotels and motels in the Homestead area. Also included are the only lodgings inside either park. The rate categories in the list are based on the all-year or peak-season price; off-peak rates may be a category or two lower.

Category	Cost*
Very Expensive	over $120
Expensive	$90–$120
Moderate	$50–$90
Inexpensive	under $50

**per room, double occupancy, without 6% state sales tax and modest resort tax*

The following credit card abbreviations are used. AE, American Express; CB, Carte Blanche; DC, Diners Club; MC, MasterCard; V, Visa.

Flamingo Lodge Marina & Outpost Resort. This rustic low-rise wilderness resort, the only lodging inside Everglades National Park, is a strip of tentative civilization 300 yards wide and 1½ miles long. Accommodations are basic but attractive and well kept. An amiable staff with a sense of humor helps you become accustomed to alligators bellowing in the sewage-treatment pond down the road, raccoons roaming the pool enclosure at night, and the flock of ibis grazing on the lawn. The rooms have wood-paneled walls, contemporary furniture, floral bedspreads, and art prints of flamingos and egrets on the walls. Most bathrooms are near the door, so you won't track mud all over the room. Television reception varies with wind conditions and vultures perching on the antenna, but you don't come here to watch TV. All motel rooms overlook Florida Bay. The cottages are in a wooded area on the margin of a coastal prairie. Ask about reserving tours, skiffs, and canoes when you make reservations. *Box 428, Flamingo 33030, tel. 305/253–2241 from Miami, 813/695–3101 from Gulf Coast. 121 units with bath, including 102 motel rooms, 2 2-bath suites for up to 8 people, 17 kitchenette cottages (2 for handicapped guests). Facilities: screened outdoor freshwater swimming pool, restaurant, lounge, marina, marina store with snack bar, gift shop, coin laundry. AE, CB, DC, MC, V. Lodge, marina, and marina store open all year; restaurant, lounge, and gift shop closed May 1–Oct. 31. Moderate.*

Greenstone Motel. Centrally located low-rise motel, in downtown Homestead's Historic District, this place was built in 1960 and remodeled in 1987. Rooms decorated in earth tones, with photos of waves and seagulls over the beds, which are medium-firm. The best rooms face south, overlooking a vest-pocket park with benches and shrubbery. The second-floor balcony in front is a good vantage point to see the magnolia design in the pavement on the street below. *304 N. Krome Ave., Homestead 33030, tel. 305/247–8334. 24 rooms. Facilities: free HBO, coffee bar in lobby. AE, CB, DC, MC, V. Moderate.*

Holiday Inn. Low-rise motel on a commercial strip. The best rooms look out on the landscaped pool and adjoining Banana Bar. Rooms have contemporary walnut furnishings and firm, bouncy mattresses. *990 N. Homestead Blvd., Homestead*

33030, tel. 305/247–7020 or 800/HOLIDAY. 139 rooms with bath. Facilities: outdoor freshwater swimming pool, restaurant and lounge with entertainment Wed.–Sat., poolside bar, radio and cable TV, massage shower heads. AE, CB, DC, MC, V. Moderate.

Knights Inn. This low-rise motel opened in 1987 on a commercial strip next door to a McDonald's. Beds are a foot longer than normal, and the mattresses are firm. The inn is decorated in English half-timber style, inside and out. *401 U.S. 1, Florida City 33034, tel. 305/245–2800. 108 rooms, including 7 suites, 11 fully equipped kitchenettes, 27 for handicapped guests. Facilities: outdoor freshwater swimming pool, free HBO and TV movies, free ice, free local phone calls, coffee bar in lobby, security at night. AE, CB, DC, MC, V. Moderate.*

Park Royal Inn. This low-rise motel on a commercial strip has rooms with a rough wood wall, flower bedspreads, blue or gray carpet, gray chairs and dressers, and lamps with a shell or pelican design. No closet, very small clothes rack. *100 U.S. 1, Florida City 33034, tel. 305/247–3200 or 800/521–6004. 163-unit motel, including 1 efficiency apartment, 7 rooms for handicapped guests. Facilities: outdoor freshwater swimming pool, minirefrigerator in each room, color TV, phone. AE, CB, DC, MC, V. Moderate.*

Camping

Biscayne National Park

You can camp on designated keys seven miles offshore at primitive sites or in the back country. Carry all your food, water, and supplies onto the keys, and carry all trash off when you leave. Bring plenty of insect repellent. *Free. No reservations. No ferry or marina services. For back-country camping, obtain a free permit from rangers at Adams Key, Convoy Point, or Elliott Key.*

Everglades National Park

All campgrounds are primitive, with no water or electricity. Come early to get a good site, especially in winter. Bring plenty of insect repellent. *Open all year. Check-out time 10 AM. Admission: $7 per site in winter, free in summer. Stay limited to 14 days Nov. 1–Apr. 30. Register at campground.*

Long Pine Key. 108 campsites, drinking water, sewage dump station.

Flamingo. 235 drive-in sites, 60 walk-in sites, drinking water, cold-water showers, and sewage dump station.

Back country. 34 designated sites, most with chickees (raised wood platforms with thatch roofs). All have chemical toilets. Carry all your food, water, and supplies in; carry out all trash. Get free permit from rangers at Everglades City or Flamingo. Permits issued for a specific site. Capacity and length of stay limited.

5 Fort Lauderdale

Introduction

If you think of Fort Lauderdale only as a spring-break mecca for collegians seeking sun, suds, and surf, your knowledge is both fragmentary and out of date. The 1960 film, *Where the Boys Are,* attracted hordes of young people to the city's beaches for more than two decades, but now the center of spring-break activity has shifted north to Daytona Beach.

Fort Lauderdale today emphasizes year-round family tourism focused on a wide assortment of sports and recreational activities, an extensive cultural calendar, artistic and historic attractions, and fine shopping and dining opportunities.

Sandwiched between Miami to the south and Palm Beach to the north along southeast Florida's Gold Coast, Fort Lauderdale is the county seat of Broward County. The county encompasses 1,197 square miles—17 square miles less than the state of Rhode Island. Broward County has 23 miles of Atlantic Ocean beach frontage, and it extends 50 miles inland to the west. A coastal ridge rising in places to 25 feet above sea level separates the coastal lowlands from the interior lowlands of the Everglades.

Broward County is named for Napolean Bonaparte Broward, Florida's governor 1905–09. His drainage schemes around the turn of the century opened much of the marshy Everglades region for farming, ranching, and settlement. In fact, the first successful efforts at large-scale Everglades drainage took place within Broward County's boundaries.

Fort Lauderdale's first known white settler, Charles Lewis, established a plantation along the New River in 1793. The city is named for a fort which Major William Lauderdale built at the river's mouth in 1838 during the Seminole Indian wars.

The area was still a remote frontier when Frank Stranahan arrived in 1892 to operate an overnight camp on the river. Stranahan began trading with the Indians in 1901 and built a store, which later became his residence. It's now a museum.

Fort Lauderdale incorporated in 1911 with just 175 residents, but it grew rapidly during the Florida boom of the 1920s. Today the city's population of 160,000 remains relatively stable, while suburban areas bulge with growth. Broward County's population is expected to exceed 1.35 million by 1990—more than double its 1970 population of 620,000. The county has become a haven for retirees; more than a third of the new arrivals are over the age of 55.

New homes, offices and shopping centers have filled in the gaps between older communities along the coastal ridge. Now they're marching west along I–75, I–595, and the Sawgrass Expressway, transforming the Everglades. Meanwhile, Fort Lauderdale is building skyscrapers downtown to cement its position as the county's financial and commercial hub.

Broward County is developing a concentration of clean high-technology industries, including computer manufacturing, data processing, and electronics. Port Everglades, a major deep-water seaport, handles refined petroleum products and general cargo. A cruise terminal at Port Everglades caters to luxury liners, leaving the mass-market cruise business to the Port of Miami.

To accommodate the traffic which comes with all this growth, the Florida Department of Transportation is expanding Broward County's road system. During 1989, construction on I–95 and I–595 threatens to create gridlock during rush hours. A tri-county commuter train scheduled to run through Broward County from Miami to West Palm Beach will take some cars off the highways, but you should still expect traffic delays and allow extra time to move around the county.

Even when you're stuck in traffic, you can still enjoy Broward County's near-ideal weather. The average temperature is 75 degrees (winter average 66 degrees, summer average 84 degrees). Rainfall averages 65 inches a year, with 60% of the total occurring in afternoon thunderstorms June–October. The warm, relatively dry winters help to give the county about 3,000 hours of sunshine a year.

Arriving and Departing

By Plane **Fort Lauderdale–Hollywood International Airport (FLHIA),** four miles south of downtown Fort Lauderdale, is Broward County's major airline terminal. To get there off I–95, take the Griffin Road east exit to U.S. 1 and turn left to the airport entrance, about ¼ mile north.

Between the Airport and Center City Broward Transit's bus route No. 1 operates between the airport and its main terminal at N.W. 1st Street and 1st Avenue in the center of Fort Lauderdale. The fare is 75 cents. Limousine service is available from *Yellow Airport Limousine Service* (tel. 305/527–8690) to all parts of Broward County. Fares range from $6 to $13 or more per person, depending on distance. Fares to most Fort Lauderdale beach hotels are in the $6–$8 range. Pickup points are at each of the new terminals.

Rental Cars Six rental-car companies have booths near FLHIA's baggage claim area: **Avis** (tel. 305/920–2841), **Budget** (tel. 305/921–8585), **Dollar** (tel. 305/525–7031), **General** (tel. 305/524–4635), **Hertz** (tel. 305/525–5281), and **National** (tel. 305/525–3633).

Six other rental-car companies have offices near the airport: **Alamo** (tel. 800/327–9633), **American International** (tel. 305/522–6400), **Payless** (tel. 305/467–8544), **Snappy** (tel. 305/486–8808), **Thrifty** (tel. 305/525–4355), and **USA** (tel. 305/763–7369).

By Train **Amtrak** provides daily service to Broward County, with stops at Hollywood, Fort Lauderdale, and Deerfield Beach. The Silver Star also stops at these cities daily on its Miami–Tampa route, offering deep, reclining seats in modern coaches, and sandwiches and beverages in its cafe lounge. Fort Lauderdale station (200 S.W. 21st Terr., tel. 305/463–8251). Reservations (tel. 800/872–7245).

By Bus **Greyhound** Bus Lines (513 N.E. 3rd St., Ft. Lauderdale, tel. 305/764–6551 or 800/872–6242).

By Car The access highways to Broward County from the north or south are Florida's Turnpike, I–95, U.S. 1, and U.S. 441; for a more scenic—and slower—drive, Rte. A1A, which generally parallels the beach area. The primary access road to Broward County from the west is Rte. 84.

Getting Around

By Car In June 1988, the Florida Department of Transportation (FDOT) began to build the last stage of the I–595/Port Everglades Expressway Project, which runs east–west through the middle of Broward County. By 1990, 15 interchanges will be improved and local roads will be linked to I–595, which follows the Rte. 84 corridor from I–75 east to the port.

At the same time, I–95 is being widened, disrupting north-south traffic for 46 miles from Yamato Road, in southern Palm Beach County, through Broward County to Rte. 836, in northern Dade County.

If you're driving into Florida, stop at a visitor center near the state line for a traveler advisory card on the current status of I–95 construction. Ask for current information on travel time and alternative routes.

FDOT officials urge you to take Florida's Turnpike or the Sawgrass Expressway through Broward County to avoid I–95. A new interchange at S.W. 10th Street in Deerfield Beach was being built in 1988 to connect the Sawgrass Expressway directly to I–95. Other alternatives include crowded local roads such as A1A, U.S. 1, U.S. 441, and University Drive (Rte. 817).

Listen to radio traffic reports on the status of I–95 construction. Your hotel clerk should know which stations have them.

Try to avoid driving anywhere in Broward County—and especially on I–95—in the morning and evening rush hours (7–9 AM and 3–6 PM). Allow plenty of time to get where you're going, be patient, and stay calm. South Florida drivers can be among the world's worst.

FDOT has set up a consumer service organization to issue free publications and to provide traffic reports by phone. *Gold Coast Commuter Services, 6261 N.W. 6th Way, Suite 100, Fort Lauderdale, tel. 305/771–9500 or in FL 800/234–7433. Open 8–5.*

By Bus **Broward County Mass Transit** serves the entire county. The fare is 75 cents plus 10 cents for a transfer, with some bus routes starting as early as 5 AM; most end at 10 PM. Call for route information (tel. 305/357–8400). There are also special seven-day tourist passes for $8 that are good for unlimited use on all county buses. These are available at most major hotels.

By Taxi It's difficult to hail a taxi on the street; sometimes you can pick one up at a major hotel. Otherwise, phone ahead. Fares are not cheap; meters run at the rate of $1.75 for the first mile and $1.20 for each additional mile. Major companies include Yellow Cab (tel. 305/527–8600) and Broward Checker (tel. 305/485–3000).

Important Addresses and Numbers

Tourist Information The main office of the Fort Lauderdale Chamber of Commerce (tel. 305/765–4466) is at 500 E. Broward Boulevard. The office is open weekdays 8:30–5. A new information booth—the first of four—has been established at the Delta Terminal of the Fort

Lauderdale International Airport and is scheduled to be open daily 10–10. Other communities in Broward County also have individual chambers of commerce, including Dania (tel. 305/927–3377), Hollywood (tel. 305/776–1000), Oakland Park–Wilton Manors (tel. 305/564–8300), and Pompano Beach (tel. 305/941–2940). A recorded message of local events, updated weekly, is also available (tel. 305/765–8068).

Emergencies Dial 911 for **police** and **ambulance** in an emergency.

Poison Control (tel. 800/282–3171).

Crisis Intervention. 24-hour hotline (tel. 305/523–8553).

Doctors. Many hospital emergency rooms are open 24 hours day, seven days a week, including Holy Cross Hospital (4725 N. Federal Hwy., Fort Lauderdale, tel. 305/771–8000) and Broward General Medical Center (1 Corporate Plaza, Fort Lauderdale, tel. 305/355–4400). Physician Information Service (tel. 305/966–DOCS).

Dentists. Lake Side Dental Center (5473 Rte. 7, Tamarac, tel. 305/486–7025); Family and General Dentistry (7420 N.W. 5th St., Suite 101, Plantation, tel. 305/791–0330).

24-Hour Pharmacy. Cunningham Drugs (3101 N. Ocean Blvd., Fort Lauderdale, tel. 305/564–8424 or 305/563–3800).

24-Hour Doctors' House Calls. Many Broward hotels use this referral service, which will send a physician to you. Medical services available include general medicine, pediatrics, and geriatrics. In-office dental referrals. Translators available. *3801 N. University Dr., Suite 507, Sunrise, tel. 305/748–5900.*

Guided Tours

Orientation Tours **The Voyager Sightseeing Train** tours the streets of Fort Lauderdale and Port Everglades, departing daily at 10, noon, 2, and 4 from 600 Seabreeze Boulevard, Fort Lauderdale (tel. 305/463–0401). This rubber-wheeled "train" offers nine different tours, including an 18-mile swing around Fort Lauderdale and the port, with visits to luxurious homes, the historic sections of Fort Lauderdale, and the exclusive shops on Las Olas Boulevard. You can also take this open-air tram on shopping tours and to Ocean World, Flamingo Gardens, air-boat rides, and even the Everglades. Cost: $5.95 adults, $3 children 3–12.

The ***Paddlewheel Queen,*** a flat-bottom luncheon and sightseeing cruise boat, visits major spots along Fort Lauderdale's Intercoastal Waterway, including Millionaires' Row, Old Fort Lauderdale, downtown Fort Lauderdale, Little Florida, and Port Everglades, sailing daily at 2 with a capacity for 400 passengers from 2950 N.E. 30th Street, one block south of Oakland Park Beach Bridge, two blocks west of A1A. Reservations and dinner information, tel. 305/564–7659.

Special-Interest Tours **Bonnett House** (900 N. Birch Rd., tel. 305/563–5393), also known as the Bartlett Estates, is now open to the public for the first time. One of Fort Lauderdale's oldest and most exotic estates, valued at more than $36 million, it is furnished with its original antique furniture. Ninety-minute guided tours are available at 10 and 1:30 Tuesdays, Thursdays, and Saturdays. Cost: $7.50 per person.

Exploring Fort Lauderdale

Central Fort Lauderdale is diverse, picturesque, and surprisingly compact. Within a few blocks you'll find modern high-rise office buildings; a historic district with museums, restaurants and antique shops; a scenic riverfront drive; upscale shopping; and the only tunnel in Florida—all within two miles of the beach.

Numbers in the margin correspond with points of interest on the Fort Lauderdale map.

This tour begins on the beach at Las Olas Boulevard and Rte. A1A. Go north on Rte. A1A along **the beach,** with hotels, restaurants and shops on your left, the ocean on your right. Turn
1 left at Sunrise Boulevard, then right into **Hugh Taylor Birch State Park.** Amid the 180-acre park's tropical greenery, you can stroll along a nature trail, picnic, and canoe. *3109 E. Sunrise Blvd., tel. 305/564–4521. Open 8–5:30. Admission: $1 per car and driver, 50¢ per passenger.*

Leaving the park, go south on Birch Road to Las Olas Boulevard, turn right, and cross the Intracoastal Waterway. You're
2 now westbound through **The Isles,** Fort Lauderdale's most expensive and prestigious neighborhood, where the homes line a series of canals with large yachts beside the seawalls. When you reach the mainland, Las Olas becomes an upscale shopping street with Spanish-Colonial buildings housing high-fashion boutiques, jewelry shops and art galleries. The heart of the **Las Olas Shopping District** is from S.E. 12th Avenue to S.E. 6th Avenue.

3 Turn left on S.E. 6th Avenue, and visit **Stranahan House,** home of pioneer businessman Frank Stranahan. He arrived in 1892 and began trading with the Seminole Indians. In 1901 he built this building as a store, later made it his home. Now it's a museum with many of the Stranahans' furnishings on display. *1 Stranahan Pl. (S.E. 6th Ave.), tel. 305/524–4736. Open Wed., Fri., Sat. 10–4, Sun. 1–4. Admission: $3.*

Return to Las Olas Boulevard, go to S.W. 1st Avenue, and turn left beside the *News & Sun-Sentinel* building. Go a block south to New River Drive, where you can park and stroll a portion of
4 the palm-lined **River Walk,** a linear park with walkways and sidewalk cafes along both banks of the New River. As part of a $44-million redevelopment program, Fort Lauderdale is improving and extending the River Walk. Unlike the Miami River, which carries a heavy load of commercial shipping, New River traffic is primarily recreational yachts and tour boats. This portion of New River Drive returns you to Las Olas Boulevard at S.W. 5th Avenue.

Turn left, and go to the **Museum of Art,** which features a major collection of works from the CoBrA (Copenhagen, Brussels and Amsterdam) movement, plus American Indian, Pre-Columbian, West African and Oceanic ethnographic art. Edward Larabee Barnes designed the museum building, which opened in 1986. *1 E. Las Olas Blvd., tel. 305/525–5500. Open Tues. 11–9, Wed.–Sat. 10–5, Sun. noon–5. Admission: $3 adults, $2 seniors, $1 students, free under 12. Free 1-hour tours Tues. noon and 6:30 PM, Wed.–Sat. noon, Sun. 2 PM. Parking nearby in municipal garage.*

Fort Lauderdale Area

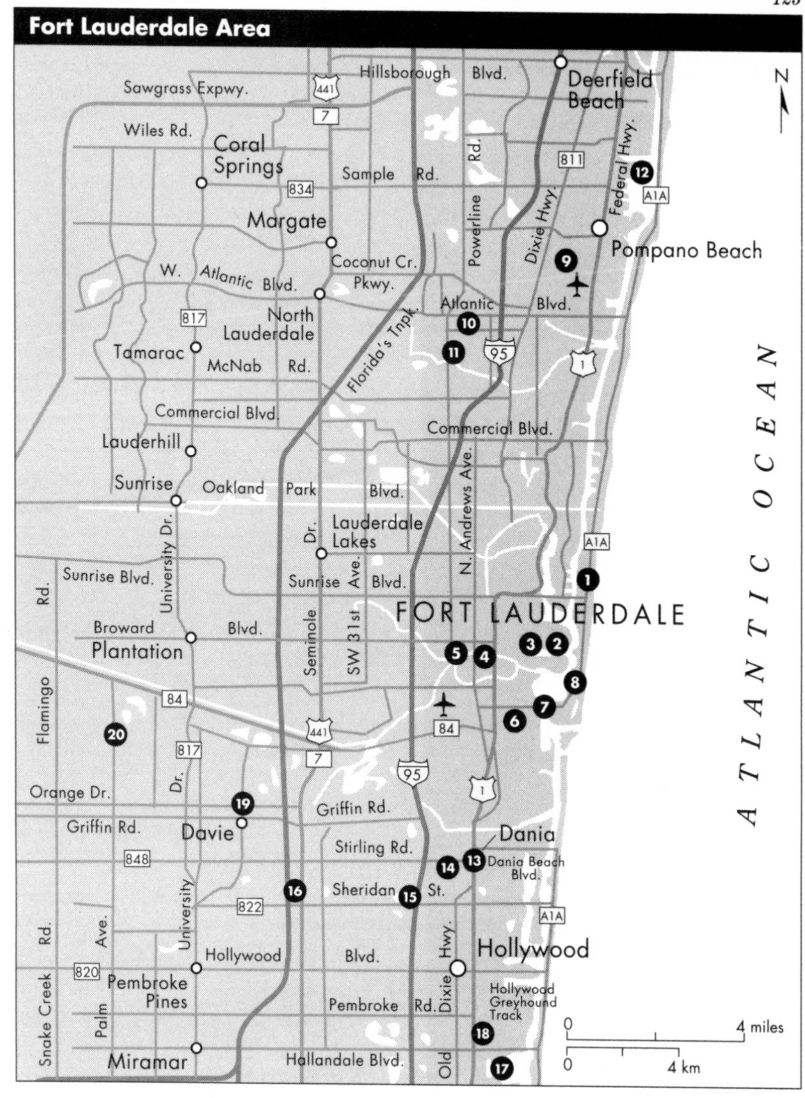

Brooks Memorial Causeway, **7**
Broward County Museum of Archaeology, **5**
Dania, **13**
Davie, **19**
Flamingo Gardens, **20**
Goodyear blimps, **9**
Gulfstream Park, **17**
Hillsboro Lighthouse, **12**
Hollywood Greyhound Track, **18**
Hugh Taylor Birch State Park, **1**
The Isles, **2**
Ocean World, **6**
Pompano Harness Track, **10**
Quiet Waters Park, **11**
River Walk, **4**
Seminole Okalee Indian Village, **16**
Six Flags Atlantis, **14**
Stranahan House, **3**
Swimming Hall of Fame Museum, **8**
Topeekeegee Yugnee Park, **15**

Go west on Las Olas Boulevard to S.W. 1st Avenue, and stop at
5 the **Broward County Museum of Archaeology.** Featured here are a 2,000-year-old skeleton of a Tequesta Indian girl, remains of Ice Age mammals, a diorama of Indian life, and information on archaeological techniques. Special shows display artifacts of African, pre-Columbian and other cultures. *203 S.W. 1st Ave., tel. 305/525-8778. Open Tues.–Sat. 10–4, Sun. 1–4. Admission: $1 adults, 50¢ children and seniors. Tours Tues.–Sat. 1:30, Sun. 2.*

Take S.W. 1st Avenue north to S.W. 2nd Street, turn left, cross the Florida East Coast Railway tracks, and turn left onto S.W. 2nd Avenue. You're now in **Himmarshee Village,** an eight-square-block historic district. Park and walk to explore several fascinating museums.

The **Fort Lauderdale Historical Society Museum** surveys the city's history from the Seminole Indian era to World War II. A model in the lobby depicts old Fort Lauderdale. The building also houses a research library and a bookstore. *219 S.W. 2nd Ave., tel. 305/463-4431. Open Mon.–Sat. 10–4, Sun. 1–4. Admission free.*

The **Discovery Center** includes a science museum in the three-story **New River Inn,** Fort Lauderdale's first hotel, and a pioneer residence museum in the restored **King-Cromartie House.** The Discovery Center Museum is a child-oriented place with hands-on exhibits that explore optical illusions and bend rays of light, an insect zoo, a glass-front beehive, a loom, a computer center, and a small planetarium. *229 and 231 S.W. 2nd Ave., tel. 305/462-4115. Open Tues.–Fri. 2–5, Sat. and school holidays 10–5, Sun. 1–5. Admission (includes both museums): $2, under 3 free.*

A brick drive between the King-Cromartie House and the New River Inn brings you one block west to S.W. 3rd Avenue. On your left is the **Bryan House,** a 1904 dwelling which is now a restaurant.

Go north on S.W. 3rd Avenue past an assortment of antique shops and restaurants in some old commercial buildings that are also part of the Himmarshee Village historic district. At Broward Boulevard, turn right and go east to Federal Highway (U.S. 1). Turn right and go south through the **Henry E. Kinney Tunnel,** named for a founder of Fort Lauderdale. It dips beneath Las Olas Boulevard and the New River.

Continue south on Federal Highway to S.W. 17th Street, then
6 turn left again about a mile east at the entrance to **Ocean World.** Continuous shows daily feature trained porpoises and sea lions. Display tanks hold sharks, sea turtles, alligators, and river otters. You can feed and pet a dolphin here. *1701 S.E. 17th St., tel. 305/525-6611. Open 10–6, last show starts 4:15. Admission: $7.95 adults, $5.95 children 4–12, under 4 free. Boat tour admission: $4 adults, $3 children 4–12, under 4 free.*

7 Go east on S.E. 17th Street across the **Brooks Memorial Causeway** over the Intracoastal Waterway, and bear left onto Seabreeze Boulevard (Rte. A1A). You'll pass through a neighborhood of older homes set in lush vegetation before emerging at the south end of Fort Lauderdale's beachfront strip. On your left at **Bahia Mar Resort & Yachting Center,** novelist John McDonald's fictional hero, Travis McGee, is honored with a

plaque at the marina where he allegedly docked his houseboat (*see* Lodging). *801 Seabreeze Blvd., tel. 305/764–2233 or 800/327–8154.*

8 Three blocks north, visit the **Swimming Hall of Fame Museum,** featuring photos, medals, and other souvenirs from major swimming events around the world. Included are memorabilia from Johnny Weissmuller, Mark Spitz, and other swimming champions. An Olympic-size pool hosts special events and is open to the public for swimming at other times. *501 Seabreeze Blvd., museum tel. 305/462–6536, pool tel. 305/523–0994. Open Mon.–Sat. 10–5, Sun. 11–4. Museum admission: $1.25 adults, $1 children 6–21 and seniors, $3 family. Pool admission: $2 adults, $1.50 seniors, $1 students.*

This concludes the central Fort Lauderdale tour. To return to the starting point, continue north on Seabreeze Boulevard to Las Olas Boulevard.

Exploring North Beach

The northeast section of Broward County includes the communities of Pompano Beach, Sea Ranch Lakes, Lighthouse Point, Deerfield Beach, and Hillsboro Beach.

9 The home of one of only four remaining **Goodyear blimps** (1500 N.E. 5th Ave., Pompano Beach, tel. 305/946–8300) is off I–95. Rides are available when the blimp is in town and not booked for a special sports or promotional event at Pompano Beach Airport. So if you're hoping for a ride call ahead.

Heading south on I–95, take the Atlantic Boulevard exit, then
turn onto Power Line Road, which will lead you to the popular
10 **Pompano Harness Track.** The track is open from November to
early April for harness racing, and from June to early August
for quarter-horse racing. The Top 'O The Park restaurant overlooks the finish line. Post time: 7:30 nightly.

A unique water skiing cableway is at **Quiet Waters Park,** just
11 south of the racetrack, on Power Line Road. **Ski Rixen** offers
lessons for beginners, plus skis and life vests. A cable pulls the skiers. If you're skilled enough, there are all sorts of variations to the two-hand, two-ski way of skimming across the water. *Open daily, 8–sunset. Admission: free Mon.–Fri., 50 cents Sat. and Sun. Children under 4 free at all times.*

Take Hillsboro Boulevard east to Rte. A1A, turn right, and go
12 south to Hillsboro Beach and the **Hillsboro Lighthouse,** a major
historic landmark since 1907 and one of the most powerful lighthouses in the United States. It marks the eastern tip of the Hillsboro inlet, which provides easy access to the ocean from the Intracoastal Waterway.

Exploring Southern Broward

In southern Broward County, an exploration can include native Indian crafts and lifestyles, high-stakes pari-mutuel wagering, and a unique natural park, all within the same driving loop.

13 Start with the **Dania Jai-Alai Palace** (301 E. Dania Beach Blvd., Dania, tel. 305/428–7766), offering one of the fastest games on the planet from early November through April.

Take Dania Beach Boulevard west to U.S. 1, turn left, go south
14 to Sterling Road, turn right, and go west to **Six Flags Atlantis** (2700 Stirling Rd., Hollywood, tel. 305/926–1000), one of the world's largest water-theme parks. It has 2 million gallons of water in 45 pools and water slides up to 7 stories high, plus seven amusement rides, and water ski and diving shows. Highlights include a wave pool and an activity pool with trollies, slides and rope ladders. Riders on Thunderball, the steepest water slide, reach speeds near 40 mph. The park sets minimum and maximum height requirements for participants in some activities. *2700 Stirling Rd., Box 2128, Hollywood, tel. 305/926–1101. Summer hours 10 AM–10 PM; phone for hours at other times of year. Admission $11.95 adults, $4.95 seniors over 55, $9.95 children 3–11.*

Take I–95 south to the Sheridan Street exit, then west, where
15 you'll find **Topeekeegee Yugnee Park.** Rentals include sailboats, Windsurfers, paddleboats, and canoes. *Open daily 8–8. Admission: $1 adults, 50 cents children 6–12, children under 6 free.*

Take Sheridan Street west to U.S. 441/Rte. 47, turn right, and
16 go north through the **Seminole Okalee Indian Village.** The never-conquered Seminole Indian tribe has been divided into four groups, and one of the groups lives here, selling native arts and crafts and running a megabuck bingo game. *Bingo nightly 6:45–1. Matinee games Mon.–Sat. noon–6. Admission: $15 and $25 on Tues., Fri., and Sun.; $20, $30, and $40 on Mon., Thurs., Sat. The more you pay, the more you stand to win. All prices include 12 Bingo cards. 4150 Rte. 7, corner of Sterling Rd., tel. 305/961–5140.*

17 At the **Gulfstream Park Racetrack** (901 S. Federal Hwy., tel. 305/454–7000) in Hallandale. Thoroughbred racing is offered from early January to early March. During the off-season, there are free tours. This track is the home of the Florida Derby, one of the premier racing events in the southeast.

18 Also in Hallandale on U.S. 1 is the **Hollywood Greyhound Track** (tel. 305/454–9400). Simply reverse your direction and head north to 831 N. Federal Highway. The greyhounds race from the day after Christmas to late April.

Exploring Inland

Broward County extends toward the center of Florida, toward the Everglades, and, as you move inland, the choices—with one all-weather, man-made exception—reflect the more natural, less developed parts of the county.

19 The **Davie Rodeo Complex** is at Orange Drive and Davie Road in Davie, where rodeos have been held for more than 40 years. The championship rodeos are held in March and December. Just north, on Davie Road, is the **Buehler Planetarium,** where star-studded skies are on view, regardless of the weather or time of day. *Broward Community College campus, 3501 S.W. Davie Rd., tel. 305/475–6680. Shows held 7:30 PM Thurs., 2:30 and 3:30 PM Sun. Admission free.*

Back on Orange Drive, west to Griffin Road, at **Spykes Grove & Tropical Gardens,** the entire family can hop aboard an hourly 15-minute, tractor-pulled tram through working citrus groves. *7250 Griffin Rd. Open daily, 9–5:30. Admission free.*

20 Head west on Griffin Road and on to Flamingo Road to **Flamingo Gardens.** Weekly events held every Friday at 7:30 PM. *Tel. 305/584–4537. Admission: $3 adults, $2 children 3–12.* There are crocodiles, alligators, monkeys, pink flamingoes, and other exotic birds, along with a petting zoo, a mini-botanical garden, 60 acres of orange groves, antique car and historical museums, and a tram ride. *3750 Flamingo Rd., tel. 305/473–0010. Open daily 9–5:30. Admission to the park is free, but there is an all-inclusive charge of $5 for adults, $2.50 for children 4–17, for Gator World, the petting zoo, tram ride, botanical gardens, and museums.*

Fort Lauderdale for Free

Manatees

During the winter, manatees frolic in the warm-water discharge from Florida Power & Light Company's Port Everglades power plant. The massive marine mammals, which may be 15 feet long and weigh three-quarters of a ton, are susceptible to cold and congregate around the outfall when the temperature in local waters falls below 68 degrees.

An observation deck at the plant's intake pipe is open to the public, without charge, at all times. There you may see angelfish, reef fish, and sea turtles as well as manatees. Take Rte. 84 east to its end inside the port, turn right at Eisenhower Boulevard, and look on your right near some railroad tracks for the observation deck and a nearby parking area.

One weekend a year, usually in late January, FP&L invites the public onto the plant grounds for a closer look at the manatees. Hourly viewings, film showings. *For schedule information, phone the Broward Parks & Recreation Division's recorded special-events number, tel. 305/563–PARK, or the administrative office, tel. 305/357–8100.*

What to See and Do with Children

Butterfly World. This attraction in Tradewinds Park is a screened-in tropical rainforest on 2.8 acres of land, where thousands of caterpillars pupate and emerge as butterflies. Up to 150 species flit through the shrubbery. Many are so tame they will land on you. Guides offer a 56-minute tour. Best time to go is in the afternoon; school groups fill the place in the mornings. *3600 W. Sample Rd., Coconut Creek, tel. 305/977–4400. Open Mon.–Sat 9–5, Sun. 1–5. Admission: $6 adults, $4 children 3–12.*

Shopping

Shopping Districts

Major malls: *Galleria Mall* on Sunrise Boulevard, just west of the Intracoastal Waterway, occupies more than one million square feet and includes Neiman-Marcus, Lord & Taylor, Saks Fifth Avenue, and Brooks Brothers (open 10–9 Mon.–Sat., noon–5:30 Sun.). *Oceanwalk* (101 N. Ocean Dr., Hollywood) is in a seashore environment with shops, restaurants, food, and entertainment. The building is a historic landmark.
Antiques: More than 75 dealers along U.S. 1 (Federal Hwy.), a half mile south of the Fort Lauderdale International Airport and a half mile north of Hollywood. Open 10–5 every day but Sunday. Exit Griffin Road East off I–95.
Trendy: *Las Olas Boulevard.* From S.E. 5th Avenue to a block

east of the Himmarshee Canal. A tree-lined boulevard with a divided grassy median and bricked crosswalks, with some of the finest shops in Fort Lauderdale.

Beaches

The Fort Lauderdale area boasts an average temperature of 75.5 degrees and 25 miles of oceanfront beach. Parking is readily available, often at parking meters. At the southern end of Broward County, **John U. Lloyd Beach State Recreation Area** (6503 N. Ocean Dr., Dania) offers a beach for swimmers and sunners, but also 244 acres of mangroves, picnic facilities, fishing, and canoeing.

Throughout Broward County, each municipality along the Atlantic has its own public beach area. Hollywood also has a 2.5-mile boardwalk, edged with shops and eateries. Dania, Pompano Beach, Deerfield Beach, and Lauderdale-by-the-Sea have fishing piers in addition to the beaches.

The most crowded portion of beach in this area is along the **Fort Lauderdale "Strip,"** which runs from Las Olas Boulevard north to Sunrise Boulevard. When heavy thunderstorms are in the area, there are actually some surfing possibilities (generally not available in this area), but the threat of being hit by lightning keeps most sensible people out of the water.

In past years, there have been some serious oil spills and dumpages by freighters and tankers at sea, and the gunk has washed ashore in globules and become mixed with the beach sand. The problem has been somewhat eased, but some hotels still include a tar-removal packet with the toilet amenities. If you're concerned, ask at the desk of your hotel or motel.

Participant Sports

Biking Bicycling is popular throughout Greater Fort Lauderdale. Young children should ride accompanied by their parents, because of heavy traffic and older drivers who have difficulty in seeing children on low bicycles. Some south Florida auto drivers resent bike riders. Ride defensively to avoid being pushed off the road.

International Bike Shop. Just off the beach, behind McDonald's. *101 S. Atlantic Blvd., Fort Lauderdale tel. 305/463–8707. Open daily 9–8. Rents 3-, 5- and 10-speed English racers, tandems, and beach cruisers. Bikes come with lock and chains. $5 for 2 hours, $10 for 5 hours, $15 for 24 hours, $50 per week.*

Diving Good diving can be enjoyed within 20 minutes of shore along Broward County's 25-mile coast. Among the most popular of the county's 80 dive sites is the two-mile-wide, 23-mile-long Fort Lauderdale Reef.

South of Port Everglades Inlet, experienced divers can explore Barracuda and Hammerhead reefs. North of the port, three parallel coral reefs extend most of the way to the Palm Beach County line. The reef closest to shore comes within 100 yards of the beach a block north of Commercial Boulevard; the most distant is in 100 feet of water about a mile offshore. Snorkelers and beginning divers should stay on the first reef.

Dive Boats and Instruction All **Force E** stores rent scuba and snorkeling equipment. Instruction is available at all skill levels. Dive boat charters are available. *2700 E. Atlantic Blvd., Pompano Beach, tel. 407/943–*

3483 or 800/527–8660 (answered by West Palm Beach store). Open winter weekdays 10–9, summer weekdays 8 AM*–9* PM*, Sat.–Sun. 8–4. 2104 W. Oakland Park Blvd., Oakland Park, tel. 305/735–6227. Hours same as Pompano Beach store.*

Spas If you watch "Lifestyles of the Rich and Famous" on TV, you'll recognize the names of Greater Fort Lauderdale's two world-famous spas, the Bonaventure Resort & Spa and Palm-Aire Resort & Spa. At each resort, women comprise 75–80% of the spa clientele.

Both resorts offer single-day spa privileges to non-guests. Price and availability of services vary with seasonal demand; resort guests have priority. At each resort, day users may receive a body massage, exercise class, facials, herbal wrap, spa-cuisine lunch, and other spa facilities and services.

Bring your own sneakers and socks. The spa provides everything else you'll need. Each spa will help you design a personal exercise-and-diet program tied to your lifestyle at home. If you already have an exercise program, bring it with you. If you have a medical problem, bring a letter from your doctor.

Bonaventure Resort & Spa (250 Racquet Club Rd., Fort Lauderdale, tel. 305/389–3300) is part of a hotel and convention complex near the Sawgrass Expressway interchange with I–595 in western Broward County. Free caffeine-free herbal teas served in the morning, fresh fruit in the afternoon. Staff nutritionist follows American Heart Association and American Cancer Society guidelines, and can accommodate macrobotic and vegetarian diets. Full-service beauty salon open to the public.

Palm-Aire Resort & Spa (2501 Palm-Aire Drive N., Pompano Beach, tel. 305/975–6122 or 800/327–4960). This health, fitness and stress-reduction spa offers exercise activities, personal treatments, and calorie-controlled meals. 15 minutes from downtown Fort Lauderdale.

Spectator Sports

Baseball Home games played by the New York Yankees in spring training are available at Lockhart Stadium (5301 N.W. 12th Ave., Fort Lauderdale, tel. 305/776–1921).

Football The Fort Lauderdale Rattlers play semipro ball at Lockhart Stadium (530 N.W. 12th Ave., tel. 305/776–5159 or 305/776–2621).

Rugby The Fort Lauderdale Knights play rough and ready on the green at Holiday Park (off Federal Hwy., 2 blocks south of Sunrise Blvd., Fort Lauderdale, tel. 305/561–5263).

Dining

The list below is a representative selection of independent restaurants in Fort Lauderdale and Broward County, organized geographically, and by type of cuisine within each region of the county. Unless otherwise noted, they serve lunch and dinner.

The most highly recommended restaurants are indicated by a star ★.

The following credit card abbreviations are used: AE, American Express; CB, Carte Blanche; DC, Diners Club; MC, MasterCard; and V, Visa.

Category	Cost*
Very Expensive	over $55
Expensive	$35–$55
Moderate	$15–$35
Inexpensive	under $15

**per person, without 6% state sales tax, service, or drinks*

Bonaventure
American

The Garden. Coral-rock walls and earth-tone rattan furnishings, and terraced seating gives this restaurant in the Bonaventure Resort and Spa an inviting, outdoorsy appearance. It's a relaxed family restaurant, catering primarily to a resort clientele but welcoming others as well. Specialties include seafood salad appetizer (shrimp, crab, scallops) served with mustard sauce on a bed of greens, veal Milanese (medallion of veal sautéed in egg batter, with a sauce containing tomatoes, ham, mushrooms, dill pickles, and cream), and tall cheesecake (chocolate, marble, blueberry, strawberry, and plain). *250 Racquet Club Rd., tel. 305/389–3300 or 800/327–8090. Dress: informal. Reservations not accepted. AE, DC, MC, V. Moderate.*

Italian
★

Casa Vecchia. This old house (*casa vecchia*) stands beside the Intracoastal Waterway, surrounded by a formal garden where you can watch boats cruise past. The garden also grows herbs which flavor the restaurant's fare. Casa Vecchia was built in the late 1930s. Diners are encouraged to roam through the building to admire antique furnishings and original statuary and paintings. Spanish tiles decorate Casa Vecchia's walls and many tabletops. Specialties include meat canneloni, fettuccine funghi (mushroom-flavored noodles tossed with butter, basil, and porcini), and *granchio* Casa Vecchia (Maryland lump crabmeat served with scallions, a splash of cognac, and red linguine). Desserts include full-flavored sorbets of fresh seasonal fruit prepared on the premises and poached pear with mascarpone cheese. *209 N. Birch Rd., tel. 305/463–7575. Jacket preferred. Reservations advised. AE, CB, MC, V. Expensive.*

Natural

Spa Restaurant. In the Bonaventure Resort and Spa, this 70-seat restaurant caters primarily to spa guests. Menus state the number of calories in each item. Tropical pastels and white rattan furniture seem to match the healthful, low-calorie natural fare prepared in a separate kitchen by chefs attuned to special dietary needs. Specialties include cream of cauliflower soup, a broad variety of salads, medallions of turkey Santa Barbara with a tangy-sweet apricot-lingonberry sauce, peach cobbler topped with granola, and strawberry-rhubarb crustless pie. *250 Racquet Club Rd., tel. 305/389–3300 or 800/327–8090. Dress: informal. Breakfast, lunch, dinner. Reservations advised. Non-smoking seating available. Closed last 2 weeks in Aug. AE, DC, MC, V. Moderate.*

Seafood

Renaissance Seafood Grill. This gourmet restaurant, in the Bonaventure Resort and Spa, 5-star-rated by the Confrerie de la Chaine des Rotisseurs, features mesquite-grilled seafood and California cuisine with Florida adaptations. You dine in a rain forest, with views of a waterfall surrounded by palm and

Fort Lauderdale Area Lodging and Dining

Lodging

Bahia Mar Resort & Yachting Center, **10**

Bonaventure Resort and Spa, **6**

Casa Alhambra, **7**

De Vito by the Sea, **15**

Fort Lauderdale Marriott Hotel & Marina, **13**

Marriott's Harbor Beach Resort, **12**

Palm-Aire Resort & Spa, **1**

Pier 66 Hotel and Marina, **11**

Riverside Hotel, **9**

Royce Resort Hotel, **4**

Sheraton Design Center Hotel, **14**

Westin Cyprus Creek, **3**

Dining

Boodles, **14**

Cafe Max, **2**

Casa Vecchia, **5**

Down Under, **14**

The Garden, **6**

Renaissance, **6**

Shirttail Charlie's, **8**

Spa Restaurant, **6**

ficus trees, ferns and blooming flowers, and a pond with variegated foot-long carp. Specialties include chilled cream of avocado and cucumber soup; hot cream of popleno pepper soup with chunks of brie cheese; a spinach-and-beansprout salad with pickled eggs and rosemary vinaigrette dressing; whole-wheat fettuccine sautéed with chunks of Maine lobster, scallops, and chives in a lobster sauce; mako shark in a lime-parsley-butter sauce. *250 Racquet Club Rd., tel. 305/389–3300 or 800/327–8090. Jacket preferred. Dinner only. Reservations required. AE, DC, MC, V. Expensive.*

Dania
American

Boodles. In Sheraton Design Center Hotel, you may dine on a "porch" with a fountain, overlooking the lobby; or in a wine room, an intimate "plum room," or the main dining room. Specialties include a spicy-sweet alligator chili; Boodles's house salad with Boston Bibb lettuce, sliced green pepper, radicchio, a tomato wedge, Japanese *enoki* mushrooms, and a rose-petal vinaigrette dressing; mesquite-grilled prawns wrapped in bacon and dipped in Cajun barbecue sauce, with wild rice, sliced apples, and mixed vegetables; grilled filet mignon filled with a creamy *boursin* herb cheese. *1825 Griffin Rd., tel. 305/920–3500. Dress: informal. Breakfast, lunch, dinner, Sunday brunch. Reservations accepted. Non-smoking seating available. AE, CB, DC, MC, V. Expensive.*

Fort Lauderdale
Continental

Down Under. When Al Kocab and Leonce Picot opened Down Under in 1968, the Australian government sent them a boomerang as a gift. The name actually describes the restaurant's location, below a bridge approach at the edge of the Intracoastal Waterway. The two-story structure was built to look old, with walls of antique brick deliberately laid off-plumb. Specialties include fresh Belon oysters and littleneck clams from Maine; Florida blue crab cakes; Brutus salad (Down Under's version of Caesar salad); fresh Idaho trout lightly sautéed and topped with Florida blue crab and Hollandaise sauce; and Florida lobster and stone crab in season. Desserts include Key-lime pie with meringue and amaretto tart with a thin layer of raspberry filling and a light apricot sauce. *3000 E. Oakland Park Blvd., tel. 305/563–4123. Jackets preferred. Reservations advised. AE, CB, MC, V. Expensive.*

Seafood
★

Shirttail Charlie's. You can watch the world go by from the outdoor deck or upstairs dining room of Shirttail Charlie's. Boats glide up and down the New River. Monday–Thursday diners may take a free 45-minute after-dinner cruise on the 24-passenger launch *Cavalier,* which chugs upriver past an alleged Al Capone speakeasy. Charlie's itself is built to look old, with 1920s blue-and-white five-sided tile on a floor that leans toward the water. The menu reflects Caribbean cuisine. Specialties include an alligator-tail appetizer served with Tortuga sauce (a béarnaise with turtle broth and sherry); conch served four ways; crab balls; shark bites; blackened tuna with Dijon mustard sauce; crunchy coconut shrimp with a not-too-sweet piña colada sauce; and a superbly tart Key-lime pie with graham-cracker-crust. *400 S.W. 3rd Ave., tel. 305/463–3474. Jacket preferred upstairs, casual downstairs. Reservations advised upstairs. AE, MC, V. Moderate.*

Pompano Beach
American
★

Cafe Max. Dennis and Patti Max have established four south Florida restaurants—Cafe Max in Pompano Beach, Maxaluna in Boca Raton, The Brasserie in Plantation, and Max's Place in north Miami (now owned by its chef, Mark Militello). As you enter Cafe Max, you're greeted by the aroma of fragrant spices issuing from the open theater kitchen. The decor includes art deco–style black wood chairs, original art work, and cut flowers. Booth seating is best; the tables are quite close together. The chef combines the best of new American cuisine with traditional *escoffier* cooking. Specialties include stuffed poblano peppers stuffed with Monterey Jack and goat cheeses, cilantro and almonds, and served with green tomatillo salsa; fresh Okeechobee heart-of-palm salad with pink peppercorns, orange slices, a radicchio garnish, and citrus vinaigrette dressing; soft-shell crab with fresh tomato-jicama relish; grilled veal chops with cucumber polenta (a cornmeal custard with diced vegetables); and chicken with homemade pasta. Daily chocolate dessert specials include hazelnut chocolate cappuccino torte and white-chocolate mousse pie with fresh raspberries. Other desserts include fresh fruit sorbets and homemade ice cream served with sauce *Anglais* and fresh raspberries. *2601 E. Atlantic Blvd., tel. 305/782–0606. Jacket preferred. Dinner only. Reservations advised. AE, DC, MC, V. Expensive.*

Lodging

In Fort Lauderdale, Pompano Beach, and the Hollywood-Hallandale area, dozens of hotels line the Atlantic Ocean beaches. You can find a full spectrum of accommodations, from economy motels to opulent luxury hotels with posh, pricey suites.

Inland, the major chain hotels along I–95 north and south of the airport cater primarily to business travelers and overnight visitors en route to somewhere else.

Wherever you plan to stay in Broward County, reservations are a good idea throughout the year. Tourists from the northern U.S. and Canada fill up the hotels from Thanksgiving through Easter. In summer, southerners and Europeans create a second season that's almost as busy.

The list below is a representative selection of hotels and motels, organized geographically. The rate categories in the list are based on the all-year or peak-season price; off-peak rates may be a category or two lower.

The most highly recommended hotels are indicated by a star ★.

Category	Cost*
Very Expensive	over $120
Expensive	$90–$120
Moderate	$50–$90
Inexpensive	under $50

**per room, double occupancy, without 6% state sales tax and nominal tourist tax.*

The following credit card abbreviations are used: AE, American Express; CB, Carte Blanche; DC, Diners Club; MC, MasterCard; V, Visa.

Bahia Mar Resort & Yachting Center. Naval architect J. H. Phillpot designed the Bahia Mar marina in 1949; it was the first in Fort Lauderdale to accommodate boats longer than 30 feet. Travis McGee, fictional hero of mystery author John McDonald, "lived" at Bahia Mar aboard a boat called *The Busted Flush.* Two months after McDonald died in December 1986, the Literary Landmark Association dedicated a plaque at slip F–18 in memory of McDonald and McGee. Ironically, McDonald never stayed on the premises. Marina wing rooms are furnished in tropical posters; tower rooms have a soft blue-white color scheme. Upper floors of the 16-story tower provide spectacular views of the ocean and Intracoastal Waterway. *801 Seabreeze Blvd., Fort Lauderdale 33316, tel. 305/764–2233 or 800/327–8154. 298 rooms with bath, including 9 suites, 30 nonsmokers rooms, 3 rooms for handicapped guests. Facilities: outdoor freshwater swimming pool, 350-slip marina where 15 deep-sea-fishing charter boats dock, power-boating and sailing instruction, dive boat and shop, 4 tennis courts, conference center, shopping arcade, restaurants. AE, CB, DC, MC, V. Expensive.*

Bonaventure Resort and Spa. Mid-rise resort with spa and conference center on 1,250 acres, 17 miles west of Fort Lauderdale. The hotel lobby is light and airy, with colorful angelfish and a cuddly-looking sand shark in a large aquarium just inside the front entrance. All guest rooms are in nine four-story buildings. Room views look out on the pools, lake, and golf courses. Bathroom amenities include bidets in many rooms, heat lamps, and full-size bath towels. *250 Racquet Club Rd., Fort Lauderdale 33326, tel. 305/389–3300 or 800/327–8090. 504 rooms include 8 suites. Facilities: 5 outdoor solar-heated freshwater swimming pools; 2 18-hole golf courses; 24 tennis courts, 43,000-square-foot spa with separate facilities for men and women (see* Participant Sports*); canoes, paddleboats, and a small sailboat on a half-mile-long lake which winds through the resort; bicycles and bicycle paths, saddle club, bowling alley, roller-skating rink, 4 restaurants, 2 lounges. AE, DC, MC, V. Expensive.*

★ **Casa Alhambra Bed & Breakfast Inn.** Victoria Feaman, co-owner and manager of this guest house, lives on the premises and treats customers as honored guests in her home. In fact, Casa Alhambra was a private home, built in 1932–36 and restored in 1986–87. The white-stucco dwelling retains such charming touches as a red-tile roof, stained-glass windows, hardwood floors, and a working brick fireplace. Vicky serves a complimentary Continental breakfast each morning and cocktails and hors d'oeuvres each evening in the living room. The large upstairs bedroom has a medium-firm king-size bed overlooking the tile roof and deck; two smaller bedrooms upstairs share a bath, an arrangement ideal for a foursome. *3029 Alhambra St., Fort Lauderdale 33304, tel. 305/467–2262. 5 rooms with bath. Facilities: outdoor freshwater hot tub with Jacuzzi, bicycles, piano, library, refrigerator privileges. No children under 10. AE. Moderate.*

Di Vito By the Sea. This eccentric low-rise beachfront hotel was built by Anthony Di Vito to express his love for his wife and exalt their Italian origins. Its architecture incorporates a reproduction of the Leaning Tower of Pisa with sea-horses, mermaids, and friezes with mythological heroes. Most guests rent by the week. There is no lobby, just an office and a patio facing the boardwalk in front of the building. *3500 N. Boardwalk, Hollywood 33019, tel. 305/929–7227. 20 rooms with bath, 4 yearly-rental apartments in an adjoining building. Facilities: 200 feet of beach frontage, efficiency kitchens in some rooms. No credit cards. Moderate.*

Fort Lauderdale Marriott Hotel & Marina. This hotel's 13-story tower beside the Intracoastal Waterway commands a striking view of the beach and the entrance to Port Everglades. Most rooms have balconies overlooking the water and standard Marriott furnishings in natural dark woods with pink, mauve, and green fabrics and wall coverings. *1881 S.E. 17th St., Fort Lauderdale 33316, tel. 305/463–4000 or 800/228–9290. 583 rooms with bath, including 19 suites, 26 nonsmokers rooms, 17 rooms for handicapped guests. Facilities: outdoor freshwater swimming pool and whirlpool, free shuttle to beach, 32-slip marina for yachts up to 200 feet long, 4 tennis courts, fitness center, game room, in-room minibars and safes, pay-TV movies, AE, CB, DC, MC, V. Very Expensive.*

Marriott's Harbor Beach Resort. Fort Lauderdale's only AAA-rated 5-diamond hotel is a 14-story tower on 16 acres of oceanfront. Built in 1984, it is scheduled to undergo renovations in summer 1989. The free-form pool has a cascading waterfall. Room furnishings are light wood with mauve, pink, blue, and green hues; each room has a balcony, with the best views facing the ocean. *3030 Holiday Dr., Fort Lauderdale 33316, tel. 305/525–4000 or 800/228–9290. 645 rooms with bath, including 36 suites, 7 rooms for handicapped guests. Facilities: 1,100 ft of beach frontage, cabanas, windsurfing, Hobie cats, 65-foot catamaran, parasailing, outdoor heated freshwater swimming pool and whirlpool, 5 tennis courts, fitness center, men's and women's saunas, 3 boutiques, 5 restaurants, 3 lounges, in-room minibars, HBO, TV movies. AE, DC, MC, V. Very Expensive.*

Palm-Aire Resort & Spa. This mid-rise resort with spa and conference center on 1,500 acres 15 miles north of Fort Lauderdale is lushly landscaped, and planters on each terrace make the four-story main building resemble a hanging garden. The rooms have big closets, a separate dressing alcove, and choice of soft or firm pillows. *2501 Palm-Aire Dr. N, Pompano Beach 33069, tel. 305/972–3300 or 800/327–4960. 194 rooms with bath and private terrace, 4 outdoor freshwater swimming pools, 3 golf courses, half-mile jogging trail with exercise stations, 37 tennis courts, Continental and spa restaurants, boutique. AE, DC, MC, V. Very Expensive.*

Pier 66 Hotel and Marina. Phillips Petroleum built Fort Lauderdale's original high-rise luxury hotel on the eastern bank of the Intracoastal Waterway. An octagonal rooftop cocktail lounge rotates slowly, offering patrons a spectacular view. Rooms are attractively furnished in tropical pastels. *2301 S.E. 17th St., Fort Lauderdale 33316, tel. 305/525–6666, FL 800/432–1956, rest of USA 800/327–3796. 388 rooms, including 8 suites. Facilities: water taxi and van shuttle to beach, outdoor heated freshwater swimming pool, full-service marina with 142 wet slips for boats up to 200 ft long, scuba diving, snorkling, parasailing, small boat rentals, waterskiing, fishing and sailing yacht charters, 2 hard-surface tennis courts, indoor and outdoor health clubs with saunas and exercise equipment, men's and women's saunas, massage therapy. AE, CB, DC, MC, V. Very Expensive.*

★ **Riverside Hotel.** This six-story hotel, on Fort Lauderdale's most fashionable shopping thoroughfare, was built in 1936, and was extensively remodeled in 1987. An attentive staff includes many veterans of two decades or more. Each room is unique, with antique oak furnishings, framed French prints on the walls, in-room refrigerators, and European-style baths. Best rooms face south, overlooking the New River; worst rooms, where you can hear the elevator, are the 36 series. *620 E. Las Olas Blvd., Fort Lauderdale 33301, tel. 305/467–0671, in USA 800/325–3280, in FL 800/421–7666. 116 rooms with bath, including 12 suites, 15 nonsmokers rooms. Facilities: kidney-shaped heated outdoor freshwater swimming pool beside the New River, 540 ft of dock with mooring space available by advance reservation, volleyball court, two restaurants, poolside bar. AE, DC, MC. Expensive.*

Royce Resort Hotel. Built in 1966, this nine-story hotel has been undergoing renovation since 1986. All rooms have balconies, dehumidifiers, and triple dressers. In some, the color scheme is off-white and pastels; others have burgundy carpeting with mauve curtains and matching bedspreads. *4040 Galt Ocean Mile, Fort Lauderdale Beach 33308, tel. 305/565–6611, or 800/237–6923. 224 rooms with bath, including 14 suites, 4 rooms for handicapped guests. Facilities: 225 ft of beach frontage on Atlantic Ocean, outdoor heated freshwater swimming pool, sailboat rentals, shuffleboard, video game room, 2 restaurants, nightclub, poolside bar, ice cream shop, tropical juice bar, free cable TV, plus pay-TV movies. AE, DC, MC, V. Expensive.*

Sheraton Design Center Hotel. This high-rise business hotel is near the airport, across a landscaped plaza from the interior-design showrooms in Design Center of the Americas. The hotel's color theme is mauve, with variations of peach, wine, and pink. In the two-story atrium lobby, art deco–style hanging chandeliers with double-round diffusers hang from a skylight; pale beige, peach, and gray fabrics predominate. *1825 Griffin Rd., Dania 33004, tel. 305/920–3500 or 800/325–3535. 250 rooms with bath, including 5 suites, 20 nonsmokers rooms, 20 rooms for handicapped guests. Facilities: outdoor heated freshwater swimming pool and whirlpool, 2 lighted tennis courts, fitness center, men's and women's saunas, 2 racquetball courts, 2 restaurants, 2 lounges, complimentary shuttle to airport, AE, CB, DC, MC, V. Very Expensive.*

Westin Cypress Creek. Built in 1986, this high-rise business hotel is in Radice Corporate Center, a suburban office park surrounding a lagoon with a fountain in the center. The hotel's three-story atrium lobby was inspired by the Great Temple at Karnak, Egypt; eight weathered-looking concrete columns with a rough pink-stucco finish rise to a skylight through which you can see the building's facade. Best rooms are on the 14th and 15th floors, where concierge service includes a Continental breakfast and a cocktail hour. *400 Corporate Dr., Fort Lauderdale 33334, tel. 305/772–1331 or 800/228–3000. 294 rooms with bath, including 25 suites, 34 nonsmokers rooms, 19 rooms for handicapped guests. Facilities: outdoor heated freshwater swimming pool and Jacuzzi, poolside bar with lunchtime barbecue, health club with Nautilus equipment, men's and women's saunas, jogging trail, volleyball, basketball, 2 restaurants, 2 lounges, in-room minibars. AE, CB, DC, V. Very Expensive.*

The Arts and Nightlife

For the most complete weekly listing of events, get the *Fort Lauderdale News/Sun Sentinel* on Friday and read the "calendar" entertainment insert, "Showtime!"

Tickets are sold at individual box offices, and through BASS Tickets, a computerized sales system. Call for tickets or information (tel. 305/741–3000 in Broward or 305/428–BASS in North Broward). There's also a concert line in Broward (tel. 305/493–8811).

The Arts

Theater

Pompano Players Theatre (1300 N.E. 6th St., Pompano Beach, tel. 305/946–4646) provides a venue for Broadway shows and pre-Broadway shows by name stars during the tourist season. Performances Tuesday–Sunday at 8 and Wednesday and Saturday at 2.

Sunrise Musical Theatre (5555 N.W. 95th Ave., Sunrise, tel. 305/741–7300) stages Broadway musicals, some dramatic plays with name stars, and concerts by well-known singers throughout the year. The theater is 14 miles west of Fort Lauderdale Beach via Commercial Boulevard.

Broward Community College (Central Campus, 3501 S.W. Davie Rd., Fort Lauderdale, tel. 305/761–7412) offers its International Showcase October–April. The showcase features a mixture of Broadway productions with name stars, dance companies, jazz bands, and individual concerts. Performances are held in several different halls, usually on Saturday and Sunday at 2:15 and 8:15 PM.

Concerts

The Broward Symphony presents a six-concert series October–May at the Baily Hall of Broward Community College (3501 S.W. Davie Rd., tel. 305/368–6875). The office is open weekdays 9–5.

The Philharmonic Orchestra of Florida presents a 10-concert celebrity series in Fort Lauderdale and in Boca Raton and a nine-concert classic hits series in Fort Lauderdale. Performances, usually on weeknights at 8:15, are given at Fort Lauderdale's War Memorial (800 N.E. 8th St., just off Federal Hwy. at Holiday Park) and at the Florida Atlantic University in Boca Raton (500 N.W. 20th St.). The symphony office (1430 N. Federal Hwy., Fort Lauderdale, tel. 305/561–2997) is open weekdays 9–5.

The Fort Lauderdale Opera Guild schedules one major production each month January–April. Performers are drawn from major international and national opera companies, and performances are usually given at 8 in the War Memorial Auditorium (800 N.E. 8th St., Fort Lauderdale). Tickets may be obtained at the Guild office (1040 Bayview Dr., tel. 305/566–9913 or 305/728–9700) weekdays 9–5.

Nightlife

Bars and Nightclubs

Pier Top Lounge. A rotating 125-seat lounge atop the 17-story tower of the Pier 66 Hotel & Marina, this contemporary/pop lounge offers a 360-degree view of the Atlantic Ocean and Intracoastal Waterway. A complete revolution takes 66 minutes. It's a great place to watch the sunset. The lounge is decorated with brass railings and a hardwood bar. Small wood dance floor. Casual dress. No minimum. *2301 S.E. 17th St., Fort Lauderdale, tel. 305/525–6666. Open noon–2 AM. Live entertainment from a top-40 band Tues.–Sun.*

Musician Exchange Downtown Cafe. As you drive down Andrews Avenue, the main north–south artery in downtown Fort Lauderdale, you can hear the mellow jazz emanating from the Musician Exchange. The 200-seat pale-pink-and-gray cafe and club offers jazz, blues, and rhythm-and-blues. Phone for schedule information. Six booths on the upstairs balcony are the best seats in the house. No minimum. *200 S. Andrews Ave., Fort Lauderdale, tel. 305/764–1912. Admission price varies with show. National big-name acts Fri.–Sat. Showtimes 8:30 and 11:30.*

Shirttail Charlie's Downstairs Bar. A scenic place to have a beer or snack and watch boat traffic on the New River through downtown Fort Lauderdale. No entertainment. Informal. *400 S.W. 3rd Ave., Fort Lauderdale, tel. 305/463–3474. Open Mon.–Fri. 11:30–10, Sat. 11:30–10, Sun. 11:30 –9.*

Penrods on the Beach. Opened in 1980 in the Sheraton Yankee Trader's south tower, Penrods quickly became a favorite with young visitors to Fort Lauderdale. It features a sports room large enough for 350 people, with video games, four pool tables, an electronic dart game, compact-disk jukebox, 10-foot TV screens, wood dance floor, and stage. A small disco for 270 people, open nightly, has a double-deck wood dance floor. No cover for people over 21 during the week, people 18–21 pay $3 cover. Friday and Saturday people over 21 pay $3 cover, 18–21 pay $5 cover. No cover in the daytime. *303 N. Atlantic Blvd., Fort Lauderdale, tel. 305/763–1359. Open Sun.–Fri. noon–2 AM, Sat. noon–3 AM.*

Peppers. High-energy nightclub with art-deco decor in Westin Cypress Creek Hotel. Features rock-and-roll DJs most weekend nights, with videos produced in-house; occasional live jazz. Wood dance floor. *400 Corporate Dr., Fort Lauderdale, tel. 305/772–1331. Open Mon.–Thu. 5 PM–1:30 AM with complimentary buffet 5–7 PM, Fri.–Sat. 7 PM–1:30 AM. No cover or minimum.*

Comedy Clubs

The Comic Strip. Stand-up comedians from New York work surrounded by framed old newspaper funnies—Katzenjammer Kids, Superman, Prince Valiant, L'il Orphan Annie, Hubert, etc. Deli-style restaurant serves soups and sandwiches, two-drink minimum, alcoholic and nonalcoholic beverages. Amateur night Sunday and Monday, phone ahead to sign up. *1432 N. Federal Hwy., Fort Lauderdale, tel. 305/565–8887. Showtime Sun.–Thurs. 9:30, Fri. 10, Sat. 8:30 and 11:30.*

Country/Western

Do-Da's Country Music Emporium. The Frontier Room seats 800 at buckboard tables and has a 2,100-square-foot wood dance floor; the smaller pecky-board Tennessee Room seats 100. Glass-and-brick arches enclose the Tex-Mex dining area, Rosa's Cantina. The shoot-'em-down corral bar in the Frontier Room has an old-fashioned barber chair. *700 S. U.S. 441, Plantation, tel. 305/791–1477. Open 11 AM–4 AM. Live country/western music, with name bands on weekends 8 PM–3 AM.*

6 Palm Beach

Introduction

Wealth has its privileges. That's the continuing reality of Palm Beach.

Those privileges include the finest homes, cars, food, wine, furniture, jewelry, art, clothing, and toys that money can buy—and the right to stare back at the tourists who visit this elegant barrier-island enclave 70 miles north of Miami.

Henry Morrison Flagler created Palm Beach in 1894. He helped John D. Rockefeller establish the Standard Oil Company, then retired and put his money into Florida railroads and real estate. He bought a small railroad between Jacksonville and St. Augustine, renamed it the Florida East Coast Railroad, and extended it southward. Along the rail line he built hotels to generate traffic, including a huge wooden structure, the 2,000-room Royal Poinciana, beside a tidal bay called Lake Worth.

Flagler created an international high-society resort at Palm Beach, attracting the affluent for the Season, December 15 to Washington's Birthday (Feb. 22). Then they departed for Europe, extolling Palm Beach's virtues and collecting great art to ship back to the mansions they were building on the island.

A workman told Flagler that people liked to picnic along the beach "down by the breakers," so he built a second hotel there in 1896. It burned, was rebuilt, and burned again. The third structure to bear the name The Breakers rose in 1926 and stands today as the grande dame of Palm Beach hostelries.

Socialites and celebrities still flock to The Breakers for charity galas. They browse in the stores along Worth Avenue, regarded as one of the world's classiest shopping districts. They swim on secluded beaches that are nominally public but lack convenient parking and access points. They pedal the world's most beautiful bicycle path beside Lake Worth. And what they do, *you* can do—if you can afford it.

Despite its prominence and affluence, the Town of Palm Beach occupies far less than 1% of the land area of Palm Beach County, which is 521 square miles larger than the state of Delaware and is a remarkably diverse political jurisdiction.

West Palm Beach, on the mainland across Lake Worth from Palm Beach, is the city Flagler built to house Palm Beach's servants; today it's the county seat and commercial center of Palm Beach County, with a population of about 70,000.

To the south in Lake Worth, the Lannan Museum features a major collection of contemporary art. Lantana has a large Finnish population and is the headquarters of the *National Enquirer*, which erects a huge Christmas tree on its grounds each December. Delray Beach began as an artists' retreat and a small settlement of Japanese farmers, including George Morikami, who donated the land for the beautiful Morikami Museum of Japanese Culture to the county park system. Boca Raton, an upscale community developed by pioneer architect Addison Mizner as a showcase for his Spanish Revival style, retains much of its 1920s ambience through strict zoning.

To the north, Palm Beach Gardens is a golf center, home of the Professional Golfer's Association. Jupiter boasts the Burt

Reynolds Jupiter Theater and a dune-fringed beach that remains largely free of intrusive development.

Many visitors to Palm Beach County don't realize that it extends 50 miles inland to encompass the southeastern quadrant of 448,000-acre Lake Okeechobee, the fourth-largest natural lake in the United States. Its bass and perch attract fishermen; catfish devotees prize the hearty flavor of succulent Okeechobee "sharpies."

To reach Lake Okeechobee from the Atlantic coast, you'll drive west past vast fields of sugar cane and vegetables growing on drained Everglades muck soils. The lakeshore towns nestle in the shadow of 36-foot-high Hoover Dike, which runs 112 miles around the perimeter of the lake for flood control.

Marinas at Pahokee and Belle Glade provide lake access. Pahokee has a 125-foot tower, which you can climb for a view of the lake. In Lake Harbor, about as far west as you can go in Palm Beach County, the state is restoring a lock and lockmaster's house built early in the 20th century on the Miami Canal.

Palm Beach County is also the main gateway to the Treasure Coast, consisting of Martin, St. Lucie, and Indian River counties along the Atlantic coast to the north.

Arriving and Departing

By Plane **Palm Beach International Airport,** located between Southern Boulevard and Belvedere Road on Australian Avenue, is about five miles from the Atlantic beaches.

Between the Airport and City Center There is no bus service from Palm Beach International to the rest of the county. **Airport Limo/Yellow Cab Co.** (tel. 407/689–4222) offers transportation.

By Train **Amtrak** (201 S. Tamarind Ave., West Palm Beach, tel. 800/872–7245) connects West Palm Beach with cities along Florida's east coast daily.

By Car Most visitors explore Palm Beach County by car. I–95 runs north–south, to link West Palm beach with Miami and Fort Lauderdale to the south. To get to central Palm Beach, take exits at Belvedere Road or Okeechobee Boulevard. Southern Boulevard (U.S. 98) runs east–west.

Getting Around

By Bus Buses require exact changes (80 cents, plus 15 cents for a transfer). Service is from 5:55 AM to 8:55 PM daily. For information tel. 407/686–4560.

By Taxi Rates start at $1.25 for the first mile and 25 cents for each additional ⅙ mile, or for every 30 seconds of waiting time. Some privately owned cabs charge more.

Important Addresses and Numbers

Tourist Information The **Chamber of Commerce** for the Palm Beaches (501 N. Flagler Dr., West Palm Beach, tel. 407/833–3711) is open weekdays 8:30–5.

Emergencies Dial 911 for **police** and **ambulance** in an emergency.

Hospitals Two hospitals in West Palm Beach with 24-hour emergency rooms are **Good Samaritan Hospital** (Flagler Dr. and Palm Beach Lakes Blvd., tel. 407/655–5511) and **St. Mary's Hospital** (901 45th St., tel. 407/844–6300). There is also a doctor-referral number for visitors (tel. 407/433–3940).

24-Hour Pharmacy **Eckerd Drugs** (3343 S. Congress Ave., Palm Springs—southwest of West Palm Beach—tel. 407/965–3367).

Exploring Palm Beach and West Palm Beach

Palm Beach is an island community 12 miles long and no more than a quarter-mile across at its widest point. Three bridges connect Palm Beach to West Palm Beach and the rest of the world. This tour takes you through both communities.

Numbers in the margin correspond with points of interest in the Palm Beach and West Palm Beach map.

Begin at Royal Palm Way and County Road in the center of
1 Palm Beach. Go north on County Road past **Bethesda-by-the-Sea Church,** built in 1927 by the first Protestant congregation in southeast Florida. Inspiring stained-glass windows and a lofty, vaulted sanctuary grace its Spanish-Gothic design. A stone bridge with an ornamental tile border spans the pond; bubbling fountains feed it. *141 South County Rd., Palm Beach, tel. 407/655–4554. Gardens open 8–5. Services Sun. 8, 9, and 11 AM in winter, 8 and 10 June–Aug.; phone for weekday schedule.*

2 Continue north on County Road past **The Breakers** (1 S. County Rd., Palm Beach), an ornate Italian Renaissance hotel built in 1926 by railroad magnate Henry M. Flagler's widow to replace an earlier hotel, which burned (*see* Lodging). Explore the elegant public spaces—especially on a Sunday morning, when you can enjoy the largest champagne brunch in Florida at The Beach Club.

Continue north on County Road to Royal Poinciana Way. Go
3 inside the **Palm Beach Post Office** to see the murals depicting Seminole Indians in the Everglades and royal and coconut palms. *95 N. County Rd., Palm Beach, tel. 407/832–0633 or 1867. Open weekdays 8:30–5.*

Continue north on County Road to the north end of the island,
4 past the very-private **Palm Beach Country Club** and a neighborhood of expansive (and expensive) estates.

5 You must turn around at **E. Inlet Drive,** the northern tip of the island, where a dock offers a view of Lake Worth Inlet, the U.S. Coast Guard Reservation on Peanut Island, and the Port of Palm Beach across Lake Worth on the mainland. Observe the no-parking signs; Palm Beach police will issue tickets.

Turn south and make the first right onto Indian Road, then the first left onto Lake Way. You'll return to the center of town through an area of newer mansions, past the posh, private Sail-
6 fish Club. Lake Way parallels the **Palm Beach Bicycle Trail** along the shoreline of Lake Worth, a palm-fringed path through the backyards of some of the world's priciest homes.

Palm Beach and West Palm Beach

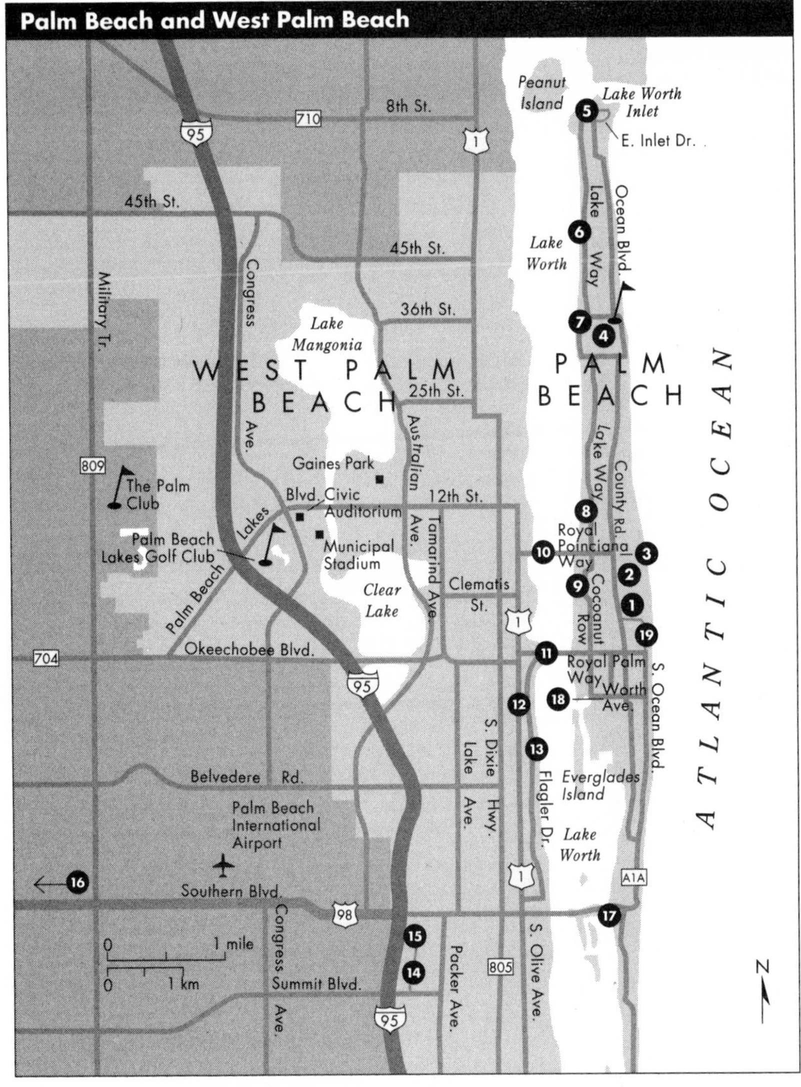

Ann Norton Sculpture Gardens, **13**
Bethesda-by the-Sea Church, **1**
The Breakers, **2**
Canyon of Palm Beach, **7**
Dreher Park Zoo, **14**
E. Inlet Drive, **5**
Flagler Memorial Bridge, **10**
Lion Country Safari, **16**
Mar-A-Lago, **17**
Norton Gallery of Art, **12**
Palm Beach Bicycle Trail, **6**
Palm Beach Biltmore Hotel, **8**
Palm Beach Country Club, **4**
Palm Beach Post Office, **3**
Public beach, **19**
Royal Palm Bridge, **11**
South Florida Science Museum, **15**
Whitehall, **9**
Worth Ave., **18**

Watch on your right for metal posts topped with a swatch of white paint, marking narrow public-access walkways between houses from the street to the bike path.

Lake Way runs into Country Club Road, which takes you
7 through the **Canyon of Palm Beach,** a road cut about 25 feet deep through a ridge of sandstone and oolite limestone.

As you emerge from the canyon, turn right onto Lake Way and continue south. Lake Way becomes Bradley Place. You'll pass
8 the **Palm Beach Biltmore Hotel,** now a condominium. Another flamboyant landmark of the Florida boom, it cost $7 million to build and opened in 1927 with 543 rooms.

As you cross Royal Poinciana Way, Bradley Place becomes Co-
9 conut Row. Stop at **Whitehall,** the palatial 73-room mansion that Henry M. Flagler built in 1901 for his third wife, Mary Lily Kenan. After the couple died, the mansion was turned into a hotel. In 1960, Flagler's granddaughter, Jean Flagler Matthews, bought the building. She turned it into a museum, with many of the original furnishings on display. The art collection includes a Gainsborough portrait of a girl with a pink sash, displayed in the music room near a 1,200-pipe organ. Exhibits also depict the history of the Florida East Coast Railway. Flagler's personal railroad car, "The Rambler," is parked behind the building. A tour by well-informed guides takes about an hour; afterwards, you may browse on your own. *Coconut Row at Whitehall Way, Palm Beach, tel. 407/655–2833. Open Tues.–Sat. 10–5, Sun. 1–5, closed Mon. Admission: $3.50 adults, $1.25 children.*

Turn left on leaving Whitehall. Take Coconut Row back north
10 to Royal Poinciana Way, turn left, and cross the **Flagler Memorial Bridge** into West Palm Beach. On the mainland side of the bridge, turn left onto Flagler Drive, which runs along the west
11 shore of Lake Worth. A half-mile south of the **Royal Palm Bridge,** turn right onto Acteon Street, which is the north edge
12 of a sloping mall leading up to the **Norton Gallery of Art.**

Founded in 1941 by steel magnate Ralph H. Norton, the Norton Gallery boasts an extensive permanent collection of French impressionist and 20th-century American paintings, Chinese bronze and jade sculptures, a sublime outdoor patio with sculptures on display in a tropical garden, and a library housing more than 3,000 art books and periodicals. The Norton also secures many of the best traveling exhibits to reach south Florida. *1451 S. Olive Ave., West Palm Beach, tel. 407/832–5194. Open Tues.–Sat. 10–5, Sun. 1–5. Admission free; donations requested.*

Return to Flagler Drive down Diana Street at the south edge of the mall, turn right, go a half-mile south to Barcelona Road, and
13 turn right again. You're at the entrance to the **Ann Norton Sculpture Gardens,** a monument to the late American sculptor Ann Weaver Norton, second wife of Norton Gallery founder Ralph H. Norton. The gardens display, in a tropical jungle, seven granite figures and six brick megaliths. The brick forms reflect their creator's girlhood in Selma, AL, in a pre–World War I southern landscape dotted with the brick chimneys of burned-out farmhouses and haunted by memories of General Sherman's Civil War march to the sea. The garden also contains native plants and 132 different kinds of palms. Other sculptures in bronze, marble, and wood are on display in Norton's studio. *253 Barcelona Rd., West Palm Beach, tel. 407/832–5328. Open*

Tues.–Sat. noon–4 or by appointment. Admission: $2 adults, children under 12 free.

Return again to Flagler Drive and continue south to Southern
Boulevard (U.S. 98). Turn left and go west almost a mile, turn
left onto Parker Avenue, and go south about three-quarters of
a mile. Turn right onto Summit Boulevard, and right again at
14 the next stoplight into the parking lot at the **Dreher Park Zoo.**
The 32-acre zoo has nearly 100 different species of animals, including an endangered Florida panther. Of special interest are
the reptile collection and the petting zoo. *1301 Summit Blvd.,
West Palm Beach, tel. 407/533–0887. Open daily 9–5. Admission: $4 adults, $2 children 3–12 and seniors over 60, under 3
free.*

As you leave the zoo parking lot, turn left and follow a winding
15 road for about a quarter-mile to the **South Florida Science Museum.** Here you'll find hands-on exhibits in a science arcade,
aquarium displays with touch-tank demonstrations and
feedings daily at 4 PM, planetarium shows, and a chance to observe the heavens at night through the most powerful telescope
in south Florida. *4801 Dreher Trail N, West Palm Beach, tel.
407/832–1988. Open Tues.–Sat. 10–5, Sun.–Mon. noon–5. Admission: $3 adults, $2.50 seniors over 62, $1.50 children 4–12,
$8 family. Planetarium admission: $1.*

Leaving the science museum, retrace your path on Summit
Boulevard and Parker Avenue to Southern Boulevard, turn
16 left, and go about 16 miles west to **Lion Country Safari,** where
you drive (with car windows closed) on eight miles of paved
roads through a 500-acre fenceless zoo where 1,000 wild animals roam free. Lions, elephants, white rhinoceroses, giraffes,
zebras, antelopes, chimpanzees, and ostriches are among the
species in residence. Try to go early in the day, before the park
gets crowded. If you have a convertible or a new car on which
you don't want animals to climb, the park will rent you a zebra-
stripe, air-conditioned sedan. An adjacent KOA campground
offers campers a park discount. *Box 16066, West Palm Beach
33416, tel. 407/793–1084. Open daily 9:30–5:30. Admission:
$12.14 adults, $10.45 children 3–16, $8.55 seniors over 65, un-
der 3 free, car rental $5 per hour plus tax.*

Returning to town on Southern Boulevard, look for the Italian-
17 ate towers of **Mar-A-Lago** (1100 S. Ocean Blvd., Palm Beach)
silhouetted against the sky as you cross the bridge to Palm
Beach. Mar-A-Lago, the former estate of breakfast-food heir-
ess Marjorie Meriweather Post, is now owned by real estate
magnate Donald Trump. It's closed to the public, but you can
catch a glimpse as you drive past.

Turn north on Ocean Boulevard, one of Florida's most scenic
drives. The road follows the dune top, with the beach falling
away to surging surf on your right, and some of Palm Beach's
18 most opulent mansions on your left. You will pass the east end
of **Worth Avenue,** regarded by many as the world's classiest
shopping street (*see* Shopping).

19 As you approach Worth Avenue, the **public beach** begins. Parking meters along Ocean Drive between Worth Avenue and Royal Palm Way signify the only stretch of beach in Palm Beach with convenient public access.

This concludes the tour. To return to its starting point, turn left on Royal Palm Way and go one block west to County Road.

Palm Beach for Free

Concerts The *Palm Beach Post,* in its "TGIF" entertainment insert on Fridays, lists all events for the weekend, including concerts. Admission is often free or by donation.

Nature Guided and self-guided tours through botanical gardens with tropical and subtropical plants are conducted at Mounts Botanical Gardens, Military Trail. *North of Southern Blvd., West Palm Beach. Open Mon.–Sat. 8:30–5, Sun. 1–5; guided tours Sun. at 2.*

What to See and Do with Children

Gumbo Limbo Nature Center. At this unusual nature center, you can stroll a 1,628-foot boardwalk through a dense tropical forest and climb a 50-foot tower to overlook the tree canopy. The forest is a coastal hammock, with tropical species growing north of the tropics. One tree species you're sure to see is the gumbo-limbo, often called "the tourist tree" because of its red, peeling bark. Ask for a guide to the hammock's flora, with photos and brief text keyed to numbered posts along the trail. In the nature center building, a diorama depicts the nest of a loggerhead sea turtle along the nearby beach. The center's staff leads guided turtle walks to the beach to see nesting mothers come ashore and lay their eggs. *1801 N. Ocean Blvd., Boca Raton, tel. 407/368–4776. Open Mon.–Sat. 9–4, fall–spring; Mon.–Fri. 4–8 PM in summer. Admission free. Turtle walks early June–late July Mon.–Thurs. 9 PM–12:30 AM. Admission: $2. Reservations required.*

Off the Beaten Track

Arthur R. Marshall Loxahatchee National Wildlife Refuge Loxahatchee Refuge is 221 square miles of saw-grass marshes, wet prairies, sloughs, and tree islands. You go there to stroll the nature trails, see alligators and birds (including the rare snail kite). You can also fish for bass and panfish, ride an airboat, or paddle your own canoe through this watery wilderness.

Loxahatchee refuge recently was renamed in memory of Art Marshall, a Florida environmental scientist instrumental in Everglades preservation efforts.

Refuge entrance fee $3 per car, $1 per pedestrian. Open 1 hr before sunrise–1 hr after sunset.

The refuge has three access points, each with its own facilities and services:

Headquarters The ranger at the visitor center will show a seven-minute slide presentation on request. Walk both nature trails—a boardwalk through a dense cypress swamp, and a marsh nature trail to a 20-foot-tall observation tower overlooking a pond. A seven-mile canoe trail starts at the boat-launching ramp here. *Entrance off U.S. 441 between Boynton Blvd. (Rte. 804) and Atlantic Ave. (Rte. 806), west of Boynton Beach. Mailing address: Rte. 1, Box 278, Boynton Beach, tel. 407/732–3684 or 407/734–8303.*

Hillsboro Recreation Area A concessionaire offers airboat rides, boat rentals, guide services, and a store with snacks, fishing tackle, and bait. The airboat ride lasts a half hour, in a 20-passenger craft with a

Cadillac engine. The driver, an interpretive naturalist with a biology degree, will take you into the middle of the Everglades, then shut off the engine and explain the unique ecosystem around you. *Entrance off U.S. 441 on Lox Rd. (Rte. 827), 12 mi south of Headquarters and west of Boca Raton. Loxahatchee Recreation, Inc., Rte. 1, Box 642–S, Pompano Beach 33060, tel. 305/426–2474. Concessionaire open 6* AM*–30 min before park closing. Airboat rides 9–4:30, $7.50 adults, $4 children under 12, under 3 free. Rental for 14–ft. boat with outboard engine $27.50 for 5 hours, $13.75 evening special for last 3 daylight hours; for rowboat, $10 for 5 hours. Fishing and hunting guide $150 per half-day, $200 per day. MC, V.*

20-Mile Bend Recreation Area Boat ramp and fishing area at north end of refuge. *Entrance off U.S. 98 and 441, due west of West Palm Beach. No services.*

Shopping

Worth Avenue One of the world's last strongholds for quality shopping, Worth Avenue runs a quarter-mile east–west across Palm Beach, from the beach to Lake Worth.

The street has more than 250 shops. The 300 block, with a maze of Italianate villas designed by Addison Mizner, retains a quaint charm. The 100 and 200 blocks are more overtly commercial. Most merchants open at 9:30 or 10 AM, and close at 5:30 or 6 PM. Summer hours may be shorter.

Parking on and around Worth Avenue is quite limited. On-street parking has a one- or two-hour limit, strictly enforced. An alternative is Apollo Valet Parking at Hibiscus and Peruvian avenues, a block off Worth Avenue. Merchants will stamp your parking ticket if you buy something (or if you look like a prospective customer); each stamp is good for an hour of free parking.

Apollo's parking deal is just one reason to look presentable when you tour Worth Avenue. Come dressed to feel comfortable, blend in, and indulge your fantasies.

The Worth Avenue Association has strict rules to keep the street classy: no renovations are allowed from October to May, and special sales are limited to 21 consecutive days anytime between April and October.

Many "name" stores associated with fine shopping have a presence on Worth Avenue, including Bonwit Teller, Brooks Brothers, Cartier, Elizabeth Arden, Gucci, Pierre Deux, Saks Fifth Avenue, and Van Cleef & Arpels. No other street in the world has such a dense concentration of these upscale firms—and they tend to send their best merchandise to Worth Avenue to appeal to the discerning tastes of their Palm Beach clientele.

Beaches

The best beaches in Palm Beach County are in the Jupiter area, on Singer Island, and in Boca Raton. Surfing isn't a major draw for this portion of the Atlantic, but wading and surf diving into the shallow waves are.

Sunshine at the beaches can be murder. Use sunscreens and monitor your sunning. You can get a severe sunburn on a cloudy day; ultraviolet rays aren't slowed down by an overcast sky.

Participant Sports

Biking Because of traffic, bicycle with caution while on city and county roads. A nice bike path is in *John D. MacArthur Park* (alongside PGA Blvd.) as it runs east toward Singer Island. Rentals: **Palm Beach Bicycle Trail Shop** (105 N. County Rd., Palm Beach, tel. 407/659–4583).

Diving You can drift-dive or anchor-dive along Palm Beach County's 47-mile Atlantic coast.

Drift divers take advantage of the Gulf Stream's strong currents and proximity to shore—sometimes less than a mile. A group of divers joined by nylon line may drift across coral reefs with the current; one member of the group carries a large, orange float which the charter-boat captain can follow. Drift diving works best from Boynton Beach north.

South of Boynton Beach, where the Gulf Stream is farther from shore, diving from an anchored boat is more popular.

Breakers Reef (off The Breakers, a historic Palm Beach hotel). Diners at the hotel's Beach Club can count the dive boats within a half-mile of their lunch table.

Dive Boats and Instruction The following **Force E** stores rent scuba and snorkeling equipment and have PADI affiliation. Instruction available at all skill levels. Dive-boat charters are also available.

1399 N. Military Trail, West Palm Beach, tel. 407/471–2676 or 800/527–8660. Open winter weekdays 10–9, summer weekdays 8–9, Sat. 8–7, Sun. 8–4.

155 E. Blue Heron Blvd., Riviera Beach, tel. 407/845–2333. Open weekdays year-round 8–7, Sat. 6:30–7, Sun. 6:30–5.

39 S. Ocean Blvd., Delray Beach, tel. 407/272–0311. Open Nov.– May. Contact store for hours.

877 E. Palmetto Park Rd., Boca Raton, tel. 407/368–0555. Hours same as West Palm Beach store.

7166 Beracasa Way, Boca Raton, tel. 407/395–4407. Hours same as West Palm Beach store.

Golf There are more than 74 public, private, and semiprivate golf courses in the Palm Beach County area. The **PGA Sheraton Resort** (400 Ave. of the Champions, Palm Beach Gardens, tel. 407/627–2000), west of the city, has one of the most famous golf courses in the area.

Hunting **J. W. Corbett Wildlife Management Area.** More than 55,000 acres for hunting deer, wild hog, squirrel, and quail in season. Access off Indiantown Road and Beeline Highway, west of Jupiter. For information on licensing, call the Florida Game and Fresh Water Fish Commission (tel. 407/683–0748).

Spas The first alternative lifestyle center in the United States, the **Hippocrates Health Institute** (1441 Palmdale St., West Palm Beach, tel. 407/471–8876), was founded in Boston in 1963 by Ann Wigmore, and it moved to its present 10-acre site in 1987. Guests receive complete examinations by traditional and alternative health-care professionals. Personalized programs include juice fasts and the eating of raw foods.

Tennis For information on public tennis courts, call either the West Palm Beach City Parks and Recreation Department (tel.

407/659–8077) or the Palm Beach County Parks and Recreation Department (tel. 407/964–4420).

Spectator Sports

Baseball Spring-training headquarters for the Atlanta Braves and the Montreal Expos are in West Palm Beach at the Municipal Stadium (Lakes Blvd. and Congress Ave.). Also home for the West Palm Beach Expos summer baseball team. Call for tickets (tel. 407/684–6801).

Greyhound Racing Racing open late October–April at the Palm Beach Kennel Club. Dining in the Paddock Room. *Belvedere Rd. and Congress Ave., tel. 407/683–2222. Races nightly at 8 except Sun. and Wed.; matinees at 12:30 Thurs. and Sat., and on Mon. from Dec. 28 to June 6. General admission: 50 cents; dining room admission: $2.*

Jai Alai Thirteen games per performance, January 1–mid-May. *45th Street, 1 mi west of U.S. 1, ¼ mile east of I–95, tel. 407/844–2444. Open nightly Tues.–Sat., 7:15. Matinees Wed. and Sat. at noon. Admission: 50 cents; must be over age 18.*

Polo Played November–April at three locations: **Palm Beach Polo and Country Club** (Wellington, tel. 407/793–1113), **Gulfstream Polo Grounds** (Lake Worth Rd., tel. 407/965–9924), and **Royal Palm Polo** (Boca Raton, tel. 407/994–1876). Sunday is the featured game day, but games are also played during the week. Also check The *Palm Beach Post*'s "TGIF" on Friday for additional local games.

Rugby The **Palm Beach Rugby Club** (tel. 407/747–5978 after 6 PM) practices Tuesdays and Thursday nights at 7:30 during tourist season at Lake Lytal Park (3045 Gun Club Rd.).

Dining

The list below is a representative selection of independent restaurants in Palm Beach County, organized geographically, and by type of cuisine within each region of the county. Unless otherwise noted, they serve lunch and dinner.

The most highly recommended restaurants are indicated by a star ★.

Category	Cost*
Very Expensive	over $55
Expensive	$35–$55
Moderate	$15–$35
Inexpensive	under $15

**per person without 6% state sales tax, service, or drinks*

The following credit card abbreviations are used: AE, American Express; CB, Carte Blanche; DC, Diners Club; MC, MasterCard; V, Visa.

Boca Raton
Continental

Gazebo Cafe. The locals who patronize this popular restaurant know where it is, even though there is no sign. You'll probably circle the block three times. Look for the Barnett Bank in Sun Plaza, a block north of Spanish River Drive. Once you find the place, await your table in the open kitchen where Greek-born owner-chef William Sellas and his staff perform a gastronomic ballet. The main dining room has a high noise level. You may be happier in the smaller back dining room. Specialties include lump crabmeat with an excellent glaze of Mornay sauce on a marinated artichoke bottom; smoked spinach salad with *fresh* heart of palm, egg white, bacon, croutons, mushrooms, fruit garnish, and a dressing of olive oil and poupon mustard; Paul Sellas's (the chef's young son) "classic" bouillabaisse with Maine lobster, shrimp, scallops, clams, and mussel topped with julienne vegetables in a robust broth flavored with garlic, saffron, and tomatoes; and raspberries with a Grand Marnier–Sabayon sauce. The staff can accommodate travelers in seven languages. *4199 N. Federal Hwy., Boca Raton, tel. 407/395–6033. Jacket preferred. Reservations advised. Closed Sun. and Aug.–mid-Sept. AE, DC, MC, V. Moderate.*

French ★ **La Vieille Maison.** This elegant French restaurant occupies a two-story dwelling, which architect Addison Mizner may have designed. The structure dates from the 1920s, hence the name, which means old house. It has been renovated repeatedly, but it retains features typical of Mizner's work. Closets and cubbyholes have become intimate private dining rooms. Every table is set with a complimentary appetizer, a rillette of salmon with toast rounds. You may order from a fixed-price or an à la carte menu throughout the year; in summer, a separate fixed-price menu available Sunday through Thursday offers a sampling of the other two at a more modest price. Specialties include saucisson chaud (pork-and duck sausage with pistachios, baked in a phyllo pastry and served with a truffle sauce), fresh Florida red snapper (sautéed with onions, tomatoes, and fresh basil —executive chef Christian Planchon's favorite dish), and tranche de boeuf a la bourgeoise (beef pot roast braised in red wine and served with carrots, pearl onions, potatoes, and turnips). Dessert specialties include gateau praline (a white cake with a crunchy pecan filling), and tarts with a thin crust and lightly glazed fresh seasonal fruit. *770 E. Palmetto Park Rd., tel. 407/391–6701 in Boca Raton, 407/737–5677 in Delray Beach and Palm Beach, 305/421–7370 in Ft. Lauderdale. Jackets required. Reservations required. Closed Memorial Day, Labor Day, July 4th. AE, CB, MC, V. Expensive.*

Jupiter *American* **Sinclair's American Grill.** This 140-seat restaurant overlooking the ocean and hotel pool has louvered shutters, paddle fans, ceramic banana-tree table lamps, light wood furnishings, and hanging plants. Most of the cooking takes place in an open theater kitchen with a woodburning grill and a French rotisserie. Executive chef Granville Wood plans to switch from mesquite to other scented woods. The menu favors Florida seafood and tropical fruits and vegetables in season. Seafood specialties include conch fritters; grilled swordfish with fresh pineapple cilantro salsa; salmon with a glaze of Chinese mustard and soy sauce; marinated and grilled cobia (a Florida species of sea catfish) with cold tomato salad; and mako shark with papaya and macadamia-nut vinaigrette. Other specialties include rack of lamb; grilled venison (in winter only) with cranberries and ginger; crème de menthe, meringue, and chocolate sauce in a graham-cracker crust; and Key-lime mousse and cheesecake. For grazers, half-portions are available at half the menu price plus $1. *Indiantown Rd., and Rte. A1A, Jupiter, tel. 407/746–2511, in FL 800/432–1420, elsewhere 800/821–8791. Dress: in-*

formal, jacket preferred. Reservations advised. AE, CB, DC, MC, V. Expensive.

Seafood

Charley's Crab. A sister restaurant to the Palm Beach Charley's Crab, this one opened in March 1988, in a lofty tin-roofed Florida Cracker-style structure. Its high ceilings—with beams and air-conditioning ducts exposed and painted pale hues of blue, gray, and beige—evoke feelings of sea, sky, and sand. The restaurant's centerpiece—a gilded nude statue, *Women Bathing*, by Edward Kasprowicz—stands on a six-foot-high pedestal in the main dining room. Menus change daily. Specialties include chilled crab bisque; swordfish *picatta* (sautéed in a lemon and sherry sauce); seafood paella with salmon, swordfish, littleneck clams, mussels, sausage, chicken, and rice with saffron; a pungently spiced seviche; a tangy Key-lime pie rich with extra egg yolks; and a French apple tart with cinnamon ice cream. *1000 N. Federal Hwy., Jupiter, tel. 407/744–4710. (Also in Stuart at 423 S. Federal Hwy., tel. 407/288–6800.) Dress: informal in cafe; jackets preferred at night in restaurant. Reservations suggested. AE, CB, DC, MC, V. Moderate.*

Harpoon Louie's. The best view of the historic Jupiter Lighthouse is from Harpoon Louie's outdoor terrace and dock. The menu emphasizes huge portions of fresh local fish, competently spiced. Specialties include a mild tomato-based conch chowder; conch fritters; snapper belle meunière; shrimp Bombay; and Key-lime pie. *1065 Rte. A1A, on Jupiter Inlet, Jupiter, tel. 407/744–1300. Dress: casual. Reservations not accepted. AE, DC, MC, V. Moderate.*

Palm Beach

American

Chuck & Harold's. Boxer Larry Holmes and thespians Brooke Shields and Burt Reynolds are among the celebrities who frequent this combination power-lunch bar, celebrity sidewalk cafe, and nocturnal big-band/jazz garden restaurant. A blue-and-yellow tent on pulleys rolls back in good weather to expose the garden to the elements. Local business people wheel and deal at lunch in the bar area while quaffing Bass Ale and Harp Lager on tap. Locals who want to be part of the scenery frequent the front-porch area, next to pots of red and white begonias mounted along the sidewalk rail. Specialties include a mildly spiced conch chowder with a rich flavor and a liberal supply of conch; an onion-crunchy gazpacho with croutons, cucumber spear, and a dollop of sour cream; an outrageous charcoal-grilled pizza topped with sun-dried tomato, smoked turkey, and grilled red onions; and a tangy Key-lime pie with a graham-cracker crust and a squeezable lime slice for even more tartness. *207 Royal Poinciana Way, Palm Beach, tel. 407/659–1440. Dress: casual. Reservations suggested. AE, CB, DC, MC, V. Moderate.*

Doherty's. This local restaurant-pub feels like an old shoe, comfortable and unpretentious. Specialties include chicken hash Doherty with a secret cream sauce and sherry or currant jelly, eggs Benedict, a creamy oyster stew, and fish and chips (Wed.–Fri. only). *288 County Rd., Palm Beach 33480, tel. 407/655–6200. Dress: Informal. Reservations not accepted. AE, MC, V. Moderate.*

Continental

The Breakers. The main hotel dining area at The Breakers consists of the elegant Florentine Dining Room, decorated with fine 15th-century Flemish tapestries; the adjoining Celebrity Aisle where the maître d' seats his most honored guests; and the Circle Dining Room, with a huge circular skylight framing a bronze-and-crystal Venetian chandelier. Specialties include rack of lamb Dijonnaise; salmon *en croute* with spinach, herbs and sauce Véronique (a grape sauce); *vacherin glacé* (praline-flavored ice cream encased in fresh whipped cream and frozen in a baked meringue base); and Key-lime pie. The Breakers also serves less formally at its Beach Club, where locals flock for the most sumptuous Sunday champagne brunch in Florida, and at the Fairway Cafe in the golf-course clubhouse. *1 S. County Rd., Palm Beach, tel. 407/655–6611 or 800/833–3141. Jacket and tie required. Reservations required. AE, CB, DC, MC, V. Expensive.*

International ★ **The Dining Room.** Since it opened in 1926, this formal hotel dining room in the Brazilian Court has been a favorite with the Palm Beach elite. The 94-seat dining room, with Romanesque arches and a sunny yellow color scheme, opens onto the outdoor Fountain Court. David Woodward, executive chef, uses only fresh ingredients and prepares all sauces from scratch. Specialties include Brazilian black-bean soup, a hotel standard throughout its history; pizza topped with sun-dried tomatoes and smoked duck; fillet of fresh Norwegian salmon with lobster mousseline; sautéed Florida red snapper fillet with fresh basil; roast rack of baby lamb with fried cheese polenta of Mexican corn meal; and kiwi, mango, and raspberry sorbet on a bed of cantalope puree. *301 Australian Ave., Palm Beach, tel. 407/655–7740 or 800/351–5656. Jacket and tie required. Reservations required. AE, CB, DC, MC, V. Very Expensive.*

Seafood **Charley's Crab.** Audubon bird prints, silk flowers, and French posters accent the walls of this restaurant across the street from the beach. During the season, the dinner line forms early. The raw bar in front is noisy and crowded, the back dining rooms more relaxed. Menus change daily. Specialties include chilled basil fussili, an appetizer with octopus, squid, fresh herbs, garlic, olive oil, tomato, and bell pepper; and Charley's Bucket (steamed whole live Maine lobster, Dungeness crab, mussels, clams, corn on the cob, and broiled redskin potatoes). *456 S. Ocean Blvd., Palm Beach, tel. 407/659–1500. Dress: informal. Reservations suggested. AE, DC, MC, V. Expensive.*

Palm Beach Gardens
Continental **The Explorers.** You sit in red leather hobnail chairs at tables lit with small brass and glass lanterns. The à la carte menu includes big-game items. Specialties include a French apple-smoked *barbarie* duck appetizer with strawberry rhubarb chutney; braised lion loin and black buck antelope; and almond snow eggs, an egg-shaped meringue poached in almond cream, plated between three-fruit coulees (boysenberry, mango, and tamarillo) and garnished with a nest of butter caramel. The Explorers Wine Club meets monthly for wine and food tastings and is open to the public for a one-time $5 membership. Contact the club for a schedule of events. *400 Ave. of the Champions, Palm Beach Gardens, tel. 407/627–2000. Jacket required. Reservations advised. Closed Sun.–Mon. May–Sept. AE, MC, V. Expensive.*

Lodging

The list below is a representative selection of hotels and motels in Palm Beach County. The rate categories in the list are based on the all-year or peak-season price; off-peak rates may be a category or two lower.

The most highly recommended hotels are indicated by a star ★.

Category	Cost*
Very Expensive	over $120
Expensive	$90–$120
Moderate	$50–$90
Inexpensive	under $50

**per double room without 6% state sales tax and modest tourist tax*

The following credit card abbreviations are used: AE, American Express; CB, Carte Blanche; DC, Diners Club; MC, MasterCard; V, Visa.

Very Expensive

Boca Raton Hotel & Club. Architect and socialite Addison Mizner designed and built the original. The tower was added in 1961, the ultramodern Boca Beach Club, in 1981. Room rates during the winter season are based on the modified American plan (including breakfast and dinner). The rooms in the older buildings tend to be smaller and cozily traditional; those in the newer buildings are light, airy and contemporary in color schemes and furnishings. *501 E. Camino Real, Boca Raton 33432, tel. 407/395–3000 or 800/327–0101. 1,000 rooms: 100 in the original 1926 Cloister Inn, 333 in the 1931 addition, 235 in the 27-story Tower Building, 212 in the Boca Beach Club, 120 in the Golf Villas. Facilities: 1½ mi of Atlantic Ocean beach, 4 outdoor freshwater swimming pools, 22 tennis courts (2 lighted), health spa, 23-slip marina, fishing and sailing charters, 7 restaurants, 3 lounges, in-room safes. AE, DC, MC, V.*

Brazilian Court. Built in 1926, the Brazilian Court received new owners and an extensive renovation in 1984–85. The yellow Mediterranean-style buildings still surround a pair of courtyards, where much of the original landscaping survives today. An open loggia with ceiling beams of exposed pecky cypress was enclosed to provide a gracious European-style lobby. A concierge at an antique desk greets you for check-in. All guest rooms feature gold-plated plumbing fixtures, firm mattresses, and valances above the beds and windows. However, no two rooms are alike. *301 Australian Ave., Palm Beach 33480, tel. 407/655–7740 or 800/351–5656. 134 rooms with bath, including 6 suites, rooms for nonsmokers and handicapped guests. Facilities: outdoor heated freshwater swimming pool, cable TV, two restaurants, lounge, 24-hr room service. AE, CB, DC, MC, V.*

The Breakers. This historic seven-story oceanfront resort hotel, built in 1926 and enlarged in 1968, is currently undergoing renovation. At this palatial Italian Renaissance structure, cupids wrestle alligators in the Florentine fountain in front of the main entrance. Inside the lofty lobby, your eyes rise to majestic ceiling vaults and frescoes. The hotel's proud tradition of formality remains. After 7 PM, men and boys must wear jackets and ties in the public areas. (Ties are optional in summer.) The new room decor comes in two color schemes: cool greens and soft pinks in an orchid-patterned English cotton chintz fabric; the other is in blue, with a floral and ribbon chintz. Both designs include white plantation shutters and wall coverings, Chinese porcelain table lamps, and original 1920s furniture restored to its period appearance. The original building has 15 different sizes and shapes of rooms, many a bit cramped by today's standards. If you like a lot of space, ask to be placed in the newer addition. *1 S. County Rd., Palm Beach 33480, tel. 407/655–6611 or 800/833–3141. 528 rooms with bath, including 40 suites. Facilities: 1/2 mi of Atlantic Ocean beachfront, outdoor heated freshwater swimming pool, 19 tennis courts, 2 golf courses, health club with Keiser and Nautilus equipment, men's and women's saunas, lawn bowling, croquet, shuffleboard, shopping arcade with upscale boutiques, 3 restaurants, lounge. AE, CB, DC, MC, V.*

The Colony. Located a block off Worth Avenue, this mid-rise luxury city hotel caters to an older, upscale clientele. The Duke and Duchess of Windsor stayed here. John Lennon once was turned away from the dining room because he arrived tieless. Hotel built in 1947, restored in 1987–88; low-rise maisonettes built in mid-1950s, apartments built in 1960s. A striking lobby mural by Phil Brinkman depicts turn-of-the-century Palm Beach. Room decor is tropical chic, with rattan furnishings and pink, blue, and tropical green pastel fabrics in floral patterns. *155 Hammon Ave., Palm Beach 33480, tel. 407/655–5430, fax 407/659–1793, cable Prestige/Palm Beach. 106 rooms, including 36 suites and apartments. Facilities: outdoor heated freshwater swimming pool, restaurant serves 3 meals daily, dancing nightly with live band, beauty parlor. AE, MC, V. Open Oct. 29–May 1.*

PGA Sheraton Resort. This sportsperson's mecca at PGA National Golf Club underwent a $1.8-million renovation in 1987–88 by an interior designer who likes mauve, peach, and aqua. The resort is headquarters for the Professional Golfer's Association and the U.S. Croquet Association, and hosts many major golf, tennis, and croquet tournaments. *400 Ave. of the Champions, Palm Beach Gardens 33418, tel. 407/627–2000 or 800/325–3535. 358 rooms with bath, including 25 suites, 36 nonsmokers rooms, 14 handicapped rooms, 80 2-bedroom, 2-bath cottages with fully equipped kitchen. Facilities: 4 golf courses, 19 tennis courts (10 lighted), 5 croquet courts, 6 indoor racquetball courts, outdoor freshwater swimming pool, sand beach on 26-acre lake, sailboats and aquacycles for rent, fitness center, sauna, whirlpool, aerobic dance studio, 4 restaurants, 2 lounges, in-room minibars and safes. AE, MC, V.*

Palm Beach Polo and Country Club. Individual villas and condominiums are available in this exclusive 2,200-acre resort where Britain's Prince Charles comes to play polo. Arrange to rent a dwelling closest to the sports activity which interests you: polo, tennis, or golf. Each residence is uniquely designed and furnished by its owner according to standards of quality set by the resort. *13198 Forest Hill Blvd., West Palm Beach 33414, tel. 407/798–7000 or 800/327–4204. 140 privately owned villas and condominiums available for rental when the owners are away. Facilities: 10 outdoor freshwater swimming pools, 24 tennis courts, 2 18-hole golf courses and 1 9-hole course, men's and women's saunas, 10 polo fields, equestrian trails through a nature preserve, 5 stable barns, 2 lighted croquet lawns, squash and racquetball courts, sculling equipment and instruction, 5 dining rooms. AE, DC, MC, V.*

Expensive ★ **The Jupiter Beach Hilton.** This high-rise oceanfront resort hotel is frequented by celebrities and sea turtles. Robby Benson and Carol Burnett, are among the stars who stay here while performing at the nearby Burt Reynolds Jupiter Theater. The sea turtles come ashore each summer to lay their eggs in the sand along this stretch of unspoiled beach. The Jupiter Beach Hilton's beach director leads turtle walks at night to look for nesting mothers. In the morning, he collects the eggs in a holding pen by the beach hut to protect them from predators. When the eggs hatch, he helps the baby turtles dig out and guards them as they scramble into the surf. Human guests are at least as well-pampered by a friendly and efficient staff. The nine-story hotel has interior decor of sophisticated informality. The lobby suggests Singapore, with wicker and bamboo furniture, white-washed wood floors, white ceiling fans, and a plethora of palms, orchids, and other tropical plants. *Indiantown Rd. and Rte. A1A, Jupiter 33477, tel. 407/746–2511, in FL 800/432–1420, elsewhere in the USA 800/821–8791, in Canada 800/228–8810. 197 rooms with bath, including 4 suites, 26 nonsmokers rooms, 2 rooms for handicapped guests. Facilities: outdoor heated freshwater swimming pool, 400 ft of beachfront, 60 cabanas, snorkeling, windsurfing, lighted tennis court, poolside snack bar, boutique, fitness center, restaurant, lounge, cable TV, in-room minibars. AE, CB, DC, MC, V.*

Excursion: Treasure Coast

Numbers in the margin correspond with points of interest on the Treasure Coast map.

1 This excursion north from **Palm Beach** through the Treasure Coast counties of Martin, St. Lucie, and Indian River traverses an area which was remote and sparsely populated as recently as the late 1970s. Resort and leisure-oriented residential development has swollen its population. If you plan to stay overnight or dine at a good restaurant, reservations are a must—here
2 as well as in **West Palm Beach.**

The interior of all three counties is largely devoted to citrus production, and also cattle ranching in rangelands of pine-and-palmetto scrub. St. Lucie and Indian River counties also contain the upper reaches of the vast St. Johns Marsh, headwaters of the largest northward-flowing river in the United States. The St. Johns drains the backside of the Atlantic coastal ridge along two-thirds of the Florida peninsula, and it flows through downtown Jacksonville before emptying into the ocean. If you take Florida's Turnpike from Palm Beach north to the Orlando—Disney World area, you will dip into the edge of St. Johns Marsh about eight miles north of the Fort Pierce exit.

Along the coast, completion of I–95's missing link from Palm Beach Gardens to Fort Pierce in December 1987 eliminated the Treasure Coast's last vestiges of relative seclusion. Hotels, restaurants, and shopping malls already crowd the corridor from I–95 to the beach throughout the 70-mile stretch from Palm Beach north to Vero Beach. The Treasure Coast has become another link in the chain of municipalities that some Floridians call "the city of U.S. 1."

What remains of the old Treasure Coast are limited resources of beaches, boating waters, fishing, and wildlife. Demand for those resources has increased, but there's still enough to go around if everyone will be polite and respect Mother Nature.

Of special interest in this area are the sea turtles which come ashore from April to August to lay their eggs on the beaches. Volunteers collect freshly laid turtle eggs and take them to protected hatcheries. The young turtles are most vulnerable when they emerge from the eggs and crawl to the water, so several groups maintain saltwater tanks to hold the hatchlings for up to a year. Their growth during this period gives them a better chance to survive after being returned to the sea.

Exploring Treasure Coast

This tour takes you north from Palm Beach along the coast as far as Vero Beach but you can break away at any intermediate point and return to Palm Beach on I–95.

From downtown West Palm Beach, take U.S. 1 about five miles north to Blue Heron Boulevard (Rte. A1A) in Riviera Beach, turn right, and cross the **Jerry Thomas Bridge** onto Singer Island. Sightseeing boats depart from **Phil Foster Park** on the island side of the bridge.

Continue on Rte. A1A as it turns north onto Ocean Blvd. past hotels and high-rise condominiums to **Ocean Reef Park** (3900 N. Ocean Dr., Riviera Beach, tel. 407/964–4420), a snorkeling spot

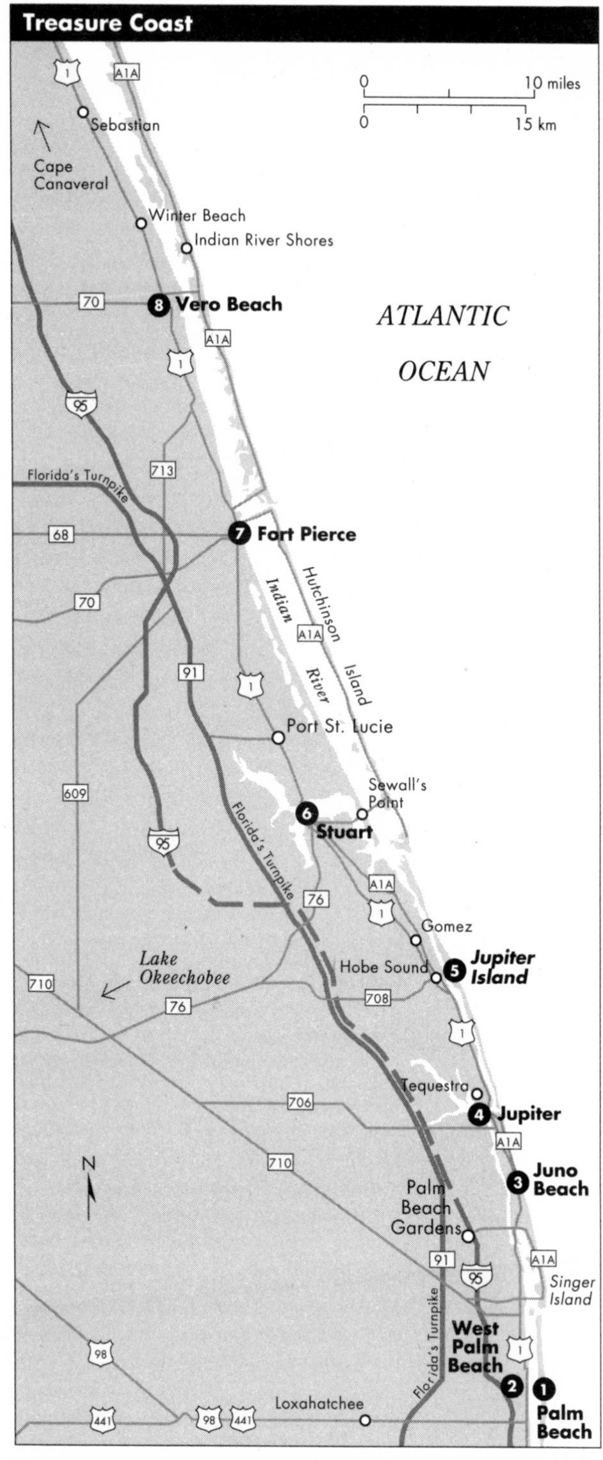
Treasure Coast
0
10 miles
0
15 km
1
A1A
Sebastian
Cape Canaveral
Winter Beach
Indian River Shores
70
8 Vero Beach
ATLANTIC
OCEAN
A1A
1
95
713
Florida's Turnpike
68
7 Fort Pierce
Hutchinson
Island
Indian
River
A1A
70
91
1
Port St. Lucie
Sewall's Point
609
6 Stuart
Florida's Turnpike
95
A1A
76
1
Gomez
Lake Okeechobee
Hobe Sound
5 Jupiter Island
710
708
76
1
Tequestra
706
4 Jupiter
A1A
3 Juno Beach
710
N
Palm Beach Gardens
91
95
A1A
Singer Island
West Palm Beach
1
98
Florida's Turnpike
2
1
Palm Beach
441
98
441
Loxahatchee

where the reefs are close to shore in shallow water. You may see angelfish, sergeant-majors, rays, robin fish, and occasionally a Florida lobster (actually a species of saltwater crayfish). Wear canvas sneakers and cloth gloves.

Go north on Rte. A1A to **John D. MacArthur State Park** 10900 Rte. A1A, North Palm Beach, tel. 407/964–4420), which offers more good snorkeling along almost two miles of beach, and access to the mangrove swamps in the upper reaches of Lake Worth.

North of MacArthur State Park, Rte. A1A rejoins U.S. 1, then veers east again 1½ miles north at Juno Beach. Take Rte.
3 A1A north to the **Children's Museum of Juno Beach,** established by Eleanor N. Fletcher, "the turtle lady of Juno Beach." Museum displays interpret the sea turtles' natural history; hatchlings are raised in saltwater tanks, tagged and released into the surf. The museum conducts guided turtle watches June 1–July 15, at the height of the nesting season. *1111 Ocean Dr., Juno Beach, tel. 407/627–8280. Admission free. Open Tues.–Sat. 10–3, Sun. 1–3.*

4 From Juno Beach north to **Jupiter,** Rte. A1A runs for almost four miles atop the beachfront dunes. West of the road, about half the land is undeveloped, with endangered native plant communities. The road veers away from the dunes at **Carlin Park** (400 Rte., A1A, Jupiter, tel. 407/964–4420), which provides beach frontage, covered picnic pavilions, hiking, and cardiovascular fitness trails, two tennis courts, and fishing sites.

At the northwest corner of Indiantown Road and Rte. A1A is **Burt Reynolds Jupiter Theater.** Reynolds grew up in Jupiter; his father was Palm Beach County sheriff. His contacts and friendships have attracted more than 150 Broadway and Hollywood stars to perform here since the theater opened in 1979. The theater presents 10–12 productions a year; Reynolds himself sometimes acts and/or directs. Of the 449 seats, 254 are Las Vegas–style: you dine and watch the show from your table (rows G–M); the other 195 are standard front-of-the-house theater seats (rows A–F) for patrons who dine in a separate room decorated with tropical fish tanks and etched-glass art representing each year's productions. *1001 E. Indiantown Rd., Jupiter, tel. 407/746–5566. Ticket price includes 3-course meal. Open Tues.–Sat., dinner at 6, performance 8:30; Wed., Sat., Sun. matinees, lunch (or Sun. brunch) 11:30 AM, performance 1:30 PM. Jackets required. Reservations 2 wks in advance advised. AE, MC, V.*

Leave the theater grounds on Indiantown Road, go west to U.S. 1, and turn right. About a mile north of Jupiter Island, the Loxahatchee Historical Society's new 4,800-square-foot museum opened in the summer of 1988. Permanent exhibits in preparation will emphasize Seminole Indians, the steamboat era, pioneer life on the Loxahatchee River, shipwrecks, railroads and modern-day development. A pioneer dwelling at the mouth of the river, the Dubois Home, is open Sunday afternoons; ask for directions at the museum. *In Burt Reynolds Park, Box 1506, Jupiter, tel. 407/747–6639.*

Continue north on U.S. 1 across the Loxahatchee River. The 105-foot-tall **Jupiter Lighthouse,** east of the bridge, is the oldest structure in Palm Beach County, built 1855–59. To reach the lighthouse and a small museum of local history on the ground floor, turn east on Route 707, then take the first right into Lighthouse Park. *No phone. Admission free. Open Sun. noon–2:30.*

5 Take Rte. 707 north from the lighthouse onto **Jupiter Island.** Just north of the Martin County line, stop at the Nature Conservancy's 113-acre **Blowing Rocks Preserve,** with plant communities native to beachfront dune, strand (the landward side of the dunes), marsh, and hammock (tropical hardwood forest). Sea grape, cabbage palms, saw palmetto, and sea oats help to anchor the dunes. The floral beauty of Indian blanket, dune sunflower, and goldenrod carpets the ground. You may see pelicans, seagulls, ospreys, redbellied and pileated woodpeckers, and a profusion of warblers in spring and fall. A trail takes you over the dune to the beach. At high tide, spray shoots up through holes in the largest Anastasia limestone outcropping on the Atlantic coast. At dead low tide, you can walk on the seaward side of the rocks and peer into caves and solution holes. Best time to go is early morning, before the crowds. The parking lot holds just 18 cars, with room for three cars to wait; Jupiter Island police will ticket cars parked along the road shoulder. *Box 3795, Tequesta, tel. 407/575–2297. Open 6–5. Admission by donation. No food, drink, ice chests, pets, or spearfishing allowed. No rest rooms.*

At the north end of Jupiter Island, **Hobe Sound National Wildlife Refuge** (13640 S.E. Federal Hwy., tel. 407/546–6141) has a 3½-mile beach where turtles nest and shells wash ashore in abundance. To visit the Hobe Sound Nature Center (tel. 407/546–2067) at refuge headquarters, turn south where Rte. 707 rejoins U.S. 1 in the town of Hobe Sound. The nature center's interpretive displays include turtle skeletons; guided wilderness tours are available by reservation.

Just south of the nature center is the entrance to **Jonathon Dickinson State Park,** 10,284 acres of pine and palmetto flatwoods, mangrove river swamp, and the winding upper northwest fork of the Loxahatchee River—part of the federal government's wild and scenic rivers program. *14800 S.E. Federal Hwy., Hobe Sound, tel. 407/546–2771. Open daily 8–sundown. Admission: $1 driver, 50 cents per passenger. Facilities: bicycle trail, cabins, camping, rental canoes and rowboats, snack bar.*

6 Turn north and take U.S. 1 through some unavoidable commercial development to **Stuart,** then rejoin Rte. A1A northbound to Hutchinson Island. Stop at the pastel-pink **Elliott Museum,** built in 1961 in honor of inventor Sterling Elliott. On display is an early model of his Elliott Addressing Machine, forerunner of today's Addressograph machines. He also invented a four-wheel bicycle, the quadricycle; the mechanism that makes its wheels turn is the basis of the automobile differential. In addition to Elliott's inventions, the museum features antique automobiles, dolls and toys, and fixtures from an early general store, blacksmith shop, and apothecary shop. Children enjoy feeding coins to a voracious collection of 19th-century mechanical banks. *825 N.E. Ocean Blvd., Stuart, tel. 407/225–1961. Open daily 1–4. Admission: $2.50 adults, 50 cents children 6–13, under 6 free.*

A mile south of the Elliott Museum stands the **House of Refuge Museum,** built in 1875 and now restored to its original appearance. It's one of 10 such structures erected by the U.S. Life Saving Service (an ancestor of the Coast Guard) to aid stranded sailors along Florida's then-remote Atlantic Coast. The keeper here patrolled the beach looking for shipwreck victims whose vessels foundered on Gilbert's Bar, an offshore reef. Exhibits include antique lifesaving equipment, maps, ships' logs, artifacts from nearby wrecks, and boatmaking tools. Turtle pens in an old cistern nurture hatchlings from eggs collected along Hutchinson Island's beach. A 35-foot watchtower in the front yard was used during World War II by submarine spotters. *301 S.E. MacArthur Blvd., Stuart, tel. 407/225–1875. Open Tues. –Sun. 1–4, closed Mon. Admission: $1 adults, 50 cents children 6–13, under 6 free.*

7 Other artifacts of the region's history are on display in **Fort Pierce Inlet State Recreation Area,** at the St. Lucie County Historical Museum. To get there, take Rte. A1A across South Beach Causeway into Fort Pierce for a mile of U.S. 1, bypassing Fort Pierce Inlet (which divides Hutchinson Island), then veer east across North Beach Causeway into the recreation area. Museum exhibits include treasure from a Spanish fleet wrecked in a 1715 hurricane. A diorama illustrates a Seminole Indian encampment with a *chickee* (palm-thatched shelter) and dugout canoe. On the grounds is a restored and furnished pioneer Cracker-style house dating from 1907. The recreation area also includes a small museum dedicated to World War II frogmen, Pepper Beach, and a wildlife refuge on Jack Island accessible only by footbridge. *414 Seaway Dr., Fort Pierce, tel. 407/464–6635. Open Tues.–Sat. 10–4, Sun. noon–4. Admission: $1 adults, 50 cents children 6–12, under 6 free.*

North of Pepper Beach, development increases along Rte.
A1A as you approach Vero Beach, but the city provides beach-
8 access parks at intervals. Stop at **The Driftwood Resort** (3150 Ocean Dr., Vero Beach, tel. 407/231–0550), an unusual-looking beachfront hotel and restaurant built largely of driftwood by its eccentric founder, Waldo Sexton.

This concludes the Treasure Coast excursion. Take Rte. 60 west through Vero Beach to I–95 for the return to Palm Beach.

7 The Florida Keys

Orientation
by Kathryn Kilgore

The Florida Keys stretch southwest from mainland Florida for 180 miles, from Biscayne Bay to the Dry Tortugas. If you take U.S. 1 south out of Miami, you enter the Keys at Key Largo, just after the southernmost "Crocodile Crossing" sign. Past this point, there are only alligators. As you drive down U.S. 1 through the islands, the silvery blue and green Atlantic, with its great living reef, are on your left, and the Gulf of Mexico and the back country are on your right. Sometimes, the ocean and the gulf are a mile or so apart. At other times, on the narrowest landfill islands, they are separated only by the road, much of which was built on top of Henry Flagler's old railroad, which was constructed between 1905 and 1916 but was washed away by a hurricane after only 20 years.

The road varies from a frustrating traffic-clogged trap to a mystical pathway skimming across the sea. There are more islands than you will be able to remember, 42 bridges, and a lot of landfill. Follow the little green mile markers (also left over from the railroad) by the side of U.S. 1, and even if you lose track of the names of the islands, you won't get lost. There are many places to stop and swim, snorkel, fish, walk, bike, picnic, or take a boat out into the back country or the ocean. When the sun isn't bright and directly overhead, the little mangrove islands can be haunting.

The Keys are subtle and take getting used to. Their beauty is bound to the changes in the light and in the sea. Low, plant-covered islands lie scattered in the shallow, clear water, mysterious and deserted. There's a funky feeling of decay everywhere. The ocean is as omnipresent and inviting as the land, perhaps even more so: docks, boats, shore, and shallow water lure you. People find themselves stopping to swim and fish along the side of the road. The peacefulness of the Keys comes from the water—so close, waveless, and almost always within view. Be prepared: This place doesn't look like Florida.

Along the reefs and among the islands, there are over 600 kinds of fish to swim with, catch, or eat. There are strange trees and plants: poisonwood, strangler fig, gumbo- limbo, Jamaica dogwood, lignum vitae, marberry, pigeon plum, satin leaf, shortleaf fig, stopper, West Indian mahogany, wild lime, wild tamarind, and willow bustic. There are miniature deer. There are state parks and places to camp. There is a sky full of blue, and a mirror for an ocean. People will lie to you about the weather; in the summer the temperature rarely goes over the low 90s, but in the winter, although it never freezes, it can be damp and cold, with temperatures occasionally hitting the low 40s.

There are many things to see in the Keys, but first you have to remind yourself to get off the only highway, U.S. 1, which is lined with junk and has the strange seductive power of keeping you to itself. If you can manage to leave this road, you will meet the local people—among the more interesting remaining attractions in the Keys, because so much else has become commercial. (In Key West, they will even try to sell you the sunset.) The old road that U.S. 1 replaced is an easy detour to start with, especially in the Upper Keys (sometimes it almost parallels the highway), and wherever it goes, it comes back eventually to U.S. 1.

The Upper, Middle, and Lower Keys are essentially different from Key West, the final island accessible by road. Key West was a 19th-century salvaging boomtown with a deep-water port, at a time when the rest of the Keys were mangrove thickets and hammocks (subtropical hardwood forests) inhabited by pirates and Indians and infested with mosquitoes. Today, except for the much vaster confluence of ethnic, sexual, and social backgrounds and its old buildings and Conch houses in Key West, you might almost miss this difference because all the Keys have been built up in a similar fashion in the past 15 years. The old Key West is history (*see* Key West).

Getting Around

By Plane Piedmont, Eastern, and Delta have flights (some hourly) from Miami (with connections to other Florida cities) to Marathon or Key West. *Marathon Airport* (tel. 305/743–2155) and *Key West Airport* (tel. 305/296–5439) are the two airports in the Keys.

By Car You can get down the Keys by car via U.S. 1. Take the highway south out of Homestead, and you will end up in Key West in about 3½ hours. For a scenic tree-lined detour, take the left fork off U.S. 1, just past Florida City, to the Card Sound toll bridge, which ends in north Key Largo. Go right on Rte. 905, which rejoins U.S. 1, heading south to Key West.

When driving on the Keys, watch for the mile markers—little green-and-white markers (MM) that appear on the right of the road. These markers begin with zero at Key West and tell you how much farther you have to go. They are generally the *only* addresses you'll find along the Keys. If you ask for directions, residents will respond by telling you which mile marker a place is at or near.

Maps: The most readily available maps are *Teall's Guides* of the Upper, Middle, and Lower Keys. Nationwide Distributors (12027 S.W. 117 Ct., Miami 33186) also puts out two roadmaps, one for the Upper and one for the Lower Keys, that are the best maps if you can find them.

By Bus You can take the Greyhound/Trailways bus (tel. 305/871–1810 in Miami, tel. 305/296–9072 in Key West) from Miami, which stops at many points along the Keys and ends in Key West.

Key Limo (tel. 305/743–6939 or 800/531–4772 in FL, 800/-826–6754 in rest of USA) is a passenger van that goes forth and back twice a day from Miami Airport to Marathon and Key West, stopping wherever you want to go in between.

By Boat If you go in your own boat down the Keys, there are, of course, charts and marine guides.

To explore the waters off the Keys, you can rent sailboats (try **Tropical Sailboats** on Higgs Beach in Key West, tel. 305/294–2696). Motorboats, canoes, and other watercraft are also available at many of the northern Keys.

En Route and in Key West Once you get to Key West, transportation by bike or moped is easy (there are rentals on almost every block). You can also walk to most places.

Cars are rented at **Thrifty** (2516 N. Roosevelt Blvd., tel. 305/296–6514). There are also buses and taxis to take you around Key West (tel. 305/296–6666). Information on all forms of transportation is available through local chambers of commerce (see Important Addresses and Numbers) or through Florida Keys Information (tel. 800/FLA–KEYS).

Guided Tours

John Pennekamp Reef State Park (MM 102.5) has snorkeling tours. The park also has a glass-bottom boat that goes out for 2½ hours three times a day. For information, *tel. 305/451–3200.*

Theater of the Sea (MM 84.5) has a continuous guided tour of its fish tanks and a porpoise show. *Tel. 305/664–2431. Admission: $8.50 adults, $5 children.*

The Park Service (MM 79) has tours of Lignumbille Key and Indian Key at 8:30 and 1:30, except Tuesday and Wednesday. *Tel. 305/664–4815. Admission: $5 adults, $2.50 children under 12.*

Within Key West

The Conch Train, which leaves from Mallory Square, tours the whole island, giving the general story of Key West in 1½ hours. *303 Front St., tel. 305/294–5161. Admission: $9 adults, $3 children 3–11.*

The Trolley does much the same as the Conch Train, except it will go down smaller, narrower streets. It also leaves from Mallory Square *(tel. 305/296–6685).*

Conch Classic Tours's red Waco biplane, with a loop-loving pilot, will take you around the island by air *(tel. 305/296–0727).* Rides start at $20.

Key West Seaplane Service offers a four-hour round-trip excursion to Fort Jefferson on Dry Tortuga with low-altitude viewing of the Gulf of Mexico and the Keys. During the two-hour stopover, you can take a self-guided tour of the fort or snorkel in the waters. *On Stock Island behind the golf course on Junior College Rd., tel. 305/294–6978. Cost: $99 adults, $55 children 3–6.*

Special-Interest Tours

Each January and February, the Old Island Restoration Foundation (OIRF) sponsors a three-weekend **House and Garden Tour** that takes you to five or six different homes per weekend for $8. The four categories of houses shown are Old Historic, Uniquely Located, Famous Occupants, and Island Living, which about covers it. *OIRF, Hospitality House, Mallory Sq., or Box 689, Key West 33040, tel. 305/294–9501.*

There is also the Annual Key West Literary Seminar, each January. For information, contact the *Literary Seminar, Box 391, Sugarloaf Shores 33044, tel. 305/745–3640.*

Important Addresses and Numbers

Tourist Information

Florida Keys Information (tel. 800/FLA–KEYS) offers information on all the Keys—places to stay and things to do, entertainment schedules, transportation, and guides.

Maps, fishing data, transportation, lodging information, guides, and scheduled events are also available from the following chambers of commerce, open 9–5, Mon.–Sat. (Key West is open Sun.):

The Upper Keys Chamber of Commerce (MM 105.5, Key Largo, tel. 305/451–1414);

Islamorada Chamber of Commerce (MM 82.5, Box 915, Islamorada, tel. 305/664–4503);

Greater Marathon Chamber of Commerce (3330 Overseas Hwy., Marathon, tel. 305/743–5417);

Lower Keys Chamber of Commerce (Big Pine Key, tel. 305/872–2411);

Greater Key West Chamber of Commerce (off Mallory Sq., tel. 305/294–2578).

Emergencies Dial 911 for **police** and **ambulance** in an emergency.

Hospitals **Mariner's Hospital** (MM 88.5, tel. 305/852–9222). **Fisherman's Hospital** (MM 49, tel. 305/743–5533) has a 24-hour emergency room. For the Key West area: **Florida Keys Memorial Hospital** (5900 Junior College Rd., Stock Island, tel. 305/ 294–5531) and **De Poo Hospital** (1200 Kennedy Dr., Key West, tel. 305/294–5183).

Helpline (Upper and Middle Keys, tel. 800/341–4343; Lower Keys, tel. 305/296–HELP) offers counseling and information on community services.

Miami to Key West

As noted above, attractions are listed by island or mile marker, written as MM. Numbers in the margin correspond with points of interest on the Florida Keys map.

Exploring the Upper Keys

1 **Key Largo** (MM 110) was known as Rock Harbor, but the town was renamed after John Huston shot a few scenes of his 1948 Bogart-Bacall film here in the Caribbean Club. Although most of *Key Largo* was shot in Hollywood, Bogart became an instant celebrity here. Now you can see the original riverboat from *The African Queen* rotting alongside the highway in front of a totally unrelated restaurant.

The Caribbean Club (MM104) is a bikers' bar, with a nice view, through the Harley-Davidsons, of the Gulf.

2 The **John Pennekamp Reef State Park** (MM102.5) is the first place on U.S. 1 where you can stop to snorkel or dive off the Keys' barrier reef. This reef, the only living coral reef in North America, runs four to seven miles offshore from Key Largo to the Dry Tortugas, and it is, for many, the main event in the Keys. Even if you don't go diving, you'll notice the reef, which causes the absence of waves on the Keys' Atlantic beaches and, therefore, the bone-jarring lack of sand. Pennekamp Park covers 2,289 acres of land, 52,722 acres of water, and 21 miles of reef. There are nature trails and guided underwater tours. Sections of the reef differ, depending on the depth of the sea and human or natural damage. In December 1987, two U.S. Coast Guard cutters were sunk in 125 feet of park water to make more (artificial) reef. An underwater statue here is called *Christ of the Deep.* Call about camping information and reservations (tel. 305/451–1202). For information on snorkeling, scuba tours, and boat and equipment rental, contact *Coral Reef Park Co., Box 1560, Key Largo 33037, tel. 305/451–1621 or 800/432–2871.*

In addition to the day-long scuba-diving course Fridays ($70), the park has week-long courses ($210). Snorkeling tours are at 9 AM, noon, and 3 PM ($18). There's a snorkeling and sailing trip ($50 a day). Scuba trips ($27.50) are at 9:30 and 1:30. The park dive shop rents equipment, boats, and houseboats. Pennekamp's glass-bottom boat, the *Discovery,* does a 2½-hour tour over the reef three times a day. *Tel. 305/451–1621. Cost: $10 adults, $5 children.*

Because of Pennekamp's popularity, if you want to sleep in the Key Largo area, make reservations in advance.

Between MM 106 and MM 99.5 north of Tavernier are several dive shops, including *American Diving Headquarters* (MM 106, tel. 305/451–0037), *Quiescence* (MM 103.2, tel. 305/451–2440), *Sea Dwellers* (MM 100, tel. 305/451–3640), *Ocean Divers* (MM 100, tel. 305/451–1113), and *Diver's World* (MM 99.5, tel. 305/451–3200).

3 The town of **Tavernier** was named after a pirate. Harry Harris Park is on the ocean side, north of Tavernier. Turn left at Burton Drive near MM 92.5 and head past the trailers. There's a shopping mall, Tavernier Towne, at MM 91. You'll end up in the vanished town of Planter, settled in 1866 but abandoned when

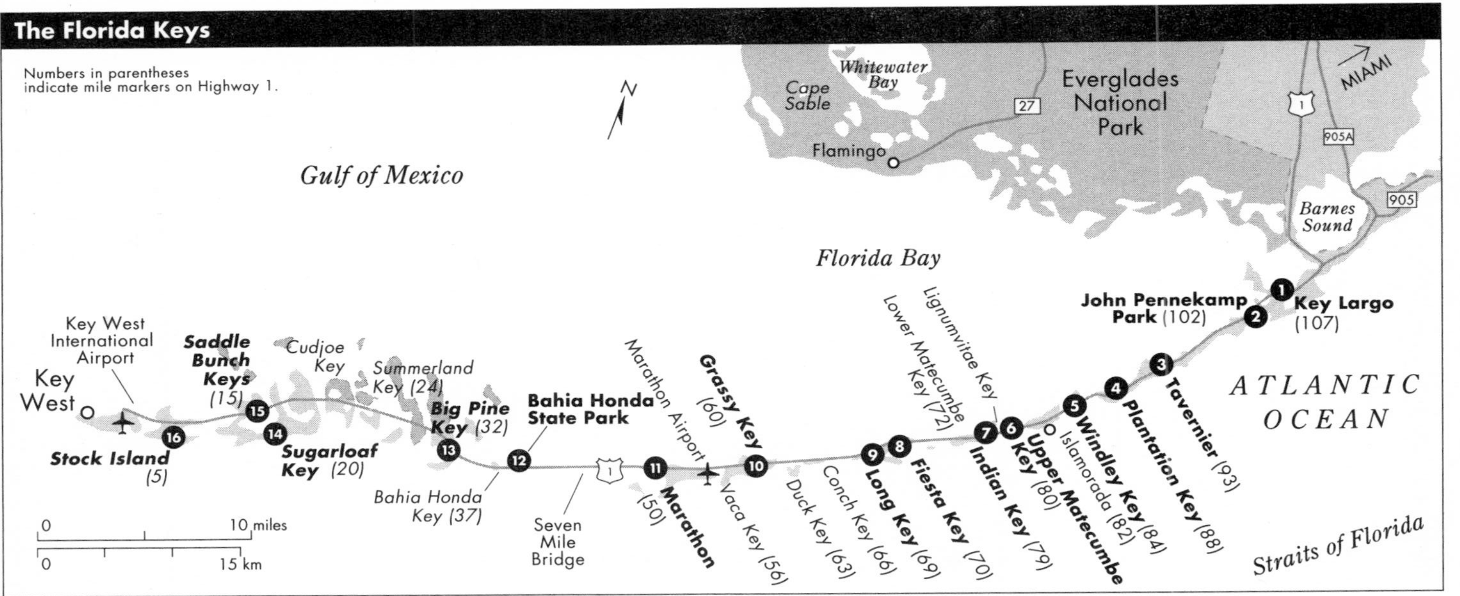
The Florida Keys
Numbers in parentheses
indicate mile markers on Highway 1.
N
Gulf of Mexico
Cape Sable
Whitewater Bay
Flamingo
27
Everglades National Park
1
905A
MIAMI
Barnes Sound
905
Florida Bay
Key Largo (107)
John Pennekamp Park (102)
Tavernier (93)
Plantation Key (88)
Windley Key (84)
Islamorada (82)
Upper Matecumbe Key (80)
Lignumvitae Key
Lower Matecumbe Key (72)
Indian Key (79)
Fiesta Key (70)
Long Key (69)
Conch Key (66)
Duck Key (63)
Grassy Key (60)
Vaca Key (56)
Marathon Airport
Marathon (50)
Seven Mile Bridge
Bahia Honda State Park
Bahia Honda Key (37)
Big Pine Key (32)
Summerland Key (24)
Cudjoe Key
Sugarloaf Key (20)
Saddle Bunch Keys (15)
Stock Island (5)
Key West International Airport
Key West
ATLANTIC OCEAN
Straits of Florida
0
10 miles
0
15 km
1
2
3
4
5
6
7
8
9
10
11
12
13
14
15
16

the railroad came through. Tavernier also has some "hurricane-proof" reinforced-concrete houses, built after the 1935 hurricane with the aid of the Red Cross. The houses were windproof, but because the cement was mixed with seawater, the rods inside the concrete rusted and cracked the walls.

Pineapple and banana plantations, owned by Conchs (early Tory settlers from the Bahamas) who moved up from Vaca Key,
4 once covered **Plantation Key** (MM 90), but the remote settlers could not compete with the Cuban market and the soil became depleted. There's a reef off Plantation Key, and there's a midden (a pile of stones and shells from a Caloosa Indian feast).

5 The Theater of the Sea (MM 84.5) by the highway on **Windley Key** has a guided tour that will introduce you to the Keys fish and a wacky dolphin show, where you can see a dolphin imitate an airplane—noise and all. The theater is set in a 1907 railroad quarry and is one of the oldest marine parks in the world. The quarries here once produced Key limestone, which was used as trim for buildings all over the United States. *Tel. 305/664–2431. Admission: $8.50 adults, $5 children 4–12. Continuous shows 9:30–4. You can swim with the dolphins (cost: $50).*

6 **Upper Matecumbe Key** (MM 80) was the target of the monster 1935 hurricane. (Matecumbe means "kill man" in a mixture of Spanish and the native Indian tongue.) When the hurricane struck, a train full of people fleeing Islamorada (many of them WPA workers building the new highway) was hit by a tidal wave and 200-mph winds, which knocked the cars off the rails. Altogether some 800 people died in the hurricane, and it was the end of Flagler's railroad.

For fishing and tournament information: *Holiday Isla* (MM 84.5, tel. 305/664–2321) or *Whale Harbor Marina* (MM 84, tel. 305/664–4511).

The Cheeca Lounge (tel. 305/664–4651) was once the last of the elegant fishing clubs in the Keys, but it's been totally rebuilt. It's in the town of **Islamorada** (MM 82), still on Upper Matecumbe, which has a reputation as a fishing spot. There are a lot of restaurants here (*see* Dining) and some good coral offshore for diving.

Around MM 81.5 is the WPA hurricane monument to the dead. Its design depicts wind-whipped palms.

There are tours of **Lignumvitae** (offshore at MM 79), an uninhabited virgin hammock, with vegetation that was once typical of Florida's original forest. (Lignum vitae, a dense-wood tree, was once used as the wood for boat hulls.) For information and reservations, contact *Long Key State Recreation Area* (tel. 305/664–4815). Park Service ferry-operated tours to Lignumvitae run daily except Tuesday and Wednesday, leaving at 8:30 and 1:30. Cost: $5 adults, $2.50 children. *Bud 'n' Mary's* rents boats and conducts tours. Cost for a 16-foot, 25-HP boat for four persons: $25 half-day, $70 a day.

A lot of shipwrecked Frenchmen were supposedly killed by the
7 Caloosa Indians on **Indian Key** (out in the water to the left near MM 79). Later, in 1840, a number of refugees from another Indian attack here (this time by Seminoles) fled to Key West. One of them was wrecker Jacob Houseman, who had established his personal salvaging station and resort hotel on Indian Key. It was in 1832 that John J. Audubon, while anchored off Indian Key, discovered some new (to him) species of birds, including

the roseate tern. You can take your own boat out to Indian Key, or you can rent one from Bud 'n' Mary's.

Off the **Lower Matecumbe Keys** (MM 75), Alligator Reef Lighthouse, built in 1873, is visible.

8 Craig Key and Fiesta Key were made from landfill. **Fiesta Key** (MM 70) has trailer and tenting facilities and snorkeling. **Layton,** on the northwestern side of Long Key (MM 67.5), is a city incorporated in 1963. It was run by its mayor and incorporator, Del Layton, until his death in 1987.

9 **Long Key** is the home of the Long Key State Recreation Area (MM 67.5), which has rangers, a camping area, facilities for camper-trailers, and many birds. It's a long walk into shallow water and is, thus, less than perfect for swimming. You can take a guided overnight canoe trip on the second Saturday of each month if you bring your own canoe and equipment (tel. 305/664–4815 for canoe-trip reservations and park information).

Long Key was the site of the Long Key Fishing Club, where Zane Grey, writer of Westerns, used to vacation and fish. The old club was built in 1906 by Henry M. Flagler from an abandoned construction camp, but the 1935 hurricane destroyed it.

Exploring the Middle and Lower Keys

Flagler's now-abandoned railroad bridge, the Long Key Viaduct, with its 180 arches, parallels the new bridge into Conch Key (MM 65.5), where you can see stacks of lobster and crab traps.

10 On **Grassy Key** (MM 59) is the chipped dolphin monument, a leftover from Flipper's Sea School, now the Dolphin Research Center. There is no sign, but if you go in, you'll find that the center is working on human/dolphin interaction. The staff will take you on a tour. "Educational walking tours" are conducted Wednesday–Sunday at 9:30, 11, 1, and 3:30. For $50, you can (by booking on the first day of the month) have a "dolphin encounter" and swim with the dolphins. For $630, you can participate in Dolphinlab, a one-week program (including room and board) on the biology, behavior, husbandry, research, and training of dolphins by hands-on experience. *Box Dolphin, Marathon Shore 33052, tel. 305/289–1121 or 305/289–0002.*

For the next few miles (MM 58–54), as you get ready for a Marathon traffic jam, you have a chance to spend time with the mangroves and the above-ground water pipeline that ever so slowly pumps the Keys' water supply all the way down to Key West.

After the bridge into **Vaca Kay** there's Captain Hook's Marina (MM 33, tel. 305/743–2444), which has charter boats, particularly for spearfishing. Vaca Key once had farmlands, freshwater wells, and cows. It was the end of Flagler's railroad for three years (1908–11) while construction proceeded on the great **Seven Mile Bridge.** Now, Vaca Key is mostly the community of Marathon. If you're not ready for Marathon's shopping-mall architecture and endless highway reconstruction work, you can drive Sombrero Road at MM 50 past the S.S. *Winter Queen* (which goes to the Tortugas for fishing, tel. 305/743–6969) to Sombrero Beach, a long and pretty beach with some ancient pitted shoreline coral that you might mistake for mud. There's sand, Australian pines, lots of grass, picnic tables, and many signs telling you what you can't do. Straight out from the shore is Sombrero Lighthouse.

11 The Gulf Stream, five miles offshore from **Marathon** (MM 50), is the site for famous shark, sailfish, and marlin sportfishing tournaments. You can hunt lobsters in season (Aug.–Mar.) and can legally spear fish one mile offshore. Hurricane Resort (MM 49.5) has charter information (tel. 305/743–2393), as does the Marathon Chamber of Commerce (tel. 305/743–5417).

In 1982, Flagler's railroad bridge was replaced with the longest continuous bridge in the U.S. (65 feet high), where, every April, the **Seven-Mile-Bridge Run for Marathon marathon** is held. Part of the original bridge still exists, rising over tiny Pigeon Key, where old houses built by the railroad sit empty among the palms, inhabited by a caretaker, awaiting fate (rumor has it that the island may become a park).

12 **Bahia Honda** ("deep bay" in Spanish) **Key** (MM 37) has one of the two best beaches on the Keys, at Bahia Honda State Park (tel. 305/872–2353). There is *sand* on this beach, and a picnic area. The swimming is quite good. There are big palms and the piers of the old railroad bridge. There's camping, a nature trail, a marina, a boat ramp, a dive shop, Windsurfer rentals, and several new cottages for rent. The park borders on the fastest, deepest channel between any of the Keys.

When you cross over the Bahia Honda Bridge, you're in the **Lower Keys.**

13 **Big Pine Key** (MM 32) has deserted dead-end roads that have a creepy feel to them. Big Pine (eight by two miles) is second in size to Key Largo. It is limestone-based and covered in pines, scrub, and cacti. It feels far less than tropical, although it's deep in the only tropical part of the continental United States. It has been burned and bulldozed by settlers for centuries, and it doesn't look quite right. Some geologists theorize that Big Pine is part of the Appalachian Ridge, unlike the rest of the Keys.

It's worth going to the National Key Deer Refuge (at MM 31, turn right onto Rte. 940, then take the left fork, otherwise known as Big Pine Rd. or Prison Rd.) to see the little Key deer; the pine and palm forest; Watson's Hammock, full of large tropical hardwood trees; and the blue hole, with its alligator. The Key deer, an endangered species, are thought to be a subspecies of the white-tail deer. They are about 2½ feet tall. Drive through the inhabited areas of Big Pine Key, and you will eventually come to the **No Name Key Bridge,** a nice place to lean over Bogie Channel with everybody else and fish with a hand line. On No Name Key, the one paved road dead-ends at a pile of rocks. There are a few spooky houses and no electricity on this island.

Little Torch Key, Middle Torch, and **Big Torch** (MM 28) were named for the torchwood tree, which burns easily when green. The soapberry tree grows here, too; if you sprinkle its seeds on calm water, the fish will get "stoned" and float to the surface to be grabbed (they say). You can still find Key limes growing wild in the Torches. There's a long road to nowhere on Big Torch Key. On Little Torch, the Torch Tides Bar (once the Island Woman Bar) has a sign in front that reads Harley Parking Only: All Others Will Be Crushed.

Seven miles off the coast of **Ramrod Key** is a reef called **Looe Key,** a national marine sanctuary, considered the most beautiful reef in the Keys. Among other dive shops, *Reef Divers* (tel. 305/872–4145) at the Looe Key Reef Resort (MM 27) will take you there. The Looe Key Reef Resort is an inexpensive, popular place to stay (*see* Lodging).

14 On **Sugarloaf Key** (MM 20), which used to have a sponge farm and a famous old fishing camp called Pirate's Cove, you'll find the Sugarloaf Lodge (MM 17), only somewhat decayed, with a marina, gas station, tennis courts, swimming pool, an airstrip, and a lagoon with *one* old porpoise (called Sugar) in it (*see* Lodging).

In the driveway of the Sugarloaf Lodge is a replica of the bat tower, which might remind you to visit the real Bat Tower (MM 17) down the dirt road past the lodge. Built in 1929 by a Mr. Perky, it was supposed to attract the bats that would eat the mosquitoes, but it never attracted anything.

15 In the **Saddlebunch Keys,** above Saddlebunch No. 3, you'll find the Bay Point Inn (MM 15), a slightly run-down roadside bar and restaurant. They used to burn mangroves in these keys to make Key West's charcoal. Smugglers and the hijackers of smugglers lay low here.

Next is **Big Coppitt** and then **Boca Chica Key** (MM 10), the Navy base. You may not notice the Navy until later, when a sonic boom jars an island or a high wedge of fighters crosses the sky.

16 Soon you will enter **Stock Island** (MM 5), just before Key West. You should now notice Mount Trashmore, a smoldering local garbage dump that is the highest point in the Lower Keys. When you arrive in Stock Island, you may want to go to the Cow Key Marina (at 5th Ave. and 5th St.). Here, you'll find the Boca Chica Bar, which is a very-late-night sleazy bar. This is where Tom McGuane's *92 In the Shade* was filmed.

Stock Island has *a lot* of trailers. Some of the people who once lived in Key West, but who no longer can afford it, now live here in their trailers. Stock Island is a service island, without any town. There's no old conch houses to look at, no beaches, and not much to attract tourists, even though it does house the 18-hole Key West Resort Golf Course (tel. 305/294–5232); the Florida Keys Memorial Hospital (tel. 305/294–5531); the Tennessee Williams Fine Arts Center (tel. 305/294–6232), which brings all sorts of interesting music and dance and theater to the Lower Keys; Florida Keys Community College; the Key West Seaplane Service (tel. 305/294–6978), which has daily flights to Fort Jefferson and the Dry Tortugas; the Oceanside Marina, which has charter boats; and the Key West Kennel Club (tel. 305/294–9517), the dog-racing track. Most of the Key West fishing and shrimping fleet has moved to Stock Island's Safe Harbor, where you can walk around and peer at the boats or buy fresh fish. The mysterious Key West Botanical Garden (take the last road to the right before Key West) has narrow paths wandering among labeled trees. It is a restful place to visit.

What to See and Do with Children

If your children like to fish, there are plenty of bridges along U.S. 1 to hang a line over. Some of the original railroad bridges, like the old Seven Mile Bridge, are fun for fishing, too. The *Theater of the Sea* (MM 84.5) has a great tour for kids and a porpoise show in which children may participate. In general, there is little distinction in the Keys between what children and adults do; the place has a way of turning everyone into children.

Shopping

If you like "Retired and Living on My Children's Inheritance" T-shirts, the stores in the Keys are for you. If beads from the Philippines, shells from the Caribbean, straw hats from Mexico, antiques from New Jersey, and clothes from India appeal to you, shop in the Keys. And if you want to pay double the mainland price for the usual things, you'll be in shopper's heaven. There are some good finds, however. When the Caloosas and Seminoles were run off the islands, they didn't leave many artifacts, and hurricanes, mold, termites, and the ocean have taken away much of what was old. But what is left is fabulous, once you find it. There are beautiful 17th-century silver and gold coins around, or you can buy a 200-year-old Conch house, a real cannonball, a ship's copper fittings, or a rare old gin bottle dropped by a drunken sailor into the sea 90 years ago.

Beaches

In the Keys, there are few sandy beaches, but there are lots of places to swim if you don't mind the floating plastic. Many good places to stop are unmarked but are right along the road; you'll see them. There are also **Pennekamp State Park** (MM 102.5), **Long Key State Park** (MM 69–68), **Bahia Honda State Park** (MM 34), and **Fort Taylor** in Key West (*see* Key West Beaches).

Sports

Biking Bicycles are for rent everywhere. Best bet is the *Upper Keys Hike-or-Bike Trail (see* Key Largo).

Boating For sailing and fishing in the upper and lower Keys, check with the *Whale Harbor Marina* (MM 84), the *Whale Harbor Docks* (MM 84), the *Holiday Isle Marina* (MM 84.5), *Caloosa Cove Marina* (MM 73.5), and *Hurricane Resort* (MM 49.5).

Diving There are so many dive shops that you only have to decide where you want to be, then check with the area Chamber of Commerce (*see* Important Addresses and Numbers).

Golf and Tennis The **Cheeca Lodge Resort** at Islamorada (tel. 305/664–4651) and **Key Colony Beach** (tel. 305/289–0821) at Marathon have golf courses and tennis courts. **Plantation Yacht Harbor** (tel. 305/852–2381) and **Tennis Island** at Windly Key, Islamorada (tel. 305/664–9808), have tennis.

Camping

Campsites for recreational vehicles and tents are situated all along the keys, with rates ranging from $14 to $40, depending on the facilities. Among them, heading southward, are **Calusa Camp Resort** (MM 101.5, tel. 305/451–0232), **American Outdoors** (MM 97.5, tel. 305/852–8054), **Fiesta Resort KOA Campground** (MM 70, tel. 305/664–4922), **Pelican Motel & Trailer**

Park (MM 59, tel. 305/289–0011), **Gulfstream Trailer Park & Marina** (MM 49, tel. 305/743–5619), **Sunshine Key Camping** (MM 39, tel. 305/872–2217), and **Big Pine Key Fishing Lodge** (MM 33, tel. 305/892–2351).

Dining

It might be possible to live on conch, stone-crab claws, and Key-lime pie. Conch is versatile: It is made into conch dip; conch fritters; conch salad; conch chowder; conch Parmesan; conch Creole; conch stew; curried conch; cracked conch, pounded, breaded, and fried; conchburgers, and so on. Because of all this conch eating, there was a conch-shortage crisis. The conch you eat now is not native; it was harvested in the Bahamas. Stone-crab claws are cracked and served hot or cold, and you get to deal with their shells. If you don't want to, order yellowtail and various snappers, grouper, jewfish, permit (a wonderful species), grunt (not recommended), shrimp, crayfish, shark, dolphin, and so on. Key-lime pies vary greatly, and which is the best is a hotly debated topic. Key West also has native Cuban foods; when you get sick of fish, you can have *bollas* (fried vegetables), *plantanos* (plantains), *frijoles negros* (black beans), *arroz con pollo* (chicken with rice). And, of course, there are Burger Kings and other fast-food chains, just like on the mainland.

Restaurants are listed by MM, from north to south. (For dining in Key West, *see* Key West section.)

Category	Cost*
Expensive	over $40
Moderate	$20–$40
Inexpensive	under $20

**per person without sales tax (6% in Florida), service, or drinks*

The following credit card abbreviations are used: AE, American Express; CB, Carte Blanche; DC, Diners Club; MC, MasterCard; V, Visa.

The Upper Keys
Expensive

Marker 88. Famous in the Keys for its food, this restaurant is in a low rambling building underneath big trees. It's noisier than it looks, but it has very good fish and Continental food. *MM 88, Plantation Key, tel. 305/852–9315. Dress: dressy to informal. Reservations needed. AE, CB, DC, MC, V. Closed Mon.*

Moderate

The Italian Fisherman. This is a rather large place for the Keys, with four floors of dining overlooking the Gulf of Mexico. The service is impersonal (orders are handled through computers), but the restaurant has the best food in Key Largo. Both the seafood and pasta dishes are superb. *MM 104, Key Largo, tel. 305/451–4471. Dress: informal. Reservations advised. AE, MC, V.*

The Quay. The food is indifferent here, except for the native (endangered) alligator sautéed in garlic lemon butter. The ambience, however, is jolly and relaxed in a typical nautical setting. *MM 102, Key Largo, tel. 305/451–0943. Dress: informal. Reservations. AE, MC, V.*

Ziggy's Conch Restaurant. With its green and black facade,

Ziggy's will make you feel like you've driven into the 1940s. It's extremely popular and serves good fish. Although some believe it's overrated, we can't knock it. *MM 83, Islamorada, tel. 305/664–4590 or 305/664–3391. Dress: informal. Reservations needed. AE, MC, V. Opens 5 PM, closed Thurs.*

Inexpensive

The Grassy Key Dairy Bar. Famous for miles around for good food, this restaurant thrives on variety. Every night there is a different theme and menu: Mexican night, Italian night, barbecue night, and so on. A small and casual place, this restaurant has an intimacy that can make you feel like you're eating in a kitchen. *MM 58.5, Marathon, tel. 305/743–3816. No credit cards. Closed Sun. and Mon.*

Island Jim's. Next to the Big Pine meat market, this place serves tender steaks and prime rib as well as seafood. Other than that, it's another typical Keys restaurant; small (two rooms, with a bar), with a nautical but homey decor. *MM 31.2, Big Pine, tel. 305/872–2017. Dress: casual. No credit cards.*

Lor-e-lei on the Gulf. This restaurant overlooks a small harbor full of boats, and off to one side is a pier with a ramshackle open bar where you can watch the sunset. A wide variety of seafood is served here, including blackened fish, grilled shrimp, broiled or steamed lobster, and crab Lor-e-lei (crab in a tomato base with cheese), as well as filet mignon, lamb, and ribs. *MM 82, Islamorada, tel. 305/664–4657. Dress: informal. Reservations advised. AE, MC, V.*

Mangrove Mama's. This endangered species in the Keys is a low wood shack of a restaurant with a glassed-in porch, checkered tablecloths, fireplace, classic rock and roll, fresh local seafood, natural foods, beer served in jars, and a clientele consisting largely of dropouts from society. *MM 28, Sugar Loaf, tel. 305/745–3030. Dress: informal. Reservations suggested, except Sun. Closed Thurs. MC, V.*

Mrs. Mac's Kitchen. This is a small, simple shack with a counter and a few tables, right off the edge of the highways. It serves homemade soups, chili, sandwiches, fish, and is a good place for lunch and eavesdropping. *MM 99.5, Key Largo, tel. 305/451–3722. No credit cards.*

Papa Joe's. Perched on the edge of Tea Table Channel, this restaurant presents a fine view of the Gulf. Just as fine are its seafood dishes, as well as its zesty Italian food. *MM 80, Islamorada, tel. 305/664–8109. Dress: informal. MC, V.*

Lodging

If you like chain hotels, they're here, and new ones pop up all the time. Rest assured, a computer can reserve you a room. Call 800/FLA–KEYS to get a fairly complete accommodations guide. But the smaller, older hotels, many listed here, have more atmosphere and better beaches.

Category	**Cost***
Very Expensive	over $125
Expensive	$100–$125
Moderate	$50–$100
Inexpensive	under $50

**per room, double occupancy, without 6% state sales tax and nominal tourist tax*

As in the dining section, hotels are listed here by Mile Marker (MM), from north to south. Rates quoted in this chart are those charged in season, December 15–April 30. You can expect to pay $10–$20 less in each category during the off-season.

The following credit card abbreviations are used: AE, American Express; CB, Carte Blanche; DC, Diners Club; MC, MasterCard; V, Visa.

Hotels
Expensive

Cheeca Lounge. This attractive and popular old fishing resort was just remodeled in 1988, with no loss in its charm. The resort has suites, villas, large grounds, and rooms facing the water. *MM 82, Islamorada 33036, tel. 305/664–4651. 86 units. Facilities: restaurants, lounge, pool, tennis courts, and golf course. AE, CB, DC, MC, V.*

Hawks Cay. Looking more like a Caribbean resort than any other property on the Keys, this is a 60-acre self-sufficient pink-and-green "tropical resort island." It seems to attract a youngish crowd, with a lagoon off the Atlantic for swimming. *Off MM 61, Marathon 33050, tel. 305/743–7000 or 800/327–7775. 177 units. Facilities: tennis and golf, fitness trail, restaurants and bars, conference rooms. AE, CB, DC, MC, V.*

Sheraton Key Largo. This large chain hotel puts its best face toward the gulf, which is what most people want when they visit the Keys. Most visitors also find the hotel relaxing because of the self-contained services offered at a chain. *MM 97, Key Largo 33037, tel. 305/852–5553. 200 rooms with bath. Facilities: pool, bars, tennis courts, restaurant, gift shop. AE, CB, MC, V.*

Moderate–Expensive

The Buccaneer. A heavy-handed pirate theme is much in evidence here, where many of the guests favor gold chains. There are rooms, cottages, and two-bedroom villas with Jacuzzis and dishwashers. *MM 48.5, Marathon 33050, tel. 305/743–9071 or 800/237–3329. 75 units. Facilities: pool, gulf dock, tennis, charter boats, Windsurfers, sailboats, powerboats, sailing, bars, restaurants. AE, DC, MC, V. Moderate for cottages; Expensive for villas.*

Caloosa Cove Resort. Although this place looks like a cement block, at least it's on the ocean and its rooms are quite cozy. Available are time-shares and short- and long-term rental efficiencies and suites. *MM 73.8, Lower Matecumbe 33036, tel. 305/664–8811. 30 units. Facilities: tennis and water sports. AE, CB, DC, MC, V.*

Holiday Isle. This huge complex can prove to be a haven if you're driving up the Keys and the Snake Creek drawbridge get stuck. The hotel usually has enough partying people to cause a traffic jam of its own. *MM 84, Islamorada 33036, tel. 305/664–2321 or 800/327–7070. 71 units, including all sorts of suites. Facilities: a sandy beach, all water sports, 5 restaurants, lounge, bar, nightclub, marina with charter boats for hire. AE, CB, DC, MC, V.*

Moderate

The Drop Anchor. This comfortable, pink, old place has a pleasant ambience and is very well maintained. There are both rooms and efficiencies, and also a fine ocean beach. *MM 85, Islamorada 33036, tel. 305/664–4863. 12 units. Facilities include a pool. AE, MC, V.*

Largo Lodge. Very comfortable large two- and three-room cottages are set in a jungly garden of palms and orchids here. And there's a wide dock where you can watch the sun set over the gulf. *MM 102, Key Largo 33037, tel. 305/451–0424. 6 units. No pets or children. AE, MC, V.*

Lime Tree Bay Resort. Sitting on a big semicircle of land in the gulf, Lime Tree has cottages, efficiencies, a treehouse, penthouses with skylights, and small older rooms recently redone, each in a different theme. Friendly and Keys-ish ambience. *MM 68.5, Layton 33001, tel. 305/664–4740. 30 units. Facilities: restaurant, scuba boat, sailboats, canoes, barbecue area, and pool. AE, CB, DC, MC, V.*

Inexpensive–Moderate

The Islander. This is one of the Keys's wonderful originals, in operation for some 32 years. There are 16 separate buildings spread on 25 acres along a beach. Rooms, all on one floor, have high-beamed ceilings and Italian tile floors. *MM 82.1, Islamorada 33036, tel. 305/664–2031. 114 rooms, 92 with full kitchens. Facilities: beach, fishing pier, restaurant, both fresh- and saltwater pools. AE, MC, V.*

Inexpensive

Looe Key Reef Resort. On a canal with a boat dock, this resort is famous for its diving expeditions to Looe Key. It also has an old-fashioned motel with rooms that look motelish, complete with vinyl appointments. It's a very popular place, so book ahead. The Reef Divers store is on premises, and a 40-foot dive boat offers diving expeditions to Looe Key as well as nature expeditions and trips to Tortugas. *MM 27, Ramrod Key 33042, tel. 305/872–2215. 20 rooms. Facilities: pool and informal restaurant. AE, MC, V.*

Rock Reef Resort. Pleasant efficiency cottages, one- and two-bedroom suites, houses, and a boat dock face the bay side of Key Largo. *MM 98, Key Largo 33037, tel. 305/852–2401. 20 units. No credit cards, but checks are accepted.*

Sugarloaf Lodge. Right on the gulf, Sugarloaf features rooms with a water view. It may look nondescript, but its rooms are cozy and the place is a favorite hangout for some writers. Perhaps it's the performing porpoise in the lagoon that attracts them. Or it might be the gas station with tacky souvenirs. *MM 17, Sugarloaf Key 33044, tel. 305/745–3211. 55 rooms. Facilities: marina with charter boats and guides, airstrip for light planes, pool, restaurant, bar.*

Valhalla Beach Motel. This place boasts the wonderful advantage of being far off U.S. 1—far from the sounds of traffic. It's a simple old motel, on a beautiful point of oceanside land, with deep water for swimming. *MM 56.5, Marathon 33052, tel. 305/289–0616. 12 rooms and efficiencies; weekly rates. Facilities: dock, swimming. No credit cards.*

Houseboats

Houseboats at Pennekamp Park are $100 a day, $425 a week. Camping with a tent or camper is also available at three of the four state parks: Pennekamp (MM 102, tel. 305/451–1202), Long Key (MM 69, tel. 305/664–4815), and Bahia Honda (MM 37, tel. 305/872–2353); $12 per night, reservations accepted no less than 14 or more than 60 days in advance.

The Boot Key Marina (MM 48, tel. 305/743–4200) has houseboats with bathrooms and kitchens, air-conditioning, and decks. Moderate.

Key West

Key West never stops. It still seems to be able to support a rotating and varied population. Waking up in their wooden houses under the sapodilla and banyan trees are the Conch natives and near-natives, the part-time snowbirds, the fishermen and shopkeepers, artisans and scam artists, dealers and writers, recluses and carpenters, blacks, Cubans, gays, Navy personnel, tourists—the rich and the poor. But the city is seriously becoming gentrified and homogenized. Its major industry is itself.

Whereas the rest of the Keys don't really have much history, Key West certainly does. The island joined the future state of Florida when, in 1822, John Simonton bought it in a Cuban bar for $2,000. U.S. Navy Commodore David Porter and his fleet then spent several years getting rid of the so-called brethren of the coast—the pirates. In 1829, William Whitehead laid out the still-intact streets of Old Town, where, throughout the 19th century, ship captains built and rebuilt their houses after each fire. Until 1852, when the lighthouses were constructed, the 600-some residents earned a collective $1.5 million per year from grounded ships. By 1890, some 6,000 people here earned their living rolling cigars, and a certain panache had vanished. But by 1934, the city was broke, 80% of the people were on welfare, and Key West threw itself on the mercy of the state. The state sent Julius Stone, who promoted the tourist trade, proclaiming that "unless a visitor is prepared to spend at least three full days here, the Key West Administration would rather he did not come." Six months later, after the 1935 hurricane blew away Flagler's 20-year-old railroad, nobody could get here anyway.

There are so many facts and explainers of facts on Key West that you can't miss learning something from them. Passing tour trolleys and trains will shout information at you about the oldest or the best while you're standing on the curb. Key West is 150 miles from Miami and 90 miles from Cuba. It is four miles long and two miles wide, double its original size; you can go from here by boat to the Marquesas or the Dry Tortugas. It has three forts and was a Union outpost in the Civil War. It has an inland lighthouse that was built up from 58 to 78 feet as the island grew. Key West has beaches all along the south side, with no waves and little sand. It has a cemetery with a gravestone in it that reads I Told You I Was Sick. It *does* have a lot of writers, but they always have one foot out the door. It has a daily newspaper known as the "Mullet Wrapper," three shopping malls, a large Navy base, and an astounding number of condominiums, hotels, guest houses, bars, and restaurants. Almost every termite-ridden, unpainted Old Town Conch house, from mansion to shack, has been or is being "restored." Read the old WPA guide and weep: The Conch Republic is no longer the little sleepy fishing village it was when Ernest Hemingway first arrived.

The history of Key West survives in its architecture more than in the landscape. Buildings have often been moved; Pepe's on Greene Street came from Duval Street lock, stock, and barrel. The Bahamas houses came from the Bahamas, and the Oldest House from England. The Fisherman's Cafe was moved from

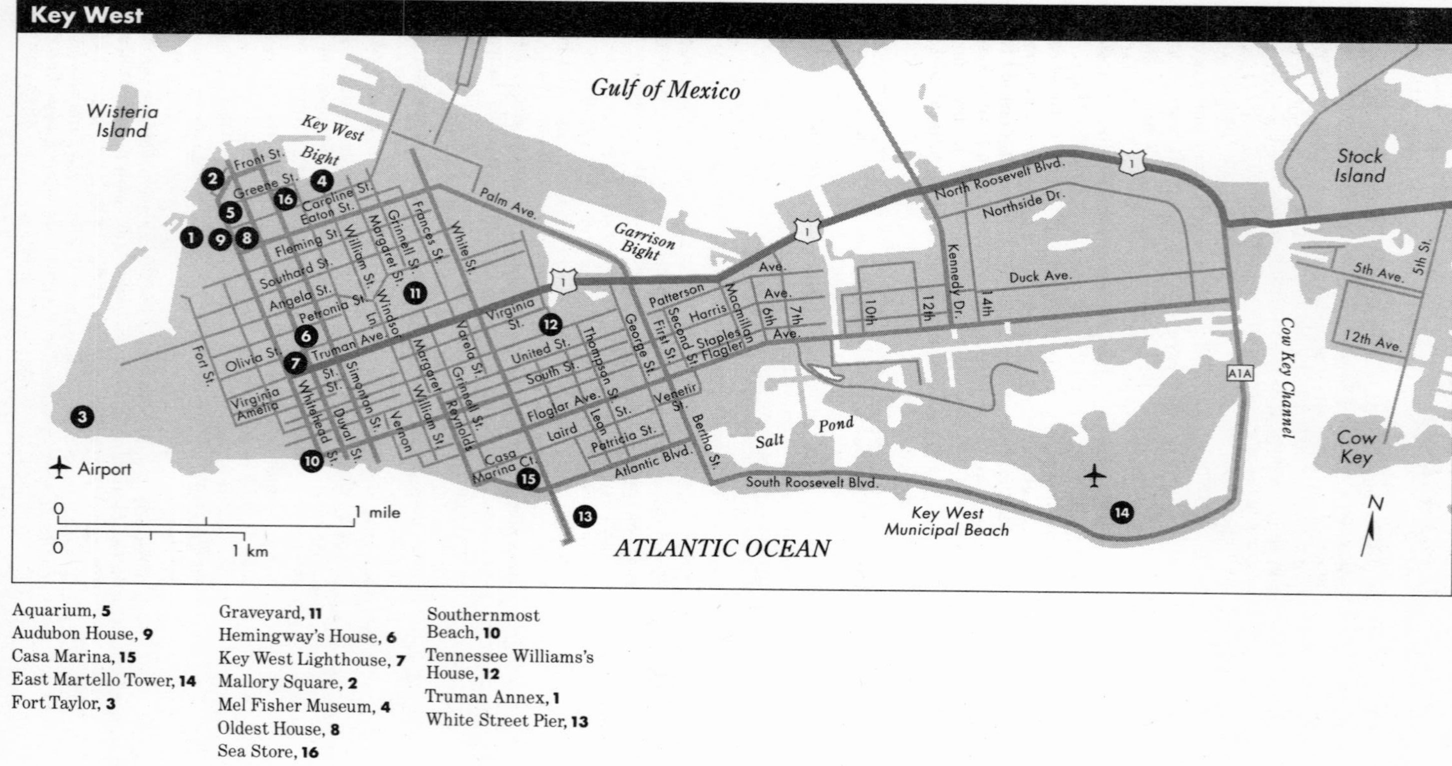

Aquarium, **5**
Audubon House, **9**
Casa Marina, **15**
East Martello Tower, **14**
Fort Taylor, **3**
Graveyard, **11**
Hemingway's House, **6**
Key West Lighthouse, **7**
Mallory Square, **2**
Mel Fisher Museum, **4**
Oldest House, **8**
Sea Store, **16**
Southernmost Beach, **10**
Tennessee Williams's House, **12**
Truman Annex, **1**
White Street Pier, **13**

Front Street and is now the Conch Train ticket office. One house on the end of Duval Street was turned around so the light would be better. Gato's mansion, built on Truman Street, was moved to Virginia Street. In 1987, a series of big Conch houses were mysteriously rearranged on Front Street. If you bike along Caroline Street or William Street or any other Old Town street, you can see how many of these two-story houses with gingerbread trim and deep porches and balconies there are: wood became a rare commodity, so hundreds of the old buildings are still here. Visit the cemetery with condolike graves (as in New Orleans, people are buried above ground and, more recently, in stacks) and tilting old headstones; More Conchs (descendants of the original Bahamian settlers) now rest in the cemetery than in their original houses. Walk along the harbor and see the boats of shrimpers, wreckers, smugglers, and the Navy, half hidden behind the proliferating tourist traps. You can think about the Mariel boatlift, when many of these same boats brought over human cargo from Havana. You can contemplate the fact that the ex-mayor of Key West water-skied from this island to Cuba in about six hours. After you've baked on the beach or caught your limit of snappers or had enough shrimp to eat, you can walk or rent a bike and ride in almost any direction and play the tourist.

Exploring Key West

Numbers in the margin correspond with points of interest on the Key West map.

1 **Truman Annex.** In 1986, an American Sikh named Pritam Singh bought, for $17.5 million, Truman Annex, the last large abandoned piece of land on Key West: a haunting, tree-filled, 42-acre section of the old Navy base with a deep-water harbor. The Navy had moved out of the annex 12 years before. During the intervening years, the land was occupied by only the 100 or so lucky people who had workshops or office space on the grounds. Harry Truman's Little White House (where the former president vacationed) is here, as are a large crumbling building once leased to artists and writers, the Key West Customs House, and a Marine Hospital, built in 1844, where Dwight D. Eisenhower once stayed. There are fields, banyans, sapodillas, palms, the mental-health center, the old foundery, the big machine-tooling shop, four swimming pool–size cisterns, many old Navy barracks, and a wide crumbling pier where the Treasure Salvagers unloaded King Philip's 350-year-old cannons and silver bars in 1985. Mel Fisher of the Treasure Salvors stored millions of dollars of salvaged gold, silver, and emeralds in a little warehouse at the edge of the Annex.

Fifteen or 16 of the original ruined buildings have been saved by the new owner, Pritam Singh (including Fisher's museum, which still holds what gold and silver wasn't distributed to those who found it). These days, what you can see under construction, if that's the word for it, are some 50 single-family town houses and about 214 condominiums, plus 200 units of what is called "affordable housing," a 110-unit hotel, parking lots, a "multiuse structure" with stores for rent, a new pier that will hold six or seven restaurants and the same number of bars, an 80-slip marina, a new cruise-ship marina, and a bit of room in the back of all this for the mental-health center and the artists.

Before long, people will be able to sleep in new presidential suites upstairs in Truman's old house.

Pritam Singh also managed to buy the island across the harbor
from the Annex. **Tank Island** is the island that is sometimes di-
2 rectly in the way of the sunset off **Mallory Square,** next to
Christmas Tree Island where sleeping-bag-quality "affordable housing" exists. Tank Island consists of 27 tree-covered acres, plus 31 acres of sea-bottom, bringing Singh's land holdings to a total of some 108 acres, all approved for new development by the South Florida Regional Planning Council. Tank Island is to be developed in an upscale, exclusive fashion, with tennis courts, landscaped parks, and a ferry to transport you there. As the representative of the Truman Annex Company says, "People will pay for the privilege of going to the island, period."

Leave Truman Annex via the Fleming Street entrance, turn
right on Fleming Street going toward the Navy Air Base, take
3 a left (following the small signs), and you will find **Fort Taylor.**
The park here has Key West's best swimming beach. In 1845, the year before the hurricane that destroyed the lighthouse, work was begun on Fort Taylor, and it was not yet finished 21 years later when the fort was declared obsolete. Fort Taylor, which was in the only city south of the Mason-Dixon line to be held by the Union throughout the Civil War, was built mostly by slaves. Its trapezoid shape rose 50 feet above the water, 1,200 feet out from shore (by now it is inland). During the Civil War, hundreds of blockade-running ships were detained here. In 1898, the walls were lowered and the fort was rearmed for the Spanish-American War. In 1976, Fort Taylor became a National Historic Site. Recently, half the fort was painted a dreary black. Grass grows in the center court, and cannons rest on the deserted wide ledges. There's a great view of the port from these walls. You can sit up here and, if you're lucky, there'll be nobody else around. *Western end of Southard St., tel. 305/292–6713. Open daily 8 AM–sunset. Admission to park: $1.50 per vehicle and driver, $1 each additional passenger. Fort tours daily 2 PM, free.*

4 **Mel Fisher Museum.** Enjoy lunch near the docks one day and then stroll down to the pier between the Turtle Kraals and the Half-Shell Raw Bar (at Land's End Village). If you walk out a ways; you may be able to see, at the pier to the right, the scruffy old green ***Dauntless.*** The *Dauntless* was the Mel Fisher boat that in 1985 found the $400-million motherlode of the shipwrecked *Atocha,* which went down in 1622. Fisher spent 20 years searching for what was then considered the most valuable ship ever recovered. According to the ship's manifest, it contained, besides the long-forgotten 550 passengers, a full load of 1,038 silver ingots, 7,175 ounces of gold, and 230,000 hand-stamped silver coins, all belonging to King Philip and all en route from the New World to satisfy the Spanish national debt and to subsidize the Spanish military.

Those things at the stern of the *Dauntless* that look like the elbows of huge heating ducts are called "mailboxes"; they blow the sand off the unyielding sea bottom or off underwater treasure. The *Dauntless* continues to explore the grave of the *Atocha*'s sister ship, the *Santa Margarita,* bringing up many millions of dollars worth of gold, silver, jewels, and gems. This largest treasure cache in the world is displayed at the museum on Front Street at the edge of the Truman Annex. *Mel Fisher*

Maritime Heritage Society, 200 Greene St., tel. 305/296–9936. Admission: $5 adults, $1 children under age 6. Open daily 10–5:15.

5 Near the Mel Fisher Museum is the WPA-built **Aquarium,** Key West's oldest tourist attraction, a good diversion for children or on a rainy day. The old open tanks have been turned into a touch tank, from which you can pick up and squirt a sea cucumber or poke at other invertebrates, and a feeding tank that contains a sandpapery skinned shark and an aged barracuda with a missing fin. *1 Whitehead St., off Mallory Sq., tel. 305/296–2051. Admission: $3.50 adults, $1.75 children. Fish and shark feeding at 11, 1, 3, and 4.*

You will probably want to get out on the water and explore the islands off Key West. Among the most restful boats is *The Wolf*, a 74-foot three-masted Southern Coastal Schooner with (usually) a salty all-woman crew, who will take you on a daytime reef-snorkeling trip ($35) or a sunset sail ($20). It's great in a strong wind—a beautiful ride and lots of fun. Docked behind the A & B Lobster House (700 Front St., tel. 305/296–WOLF). Ice provided, bring your own whatever.

6 **Hemingway's House** is something you should see because everyone will ask you if you did. What you'll see are 100 cats, the island's first swimming pool, and not a sign left of Hemingway. *907 Whitehead St., tel. 305/294–1575. Open daily 9–5. Admission: $4 adults, $1 children 6–12.*

7 From the top of the **Key West Lighthouse** (88 steps to climb its 78 feet), you can see down across the street into Hemingway's bedroom. You can also enjoy a sweeping view of the island. The lighthouse was built in 1846 to replace the one on Whitehead Point that was destroyed by a hurricane. It started at 58 feet and was built up as the land around it. Its light was extinguished, or "decommissioned," in 1969. *Lighthouse and Museum, 938 Whitehead St., tel. 305/294–0012. Admission: $2.50 adults, 50 cents children 7–15. Open 9:30–5.*

If you want to see how people in Key West used to live, and where they put their kitchens (outside), walk up to Duval
8 Street and see the **Oldest House** (which isn't the oldest; the bottle lady's house on the corner of Angela and Margaret reportedly is older). *Oldest House and Wreckers' Museum, 322 Duval St., tel. 305/294–9502. Admission: $2 adults, 50 cents children. Open 9–5.*

9 The **Audubon House** is really the Geiger house, because Audubon never lived here (although he visited, and many of his prints are on display). Geiger was a wrecker, and his house is notable because its once-slated destruction resulted in the formation of OIRF (Old Island Restoration Federation), the organization that saved quite a bit of Key West. Many properties that the OIRF has saved, are listed in the walking tours which you can pick up at the Chamber of Commerce. *205 Whitehead St., tel. 305/294–2116. Admission: $4 adults, $1 children. Open 9:30–5.*

It's worth going down Whitehead back past Hemingway's
10 house to the **Southernmost Beach,** at least to watch the nonstop picture taking. Swimming is less desirable. From here, it's only 90 miles to Cuba.

11 Go to the **Graveyard**—alone or with a good friend, either at dawn or at sunset (when they lock the gates on you, so beware).

To get to the graveyard, go north on Truman Avenue and turn left on Francis Street.

12 **Tennessee Williams' House** (1431 Duncan St.) is a little out of the way, has no tour, and nobody's there; but you can look at the outside. It's a much more modest structure than Hemingway's. "Tenny was quiet," a friend of his says. "I think he was shy."

If you want to take a longish (five to six miles, roundtrip) bike ride, pedal out along the Atlantic on Rte. A1A, past the airport, until you get to the houseboats. Some of the houseboats are small and whimsical; some are trashy and suspicious looking.

13 On your way out to the houseboats, you'll pass the **White Street Pier.** Visit the pier at night and, if you can, take a fishing rod. (The pier is on the Atlantic end of White Street.)

Shortly after you pass the airport on Rte. A1A, you will see
14 **East Martello Tower,** one of three unfinished Civil War forts. The tower houses the Art Museum, where you can see the collected works of Stanley Papio, a Canadian welder who moved to Key Largo in 1949. Soon after his move, huge homemade sculptures fashioned from junk began to fill his yard, much to the horror of his neighbors, who had him arrested six times for his "eyesores." He's been called macho, playful, and crazy, and he has also been likened to Picasso, Dali, Warhol, and Hopper—decide for yourself. The museum also has a collection of painted wood carvings of old Key West street scenes by local Cuban primitive artist Mario Sanchez. *3501 S. Roosevelt Blvd., tel. 305/296–6206. Admission: $2.50. Open daily 9:30–5.*

Returning from Martello Tower, you can drive on Flagler Street and, at 1500 Reynolds Street, view the last of Henry Flagler's hotels, which he developed along his train route. The
15 **Casa Marina** was opened in 1922, a Spanish renaissance retreat for the rich. Succeeding waves of military and tourists occupied it. It was closed in the early 1960s, but in 1980 Marriott acquired the resort, refurbished it, and added two wings (*see* Lodging). The impressive old building still sits on its tropical site, facing one of the rockiest and prettiest beaches on the island.

Once you get oriented, you should visit one of Key West's best
16 stores: Bill and Fran Ford's **Sea Store** (614 Greene St., tel. 305/294–3438). The Fords are salvagers of the cultural and natural history of the Keys. Their store contains a joyful miscellany of old bottles (including the beautiful Vanden Bergh Gin bottles made in Holland until 1904 and dropped around the Keys by drunks), remnants of old boats, and household objects handmade out of native wood. If you ask to see old coins, the Fords will show you the Silver Rider, a Dutch coin made in 1677; cobs (pieces of eight) from the *Atocha* and from 1715 and 1733 wrecks off the Keys; Spanish pillar dollars, with the pillars of Hercules at the Straits of Gibraltar on either side of two overlapping worlds under one crown with the sea beneath them. This coin was first made for Philip V in 1732 and used in the New World as legal tender until 1865. There are gold coins, too.

Off the Beaten Path

Fort Jefferson was built supposedly to control the Gulf of Mexico. It is an enormous structure on Garden Key in the Tortugas, 70 miles off Key West. Slaves, prisoners, and U.S. Army deserters began construction on the massive hexagon in 1846. By 1856, it had reached a height of a few feet above sea level. In 1866, while the work still continued, its huge, eight-foot-thick walls began sinking; the island, it was discovered, was sand—not coral. Samuel Mudd, the doctor who set John Wilkes Booth's broken leg after Booth assassinated Lincoln, was imprisoned here. He was the only doctor at the fort to survive the 1867 yellow-fever epidemic and, therefore, for some reason, he was pardoned. The fort was abandoned in 1874 without its men ever seeing battle. There's good snorkeling off Fort Jefferson, and silence, sea turtles, and many birds. You can make arrangements to camp overnight or longer, but you have to bring everything with you, even water. You can fly or take a boat to Fort Jefferson; several outfitters in Key West offer trips, including Key West Seaplane Service (tel. 305/294–6978).

Shopping in Key West

Unless it's raining or the airline has lost your suitcase, you might want to avoid a lot of shopping. Duval Street has many pleasant stores that sell resort items, souvenirs, and clothes for prices higher than on the mainland. **Fast Buck Freddies** (500 Duval St.) is probably the most visually interesting store to prowl through. Though Freddies sells resort wear and fancy kitchen-ware, it's known mostly for its camping gear and gift items.

The **Sea Store** (*see* Exploring) is your best bet for goods that are native to the Keys, especially salvaged objects, woodwork, and old bottles and coins.

For home decoration, go to **Gingerbread Square Gallery** (910 Duval St.). The **Lucky Street Gallery** (Olivia and Duval Sts.), the most interesting gallery in town, features contemporary paintings, sculpture, ceramics, glass, and handmade jewelry, primarily by Keys artists. The gallery is located in a renovated old Conch building.

The **White Street Gallery** (901 White St.) occasionally shows paintings by French artists who have come here to paint scenes of Key West.

The **Key West Island Bookstore** (on Fleming St. opposite Fausto's) and the **Monroe County Library** (700 Fleming St.) have many books on the Keys and on Florida.

Beaches

Fort Taylor State Park (*see* Exploring) has the best (deepest) swimming water on Key West, off a beautiful but astonishingly hard coral beach under Australian pines, with picnic tables and grills, fishing, showers, and a view of the harbor. It closes at sunset. *Tel. 305/292–6713. Admission: $1.*

Smathers Beach, west of the airport and opposite a few condominiums, is a shallow, sandy, Coney Island–type beach (built at a cost of $95 a foot) lined with cars, trucks renting rafts and selling snacks, Windsurfers and Hobie Cats for rent, a parasail outfit, and public bathrooms. Across Rte. A1A is a line of palms planted by the WPA. *Admission free.*

Higgs Memorial Beach has a playground for children, a wind-free place to lurk beneath the old West Martello Tower on cool days, a sandwich shop, bathrooms, and picnic tables. *Admission free.*

Participant Sports

Biking **Ray's** (906 Truman St., tel. 305/294–0553) rents bikes, mopeds, and scooters. **The Bike Shop** (1110 Truman St., tel. 305/294–1073) and the **Bicycle Center** (523 Truman St., tel. 305/294–4556) both rent bikes.

Boating and Fishing **Key West Boat Rentals** (617 Front St., tel. 305/294–2628) rents boats. Arrangements for charter and party fishing boats can be made at the **Garrison Bight Marina.** For bonefishing, try **Jeffrey Gardens** (tel. 305/294–3248).

Diving The ***Coral Princess*** fleet (tel. 305/296–3287) will take you out to the reef; the diving locations depend on the weather. **Key West Pro Dive Shop** (tel. 305/296–3823) and **Reef Raiders** (tel. 305/294–3635) do also, and they arrange dives, give scuba lessons, and rent equipment.

Exercise All sorts of aerobics and dance classes are available at **The Coffee Mill** (916 Ashe St., tel. 305/296–9982). The **Reach Hotel** (tel. 305/296–5000) has a fitness center.

Golf The 18-hole **Key West Resort Golf Course** is on Stock Island (tel. 305/294–5232).

Tennis There are public courts across from Higgs Beach and at **Island City Tennis** (Truman Ave., tel. 305/294–1346). The **Casa Marina** (tel. 305/204–3535) also has tennis courts.

Spectator Sports

Dog Racing **Key West Kennel Club** on Stock Island (tel. 305/294–9517). Open Dec.–Apr.; races Mon.–Sat. 8 PM and Sat. 1:15 PM. Admission $1, matinee free, women free Tues. night. For additional weekly events at the club, pick up a booklet at the Chamber of Commerce on Mallory Square.

Dining

"Grunts, grits and gravy" were once your typical meal here. In case you don't want that, try the following.

Category	Cost*
Expensive	over $40
Moderate	$20–$40
Inexpensive	under $20

**per person without sales tax (6% in Florida), service, or drinks*

The following credit card abbreviations are used: AE, American Express; CB, Carte Blanche; DC, Diners Club; MC, MasterCard; V, Visa.

Expensive

Cafe des Artistes. Southern French and Caribbean French are featured in this multilevel restaurant with several cozy and quiet rooms—a favorite of wealthier locals. Pâté, escargot, lobster, fish, and vegetables are all perfectly cooked and artistically presented. *1007 Simonton St., tel. 305/294–7100. Dress: dressy to informal. Reservations advised. AE, MC, V.*

La-Te-Da. This "Stork-Club-gone-tropic" has a lot going on: twinkling lights, a choice of oriental or western cuisine, tea-dances, brunches. There are two restaurants: the **Crystal Cafe** upstairs, **La-Te-Da** downstairs. It's a cheerful extravaganza, with very good food, especially the duck pâté, snapper, yellowtail, quail, and the popular four-course prix fixe dinner. *1125 Duval St., tel. 305/294–8435. AE, CB, DC, MC, V. Downstairs restaurant is closed Sun. night.*

Louie's Back Yard. This restaurant has a wide oceanside dining deck on three levels surrounded by trees full of twinkling lights. Inside the big Victorian Conch house are two bars, and two more rooms for dining. Louie's is considered to be the best restaurant in Key West; it also has a fantastic view of the Atlantic. Its menu is exotic: pan-cooked potato cakes with sour cream and caviar; wild mushroom terrine with walnuts and Stilton cheese; smoked barbecue duck salad with oriental noodles; also roast duck, grilled swordfish, fillet of beef, even nonnative salmon. *Corner of Vernon and Waddell Sts., tel. 305/294–1061. Dress: dressy, but jackets are not required. Reservations advised. AE, CB, DC, MC, V.*

Moderate–Expensive

Jordan's. The atmosphere here is as cozy as an English pub. The dining room is small, but there's plenty of space between tables, and you can also eat in the tiny garden-terrace in the back. The menu changes nightly but there is always fresh fish, sometimes served with spicy light sauces; unusual salads, often with artichokes; and always excellent service. Wine and beer only. *808 Duval St., tel. 305/296–5858. Dress: informal or your choice. Reservations. AE, MC, V.*

Kyushu. Unfailingly fresh sushi and sashimi are served here as well as cooked Japanese dishes, such as chicken teriyaki and tempura. You can eat outside under a straw roof, in one of two indoor rooms, or in a tatami room. The service is excellent unless too many groups of people arrive at once. *921 Truman St., tel. 305/294–2995. Dress: casual. AE, MC, V.*

Moderate

The A & B Lobster House. This old standby since 1947 is located upstairs in a former fish house. It has changed over the years, but the room is still plain and located in the marina, with a great view of the harbor. It is a kind of midwestern place in atmosphere and menu, serving shrimp, lobster, yellowtail, and shark, as well as filet mignon, prime rib, and New York strip steak. Entrees are served with rice and beans or a baked potato and Key-lime pie is available for dessert. *700 Front St., tel. 305/294–2536. Dress: informal. AE, DC, MC, V.*

Dickies. The atmosphere is refined here, but the prices are moderate, the ambience warm, and the food tasty and attractively presented. The food ranges from French traditional—such as beef bongo—to fried chicken to fish to the humble meatloaf. There's a fine wine list and a good piano bar. Though the restaurant is popular, it is never unbearably crowded. *320 Grinnell St., tel. 305/294–4046. Dress: whatever you fancy, including informal. Reservations advised. MC, V.*

Harbor View Cafe. Dining here is provided in a setting of wicker furniture, ceiling fans, flowered cushions, conch-shell centerpieces, and soft lighting. The fare includes a Caribbean catch, which varies daily, and pasta dishes such as spinach and cheese tortellini, gulf shrimp on linguini, and pasta with garlic clams. Large selection of pies and cakes for dessert. *1 Duval St., tel. 305/294–9541. Dress: casual. Reservations advised. AE, MC, V.*

Pepe's Cafe. This old-time restaurant and bar is located near the old waterfront. It's a small place, off the beaten track, with wooden booths and tables and the biggest ceiling fan you ever saw. Pepe's was once a shrimpers' cafe, and it still has good home-style meals: fried chicken, steak, roast beef, or fish, almost always served with mashed potatoes, gravies, and broccoli. A turkey dinner is served once a week. *806 Caroline St., tel. 305/294–7192. Dress: informal. MC, V.*

The Pier House. This is a place for tourists, but the quality of the food doesn't suffer. There are three restaurants here: **Pier House Restaurant, Harbor View Cafe,** and **Pete's Raw Bar.** Pier House Restaurant has water on three sides and faces Key West Harbor and the sunset. The menu of "new American cuisine" changes monthly and features grilled fish, duckling, rack of lamb, a fresh catch with avocado, papaya and Key-lime butter, and, for dessert, Key-lime pie topped with meringue. *1 Duval St., tel. 305/294–9541. Dress: casual to informal.*

Inexpensive

The Crab Shack. Good, spicy, steamed shrimp, incredible crab platters, and other local seafood dishes are served here with black beans, baked potato or corn, and a salad. Diners have a choice of a large covered terrace or an indoor dining room decorated in nautical kitsch. The food is fresh and the portions are hefty. *908 Caroline St., tel. 305/294–9658. Dress: informal. AE, CB, DC, MC, V.*

Dim Sum. Various Asian dishes are served in a peaceful, oriental, wood-paneled room. Specialties include hot-and-sour soup, chicken curries, and a vegetable dish served with a peanut sauce. Sake and unusual beers are available. The only complaint is that some of the tables are rather small. Brunch served Wednesday–Sunday. *613 Duval St., tel. 305/294–6238. Dress: casual. Reservations advised. MC, V.*

Full Moon Saloon. This dark, comfortable barroom-restaurant is a local hangout where you can drink or eat until 4 AM under a large sailfish caught by writer Phil Caputo. Meals are surprisingly good—particularly the giant salads, fish platters and fish sandwiches, hamburgers, and conch fritters. *1202 Simonton St., tel. 305/294–4040. Dress: informal. MC, V.*

El Loro Verde. The best Mexican food in Key West is served at cozy wooden booths here. The burritos, tacos, tostadas, and other Mexican standards are all freshly prepared, and the portions are large. *404 Southard St., tel. 305/296–7298. Dress: informal. Reservations advised. No credit cards.*

El Siboney. Good Cuban food is what you'll find here. The dinerlike atmosphere is cheery and aromatic. Popular dishes include roast pork, paella, fresh fish, and, for dessert, flan. Dinner comes with black beans, rice, and plantain or yucca. *900 Catherine St., tel. 305/294–2721. Dress: informal. No credit cards.*

Lodging

Houses

If you're staying for a week or so or if you travel with family or friends, it's worth renting a house. **Property Management of**

Key West (517 Eaton St. 33040, tel. 305/296–7744) specializes in vacation rentals.

Other agencies with some furnished houses are **Island Properties** (400 Simonton St. 33040, tel. 305/296–7766), **Key Lime Realty** (507 Whitehead St. 33040, tel. 305/296–8516), **Knight Realty** (336 Duval St. 33040, tel. 305/294–5155), and **Old Town Realty** (605 Simonton St., tel. 305/294–1012).

Category	**Cost***
Very Expensive	over $150
Expensive	$125–$150
Moderate	$100–$125
Inexpensive	under $100

**per room, double occupancy, without 6% state sales tax and nominal tourist tax*

The following credit card abbreviations are used: AE, American Express; CB, Carte Blanche; DC, Diners Club; MC, MasterCard; V, Visa.

Hotels

Expensive–Very Expensive

The Casa Marina Resort. Though a Marriott hotel now, the Casa Marina retains much of the character of the original 1920s Flagler resort. The huge Spanish-Moorish structure has its own long beach lined with palm trees. Rooms are decorated in bamboo and Spanish-style furniture. People who seem to be exhausted by success lounge on the veranda or at one of the outside bars. *1500 Reynolds St. 33040, tel. 305/296–3535 or 800/626–0777 in USA, 800/235–4837 in FL. 314 rooms and suites. Facilities: tennis, pool, Jacuzzi, sauna, sailboats and Windsurfers, swimming, fishing off pier. AE, CB, DC, MC, V.*

Hyatt Key West. This brand-new (opened spring 1988) resort and marina is typical of all Hyatt properties, but without the Hyatt signature—a zooming atrium. Each of its 120 guest rooms, however, has a balcony and water view. There's also a private beach with a deck area and an oversized whirlpool. *901 Front St. 33040, tel. 305/296–9900 or 800/228–9000. AE, CB, DC, MC, V.*

Ocean Key House. Looming over the Gulf, this hotel seems to lack color and warmth, but it has luxury suites with kitchens and living-dining rooms. Each suite has a balcony, its own Jacuzzi, near full-size kitchen equipped with electric coffee maker. The suites are tastefully decorated in pastel colors, thick carpets, and art-deco reproductions. *0 Duval St. 33040, tel. 305/296–7701 or 800/328–9815. 100 units. Facilities: pool, gulf pier for boat docking, fishing or swimming. AE, CB, DC, MC, V.*

Moderate–Expensive

Best Western Key Ambassador. It's best to specify whether you want a standard room, which looks out over a pine grove, or ocean-view or harbor-view room. The view inside each room is pleasant—tastefully decorated and with wall-to-wall carpeting. There are five two-story buildings in this complex, with the three originally built (1950s) facing poolside; the other two were built in 1980. *1000 S. Roosevelt Blvd. 33040, tel. 305/296–3500. 100 rooms. Facilities: refrigerators and balconies for all second-story rooms; pool with poolside bar; outdoor fitness center, shuffleboard courts. AE, CB, DC, MC, V.*

Moderate

Days Inn. A comfortable place for the whole family, with a pool, children's playground, and pet facilities (at an extra charge). *U.S. 1 and N. Roosevelt Blvd. 33040, tel. 305/296-3742. AE, CB, DC, MC, V.*

EconoLodge Resort. Facilities are what separates this EconoLodge from the other moderate-price hotels. Facing the gulf side, this place has popular barbecue pits, a pool, sun deck, and tennis courts, as well as nicely appointed rooms. *3820 N. Roosevelt Blvd. 33040, tel. 305/294-5511. AE, CB, DC, MC, V.*

Quality Inn. Visitors to this hotel don't have to go far to catch the Conch Tour Train, for the train's depot is right on the premises. The inn, although a part of a chain, is very friendly—another reason for attracting families. *3850 N. Roosevelt Blvd. 33040, tel. 305/294-6681. AE, CB, DC, MC, V.*

The 1950s-Style Motels

These old motels have more character, sometimes more amenities, and are usually cheaper than the chain hotels. They are only a block or two from the beach and are ideal for families on a tight budget.

Atlantic Shores. A location on the ocean, a pier, and a pool make this motel very popular with college students. *510 South St. 33040, tel. 305/296-2491. AE, CB, DC, MC, V. Inexpensive–Moderate.*

The Hibiscus. Recently bought by Best Western and then remodeled, this motel boasts rooms with two queen-size beds and a refrigerator. *1313 Simonton St. 33040, tel. 305/296-6711. AE, CB, DC, MC, V. Moderate.*

The Santa Maria. The fact that it's very '50s-looking is part of this motel's charm. *1401 Simonton St. 33040, tel. 305/296-5678. AE, CB, DC, MC, V. Inexpensive.*

The South Beach Motel. This is a pleasant motel with a pool and a pier for boating or fishing. *500 South St. 33040, tel. 305/296-5611. AE, CB, DC, MC, V. Inexpensive.*

Guest Houses

The Artist House. Built in 1898, this Queen Anne–Victorian mansion was newly renovated, but its old-fashion decor was kept intact. There are antique furnishings, brass and mahogany poster beds, oriental rugs, and hand-painted William Morris wallpaper reproductions. Guests are served juice and coffee daily. Five guest suites with private bath, air-conditioning, TV, and full kitchen facilities. *534 Eaton St. 33040, tel. 305/296-3977. No children. AE, CB, MC, DC, V. Moderate–Expensive.*

Duval House. Decorated pleasantly in pink and white, this place is so centrally located that it may make you feel claustrophobic. There are 22 rooms with private baths found in five different buildings surrounding a garden and swimming pool. The main building is 130 years old, and some of its rooms are furnished with antiques. All rooms have ceiling fans, and most have balconies. *815 Duval St. 33040, tel. 305/294-1666. AE, CB, DC, MC, V. Moderate.*

Eden House. Built in 1924, this is the oldest continuously operated hotel in Key West. The rooms are furnished in the 1920s style, with white wicker furniture and accents of blue and pink. All rooms have ceiling fans. Continental breakfast is included. *1015 Fleming St. 33040, tel. 305/296-6868 or 800/533-KEYS. 31 rooms, 10 with private bath. AE, CB, DC, MC, V. Moderate.*

Island City House. Three guest houses, enclosed by gingerbread fences for privacy, share a common tropical garden area. There is also an outdoor gas grill, picnic table, and breakfast bar. *441 Williams St. 33040, tel. 305/294-5702 or*

800/634–8230. 24 suites with kitchens. AE, CB, DC, MC, V. Moderate.

The Arts and Nightlife

Every evening, without fail, there's **Sunset at Mallory Square.** As the sun sets, there are fire-eaters, jugglers, conga drummers, bagpipe players, and much more. It's an interesting show, if only for people-watching. And, of course, there's the sunset, which everyone applauds. Free unless you bring a car.

Plays, Dance, and Music **Jan McArt's Cabaret Theater** (tel. 305/206–2120), the **Tennessee Williams Fine Arts Center** (tel. 305/294–6232), the **Red Barn Theatre** (tel. 305/296–9911), and the **Waterfront Playhouse** (tel. 305/294–5015) all stage productions. The entertainment schedule for Key West is listed in the *Key West Citizen, Solaris Hill, Florida Keys Magazine*, and *Humm's Guide*.

Movies There are two movie complexes at the malls: **Cinema Four** (Searstown Shopping Center, tel. 305/294–0000) and the **Plaza Twin** (Key Plaza, tel. 305/296–8810). Old films are screened at **The Picture Show** (620 Duval St., tel. 305/294–1448).

Bars Live bands, from rock to reggae, are featured throughout Key West. The *Key West Citizen* lists which bands are playing, and where. Among the bars, don't miss **Captain Tony's** (428 Greene St.), which was the original Sloppy Joe's, Ernest Hemingway's favorite. Ex-gun runner Captain Tony, who has run for mayor in three recent elections, also might interest you. **Louie's Backyard** (corner of Vernon and Waddell Sts.) has an outside deck, which is great for a drink at sunset—and beyond.

8 Disney World and the Orlando Area

Introduction

by David Wilkening

A freelance writer who lives in Orlando, David Wilkening is a contributing editor of Orlando Magazine. *He writes for several local and national publications, including travel books and travel magazines.*

Orlando, a high-profile city of fast growth boosted by a robust business climate and thriving tourist trade, seems to be an area touched by pixie dust. A magical city. But it was not always that way.

A military outpost was established here in 1838, and the area became known as Fort Gatlin. In 1850, that name gave way to Jernigan, in deference to one of the region's most prosperous residents. It wasn't until 1875 that the one square-mile-wide city was incorporated as Orlando. There are various theories why the name was chosen, but the most popular is that the new city was named after Orlando Reeves, a soldier killed fighting the Seminole Indians.

Upon its incorporation, Orlando had less than 100 residents. The town had no seaport or major waterway. There was no railroad to spur its growth. In short, there was little to stimulate or sustain any prosperity. But Orlando had a sunny year-round climate. And it had something else, the importance of which would become evident much later—a location in the very center of what would become one of the fastest-growing states in the country.

Citrus and cattle were the dominant industries in Orlando's early years. The English arrived in the mid-1860s, bringing with them tennis, polo, and afternoon tea. The great freezes of 1884 and 1885 virtually ruined the citrus industry, and traditional farming returned. Orlando remained a clean, sleepy, handsome city, known for its lakes and for its sprawling oak trees planted by northerners who wanted to remember the world they had left behind.

In the 1950s, large corporations gave the area a solid business base on which to build. Today, in large part because of Walt Disney World, Orlando is known for its tourism. But it's also a growing center of national and international business activity.

In its graceful and quiet past Orlando enjoyed a small-town pace that earned it the title of "The City Beautiful." The city today is far more metropolitan, even cosmopolitan, but much of the original charm remains. Many residents have homes near the hundreds of clear spring-fed lakes, far from the south Orlando-based tourist corridor. The aroma here is often that of orange blossoms and citrus trees. The city has retained its parklike atmosphere.

The population of the greater metropolitan area that includes Orange, Seminole, and Osceola counties is now approaching one million. Various surveys cite the greater Orlando area as among the fastest growing in the country.

With all its business activity, however, Orlando is better known as the world's Number One tourist destination. Disneyland had long been a successful staple in California when Disney decided, in the early 1960s, to build another theme park in the eastern United States. By 1963, Florida was chosen as the best state. Orlando was chosen for a variety of reasons, including its transportation system and its large amounts of open, available land.

By 1964, property was quietly purchased. Eventually, a huge tract of 28,000 acres was bought. But, it wasn't until late

1965 that news reports leaked out that Disney was buying those parcels of land in anticipation of a large-scale theme park.

The accumulation of the land, often in small parcels purchased by agents working silently for Disney, was a dramatic story in itself. But seeing how the surrounding tourist areas around his California park had suffered rampant commercial sprawl, Disney was determined to buy enough land in Orlando to prevent that from happening again. This time, he would have **control** of the surrounding area.

On November 16, 1965, Walt Disney outlined his dream of an innovative working and living center that would provide a new way of life. He called it Experimental Prototype Community of Tomorrow (Epcot). The first phase: the Magic Kingdom and a vacation complex. Walt Disney died the next year and never saw his dream come true. But construction began in 1969 on the park, which opened in 1971. New attractions were added continually, and, by the end of the fifth year, almost 11 million visitors annually were parading through the Magic Kingdom.

Plans were announced for another phase of the Disney master plan in 1975. That was Epcot. On October 1, 1982, Epcot Center, as it was now called, opened its gates. It was not a quiet opening but included a month-long celebration that featured the West Point Glee Club, the 450-piece All American Marching Band, and World Showcase Festival performers representing 23 countries. The Epcot Center that emerged after Disney's death was not the one he envisioned—a living, working community set next to theme parks—apparently because it was later determined that the concept was not practical. But Epcot Center, standing on its own, was an immediate success. Almost 23 million visitors passed through its gates the very first year.

Walt Disney World is now the most-popular man-made attraction on Earth. A slow day brings in 25,000 visitors, while a busy day can bring 150,000. The attraction's vast, varied complex occupies 43 square miles. There's something for everyone.

The Magic Kingdom itself offers 98 acres of amusement. Disney's vision is everywhere as visitors encounter the nostalgia of Main Street, the good times at Adventureland, the down-home atmosphere of Frontierland, the dignity and history of Liberty Square, the magic of Fantasyland, and the world of the future in Tomorrowland.

Three miles south of the Magic Kingdom, and only a few minutes by tram, is Epcot Center—a 260-acre complex of entertainment. The two distinct dimensions here are Future World, which features the latest ideas in everything from lifestyles to communications, and World Showcase, where nations display their cultures through films and other displays.

Arriving and Departing

By Plane More than 33 scheduled airlines operate in and out of Orlando's airport, with direct service to more than 50 U.S. cities. At last count, Delta, the official airline of Disney World, had 56 flights to and from the airport every day! Travel packages to Disney World are offered by Delta (tel. 800/872–7786) and Pan Am (tel. 800/221–1111). Other U.S. airlines that serve Orlando include American, American Trans Air, Continental, Delta, Eastern,

Florida Express, Midway Express, Northwest, Piedmont, Trans World Airlines, United, USAir, and Suncoast Airlines.

From the Airport to the Hotels For Disney World, Lake Buena Vista Village, and International Dr., but not Rte. 192, the cheapest transportation is by **Gray Line of Orlando** (tel. 407/422–5550). The 47-passenger buses leave for Disney World every 30 minutes. The cost is $10 one-way, $15 round-trip, free for each child under 15 accompanied by an adult. **Airport Limousine Service of Orlando** (tel. 407/423–5566) sends 11-passenger vans to Disney World and along Rte. 192 every 30 minutes. One-way $11, round-trip $20. The trip takes about 35 minutes.

Taxis Taxis are the fastest way to travel (25–30 minutes to hotels), but the ride won't be cheap. To Walt Disney World hotels or to hotels along West 192, a cab trip will cost about $35 plus tip. To the International Drive area, it will cost about $25 plus tip.

By Car When leaving the airport, a left turn onto the Beeline Expressway (Rte. 528) leads you past Sea World to I–4. A left turn on I–4 takes you to Walt Disney World Village and Epcot Center or to U.S. 192 and the Magic Kingdom entrance. A right turn on I–4 from the Beeline takes you past Hwy. 482 and into downtown Orlando.

By Train **Amtrak** (tel. 800/USA–RAIL) stops both in Orlando (1400 Sligh Blvd.) and in Kissimmee (416 Pleasant St.).

By Bus Contact **Greyhound/Trailways** (tel. 407/843–7720) or consult your phone book or directory assistance for a local number that will automatically connect you with the national Greyhound/Trailways Information Center.

Getting Around

By Car The most important artery in the Orlando area is **Interstate 4 (I–4)**, which many locals simply refer to as "the Expressway." This interstate ties everything together, and you'll invariably receive directions in reference to it. The problem is that I–4 is considered an east–west expressway in our national road system (the even numbers refer to an east–west orientation, the odd numbers to a north–south orientation). I–4 does run from east to west *if* you follow it from the Atlantic Coast to Florida's Gulf of Mexico. But in the Orlando area, I–4 actually runs north–south. Always remember, therefore, that when the signs say north, you are often going east, and when the signs say south, you are often going west. Think north–east and south–west. Another main drag is **International Drive,** which has several major hotels, restaurants, and shopping centers. You can get onto International Drive from I–4 Exits 28 and 29.

The other main road, Irlo Bronson Memorial Highway (U.S. 192), cuts across I–4 at Exits 25A and 25B. This highway goes through the Kissimmee area and crosses Walt Disney World property.

By Bus If you are staying along International Drive in Kissimmee or in Orlando proper, you can take advantage of the limited public bus system, but only to get places locally. To find out which bus to take, ask your hotel clerk or call the Tri-County Transit Authority Information Office (tel. 407/841–8240) during business hours. A transfer will add 5¢ to the regular 75¢ fare.

By Taxi Taxi fares start at $2.25 and cost $1.30 for each mile thereafter, with slightly higher rates during nighttime hours. Call **Yellow Cab Co.** (tel. 407/699–9999 or 423–4455) or **Town and Country Cab** (tel. 407/828–3035).

From the Hotel to the Airport From downtown Orlando, you can catch a public bus to the airport from the main terminal of the **Tri-County Transit Authority** (438 Woods Ave., Orlando, tel. 407/841–8240). Because downtown Orlando is far from most tourist hotels, you will probably want to use a private shuttle service ($10 adults, $5 children). Ask at your hotel desk for the most convenient service, or contact **Airport Limousine** (tel. 407/422–4561 or 407/423–5566) or **First Class Transportation** (tel. 407/351–5590).

Guided Tours

General-Interest Tours **Cosmos/Globus Gateway** (150 S. Los Robles Ave., Suite 860, Pasadena, CA 91101, tel. 818/449–0919 or 800/556–5454) offers a comprehensive eight-day tour that includes entry to Disney World and Epcot Center. If you live on the East Coast of the country, **Domenico Tours** (751 Broadway, Bayonne, NJ 07002, tel. 800/554–TOUR) will take you to Orlando via coach tour or direct flight; from the west, it's air only.

Special-Interest Tours

Boat Tours **Rivership Romance.** A 110-foot, triple-decker catamaran takes visitors up the cypress-lined, densely forested St. John's River for either a few hours or a couple of days. The day trips take you through a peaceful, tropical landscape. You may see some interesting wildlife, such as manatees (the endangered sea cows), blue herons, and bald eagles, but most of the time you'll be listening to the silence. The cost ranges from $15 to over $30 per person ($190 for the overnight trip), including some meals. *Monroe Harbour, 433 North Palmetto Ave., Sanford. From I–4 take Exit 51 and drive east 4 mi., tel. 407/321–5091. Dress: casual. Reservations required. MC, V. Moderate.*

Balloon Tours **Balloon Flights of Florida** (129 W. Church St., Orlando, tel. 407/422–2434). This Church Street Station event is not cheap, but it's an experience you'll never forget. The flight, led by a balloonist who made the first trip across the Atlantic, is followed by brunch at Lili Marlene's. $135 per person.

Rise and Float Balloon Tours (5931 American Way, International Plaza, Orlando, tel. 407/352–8191). Depart at dawn and indulge yourself with an in-flight champagne breakfast.

Helicopter Tours **J. C. Helicopters.** Sign up for aerial tours of Walt Disney World, Sea World, and other attractions. The flights at dark are spectacular. Prices start at $20 for adults, $10 for children. *Orlando Hyatt Heliport at I–4 and U.S. 192 (next to Walt Disney World), tel. 407/847–7222.*

Important Addresses and Numbers

Visitors to **Mickey's Kingdom** can direct all inquiries to Walt Disney World (Box 10000, Lake Buena Vista, FL 32830. Attention: Guest letters. Tel. 407/824–4321.) Request a free copy of the *Walt Disney World Vacation Guide.*

For information on the greater Orlando area, contact the **Tourist Information Center,** 8445 International Drive, Orlando 32819, tel. 407/351–0412. Open 8–8. Ask for the free *Discover Orlando* guidebook.

Visitors to the Kissimmee area on U.S. 192 can get brochures from the **Kissimmee/St. Cloud Convention and Visitors' Bureau,** 1925 E. Spacecoat Hwy., E. U.S. 192, Kissimmee 32742, tel. 407/849–5000, in FL 800/432–9199, outside FL 800/327–9159.

Emergency Dial 911 for **police** and **ambulance** in an emergency.

Doctor Hospital emergency rooms are open 24 hours a day. The most accessible hospital, located in the International Drive area, is the **Orlando Regional Medical Center/Sound Lake Hospital** (9400 Turkey Lake Rd., tel. 407/351–0550).

For hotel-room visits by physicians for minor medical care, contact a mobile minor emergency service called **Housemed** (tel. 407/648–9234).

24-Hour Pharmacies **Dyer's Apothecary** (201 Hilda St., Suite 16, Kissimmee, tel. 407/846–6565, 24-hour emergency service, 407/847–4604) offers delivery service.
Eckerd Drugs (908 Lee Rd., Orlando, tel. 407/644–6908).

Road Service **AAA Emergency Road Service** (tel. 407/893–3333).

Disney World Walt Disney World Information, tel. 407/824–4321
Accommodations Reservations, tel. 407/824–8000
Dinner Show Reservations, tel. 407/824–8000
Walt Disney World Resort Dining/Recreation Information, tel. 407/824–3737
Tours (Magic Kingdom and Epcot Center), tel. 407/827–8233
Magic Kingdom Lost and Found, tel. 407/824–4521
Epcot Center Lost and Found, tel. 407/827–8236
Car Care Center, tel. 407/824–4813
Western Union at Walt Disney World, tel. 407/824–3456
Banking Information (Sun Bank), tel. 407/824–5767
Time and Weather, tel. 407/422–1611
Walt Disney World Shopping Village Information, tel. 407/828–3058
KinderCare Child Care, tel. 407/827–5444

Exploring Walt Disney World and the Orlando Area

Walt Disney World has its own complete transportation system to get you wherever you want to go. Because the property is so extensive, however—27,400 acres, 98 of them for the Magic Kingdom and another 260 for Epcot—the system can be a bit confusing, even for an experienced visitor. Best-known is the elevated monorail, which connects Walt Disney World's biggest resorts and attractions. There are also extensive bus, motor-launch, and ferry systems. If you are staying at an on-site resort or a Walt Disney World Village hotel or if you hold a combination Magic Kingdom–Epcot Center ticket, transportation is free. If not, you can buy unlimited transportation within Walt Disney World for $2.50 a day.

By Monorail This elevated train of the future operates daily 7:30 AM–11 PM (or until 1 hour after the Magic Kingdom closes). It does not go everywhere. The central connecting station for the monorail is called the **Transportation and Ticket Center** (TTC). One monorail line goes from the TTC to the Magic Kingdom and back in a loop around Seven Seas Lagoon. This line is primarily for visitors who are not guests at the on-site resorts. Another line

Orlando Area

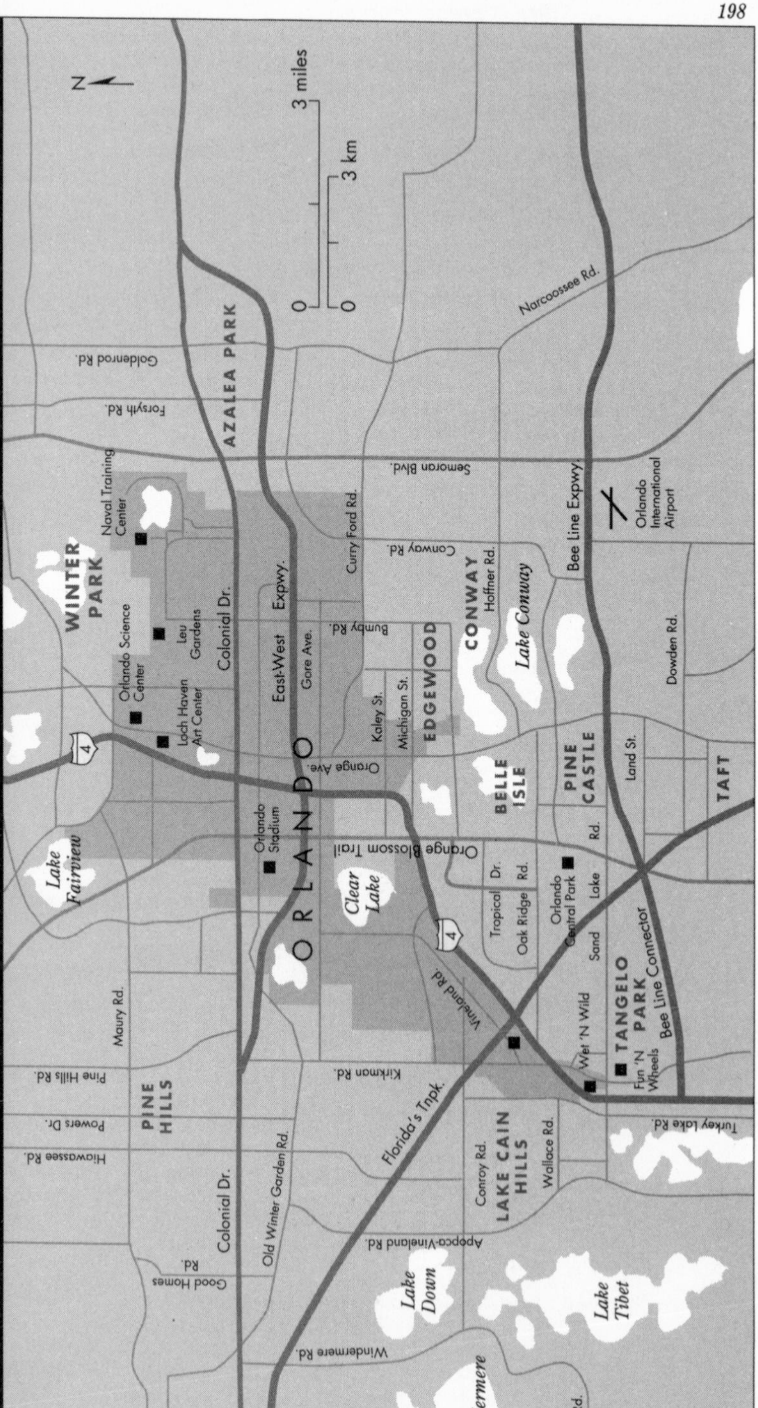

connects the TTC with the Contemporary Resort, the Magic Kingdom, the Grand Floridian, and the Polynesian. A third line goes directly from the TTC to Epcot Center. The TTC is where you can transfer between the Disney bus system and the monorail. When you get to a monorail station, ask an attendant if you can sit in the conductor's cabin, called "the nose" by the crew.

By Bus Each bus carries a small color-coded or letter-coded pennant on the front and sides. Here's where the buses take you:

Green—Connects Disney Inn and Polynesian Village Resort with the TTC. This line operates every 15 minutes 8 AM–2 AM.

Blue–Connects Fort Wilderness Resort Area with the TTC. These buses operate every eight minutes 8 AM–2 AM.

Green and **Gold**—If the pennant has the letters EC/V on it, the bus connects the TTC to the villas, Lake Buena Vista, and World Disney World Village. If the bus has the letters MK on it, it travels only between the TTC and the villas. These lines operate every 20 minutes 8 AM–2 AM.

Silver and **Red Stripe**—Connects Walt Disney World Village Hotel Plaza, Lake Buena Vista, and Epcot Center. This bus operates every 20 minutes from 8 AM until two hours after Epcot closes.

Red and **White**—Connects Walt Disney World Village Hotel Plaza and Lake Buena Vista with the TTC. This line operates every 20 minutes, 8 AM until about two hours after the Magic Kingdom closes.

By Motor Launch These boats depart about every 20 minutes and use color-coded flags to identify their route. They are for the use of Disney resort guests only, with the exception of day guests with special activity tickets to such places as Discovery Island and River Country.

Blue—Connects the Contemporary Resort with the Fort Wilderness Resort Area and Discovery Island every 15 minutes 10 AM–10 PM.

Green—Connects the Magic Kingdom, Fort Wilderness Resort Area, and Discovery Island (when it is open) every 20–25 minutes from half an hour before opening until closing time.

By Ferry A ferry service runs across Seven Seas Lagoon connecting the TTC with the Magic Kingdom. It departs from each side of the lagoon about every 12 minutes when the Magic Kingdom is open. It often gets you to the Magic Kingdom faster than does the monorail. It is a comfortable ride, gliding over the lagoon's silky waters. Most people heading for the Magic Kingdom opt for the monorail and then take the ferry back at day's end, so if you want to avoid the worst of the lines for both the monorail and ferry, take the opposite tack.

By Car If you arrive at either the Magic Kingdom or Epcot Center by car, there is a $3 parking charge. If you're staying at a Disney World hotel, show your guest ID for free parking. Remember or write down *exactly* where you park; you'll have a long wait before the sea of automobiles has departed and yours is the only one left. Trams make frequent trips between the parking areas and the front gate.

Car Care: If your car won't start or it breaks down in Disney World, the **Car Care Center** near the Toll Plaza to the Magic

Walt Disney World

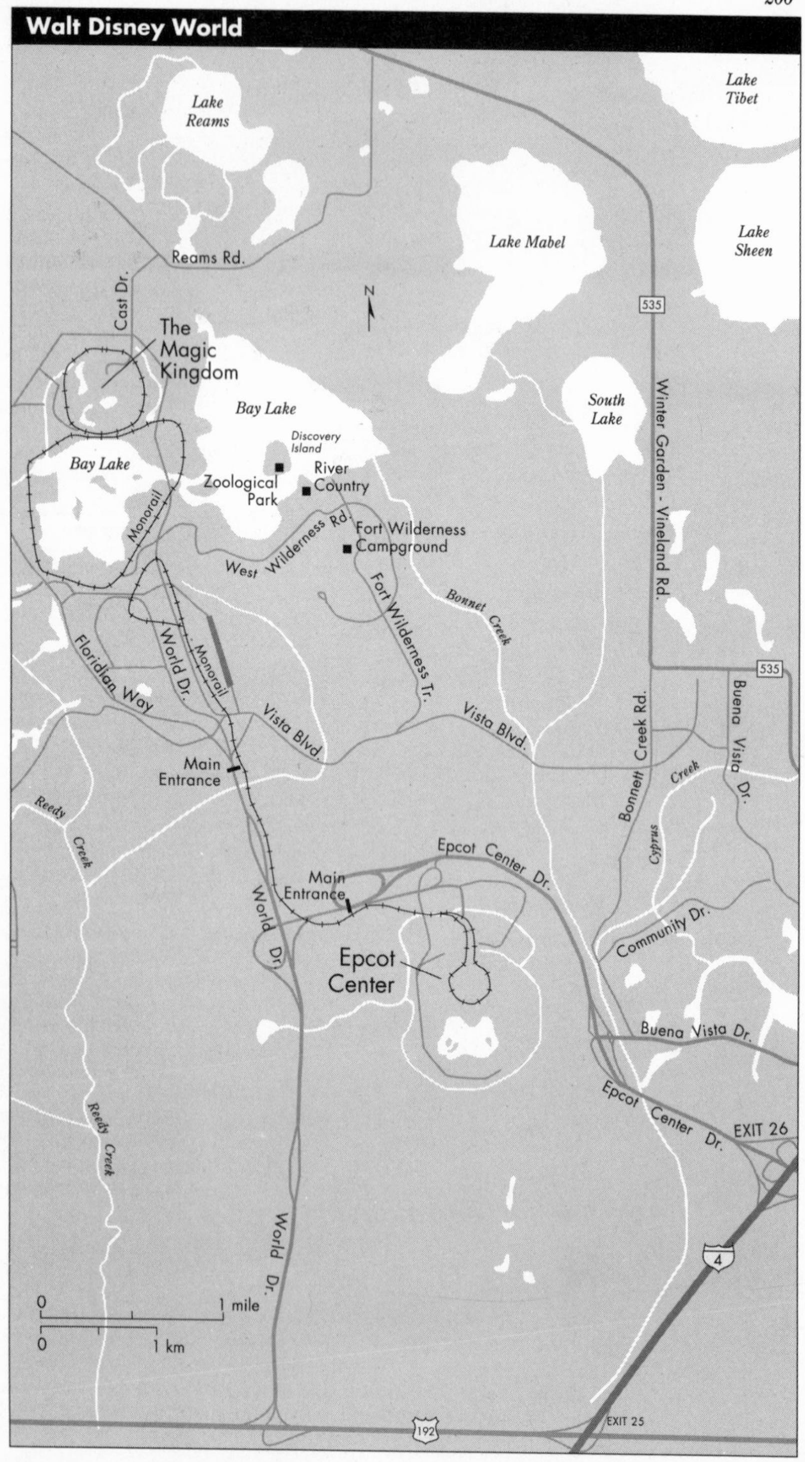

Kingdom offers emergency road service. Open Mon.–Fri, 7 AM–6 PM, tel. 407/824–4813.

Admission Visiting Walt Disney World is not cheap, especially if you have a child or two along. There are no discounted family tickets. Seven different types of admission tickets are sold in one of two categories—adult, meaning everyone aged 10 and older, and children aged 3–9. Children under age 3 get in free.

The word "ticket" is used by Disney World only to mean a single day's admission to either the Magic Kingdom or Epcot Center. The price is $28 for adults and $22 for children. If you want to spend two days visiting either or both attractions, you have to buy a separate ticket each day. For more than two days, Disney World offers what it calls the Passport, which admits you to both the Magic Kingdom and Epcot Center, along with unlimited use of the internal transportation system.

Here is a list of prices. They are subject to change, so call for confirmation.

One-day ticket	$28 adults, $22 children
Three-day passport	$78 adults, $63 children; *$77/$62**
Four-day passport	$96 adults, $77 children; *$94/$75**
Five-day passport	$110 adults, $88 children; *$107/$85**
River Country, one day	$11.75 adults, $9.25 children; *$10.75/$8.25**
River Country, two days	$17.75 adults, $13.75 children; *$16.75/$12.75**
Discovery Island, one day	$7.50 adults, $4 children; *$6/$3**
Combined River Country/Discovery Island, one day	$15 adults, $11 children; *$14/$10**
Annual pass	$165 adults, $140 children

**visitors staying in a Disney World Resort or in a resort in the WDW Village Hotel Plaza*

Passports are available for three, four, or five days. They can save you a great deal of money and may be advisable even if you're staying in the area for only two days. Each time you use a Passport, the entry date is stamped on it; the remaining days may be used any time in the future. If you buy a one-day ticket and later decide to extend your visit, you can get full credit for it toward the purchase of any Passport. Exchanges can be made at City Hall in the Magic Kingdom or at Earth Station in Epcot Center. Do this before leaving the park; once you've left, the ticket is worthless.

Tickets and Passports to Walt Disney World and Epcot Center may be purchased at admission booths at the TTC, in on-site or Hotel Plaza resorts (if you're a registered guest), or at the Walt Disney World kiosk on the second floor of the main terminal at Orlando International Airport. If you want to buy tickets before you arrive in Orlando, send a check or money order to Admissions, Walt Disney World, Box 10000, Lake Buena Vista, FL 32830. Remember, it usually takes four to six weeks for the order to be processed, so write well in advance.

If you want to leave the Magic Kingdom or Epcot Center and return on the same day, be sure to have your hand stamped on the way out. You'll need your ticket *and* the hand stamp to be readmitted.

Operating Hours Hours vary widely throughout the year and change for school and legal holidays. In general, the longest hours are during the summer months, when the Magic Kingdom is open until midnight and Epcot Center is open to 11 PM. At other times of year, Epcot Center is open until 8 PM, and the Magic Kingdom to 6 PM, with Main Street remaining open until 7. Though both parks usually open at 9 AM, visitors can enter the grounds up to an hour earlier and get a significant head start on the crowds. A good bet for breakfast before 9 AM is the **Crystal Palace** (turn left at the end of Main St.). For current hours, tel. 407/824–4321.

When to Go The busiest days of the week are Monday, Tuesday, and Wednesday. You would think the weekend would be busiest, but it's not. Perhaps everyone tries to beat the crowds by going in the early part of the week, or perhaps vacationers leave on Friday, travel over the weekend, and begin their visits on Monday. Whatever the reason, Friday and Sunday are the slowest days, and Thursdays and Saturdays are only moderately busy.

The best time of the day to be at the parks is in the late afternoon and evening—especially during the summer months and holidays, when the attractions stay open late. It also helps to arrive as soon as the gates open, up to an hour before the "official" opening time. The most crowded time of the year is from Christmas through New Year's Day. The parks are also packed around Easter.

Memorial Day weekend is not only crowded, but hot. Other busy times of the year are mid-June–mid-August, Thanksgiving weekend, the week of Washington's Birthday in mid-February, and the weeks of college spring break in late March. The rest of the year is generally hassle-free, particularly from early September until just before Thanksgiving. The best time of all is from just after Thanksgiving weekend until the beginning of the Christmas holidays. Another excellent time is from early January through the first week of February. If you must go during summer, late August is best.

Magic Kingdom

You'll first see Town Square City Hall is on your left. MGM studios are on your right. The railroad station is directly behind you.

Sprawling before you is Main Street—a shop-filled boulevard with Victorian-style stores, and dining spots. Walk two blocks along Main Street and you'll enter Central Plaza, with **Cinderella's Castle** rising directly in front of you. This is the hub of the Kingdom; all the "lands" radiate out from it.

This is as good a place as any to see the daily parade at 3 PM. All Disney's characters are featured in the 20-minute show. In summer and during holidays, there's also an Electrical Parade of giant floats at 9 and 11 PM.

City Hall is a good place to pick up the *Magic Kingdom Guide Book* and a schedule of daily events. It is also the lost-and-found point for property and people. Nearby, beneath the railroad, are lockers where bags and gifts may be stored.

A great way to get an overview of the Kingdom is to hop aboard the railroad and take a 14-minute, 1½-mile ride around the perimeter of the park. You can board at the Victorian-style station you pass beneath to enter Town Square. The only other station is at Frontierland. The Magic Kingdom is the home of Mickey and Minnie Mouse, Goofy, Pluto, and dozens of other Disney characters. Seen on the streets, they're a child's delight, and even adults beam with pleasure as they shake hands with the fantasies they've grown up with. Characters are always willing to pose for photos. They're most often found next to City Hall.

The Magic Kingdom is divided into six lands. Stories are told of tourists who spend an entire day in one land, thinking they have seen all the park; don't let that happen to you.

Adventureland These soft adventures to far-off lands are among the most crowded in the Kingdom. Visit as late in the afternoon as possible or, better yet, in the evening. Adventureland is the worst place to be in the morning, because other travel guides recommend it as a first stop.

Swiss Family Robinson Treehouse (popular; all ages) is a good way to get some exercise and a panoramic view of the park. Visitors walk up the many-staired tree in single file, a trip that can take up to a half hour.

Jungle Cruise (popular; all ages) takes visitors along the Nile, across an Amazon jungle, and so on. The tour guide's narration is corny but nevertheless brings laughs. The ride itself takes only 10 minutes, but the line can take as long as an hour. Go during the parade time at 3 PM or after 5 PM. Avoid 10 AM–noon.

Pirates of the Caribbean (very popular; all ages) is a journey through a world of pirate strongholds and treasure-filled dungeons. The Audio-Animatronics pirates are first rate.

Tropical Serenade-Enchanted Tiki Birds (not very popular; for children) was one of the first Audio-Animatronic creations. The show's talking birds are somewhat charming, but the show itself can be confusing because it's difficult to tell what bird is speaking at any time. If you're in a hurry, you can safely skip this one.

Fantasyland This is a land in which storybook dreams come true and children are very much in their element.

There are a few traditional amusement-park rides with Disney themes, such as the Mad Tea Party, where teacups spin around a large teapot. Other favorites are Dumbo the Flying Elephant and a spectacular merry-go-round. There are also several indoor rides that spook and enchant children as they pass through a cartoon world filled with many familiar fairy-tale characters.

20,000 Leagues Under the Sea (very popular; all ages) is an underwater cruise inspired by the Jules Verne novel. Lines move slowly, but how often do you get to ride in a submarine and explore the world beneath the sea?

Frontierland "Frontier Fun" is the theme of this gold-rush town of the Southwest.

Big Thunder Mountain (very popular) is a scream-inducing roller coaster. Children must be at least 4′2″. For real roller-coaster fans, the ride is somewhat tame, but it's one of two fast rides in Walt Disney World (Space Mountain is the other one). Try to go in the evenings when the mountain is lit up and lines are relatively short.

Country Bear Jamboree (moderately popular; for children) is a somewhat dated show with furry bears who sing and dance. A better show is put on at **Diamond Horseshow Jamboree** (popular; all ages)—a live stage show with singing, dancing, and innocently rowdy entertainment. You must make reservations early in the morning at the Hospitality House on Main Street, because there are only five shows daily. The strongest demand is usually for the noon and 1:30 shows. Other performances are at 3, 4:30, and 6 PM.

Tom Sawyer's Island (not very popular; all ages) has little to see but offers a happy respite from the crowds on the mainland. Adults can relax at **Aunt Polly's Porch** with lemonade and lunch while the kids scramble up Harper's Mill (a working windmill) or explore the caves and bridges.

Liberty Square This is a small land adjoining and blending into Frontierland. It's theme is Colonial history and it has a few decent but tame attractions.

Haunted Mansion (very popular; all ages) is the most popular attraction here. The spine-tingling effects, with ghosts, goblins, and graveyards, are realistic and may be too intense for the very young. The best time to go is in the morning when the lines are short. Avoid the noon–4 PM rush.

Liberty Square Riverboats (moderately popular; all ages) take visitors on a quiet, half-mile cruise through the rivers of America, passing Wild West scenes. It's not great entertainment, but it can be a comfortable escape from the crowds and the sun.

Hall of Presidents (moderately popular; adults or mature children) was a sensation when it first opened, but now it seems a bit slow and unexciting. Still, visitors of all ages find it interesting to see the Audio-Animatronics presidents in action. Adults find it educational; young children find it boring.

Tomorrowland "Fun in the Future" is the motto of this land. Save it for the future if your time is limited because, except for Space Mountain, its rides are lackluster compared to others in the park. One major problem is that most attractions are sponsored by major corporations, and audiences are bombarded by commercial advertising.

Space Mountain (very popular; children must be at least age 3) is the main attraction, though children under 7 must be accompanied by an adult. The space-age roller coaster may never go over 20 miles an hour, but the experience in the dark, with everyone screaming, is thrilling, even for hardcore roller-coaster fans.

American Journey, including **CircleVision, Carousel of Progress,** and **Mission to Mars** (unpopular; all ages), is a series of 20-minute attractions that may be 20 minutes too long. Circlevision's patriotic look at the landscape of America on nine movie screens is perhaps the best bet.

Grand Prix Raceway (popular) takes children in mini race cars to speeds up to seven miles per hour. The ride is confining with little room to maneuver your vehicle. Children must be at least age 7 to ride alone, and there are usually long lines.

Epcot Center

Epcot Center is divided almost equally into two distinct areas separated by the 40-acre World Showcase Lagoon. The northern half, which is where the admission gates are, is filled with the Future World pavilions, sponsored by major American corporations. The southern half is World Showcase. If you want to minimize the time spent waiting in line, do the opposite of what most people do. In the morning, visitors head for what's closest, which is Future World, so you should begin at World Showcase. In the afternoon, come back and explore Future World when the crowds have shifted to World Showcase. Evening hours, of course, are the best times for visiting either area.

Visitors who are familiar with the Magic Kingdom find something entirely different at Epcot Center. For one thing, Epcot is twice as large. For another, Epcot's attractions all have an educational dimension. **Future World** explores technological concepts, such as energy and communications, in entertaining ways. **World Showcase** is a series of pavilions in which various nations portray their cultures through a combination of films, exhibits, and seemingly endless shops. Bring a hearty appetite, because ethnic cuisines are featured in each foreign pavilion.

As you enter Epcot Center, you'll pass beneath **Spaceship Earth,** a 17-story sphere that marks the start of Future World. World Showcase is behind Future World. Stop first at Earth Station to pick up a guidebook and entertainment schedule. Also, make reservations for the busy, full-service restaurants here. Remember that it's not unusual for most restaurants to be fully reserved by 10 AM in the peak season. Remember also that guests who are staying in on-site properties can make their reservations ahead of time.

Future World The subjects explored at Future World include the ocean, agriculture, communications, energy, imagination, and transportation.

Communicore East and West (popular; all ages). These two buildings house exhibits by the various sponsoring companies of Epcot Center. The educational computer games are very popular with children.

Horizons (popular; all ages). A journey into the lifestyles of the next century, with robitic-staffed farms, ocean colonies, and space cities.

Journey Into Imagination (popular; for children). Two of the most popular characters, Dreamfiner and Figment, are your guides on a tour of the creative process that depicts how literature and art come from the sparks of ideas. Particularly popular with teenagers is **Captain EO,** a $17 million, 3-D film starring singer Michael Jackson. The experience here is well worth the wait in line, but try to go in the late afternoon when there are fewer people. Also be sure to see the "dancing waters" display in front of the entrance to Captain EO.

Listen to the Land (popular; for adults and mature children). The main event here is a boat ride through the experimental greenhouse that demonstrates how plants may be grown in the future, not only on Earth but in outer space. It's provocative for adults but somewhat dull for children. Those who are interested can arrange to join one of several walking tours. Reservations can be made in the morning on the lower floor, in the corner opposite the boat ride, behind the *Broccoli and Company* kiosk.

The Living Seas (popular; all ages). This is a new attraction and one of the most popular. It's the largest facility ever dedicated to the relationship of humans with the ocean and is sometimes known as the "eighth sea." Visitors take a gondola ride beneath the sea for a dynamic close-up look at marine life in a six-million-gallon aquarium more than four fathoms deep. There are more than 200 varieties of sea life among the 5,000 inhabitants. You can easily spend a half day here.

Spaceship Earth (very popular; all ages). This million-pound silver geosphere is so large that on clear days airline passengers on both coasts of Florida can see it. Inside the dome, visitors take a highly praised journey through the dramatic history of communications, from cave drawings to space-age technology. Visitors see the dome when they first get to Epcot Center and routinely make their way here. You would be well advised to wait until the late afternoon when the crowds have thinned.

Universe of Energy (very popular; all ages). This is a fast-paced exploration of the forces that fuel our lives and the universe. You'll ride on theater seats through a display on the Earth's beginnings, past battling dinosaurs, through earthquakes, and beneath volcanoes.

World Showcase

World Showcase offers an adventure that is very different from what you will experience in either the world of the future in Epcot Center or the world of fairy tales in the Magic Kingdom. The Showcase presents an ideal image—a Disney version—of life in 10 countries. Native food, entertainment, and wares are on display in each of the pavilions. Most of the nations have done an imaginative and painstaking job of re-creating scale models of their best-known monuments, such as the Eiffel Tower in France, a Mayan temple in Mexico, and a majestic pagoda in Japan. During the day, these structures are impressive enough, but at night, when the darkness inhibits one's ability to judge their size, you get the sense that you are seeing the real thing. It's a wonderful illusion, indeed.

Unlike Future World and the Magic Kingdom, the Showcase doesn't offer amusement-park-type rides (except in Mexico and, in late 1988, Norway). Instead, it features breathtaking films, ethnic art, cultural entertainment, Audio-Animatronics presentations, and dozens of fine shops and restaurants featuring national specialities. The most enjoyable diversions in World Showcase are not inside the national pavilions but in front of them. At various times of the day, each pavilion offers some sort of live street show, featuring comedy, song, or dance routines and demonstrations of folk arts and crafts. Don't be shy about trying to improve your foreign-language skills!

The only unfortunate note in this cultural smorgasbord is that with so many shops and restaurants, there seems to be more of an emphasis on commercialism than on education or entertainment. Know in advance that a taste of a nation may mean a bite out of your bank account.

The focal point of World Showcase, on the opposite side of the lagoon from the entrance area, is the host pavilion, the **American Adventure.** The pavilions of the other countries fan out from the right and left of American Adventure, encircling the lagoon. Going clockwise from the left as you enter World Showcase are the pavilions of Mexico, Norway, People's Republic of China, Germany, Italy, the United States, Japan, Morocco, France, United Kingdom, and Canada.

Mexico: This tame "boat ride" inside the pavilion is much like rides you have seen in the Magic Kingdom. The major tourist attractions of Mexico are its theme. Windows and doorways are filled with colorful video images, and rooms are full of dancing, costumed puppets, and Audio-Animatronics landscapes that roar, storm, and light up as you journey from the jungles of the Yucatan to the skyline of Mexico City. In front of the pavilion is **Cantina de San Angel**—a fast-food joint and bar that's good for burritos, margaritas, and, at night, a great view of the laser show.

Norway: Scheduled to open in late 1988, this pavilion will take visitors on a ride in small Viking vessels through the landscape and history of this Scandinavian country. Visitors will tour a 10th-century Viking Village, sail through a fjord, and experience a storm and the midnight sun. The main spectacle of this pavilion will be a re-creation of a 14th-century coastal fortress in Oslo called Akershus.

China: The much-talked about film should not be missed. It is a CircleVision presentation on the landscape of China, taking viewers on a fantastic journey from inner Mongolia to the Tibetan mountains, along the Great Wall, into Beijing, and through some of the most glorious landscape on Earth. The Chinese pavilion also has a wonderful shopping gallery with ivory goods, jade jewelry, hand-painted fans, opulent carpets, and inlaid furniture.

Germany: The main event in this replica of a small Bavarian village is the restaurant's oompah band show, with singers, dancers, and musicians. The indoor village is worth a quick look. There are four shows daily. You'll also find plenty of German wines, sweets, glassware, and porcelain for sale.

Italy: The main attraction is the architecture—a reproduction of St. Mark's Square in Venice, with the Campanile (bell tower) di San Marco as its centerpiece, and, behind it, the elegant and elaborately decorated Doges Palace. Complementing these buildings are Venetian bridges, gondolas, colorful barber poles, and the sculpture of the Lion of St. Mark atop a column. In the plaza of this pavilion, you can watch and participate in a comedy show put on by an Italian theater troupe. The show can be amusing, but only if there is a full, lively audience.

American Adventure: This is a 30-minute Audio-Animatronics show about the making of the United States. The huge, colonial-style theater features the most sophisticated and realistic animatronics characters in Disney World. The show takes visitors from the arrival of the Pilgrims through the revolutionary war, the Civil War, the taming of the West, the two world wars; and so on. The voyage is hosted by Benjamin Franklin and Mark Twain. Some will find the presentation a bit long, even though 30 minutes is not much time to cover 200 years of history. Many people find it inspiringly patriotic, but children may take this opportunity to catch a few winks—the dramatic music often puts them right to sleep.

Directly opposite the American Adventure pavilion, on the lagoon, is the open-air **American Gardens Theater by the Shore,** where live, high-energy, all-American shows are performed about four times a day. Show times vary but are posted each day on boards in front of the theater's entrances.

Japan: Elegant landscaping of rocks, streams, trees, and shrubs combines with traditional architecture to create this peaceful and charming pavilion. Inside the *torii* gates are monumental bronze sculptures and a pagoda. Of special interest are the Mitsukoshi Department Store, where lacquered dinnerware, teapots, vases, bonzai trees, and Japanese dolls and toys are for sale, and the Bijutsu-kan Gallery, featuring temporary exhibits of traditional Japanese crafts. The Yakitori House serves inexpensive Japanese fast food in a pleasant garden—a good bet for lunch.

Morocco: This is one of the more spectacular-looking of the pavilions. It has a replica of the Koutoubia Minaret from a famous prayer house in Marrakesh; a gallery of Moroccan art, tapestries, and traditional costumes; and a street with shops selling basketry, leather goods, samovars, and exquisite jewelry. Dancers move to the exotic rhythms of North Africa.

France: This 18-minute film is projected on a five-panel semicircular screen and takes viewers on a romantic tour of France—through the countryside, into the Alps, along the coast, and, of course, into Paris. It is a sophisticated visual adventure with little narration but much lyrical poetry and classical music.

The pavilion itself resembles a French boulevard, lined with shops and cafes. Of special interest are **Tout Pour le Gourmet** and **Les Vins de France,** two shops featuring French culinary specialties, such as wines, cheeses, mustards, herbs, and pâtés. A little patisserie/boulangerie prepares all kinds of baked goods. Two restaurants, **Bistro de Paris** and **Au Petit Cafe,** are ideal for lunch. Also in this pavilion is an impressive model of the Eiffel Tower that was constructed using Alexandre-Gustave Eiffel's original blueprints.

United Kingdom: On this street from Old London are a variety of architectural styles, from thatched–roof cottages to Tudor and ornate Victorian homes. The city square and rural streets are filled with numerous food, toy, and souvenir shops. The very British **Rose and Crown** pub serves Stilton cheese, ales, and simple English fare. Street artists and a minstrel troupe perform throughout the day.

Canada: This CircleVision film takes its audience into Canada's great outdoors, from the magnificent snow-peaked Rockies, down sprawling Arctic glaciers, and across the plains to Montreal. Peaceful gardens, a rocky gorge, an emporium selling everything from sheepskins to lumberjack shirts and maple syrup, and a cafeteria-style restaurant called **Le Cellier** are other highlights of this quaint pavilion.

Other Attractions in Disney World

Typhoon Lagoon Scheduled to open in mid-1988, this 50-acre aquatic entertainment complex will feature the largest water-slide mountain in the world and a huge wave-making lagoon for swimming and surfing. The water park will include a Swiss Family Robinson–type tropical island, covered with lush greenery, where guests may play at being shipwrecked. A saltwater pool will contain a coral reef, where snorkelers can come mask to face with all sorts of Caribbean sea creatures, such as groupers, parrotfish, and even baby sharks.

Disney–MGM Studio Tour The biggest new addition to Disney World will be the Disney-MGM studios (now scheduled to open in April 1989), a complete working film-production facility that will consist of an animation complex, four massive sound stages, a back lot of streets and sets, and numerous film and television postproduction facilities, including some of the most technologically advanced special-effects studios in the business. Guests will be able to visit the Animation Building and get a firsthand view of Disney artists at work in the many stages of creating a Disney animated feature.

River Country In the backwoods setting of the Fort Wilderness Campground Resort, kids can slide, splash, and swim about in an aquatic playground, complete with whitewater inner-tubing channels and corkscrew water slides that splash down into a 300,000 gallon pond. The pool is heated during the winter, so kids can take a dip here year-round. During the summer, River Country can get very congested, so it's best to come late in the afternoon. *Fort Wilderness Resort, tel. 407/824–3737. Admission: adults 1 day $10.75, 2 days $16.75; children aged 3–9, 1 day $8.25, 2 days $12.75.*

Discovery Island Covered with exotic flora; small, furry animals; and colorful birdlife, this little island makes a great escape from the man-made tourist attractions of Walt Disney World. Visitors listen to nature as they stroll along winding pathways and across footbridges. Disney did not create these creatures—he just brought them here. Keep an eye out for the Galapagos tortoises, trumpeter swans, scarlet ibis, and bald eagles. Tickets are sold at Fort Wilderness's River Country, at the TTC, at guest service desks in the Disney resorts, and on the island itself. You can get there by watercraft from the Magic Kingdom, Contemporary Resorts, Polynesian Village, Grand Floridian, and River Country in Fort Wilderness. *Discovery Island: $6 adults, $3 children aged 3–9. River Country/Discovery Island combination ticket: $13 adults, $9 children aged 3–9.*

The Orlando Area

1. **Alligatorland Safari Zoo.** More than 1,600 exotic animals and birds in a natural setting. *U.S. 192 between Kissimmee and Walt Disney World, tel. 407/396–1012. Admission: $4.20 adults, $3.15 children 4–11. Open daily 8:30–8.*

2. **Boardwalk and Baseball.** Live entertainment, shows, and some 30 rides in a 135-acre theme park. The highlight is the largest wooden roller coaster in the southeast. *U.S. 27 near I–4 interchange. Box 800, Orlando, FL 32802, tel. 407/422–0643. Admission: $16.95 adults, $12.95 children under 46".*

3. **Bok Tower Gardens.** A 128-acre garden with pine forests, shady paths, and a bell tower that rings daily at 3 PM. *Between Haines City and Lake Wales off U.S. 27, tel. 813/676–1408. Admission: $2 per person; children under 12 free. Open daily 8–5:30.*

Alligatorland Safari Zoo, **1**
Boardwalk & Baseball, **2**
Bok Tower Gardens, **3**
Central Florida Zoological Park, **4**
Cypress Gardens, **5**
Fun 'n Wheels, **6**
Gatorland Zoo, **7**
Mystery Fun House, **8**
Places of Learning, **9**
Sea World, **10**
Wet 'n Wild, **11**
Xanadu, **12**

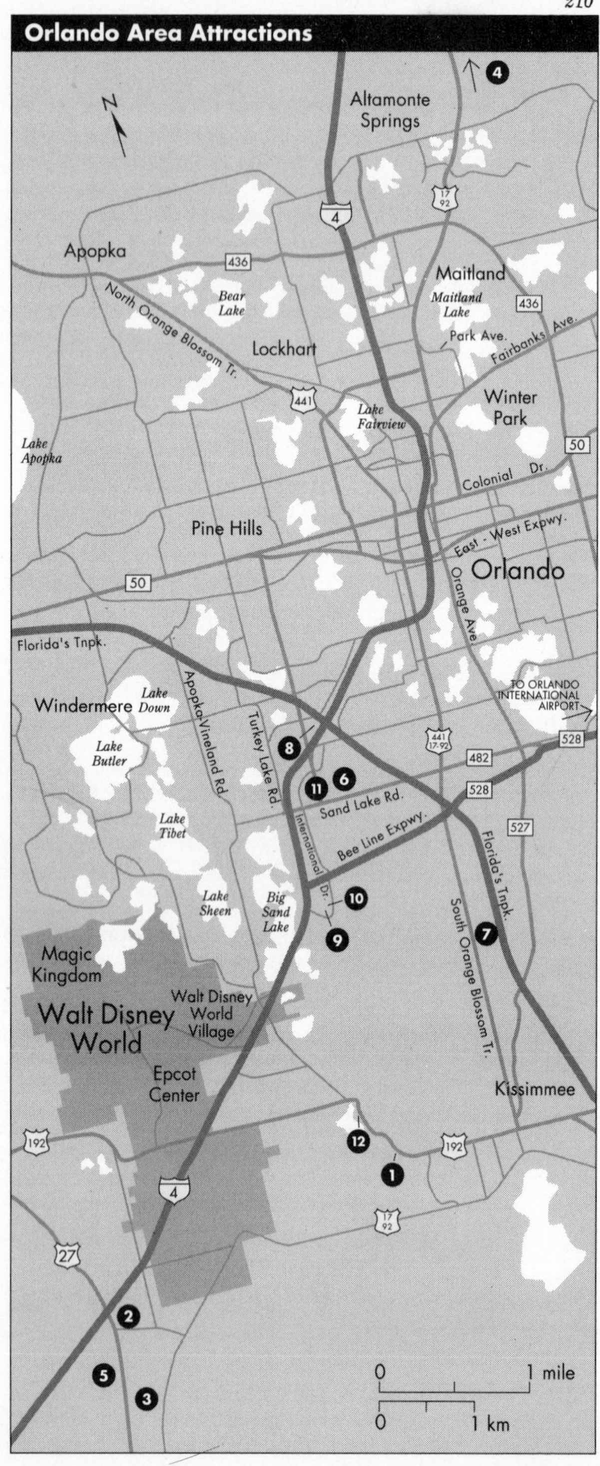

4 **Central Florida Zoological Park.** A 110-acre zoo. *U.S. 17–92, 1 mi east of I–4 and 4 mi west of Sanford, tel. 407/323–6471. Admission: $3.50 adults, $1.50 children 3–12. Open daily, 9–5.*

5 **Cypress Gardens.** Central Florida's original theme park features exotic flowers, waterskiing shows, and bird and alligator shows. *East of Winter Haven off Rte. 540, tel. 407/351–6606. Admission: $14.95 adults, $9.95 children 3–11. Open daily 8* AM*–dusk.*

6 **Fun 'n Wheels.** An expensive but active family theme park with go-cart tracks, rides, minigolf course, bumper boats, and cars. No general admission charge. *6739 Sand Lake Rd. at International Dr., Orlando, tel. 407/351–5651. Open daily 10* AM*–midnight.*

7 **Gatorland Zoo.** Thousands of alligators and crocodiles, sleeping in the sun are viewed from a walkway. Also snakes, flamingos, monkeys, and other Florida critters. *South of Orlando on U.S. 17–92 near Kissimmee, tel. 407/855–5496. Admission: $4.75 adults, $3.50 children aged 3–11. Open daily 8–6.*

8 **Mystery Fun House.** Magic mirrors, moving floors, laughing doors, barrels that roll, a shooting arcade—all are favorites with children, though the price is high for not much more than few minutes' entertainment. *5767 Major Blvd., off Kirkman Rd. near International Dr., tel. 407/351–3355. Admission: $5.95 adults, $4.95 children. Open daily 10–9.*

9 **Places of Learning.** Great selection of children's books and educational games. Recommended for the non-bookish, too. *6825 Academic Dr., Orlando, tel. 407/345–1038. Admission free. Open daily 9–6.*

10 **Sea World.** A major theme park celebrating sea life, including popular Baby Shamu and the awesome Shark Encounter. Marine animals perform in seven major shows. The park also has tropical fish, otter habitats, walrus training exhibits, botanical gardens, and other educational diversions in a setting more tranquil than that of most theme parks. *Located 10 mi south of Orlando at the intersection of I–4 and the Beeline Expressway, 7007 Sea World Dr., Orlando, tel. 407/351–3600 or 800/327–2420. Admission: $18.95 adults, $15.95 children aged 3–11. Open daily 8:30* AM*–9:30* PM*, with extended summer and holiday hours.*

11 **Wet 'n Wild.** Water slides, flumes, lazy rivers, and other water-related activities for swimmers and sunbathers. *6200 International Dr., Orlando, tel. 407/351–3200. Admission: $12.95 adults, $10.95 children aged 3–12, under age 2 free. Open daily 10–5, except in winter.*

12 **Xanadu.** A dome-shaped home showcasing technological and electronic devices. Guided tours daily. *Located at the intersection of U.S. 192 and Rte. 535, Kissimmee, tel. 407/396–1992. Admission: $4.75 adults, $3.50 children aged 4–17, under age 3 free.*

Orlando for Free

Citrus World, Inc. Free film showing citrus processing from tree to grocer; free samples. The film is shown every 40 minutes. *U.S. 27S, Lake Wales, about 1 hr south of Orlando, tel. 813/676–1411. Open Nov.–June, weekdays 9–4:30.*

Florida Cactus. Self-guided tours through a cactus nursery in Plymouth, 30 minutes north of Orlando. *Tel. 407/886-1833. Open weekdays 7:30–4:30, Sat. 7:30–11:30.*

Kissimmee Livestock Market, Inc. Going, going, gone in a real cattle auction, one of the oldest in Florida. *Box 2329, Kissimmee, FL 32742, tel. 407/847-3521. Open Wed. at 1 PM.*

Lake Wales Museum. Railroad memorabilia and area history. *325 S. Scenic Hwy., Lake Wales, tel. 813/676-5443. Open weekdays 9–5, Sat. 10–4.*

Monument of the States. A 50-foot-tall step pyramid built in the 1940s from concrete and stones donated by every state in the union. *Monument St., Lake Front Park, Kissimmee, tel. 407/847-3174.*

Orange County Historical Museum. Local memorabilia. *Loch Haven Park, 812 E. Rollins St., Orlando, tel. 407/898-8320. Open Tues.–Fri. 10–4, weekends 2–5. Closed Mon.*

Slocum Water Gardens. An extensive display of water plants. *1101 Cypress Gardens, Winter Haven, FL 33880, tel. 813/293-7151. Open weekdays 8–noon and 1–4, Sat. 8–noon.*

Tupperware World Headquarters. Narrated tours and displays depicting the evolution of food storage since the days of the ancient Egyptians. *U.S. 441 south of Orlando near Kissimmee, tel. 417/847-3111. Open weekdays 9–4.*

Water Ski Museum and Hall of Fame. Waterskiing fans will love what is probably the world's largest collection of equipment and memorabilia. *799 Overlook Dr., Winter Haven, tel. 813/324-2472. Open weekdays 10–5.*

Off the Beaten Track

Big Tree Park. One of the oldest and largest bald cypress trees in the country in a moss-draped park with picnic tables. *U.S. 17–92 on General Hutchinson Pkwy., Longwood, tel. 407/323-2500. Admission free. Open daily from 9 AM.*

Cassadaga. The mystic's mecca, an eerily tree-shaded village started by Spiritualists. Many of the residents read palms, peer into the future, and relay messages from the world beyond. When the psychics meet from January to March, many of the lectures and seminars are open to the public. Visit anytime. *Located off I-4, 7 miles south of DeLand. First Spiritualist Church of Cassadaga, Box 152, Cassadaga, FL 32706, tel. 904/228-2880.*

Hontoon Island State Park. Take a ferry-boat ride to a 1,650-acre park and campground with six rustic cabins, 22 campsites, a floating marina with slips for 54 boats, and an 80-foot observation tower. The park is off Rte. 44 on Hontoon Rd. *Hontoon Island, 2309 Riverride Rd., DeLand, FL 32720, tel. 904/736-5309. Open daily 8 AM–sunset. The ferry operates from 9 AM until an hour before the park closes.*

Navy Graduation. Recruit graduation parade every Friday at 9:45 AM. *Orlando Naval Training Center, General Rees Rd., entrance off Corrine Dr., Orlando, tel. 407/646-5054. Admission free.*

Pioneer Settlement for the Creative Arts. Folk museum with demonstrations of day-to-day pioneer lifestyles, a turn-of-the-century country store, and a train depot. *Intersection of U.S.*

40 and 17 in DeLand, about 40 miles from Orlando, tel. 904/749–2959. Admission: $2.50 adults, $1 children under age 16. Open weekdays 9–4, weekends by appointment.

Shopping

Altamonte Mall. Of the many regional retail centers, this is the largest and best known. The 30-acre, two-level, totally enclosed and air-conditioned mall has some 165 stores, including a huge Burdines, Jordan Marsh, Robinsons, and Sears. *A half mile east of I–4 on Rte. 436 in Altamonte Springs. Open Mon.–Sat. 10 AM–9 PM, Sun. noon–5:50 (except holidays).*

Florida Mall. This is a newer, large-scale center in Orlando, closer to the Walt Disney World tourism corridor. More than 160 stores in an enclosed mall that has three distinctive shopping areas—Victorian, Mediterranean, and Art Deco. *On the corner of Sand Lake Rd. (Rte. 482) and S. Orange Blossom Trail and near International Dr. Open Mon.–Sat. 10–9, Sun. noon–5:30.*

Flea World. Flea markets are scattered across the Orlando area, but this is the largest and most popular. Well over 1,000 booths, some air-conditioned, offer arts and crafts, auto parts, citrus produce, and so on. *Highway 17-92 between Orlando and Sanford. Admission free. Open Fri., Sat., and Sun. 8–5.*

Park Avenue. This is the place to go for fashionable, upscale shopping in Winter Park. Most stores are open weekdays 9–5, but you can window-browse anytime and enjoy the many restaurants and ice cream shops along the avenue. The shops range from the Ralph Lauren Polo Shop to small antique shops.

Mercado. The latest trend in Orlando is "festive retail," where shopping is combined with entertainment. At Mercado, visitors wander along brick streets and browse through more than 50 specialty shops in the atmosphere of a Mediterranean village. Free entertainment nightly includes the animated "Mugsy's Merry Medley." Exotic foods are all under one roof at the International Food Pavilion. *8445 International Dr. Open 10–10 daily.*

Old Town. Also in the tourist corridor is this collection of more than 70 specialty shops and restaurants along pedestrian walks. Tethered balloon rides are available. *5770 Spacecoast Pkwy., Kissimmee. Open daily 10–10.*

Walt Disney World. For unusual and sophisticated shopping, try World Showcase, where each country offers unique native merchandise. Walt Disney World Village in Lake Buena Vista, only two miles from Epcot Center and six miles from the Magic Kingdom, is a collection of some 20 shops that offer everything from Christmas tree ornaments to Disney memorabilia.

Participant Sports

Many resort hotels let nonguests use their golf and tennis facilities. Some hotels are affiliated with a particular country club and offer preferred rates. If you are staying near a resort with facilities you want to use, call and inquire about its policies. Be sure to call in advance to reserve courts and tee times. What follows is a list of the best places that are open to the public.

Bicycling The most scenic bike riding in Orlando is on the property of Walt Disney World, along roads that take you past forests, lakes, golf courses, and Disney's wooded resort villas and campgrounds. Bikes are available for rent at **Fort Wilderness Bike Barn** (tel. 407/824–2742). Bike rental $2.10 per hour, $5.25 per day.

Fishing **Fort Wilderness Campground** (tel. 407/824–2760) is the starting point for two-hour fishing trips, departing at 8 AM and 3 PM. Boats, equipment, and guide for up to five anglers cost $100.70.

Bass Challenger Guide (6710 Gibralter Rd., Orlando, tel. 407/273–8045) rents Ranger boats equipped with drinks and tackle. Transportation can be arranged to and from their location. Half day (1 or 2 persons) $100, full day $150.

Bass Bustin' Guide (5953 Swoffield Dr., Orlando, tel. 407/281–0845) provides boat, tackle, transportation, and amenities for bass fishing on local lakes. And it guarantees fish! Half day $100, full day $150.

Golf **Golfpac** (Box 484, Maitland, FL 32751, tel. 407/660–8559 or 800/327–0878) packages golf vacations and prearranges tee times at over 25 courses around Orlando.

Poinciana Golf & Racquet Club (500 Cypress Pkwy., tel. 407/933–5300) has a par-72 course about 18 miles southeast of Walt Disney World.

Walt Disney World's three championship courses—all played by the PGA Tour—are among the busiest and most expensive in the region. Greens fees are $45 for guests staying in Disney World properties; $55 for nonguests; $25 after 3 PM.

Golf lessons are given in small groups at the Disney Inn courses, the Magnolia and the Palm. Private lessons are available both at these courses and at the Lake Buena Vista Club. There is also a six-hole, 1,115-yard course on artificial turf for children ($7) and adults ($9). For private lessons at the Lake Buena Vista Club, phone 407/828–3741. For all other information, phone the starter's number 407/824–2270.

Horseback Riding **Hyatt Grand Cypress Equestrian Center** (tel. 407/239–1234) offers hunter/jumper private lessons and riding trails for guided outings. Private lesson $35 an hour, trailside $20 an hour.

Fort Wilderness Campground (tel. 407/824–8000) in Walt Disney World offers tame trail rides through the backwoods and along lakesides. Open to the general public. Call in advance to arrange an outing. Rides at 9, 10:30, noon, 1, and 2. Cost: $10 per person for 45–60 minutes. Children must be over age 9.

Ice Skating **Orlando Ice Skating Palace** (3123 W. Colonial Dr., Parkwood Shopping Plaza Orlando, tel. 407/299–5440) isn't the most attractive rink, but if you are homesick for a winter chill, this should do the trick. Open Wed.–Sun. 7:30–10:30 PM. Call for daytime hours.

Jogging Walt Disney World has several scenic jogging trails. Pick up jogging maps at any Disney resort. **Fort Wilderness** (tel. 407/824–2900) has a 2.3-mile jogging course, with plenty of fresh air and woods, as well as numerous exercise stations along the way.

Tennis **Disney Inn** has two courts, **Lake Buena Vista Club** has three, and the **Contemporary Resort Hotel** has six. Private and group lessons are available at the Contemporary (tel. 407/824–3578). Racquets may be rented by the hour.

Orange Lake Country Club (tel. 407/239–1050) offers golf, inexpensive tennis, and a variety of water sports. Greens fee $35, tennis $4 per hour.

The Orlando Vacation Resort (west of I–4 on U.S. 27, tel. 407/394–6171) has 17 asphalt courts open only to guests.

The Vistana Resort (Lake Buena Vista, Rte. 535, about 5 minutes from Disney Village, tel. 407/239–3100) has 10 clay and four Deco-Turf courts open to nonguests for $5.

Grand Cypress Racquet Club (tel. 407/239–4604) has the most expensive courts around, but the club is beautiful. Games can be arranged. Singles $12 per hour; doubles $16 per hour.

Water Sports Marinas at **Contemporary Resort, Fort Wilderness, Polynesian Village,** and **Walt Disney World Village** rent Sunfish, catamarans, motor-powered pontoon boats, pedal boats, and Water Sprites for the 450-acre Bay Lake, the adjoining 200-acres of the Seven Seas Lagoon, Club Lake, Lake Buena Vista, and Buena Vista Lagoon. The Polynesian Village marina rents outrigger canoes. Fort Wilderness rents canoes. For waterskiing ($65 per hour) reservations, phone 407/824–2222, ext. 2757.

Airboat Rentals (4266 Vine St., Kissimmee, tel. 407/845–3672) rents airboats ($14 per hour) and canoes for use on Shingle Creek, with views of giant cypress trees and Spanish moss.

Ski Holidays (tel. 407/239–4444) has waterskiing, jetskiing, and parasailing on a private lake next to Walt Disney World. Boats $50 per hour, $180 for four hours. Parasailing $30. To get there take I–4 to the Lake Buena Vista exit, turn east on Rte. 535 toward Kissimmee, and, about 200 yards east, you will see a sign to Lake Bryan.

Rent a powerful seven-seater ski boat at **Sanford Boat Rental** (tel. 407/321–5906, in Florida 800/237–5105, outside Florida 800/692–3414) up the St. John's river. Bring your own equipment for bass fishing or rent waterski equipment. Very good rates for whole-day outings. Houseboats and pontoons are available for day or overnight trips. Pontoon and ski boats $60 for four hours; 44-foot houseboat $350 per day, $560 for two days.

Carefree Sailing of Florida (3630 Silver Star Rd., Orlando, tel. 407/298–1584) offers one-day excursions on private yachts, complete with crew. Boats depart from Sanford, Daytona, and Cocoa Beaches. From $50 per person.

Spectator Sports

Orlando Seminole Jai Alai. This sport originated in Spain but is now played all over the world, particularly in Latin America. It is a fast, exciting, and dangerous game played with a hard ball that is hurled against a wall (fronton) at high speed. *Fern Park, off I–4 about 20 min north of Orlando, tel. 407/339–6221. Admission: $1. Open afternoons noon–4:30, evenings 6–11:30. Closed selected weeks in Apr., Sept., Oct. Phone for the latest schedule.*

Sanford Orlando Kennel Club (301 Dog Track Rd., Longwood, tel. 407/831–1600) has dog racing and betting nightly except

Sun. at 7:30. Matinees Mon., Wed., and Sat. at 1. *Admission: $1. Open Dec. 26–May 2.*

Dining

If you want to try some local specialties, consider stone crabs, pompano (a mild white fish), Apalachiocola oysters, small but tasty Florida lobsters, and conch chowder. Fresh hearts of palm are a treat, too.

The most highly recommended restaurants in each price category are indicated by a star★.

Category	Cost*
Very Expensive	over $40
Expensive	$30–$40
Moderate	$20–$30
Inexpensive	under $20

**per person without tax, service, or drinks*

Credit card abbreviations: AE, American Express; DC, Diners Club; MC, MasterCard; V, Visa.

In Epcot Center World Showcase offers some of the finest dining to be found not only in Walt Disney World but in the entire Orlando area. The problem is that the restaurants are often crowded and difficult to book. Many of them are operated by the same people who own internationally famous restaurants in their home countries. The top-of-the-line places, such as those in the French, Italian, and Japanese pavilions, can be expensive, but they are not as pricey as comparable restaurants in large, cosmopolitan cities such as Paris or New York. One good thing about Epcot's restaurants, besides the food, is that most of them have limited-selection children's menus with drastically lower prices, so bringing the kids along to dinner won't break the bank.

Visitors are not expected to go all the way back to their hotels to change and clean up and then return for dinner, so casual dress is expected in all the restaurants, even the finest.

If you want to eat in one of the more popular restaurants, it will be much easier to get a reservation for lunch than for dinner. It won't be quite the same experience, but it will be cheaper. Another way to get a table is to have lunch before noon and dinner before 6 or after 8.

Both lunch and dinner reservations are strongly recommended at all the finer restaurants in Epcot. Unless you are staying at one of the Walt Disney World hotels, you cannot reserve in advance of the day on which you wish to eat, and you can't book by phone. Instead, you must reserve in person at each restaurant or head for Earth Station at the base of Spaceship Earth as soon as you get to Epcot Center. There you will find a bank of computer screens called WorldKey Information. You need to stand in line to get to one of these screens and place the reservation, and the lines form very early. On busy days, most top restaurants are filled within an hour of Epcot's opening time, so you may have to line up at the Epcot admissions booth before opening time and then, once you're through the gate, make a mad dash for the WorldKey computer terminals. If there is a long line when you get to Earth Station, remember that on the far side of Future World, just before the bridge to World Showcase, is an outdoor kiosk with five WorldKey terminals that few people notice. There is also another WorldKey kiosk on the far side of the Port of Entry gift shop, near the boat dock for the water taxi to the Moroccan pavilion. Having made the reservations, you can begin to enjoy your day at Epcot.

If you are a guest at an on-site Walt Disney World resort or at one of the Walt Disney World Village hotels, avoid the battle of the WorldKey by booking a table by phone (tel. 407/824–4000). Remember that if you are staying at one of these resorts, you cannot make a same-day reservation by phone but must book either one or two days in advance between noon and 9 PM. The restaurant will ask to see your resort identification card, so don't leave it in your hotel room. No matter how you book, try to show up at the restaurant a bit early to be sure of getting your table. You can pay with American Express, Visa, MasterCard, or, of course, cash. If you're a guest of a Disney hotel, you can charge the tab to your room.

British **Rose and Crown.** This is a very popular, friendly British pub, where visitors and Disney employees come at the end of the day to knock off a pint of crisp Bass Ale or blood-thickening Guinness Stout with a few morsels of Stilton cheese. "Wenches" serve up simple pub fare, such as steak-and-kidney pie, beef tenderloin, and fish and chips. The Rose and Crown sits on the shore of the lagoon, so on warm days it's nice to lunch on the patio at the water's edge and enjoy the soft breezes and the homiest atmosphere in Epcot Center. *Moderate.*

French **The Bistro de Paris.** Located on the second floor of the French pavilion, above Les Chefs, this is a relatively quiet and charming spot for lunch or dinner. The bistro specializes in regional cooking from southern France. A favorite is steamed filet of fresh grouper with tomato, mushrooms, fresh herbs, and white wine sauce, served with rice pilaf. Wines are moderately priced and available by the glass. *Moderate.*

★ **Les Chefs de France.** Three of France's most famous culinary artists came together to create this French restaurant. The most renowned of the three, Paul Bocuse, operates one restaurant north of Lyon and two in Tokyo and has published several famous books on French cuisine. Another, Gaston Lenôtre, has gained eminence for his pastries and ice creams. The third of this culinary triumvirate, Roger Vergé, operates one of France's most highly rated restaurants, near Cannes. The three don't actually prepare each meal, but they were the ones who created the menu and carefully trained the chefs. Some of their most popular classic dishes are roast duck with prunes and wine sauce; beef filet with fresh ground pepper, raisins, and Armagnac sauce; and filet of grouper topped with salmon-vegetable mousse and baked in puff pastry. *Moderate.*

German **Biergarten.** This popular spot boasts Oktoberfest 365 days a year. Visitors sit at long communal tables and are served by waitresses in typical Bavarian garb. The cheerful—some would say raucous—atmosphere is what one would expect from a place where performers yodel, sing, and dance to the rhythms of an oompah band. The crowd, pounding pitchers of beer or wine while consuming hot pretzels and hearty German fare, is usually pretty active when audience participation is called for and just as active when it is not. *Moderate.*

Italian **Alfredo's.** This is a World Showcase hot spot, with some of the finest food in Walt Disney World. During dinner, waiters skip around singing Italian songs and bellowing arias. The restaurant is named for the man who invented the now-classic fettuccine Alfredo, a pasta served with a sauce of cream, butter, and loads of freshly grated Parmesan cheese. Another popular dish is *Lo Chef Consiglia* (the chef's selections), which consists of an appetizer of spaghetti or fettuccine, a mixed green salad, and a chicken or veal entree. The most popular veal dish is *Piccata di Vitello*—veal thinly sliced and panfried with lemon and white wine. *Moderate.*

Japanese **Mitsukoshi.** This isn't just a restaurant, it's a complex of dining areas on the second floor above the Mitsukoski Department Store. Each of the five dining rooms (on your left as you enter) has four tables, each seating eight and each with its own grill on which chefs prepare meats and fish with acrobatic precision. It's an American's idea of the real Japan, but fun nonetheless. *Moderate.*

Mexican **San Angel Inn.** The lush, tropical surroundings—cool, dark, almost surreal—make this one of the most exotic restaurants in Disney World. The ambience is at once romantic and lively. Tables are candlelit, but close together, and the restaurant is open to the pavilion, where folk singers perform and musicians play guitars or marimbas. One of the specialties is *Langosta Baja California*—Baja lobster meat, sautéed with tomatoes, onions, olives, Mexican peppers, and white wine, and baked in its shell. Try the margaritas, and, for dessert, don't miss the chocolate Kahlúa mousse pie. *Moderate.*

Moroccan **Marakesh.** Belly dancers and a three-piece Moroccan band set the mood in this exotic restaurant, where you may feel as though you have stumbled onto the set of *Casablanca.* The food is only mildly spicy and relatively inexpensive. At lunch, you may want to try the national dish of Morocco, *couscous,* served with garden vegetables. For dinner, try the *bastila,* an appetizer of sweet and spicy pork between many layers of thin pastry, with almonds, saffron, and cinnamon. *Moderate.*

The Walt Disney World Area These are restaurants close to Disney World, situated along International Drive or near Kissimmee, Disney Maingate, or Lake Buena Vista.

American **Bennigan's.** This adequate, upscale chain restaurant has lots of simple American favorites, such as nachos, potato skins, steaks, burgers, sandwiches, and quiches. The atmosphere is friendly and comfortable, with dark wood walls covered with collector's items from the early 1900s. This is a convenient place to get a drink and relax, particularly later in the evening, when a young singles crowd arrives. *6324 International Dr., Orlando, tel. 407/351–4436. Dress: casual. Reservations not necessary. AE, MC, V. Inexpensive.*

Empress Lilly. Disney's 220-foot, 19th-century Mississippi-style riverboat is a popular tourist dining spot at the far end of Walt Disney World Shopping Village, right on Buena Vista Lagoon. Though the boat is permanently moored, it looks like an elegant old-fashioned Victorian showboat, complete with brass lamps, burgundy velvet love seats, and mahogany wood. The boat has several restaurants and lounges. Beef is served in the *Steerman's Quarters* and seafood in *Fisherman's Deck.* Only 5% of the tables are open for reservations, two days in advance.

Visitors without reservations should arrive early, add their names to the list, then go and listen to banjo music in the *Baton Rouge Lounge*. The food is as predictable as it is expensive, but dining here can be an enjoyable experience for large families or groups who want a decent meal but do not want to feel inhibited by a stuffy atmosphere. The third restaurant on the showboat is the *Empress Room*, a plush, Victorian dining room filled with gilded reminders of another age. It is a luxurious (if gaudy) setting that might bring out the Rhett Butler or Scarlett O'Hara in you, but you will wish that the food were more palatable, especially at these prices. The menu reads elegantly, featuring such specialties as duck, pheasant, venison, and various seafood dishes, but the food is unlikely to live up to your elegant expectations. *Steerman's Quarters and Fisherman's Deck: Walt Disney World Shopping Village, tel. 407/828–3900. Dress: casual. Only a few reservations accepted. AE, CB, DC, MC, V. Moderate. Empress Room: Jacket required. Reservations required, up to a month in advance. AE, CB, DC, MC, V. Expensive.*

Australian

The Outback. A glass elevator descends into this huge restaurant beside a waterfall and pool, located behind the Buena Vista Palace Hotel. In the middle of the room are the grills and barbecue pits, where the chefs cook up surf-and-turf Aussie specialties such as rack of lamb and lobster tail. Ninety-nine brands of beer are served in this fun, relaxed, family restaurant, where waiters serve you in outback safari outfits and the kids don't have to sit on their hands. *Buena Vista Palace, WDW Village, Lake Buena Vista, tel. 407/827–3430. Dress: casual. Reservations accepted. AE, DC, MC, V. Moderate.*

Cajun/Creole

Royal Orleans. Some of the most authentic Louisiana cooking outside New Orleans is prepared under the direction of the award-winning Cajun chef, "Beany" MacGregor. Specialties include sherried turtle soup and *la truite roulee* (small slivers of trout fillet, shrimp, Louisiana blue crab, and fresh artichoke hearts wrapped in spinach leaves and topped with béarnaise sauce). Fresh seafood and crawfish are flown in daily from Louisiana. Royal Orleans is located in the back left corner as you drive into the Mercado Shopping Village on International Drive. *8445 International Dr., Orlando, tel. 407/352–8200. Jacket required. Reservations advised. AE, CB, DC, MC, V. Moderate.*

Continental

★ **Arthur's 27.** This is Orlando's most expensive restaurant, located on the top floor of the Buena Vista Palace Hotel. Visitors get not only an elegant meal, but one of the best views of the Magic Kingdom and Epcot Center. The fixed-price, seven-course Continental dinner costs $62 per person, *without* drinks; if you order à la carte, expect to pay more. Service and quality are first class, though bordering on the pretentious. The wine list is formidable, featuring everything from reasonable California wines to some vintage Bordeaux that could be sold at auction. Specialties include venison and sautéed breast of duck with honey-ginger sauce. There is only one seating per night, so reservations are at a premium and should be made at the same time that you reserve your room. *Buena Vista Palace Hotel, Walt Disney World Village, tel. 407/827–3450. Jacket required. Reservations strongly recommended. AE, CB, DC, MC, V. Very Expensive.*

Atlantis. Those who associate Stouffer with frozen dinners will be happily surprised by the tasteful and art nouveau surroundings, the subdued atmosphere, and the sophisticated French menu. The waiters, even the busboys, are formally attired and very helpful. For an appetizer, try the warm duck salad. For entrees, the specialties are rack of lamb, blackened with Cajun spices and served with an avocado cream sauce, and swordfish grilled to perfection (though you may want to order it with the port-wine sauce on the side). The rich desserts border on divinity. *Stouffer Resort, 6677 Harbor Dr., Orlando, tel. 407/351–5555. Jacket required. Reservations recommended. AE, CB, DC, MC, V. Expensive.*

Dux. In the Peabody Hotel's gourmet restaurant, some creations are innovative, such as the grilled quail with poached quail eggs, served with wild rice in a carrot turrine nest. Others are a trifle self-conscious, like the avocado with sautéed salmon, artichoke chips, and champagne caviar sauce. For an entree, consider the baked Florida lobster with chanterelle mushrooms, spinach, and champagne sauce. The selection of California wines is outstanding. *Peabody Hotel, 9801 International Dr., Orlando, tel. 407/352–4000. Jacket required. Reservations strongly recommended. AE, CB, DC, MC, V. Expensive.*

La Coquina. This is a hotel restaurant with an emphasis on seafood and serious sauces. One popular meat specialty is loin of lamb with eggplant and goat cheese in grape leaves, served with grilled *polenta* (a type of cornmeal). The best bet here is Sunday brunch—a cornucopia of fruits, vegetables, pastries, pâtés, smoked fish, and a number of dishes cooked before your eyes. The $27 brunch is served with Domaine Chandon champagne; the $52 brunch, with all the Dom Perignon champagne you can consume. If you're hungry and thirsty enough, you just might be able to put them out of business. *Hyatt Regency at Grand Cypress Resort, tel. 407/239–1234. Jacket required. Reservations suggested. AE, CB, DC, MC, V. Expensive.*

Indian **Darbar.** This lavishly decorated dining room features northern Indian cuisine. In addition to curries and pilafs, Darbar specializes in tandoori cooking—barbecuing with mesquite charcoal in a clay oven. Meats and vegetables are marinated in special sauces overnight and cooked to perfection. If you're not familiar with Indian cuisine, this is a good place to begin. The best bet is the tandoori dinner for two, with different types of lamb and chicken. *7600 Dr. Phillips Blvd., Orlando, tel. 407/345–8128. To get there, take Sand Lake Blvd. (exit 29 off I–4) and head west on to the Marketplace Shopping Center (right after the 2nd stop light). The restaurant is in the shopping center. Dress: casual. Reservations advised on weekends. AE, CB, DC, MC, V. Moderate.*

Italian **Cappriccio.** This is a smart-looking, California-chic Italian eaterie, slickly decorated with granite and marble tiles. The menu features traditional and innovative pasta dishes, such as spinach fettuccine with smoked salmon and mushrooms in a cream sauce. Also special are the exotic pizzas, cooked in old-fashioned wood-burning brick ovens. Try the *Pizza al Cinque Formaggi* (made with sun-dried tomatoes, five cheeses, fresh herbs, and tons of garlic). It's a far cry from the Pizza Hut, so be prepared for deep-dish prices. *Peabody Hotel, 9801 International Dr., Orlando, tel. 407/352–4000. Dress: casual. Reservations recommended. AE, CB, DC, MC, V. Moderate.*

★ **Christini's.** For traditional Italian cuisine, this is Orlando's finest. The restaurant is not about to win any awards for interior decoration, but the food couldn't be fresher and the service couldn't be more efficient. The restaurant makes its own pastas daily and serves them with herbs, vegetables, and freshly grated Parmesan. Specialties include fresh fish; a fish soup with lobster, shrimp, and clams; and veal chops with fresh sage. *Intersection of Sand Lake Rd. and Dr. Phillips Blvd., in the Marketplace Shopping Center, tel. 407/345–8770. Jacket required. Reservations recommended. AE, CB, DC, MC, V. Expensive.*

Japanese ★ **Ran-Getsu.** The best Japanese food in town is served in this palatial setting. The atmosphere may seem a bit self-conscious—an American's idea of the Orient—but the food is fresh and carefully prepared. Sit at the curved, dragon's tail-shaped sushi bar for the Matsu platter—an assortment of *nigiri-* and *maki-*style sushis—or, if you are with a group, sit Japanese style at tables overlooking a carp-filled pond and decorative gardens. Specialties are sukiyaki and *shab-shabu* (thinly sliced beef in a boiling seasoned broth, served with vegetables and prepared at your table). If you feel more adventurous, try the deep-fried alligator tail. *8400 International Dr., Orlando, tel. 407/345–0044. Dress: casual. Reservations accepted. AE, CB, DC, MC, V. Moderate.*

Kosher **Palm Terrace.** This is a kosher restaurant supervised by Rabbi Jakobs of the Orthodox Union. Diners who are not guests at the Hyatt Orlando pay a fixed price of just under $30 ($7 for children) for Shabbos meals. Meals must be prepaid on Friday, and reservations are required one-half hour before candle lighting. Kosher breakfast and lunch items are available next door at the Marketplace Deli from 7 AM to 1 AM (the Hyatt also has a shul, with services held twice daily.) *Hyatt Orlando. 6375 Irlo Bronson Memorial Hwy., Kissimmee, tel. 407/396–1234. Dress: informal. Reservations required. AE, CB, DC, MC, V. Moderate.*

Seafood **Hemingway's.** Located by the pool at the Hyatt Grand Cypress Resort, this restaurant serves all sorts of sea creatures, from conch, scallops, and squid to grouper, pampano, and monkfish. In addition to the regular menu, Hemingway's also has what is called a "Cuisine Naturelle" menu, featuring dishes that are low in fat, calories, sodium, and cholesterol—recipes that are approved by the American Heart Association and Weight Watchers. What more could you want other than a big hot-fudge sundae for dessert? *Hyatt Regency at Grand Cypress Resort, tel. 407/239–1234. Dress: casual. Reservations suggested. AE, CB, DC, MC, V. Moderate–Expensive.*

24 Hours **Bee Line Diner.** This is a slick 1950s-style diner that's always open. It is in the Peabody Hotel, so it's not exactly cheap, but the salads, sandwiches, and griddle foods are tops. A good bet for breakfast or a late-night snack. And for just a little silver, you get to play a lot of old tunes on the jukebox. *Peabody Hotel, 9801 International Dr., Orlando, tel. 407/352–4000. Dress casual. Reservations not necessary. AE, CB, DC, MC, V. Moderate.*

The Orlando Area The following restaurants are in or near the city of Orlando and cater mostly to a local clientele.

American **The Bubble Room.** Some visitors will get a real kick out of this upbeat, nostalgia-themed restaurant with its big-band-era music and wacky wall-to-wall decor from the 1930s, '40s, and '50s. Every inch of space is covered with bric-a-brac, framed movie stills, and magazine covers of bygone luminaries. Not only is the place fun and crazy, but the food is pretty wild as well. The menu is a hodgepodge of the Bubble Room's interpretations of recipes from around the world, from Asian to Cajun. Seafood is shipped daily from the Gulf Coast. The specialty of the house, "The Eddie Fisherman," is a fillet of local black grouper covered with a light nut-crumb topping and then poached in a brown paper bag. *1351 S. Orlando Ave. (on Rte. 17–92), Maitland, tel. 407/628–3331. Dress: very casual. Reservations recommended. AE, CB, DC, MC, V. Moderate.*

★ **Chalet Suzanne.** If you like to drive or are returning from a day at Cypress Gardens, consider dining at this award-winning family-owned country inn and restaurant. It has been expanded bit by bit since it opened in the 1930s. Today, it looks like a small Swiss village—right in the middle of Florida's orange groves. The place settings, china, glasses, chairs, and even the tables are of different sizes, shapes, and origins. Strangely, however, it all works together as the expression of a single sensibility. For an appetizer, try broiled grapefruit. Recommended among the seven entrees are chicken Suzanne, shrimp curry, lobster Newburg, shad roe, and filet mignon. Crepes Suzanne are a good bet for dessert. The seven-course meals begin at $40. This unlikely back-road country inn should provide one of the most memorable dining experiences one can have in Orlando. *U.S. 27 north of Lake Wales, about 10 mi past Cypress Gardens turnoff, tel. 813/676–6011. Jackets requested. Reservations suggested. AE, CB, DC, MC, V. Closed Mon. during summer. Expensive.*

Chinese ★ **4, 5, 6.** Pedestrian surroundings don't hide well-prepared and well-served traditional dishes, such as steamed sea bass and chicken with snow peas. Served in Chinatown fashion by cart-pushing waiters. *657 N. Primrose Dr., Orlando, tel. 407/898–1899. Dress: very informal. Reservations: Recommended on weekends. AE, CB, DC, MC, V. Open weekends to 2 AM. Inexpensive.*

Continental ★ **Park Plaza Gardens.** This popular spot is a see-and-be-seen experience for the locals of beautiful old Winter Park. At lunch, the society grand dames show their colors among an assortment of local secretaries and yuppies on business lunches. In the evening, the area's well-heeled families come here to dine. The Park Plaza is best for lunch because of its fabulous salads and quiches. The dinner menu emphasizes seafood and veal. For dessert, the baked Alaska is a must. During the day, the restaurant is a bright greenhouse filled with plants; at night it is candle lit and romantic. On Sunday, there is a good champagne brunch at bargain prices. *319 Park Ave. S., Winter Park; tel. 407/645–2475. Jackets usually worn but not required. Reservations advised. AE, CB, DC, MC, V. Moderate.*

Cuban ★ **Numero Uno.** Long regarded by food critics as the best in town. Ambience is casual plastic. Cuban roast pork with rice and black beans is one of the specialties. *2499 S. Orange Ave., tel. 407/841–3840. Dress: informal. Reservations unnecessary. AE, CB, DC, MC, V. Inexpensive.*

French **La Belle Verrière**. Dine among plants and fresh flowers in the glow of Tiffany stained glass. Specialties include leg of lamb and fresh fish dishes in delicate sauces. Save room for the crème caramel or chocolate mousse. *142 S. Park Ave., Winter Park, tel. 407/645–3377. Dress: upscale informal. Reservations recommended. AE, CB, DC, MC, V. Closed Sun. Moderate.*

Coq au Vin. The atmosphere here is Mobile Home Modern, but the traditional French fare is first class, and you can pride yourself on discovering a place few tourists know about but that is nearly always filled with a friendly Orlando clientele. Owners Louis Perotte (the chef) and his wife, Magdalena (the hostess), are a charming couple who give the place its warmth and personality. The specialties include homemade chicken liver pâté, fresh rainbow trout with champagne, and roast Long Island duckling with green peppercorn sauce. For dessert, try the crème brûlée. *4800 S. Orange Ave., Orlando, tel. 407/851–6980. Dress: informal. Reservations suggested. AE, CB, DC, MC, V. Moderate.*

Mexican

★ **Bee Line Mexican Restaurant.** It looks like another hole-in-the-wall eatery, but the burritos, taco salads, meat chalupas, and chili rellenos are among the best in the area. *4542 Hoffner Rd., Orlando (near the airport), tel. 407/857–0566. Dress: casual. No reservations. No credit cards, but checks are accepted. Inexpensive.*

★ **Paco's.** Good Mexican food in a cheerful but cramped little house. Guacomole is hand mashed from avocados on the premises; so are the refried beans. *1801 W. Fairbanks Ave., Winter Park, tel. 407/629–0149. No reservations or credit cards. Inexpensive.*

Villa Las Palomas. The building itself is a relatively faithful recreation of its parent restaurant, the San Angel Inn, built in 1692 near Mexico City. It is a shame that the restaurant's architectural charm is lost along a street lined with gas stations and shopping malls, but on entering, you feel as though you have crossed the border and stepped into an elegant Mexican inn. The food is traditional. The menu includes burritos and enchiladas, but do try more ambitious dishes, such as mole *poblano,* a roasted half chicken simmered in a sauce of more than 20 Mexican spices. The food can be a bit heavy, so you may want to stick with seafood. The margaritas are first class. Mexican guitarists will sing requests for you, and on weekends there is a 10-piece mariachi band. *3552 E. Colonial Dr., Orlando, tel. 407/894–2610. Dress: casual. Reservations accepted. AE, CB, DC, MC, V. Moderate.*

Pizza

Johnny's Pizza Palace. Red leather booths are the setting for crisp pizza and a two-crust pie that Chicagoans call a stuffed pizza. Pasta and sandwiches are also on the menu. *4909 Lake Underhill Rd., tel. 407/277–3452. Dress: pizza-parlor modern. Reservations not necessary. MC, V. Inexpensive.*

Rossi's. This is a local pizza joint—a garlic bread pepperoni pizza and a pitcher of Bud or root beer type of spot. The food is not about to win any awards, but Rossi's is a good escape from the tourist/hotel scene, and the price is right. *5919 S. Orange Blossom Trail, Orlando, tel. 407/855–5755. Dress: very informal. AE, MC, V. Inexpensive.*

Seafood

South Seas. The only problem here is knowing which of the 70 seafood dishes to order. Whatever you choose, it's likely to be fresh, for the kitchen is supplied by the restaurant's own fish market. The large, modern dining room gets no points for ambience, but the prices are the best around. Sink your teeth into alligator or shark that won't bite back, crack open some lobster or oysters, or butter up some catfish or snapper. Steak and burgers are also served, but that would be like ordering a quarter-pounder with cheese from Colonel Sanders. *3001 Curry Ford Rd., Orlando, tel. 407/898–8331. Dress: casual. Reservations not accepted. AE, MC, V. Moderate.*

Wekiwa Marina Restaurant. Plenty of local color here as everyone from three-piece-suited bankers to overall-clad farmers eat catfish, frog legs, and cheese grits in a Cracker-style wooden building on the wharf. *1000 Miami Springs Rd., Longwood (off I–4, about 20 min north of Orlando), tel. 407/862-9640. Dress: blue-jean informal. Reservations only for large parties. AE, CB, DC, MC, V. Inexpensive.*

Gary's Duck Inn. This long-time Orlando favorite is known for its knotty-pine nautical motif and its fresh shrimp, crab, and fish dishes. This was the model for a seafood chain known as Red Lobster. *3974 S. Orange Blossom Trail, Orlando, tel. 407/843–0270. Dress: casual. Reservations not required. AE, CB, DC, MC, V. Inexpensive.*

Steak

Cattle Ranch. If you're hungry and looking for a big, thick, juicy, down-home American steak, then steer for the Cattle Ranch. It's cheap and, if you're insanely hungry, it's free. Just take "The 6-pound Challenge," in which you're given 75 minutes to eat an entire six-pound steak dinner, including salad, potato, and bread. If you can do it, you won't have to pay a dime. If you can't, it will cost you just over $30. There is nothing fancy about this cowboy cafeteria except the steaks that come off the burning orangewood fire. And you won't see another tourist for miles around. *6129 Old Winter Garden Rd., Orlando (2½ blocks west of Kirkman Rd.); tel. 407/298–7334. Dress: very informal. Reservations not needed. AE, MC, V. Inexpensive.*

24 Hours

Skeeter's. After Orlando's nightclubs close, both old and young stagger over to this popular diner to sober up or to prolong the party over some fried eggs, hash browns, and pancakes. A fun diner, with lots of local character; open around the clock. *1212 Lee Rd., Orlando, tel. 407/298–7973. Dress: informal. No credit cards. Inexpensive.*

Lodging

To stay within or outside Walt Disney World—that is the question. The law of inertia seems to keep most Walt Disney World guests within its realm. And if you are coming to Orlando for only a few days and are interested solely in the Magic Kingdom, Epcot Center, and the other Disney attractions, these resorts on Disney property may be right for you. But if you plan to visit other attractions, you should at least consider the alternatives.

Let's look at the pros and cons of staying in an on-site hotel. On the positive side, you won't need to drive, and transportation within Disney World will be free. None of the hotels is within the actual confines of the Magic Kingdom or Epcot Center, but transportation is usually quick and efficient. Remember, though, that the monorail serves just three on-site hotels: the Grand Floridian, Contemporary, and Polynesian Village Resorts. If you stay anywhere else you will have to take Disney's bus to the monorail.

If you have kids, they will be able to fend for themselves more easily and stay out of trouble within Walt Disney World. Built with families in mind, rooms in the on-site resorts are large and can as a rule accommodate up to five persons. They offer cable TV with the Disney Channel and a channel providing the latest updates on special daily events.

The thrill—especially for children—of knowing you are actually staying in Walt Disney World may be worth staying here. The hotels offer many of their own special events, such as theme dinner shows and breakfasts at which Disney cartoon characters come to entertain the kids.

As a Disney guest, you get first rights to tee-off times at the busy golf courses, and you are able to call up to two days in advance to make hard-to-get reservations at any of the fine restaurants in Disney World. Outsiders can make reservations only by calling while at the park on the day they wish to dine or they must wait on line.

As an on-site guest, you also get a guest identification card that allows you to charge anything at Walt Disney World (except in the Magic Kingdom) to your room.

On the negative side, hotels with comparable facilities tend to cost more on Disney property than off it. You may have heard that by staying at a Disney hotel you get discounts on multiple-day Passports. This is little more than an advertising ploy—unless you consider the savings of a few dollars on hundreds of dollars worth of Passports a significant discount. Whatever small savings you may realize will be undercut by the higher cost of staying in an on-site property.

Reservations All on-site accommodations may be booked through the Walt Disney World Central Reservations Office (Box 10100, Lake Buena Vista 32830, tel. 407/824–8000). Reservations must often be made several months in advance and sometimes, for the best rooms during high season, a year in advance. There are always cancellations, of course, so it's worth trying even at the last minute. Keep in mind that Delta Airlines (tel. 800/872–7786) has many rooms allotted to it for its travel packages, so check with Delta, too. Visitors on a tight budget should be aware that many hotels (and attractions) offer discounts up to 40% from September to mid-December.

If the on-site resorts are full, central reservations will automatically try to book a place for you at one of the Walt Disney World Village hotels. Be sure to tell them exactly what you are looking for. You must give a deposit for your first night's stay within three weeks of making your reservation, and you can get a refund if you cancel at least five days before your scheduled stay.

Land packages, including admissions tickets, car rentals, and hotels either on or off Disney property, can be made through Walt Disney Travel Co. (1675 Buena Vista Dr., Lake Buena Vista 32830, tel. 407/828–3232).

Land/air packages, with accommodations both on and off Disney property, can be booked through **Disney Reservation Service** (tel. 800/828–0228).

Ratings The most highly recommended properties in each price category are indicated by a star ★. Rates usually include the price of two children under 18.

Category	Cost*
Very Expensive	over $150
Expensive	$120–$150
Moderate	$65–$120
Inexpensive	under $65

**double room; add 9% taxes or service*

The following credit card abbreviations are used: AE, American Express; CB, Carte Blanche; DC, Diners Club; MC, MasterCard; and V, Visa.

Walt Disney World Hotels

Visitors have a choice of staying at (1) hotels that are owned and operated by Disney, (2) hotels that are privately owned but that are located on Disney property, and (3) hotels in the Orlando area.

Let's look at the Disney-run hotels first. In brief, the *Contemporary* is the biggest and busiest resort—the one that is most crowded with children and conventioneers. Yet it is also the center of action, with the most entertainment, shops, and restaurants.

The *Polynesian Village* is the most popular, particularly with families and couples. It has a relaxed environment with low, tropical buildings and walking paths along the Seven Seas Lagoon. It can be difficult to find a place to be alone, however. The charm of the *Grand Floridian* will survive the crowds. The waterfront location makes it particularly attractive.

The most relaxed and low-key of the hotels is the *Disney Inn*. It is the smallest, and, because it is between two golf courses, it is the quietest. The *Resort Villas* are especially attractive for families or groups of two or more couples. There are four different types of villas in relatively isolated woodland settings. Least formal are the trailer and camp sites that are in an even more wooded setting in the Fort Wilderness Resort area.

Reservations sometimes become available at the last minute. For same-day reservations, phone each Disney property directly. For advance reservations, tel. 407/824–8000.

Contemporary Resort Hotel. This high rise in the heart of Walt Disney World has a slick, space-age impersonality. Shops, lounges, and restaurants bustle under the 15-story atrium, creating an urban atmosphere not found in other, more easygoing Disney facilities. The futuristic monorail running right through the lobby contributes to the stark, modernistic mood. Rooms in the front are at a premium because they look out toward the Magic Kingdom. *Central Reservations, Box 10100, Lake Buena Vista 32830, tel. 407/824–8000 or 407/824–1000 for same-day reservations. 1,052 rooms. AE, MC, V. Expensive–Very Expensive.*

Disney Inn. Golfers are "fore" it, of course, but anyone who wants to get away from the crowds will appreciate this hotel once known as the Golf Resort. It's the smallest and quietest resort among the on-site hotels. The golf is world class, but since its name change the inn has also been discovered by couples who want some quiet time (with or without children). The most expensive rooms overlook the pool. Rooms on the first floor have direct access to the pool but can be noisy at times. Rooms with a view of the golf fairways are particularly pleasant. One of the quietest places to eat within Walt Disney World is located here—a new restaurant called the Garden Gallery, serving American cuisine. *Central Reservations, Box 10100, Lake Buena Vista 32830, tel. 407/824–8000. 855 rooms. AE, MC, V. Expensive–Very Expensive.*

★ **Grand Floridian Beach Resort.** This Palm Beach-style coastal hot spot offers old-fashioned character with all the conveniences of a modern hotel. The gabled red roof, brick chimneys, and long ambling verandahs were built with loving attention to detail. Small touches, such as crystal chandeliers and stained-glass domes, create the feeling of a more sedate and leisurely era. As might be expected from a beach resort, there are all sorts of water sports in the marina. The Floridian also has its own monorail stop that links it to the TTC. Even the resort's monorail station elegantly carries off the Victorian theme. *Central Reservations, Box 10100, Lake Buena Vista 32830, tel. 407/824–8000. AE, MC, V. 900 rooms, including 69 concierge rooms and 12 suites. Expensive–Very Expensive.*

Polynesian Village Resort. You are supposed to get the feeling that you are on a tropical island when you come here, so everything at The Poly, as it's called, has a South Pacific slant to it. The focal point of the resort is the Great Ceremonial House, where visitors check in. The atrium sets the tone, with its lush tropical atmosphere complete with volcanic rock fountains, blooming orchids, and coconut palms—the whole bit. You might think you were at a resort in Fiji if you didn't notice all the kids running around wearing Mickey Mouse caps.

Stretching from the main building are 11 two- and three-story "longhouses," each of which carries the name of some exotic Pacific Island. All rooms offer two queen-size beds and a small sleeper sofa, accommodating up to five people. Except for some second-floor rooms, all have a balcony or patio. If you don't like to walk too much and want to be near the main building, with its shops and entertainment, request a room in the Bora Bora or Maui longhouses. For the best view of the Magic Kingdom and the Seven Seas Lagoon, with its sandy palm-trimmed beaches, stay in the Samoa, Moorea, or Tonga.

The least expensive rooms look out at the other buildings, the monorail, and the parking lot across the street. Slightly more expensive are the garden- and pool-view rooms. Rooms overlooking the lagoon are the priciest, but they are also the most peaceful and include a host of upgraded amenities and services that make them among the most sought after in Disney World. Recreational activities center around the hotel's large sandy beach and marina, where you can rent boats for sailing, waterskiing, and fishing. If you can pull together a group of eight, you can even rent an outrigger canoe. The two swimming pools can be overrun by children; you may want to go to the beach for a dip instead. *Central Reservations, Box 10100, Lake Buena Vista 32830, tel. 407/824–8000 or 407/824–2000 for same-day reservations. AE, MC, V. 855 rooms. Expensive–Very Expensive.*

The Resort Villas

There are a few good reasons why you may prefer the Resort Villas to the four resort hotels:

- You are visiting Walt Disney World with your family or with other couples, and you want to stay together and avoid the expense of separate rooms.

- You enjoy the convenience of having your own kitchen and would like to save money by preparing some of your own meals.
- You don't like big, busy hotels, but you appreciate the amenities of a resort.

There are five types of villas, each with its own character and ambience. Though they are not quite as plush as rooms in the resort hotels, they are more spacious. Since the villas are not on the monorail, transportation to the parks can be slow, and to get around within the village you may want to use your car or rented golf cart. On the positive side, you have immediate access to great golf, great fishing, shopping, and an active nightlife. Check-in for resort villas is at the entrance to Disney Village Resort. *Disney World Co., Central Reservations, 10100 Lake Buena Vista 32830, tel. 407/824–8000 or 407/827–1100 for same-day reservations.*

The Vacation Villas. They were originally built in 1971 but were refurbished in 1986. Each unit has complete living facilities with equipped kitchens and one or two bedrooms. The one-bedroom villas have a king-size bed in one room and a queen-size sofa bed in the living room (accommodating up to four). The two-bedroom units, accommodating up to six, have a king-size bed or two twin beds in each bedroom and a sofa bed in the living room (accommodating as many as six). There are two outdoor pools at the Vacation Villas. *139 1-bedroom units, 87 2-bedroom units. Expensive–Very Expensive.*

Club-Suite Villas. These are the smallest and the least memorable of the villas—and also the least expensive. Built of cedar, they each have one bedroom, a sofa bed, a wet bar, but no kitchen—the only villas that don't. Their size and ambience reflect the needs of business people attending meetings at the nearby Conference Center. Facilities include two outdoor pools, a small game room, a playground, and boat rentals. *61 units. Expensive.*

Two-Bedroom Villas. These villas are built of cedar, like those at Club-Suite, but they are more tastefully decorated and very spacious. All have two bedrooms, and a full loft accommodating up to six. They were formerly known as the Fairway Villas because the property is surrounded by several fairways of the Lake Buena Vista Golf Course. Guests may use pools at the Villa Recreation Center or Disney Village Clubhouse. *64 units. Expensive–Very Expensive.*

Lake Buena Vista Village

The formal name of this area is Walt Disney World Village Hotel Plaza at Lake Buena Vista, but most people refer to it simply as Lake Buena Vista Village or World Village. Aside from the resorts that are actually inside Walt Disney World, these seven hotels are the most popular among visitors to Walt Disney World. This is because the properties publicize themselves as official Walt Disney World Hotels and offer many of the same incentives. Many people believe these hotels are owned by Disney. Not true. They were invited to establish themselves on Disney property, and they pay for the privilege with a percentage of their revenues. Disney does keep a close eye on them, however, to ensure that they maintain certain standards.

Because these hotels are "official," there is a premium on rooms, and rates are somewhat inflated compared with what you can find off the Disney property. Many Disney fans believe, however, that the benefits of staying in these hotels make it worthwhile. You decide.

• You can avoid box-office lines at Magic Kingdom and Epcot Center by buying tickets at your hotel. However, you can also send for these tickets before leaving home. For a three-day passport, you get less than a 2% discount—a savings of only $1.
• You get free rides on Disney World transportation, but so does anyone with a Magic Kingdom/Epcot pass. Though you are very close to Disney World, the bus takes 15–20 minutes just to reach the monorail and runs every 10–15 minutes. Transportation from nonofficial hotels off Disney property is often just as fast.
• You can make telephone reservations for restaurants and dinner shows in Disney World in advance of the general public.
• You can use the tennis and golf facilities at Lake Buena Vista Village. The Buena Vista hotels are all part of an attractively landscaped complex. Each has its own restaurants and lounges, and all are within walking distance of the popular, if touristy, Walt Disney World Shopping Village (a pleasant outdoor mall filled with gift shops and restaurants).
• Unlike Disney-owned and -operated hotels, rates do not fluctuate according to season.
• All seven hotels are comfortable and convenient, and each has a character of its own. But all are usually crowded with conventions, tour groups, or just a full house of guests.

You can call each hotel's toll-free number for reservations, or you can book rooms at any of them through the **Walt Disney World Central Reservations Office,** Box 10100, Lake Buena Vista, 32830.

Three-Bedroom Villas. If you really want to get away from it all, this is the place to stay. Isolated within a peaceful, heavily wooded area, these curious villas stand on stilts. You won't exactly feel like Tarzan and Jane in these bungalows, but you may hear some howls late at night. Predictably, this out-of-the-way little forest retreat is popular among young couples.

All "tree houses" accommodate six and have two bedrooms with queen-size beds and a third bedroom with a double bed, kitchen and breakfast bar, living room, and two bathrooms. The third bedroom is on a lower level. There is also a utility room with a washer/dryer. Guests can use nearby pools at the Villa Recreation Center or Disney Village Clubhouse. *60 units. Expensive–Very Expensive.*

Fort Wilderness. If you want to rough it, stay among 730 acres of woodland, streams, small lakes, and plenty of water activities along the southeastern edge of Bay Lake, at the northern edge of Walt Disney World property.

You can rent a 42-foot-long trailer (accommodating up to six) or a 35-foot trailer (accommodating up to four). Both types have one bedroom, a bath, a full kitchen, air-conditioning, heat, and daily housekeeping services. The trailer sites are spread over 80 forested acres.

For those who are more serious about getting in touch with the great outdoors, there are campsites spread across 21 areas. Some are for visitors' own trailers, complete with electrical outlets, outdoor charcoal grills, private picnic tables, water, and waste disposal. For a real wilderness experience, full maid service is provided. There are also tent sites with water and electricity but not sewage. The most expensive sites (100–700) are nearest the lake. The least expensive (1600–1900) are far from the lake in denser vegetation. If there's a bargain, this is it. Each site accommodates up to 10 people. *Central Reservations, Box 10100, Lake Buena Vista 32830, tel. 407/824–8000, or same-day reservations 407/824–2900. Trailers, Moderate; campsites, Inexpensive.*

Buena Vista Palace. This is the largest of the Lake Buena Vista hotels, with one of its towers soaring 27 stories high. When you enter its lobby, the hotel seems smaller and quieter than its bold, modern exterior and sprawling parking lots might suggest. Don't be fooled. You have entered on the third floor; when you head down to the ground level, you'll see just how large this place truly is. Facilities include a health club, swimming pools, four tennis courts, a beauty salon, a game room, two gift shops, and a host of bars and restaurants. Rooms are unmemorable but adequate, each with a small patio and a push-button Mickey Mouse telephone. Rooms on the upper floors are more expensive; the best ones look out toward Epcot Center. Ask for a room in the main tower to avoid the late-night noise from the nightclub that reverberates through the atrium. *1900 Lake Buena Vista Dr., Lake Buena Vista 32830, tel. 407/827–2727 or 800/327–2990. 841 rooms. AE, CB, DC, MC, V. Expensive–Very Expensive.*

Grosvenor Resort. This attractive hotel is probably the best deal in the neighborhood, with a wealth of facilities and comfortable rooms for a fair price. The former Americana Dutch Resort, it was completely refurbished in British colonial-style and renamed the Grosvenor. Public areas are spacious, with high molded ceilings and columns, warm cheerful colors, and plenty of natural light.

Recreational facilities are geared toward the active life and include two heated pools; two lighted tennis courts; racquetball, shuffleboard, basketball, and volleyball courts; a children's playground; and a game room. Rooms are average in size, but colorfully decorated, with a refrigerator/bar and a videocassette player. In the lobby, you may rent movies for the VCR or cameras to make your own videos. *1850 Hotel Plaza Blvd., Lake Buena Vista 32830, tel. 407/828–4444 or 800/624–4109. 614 rooms. AE, CB, DC, MC, V. Moderate–Expensive.*

★ **Hilton at Walt Disney World Village.** The Hilton is generally considered the top hotel in the Village. It is also one of the most expensive. In contrast to the lackluster facade, the interiors are richly decorated with brass and glass and softened with tasteful carpets. Guest rooms sparkle. Rooms are not huge, but they are cozy and contemporary, with high-tech amenities. All are the same size, with a king-size bed, two double beds, or two queen-size beds. The most expensive rooms have views of the shopping village and lake. Rooms overlooking the pool are also desirable. Although all rooms are the same size, they vary dramatically in price by location and floor, as well as by season. The Hilton provides a service that many parents will consider indispensable—a **Youth Hotel** for children aged 3–12. The hotel has full-time supervisors for its playroom, a large-screen TV (with Disney Channel, of course), a six-bed dormitory, and scheduled meals. The Youth Hotel is open daily 9 AM–midnight. The cost is $4 per hour. Other facilities include two swimming pools, a health club, two lighted tennis courts, and several outdoor and indoor bars and restaurants, including the popular **American Vineyards,** serving New American cuisine. *1751 Hotel Plaza Blvd., Lake Buena Vista 32830, tel. 407/827–4000 or*

800/445–8667. 814 rooms. AE, MC, V. Expensive–Very Expensive.

Pickett Suite Resort. Walt Disney World is certainly not one to fall behind the current trends in the hotel industry, so it is not surprising that the most recent addition to the Lake Buena Vista neighborhood would be an all-suite hotel. Suites consist of a comfortable living room area and a separate bedroom with two double beds or a king-size bed. With a sofa bed in the living room, a suite can accommodate up to six people, but certainly not all comfortably. The arrangement is convenient for small families who want to avoid the hassle of cots and the expense of two separate rooms. Each unit has a TV in each room (including a small one in the bathroom!), a stocked refrigerator, a wet bar, a coffee maker and, on request, a microwave oven. The hotel attracts a quiet, family-oriented crowd and few of the noisy conventioneers one finds at the larger, splashier properties. Facilities include a whirlpool spa, heated swimming and wading pools, two tennis courts, a game room, and a children's play area. *2305 Hotel Plaza Blvd., Lake Buena Vista 32830, tel. 407/934–1000 or 800/742–5388. 229 units. AE, CB, DC, MC, V. Expensive–Very Expensive.*

Royal Plaza. From the lobby, this hotel seems a bit dated in comparison with the slick, modern hotels in the neighborhood. But the extremely casual, fun-loving atmosphere makes it popular with families who have young children and teenagers. The rooms are generous in size, the best ones overlooking the pool. If you have any interest in afternoon naps, make sure your room isn't too close to the ground floor. The hotel has several restaurants and bars, a few shops, a hair salon, four lighted tennis courts, a sauna, pool, and putting green. *1905 Hotel Plaza Blvd., Lake Buena Vista 32830, tel. 407/828–2828 or 800/248–7890. 396 rooms. AE, CB, DC, MC, V. Expensive–Very Expensive.*

Maingate Resorts

Maingate refers to an area full of large hotels that are not affiliated with Walt Disney World but are clustered around its northernmost entrance, just off I–4. These hotels are mostly resort hotels on sprawling properties, catering to Disney World vacationers. All are good-quality hotels with a resort sameness one can find the world over. However, they vary in size and price. As a simple rule of thumb, the bigger the resort and the more extensive the facilities, the more you can expect to pay. If you're looking for a clean, modern room, you cannot go wrong with any of them. All are equally convenient to Walt Disney World, but one may emphasize a particular recreational activity over others. Where you stay may depend on how much time you plan to spend at your hotel or on which stroke—drive or backhand—you feel needs most improving.

Hyatt Orlando Hotel. This is another very large hotel, but without the extensive resort facilities. Instead of a single towering building, the hotel consists of 40 two-story buildings in four clusters. Each cluster is a community with its own pool, Jacuzzi, park, and playground at its center. The rooms are spacious but otherwise unmemorable.

The lobby and convention center are in a building at the center of the clusters. The lobby is vast and mall-like, with numerous shops and restaurants. One of the restaurants, the **Palm Terrace,** features a full kosher menu supervised by the Orthodox

Buena Vista Palace, **9**
Casa Rosa Inn, **26**
Chalet Suzanne, **6**
Contemporary Resort Hotel, **7**
Disney Inn, **2**
Embassy Suites, **21**
Fort Wilderness, **8**
Grand Floridian Beach Resort, **1**
Grosvenor Resort, **10**
Hilton at WDW Village, **17**
Hyatt Orlando, **12**
Hyatt Regency Grand, **13**
Knight's Inn Orlando Maingate West, **4**
Orlando Heritage Inn, **24**
Park Plaza, **27**
Peabody Orlando, **23**
Pickett Suite Resort, **15**
Polynesian Village Resort, **3**
Radisson Inn, **22**
Radisson Inn Maingate, **5**
Ramada Resort Maingate East, **19**
Residence Inn, **20**
Resort Villas, **11**
Royal Plaza, **16**
Sonesta Village, **14**
Stouffer Orlando Resort, **25**
Vistana, **18**

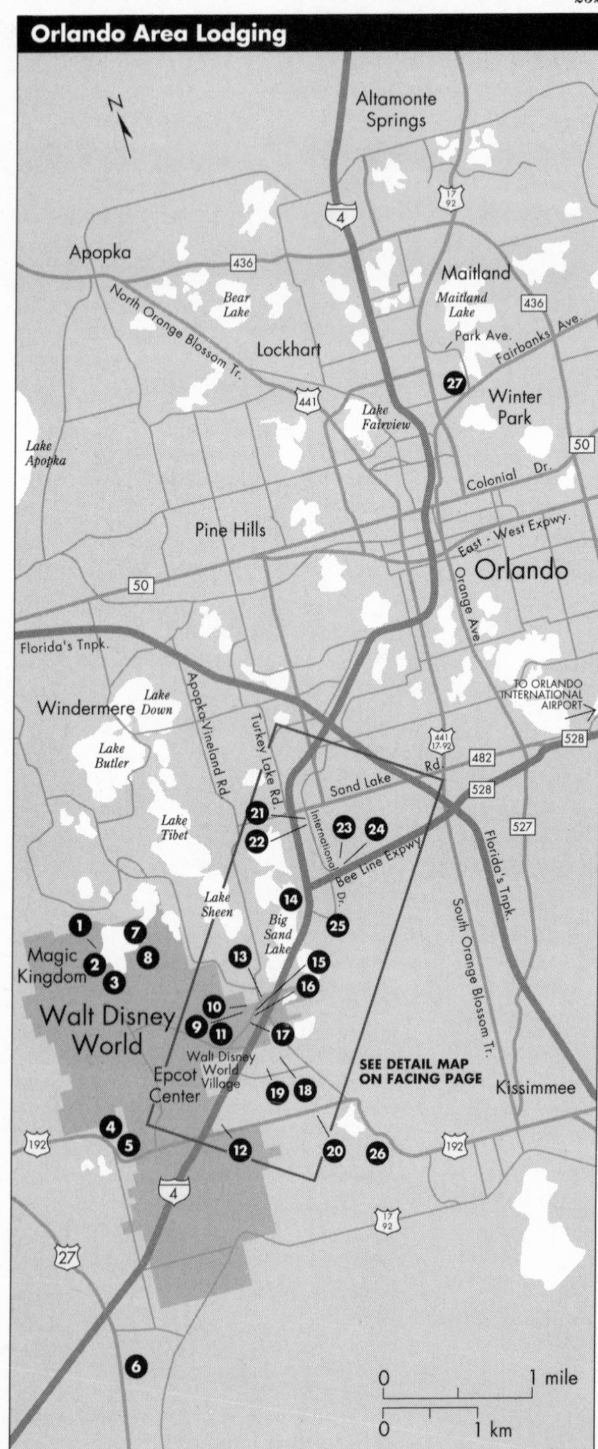

Orlando Area Lodging (detail)

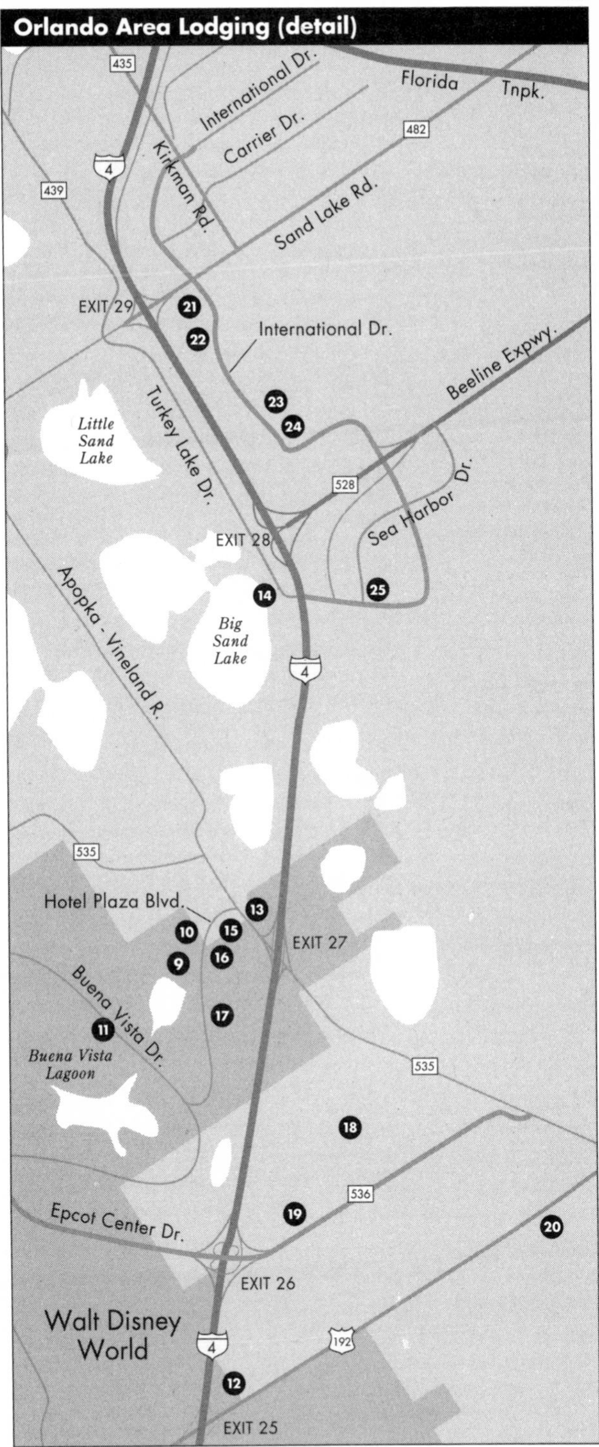

Union. There is also a very good take-out deli, with great picnic snacks for those who are wise enough to avoid the lines and prices at amusement-park fast-food stands. There are a few tennis courts, but not much else in the way of recreation. However, for busy travelers who will be spending most of their time attacking Orlando's attractions, this is a convenient, not-too-expensive headquarters. *6375 W. Irlo Bronson Memorial Hwy., Kissimmee 32741, tel. 407/396–1234 or 800/228–9000. 946 rooms. AE, CB, DC, MC, V. Moderate.*

★ **Hyatt Regency Grand Cypress.** If you were to ask someone familiar with the Orlando area which hotel is the most spectacular, few would hesitate to name the Grand Cypress. The hotel property is so extensive—over 1,500 acres—that guests need a trolley system to get around. There is virtually every activity you can imagine at a resort: a dozen tennis courts, boats of all shapes and varieties, scenic bicycling and jogging trails, a full health club, dozens of horses, a 600,000-gallon, triple-level swimming pool fed by 12 cascading waterfalls, a 45-acre Audubon nature reserve, 47 holes of golf, and a golfing academy for a high-tech analysis of your game. This huge resort has just two drawbacks: the king-size conventions that it commonly attracts, and the king-size bite it will take out of your wallet. *1 Grand Cypress Blvd., Orlando 32819, tel. 407/239–1234 or 800/228–9000. 750 rooms. AE, CB, DC, MC, V. Very Expensive.*

Knight's Inn Orlando Maingate West. There's a good selection of rooms here for a budget motel, including rooms with two double beds and efficiency apartments. Nonsmoking rooms are available. *7475 W. Irlo Bronson Hwy., Kissimmee 32741, tel. 407/396–4200. 120 units. AE, CB, DC, MC, V. Inexpensive.*

Ramada Resort Maingate East at the Park. The Ramada may offer the best deal in the neighborhood—a more attractive setting at more competitive prices. It has a few tennis courts, a swimming pool with a waterfall, a few shops and restaurants, and a delicatessen for picnickers. The rooms, like the rest of the hotel grounds, are spacious and bright, decked out in tropical and pastel colors. The best rooms, because of the view and light, face the pool. *2900 Parkway Blvd., Kissimmee 32741, tel. 407/396–7000 or 800/634–4774. 592 rooms. AE, CB, DC, MC, V. Moderate.*

Vistana Resort. Anyone interested in tennis should consider staying at this peaceful resort spread over 50 beautifully landscaped acres. It is also popular with families or groups who are willing to share a spacious, tastefully decorated villa or town house, each with at least two bedrooms and all the facilities of home—a full kitchen, living room, a washer/dryer, and so on. The price may seem high, but considering the number of people each condominiumlike unit can accommodate (up to six or eight), the rates can be a bargain. The 14 clay and all-weather tennis courts can be used without charge. Private or semi-private lessons are available for every type of player. Other facilities include a huge, free-form swimming pool and a full health club. *13800 Vistana Dr., Lake Buena Vista 32830, tel. 407/239–3100 or 800/237–9152. 458 units. AE, CB, DC, MC, V. Very Expensive.*

Orlando Area
International Drive

The International Drive area, referred to by locals as "The Drive" and formally labeled "Florida Center," is a main drag for all sorts of hotels, restaurants, and shopping malls. As you head north along The Drive, the hotels get cheaper, the restaurants turn into fast-food joints, and malls translate into factory outlets. The southern end of The Drive is more classy, but the northern end may be more congenial to your budget—particularly if all you need is a place to put your head at night.

You will be hard pressed to find any structure around here older than you are, even if you are a teenager, because the area has been built up mostly in the past 10 years as an alternative to the Disney properties. For those who are not interested exclusively in Disney World, The Drive is a convenient point of departure for Orlando's countless other attractions. The Drive immediately parallels I–4 (at Exits 28 and 29), so a few minutes' drive north puts you in downtown Orlando, while a few minutes south on I–4 puts you in Disney World.

International Drive showcases such local attractions as Sea World, Universal Studios, the labyrinth water-slide park, Wet 'n Wild, and many popular dinner shows. Many veteran Orlando visitors consider The Drive the territory's most comfortable home base, featuring some of the best hotels around.

Peabody Orlando. From afar, the Peabody looks like a high-rise office building. Don't let its austere exterior scare you away. Once inside, you will discover a very impressive, handsomely designed hotel. If you ignore the soaring numbers in the elevators and the sweeping view from your room, you will never know you are in a 27-story hotel. The Peabody's lobby has rich marble floors and fountains, and the entire hotel is decorated with modern art, giving it much color and flare. The rooms with the best views face Walt Disney World and a sea of orange trees that extends as far as the eye can see. If you want to be pampered, stay in the Peabody Club on the top three floors and enjoy special concierge service. The Peabody has a pool, a health club, and four lighted tennis courts. There are also two fine restaurants. *9801 International Dr., Orlando 32819, tel. 407/352–4000 or 800/262–6688. 891 rooms. AE, CB, DC, MC, V. Expensive–Very Expensive.*

★ **Sonesta Village Hotel.** The Sonesta, located off I–4 near International Drive, is a string of multiunit town houses on a lakefront. Following the lead of the all-suite hotels, the Sonesta "villas" consist of small apartments, some of which are bilevel with a fully equipped kitchenette, dining room/living room area, small patio, and bedroom. The units are comfortable and homey, each with its private, ground-floor entrance. One bonus of staying at the Sonesta is the outdoor facilities, including tennis courts, mini health club, swimming pool, and whirlpools convenient to each villa. Guests can sail and water-ski on the lake or offer themselves to the sun on a sandy beach. There is a restaurant and bar, but the only action is the nightly outdoor barbecue buffet. If you want to cook at "home" but are too busy to go shopping, the hotel offers a grocery delivery service. Laundry, however, is self-service. *10000 Turkey Lake Rd., Orlando 32819, tel. 407/352–8501 or 800/343–7170. 369 units. AE, CB, DC, MC, V. Expensive.*

Stouffer Orlando Resort. This first-rate resort was originally the Wyndham Hotel Sea World, until it was sold to the Stouffer chain in 1987. Located directly across the street from Sea World, this bulky, severe-looking, 10-story building looks more like a Federal Reserve Bank than a comfortable hotel. When you enter, you step into what is billed as the largest atrium lobby in the world. Facilities include an 18-hole golf course, six lighted tennis courts, a swimming pool, a whirlpool, and a child-care center and game room. On the second floor are a Nautilus-equipped fitness center and a beauty salon where you can work off or hide the effects of dinner.

Guest rooms are all large and spacious. The most expensive rooms face the atrium, but if you are a light sleeper, ask for an outside room to avoid the music and party sounds of conventioneers that rise through the atrium. *6677 Sea Harbour Dr., Orlando 32821, tel. 407/351–5555 or 800/327–6677 or 800/468–3571. 778 rooms. AE, CB, DC, MC, V. Expensive.*

Embassy Suites Hotel at Plaza International. The concept of the all-suite hotel has become very popular in the Orlando area, and the Embassy Suites, a chain hotel, was the first to offer it. All suites have a bedroom and a full living room equipped with wet bar, refrigerator, desk, pull-out sofa, and two TVs. It is a comfortable and economical arrangement, somewhat less expensive than a single room in the top-notch hotels. Because the bedroom can be closed off, it is ideal for small families. The core of the hotel is a wide atrium. It is not nearly as large as the atrium at the Stouffer, but it is much cozier, with a relaxing lounge and a pianist as its centerpieces. The hotel has both an indoor and an outdoor pool, an exercise room with Jacuzzi, sauna, steam room, and game room, but with none of the other recreational facilities that the larger hotels have. The Embassy has its own restaurant, but couples can arrange to have a full-service dinner served in the privacy of their living room. *8250 Jamaica Court, Orlando 32819, tel. 407/345–8250 or 800/327–9797. 246 rooms. AE, CB, DC, MC, V. Moderate–Expensive.*

Orlando Heritage Inn. If you are looking for a simple, small hotel with reasonable rates but plenty of deliberate charm, the Heritage is the place to stay. Located next to the towering Peabody, this newly built inn creates the atmosphere of Victorian-style Florida, complete with reproduction turn-of-the-century furnishings, rows of French windows and brass lamps, and a smattering of genuine 19th-century antiques. The guest rooms are decorated with a colonial accent—lace curtains on double French doors, folk-art prints on the walls, and quilted bed covers. The hotel has a small saloon-type lounge, and there is a dinner theater in the large Victorian rotunda several nights a week. With the exception of a swimming pool, there are few facilities. The whole place has a kitsch quaintness, in contrast to the area's other hotels, and a staff that is strong on southern hospitality. *9861 International Dr., Orlando 32819, tel. 407/352–0008 or in FL 800/282–1890 or outside FL 800/447–1890. AE, DC, MC, V. Moderate.*

Radisson Inn and Justus Aquatic Center. If you want to get in shape while visiting Orlando but want to avoid fancy resort prices, this is the place for you. Radisson is a big, modern, moderately priced hotel offering comfortable rooms (the best ones face the pool), but what makes it truly special are its outstanding athletic facilities. The hotel has a fine outdoor pool, but for those who are serious about swimming, there is also an indoor Aquatic Center with an Olympic-size swimming and diving pool. The center was built for competitive swimming and diving events and has a high-tech Human Performance Lab for personal health assessment. Other hotel facilities include a complete Nautilus center with weights and aerobicycles; tennis, raquetball, and handball courts; a jogging track; aerobics and swimmercise classes; and plenty more, including access to a local country club for golf. *8444 International Dr., Orlando 32819, tel. 407/345–0505 or 800/752–0003. 300 rooms. AE, CB, DC, MC, V. Moderate.*

U.S. 192 Area If you are looking for anything remotely quaint, charming, or sophisticated, head elsewhere. The U.S. 192 strip, formally called Irlo Bronson Memorial Highway and referred to as the Spacecoast Parkway, is generally known as Kissimmee, but whatever you call it, it is an avenue crammed with bargain-basement motels and hotels, inexpensive restaurants, fast-food chains, nickel-and-dime attractions, gas stations, and mini-marts. If all you are looking for is a decent room with perhaps a few extras for a manageable price, this is your wonderland. The number of motels here is mind boggling. It is a buyer's market, and room rates start as low as $20 a night—or lower if it is the right time of year and you can cut the right deal. But most rooms will run about $30–$70 a night, depending on the hotel's facilities and its proximity to Disney World. Among the chain hotels—Travelodge, Econolodge, Comfort Inn, Holiday Inn, Radisson, Sheraton, Best Western, and so on, plus a pride of family-operated motels, many of which are run by recent immigrants: a Norwegian couple at the Viking Motel, say, or a Chinese family at the Casa Rosa.

The Residence Inn. Of the all-suite hotels on U.S. 192, this one is probably the best. It consists of a row of four-unit town houses with private stairway entrances to each suite. One side of the unit faces the highway, the other overlooks an attractive lake, where visitors can sail, water-ski, jet ski, and fish. Forty of the units are penthouses, with complete kitchens, small living rooms, loft bedrooms, and even fireplaces. The other units are set up like studio apartments, but they still contain full kitchens and fireplaces. Regular studio suites accommodate two people; double suites accommodate up to four. Both Continental breakfast and a grocery shopping service are complimentary. The price may seem expensive, considering the location, but there is no charge for additional guests, so you can squeeze in the whole family at no extra cost. *4767 W. Irlo Bronson Memorial Hwy., Kissimmee 32741, tel. 407/396–2056 or 800/468–3027. 160 units. AE, CB, DC, MC, V. Moderate–Expensive.*

Radisson Inn Maingate. This is one of the newest hotels on the strip, located just a few minutes from the Magic Kingdom's front door. It is a very sleek, modern building with cheerful guest rooms, large bathrooms, and plenty of extras for the price. Facilities include a swimming pool, a whirlpool, a few tennis courts, and a jogging trail. Not fancy, but sufficient. The best rooms are those with a view of the pool. One floor is reserved for nonsmokers. *7501 W. Irlo Bronson Memorial Hwy., Kissimmee 32741, tel. 407/396–1400 or 800/333–3333. 580 rooms. AE, CB, DC, MC, V. Moderate.*

★ **Casa Rosa Inn.** For simple motel living—no screaming kids or loud music, please—this is your place. The pink, Spanish-style motel does not have much in the way of facilities other than a little swimming pool and free in-room movies, but it is a good, serviceable place to hang your hat. *4600 W. Irlo Bronson Me-*

morial Hwy., Kissimmee 32741, tel. 407/396–2020 or 800/ 874–1589. 50 rooms. AE, MC, V. Inexpensive.

Off the Beaten Track Mention should be made of two hotels that are off the beaten track—close enough to be part of the immediate Orlando area, but not so close that they fit into one of our categories.

Winter Park ★ **Park Plaza Hotel.** Located in Orlando's very posh, established suburb of Winter Park, the Park Plaza is an old-fashioned, wood-and-wicker Southern hotel, built in 1922. If you are in need of recreational facilities or special amenities, look elsewhere, but if you are hoping to find real Southern charm and hospitality, this is perhaps the only place in the Orlando area to find it. You are as far from the world of tourism as you can get and still be within a short driving distance of all the major attractions. It is a small, intimate hotel that gives you the feeling that you are a guest in somebody's home. All rooms open up onto one long balcony, covered with ferns, flowers, and wicker furniture. *307 Park Ave., Winter Park 32789, tel. 407/ 647–1072. To get there, drive east on I–4 and exit at Fairbanks Ave. Turn right for 1 mi until you reach Park Ave. The hotel is on your left. 18 rooms. AE, CB, DC, MC, V. Moderate–expensive.*

Lake Wales **Chalet Suzanne.** You'll find this conversation piece of a hotel in orange-grove territory, in what seems the middle of nowhere. A homemade billboard directs you down a country road that turns into a palm-lined drive. Cobblestone paths lead to a row of chalet-style houses and cabins, complete with balconies and thatched roofing. The Chalet Suzanne has been built bit by unlikely bit over the years, and the furnishings range from the rare and valuable to the garage-sale special. Bathrooms are tiled and have old-fashioned tubs, and wash basins. The most charming rooms face the lake. *U.S. Highway 27S, Drawer AC, Lake Wales 33859, tel. 813/676–6011. To get there, either land your Cessna or Lear jet on their private airstrip, or drive. Go west on I–4 from Orlando to the Rte. 27 exit and head toward Cypress Gardens. The Chalet's billboard is past the Cypress Gardens turnoff, just after Lake Wales. 30 rooms. AE, CB, DC, MC, V. Moderate–Expensive.*

Nightlife

Walt Disney World Dinner Shows **Top of the World.** This is Disney's sophisticated nighttime entertainment spot, located on the top floor of the Contemporary Resort. A spirited show called "Broadway at the Top" runs for about an hour after the two nightly seatings for dinner. A cast of high-energy dancers and singers bring to life some of Broadway's greatest hits. A single price includes the show, dinner, and taxes. Gratuity and alcoholic drinks are extra. *Contemporary Resort, tel. 407/824–8000. Reservations necessary months in advance. Jackets required. Admission: $35 adults, $17 children 3–11. Seatings at 6 and 9:15.*

Polynesian Revue and Mickey's Tropical Revue. Put on some comfortable, casual clothes and head over to the Polynesian Village Resort for an outdoor barbecue and a tropical luau, complete with fire jugglers and hula drum dancers. It's a colorful, South Pacific setting and an easygoing evening that families find relaxing and trouble free. There are two shows nightly of the Polynesian Revue and an earlier show for children called Mickey's Tropical Revue, where Disney characters perform decked out in costumes befitting these South Seas surroundings. *Polynesian Village Resort, tel. 407/824–8000. Dress: casual. Reservations necessary, usually months in advance. Polynesian Review: $23.50 adults, $14 children 3–11. Seatings at 6:45 and 9:30. Mickey's Tropical Revue: adults $20, juniors $16, children $10.50. Seating at 4:30.*

Hoop-Dee-Doo Revue. This family entertainment dinner show may be corny, but it is also the liveliest and most rollicking. A troupe of jokers called the Pioneer Hall Players stomp their feet, wisecrack, and make merry in this Western mess-hall setting. The chow consists of barbecued ribs, fried chicken, corn on the cob, strawberry shortcake, and all the fixins. There are three shows nightly at Pioneer Hall in the Fort Wilderness area—not the easiest place to get to. *Fort Wilderness Resort, tel. 407/824–8000. Dress: informal. Reservations necessary, sometimes months in advance. Admission: $25 adults, $16 juniors 12–20, $14 children 3–11. Seatings at 7:30 and 10.*

Pleasure Island. There will be a single admission charge to this nightlife entertainment complex scheduled to open in early 1989. The complex will feature a comedy club, teenage dance center, rock-and-roller skating-rink disco, numerous restaurants, lounges, shops, and even a 10-screen theater complex. Six themed nightclubs will offer everything from swinging jazz to foot-stompin' country and western to the latest pop video hits.

Laser Show. You won't want to miss Epcot Center's grand finale, a laser show that takes place along the shores of the World Showcase lagoon, every night just before Epcot closes. It is a show unlike any other. In the middle of the lagoon, laser projections of dancing images move across screens of spraying water. Orchestral music fills the air as multicolored neon lasers streak across the sky, pulsating to the rhythms of the music. Suddenly the night lights up with brilliant fireworks and the lagoon vibrates with the sounds of Tchaikovsky's 1812 Overture. Projections of the Earth's continents transform Spaceship Earth into a luminescent, spinning globe. The lasers used to create these images are powerful enough to project an identical image on a golf ball up to five miles away. The projections are called Illuminations, and one of them creates a towering Mt. Fuji over the Japan pavilion. When the show is over, the crowds exit as Spaceship Earth continues to revolve. It is a stellar performance that you won't want to miss.

The Orlando Area

Until a few years ago Orlando's nightlife was more like that of Oskaloosa, Iowa, than of a booming tourist haven. But slowly, an after-dark scene has developed, spreading farther and farther beyond the realm of Disney. Orlando entrepreneurs have now caught on that there is a fortune to be had by satisfying the fun-hungry night owls that flock to this city. New night spots open constantly, offering everything from flashy discos to ballroom dancing, country-and-western saloons, Broadway dinner theaters, and even medieval jousting tournaments.

The Arts

If all the fantasyland hype starts to wear thin, and you feel the need for more sophisticated entertainment, check out the local fine arts scene in the "Happenings" and "Calendar" sections of *Orlando Magazine*, or *Center Stage*, available at any newsstand. The average price of a ticket to performing arts events in the Orlando area rarely exceeds $10–$12 and is often half that price.

Orlando has an active performing arts agenda of ballet, modern dance, classical music, opera, and theater, much of which takes place at the **Bob Carr Performing Arts Center** (401 Livingston St., Orlando, tel. 407/896–7365). This community auditorium presents a different play each month (Wed.–Sat., with Sun. matinees). Productions are low budget, but performances are competent.

During the school year, **Rollins College** (tel. 407/646–2233) in Winter Park has a choral and symphonic concert series that is open to the public and usually free. The first week of March, there is a **Bach Music Festival** (tel. 407/646–2182) that has been a Winter Park tradition for over 55 years. Also at the college is the **Anne Russell Theater** (tel. 407/646–2501), which has a regular series of productions.

Across the street from the Peabody Hotel on International Drive is the newly expanded **Orange County Civic and Convention Center** (tel. 407/345–9898), which hosts many big-name performing artists.

Dinner Shows Dinner shows have become an immensely popular form of nighttime entertainment around Orlando. A set price usually buys a multiple-course dinner and a theatrical production—a totally escapist experience. The food tends to be predictable—but not the major attractions. Always make reservations in advance, especially on weekends. A lively crowd can be an asset; a show playing to a small audience can be a pathetic and embarrassing sight. What the shows lack in substance and depth, the audience makes up for in color and enthusiasm. The result is an evening of light entertainment, which kids in particular will enjoy.

Mardi Gras. This jazzy, New Orleans–style show is the best of Orlando's dinner attractions. The set menu consists of mixed vegetable soup, tossed salad, buckets of fried chicken, platters of roast beef, apple pie with ice cream, and all the beer, wine, or soda you can drink. It is not an elaborate meal, but it is as good as one can expect from a dinner theater. A New Orleans jazz band plays during dinner, followed by a one-hour cabaret with colorful song-and-dance routines to rhythms of the Caribbean, Latin America, and Dixieland jazz. Although the kids are more likely to vote for the Wild West or medieval shows, adults tend to prefer Mardi Gras because it is more of a restaurant nightclub than a fantasyland. *At the Mercado Shopping Village, 8445 International Dr., Orlando, tel. 407/351–5151 or 800/641–5151. Dress: casual. Reservations necessary. AE, CB, DC, MC, V. Admission: $23.95 adults, $15.95 children 3–11.*

Fort Liberty. Run by the same company that operates Mardi Gras and King Henry's Feast, this dinner show whisks you out to the Wild West. The entertainment is a mixed bag of real Indian dances, foot-stompin' sing-alongs, and acrobatics. A British cowboy shows what he can do with bullwhips and lassos, and a musician plays the 1812 Overture on the tuba and "America the Beautiful" on an old saw (yes, the kind that cuts wood). The show is full of slapstick theatrics and country-western shindigging that children really enjoy. The chow is what you might expect to eat with John Wayne out on the prairie: beef soup, fried chicken, corn on the cob, and pork and beans. You are served by a rowdy chorus of cavalry recruits who keep the food coming and beverages freely pouring. All tables seat 12, so unless you are in a big party, expect to develop pass-the-ketchup relationships. Fort Liberty is a stockade filled with shops and stalls selling gifts and souvenirs with a Western theme. The ambience is set by the photographers snapping photos of visitors dressed in cowboy garb. Forever trying to attract tourists, the Fort Liberty entertainers perform in the courtyard during the day. If the kids are more intent on seeing Marlboro country than you are, go at lunch time (11–2), pick up some fast-food fried chicken for $2, and see many of the acts that are in the dinner show. *5260 Irlo Bronson Memorial Hwy. (U.S. 192), Kissimmee, tel. 407/351–5151 or 800/641–5151. Dress: casual. Reservations necessary. AE, CB, DC, MC, V. Admission: $23.95 adults, $15.95 children 3–11.*

King Henry's Feast. Driving along the strip of hotels and shopping malls on I–4 or International Drive, you may notice two Tudor-style buildings. One of them is the Econolodge; the other is the home of Orlando's King Henry VIII and his court of 16th-century jesters. The entertainment includes a corny but talented magician, a daring fire-swallowing acrobat, and much singing, dancing, and revelry as King Henry celebrates his birthday and begins his quest for his seventh bridge. Saucy wenches, who refer to customers as "me lords" and "me ladies," serve potato-leek soup, salad, chicken and ribs, and all the beer, wine, and soft drinks you can guzzle. Bar drinks are extra. *8984 International Dr., Orlando, tel. 407/351–5151 or 800/641–5151. Dress: casual. Reservations necessary. AE, CB, DC, MC, V. Admission: $23.95 adults, $15.95 children aged 3–11.*

Medieval Times. In a huge, modern-medieval manor, visitors enjoy a four-course dinner while watching the struggle of good and evil in a tournament of games, sword fights, and jousting matches, including no less than 30 charging horses and a cast of 75 knights, nobles, and maidens. Sound silly? It is. Yet if you view it through the eyes of your children, this two-hour extravaganza of pageantry and meat-and-potatoes banquet fare can be amusing. Everyone faces forward along narrow banquet tables that are stepped auditorium-style above the tournament. If you and your family traveled the amusement-park route all day and are tired of looking and nagging at each other, you may get some respite, a bit of comic relief, and some vicarious pleasure from a night of crossing lances. $25 per person. *U.S. 192, Kissimmee, tel. 407/239–0214 or 407/396–1518, in FL 800/432–0768, outside FL 800/327–4024. Dress: informal. Reservations necessary. AE, MC, or V.*

Bavarian Schnitzel House. If you have any interest in German food, this fun-loving place serves the area's finest. The Red Baron would feel right at home in this kitschy Bavarian world, which none of the rowdy revelers seems to mind. The entertainment is a five-piece oompah band that shakes, rattles, and groans at its own corny jokes. They do a good job of getting the audience to sing, dance, and laugh the night away. Go on a crowded weekend night; if you're going to succumb, you may as well go all the way. There is no cover charge for the entertainment, and dinner is à la carte. Meals are hearty and not expensive. Goulash soup, Wiener schnitzel, and a few steins of German beer ought to set you up for a jovial evening. *6159 Westwood Blvd. (just off International Dr.), Orlando, tel. 407/352–8484, Dress: casual. Reservations suggested. AE, CB, DC, MC, V. Inexpensive–Moderate.*

Mark Two. This is the only true dinner theater in Orlando, with full Broadway musicals, such as *Oklahoma!*, *My Fair Lady*, *West Side Story* and *South Pacific*, staged through most of the year. During the Christmas holiday season, shorter Broadway musical revues are presented. A buffet and full-service cocktail bar open for business 90 minutes before the show. The food is nothing to write home about and should not be the reason to pay a visit. The buffet of seafood Newburg, baked whitefish, a variety of meats, and salad bar is only a few notches above cafeteria food. Best bets are the rich desserts that arrive during intermission. The shows are directed by the theater's owner, and the sets, costumes, music, and choreography are all done in-house. The actors are mostly from the Orlando area. It will not be the best performance you will ever see, but it can be a pleasure to hear the scores and see the routines of a favorite old musical while you sit comfortably at your table with a drink in hand. The cost of the show includes your meal. The buffet is served from 6:30 to 7:30. The performance starts at 8. *Edgewater Center, 3376 Edgewater Dr., Orlando (from I–4, take Exit 44 and go west), tel. 407/843–6275. Dress: casual. Reservations suggested. AE, MC, V. Closed Mon. Moderate.*

Church Street Station This downtown Orlando attraction is a complete entertainment experience. Widely popular among both tourists and locals, it single-handedly began Orlando's metamorphosis from a sleepy town to the nighttime hot spot it now boasts to be and is on its way to becoming. Unlike much of what you see in Walt Disney World, this place doesn't just look authentic—it *is* authentic. The train on the tracks is an actual 19th-century steam engine, and the whistling calliope was especially rebuilt to blow its original tunes. The buildings have been completely redecorated with collectibles and memorabilia from around the world. You can spend an evening in part of the complex, or you can wander from area to area, soaking up the peculiar characteristics of each. For a single admission price of $10, you're permitted to wander freely, stay as long as you wish, and do what you want, whether it's drinking, dancing, dining, or people-watching. Food and drink cost extra and are not cheap, but they add to the fun. Parts of the complex are open during the day, but the place is usually quiet then; the pace picks up at night, especially on weekends, with crowds thickest 10–11. *129 W. Church St., Orlando, tel. 305/422–2434. Reservations not necessary. Dress: casual. AE, MC, V.*

Rosie O'Grady's. This is a turn-of-the-century saloon with dark wood, brass trim, a full Dixieland band blaring out of a gazebo, and countertop cancan dancers, tap dancers, and vaudeville singers. Is this a set for *The Music Man* or an evening at the Moulin Rouge? It's difficult to tell at first. The 90-minute shows begin at 7 or 7:30 PM. The last show starts at 11:45. Multidecker sandwiches and hot dogs are sold in the Gay 90s Sandwich Parlour 4:30–11 PM.

Apple Annie's Courtyard. This is a relatively quiet nook that features continuous live folk and bluegrass music from about 8 PM to 2 AM. It's a good place to rest your feet, have a drink, and people-watch. Salads, fruit platters, and exotic drinks are served 11 AM–2 AM.

Lili Marlene's Aviator Pub. Here you have a relaxed, wood-paneled English-pub atmosphere and the finest dining on Church Street Food is hearty, upscale, and very American—mostly steaks, ribs, and seafood. Prices are not cheap. The walls have biplane-era memorabilia, and a large-scale model aircraft hangs from the ceiling. Open for lunch and dinner until midnight.

Phileas Phogg's Balloon Works. This is a very popular disco filled with young singles over age 21 and a sprinkling of old-timers showing off their moves on the dance floor. It is a good-looking yuppie tourist crowd, leavened with locals. Contemporary dance tunes are played on a sound system that will blow your socks off. The place is jammed by midnight and open until 2 AM. Much of the young crowd feels it is worth the price of admission into the Church Street Station just to be able to come here.

Orchid Garden. Decorative lamps, iron latticework, arched ceilings, and stained-glass windows create a striking Victorian arcade where visitors sit, drink, and listen to first-rate bands pounding out popular tunes from the 1950s to the '80s. Open until 2 AM.

Cracker's Raw Bar. Located behind the Orchid Garden, Cracker's is a good place to get a quick gumbo or chowder and slam down a few oysters with a beer chaser. Open until midnight.

Cheyenne Saloon. This is the biggest, fanciest, rootin'-tootin' saloon you may ever see. The former triple-level opera house is covered with moose racks, steer horns, buffalo heads, and Remington rifles; a seven-piece country-and-western band darn near brings the house down. This is a fun crowd to watch, with all the pickin', strummin', fiddlin', hollerin', and do-si-doin'. Make sure you come equipped with your best stompin' shoes, cowboy hat, and catcalls. An upstairs restaurant serves chicken-and-ribs saloon fare. The shows start at 7:30 PM, 11 PM, and 12:45 AM.

Church St. Exchange. The newest addition to the complex, near Church Street Station, is a razzle-dazzle marketplace filled with all sorts of specialty shops and old-fashioned theme restaurants.

Bars and Clubs

The bars and nightclubs have been divided into two sections. The first covers the tourist hotel districts in the Disney area, including Kissimmee, Lake Buena Vista, and International Drive. These places are usually filled with visitors to Disney World. The other section covers the city of Orlando and Winter Park, both of which cater to a more local crowd. Remember that clubs on Disney property are allowed to stay open later than are bars elsewhere, and many of them don't have last call until 2:45 AM.

Disney Area

Little Darlin's Rock n' Roll Palace. Shake, rattle, and roll the night away in this 1950s and '60s nostalgia nightclub. The interior looks like an opera house, with an orchestra-pit dance floor and a huge bandstand stage featuring famous old rock bands that still tour, such as The Drifters, Platters, and Bo Diddley. The crowd is a mix of young and old, singles and couples. The club features a very talented house band that serves up live music seven nights a week. The menu is vintage '50s: Philly hot dogs, cheese-steak sandwiches, banana splits, and, for some strange reason, escargots. *Old Town, 5770 Spacecoast Pkwy., Kissimmee 32741, tel. 407/396–6499. Dress: casual. AE, MC, V. Admission: $4.50–$6.50.*

Giraffe Lounge. Located inside the Hotel Royal Plaza, Lake Buena Vista (World Village), this flashy disco with spinning, colored lights is usually densely packed on weekends. It is a small place, and classy it ain't, but there's a lot going on, including live bands five nights a week. Happy hour runs daily 4–9:30 PM. Music plays and the bartender pours until 3 AM. *Hotel Royal Plaza, Walt Disney World Village, Lake Buena Vista, tel.*

407/828–2828. Dress: casual. AE, CB, DC, MC, V. Open 4 PM–3 AM. No cover.

The Laughing Kookaburra. A big hotel disco with live band music nightly and a serious singles crowd of all ages. The music is loud and the dance floor can get very crowded—a plus for some, a minus for others. The bar serves up 99 brands of beer, plus cocktails. Happy hour with free bar food runs daily 4–8 PM. The band plays six nights a week (off Mon.). *Buena Vista Palace Hotel, Walt Disney World Village, Lake Buena Vista, tel. 407/827–2727. Dress: casual. AE, CB, DC, MC, V. Open 4 PM–3 AM. No cover.*

La Cantina. This little bar in the Hotel Royal Plaza has guitar music seven nights a week and a happy hour, Sunday–Thursday, from midnight to 3 AM(!) It's a good thing most visitors are hotel guests—it's hard to get in an accident in an elevator. You probably would not come to this lackluster place unless you were hell-bent on getting tanked late at night. *Hotel Royal Plaza, tel. 407/828–2828. Open 11 AM–3 AM.*

Top of the Tower. Listen to a comedian tell jokes and play country and rock-and-roll classics on the guitar while you check out a tremendous view of Disney World. A very comfy hotel bar with a nice tame bunch of people. *Viscount Hotel, tel. 407/828–2424. Dress: casual. Open 8:30 PM–3 AM. No cover.*

Bennigan's. A young singles' spot that draws crowds in the early evening and during happy hours, from 4–7 PM and 11 PM–2 AM. It caters mostly to nontourists who work in the area. Food is served almost until closing. *6324 International Dr., Orlando, tel. 407/351–4436. Open 11 AM–2 AM.*

Orlando Area

The nightclubs in Orlando have significantly more character than those in the Disney hotel area. If you have the energy to get in your car, you will probably find these spots more satisfying and less touristy—if you can find them.

J.J. Whispers. A classy, brassy singles crowd flocks to this trendy disco, which tries hard to maintain an image of cosmopolitan class. Expect to mingle with fashion-conscious locals in their tastefully outrageous attire. The club is equally popular with the over-30 set, who listen to music from the 1940s, '50s, and '60s in the Showroom. The young people do what young people do in a massive, multilevel, state-of-the-art disco. J. J.'s has one restaurant serving bar-food fare, and another, a deli, that is open for lunch. It sometimes features comedians, magicians, and other stage acts. Live entertainment (Tues.–Sun., 8 PM–2 AM) includes all-male and all-female revues and live bands. *5100 Adanson St., Orlando 32804, tel. 407/629–4779. To get there, take I–4 to the Lee Rd. exit and go west for about half a mile on Lee Rd. Watch for a sharp left-hand turn at Adanson St. J.J.'s is located at the end of the Lee Rd. Shopping Center. Dress: tasteful but outrageous—or just a jacket. AE, MC, V. Cover charge: $3 and up.*

Cheek-to-Cheek. Monday nights are a big deal here because of the many big-name performers—mostly contemporary jazz musicians in the Class Act Lounge, and rock and reggae in Cheek-to-Cheek. Past performers have included Al Stewart, Wynton Marsalis, Rita Coolidge, and even Tommy Dorsey. The place can get very crowded; tables are crammed so close together that you will become fast friends, or enemies, with your neighbors. Other nights of the week (Tues.–Sat.) are very popular with the 35–50-year-old crowd, who dance to Top 40s music played by Cheek-to-Cheek's house band. *839 N. Orlando Ave.*

(U.S. 17–92), tel. 407/644–2060. Open 8 PM*–2* AM. *Mon. cover charge up to $20. Tues.–Sat. cover charge $4. Closed some Sun.*

Crocodile Club. This bar, inside a restaurant called Bailey's in Winter Park, collects a young, well-dressed college crowd from neighboring Rollins College. The atmosphere is more sophisticated and yuppified than most Orlando bars. Expect to hear Motown and dance to pop. *Bailey's Restaurant, 118 W. Fairbanks Ave., Winter Park, tel. 407/647–8501.*

Sullivan's Trailways Lounge. A very popular place with much right-friendly charm, where people of all ages and many families come to strut their stuff on the largest dance floor in Florida. Even Yankees are welcome in this Southern country-and-western dance hall. Big name performers entertain on occasion; local bands play nightly, except Sunday. *1108 S. Orange Blossom Trail (U.S. 441), tel. 407/843–2943. Bands play 9* PM*–2* AM. *Cover charge: $3.*

9 Central Florida

Orientation

by April Athey

Thick hardwood and pine wilderness, grassy rolling hills, spring-fed rivers, and hundreds of crystal-clear lakes are sandwiched here between the Gulf of Mexico wetlands and the beaches of Florida's mid-Atlantic coast. At least three distinct geographic areas are contained in this 60-mile-wide swath just north of Orlando that extends about 100 miles across the peninsula from coast to coast.

The Gulf of Mexico area lies west of I–75 between Crystal River and Weeki Wachee, a year-round manatee (sea cow) refuge.

The Daytona Beach area lies to the east (between I–95 and the Atlantic Ocean, from Ormond Beach to Melbourne) and includes the Kennedy Space Center. The area north of Orlando, between I–75 and U.S. 17/92, includes Ocala's horse farms, Marjorie Rawlings's Cross Creek country, and the St. Johns River.

Getting Around

By Plane Tampa International Airport is nearest the first of our regions, west of Orlando (*see* Getting Around the Southwest Coast). One-way limousine service for two from the airport to the Homosassa Springs area runs $37–$40 and requires advance reservations. You can call *Friendship Limousine* (tel. 904/746–5233) or *Aire-Dale Limo Service* (tel. 904/628–7820). Orlando International Airport and Gainesville Regional provide service into the region north of Orlando. Limousine rates from either airport to Ocala run $45–$65. *Embassy Limo* (tel. 904/373–3280) and *Town & Country Limo* (tel. 904/351–LIMO) are two available fleets. Daytona/Orlando Transit Service charges $17 per person one-way for its airport shuttle to the region east of Orlando (tel. 800/231–1965 in FL or 800/223–1965 in the rest of the USA).

By Car U.S. 19/98 is the primary north–south route following the west coast; I–75 and U.S. 27 are the primary north–south routes through the center of the region; I–95, U.S. 1 and A1A are the primary north–south routes near the east coast; east–west routes, listed from north to south, include Rtes. 40, 42, 44, 46, and 50. It's useful to remember that most of the east-coast beaches are found on a series of barrier islands strung together by Rte. A1A.

By Train *Amtrak* (tel. 800/USA–RAIL) serves Ocala, DeLand (near Daytona Beach), and Sanford.

By Bus *Greyhound/Trailways* has stations in Crystal River (200 N.E. Hwy. 19, tel. 904/795–4445), Homosassa Springs (8666 W. Halls River Rd., tel. 904/628–3066), Brooksville (512 W. Broad St., tel. 904/796–3068), Ocala (512 N. Magnolia Ave., tel. 904/732–2677), DeLand (224 E. Ohio Ave., tel. 904/734–2747), Daytona Beach (910 Volusia Ave., tel. 904/253–0692), New Symrna Beach (502 N. Orange St., tel. 904/428–8211), Titusville (20 N. Washington Ave., tel. 407/267–8760), Cocoa Beach (302 Main St., tel. 407/636–6531), and Melbourne (460 S. Harbor City Blvd., tel. 407/723–4323).

Scenic Drives

Route 46 Views of natural Florida wilderness, marked by the distinctive clumps of cabbage palms that look like islands floating in a sea of waving marsh grasses, spread out in every direction along this route between U.S. 1 and Sanford.

Riverside Drive New Symrna Beach's grand old homes line the Intracoastal Waterway along this route, also a popular bicycle path.

Tropical Drive From the skinny southern tip of Merritt Island, which lies between the Indian and Bananna rivers, drive north past the foliage-shrouded waterfront homesteads for a look at tropical island living, Florida style.

Guided Tours

Bay Point Dive Center (tel. 904/563–1040) conducts hour-long guided boat tours of Kings Bay for viewing manatees. Cost: $10 per person (two-person minimum). The center also conducts guided scuba diving tours for viewing manatees underwater. Cost: $25 per person (two-person minimum).

Talley's Pro Dive (tel. 904/795–2776) conducts day-long guided diving tours, including snorkeling with manatees in Crystal River (Nov.–Mar.) and drift diving in the Rainbow River. Cost: $30 per person (two-person minimum).

Homosassa River Guide Service (tel. 904/628–1302) will tailor a sunset cruise, fishing cruise, or sightseeing boat tour to your needs. Half-day or full-day tours are available. Rates per person, $80–$150.

Sun State Travel (tel. 904/867–8453) conducts bus tours of Ocala horse farms every Monday, Wednesday, and Friday. The six-hour narrated tours ($16 per person) depart at 9 AM from the offices of Sun State Travel (1729 N.E. 14th St., Ocala), and rates include a buffet lunch and visits to three horse farms. Reservations are required.

Capt. Tom's Complete River Tours (tel. 904/236–0872) acquaint visitors with the rivers on which steamboats cruised in the 1800s. You can choose a three-, four-, or eight-hour river cruise on the Okalawaha and Silver rivers. Rates: $10–$24 per person. Two- and three-day trips with hotel accommodations along the route also are available. Cruises are by reservation only.

Gray Lines of Daytona Beach (tel. 904/255–6506) conducts sightseeing tours of Central Florida attractions: Disney-Epcot, Sea World, Cypress Gardens, and NASA Kennedy Space Center's Spaceport USA. Rates include round-trip transportation and admission.

Important Addresses and Numbers

Tourist Information **Crystal River Chamber of Commerce** (28 N. Highway 19, Crystal River, tel. 904/795–3149). Open weekdays, 9–4. **Homosassa Springs Chamber of Commerce** (N. Highway 19, Homosassa Springs, tel. 904/628–2666). Open weekdays 9–4. **Hernando County Chamber of Commerce** (101 E. Fort Dade Ave., Brooksville, tel. 904/796–2420). Open weekdays 9–5. **Ocala/Marion County Chamber of Commerce** (Fort King Ave. and

Broadway, Ocala, tel. 904/629–8051). Open weekdays 8:30–5. **DeLand Area Chamber of Commerce** (336 N. Woodland Blvd., DeLand, tel. 904/734–4331). Open weekdays 8:30–5. **Greater Sanford Chamber of Commerce** (400 E. First St., Sanford, tel. 407/322–2212). Open weekdays 9–5. **Daytona Beach & Halifax Area Chamber of Commerce** (126 E. Orange Ave., Daytona Beach, tel. 904/255–0981). Open weekdays 9–5. **New Symrna Beach Chamber of Commerce** (115 Canal St., New Symrna Beach, tel. 904/428–2449). Open weekdays 8:30–5. **Cocoa Beach Chamber of Commerce** (400 Fortenberry Rd., Merritt Island, tel. 407/452–4390). Open weekdays 8:30–5. **South Brevard Chamber of Commerce** (1005 E. Strawbridge Ave., Melbourne, tel. 407/724–5400). Open weekdays 9–5.

Emergencies

Dial 911 for **police** or **ambulance** assistance.

Seven Rivers Community Hospital (6201 N. Suncoast Blvd., Crystal River, tel. 1 800/5–ACCESS). **Munroe Regional Medical Center** (131 S.W. 15th St., Ocala, tel. 904/351–7200 or 904/867–13 MD). **Halifax Medical Center** (303 N. Clyde Morris Blvd., Daytona Beach, tel. 904/254–4100). **Cape Canaveral Hospital** (on the 520 Causeway between Cocoa Beach and Merritt Island, tel. 407/799–7150).

Dentists

General & Family Dentistry (8800 S.W. State Road 200, Ocala, tel. 904/854–7070). **South Daytona Dental Center** (3231 S. Ridgewood Ave., South Daytona, tel. 904/788–9620).

Pharmacies

Wal-Mart Discount Pharmacies are open daily in Homosassa Springs (tel. 904/628–4334), Ocala (tel. 904/237–7103), New Symrna Beach (tel. 904/427–6030), Cocoa Beach (tel. 407/452–4340), and Melbourne (tel. 407/773–0663).

Exploring Central Florida

The Gulf of Mexico Area

Touring the tropical wilderness and wetlands between Crystal River and Weeki Wachee will make one thing perfectly clear—this is manatee (sea cow) country. These shy vegetarian mammals, which early explorers mistook for mermaids when they rose from the water, once were plentiful. But their number has dwindled to less than 1,000, putting them on the state's endangered-species list. The spring-fed rivers and sheltered bays of the area are virtually a year-round sanctuary for them, and locals are taking advantage of the rising attention these creatures bring.

Numbers in the margin correspond with points of interest on the Central Florida map.

Whether your embarkation point is Tampa or Orlando, a good
1 place to begin your tour is **Weeki Wachee,** with its spring of performing "mermaids." If sitting in a cool dark underground theater watching through thick glass as girls in mermaid suits perform underwater tricks (like peeling and eating a banana) doesn't interest you, the natural wilderness and wildlife at the attraction will. The jungle-boat cruise down the crystal-clear Weeki Wachee River is great for wildlife photography. Whatever you see peering back at you from the water or the trees is real. The "Birds of Prey" show makes you wonder if an eagle wouldn't make a fine pet, and the Animal Forest petting zoo is popular with children. *U.S. 19 South and Rte. 50, Weeki Wachee, tel. 904/596–2062. Admission: $8.95 adults, $5.95 children 3–11. Open daily 9–6.*

On a hot day, the tower slides and natural springwater pools at Weeki Wachee's **Buccaneer Bay** are appealing. *U.S. 19 South and Rte. 50, Weeki Wachee, tel. 904/596–2062. Admission: $5.95 adults, $4.95 children 3–11. Open late Mar.–early Sept., 10–5.*

2 For a leisurely side trip, head east on Rte. 50 to **Brooksville** (*see* Off the Beaten Track). Farther north on U.S. 19 is **Chassahowitzka National Wildlife Refuge,** a 30,500-acre estuarine habitat that is home to bald eagles, manatees, marine turtles, and peregrine falcons. The refuge is accessible only by boat, and rentals are available at **Lyke's Chassahowitzka River Campground** (tel. 904/382–2200).

The closer you get to the town of Homosassa Springs, the heavier the traffic on U.S. 19 becomes. At the Hall's River Road traffic light, you'll see a large brown-and-white sign pointing
3 the way to **Homosassa Springs Nature World.** Turn left at the light (Rte. 490–A), then left again on Fish Bowl Drive. This narrow road wends through a tropical landscape to an attraction that hasn't changed much since it opened in the 1940s. Focal point is the giant Fish Bowl Spring, in which a 168-ton floating underwater observatory allows close-up views of the fresh- and saltwater fish that congregate at the spring. Other residents of the spring and adjacent lagoons are manatees, otters, alligators, and a 4,000-pound hippo named Lucifer. A nature trail threads through the wilderness surrounding the

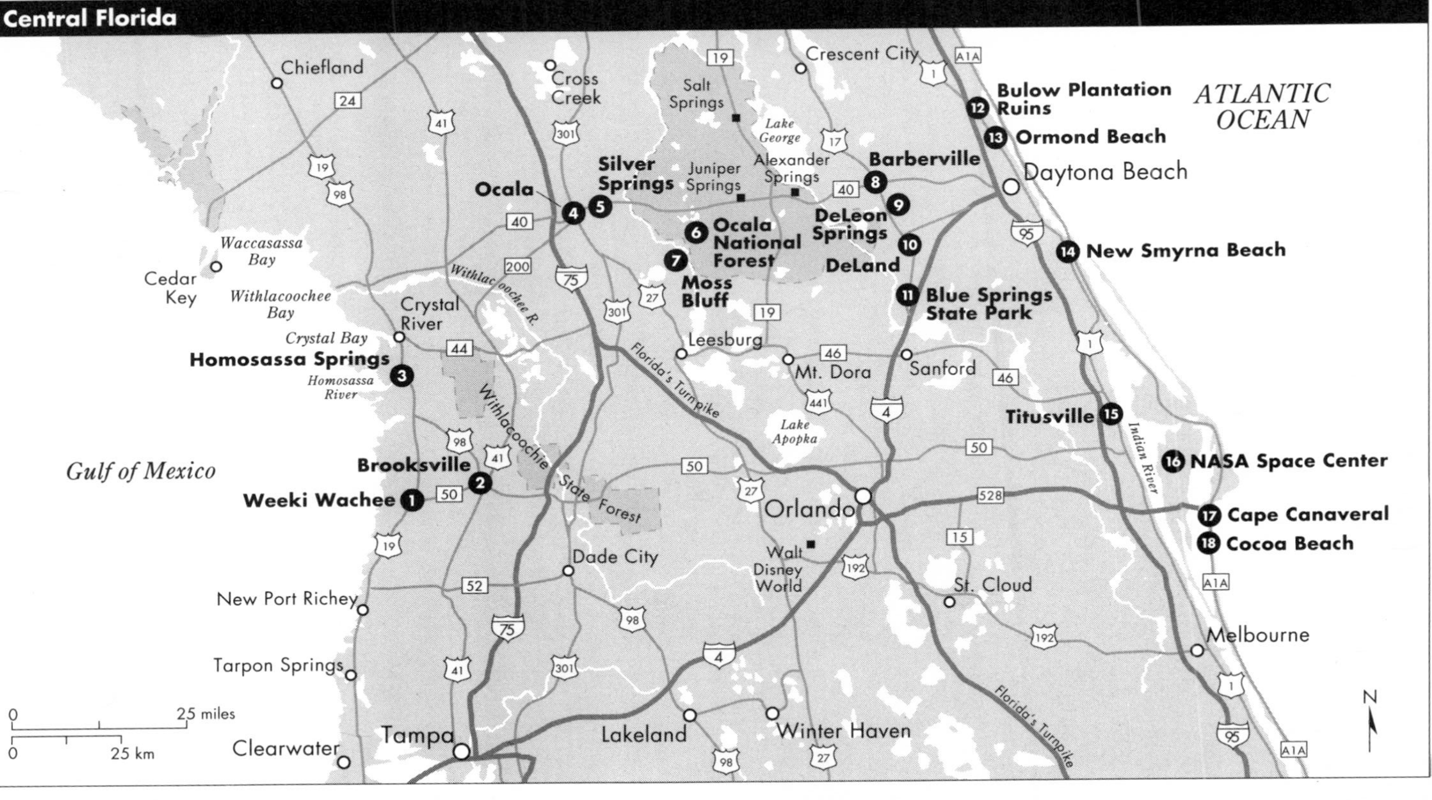
Central Florida
ATLANTIC OCEAN
Gulf of Mexico
Chiefland
Cross Creek
Salt Springs
Crescent City
Lake George
Juniper Springs
Alexander Springs
Bulow Plantation Ruins
Ormond Beach
Barberville
Daytona Beach
Ocala
Silver Springs
DeLeon Springs
Ocala National Forest
DeLand
New Smyrna Beach
Moss Bluff
Waccasassa Bay
Cedar Key
Withlacoochee Bay
Withlacoochee R.
Crystal River
Crystal Bay
Blue Springs State Park
Leesburg
Mt. Dora
Sanford
Homosassa Springs
Homosassa River
Florida's Turnpike
Lake Apopka
Titusville
Indian River
Withlacoochie State Forest
Brooksville
Weeki Wachee
NASA Space Center
Orlando
Cape Canaveral
Cocoa Beach
Walt Disney World
Dade City
St. Cloud
New Port Richey
Melbourne
Tarpon Springs
Tampa
Clearwater
Lakeland
Winter Haven
N
0
25 miles
25 km

spring, where a variety of birds and small animals roam freely. From the boat docks on Fish Bowl Drive (across from the main entrance) a cruise on the tropical Homosassa River departs every half hour. *1 mi west of traffic light on U.S. 19, Homosassa Springs, tel. 904/628–2311. Admission: $6.95 adults, $3.95 children 3–11, $5.56 senior citizens. Open daily 9–5:30.*

Beyond the attraction, Fish Bowl Drive passes the historic **Yulee Sugar Mill Ruins** and an assortment of backwoods residences before it dead-ends at the Homosassa River, where fishing devotees frequent **The Riverside Villas and Yardarm Restaurant.** Across the river, you'll see a turn-of-the-century white-frame "Old Florida" homestead and people dining alfresco.

Time Out The people you saw across the river were having lunch at **K.C. Crump's on the River** (*see* Dining).

To complete your tour of the Gulf Coast area, visit **Crystal River,** site of the Kings Bay manatee sanctuary (a holding of the Florida Nature Conservancy), and tiny **Yankeetown,** just north. Everywhere you look you'll see the distinctive red-and-white diver's flag. Diving with manatees is all the rage these days. But look, don't touch. Annoying a sea cow is against the law.

North of Orlando to Ocala

4 Dominated by **Ocala National Forest**—known to locals as the Big Scrub—this region is characterized by crystal-clear lakes, spring-fed rivers, thick hardwood forests, and grassy rolling hills that support more than 400 Thoroughbred horse farms. History recalls the days when steamboats cruised the region's St. Johns, Oklawaha, and Silver rivers. This is the Florida about which Marjorie K. Rawlings wrote so fondly, and it's the home of famed Silver Springs.

For a Sunday driving tour through the heart of Ocala's **horse farm country,** take the southwest segment of Rte. 200 between Ocala and Inverness. The well-manicured farms are neatly fenced over the grassy rolling hills. Narrated bus tours, with visits to several of the farms, are available (*see* Guided Tours).

South of Rte. 200 on I–75, take Exit 67 to Rte. 484 and visit the **Don Garlits Museum of Drag Racing.** Garlits, who was born in Florida, founded the nonprofit museum in 1976 and opened it to the public in 1984. The museum traces the history of drag racing, from its beginnings at California's Dry Lakes in the '40s to the present. On display is an array of unusual vehicles used by Garlits and other drag-racing greats, along with a collection of early-model Fords. *13700 S.W. 16th Ave., Ocala, tel. 904/245–8661. Admission: $5 adults, $3 children 6–16. Open daily 10–5.*

North of Rte. 200 on I–75, take Exit 70 to U.S. 27 and travel west 3½ miles to the new **Golden Ocala Golf Course,** worth a visit because it replicates nine famous holes. Duffers have the opportunity to play St. Andrews's 1 (the first hole played in golfing history), Baltusrol's 4, Augusta's 12 and 16, and Royal Troon's 8, among others. *7300 U.S. Hwy. 27, Ocala, tel. 904/622–0198. Starting times reserved up to 3 days in advance.*

Farther north on I–75 are the turn-of-the-century towns of **McIntosh** and **Micanopy,** pleasant stops on the way to Marjorie Kinnan Rawlings's Cross Creek country (*see* Off the Beaten Track).

The main street of **Ocala** is Silver Springs Boulevard, reached by taking Exit 69 off I–75 to Rte. 40 and heading east. The center of town is at N.E. 8th Avenue and Silver Springs Boulevard, where you can find the Chamber of Commerce and a pleasant town square park. To view the city's historic district, drive east on Fort King Avenue (a few blocks south of Silver Springs Boulevard).

Time Out **Peter Dinkel's,** on Silver Springs Blvd. (look for the weird horse-and-rider metal sculpture guarding a two-tone brown Victorian house), is a popular lunch spot. Try the fried grouper and homemade honey or cinnamon ice cream. *725 E. Silver Springs Blvd., Ocala, tel. 904/732–8003. AE, CB, DC, V.*

On the way to Silver Springs, stop at **The Appleton Museum of Art.** The palatial pink travertine marble museum houses the collection of Arthur Appleton, retired president of the Appleton Electric Co. of Chicago and owner of Bridlewood Farm, an Ocala Thoroughbred operation. Sterling-silver thrones from India, ancient oriental vases, Peruvian pottery, 12th-century Persian earthenware, and a sword presented by Napoleon to one of his soldiers are among the more than 6,000 works displayed. *Silver Springs Blvd., Ocala, tel. 904/236–5050. Admission: $2 adults, $1 children 12–18. Open Tues.–Sat. 10–4:30, Sun. 1–5.*

5 **Silver Springs,** the state's oldest attraction (established (1890), is a National Landmark that centers on the world's largest collection of artesian springs. Today, the park features wild animal displays, glass-bottom boat tours on the Silver River, a jungle cruise on the Fort King Waterway, an antique and classic car museum, and walks through natural habitats. A multimillion-dollar project has recaptured the look and atmosphere of the 1890s. New in 1989 is the Admiral Riverboat Restaurant, an authentic re-creation of a paddle wheeler that once steamed up the Silver River. The walls of its dining salon are hung with old photos of the Hart Line riverboats that provided transportation from Jacksonville to Silver Springs via the St. Johns, Oklawaha, and Silver rivers. *Rte. 40, 1 mi east of Ocala, tel. 904/236–2121. Admission to all attractions: $13.95 adults, $8.95 children 3–11. Open daily.*

Next door is Silver Springs's **Wild Waters,** a water theme park with a giant wave pool and seven water-flume rides. *Admission: $7.95 adults, $6.95 children 3–11. Open late Mar.–June 7, 10–5; June 8–Sept. 7, 10–8.*

6 Farther east on Rte. 40 is the entrance to **Ocala National Forest,** a 366,000-acre wilderness with lakes, springs, rivers, hiking trails, campgrounds, and historic sites. Area residents recall the filming of *The Yearling* at several sites within the forest. The **Visitor Information Center,** on the left just over the bridge (tel. 904/625–7470), is the site of old-fashioned sugarcane grinding and cane-syrup making during the first two weeks of November each year. The syrup is bottled and sold on the premises.

Lake Waldena Resort & Campground (tel. 904/625–2851), several miles farther east on Rte. 40, features a white-sand bathing beach and crystal-clear freshwater lake. Noncampers pay day-use fees for picnicking and access to the beach.

7 South of Rte. 40 (via Rte. 314–A) is **Moss Bluff,** on the Okalwaha River, which forms the southern boundary of Ocala National Forest. Make reservations ahead to enjoy a day-long cruise on the Oklawaha and Silver Run rivers aboard the *Osprey II,* a comfortable modern riverboat based at Moss Bluff. Cruises depart at 9:30 AM. Rate includes lunch. *Oklawaha & Silver Run River Boat Co., Box 1301, Oklawaha, tel. 904/288–2470.*

Three major recreational areas are found in the national forest: **Juniper Springs,** off Rte. 40, featuring a picturesque stone waterwheel house, campground, natural-spring swimming pool, and hiking and canoe trails; **Salt Springs,** off Rte. 40 (via Rte. 19 North), featuring a natural saltwater spring, where Atlantic blue crabs come to spawn each summer; and **Alexander Springs,** off Rte. 40 (via Rte. 445 South), featuring a swimming lake and campground.

Farther south on Rte. 19, outside the southern boundary of the national forest, is the lakeside hamlet of **Mount Dora** (*see* Off the Beaten Track).

Just outside the eastern boundary of the forest, at the cross-
8 roads of Rte. 40 and U.S. 17, are **Barberville** and the **Pioneer Settlement for the Creative Arts, Inc.** A bridge house, moved from the St. Johns River at Astor, forms the entrance to the museum. On the grounds are an old-time caboose, a railroad depot, the commissary store of a turpentine camp, and a newly constructed "post-and-beam" barn, built of wood milled on the premises. During the first weekend in May and November each year, the museum hosts a Country Jamboree, which features arts, crafts, folk music, and country cooking. *U.S. 17 and Rte. 40, Barberville, tel. 904/749–2959. Admission: $2.50 adults, $1 children 3–12. Open weekdays 9–4, weekends by appointment.*

North of Barberville on U.S. 17 is another 1800s steamboat stop, **Crescent City,** where the historic **Sprague House Inn** (125 Central Ave., Crescent City, tel. 904/698–2430) traces steamboat-era history through the inn's collection of stained-glass windows. The three-room bed-and-breakfast inn also features a full-service restaurant.

9 South on U.S. 17 is **DeLeon Springs State Recreation Area,** promoted as a fountain of youth to 1889 winter tourists. Today, visitors come to picnic, swim, fish, and hike the nature trails. *DeLeon Springs, tel. 904/985–4212. Admission: $1 per car, 50 cents per person. Open daily, 8 A.M.–sundown.*

South of DeLeon Springs, at the crossroads of U.S. 17 and Rte.
10 44, is **DeLand,** another St. Johns River steamboat stop. Founded in 1876 by Henry Addison Deland of New York, the town was incorporated in 1882, and its academy (Florida's oldest private university) was established in 1883.

A drive down the city's scenic main street (U.S. 17/Woodland Blvd.) will acquaint you with the residential-style campus of Stetson University, home of the **Gillespie Museum of Minerals.** The display of more than 25,000 specimens includes meteorites, fluorescent minerals, and Florida corals. *Michigan* *and Amelia Aves., DeLand, tel. 904/734–4121, ext. 603. Admission free. Open fall, winter, and spring sessions Mon.–Sat. 9–4; summer session Mon.–Fri. 9–4.*

The museum is one of the first points of interest on the Chamber of Commerce's self-guided scenic tour of DeLand. Copies of the map/brochure outlining the route may be obtained from the chamber's offices on Woodland Boulevard.

For a scenic tour of the St. Johns River and its special points of interest, travel west of town on Rte. 40 to Old New York Avenue and turn left; drive two miles, then take the first right onto Hontoon Road and follow it to the river. Here, you'll find **Three Buoys** (2280 Hontoon Rd., DeLand, tel. 904/736–9422), formerly Sunshine Line, offering a fleet of 46-foot luxury houseboats, each with sleeping quarters for four couples. The fully equipped "floating villas" may be chartered for about $60 per couple per day.

Hontoon Landing Marina (2317 River Ridge Rd., DeLand, tel. 904/734–2474) rents less-luxurious houseboats. The craft that sleeps 10 may be chartered for about $70 per couple per day.

11 Once a steamboat landing in the 1880s, what is now **Blue Spring State Park** is still a popular landing for explorers on the St. Johns River. Standing as a memorial to the golden age of steamboat travel is the restored 100-year-old **Thursby House,** which may be toured Thursday–Sunday, 11 AM–4 PM. The park also has boardwalks that meander through the thick forest and provide views of the springhead, where manatees congregate during the winter. Camping, hiking, fishing, and swimming also may be enjoyed here. *2100 W. French Ave., Orange City, tel. 904/775–3663. Open daily 8 AM–sundown.*

Hontoon Island (tel. 904/734–7158) is the site of a Timucuan Indian settlement and is accessible only by boat. The park features a large marina, camping, and a 35-foot-high Indian ceremonial mound. Ferry service is available from the mainland.

Daytona Beach Area

Some people refer to this 100-mile stretch of mid-Atlantic beachfront—from Ormond and Daytona Beach south to Melbourne and Sebastian Inlet—as "Orlando's beach." But it has always been more than that. Cape Canaveral was a place-name that cartographers rarely failed to include on the earliest maps of the New World. Today, it is known as the spaceport to the stars.

A good place to begin touring is along a segment of Old Dixie Highway. From I–95 north of Ormond Beach, take Exit 90 and travel east.

The first left off Old Dixie Highway (Kings Hwy.) will take you
12 to the entrance of **Bulow Plantation Ruins State Historic Site,** built in 1821. From the entrance, a winding dirt road cuts through tangled vegetation and leads to a picnic area and day-use facilities facing Bulow Creek. All that remains of the plantation are the massive ruins of the sugar mill, which may be reached either by auto or bicycle along a one-way loop road, or on foot via a scenic walking trail from the picnic area. *Tel. 904/439–2219. Open daily 9–5.*

Continue southeast on Old Dixie Highway through a tunnel of vine-laced oaks and cabbage palms. Next stop is **Tomoka State Park,** site of a Timucuan Indian settlement discovered in 1605 by Spanish explorer Alvaro Mexia. Wooded campsites, bicycle and walking paths, and guided canoe tours on the Tomoka and Halifax rivers are the main attractions. *North Beach St., Ormond Beach, tel. 904/677–3931. Open daily 8 AM–sundown.*

13 Time moves forward and the canopy thins east on Old Dixie Highway to **Ormond Beach.** Auto racing was born on this hard-packed beach back in 1902, when R. E. Olds and Alexander Winton staged the first race. The Winter Speed Carnival became an annual event, attracting enthusiasts from across the nation. Sportsmen and socialites flocked to Ormond Beach each winter and made the massive Ormond Hotel their headquarters. The grand old wooden hotel (built in 1888 to pamper Flagler's East Coast Railroad passengers) still stands watch on the east bank of the Halifax, but it is now vacant and no longer entertains guests.

Across the street from the hotel is **The Casements,** the restored winter retreat of John D. Rockefeller, now serving as a cultural center and museum. The estate and its formal gardens, on the National Register of Historic Places, are the setting for an annual lineup of special events and exhibits. Tours of the estate also are offered. *25 Riverside Dr., Ormond Beach, tel. 904/673–4701. Open weekdays 9–5, Sat. 9–12.*

To reach Daytona Beach, where Ormond's Winter Speed Carnival now takes place, follow Rte. A1A south. During spring break, race weeks, and summer holidays, expect heavy traffic along this strip of garishly painted beach motels and tacky souvenir shops. Rising above the strip is the new $45-million, 402-room Daytona Beach Marriott, which is part of a long-range downtown revitalization plan.

South of the new Marriott, on Rte. A1A, is **Ponce Inlet** beach, which is frequented by locals and visitors who are in the know. A manicured drive winds through low-growing shrubs and windblown scrub oaks to parking and picnic areas. Boardwalks traverse the delicate dunes and provide easy access to the wide beach. Marking this prime spot is a bright-red century-old lighthouse, now a historic monument and museum. *Open daily 10–5.*

Time Out **Lighthouse Landing,** only yards from the historic light, is a good place for sipping cocktails and watching the sunset (*see* Dining).

Sunset on the Halifax River may also be enjoyed aboard *The Dixie Queen.* The replica of an 1890s paddlewheeler is docked at the marina on the southwest side of the Seabreeze Bridge, north of Ponce Inlet. The 400-passenger, 65-foot vessel has a full-service galley and offers a variety of cruises.

From the marina, head south on Beach Street to Volusia Avenue (U.S. 92), drive two blocks west to U.S. 1 (Ridgewood
14 Ave.), and head south to **New Smyrna Beach.** Across the Intracoastal Waterway via Rte. 44 is New Smyrna's beach, which, like the beaches north and south of it, lies along a barrier island.

15 16 South of New Smyrna Beach on U.S. 1 are **Titusville, Merritt Island National Wildlife Refuge,** and **NASA Kennedy Space Cen-**

ter's Spaceport USA. To reach the space center, take Rte. 405 over the NASA Causeway, then follow the NASA Parkway to the entrance of Spaceport USA. Free museum exhibits and films are featured, as well as guided bus tours and an IMAX theater film presentation (*The Dream is Alive*, narrated by Walter Cronkite). *Visitors' Center TWA, Kennedy Space Center, tel. 407/452–2121. Bus tour admission: $4 adults, $1.75 children 3–12. IMAX Theater admission: $2.75 adults, $1.75 children 3–12. Open daily (except Christmas) 9–sundown.*

17 Port Canaveral, on the southern end of **Cape Canaveral,** is home to *SeaEscape* (tel. 407/784–3666), which departs on one-day cruises into the Atlantic and back from 10 to 10 every day except Friday, and **Premier Cruise Lines,** offering three- and four-night *Starcruise* experiences to the Bahamas, departing on Fridays and Mondays, respectively.

Port Canaveral also is the site of annual surfing championships, thanks to the well-formed Atlantic waves that wash the
18 beaches between **Cocoa Beach** and **Sebastian Inlet. Ron Jon's Surf Shop** (4151 North Atlantic Ave., Cocoa Beach) is almost an attraction in itself, with its massive collection of swim wear, beach gear, and T-shirts. Beach-bike rentals are available.

To the south is Cocoa Beach. When looking for a place to park your beach umbrella, keep in mind that Cocoa Beach is more crowded than the beaches farther south, such as **Satellite Beach, Indialantic,** and **Melbourne Beach.**

A good way to become acquainted with the area's waterways is to take a sightseeing or dinner cruise on *The Little River Queen*, which departs daily from **Gatsby's Dockside** in Cocoa Beach. You'll see everything from elegant residential areas to native wildlife—dolphins, manatees, and wading birds. *480 W. Cocoa Beach Causeway, Cocoa Beach, tel. 407/783–2380. Reservations are suggested.*

Exploring **Olde Cocoa Village** (201 Michigan Ave., Cocoa, tel. 407/632–1830) may convince you that there was life in Cocoa before the space program. Cobblestone walkways thread through this landscaped cluster of restored 1890s buildings in downtown Cocoa, where specialty shops display pottery, macrame, leather and silvercraft, afghans, fine art, and fashions. The **Cocoa Village Playhouse** community theater is based here and provides regular entertainment. Horse-drawn carriages can take you for a ride, and the Brevard Museum organizes village walking tours by appointment.

Time Out A walled cobblestone courtyard with lush tropical foliage and black wrought-iron dining tables draws patrons to **Mister BeauJeans** in Melbourne. It's on the grounds of the historic **Strawberry Mansion** (*see* Dining).

Sebastian Inlet marks the southern boundary of this region east of Orlando. Two recreational areas ensure the preservation of some great fishing grounds and beaches. If you like to camp, check out **Long Point Park** (tel. 407/732–3839) and **Sebastian Inlet State Recreation Area** (tel. 407/727–1752).

What to See and Do with Children

Buccaneer Bay (*see* The Gulf of Mexico Area).
Homosassa Springs (*see* The Gulf of Mexico Area).

Liberty Bell Memorial Museum. *Wells Park, west of Hickory St. and south of Hibiscus Blvd., Melbourne, tel. 407/727–1776. Open weekdays 10–4, Sat. 10–2.*
NASA Kennedy Space Center's Spaceport USA (*see* The Daytona Beach Area).
Sanford Zoo (*see* Off the Beaten Track).
Weeki Wachee (*see* The Gulf of Mexico Area).
Wild Waters (*see* The North of Orlando Area).

Off the Beaten Track

Brooksville Just east of Weeki Wachee at the intersection of Rte. 50 and U.S. 98 is **Brooksville.** This country hamlet looks like it hasn't quite caught up with the 20th century. Its quiet streets are lined with tidy cottages and an occasional imposing Victorian mansion. The town's **Heritage Museum** is housed in such a mansion. *601 S. May Ave., tel. 904/799–0129. Open Wed. and Sat. noon–3.*

About two blocks south of the museum, off Liberty Street, is **Roger's Christmas House & Village,** a cluster of cottage shops, selling everything from tree decorations to linens, stuffed animals, and gourmet kitchen utensils. *103 Saxon Ave., Brooksville, tel. 904/796–2415. Open daily (except Christmas) 9:30–5.*

Cross Creek Country North of Ocala, via I–75 or U.S. 441, are the towns of **McIntosh** and **Micanopy**—first stops on a tour of Marjorie K. Rawlings's Cross Creek country.

Less than 400 people reside in turn-of-the-century McIntosh, which didn't even bother putting up street signs until 1984. Each year in October or November (during a weekend when the Florida Gators aren't playing football at home), the townspeople dress in period clothing. Tours of Victorian homes, antique auto displays, horse-and-buggy rides, and a parade are featured. Overnight accommodations may be found at **Merrily Bed-and-Breakfast** (*see* Lodging).

Micanopy (on the National Register of Historic Districts) is home to at least 12 antique shops and **The Herlong Mansion** (built in 1875), another B&B (*see* Lodging).

Just outside Micanopy on U.S. 441 is the entrance to **Paynes Prairie State Preserve** (Rte. 2, Box 41, Micanopy, tel. 904/466–3397), an 18,000-acre basinland, where Indian artifacts have been found dating back to 10,000 BC. The prairie supported the largest cattle ranch in Spanish Florida during the 1600s; it was visited and described by William Bartram in 1774. Each April park rangers take visitors on historical tours.

Within easy driving distance of Paynes Prairie is Cross Creek and the **Marjorie K. Rawlings State Historic Site** (Rte. 3, Box 92, Hawthorne, tel. 904/466–3672). The Cracker farmhouse in which she lived and wrote *The Yearling*, *Cross Creek*, and other works is open daily 9–5.

Time Out Just up Rte. 325 from Rawlings's home is **The Yearling Inn** restaurant, which specializes in local delicacies, such as alligator tail, cooter (soft-shell turtle), quail, frogs' legs, and "fingerling" catfish (*see* Dining).

Sanford The last 1880s steamboat stop on the St. Johns River is **Sanford,** located between DeLand and Orlando on U.S. 17/92. Today, it's the celery capital of the United States, southern terminus for Amtrak's Auto Train, site of the annual Golden Age Olympic Games, and home of the **Central Florida Zoo.** *U.S. 17/92 at I-4, Lake Monroe, tel. 407/323-6471. Admission: $5 adults, $2 children 3–12. Open daily 9–5.*

Cruising the St. Johns River is still the reason why most people visit Sanford. The newest cruise operation is **St. Johns River Cruises, Inc.** (4359 Peninsula Point, Marine Park, tel. 407/330–1612), offering the only passenger tour boat that travels south of Lake Monroe on the scenic St. Johns.

The *Rivership Romance*, a 110-foot triple-deck catamaran, makes scheduled cruises on the St. Johns River from the city marina on Lake Monroe. Its most popular cruise is the 2½-hour Saturday morning Pancakes and Sausage Cruise. *433 N. Palmetto Ave., Sanford, tel. 407/321-5091. Reservations advised.*

The St. Johns may also be explored by houseboat. Contact **Sanford Boat Rentals** 4350 Orange Blvd., Sanford, tel. 407/321–5906), at the Hidden Harbour Marina.

Shopping

Gift Ideas When touring the Gulf of Mexico area, look for antiques and stuffed manatee dolls (proceeds usually support the "Save the Manatee" program). In the area north of Orlando, look for antiques at *Reeve & Howard* (105 W. Indiana Ave., DeLand; open Mon.–Sat. 9–5) and outlet merchandise at *Flechbilt Handbags, Bass Shoes*, and *Manhattan Shirts*, all in Ocala. Country crafts and horse-farm souvenirs are sold throughout the area. When touring the Atlantic beaches, look for citrus products at *Harvey's Groves* (3811 N. Atlantic Ave., Cocoa Beach), and space-program memorabilia at the Spaceport USA gift shop.

Food and Flea Markets **Flea World** has 1,200 booths under one roof selling everything from citrus fruits to jewelry and antiques. *U.S. 17–92, between Sanford and Orlando. Open Fri.–Sun. 8–5.*

Beaches

Don't expect to find sandy beaches along the Gulf coast between Crystal River and Weeki Wachee—it's more like marshland. But on the mid-Atlantic coast, between Ormond Beach and Sebastian Inlet, are about 100 miles of sandy beaches accessible to the public. The only beach area closed to the public borders the space center on Cape Canaveral. Choice beaches and parks are listed below.

The Boardwalk, at the center of Daytona Beach, is the place to see and be seen. The broad, hard-packed beach looks like a busy city sidewalk, complete with hawkers and pedestrians dodging vehicles—except everybody's wearing a bathing suit and a tan.
Ponce Inlet, about eight miles south of Daytona Beach, is a well-manicured beach park with tidy picnic pavilions, boardwalks protecting the sand dunes, and a quiet assortment of locals escaping the crunch. There's lots of space to breathe here. When swimming, keep an eye out for surf fishermen and their lines.
Canaveral National Seashore (tel. 407/867–5069), just east of New Smyrna Beach on Rte. A1A, is a 57,000-acre park

that is home to more than 250 kinds of birds and animals. The remote beach bordering the Atlantic is noted for its sand dunes and seashells. A self-guided hiking trail leads to the top of an Indian shell midden at Turtle Mound, where picnic tables are available. Free brochures and maps are available at the Visitor Center on Rte. A1A.

Paradise Beach (tel. 407/254–1764), a scenic 10-acre park north of Indialantic on Rte. A1A, has 1,600 feet of beach, picnic facilities, grills, showers, rest rooms, and a refreshment stand. A lifeguard is on duty during the summer. There is a fee for parking, and picnic tables must be reserved in advance.

Sebastian Inlet State Recreation Area (tel. 407/727–1752), about 12 miles south of Melbourne on Rte. A1A, offers three miles of beachfront for swimming, surfing, snorkeling, and scuba diving. The 576-acre park also features bathhouse facilities, campsites, a food concession, fishing jetty, and boat ramp (tel. 305/727–1752).

Participant Sports

Biking Serious cyclists tour central Florida's hilly countryside on their sleek racers; others prefer pedaling the coastal flatlands on a beach bike. In Daytona Beach, stop by **Seabreeze Surf Shop** (638 N. Grandview Ave., tel. 904/257–5136). Near New Smyrna Beach, try **Swift Cycles-Beach Concession** (1803 12th St., Edgewater, tel. 904/427–2413). In Cocoa Beach, visit **Ron Jon's Surf Shop** (4151 N. Atlantic Ave., tel. 407/784–1485).

Boardsailing The consistent ocean breezes, warm water, and sheltered waterways of Florida's mid-Atlantic coast make it a prime boardsailing site. Conditions are so good that the U.S. Boardsailing Team trains in Melbourne. There's even a vacation resort that caters to boardsailing enthusiasts—**Space Coast Sailboard Club** (2050 Rockledge Dr., Rockledge, tel. 407/632–3936). The resort is on the Indian River, between Cocoa and Melbourne, and offers accommodations, equipment rental, and instruction. Reservations are recommended.

Canoeing The gentle, spring-fed rivers that thread through this region pose no problems for beginners. Canoe trails begin upstream, so all you have to do is steer and enjoy the wildlife and wilderness. East of Brooksville, the **Withlacoochee River R.V. Park** (tel. 904/583–4778) on Rte. 575 provides livery for five river tours—including an overnight paddle to Nobleton. Janet and Tom Handley operate a canoe-rental concession at Juniper Springs Recreation Area in **Ocala National Forest** (tel. 904/625–2808 or 685–2194). The Juniper Creek trail is seven miles long and takes about three to four hours to paddle. Just outside the national park, **Katie's Wekiva River Landing** (tel. 407/322-4470) at 190 Katie's Cove in Sanford provides livery for four river tours.

Diving/Snorkeling You can scuba or snorkel with manatees in the clear spring water of Crystal River's Kings Bay (*see* Guided Tours) or do some deep wreck diving offshore from Cocoa Beach with the guys at **American Divers International** (691 N. Courtenay, Merritt Island, tel. 407/453–0600).

Fishing Both freshwater and saltwater fishing can be enjoyed here. Largemouth bass, bluegill, crappie, and other freshwater panfish are caught in the St. Johns River and its tributary lakes and streams. Fishing camps provide guides, bait, tackle, rental boats, and accommodations that range from efficiency cabins to campsites. A license, required for freshwater fishing, often can be purchased at the fishing camps. Saltwater fishing does not require a license. You can deep-sea troll in the Atlantic for blue and white marlin, sailfish, dolphin, king mackerel, tuna, and wahoo. Grouper, red snapper, and amberjack are deep-sea bottom-fishing prizes. Surf casting is popular for pompano, bluefish, flounder, and sea bass. From fishing piers, anglers hook sheepshead, mackerel, sea trout, weakfish, and tarpon. Most Atlantic beach communities have a lighted pier with a bait-and-tackle shop and rest rooms. Daytona Beach's charter fishing fleet departs from marinas near Ponce Inlet. Deep-sea charters also are found at Port Canaveral and on the gulf coast in Crystal River and Homosassa Springs.

Golf At the turn of the century, Florida boasted 14 golf courses; by 1988, it had more than 800. This region is home to at least 32, and one of them—designed by C. E. Clarke of Scotland in 1926—was among the original 14. Guests of **Mission Inn Golf and Tennis Resort** in Howey-in-the-Hills play that course today. Other noteables are **Plantation Golf Resort** in Crystal River; **Golden Ocala Golf & Country Club** (nine historic holes); **Indigo Lakes** off U.S. 92 in Daytona Beach; and **Spessard Holland Golf Course** (designed by Arnold Palmer), off Rte. A1A in Melbourne.

Horseback Riding Ocala's bluegrass horse country can be explored during trail rides organized by **Oakview Stable** (S.W. 27th Ave., behind the Paddock Mall, tel. 904/237–8844).

Skydiving Anybody who wants to jump out of an airplane when it's thousands of feet up in the air can do so with the help of **Skydive DeLand** (tel. 904/738–3539) or **Titusville Parachute Center** (tel. 407/267–0016).

Water Sports Jet skiing, boardsailing, waterskiing, sailing, and power boating are popular pastimes on the Atlantic Intracoastal Waterway. Rental equipment is available at **The Water Works** (1891 E. Merritt Island Causeway, Rte. 520, Merritt Island, tel. 407/452–2007).

Spectator Sports

Greyhound Races During the summer, you can bet on the dogs every night but Sunday at the **Daytona Beach Kennel Club** (on U.S. 92 near the International Speedway, tel. 904/252–6484).

Jai Alai The world's fastest sport, jai alai, is played September–January at the **Sports Palace** (1100 N. Wickham Rd., Melbourne, tel. 407/259–9800), January–March and June–September at **Ocala Jai-Alai** (Rte. 318, Orange Lake, tel. 904/591–2345), and February–July at **Volusia Jai-Alai** (U.S. 92, across from the Daytona International Speedway, tel. 904/255–0222).

Dining

Fresh Florida seafood is on most menus, prepared in many ways. One of the most popular fish is grouper, because of its light, sweet taste, grillable white meat, and reasonable market price. Coconut shrimp is a favorite appetizer. Gator tail, cooter (soft-shell turtle), frogs' legs, "fingerling" catfish, and quail dishes are found on the menus of rustic backwoods diners.

Family restaurants keep locals happy with simple country cooking, fresh-baked breads and cakes, and moderate prices.

The most highly recommended restaurants are indicated by a star ★.

Category	Cost*
Very Expensive	above $25
Expensive	$15–$25
Moderate	$10–$15
Inexpensive	under $10

**per person without 6% state sales tax, service, or drinks*

The following credit card abbreviations are used: AE, American Express; CB, Carte Blanche; DC, Diners Club; MC, MasterCard; V, Visa.

Very Expensive

Bernard's Surf. Don't come to Bernard's for the view; there are no windows in the two main dining rooms. Come for steaks and local fish and a few unusual dishes like alligator and buffalo. A specialty is Doc Stahl's Skillet, a combination of shrimp, crabmeat, mushrooms, and wild rice sautéed and served in the skillet. *2 S. Atlantic Ave., Cocoa Beach, tel. 407/783–2401. Dress: casual. Reservations advised. AE, DC, MC, V. Closed Christmas Day.*

★ **Churchill's.** The formal but intimate dining room at the Crown Hotel features classic French cuisine—beef, fish, and veal in a combination of sauces. Entrees are served hot from a cart that is wheeled from the kitchen to your table. A favorite is Grouper St. Pierre, featuring the light, sweet fish in a white wine and cream sauce, topped with strips of smoked Nova Scotia salmon. *109 N. Seminole Ave., Inverness, tel. 904/344–5555. Jacket and tie optional. Reservations required. AE, DC, MC, V.*

Izaak's Gourmet Restaurant. Set back in the woods by a river, Izaak Walton's Lodge (a 10-room fishing retreat built in 1924 and restored in 1987) has a 40-seat formal dining room with hunter-green wainscoting, formal black floral wallpaper, rose-colored tablecloths, and a fireplace. The chef's own favorite dish is Zuppa de Pesce: fresh lobster, crab, shrimp, scallops, and oysters in a seafood sauce, served over a bed of linguine. *1 63rd St. on Riverside Dr., Yankeetown, tel. 904/447–2311. Jacket and tie optional. Reservations advised. MC, V.*

Mango Tree Restaurant. Candles, fresh flowers, white linen tablecloths, rattan basket chairs with fluffy cushions, and eggshell-color walls adorned with tropical watercolors by local artists set a romantic mood at the Mango Tree. The intimate dining room overlooks a garden aviary that is home to exotic doves and pheasants, and the menu is a blend of American and Continental. Try the grouper broiled and topped with scallops, shrimp, and hollandaise sauce. *Cottage Row, 118 N. Atlantic Ave., Cocoa Beach, tel. 407/799–0513. Dress: smart casual. Reservations advised. AE, MC, V.*

Expensive

Arthur's. When the Ocala Hilton opened in 1987, its airy and intimate restaurant, Arthur's, garnered much attention. Light tropical colors, comfortable shellback chairs, floor-to-ceiling windows with tieback curtains, and fresh flowers complement the American/Florida regional cuisine. Special menu items include an alligator-tail appetizer, grilled swordfish, and veal split and stuffed with prosciutto and Swiss cheese, then coated with herbs and bread crumbs and panfried in peanut oil. *3600 S.W. 36th Ave., Ocala, tel. 904/854–1400. Jacket and tie at dinner, smart casual at lunch. Reservations accepted. AE, DC, MC, V.*

Gatsby's Restaurant and Lounge. This casual waterfront spot is part of a trio that includes Gatsby's Dockside and Jay Gatsby's Sports Emporium. Prime rib, steaks, and seafood are served American-style, and early-bird special dinner prices are in effect between 4:30 and 6:30. *480 W. Cocoa Beach Causeway, Cocoa Beach, tel. 407/783–2380. Dress: smart casual. Reservations advised. AE, DC, MC, V.*

K. C. Crump on the River. This 1870 Old Florida residence on the Homosassa River was restored in 1986 and reopened as a restaurant in 1987. Lemon juice, butter, and garlic season most of the seafood, and rich cream or fruit sauces complement the meat dishes. There's a small marina on the river, as well as a riverfront lounge and outdoor dining. Indoors are several airy dining rooms, with large picture windows, rattan furniture, mauve cloth napkins, and thick cotton placemats. *3900 Hall River Rd., Homosassa Springs, tel. 904/628–1500. Dress: smart casual. Reservations advised. MC, V.*

★ **Pondo's.** American and nouvelle-cuisine dishes are served in this 1921 two-story house near the St. Johns River. It has the look of an old inn and offers a choice of three intimate dining rooms (white tablecloths, seating for 150) on the ground floor. Specialties include homemade pasta, veal, vegetarian dishes, duck, prime rib, and grilled steaks. An octaganarian jazz pianist entertains. *1715 W. Old New York Ave., DeLand, tel. 904/734–1995. Jacket and tie optional. Reservations advised. AE, MC, V. Closed Tues. July–Nov.*

The Yearling Inn. Everything served in this backwoods restaurant is prepared fresh, Southern-style, including the quail dressing, hush puppies, and gravy. Specialties include alligator tail, cooter (soft-shell turtle), frogs' legs, and sweet "fingerling" catfish. During fall football weekends, just about every Formica-top table with paper placemats is taken—reservations aren't. *Rte. 325, Cross Creek, tel. 904/466–3033. Dress: casual. No reservations. AE, CB, DC, MC, V. Closed Mon.*

Moderate

★ **Alma's Italian Restaurant.** Five crowded, noisy dining rooms keep the waitresses busy. The specialties of the house are veal marsala and more than 200 imported and domestic wines. *306 N. Orlando Ave., Cocoa Beach, tel. 407/783–1981. Dress: casual. Reservations advised. AE, MC, V.*

Aunt Catfish's. Down-home seafood is featured, along with cheese grits and baked beans. This wharfside restaurant is also known for its fresh cinnamon rolls. *550 Halifax Dr., Port Orange, tel. 904/767–4768. Dress: casual. Reservations accepted. AE, DC, MC, V.*

Original Holiday House. This popular buffet-style family restaurant opened in 1959 in an old two-story house. People come for home cooking at a reasonable price. The buffet features rare roast beef, baked fish, leg of lamb, tossed green salads, baked potatoes, carrot cake, and cobbler. *704 N. Boulevard, DeLand, tel. 904/734–6319. Dress: casual. Reservations not accepted. MC, V. Closed Christmas Eve.*

Lighthouse Landing. "If it smells like fish, eat it," is the philosophy of this funky waterfront eatery. The outdoor oak tree-shaded dining deck is popular for cocktails and sunset-watching. The menu is seafood only. *4940 S. Peninsula Dr., Ponce Inlet, tel. 904/761–9271. Dress: very casual. Reservations not required. MC, V. Closed Jan.*

Marko's Heritage Inn. Its bakery, gift shop, piano parlor lounge, and down-home American cooking draw crowds. Try the Kentucky Hot Brown—thinly shaved ham and sliced turkey, topped with cream sauce, cheese and bacon. Desserts are fresh baked goods. *900 S. Ridgewood Ave., Port Orange, tel. goods 904/767–3809. Dress: casual. Reservations accepted for 20 or more. AE, DC, MC, V. Closed Christmas Eve.*

Norwood's. Since 1946, this Old Florida seafood-oyster bar has served its popular seafood platters on glass-top tables filled with seashells. Some nights it serves all-you-can-eat crab claw dinners. Try the smoked mullet and broiled fish with cheese sauce. *400 2nd Ave., New Smyrna Beach, tel. 904/428–4621. Dress: casual. No reservations. MC, V.*

★ **The Strawberry Mansion & Mister BeauJean's Restaurant.** A gingerbread-trimmed Victorian mansion with six dining rooms and a walled garden courtyard are the settings for reasonably priced California-style dishes. Try the tropical shrimp (fried in a coating of coconut and macadamia nuts) or Mrs. Brown's crab cakes (more crab than cake) for starters. Entrees include grouper with crab and scallops, homemade pasta, lamb, duck, veal, and steak. Mister BeauJean's serves breakfast and lunch in the courtyard or in its tropical-chic indoor dining room. Waffles, broccoli burritos, and Häagen-Dazs ice cream highlight the menu. *1218 E. New Haven Ave., Melbourne, tel. 407/724–8627. Dress: casual. Reservations accepted. AE, MC, V.*

Inexpensive

★ **The Blueberry Patch Tea Room.** Though most entrees are less than $5, this cottage deserves a spot in the *Most Expensive* category for its homestyle cooking with a European flair. Crab soufflé and quiche lorraine are the chef's favorites. Dessert specials include banana silk pie and coconut sour-cream cake. Look for the white-and-cornflower-blue cottage. *414 E. Liberty St., Brooksville, tel. 904/796–6005. Dress: smart casual. Reservations advised. AE, DC, MC, V. Closed Christmas Day.*

Old Spanish Sugar Mill & Griddle House. Situated inside an old stone waterwheel house by the outflow of DeLeon Springs, this restaurant and country store features freshly milled flour and baked goods and provides patrons with ingredients for making their own hot cakes and side dishes (bacon, sausage, ham) on griddles that are built into every table. All you can eat. *DeLeon Springs, tel. 904/985–5644. Dress: casual. Reservations accepted for 10 or more. No credit cards. Closed Mon. except during holidays.*

★ **The Oyster Bar.** This no-frills cinderblock seafood spot is popular with locals and features locally caught fish, oysters on the half shell, crab claws, and lobster. Beer and wine only. *224 N. U.S. 19, Crystal River, tel. 904/795–3949. Dress: very casual. Reservations not required. MC, V.*

Stavro's. This cafe is popular for its pizzas, Greek salads and desserts, pita-bread sandwiches, and baked Italian dishes. Try the Mostaccioli—ziti noodles, meat sauce, and three cheeses. *803 W. New York Ave., DeLand, tel. 904/734–5705. Dress: casual. Reservations not accepted. No credit cards.*

Lodging

Though the majority of hotels and motels in this region belong to national-chains, there is an increasing number of country inns from which to choose. Turn-of-the-century homes are being restored and converted into bed-and-breakfast establishments. The B&B concept has crept into the marketing of national chain hotels as well. New luxury, suite-style properties are including breakfast and happy-hour cocktails in their regular room rates.

Category	Cost*
Very Expensive	over $100
Expensive	$60–$100
Moderate	$40–$60
Inexpensive	under $40

**per room, double occupancy, without 6% state sales tax and nominal tourist tax*

The following credit card abbreviations are used: AE, American Express; CB, Carte Blanche; DC, Diners Club; MC, MasterCard; V, Visa

Very Expensive

Daytona Beach Marriott. This mammoth, pyramid-shape hotel is expected to open in spring 1989 and will offer 402 luxury ocean-view rooms. Amenities include a heated indoor-outdoor pool with waterfall and tropical landscaping, a sauna, health-club exercise rooms, indoor and outdoor whirlpool spas, and a children's pool and beachside playground. Incorporated into the beachfront landscaping is the city's landmark, turn-of-the-century clock tower. Facilities include two restaurants, two lounges, and a poolside bar. *1401 N. Atlantic Ave., Daytona Beach 32018, tel. 904/254–8200. AE, DC, MC, V.*

Holiday Inn Cocoa Beach Resort. When two separate beach hotels were redesigned and a promenade park landscaped between them, the Holiday Inn Cocoa Beach Resort was born. It features plush modern public rooms, an Olympic-size heated pool, tennis courts, and private access to the beach. You can choose from a wide selection of accommodations—standard, king, and oceanfront suites; villas; and bilevel lofts—all with in-room movies. Free aerobics workouts are offered, as are planned activities for children. *1300 N. Atlantic Ave., Cocoa Beach 32931, tel. 407/783–2271. AE, DC, MC, V.*

Mission Inn Golf and Tennis Resort. Courtyard fountains, stucco walls, terra-cotta roofs, and columned breezeways reflect Florida's Spanish heritage at this lakeside sports complex. Amenities include a 1926 vintage 18-hole golf course, jogging trail, exercise room, six lighted tennis courts, an outdoor pool with Hydro-spa, a 52-slip marina, and a restored 1930s river yacht. *Howey-in-the-Hills 32737, tel. 904/324–3101. AE, DC, MC, V.*

Riverview Hotel. This restored 1886 bridge tender's house, at the foot of the Rte. 44 bridge, is only four blocks from the Atlantic. Its 18 rooms feature natural wicker, antiques, and vivid watercolor paintings. The third-floor Riverview Plaza Suite has the best view of the Intracoastal Waterway and displays the tongue-and-grove pine walls of the original structure. Amenities include a courtyard swimming pool, seafood restaurant and lounge, and 10-slip marina. *103 Flagler Ave., New Smyrna Beach 32069, tel. 904/428–5858. AE, DC, MC, V.*

Seven Sisters Inn. Antique white wicker and potted red geraniums grace the wraparound veranda of this 1888 Victorian mansion. Restored in 1985, the three-story inn opened October 1987 and offers seven plush rooms with private baths. Ralph Lauren linens, antiques, fresh flowers, and gourmet breakfasts pamper guests. Sylvia's Room—with its king-size bed, expansive windows, and antique chaise—is a favorite. *820 S.E. Fort King Ave., Ocala 32671, tel. 904/867–1170. AE, MC, V.*

Expensive

Captain's Quarters Inn. It may look like just another mid-rise hotel, but inside, it's like a home away from home. An antique desk, Victorian love seat, and tropical greenery greet guests in the lobby of this 25-suite beachfront inn. Fresh-baked goodies and coffee are served in The Galley, which overlooks the ocean and looks like grandma's kitchen with a few extra tables and chairs. Each guest suite features rich oak furnishings, a complete kitchen, and private balcony. There's a heated swimming pool and sunbathing deck facing the beach. *3711 S. Atlantic Ave., Daytona Beach Shores 32019, tel. 904/767–3119. AE, MC, V.*

The Crown Hotel. In the center of rural Inverness, occupying what once was a general store, is a cozy 34-room inn. Gilt-frame mirrors, polished woods and brass, and replicas of the British crown jewels adorn the lobby. Amenities include a small backyard pool, an English pub, and a Classic French gourmet restaurant. Guest rooms are small but comfortable, with large modern baths. *109 N. Seminole Ave., Inverness 32650, tel. 904/344–5555. AE, DC, MC, V.*

Ocala Hilton. A winding, tree-lined boulevard leads to this nine-story pink tower, which opened in 1987. Nestled in a forested patch of countryside just off I–75, the 200-room hotel features a marble-floor lobby with a piano bar, a restaurant featuring regional cuisine, an outdoor heated pool and Jacuzzi, two lighted tennis courts, and a pub with live entertainment. Pickled-pine armoires hide television sets in the spacious guest rooms, which are decorated in deep tropical hues. *3600 S.W. 36th Ave., Ocala 32674, tel. 904/854–1400. AE, DC, MC, V.*

Ritz—Ocala's Historic Inn. After an extensive interior redesign and renovation—completed in 1988—this pink stucco 1925 luxury apartment building is now a 32-suite luxury hotel on the National Register of Historic Places. Kilim rugs, 19th-century carved-stone Fu lion lamps with silk shades, arched French windows, and hand-painted trompe l'oeil murals bring Boca Raton's Mizner style to central Florida. There's a courtyard swimming pool, restaurant, and lobby/piano bar. Rates include a complimentary buffet breakfast and a nightly two-hour cocktail party. *1205 E. Silver Springs Blvd., Ocala 32670, tel. 904/867–7700. AE, DC, MC, V.*

Moderate

Crossway Inn: A Cocoa Beach Resort. This 94-unit resort motel is across the street from the Atlantic and within walking distance of a surf shop and at least 16 restaurants. You can choose from standard double rooms, minisuites, or fully equipped efficiencies—all are clean, comfortable, and decorated with light tropical colors. The inn has its own video library (150 titles) and provides VCRs for the guests' use. Amenities include a lighted volleyball court, a 15-foot "mallet pool" court (you sink the 8-ball with a croquet mallet), a children's playground, and an airy Key West–style lounge with rattan furnishings and hand-painted tropical murals. *3901 N. Atlantic Ave., Cocoa Beach 32931, tel. 407/783–2221. AE, DC, MC, V.*

Crystal Lodge Resort Motel and Dive Center. A proximity to Kings Bay and the manatees that are drawing so much attention is what this two-story cinderblock roadside motel has to offer. Its 94 rooms are within a few steps of the marina, where dive boats depart for scuba and snorkeling excursions. The only rooms with a view of the water are 114 and 128. There's an outdoor pool and two restaurants, including Cracker's. *U.S. 19, Crystal River 32629, tel. 904/795–3171. CB, DC, MC, V.*

Pelican Landing Resort-On the Ocean. This tidy, two-story gray motel with royal-blue awnings features 11 efficiencies that were totally refurbished in 1987 with new appliances (including microwave ovens) and linoleum floors. Direct oceanfront views and screened porches are available in Units 1 and 6. A friendly family atmosphere, boardwalks to the beach, picnic tables, and a gas grill round out the amenities. *1201 S. Atlantic Ave., Cocoa Beach 32931, tel. 407/783–7197. MC, V.*

Inexpensive

Izaak Walton Lodge. This 1924 fishing retreat, the center supports of which are two huge trees, was completely restored in 1987. Stained black-cypress siding, white gingerbread trim, a gleaming tin roof, and red flower boxes brimming with geraniums greet those who venture off the main road to Yankeetown. There's a formal restaurant called Izaak's Gourmet and a casual seafood dining room overlooking the river. Upstairs are 10 lodge rooms with antique iron beds, carpeting, duck prints and shared baths. Out back are two very popular riverfront efficiencies decorated with natural wicker and rattan. *1 63rd Street on Riverside Dr., Yankeetown 32698, tel. 904/447–2311. MC, V.*

Merrily Bed & Breakfast. Margie Karow, one of the 400 residents of turn-of-the-century McIntosh, opened her 1888 Victorian home to guests in 1987. The pale-yellow house, with white trim and black shutters, shares an acre of land with spreading oak trees and has a screened back porch where Mrs. Karow likes to serve banana muffins for breakfast. Four guest rooms share two baths. *Ave. G and Sixth St., McIntosh 32664. tel. 904/591–1180. No credit cards.*

Sprague House Inn. Built in 1892, this Old Florida inn was used as a school for training domestics for area hotels. Renovated and reopened as a bed-and-breakfast inn in 1986, it features a full-service restaurant and three very clean rooms with private baths. Hundreds of books, stained-glass windows that depict the history of steamboat travel in Florida, and a hodgepodge of antiques and oddities decorate this unusual inn. *125 Central Ave., Crescent City 32012, tel. 904/698–2430. MC, V.*

The Arts

Oddly enough, the principal center for the arts is Daytona Beach. Side by side with pari-mutuel wagering and auto racing is **Peabody Auditorium.** The 2,560-seat center hosts internationally known artists in theater, music, and dance. The Daytona Beach Civic Ballet and the Daytona Symphony Society are also based here. *Peabody Auditorium, 600 Auditorium Blvd., Daytona Beach, tel. 904/252–0821.*

South of Daytona, the Brevard Community College each year sponsors the **Lyceum Series,** featuring a lineup of state, national, and international performing groups in the fields of music, theater, and dance. *Dr. Rosemary Layne, Brevard Community College, 1519 Clearlake Rd., Cocoa, tel. 407/632–1111, ext. 3660.*

Theater Community theater is popular throughout the region. Contact the local chamber of commerce in each community for details (*see* Important Addresses and Numbers).

Concerts South Brevard County is home to the Brevard Symphony Orchestra, the Florida Spacecoast Philharmonic, the Civic Music Association of South Brevard, and the Melbourne Chamber Music Society. *1005 E. Strawbridge Ave., Melbourne, tel. 407/724–5400.*

Nightlife

Bars and Nightclubs **FiddlestiX Spirits & Such** (2286 Rte. A1A, Canova Beach, tel. 407/773–4135). Live entertainment by Mint Condition, a rhythm and blues band that dabbles in jazz and rock and roll.

Ocean Deck (127 S. Ocean Ave., Daytona Beach, tel. 904/253–5224). Reggae bands, dancing.

Cabarets **Scallies Comedy Connection** (131 Hibiscus Ave., Melbourne, tel. 407/676–2260). Male and female revues, comedy, and variety shows, jazz Thursday.

Comedy Clubs **Mac's Famous Bar** (2000 S. Atlantic Ave., Daytona Beach, tel. 904/252–9239). Formerly a rock-and-roll spot, it now features comedy Wednesday–Sunday and live blues bands Monday and Tuesday.

The Toucan Lounge (Melbourne Hilton, 200 Rialto Place, Melbourne, tel. 407/768–0200). Three different comedy acts 8:30–11 every Wednesday night.

Country Western **Finky's** (640 N. Grandview, Daytona Beach, tel. 904/255–5059). Top-name country entertainment all year, except during spring break and race weeks, when it switches to rock and roll.

Stillwaters Saloon (1512 S.W. College Rd. [Rte. 200], Ocala, tel. 904/629–6969). Music and dancing.

Discos **Platters Lounge** (DeLand Hilton, 350 International Speedway Blvd., DeLand, tel. 904/738–5200). Multilevel sound system, flashing lights, and rock videos of '60s, '70s, and '80s hits for dancing.

For Singles **The Intra-Coastal Dispensing Co.** (531 Eau Gallie Blvd., Melbourne, tel. 407/242–9951). A two-story entertainment complex with a rooftop bar, live reggae, and comedy.

10 Southwest Florida

Introduction

by Karen Feldman Smith

A resident of Florida for the past decade, Karen Feldman Smith is the travel and consumer writer for the Fort Myers News-Press, *a contributing writer for the Gannett News Service, and a graduate of the Columbia University Graduate School of Journalism.*

Tourists and developers are fast discovering a region they formerly raced through in their haste to get to better-known Florida vacation destinations.

Southwest Florida spans some 200 miles and includes a host of diverse cities and towns. That variety satisfies the varied tastes of young singles, families, and older travelers. Sunning, shelling, sailing, and space to breathe characterize vacations on the Gulf coast.

Although the east coast of Florida may claim most of the state's historic sites—Orlando has the universally beloved Mickey Mouse gang and Key West is a shoo-in as the state's most flamboyant locale—there are lower-profile but equally worthy sites to enjoy on the Gulf coast. There are culturally rich ethnic neighborhoods, soothing natural sanctuaries harboring rare species, hotels from basic to deluxe, and some worthwhile tourist attractions. And, of course, there are the beaches, which stretch along the translucent waters of the Gulf of Mexico.

The sprawling region can be divided into three parts: the Tampa Bay area, encompassing Tampa, St. Petersburg, Tarpon Springs, and Clearwater; the Sarasota area, including Bradenton and Venice; and the Naples/Fort Myers region, from Port Charlotte south to the Everglades below Marco Island.

Tampa Bay

It's fitting that an area with a thriving international port should also be populated by a wealth of nationalities—Greeks, Scots, Hispanics, and Italians, to name a few.

Tampa is an Indian phrase meaning "sticks of fire." Indians were the sole inhabitants of the region for many years. The Spanish explorers Juan Ponce de León, Pánfilo de Narváez, and Hernando de Soto passed through in the mid-1500s but chose to settle in the eastern part of the state to protect valuable trading lanes.

The U.S. Army and civilian settlers arrived in 1824. A military presence remains in the form of MacDill Air Force Base, where the U.S. Operations Command is located.

The Cubans brought their cigar-making industry to the area in 1866 and developed Ybor City. This Tampa suburb is primarily Cuban but contains a dwindling number of cigar makers.

In Tarpon Springs, visitors should do as the Greeks do, because they are the locals. A large Greek population has lived there for decades. Sponge divers from the Dodecanese Islands of Greece moved to the area at the turn of the century. The area was the world's largest sponge center during the 1930s, but a bacterial blight wiped out the sponge beds in the 1940s. But the Greeks held on, and the sponge industry returned, though in lesser force than during its heyday. Today, the Greek influence remains evident in the churches, the restaurants, and, often, in the language spoken on the streets.

The accent is Scottish in Dunedin, just south of Tarpon Springs. Two Scots were responsible for giving the town its Gaelic name in the 1880s. If the sound of bagpipes played by men in kilts appeals to you, head to Dunedin in March or April, when the Highland games and the Dunedin Heather and Thistle holidays pay tribute to the Celtic heritage.

Tampa boasts more business suits than any other part of the region. Industry and a thriving port make it the logical spot for skyscrapers and skyrocketing commercial growth. The city's roots have not been swept away, however, in the process.

Tampa's port is the country's seventh largest, with phosphate, shrimp, and bananas the primary cargo. The city's shrimp fleet, docked at Hooker's Point, is the state's largest.

Industry flourishes as well, with millions of cigars rolled daily, phosphate mined from massive pits, and two major breweries —Busch and Schlitz—producing their products here.

But the city isn't all business. Busch Gardens affords visitors a walk on the wild side with some 3,000 exotic animals and birds in residence. The Museum of Science and Industry contains exhibits that show our striving to better understand the universe as well as our earthbound accomplishments. The Seminole Culture Center pays tribute to Indian culture and history.

Ybor City in east Tampa stubbornly clings to its Spanish roots, with a wealth of Spanish and Cuban restaurants, groceries, clubs, and cigar factories. Ybor Square, a renovated factory at Eighth Avenue and 13th Street, houses shops, restaurants, and, on some weekends, musical performances or art shows.

History buffs might find a trip to the University of Tampa's administration building rewarding. Built in 1890 as the opulent Tampa Bay Hotel, it became Teddy Roosevelt's headquarters in 1898, when some 30,000 troops were training in Tampa in preparation for the Spanish-American War.

What Tampa does not have is a gulf beach. Tampa Bay, though lovely to look at, is too polluted for swimming. For that, visitors should head to neighboring St. Petersburg.

There is water, water, everywhere around St. Petersburg; bays and the Gulf of Mexico, filled with pleasure and commercial craft, border the peninsula on three sides. On the waterfront downtown the city's two main art museums—the Museum of Fine Arts and the Salvador Dali Museum—have extensive collections. Nearby is the city pier, a five-story inverted pyramid housing restaurants and shops but currently undergoing renovation.

Sarasota and Bradenton

Sarasota is a city of two tales. Situated on the water, it is unquestionably a beach resort. But it also has a thriving cultural community, making it a suitable destination for those with a taste for the arts.

Much of the credit for the city's diversity is due to the late John Ringling, founder of the now Ringling Brothers Barnum & Bailey Circus, who chose to make Sarasota the winter home of his circus and his family. Today, his estate remains open to the public; his circus winters in Venice, about 30 minutes south of Sarasota.

Sheltering the mainland from the unpredictable gulf are several choice barrier islands, Siesta and Longboat keys, with ample beach and hotel space, and St. Armand's Key, a small circular isle lined with chic boutiques, restaurants, and stately palms.

For those who like statistics, here are a few: Sarasota County has 35 miles of Gulf beaches, 2 state parks, 22 municipal parks, and 44 golf courses, many of them open to the public.

Nearby Bradenton maintains a lower profile, but also has its share of sugar-sand beaches, golf courses, and historic sites dating back to the mid-1800s.

To the south is Venice, with its multitudinous canals crisscrossing the city. Besides being the winter home of the circus, the city contains the world's only clown college. And, though shell collecting is quite good, the beaches of Venice are best known for the wealth of shark teeth to be found.

Fort Myers, Naples, and the Resort Islands

Lee County has a split personality. Its inland communities—Fort Myers and Cape Coral—are primarily commercial and residential. Its gulf-front communities are beach resorts filled with people who are working mainly on relaxing and cultivating tans.

Fort Myers gets its nickname, the City of Palms, from the hundreds of towering royal palms that inventor Thomas Edison planted along a main residential street, McGregor Boulevard, on which his winter estate stood. Edison's idea caught on, and there are now more than 2,000 royal palms on McGregor Boulevard alone, with countless more throughout the city.

Along the county's western border are the resort islands of Estero, Sanibel, and Captiva.

Estero contains Fort Myers Beach, a laid-back beach community favored by young singles and those who want to stay on the Gulf without paying the higher prices on Sanibel or Captiva.

A few miles farther off the coast are Sanibel and Captiva, connected to the mainland by a mile-long causeway. In recent years development has threatened the charm of the islands. However, island dwellers have staunchly held the line on further development, keeping buildings low and somewhat farther apart than on the majority of Florida's barrier islands. Sanibel has long been a world-class shelling locale, with fine fishing, luxury hotels, and dozens of restaurants. You will not be able to see most of the houses, which are shielded by tall Australian pines, but the beaches and tranquil gulf waters are readily accessible.

Naples and Marco Island

Naples is smaller and on the opposite coast, but it is often likened to Palm Beach for its ambience. Fifth and Third avenues south are lined with exclusive boutiques, shops, and restaurants. Here, first-time visitors and long-time members of the city's society mingle.

For those to whom beaches are important, Naples far outstrips Palm Beach with its abundance of public beach accesses—41 miles of beach are open to the public. The yen to go shelling, sunning, and fishing can be indulged to limitless excess on the sun-drenched white shores.

South of Naples is yet another resort island, Marco. Here, high-rise condominiums and hotels line much of the waterfront, but many natural areas have been preserved, including the tiny fishing village of Goodland, where Old Florida lives on.

Getting Around

By Plane Most major carriers fly into at least one of the area's three major airports, in Tampa, Sarasota, and Fort Myers.

Tampa International is six miles from downtown. It is served by Air Canada (tel. 800/422–6232), Air Jamaica (tel. 800/523–5585), American (tel. 800/638–7320), British Airways (tel. 800/247–9297), Continental (tel. 800/525–0280), Delta (tel. 800/327–7777), Eastern (tel. 800/EASTERN), Northwest (tel. 800/225–2525), Pan Am (tel. 800/221–4433), Piedmont (tel. 800/251–5720), Transworld (tel. 800/209–2121), United (tel. 800/722–5243), and USAir (tel. 800/428–4322).

Sarasota's Airport is **Sarasota-Bradenton,** just north of the city. It is served by Air Sunshine (tel. 800/432–1744), American, Continental, Delta, Eastern, Florida Express (tel. 813/355–5323), Northwest, Transworld, and United.

The Fort Myers/Naples area's airport is **Southwest Florida Regional Airport,** about 12 miles south of Fort Myers, 25 miles north of Naples. It is served by American, Continental, Delta, Eastern, Northwest, Piedmont, United, and USAir.

Between the airports and the hotels: Major car-rental companies and taxi and limousine companies service all three airports. Many hotels also operate shuttles.

In Tampa, major transportation services include **Central Florida Limousine** (tel. 813/833–3730), serving Hillsborough and Polk counties; **The Limo** (tel. 813/822–3333 in St. Petersburg and Clearwater, or 813/442–4812 in Tarpon Springs), serving Pinellas County; and **Airport Transport of Pinellas** (tel. 813/541–5600), for Pinellas County only. Expect taxi fares to be about \$9–\$12 for most of Hillsborough County and about twice that for Pinellas County.

In Sarasota, transportation includes **Airport Limousine** (tel. 813/355–9645) and **Diplomat Taxi** (tel. 813/366–9822). Both deliver to most parts of the county. An average cab fare is \$5–\$10.

In Lee County, **Sun Lines** (tel. 813/768–0800) has an exclusive contract to keep vehicles at the airport awaiting passengers. That means you have to call any of the others if you want them, and you are likely to be charged for a round-trip—about \$40 to downtown Fort Myers or the beaches. A Sun Lines vehicle will cost about half that. Other transportation companies include **Aristocat Super Mini-Van Service** (tel. 813/275–7228), **Boca Limousine Service** (tel. 813/936–5466), **Jetport Express Co.** (tel. 813/643–1200), and **Royal Transportation of Southwest Florida** (tel. 813/394–3233).

By Car I–75 spans the region from north to south. Once you cross the border into Florida from Georgia, it should take about three hours to reach Tampa. Add an hour for Sarasota, two to Fort Myers, and three to Naples.

Alligator Alley (Rte. 84) links up with I–75 at Naples and runs east to Fort Lauderdale. U.S. 41 also runs the length of the region and serves as the business district in many communities. It's best to avoid all bridges and U.S. 41 during rush hours, 7–9 AM and 4–6 PM.

Rental car prices can vary dramatically, so it pays to shop around. Major companies serving Southwest Florida include **Alamo** (tel. 800/327–9633), **Avis** (tel. 800/331–1212), **Budget** (tel. 800/527–0700), **Dollar** (tel. 800/421–6868), **Enterprise** (tel. 800/325–8007), **Hertz** (tel. 800/654–3131), **Holiday Payless** (tel. 800/282–4682), **Sears** (tel. 800/527–0700), **Thrifty** (tel. 800/367–2277), and **Value** (tel. 800/327–2501).

By Train **Amtrak** (tel. 800/872–7245) connects the Northeast, Midwest, and much of the South to Tampa. From Tampa, Amtrak heads east, winding down to Miami and up to Jacksonville and beyond. Amtrak's Autotrain runs from Lorton, Virginia (near Washington, DC), to Sanford, Florida (near Orlando). In Tampa, the Amtrak station is at 601 N. Nebraska Avenue (tel. 813/229–2473). Within Tampa, the PeopleMover rail line provides transportation between the business district and Harbour Island. Tokens cost 25 cents each way.

By Bus **Greyhound Lines/Trailways** provides service to and throughout the state. Call the nearest office for schedules and fares (Fort Myers, tel. 813/334–1011; St. Petersburg, tel. 813/898–1496; Sarasota, tel. 813/955–5735; and Tampa, tel. 813/229–2112).

Around Tampa, the **Hillsborough Area Regional Transit** (HART), (tel. 813/254–4278, 7 AM–6 PM) system serves most of the county.

In Sarasota, **Sarasota County Area Transit** (SCAT), (tel. 813/951–5850) is the public transit company. The **Lee County Transit System** (tel. 813/939–1303) serves Fort Myers and most of the county.

Scenic Drives **I–275 between St. Petersburg** and **Terra Ceia.** Motorists get a bird's-eye view of bustling Tampa Bay along the Sunshine Skyway and its bright-yellow suspension bridge.

Rte. 679 takes you along two of St. Petersburg's most pristine islands, Cabbage and Mullet keys.

Rte. 789 carries you over several of the coast's slender barrier islands, past miles of green-blue gulf waters, beaches, and waterfront homes. The road does not connect all the islands, however. It runs from Holmes Beach off the Bradenton coast south to Lido Beach in Sarasota, then begins again on Casey Key south of Osprey and runs south to Nokomis Beach.

Rte. 867 (McGregor Boulevard), Fort Myer's premier road, passes Thomas Edison's winter home and goes southwest toward the beaches. The road is lined with thousands of royal palm trees and many large old homes.

J. N. "Ding" Darling National Wildlife Refuge. Drive along the five-mile dirt road in Sanibel and, especially at low tide, you may see raccoons; alligators; and birds, such as roseate spoonbills, egrets, ospreys, herons, and anhingas.

Head west on **Mooringline Drive** in Naples for a drive past some of the cushiest coastline property in the state. Mooring Line turns south and becomes Gulf Shore Boulevard. Condominiums, shops, hotels, and lots of beaches line this drive.

Just near the end of Gulf Shore Boulevard on Broad Avenue, you can pick up **2nd Street South,** which becomes Gordon Drive. It leads into Port Royale, where million-dollar homes are a dime a dozen. The architecture, landscaping, and statuary that are visible from the road make it a worthwhile expedition.

Guided Tours

Accelerated Coach Lines (tel. 813/442–0501) in Clearwater makes one-, two-, and three-day trips to Busch Gardens, Disney World and Epcot Center, the Kennedy Space Center, St. Augustine, and Cypress Gardens. Vans, coaches, and limousines.

Around the Town (tel. 813/961–4120) conducts tours for groups of 25 or more in the Tampa Bay area, plus Tarpon Springs and Sarasota, the dog tracks, and area theaters. Try to make reservations several weeks in advance.

Five Star Tours (tel. 800/331–8232 or 813/229–0364) conducts daily coach tours in the Tampa Bay area and to Orlando area attractions.

Gulf Coast Gray Line (tel. 813/822–3577) makes daily trips from Tampa to Disney World, Epcot Center, Sea World, Busch Gardens, and other attractions.

Travel is Fun, One Day Motor Coach Tours (tel. 813/821–9479) offers day-long tours to area sights and attractions from St. Petersburg.

Florida Adventure Tours and Charters (tel. 813/394–8870) makes daily motorcoach and van sightseeing excursions from Naples and Marco Island to the Naples–Fort Myers Greyhound Club, the Everglades, Edison's home, and Disney World. It also operates shopping tours. Free pickup and return service.

Fun Trolley Excursions (tel. 813/394–7799) conducts narrated tours of Marco Island. Visitors can travel among the larger resorts in town via a red, green, and black trolley that makes 10 trips around the island daily (five on Sundays) and allows unlimited reboarding privileges all day. Cost: $5.

Boat Tours

The Spirit of Tampa (tel. 813/273–9485) offers lunch and dinner cruises every other day. It is docked at 200 N. Ashley Street, behind the Hilton Hotel in downtown Tampa.

Sea Escape Cruises (tel. 800/432–0900) are day-long excursions into the Gulf of Mexico on full-sized cruise ships.

The ***Captain Anderson*** (tel. 813/367–7804) combines sightseeing and dinner cruises from the Dolphin Village Shopping Center, St. Petersburg Beach. The *Captain Anderson II* (tel. 813/462–2628) is docked at Clearwater Beach Marina.

The ***Starlite Princess*** (tel. 813/466–4814) is a paddlewheel excursion boat offering three-hour, five-course meals from Hamlin's Landing, Indian Rocks Beach. Old-fashioned boat adds to the fun.

The ***Miss Cortez*** (tel. 813/794–1223) departs from Cortez, just north of Bradenton, every Tuesday and Thursday for Egmont Key, a small abandoned island just north of Anna Maria Island.

The ***Bay Star*** (tel. 813/351–5897) runs two-hour narrated cruises around Longboat Key, Sarasota, and Cortez from the Holiday Inn Airport Marina and Yacht Basin, U.S. 41, one mile north of Sarasota Airport.

The ***Deliquesce*** (tel. 813/351–7839) is a 41-foot sailing yacht that makes day, sunset, and dinner cruises on Sarasota Bay. When the breeze is right you get the feeling of a seafarer on this cruise. The yacht is docked at the Holiday Inn Airport Marina and Yacht Basin, U.S. 41. Fares start at $15.

Myakka Safari Tours (tel. 813/365–0100) is at Myakka River State Park, east of Sarasota on Rte. 72. *The Gator Gal*, a large airboat, conducts one-hour tours of the 29,000-acre wildlife and bird sanctuary. Three trips daily; closed Tuesday.

Epicurean Sailing Charters (tel. 813/964–0708) conducts half- and full-day cruises from Boca Grande to Useppa Island, Cabbage Key, and other area islands.

King Fisher Cruise Lines (tel. 813/639–0969) offers cruises and island sightseeing around Charlotte Harbor from Fishermen's Village, Punta Gorda.

Everglades Jungle Cruise (tel. 813/334–7474) explores the Caloosahatchee and Orange rivers of Lee County and makes day trips to Lake Okeechobee and two-day trips across the vast inland lake. Has lunch and dinner cruises as well. Trips last three hours to two days. They depart from the Fort Myers Yacht Basin. Rates: $8–$149.

The Glass Bottom Boat (tel. 813/463–2219) offers daytime, sunset, and moonlight cruises of San Carlos Bay at Fort Myers Beach. Leaves from Gulf Star Marina. A narrated tour of the bay area with views of both above water and below.

Dalis Charter (tel. 813/262–4545) offers full- and half-day fishing and sightseeing trips and sunset cruises. Also available for private cocktail cruises. It's docked at Old Marine Market Place at Tin City (1200 Fifth Ave. S, Naples.)

Tiki Islander Boat Tours (tel. 813/262–7577) conducts a variety of tours through the northern section of the Everglades' Ten Thousand Islands, including half-day fishing and shelling expeditions to Keewaydin Island and sightseeing along Naples Bay. Tours start at the dock behind Old Marine Market Place, Naples.

Wooten's Everglades (tel. 813/394–8080) runs a variety of airboat and swamp-buggy tours through the Everglades daily from Wooten's alligator farm, 35 miles east of Naples on U.S. 41.

Eden of the Everglades (tel. 813/695–2800) travels the wilderness wetlands of the Everglades' Ten Thousand Islands, departing from Everglades City in southern Collier County six times daily.

Florida Boat Tours (tel. 813/695–4400) depart from the Captain's Table Resort in Everglades City. The 80-minute tours of the Ten Thousand Islands set off three to five times daily.

By Air

Helicopter tours of the Tampa Bay area and the west coast of Florida are offered by **Suncoast Helicopters** (tel. 813/872–6625), based at Tampa International Airport; **Topp of Tampa Airport** (6901 Rte. 54, Tampa, tel. 813/973–0056), **West Florida Helicopters** Albert Whitted Airport, tel. 813/823–5200).

Important Addresses and Numbers

Tourist Information

All the following offices are open 9–5 weekdays and closed on holidays:

Charlotte County Chamber of Commerce (2702 Tamiami Trail, Port Charlotte, tel. 813/627–2222).

Greater Clearwater Chamber of Commerce (128 N. Osceola Ave., tel. 813/461–0011).

Greater Dunedin Chamber of Commerce (434 Main St., tel. 813/736–5066).

Gulf Beaches Chamber of Commerce (105 5th Ave., Indian Rocks Beach, tel. 813/595–4575).
Lee County Tourist Development Council (2126 1st St., Fort Myers, tel. 813/335–2631).
Madeira Beach Chamber of Commerce (501 150th Ave., tel. 813/391–7373).
Pinellas Suncoast Tourist Development Council (2333 E. Bay Dr., Suite 109A, Clearwater, tel. 813/530–6452).
St. Petersburg Chamber of Commerce (401 3rd Ave. S, tel. 813/821–4069).
The Suncoast Welcome Center (2001 Ulmerton Rd., tel. 813/576–1449).
Sanibel-Captiva Chamber of Commerce (Causeway Rd., Sanibel, tel. 813/472–1080).

Tampa Bay Area **The Greater Tampa Chamber of Commerce** (801 E. Kennedy Blvd., tel. 813/228–7777). For information on current area events, call the **Visitors Information Line** (tel. 813/223–1111). For information on area accommodations, call the **Tampa/St. Petersburg Reservations Centre** (tel. 813/596–9944).
Tarpon Springs Chamber of Commerce (115 S. Ring Ave., tel. 813/937–6109).
Treasure Island Chamber of Commerce (152 108th Ave., tel. 813/367–4529).

Emergencies Dial 911 for **police** or **ambulance** in an emergency.

Hospitals Hospital emergency rooms are open around the clock. In Tampa: **University Community Hospital** (3100 E. Fletcher Ave.). In St. Petersburg: **Bayfront Medical Center** (701 6th St. S.). In Bradenton: **Manatee Memorial Hospital** (206 2nd St. E.). In Sarasota: **Sarasota Memorial Hospital** (1700 S. Tamiami Trail, U.S. 41). In Fort Myers: **Lee Memorial Hospital** (2776 Cleveland Ave.). In Naples: **Naples Community** (350 7th St. N.).

24-Hour Pharmacy **Eckerd Drugs** (11613 N. Nebraska, Tampa, tel. 813/978–0775).

Exploring Southwest Florida

Tampa

Though it's not on the Gulf of Mexico, Tampa is nearly surrounded by water. St. Petersburg, across Tampa Bay, is blessed with all the beaches; Tampa is the business and commercial hub of this part of the state, as you'll quickly notice when driving by the busy port. The major north–south route is I–75; if you're heading from Orlando, you'll likely drive in on east–west I–4.

Numbers in the margin correspond with points of interest on the Tampa-St. Petersburg-Bradenton-Sarasota map.

Day 1 Let's begin a tour of Tampa along that I–4 corridor at Exit 5 (Orient Rd., east of the city). The water tower with an arrow
1 sticking through it gives it away: this is the **Seminole Culture Center,** which contains a village and museum displaying artifacts of the Seminole Indians, who inhabited Florida long before white settlers arrived. You'll also be treated to alligator wrestling and snake shows. *5221 N. Orient Rd. Open Mon.–Sat., 9–5. Sun. noon–5. Admission: $3.50 adults, $2.75 children 3–12 and senior citizens over 60.*

2 **Ybor City** is Tampa's Cuban melting pot, which thrived on the cigar-making industry at the turn of the century. To get there, take I–4 west to Exit 1 (22nd St.) and go south five blocks to 7th Avenue. You're in the heart of Ybor City, where the smell of cigars—hand-rolled by Cuban refugees—mingles with old-world architecture. Take a stroll past the ornately tiled Columbia Restaurant and the stores lining the street, or step back to the past at **Ybor Square.** The restored cigar factory (1901 13th St.) now is a mall with boutiques, offices, and several restaurants. You can watch as artisans continue the local practice of hand rolling cigars.

For something a little more modern, head for the new skyscrapers downtown. From 7th Avenue, go west to Nebraska Avenue and turn left. That will take you to Kennedy Boulevard; turn right and drive a few blocks to the vicinity of Franklin Street. You are now in one of Tampa's booming growth areas, with a pedestrian mall down the center of Franklin Street.

3 A few more blocks to the east you'll find the **Tampa Museum of Art,** near Curtis Hixon Convention Center. Egyptian, Greek, and Roman artifacts are on display, as well as traveling exhibits. *601 Doyle Carlton Dr., tel. 813/223–8128. Open Tues. and Thurs.–Sat. 10–6, Wed. 10–9, Sun. 1–5. Donations accepted.*

Day 2 On another day, enjoy a romp through **Busch Gardens.** A safari
4 simulating a journey to the Dark Continent will let you watch free-roaming zebras, giraffes, rhinos, lions, and more—all from the comfort of a monorail. There are many other rides and attractions in this 300-acre park, so allow at least six hours here. *3000 Busch Blvd. (Rte. 580), 2 miles east of I–275, tel. 813/971–8282. Open daily 9:30–6. All-inclusive admission: $18.95, children under 2 free.*

St. Petersburg

St. Petersburg and the Pinellas Suncoast form the thumb of the hand jutting out of the west coast, holding in Tampa Bay. I–275 crosses the bay from Tampa through the heart of the city and then crosses the bay again at the Sunshine Skyway into Bradenton. U.S. 19 is the major north–south artery. Traffic can be heavy, and there are many lights, so U.S. 19 should be avoided on lengthy trips.

St. Petersburg Beaches

The bay and beaches offer two distinct communities to visit.
5 Let's start with a trip over the **Sunshine Skyway.** A $1 toll will carry you across the causeway and to the top of a sparkling new suspension bridge for a bird's-eye view of the islands and of ocean freighters and sailboats plying Tampa Bay. You can also see what's left of the original twin span that collapsed and killed more than 30 people when a ship hit it in 1980. Across the bridge, you can picnic, toss in a fishing line, or turn around and mount the summit of the bridge again. This time, you'll get a view of a series of small islands that dot the bay, and you'll see St. Petersburg Beach as you head north. *Take U.S. 19 or I–275 south from St. Petersburg.*

When you reach the end of the causeway, turn left on 54th Avenue South (Rt. 682), and follow it to Rt. 679. Turn left and cross the islands you saw from the Sunshine Skyway. You'll end up
6 eventually at **Fort Desoto Park** at the mouth of Tampa Bay. Here you can roam the fort that was built to protect gulf sea lanes during the Spanish-American War or wander the beaches of any of the islands that make up the park. *Mullet Key, 34th St. S. No admission, but tolls totaling 85 cents will be charged on the Bayway to the islands.*

Head back up the Bayway and turn left toward the beaches and then right on Gulf Boulevard (Rt. 699). The colossal pink Don CeSar Resort Hotel is off to the left. Head through St. Petersburg Beach and Treasure Island to Madeira Beach. Stop
7 here at **John's Pass Village and Boardwalk** (12901 Gulf Blvd.), a collection of shops in an old-style fishing village, where you can shop and eat at a variety of restaurants or pass the time watching the pelicans cavorting and dive-bombing for food.

When pelicans become entangled in fishing lines, locals some-
8 times carry them to the **Suncoast Seabird Sanctuary,** a nonprofit organization whose facilities are open to the public. Drive up Gulf Boulevard to Indian Shores. *18328 Gulf Blvd. Free, but donations welcome. Open daily 9–dark.*

9 Ready to get off the road and out on the water? ***The Captain Anderson II*** is the place to relax and enjoy dinner and a little dancing while sightseeing on Clearwater Bay. *Up Gulf Blvd. to Clearwater Beach Marina, tel. 813/462–2628. Open Oct.–May. Fare and dinner: $17.50. Boarding at 6:30* PM. *Reservations required.*

The Bay

For a second day in St. Petersburg, you'll enjoy a change of
10 pace along the cosmopolitan bayfront. Begin at the **Salvador Dali Museum.** To get there, take I–275 and then follow I–175

Tampa-St.Petersburg-Sarasota Area

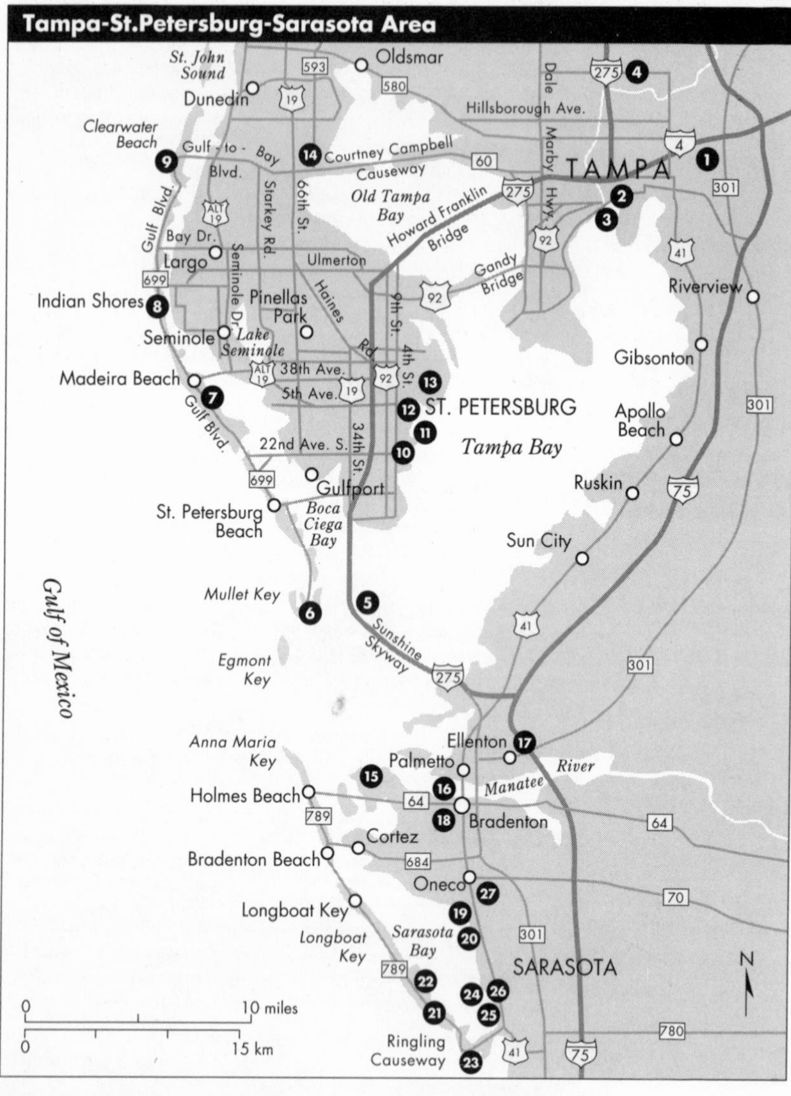

Bellm, Cars & Music, **27**
Bishop Planetarium, **18**
Busch Gardens, **4**
Capt. Anderson II, **9**
DeSoto National Memorial, **15**
Downtown Art District, **26**
Fort DeSoto Park, **6**
Gamble Plantation, **17**
John's Pass Village, **7**
Kapok Tree Restaurant, **14**
Marie Selby Gardens, **25**
Marina Jack II, **24**
Mote Marine Science Center, **22**
Museum of Fine Arts, **12**
The Pier, **11**
Ringling Museums, **19**
St. Armand's Key, **21**
Salvador Dali Museum, **10**
Sarasota Jungle Gardens, **20**
Seminole Cultural Center, **1**
South Florida Museum, **16**
South Lido Park, **23**
Suncoast Seabird Sanctuary, **8**
Sunken Gardens, **13**
Sunshine Skyway, **5**
Tampa Museum of Art, **3**
Ybor City, **2**

toward the bay. At 3rd Street South, turn right. The museum is on the left, about two blocks ahead. Inside you'll find a large collection of paintings of melting watches, colorful landscapes, and thought-provoking works of the Spanish surrealist. *1000 3rd St. S., tel. 813/823–3767. Admission: $3 adults, $2 students and senior citizens. Open Tues.–Sat. 10–5, Sun. noon–5.*

Head up 3rd Street and turn right on 2nd Avenue. You're
11 now heading for the bayfront and **The Pier,** which looks as though a hurricane has turned it upside-down. The unusual building was recently renovated and now contains a number of shops and eateries. *800 2nd Ave. NE. Admission free. Open daily 10–9.*

12 It's a short walk to the **Museum of Fine Arts,** the large building to your right along Beach Drive as you're returning from The Pier. French impressionists highlight the collection, but the museum also has outstanding examples of European, American, pre-Columbian, and Far Eastern art, as well as photography exhibits. *225 Beach Dr. NE., tel. 813/896–2667. Free, but donations are accepted. Open Tues.–Sat. 10–5, Sun. 1–5.*

From here, it's a short drive to one of Florida's most colorful
13 spots, **Sunken Gardens.** To get there, take 4th Street North (a right turn) to 18th Avenue North. Visitors can walk through an aviary with tropical birds, stroll among more than 50,000 exotic plants and flowers, and stop to smell the rare, fragrant orchids. *Admission: $5.25 adults, $3 children. 1825 4th St. N., tel. 813/896–3186. Open daily 9–5:30.*

To end the day, drive to U.S. 19, head north to Rte. 60, turn
14 right, and stop for dinner at the **Kapok Tree Restaurant.** *(see* Dining for details.)

Bradenton

Bradenton is on a finger of land enclosing the southern end of Tampa Bay; the Manatee River also borders the city's north side. The barrier island, Anna Maria, lies off the mainland and fronts the Gulf of Mexico. The combined U.S. 41 and 301 cuts north–south through the center of the city. I–75 is to the east, and Rte. 64 connects the interstate to Bradenton and Anna Maria Island.

Hernando DeSoto, one of the first Spanish explorers, set foot in Florida near what is now Bradenton. Take Rte. 64 to 75th
15 Street NW, turn north, and drive to **DeSoto National Memorial,** where park employees dressed in costumes of the period demonstrate various 16th-century weapons and show how the explorers who roamed the southeastern United States prepared and preserved food for their journeys through the untamed land. *75th St. NW, tel. 813/792–0458. Admission by donation. Open daily 8–5:30.*

Head back to the center of the city, to 10th Street West. A few
16 blocks from the river is the **South Florida Museum,** where you can find artifacts on Florida's history, including displays of Indian culture and an excellent collection of Civil War memorabilia. The museum is also home to "Snooty," the oldest living manatee (or sea cow) in captivity. In the wild, manatees are endangered, but here Snooty likes to shake hands and per-

form other tricks at feeding time. **The Bishop Planetarium** is also housed at the museum. *201 10th St. W, tel. 813/746–4132. Admission: $3 adults, $2 children and students. Open Tues.–Fri. 10–5, weekends 1–5.*

Time Out **The Pier Restaurant.** Take a lunch break on fresh-caught seafood and enjoy a view of the Manatee River in an old Spanish-style building. *At the foot of 12th St. on Memorial Pier, tel. 813/748–8087. Open daily from 11:30 AM.*

Cross the river on U.S. 41 and turn right when U.S. 301 splits off. On the left, three miles ahead, is the **Gamble Plantation**
17 **State Historical Site.** The mansion, built in 1850, is the only pre–Civil War plantation house surviving in south Florida. This is where the Confederate secretary of state took refuge when the Confederacy fell to Union forces. Some of the original furnishings are on display in the mansion. *3708 Patten Ave., Ellenton, tel. 813/722–1017. Open 9–5 Thurs.–Mon., closed Tues. and Wed. Admission: $1. Tours of the house begin on the hour; no tours from noon to 1 PM.*

18 Head back to the **Bishop Planetarium,** where, inside a domed theater, you can see star shows and special-effects laser light displays. Its location is the same as South Florida Museum, above. *Tel. 813/746–4131. Admission: $3 adults, $2 children and students; "Laser Fantasies" admission: $3.50 adults, $2.75 children. Star show Tues–Sat. at 1:30 and 3 PM. plus Fri. and Sat. at 7:30 PM.*

Sarasota

The City of Sarasota sits on the eastern shore of Sarasota Bay. Across the water lie the barrier islands of Siesta Key, Longboat Key, and Lido Key, with myriad beaches, shops, hotels, condominiums, and houses. U.S. 41 is the main north–south thoroughfare in the city; further east, I–75 carries traffic past the city to Tampa or Fort Myers. Four state roads run west from the interstate highway into Sarasota.

Day 1 Long ago, circus tycoon John Ringling found Sarasota an ideal spot to bring his clowns and performers to train and recuperate during the winter. Along the bay, Ringling also built himself a fancy home, patterned after the Palace of the Doges
19 in Venice, Italy. Today, the **Ringling Museums** include that mansion, as well as his art museum (with a world-renowned collection of Rubens paintings) and a museum of circus memorabilia. Also situated on the property is the Asolo State Theater, which was taken from an Italian castle and reassembled on-site. *Located a half mile south of the Sarasota-Bradenton Airport on U.S. 41, tel. 813/355–5101. Combined admission $4.50 ($1.75 for children 6–12) is good for the mansion and both museums. Open weekdays 9–7, Sat. 9–5, Sun. 11–6.*

From the Ringling museums, head south on U.S. 41 about 1½
20 miles to **Sarasota Jungle Gardens.** Here you can stroll through 15 acres of tropical plants and watch the bird and reptile shows. *3701 Bayshore Rd., tel. 813/355–5305. Admission: $4.95 adults, $2.95 children 6–16. Open daily 9–5.*

Time Out **Harding Circle at St. Armand's Key.** It's time to swing out across the bay. Continue south on U.S. 41 to Rte. 789. Turn right, and cross the Ringling Causeway to a little circle of shops and restaurants.

---

21 22 Just up the road from **St. Armand's Key** is the **Mote Marine Science Center,** where marine biologists work to unlock the secrets of marine life. On display are sharks, rays, fish, and other marine creatures native to the area. To get there from Harding Circle, turn north on Ringling Boulevard. Before you reach the bridge leading to Longboat Key, turn right at the sign for City Island and Mote Marine Lab. *1600 City Island Park, tel. 813/388–2451. Admission: $3 adults, $2 children 6–17. Open Tues.–Sat. 10–4, Sun. noon–4.*

You now have an option. One choice is to either head back south,
23 past the public beach at Lido Key, to **South Lido Park,** where you can try your luck at fishing, take a dip in the waters of the bay or Gulf of Mexico, roam the paths of the 130-acre park, or picnic as the sun sets through the Australian pines into the gulf. *Open 8–sunset. Admission free.*

The alternative is to turn back east across Sarasota Bay and turn right into the Marina Plaza along U.S. 41. Here you can enjoy an evening on the water in style, with a sunset dinner
24 cruise on board a stern-wheel paddleboat, the **Marina Jack II.** *Marina Plaza, Island Park, tel. 813/366–9255. Cost: $4 plus dinner. Reservations.*

Day 2 Start out your second day of exploring Sarasota at **Marie Selby**
25 **Botanical Gardens,** which are near the Island Park yacht basin. Here you can stroll through a world-class display of orchids and wander through 14 garden areas along Sarasota Bay. *800 S. Palm Ave., off U.S. 41, tel. 813/366–5730. Admission: $3.50 adults, free children under 12 when accompanied by an adult. Open daily 10–5 except Christmas.*

26 In the heart of Sarasota, you'll discover a **downtown art district,** with galleries such as Art Uptown (1367 Main St.), Adley Gallery (1620 Main St.), Corbino Galleries (69 S. Palm Ave.), Apple & Carpenter Gallery of Fine Arts (1280 N. Palm Ave.), Court of the Arts (1991 Main St.), and J. E. Voorhees Gallery (1359 Main St.).

27 On the road to the airport (U.S. 41) is **Bellm's Cars & Music of Yesterday.** The display includes 200 classic cars, such as Pierce Arrows and Auburns, and old-time music makers, such as hurdy-gurdies and calliopes. *5500 N. Tamiami Trail, tel. 813/355–6228. Admission: $4.95 adults, $2.25 children 6–16. Open Mon.–Sat. 8:30–6, Sun. 9:30–6.*

Fort Myers–Lee County

1 **Fort Myers** is the heart of the county, but only a few major roads lead through it. I–75 runs north–south, as does the more commercial thoroughfare, U.S. 41 (called Cleveland Ave. in Fort Myers). McGregor Boulevard runs from downtown Fort Myers southwest to Sanibel-Captiva. Summerlin Road runs southwest from Colonial Boulevard in South Fort Myers to Sanibel-Captiva and Fort Myers Beach. Rte. 78 (Pine Island–Bayshore Rd.) leads from North Fort Myers through north Cape Coral onto Pine Island.

Numbers in the margin correspond with points of interest on the Southwest Gulf Coast map.

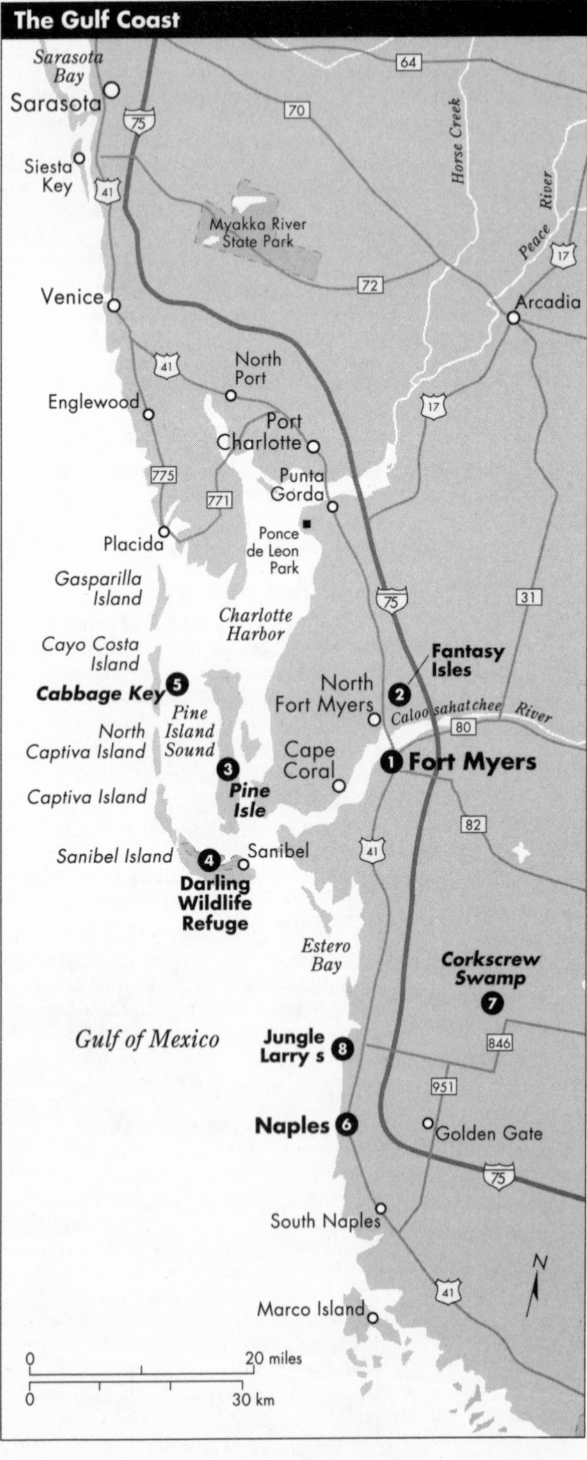
The Gulf Coast
Sarasota Bay
Sarasota
Siesta Key
Myakka River State Park
Horse Creek
Peace River
Venice
Arcadia
North Port
Englewood
Port Charlotte
Punta Gorda
Placida
Ponce de Leon Park
Gasparilla Island
Charlotte Harbor
Cayo Costa Island
Cabbage Key
Pine Island Sound
North Captiva Island
Captiva Island
Pine Isle
Fantasy Isles
North Fort Myers
Caloosahatchee River
Fort Myers
Cape Coral
Sanibel Island
Sanibel
Darling Wildlife Refuge
Estero Bay
Corkscrew Swamp
Gulf of Mexico
Jungle Larry s
Naples
Golden Gate
South Naples
Marco Island
N
0
20 miles
0
30 km
64
70
75
41
72
17
775
771
31
80
82
846
951

If you are headed downtown from the beaches, drive at least part of the way on McGregor Boulevard (from College Parkway north into town is the most scenic). Towering royal palms line both sides of the road. The originals, many of which remain, were planted by Fort Myers's most famous winter resident, Thomas Alva Edison.

Edison's Winter Home, containing a laboratory, botanical gardens, and a museum, is open for guided tours. The property straddles McGregor Boulevard (Rte. 867) about a mile west of U.S. 41 near downtown Fort Myers. The inventor spent his winters on the 14-acre estate, developing the phonograph and teletype, experimenting with rubber, and planting some 6,000 species of plants from those collected throughout the world. *2350 McGregor Blvd., Fort Myers, tel. 813/334–3614. Admission: $4 adults, $1 children 6–12. Open daily except Thanksgiving and Christmas. Tours 9–4 daily except Sun. 12:30–4.*

Just a few blocks east is the **Fort Myers Historical Museum,** which is housed in a restored railroad depot. Its displays depict the area's history dating back to 1200 BC. *2300 Peck St., Fort Myers, tel. 813/332–5955. Admission: $2 adults, 50 cents children 2–12. Open Tues.–Fri. 9–4:30, weekends 1–5.*

Head northwest to Edwards Drive, which borders the Caloosahatchee River. The **City Yacht Basin** has tour boats that offer sightseeing and luncheon cruises on the river. Also on Edwards Drive, you can find a plethora of shuffleboard courts that weather heavy use on all but the hottest days. Adjacent to the courts is the **Hall of 50 States,** where the Fort Myers Chamber of Commerce dispenses information. *1365 Hendry St. Open weekdays, 9–4.*

Take U.S. 41 north across the Caloosahatchee Bridge into North Fort Myers.

Time Out **Mariner's Inn** (3448 Marinatown Lane, tel. 813/997–8300). Head north on U.S. 41 to the light at Hancock Bridge Parkway. Turn left, and the inn is less than half a mile ahead on the left. The dining room overlooks a busy marina, and the seafood is fresh, varied, and well prepared.

Heading north on U.S. 41 once again, you will find **The Shell Factory** two miles ahead on the right. If you can't find the shells you dreamed of on the beaches, you can buy them here. The Shell Factory is a long-standing tourist attraction that sells shells, shell crafts, and other gifts, souvenirs, and clothing. *Admission free. Open daily 9:30–6.*

2 Adjacent is **Fantasy Isles,** a small amusement park with a fairytale theme. *Tel. 813/997–4204. Admission free, rides 50 cents each. Open daily 10–5 during the winter, reduced hours other seasons.*

Backtracking south on U.S. 41 about two miles, you reach the intersection of Pine Island Road. A right takes you into the
3 heart of **Pine Island,** a classic Old Florida fishing community. Go right on Stringfellow Boulevard and wend your way past mango and citrus groves. Make a left on Pineland Road, a winding palm-lined road, past a Norman Rockwell–like post office and through the village of Pineland, where fishing is still a way of life. Continue north back to Stringfellow Boulevard. In **Bokeelia,** you will enjoy a sweeping view of Charlotte Harbor, one of the country's most pristine bodies of water.

4 On Sanibel, explore the **J. N. "Ding" Darling National Wildlife Refuge**—by car, foot, bicycle, or canoe. The 5,014-acre refuge is home to some 290 species of birds, 50 types of reptiles, and various mammals. A five-mile dirt road meanders through the sanctuary. An observation tower along the road is a prime bird-watching site, especially in the early morning and just before dusk. *Tel. 813/355–5101. Admission: $3 per car or $10 for a duck stamp (which covers all national wildlife refuges).*

5 Board a boat to visit **Cabbage Key,** which sits at Marker 60 on the Intracoastal Waterway. Atop an ancient Calusa Indian shell mound on Cabbage Key is the friendly inn that novelist and playwright Mary Roberts Rinehart built in 1938. Now the inn offers several guest rooms, a marina, and a dining room that is papered in thousands of dollar bills, signed and posted by patrons over the years. *Lunch and dinner tours available through Captiva's 'Tween Waters Inn (tel. 813/472–5161), South Seas Plantation (for guests only, tel. 813/472–5111), and Fishermen's Village in Punta Gorda (tel. 813/639–0969).*

6 Naples

The city and surrounding suburbs are squeezed between the Gulf of Mexico and the wilderness of the Big Cypress National Preserve, which stretches to the Everglades. I–75 and U.S. 41 lead from the north. Alligator Alley and U.S. 41 cut through the Everglades to bring travelers from the east coast.

To get a feel for what this part of Florida was like before humans began draining the swamps, take a drive out Rte. 846 to
7 the **Corkscrew Swamp Sanctuary.** The National Audubon Society manages the 11,000-acre tract to help protect 500-year-old trees and endangered birds, such as the wood storks that nest high in the bald cypress. Visitors taking the 1¾-mile self-guided tour along the boardwalk can glimpse alligators, graceful wading birds, and unusual "air" plants that cling to the sides of trees. *16 mi east of I–75 on Rte. 846, tel. 813/657–3771. Admission: $4 adults, $2 students, children under age 6 free. Open daily 9–6.*

8 If you want to monkey around, head for **Jungle Larry's African Safari Park.** Drive south on U.S. 41 past Mooringline Drive until you see the big sign for Jungle Larry's, then turn left. Here you can see a tiglon—a cross between a tiger and a lion—and other exotic wildlife in a junglelike park. The kids will also enjoy the petting zoo. *1590 Goodlette Rd., tel. 813/262–4053. Admission: $7.95 adults, $5.95 children 3–15. Open 9:30–5:30; shows at 11:30, 2, and 4. Closed Mon., May–Nov.*

Continue along Gulfshore Boulevard and turn left on **Fifth Avenue South,** one of Naples's fashionable shopping areas.

There are additional shops along the streets of **Olde Naples** (3rd St. S).

Head south on U.S. 41 to the **Old Marine Market Place at Tin City** (1200 5th Ave. S). In a collection of former fishing shacks along Naples Bay, entrepreneurs and artisans have set up 40 boutiques, studios, and shops offering everything from scrimshaw to Haitian art.

Time Out **Merriman's Wharf** (1200 5th Ave. S, tel. 813/261–1811), in the Old Marine Market Place, is a good bet for a drink or a seafood lunch—either along the dock or indoors in air-conditioned comfort.

What to See and Do with Children

Adventure Island is a water wonderland in the heart of Tampa, complete with water slides and pools with man-made waves. There are also changing rooms, snack stands, a gift shop, and a video arcade. *1 mi northeast of Busch Gardens. 4545 Bougainvillea Ave., tel. 813/977–6606. Admission: $12.95 per person, children under 2 free. Open daily; closed Jan. and Feb.*

Busch Gardens (*see* Exploring).

Great Explorations! is a museum where you will never be told, "Don't touch!" Everything is designed for a hands-on experience. The museum, which opened in late 1987, is divided into theme rooms, such as the Body Shop, which explores health; the Think Tank, which features mind-stretching puzzles and games; the Touch Tunnel, a 90-foot-long, pitch-black maze you crawl through; and Phenomenal Arts, which displays such items as a Moog music synthesizer (which you can play) and neon-filled tubes that glow in vivid colors when touched. *1120 4th St. S, just off I–275, tel. 813/821–8885. Admission: $3.50 adults, $3 senior citizens, $2.75 children under 8.*

Sarasota Jungle Gardens (*see* Exploring).

Circus Galleries, Ringling Museum (*see* Exploring).

301 Raceway, go-cart rides and a video game room. *4050 N. Washington Blvd. (U.S. 301), Sarasota, tel. 813/355–5588. Open weekdays noon–11, weekends and holidays 11:30–11.*

Nature Center of Lee County and Planetarium offers frequently changing exhibits on wildlife, fossils, Florida Indians, and native habitats. An aviary is home to a variety of permanently disabled birds, including hawks, owls, and bald eagles. There are two miles of nature walks through the cypress swamps. The planetarium offers star shows and Cinema-360 films. *3840 Ortiz Ave., Fort Myers, tel. 813/275–3435. Nature Center admission: 50 cents; Planetarium admission: $3.50 adults, $3 senior citizens, $2.50 children under 12. Open Mon–Sat. 9–4, Sun. 11–4:30.*

Waltzing Waters and Rainbow Golf. Fountains dance with lights and music indoors during the day, outdoors at night. Adjacent is an 18-hole miniature golf course. *18101 U.S. 41 SE (at San Carlos Park), Fort Myers, tel. 813/267–2533. Admission: $6.90 adults, $3.50 children 7–12. Golf $1 with show. Open daily 11–9.*

Everglades Wonder Gardens captures the flavor of untamed Florida with its exhibit of native wildlife and natural surroundings. *U.S. 41, tel. 813/992–2591. Admission: $5 adults, $3 children 5–15. Open daily 9–5.*

Southwest Florida for Free

Bradenton **Manatee Village Historical Park.** An 1860 courthouse, 1887 church, and 1912 settler's home are situated here, as is the Old Manatee Cemetery, which dates back to 1850 and contains the graves of early Manatee settlers. (Appointments necessary to tour the cemetery.) *Rte. 64, 1 mi east of U.S. 41, tel. 813/749–*

7165. Open weekdays 9–5, Sun. 2–5 Sept.–June. Closed Sun. the rest of the year.

The DeSoto National Memorial. On the southern shore of the Manatee River, this place commemorates the first major European exploration of the area. Hernando de Soto and his conquistadors landed in 1539, somewhere between Fort Myers and St. Petersburg. The visitors' center contains relics of DeSoto's era. Films, demonstrations, and nature trail available. *5 mi west of Bradenton on Rte. 64, 2 mi north on 75th St. NW, tel. 813/792–0458. Open daily 8–5:30.*

Fort Myers Naples Area

Youth Museum of Charlotte County. Mostly animal specimens from Africa and North America, plus dolls, shells, and a variety of programs, are displayed here. *260 W. Retta Esplanade, Punta Gorda. Open weekdays 10–5.*

St. Petersburg

Fort de Soto Park. This 900-acre park is composed of six keys: Mullet, Bonne Fortune, Cunningham, Madeleine, St. Christopher, and St. Jean. Fort de Soto, begun during the Spanish-American War, is on the southern end of Mullet Key. *Reach it via 34th St. S., U.S. 19 and the Bayway. Open sunrise to sunset.*

Sarasota

Ringling Museum of Art. This is one of three museums on the grounds of the John and Mable Ringling Estate. A stipulation in the wealthy circus owner's will requires the art museum to be open free every Saturday. *On U.S. 41, 3 mi north of downtown, tel. 813/355–5101. Open 9–5.*

Tampa

Villazon and Co. cigar factory. Free 30-minute guided tours are offered. You'll see the process from the selection of tobacco through the wrapping, banding, and packaging of the cigars. *3104 Armenia Ave., tel. 813/879–2291. Open weekdays 9:30–5. Closed holidays, late Dec.–mid-Jan., and late June–mid-July.*

Shrimp Docks. By late afternoon, the shrimp boats pull in at the 22nd Street causeway to unload their catches.

University of Tampa. Tour the administration building, built in 1890, which served as Theodore Roosevelt's headquarters during the Spanish-American War. *Tours Tues. and Thurs. at 1:30, Sept.–May. Closed holidays. Reservations required, tel. 813/253–6220.*

Tampa Bay Downs and Turf Club. Women are admitted free here on Thursdays. Rte. 580 (Hillsborough Ave.) in Oldsmar. *Races Dec.–mid-Mar.; post time 1 PM. Parking $1. Tel. 813/855–4401.*

Tampa Jai Alai Fronton. This fast-paced and strenuous game is popular among Floridians, even those who don't like to bet. South Dale Mabry Highway and Gandy Boulevard (tel. 813/831–1411). Men are admitted free to Wednesday noon matinees; women to Saturday noon matinees. No one under age 18 admitted. Pari-mutuel betting.

The Suncoast Seabird Sanctuary. This refuge and rehabilitation center for injured birds houses brown pelicans, cormorants, white herons, ospreys, and many other species. Many are on exhibit for public viewing. *18328 Gulf Blvd, tel. 813/391–6211. Admission free, but the nonprofit center accepts donations. Open daily daylight hours.*

Tampa Bay Area

Railroad Historical Museum. Once a railroad station for the Orange Belt Railroad system, this place dates back to 1889. Drawings and relics from the Scottish community are on display. Walking tours of historic areas are available. *341 Main St., Dunedin, tel. 813/733–4151. Open Tues. and Sat. 10–noon, Thurs. 9:30–11:30. Closed June 1–Oct. 1.*

Heritage Park and Museum. A collection of restored pioneer homes and buildings is spread on a 21-acre wooded site. The museum is the park's centerpiece, with exhibits depicting Pinellas County's pioneer lifestyle. Spinning, weaving, and other demonstrations are held regularly. *11909 125th St. N, Largo, tel. 813/462–3474. Open Tues.–Sat. 10–4, Sun. 1–4.*

Suncoast Botanical Gardens. Small by public botanical-garden standards, but all 60 acres are populated with cacti, eucalyptus trees, palms, crepe myrtle, and other flora of the Sunshine State. *10410 125th St., Largo, tel. 813/595–7218. Open daily daylight hours.*

Off the Beaten Track

Boca Grande

Before roads to southwest Florida were even talked about, the wealthy boarded trains to get to the Gasparilla Inn on **Boca Grande.** The small community continues to be a haven for the monied who seek to stay out of the limelight. The grand inn, built in 1912, remains in operation. But the town, and the rest of Gasparilla Island, is worth a trip at any time of year. From U.S. 41 in northern Port Charlotte head southwest on Rte. 776, then south on Rte. 771 into Placida, where a causeway runs out to the island.

While condominiums and other forms of modern sprawl have begun to creep up on Gasparilla, much of Boca Grande looks as it has for a century or more. The mood is set by the old Florida homes, many made of wood, with wide, inviting verandas and wicker rocking chairs.

At the island's southern end is Old Lighthouse Beach, where a historic wooden lighthouse still stands and where there is ample parking and lots of gulf-front beach space. At mid-island is Banyan Street, so named for the huge trees that send down hundreds of shoots, shading the residential street, so that it appears to be twilight much of the day.

There is a generally sleepy ambience to the island, except in the spring, when the tarpon fishermen descend with a vengeance on Boca Grande Pass, considered among the best tarpon-fishing spots in the world.

Time Out

For sustenance, there is **The Pink Elephant** (1 Bayou Ave., tel. 813/964–0100) a casual yet serious Continental-style dining establishment in the heart of Boca Grande. Reservations accepted, but no credit cards.

Everglades City

Nestled amidst the 10,000 Islands, this tiny fishing village is the western gateway to Everglades National Park. From here, you can get a close look at the Everglades, sometimes called the river of grass. **Wooten's** (tel. 813/394–8080) offers airboat and swamp buggy rides through the swamps. Some 200 alligators are on display at Wooten's, too. To get there, drive 35 miles east of Naples on U.S. 41. Rides depart about every 30 minutes.

North Port An early-morning journey in a **hot-air balloon** gives the adventurous a bird's-eye view of a portion of southwest Florida (the portion depending on the prevailing winds). Rides commence (from North Port, south of Venice) early enough to watch the sunrise and are followed by leisurely breakfasts of quiche and champagne. *Contact Trans-America Balloons, North Port, tel. 813/426–7326. Cost: $89 per person, maximum of 3 people.*

Palmdale You aren't likely to happen upon Palmdale, a speck of a town about 40 minutes east of Punta Gorda, unless you make a point of visiting either of two singular attractions. You know you're approaching the **Cypress Knee Museum** when you see spindly hand-carved signs along Rte. 27 with sayings such as Lady, If He Won't Stop, Hit Him on Head with a Shoe. If you are younger than 6 or older than 80, you get in free; otherwise, you pay $2 for entry to Tom Gaskins's world of cypress knees. In the museum are thousands of cypress knees, the knotty, gnarled protuberances that sprout mysteriously from the bases of some cypress trees and grow to resemble all manner of persons and things. There are specimens resembling dogs, bears, ballet dancers' feet, an anteater, Joseph Stalin and Franklin D. Roosevelt. Many require Gaskins's handwritten explanations, such as Lady Hippopotamus Wearing a Carmen Miranda Hat.

After touring the museum, walk the narrow boardwalk through three-quarters of a mile of cypress swamp to see the knees and trees in an unspoiled setting. The diminutive, barefoot man wandering amid the cypress is apt to be the 79-year-old Gaskins, who has appeared twice on Johnny Carson's "Tonight" show to display—what else?—his cypress knees. *1 mi south of the U.S. 27 and U.S. 29 junction, tel. 813/675–2951. Open daily 8 AM–dusk.*

Just two miles southeast on U.S. 27, **Gatorama's** 1,000 alligators and assorted crocodiles await visitors, smiling toothily. Visitors who want to take a good long gander at gators can get their fill here, where a variety of species and sizes cohabit. It's also a commercial gator farm, so you'll see how the "mink" of the leather trade is grown for profit. *Tel. 813/675–0623. Admission: $3.50 adults, $2 children.*

Tampa Though only a mere half-acre, the **Riverside Botanical Gardens** contains a treasure trove of flora collected from around the world. The gardens are on the grounds of William Field's private home, but he and landscape designer Brett Bachelor like visitors. It's located about a mile northwest of downtown Tampa, on the banks of the Hillsborough River. *2402 Riverside Dr., tel. 813/251–6496. Open Mon.–Sat. 8–4. Closed Sun. For a guided tour, call ahead.*

Shopping

Most visitors eventually get their quota of sun, sand, and surf and find themselves in need of something else to do. For many, that something is shopping.

Gift Ideas It is a rare vacationer who does not leave the state with at least one sack of oranges or grapefruit. Most produce stands are open during the citrus season (Dec.–Mar.). Though U-pick fields are plentiful, you cannot take citrus out of state without a

USDA inspection sticker, so make sure you take only those sacks that are properly sealed.

In Tarpon Springs, natural sponges are plentiful and reasonably priced. Many shops along Dodecanese Boulevard, the town's main street, sell a variety of locally harvested sponges.

Tampa's Ybor City is a thriving Cuban community where the art of cigar making lives on. There are many small cigar shops in the area on Tampa's east side.

Shell items—jewelry, lamps, plant hangers, and such—are among the more kitschy commodities found in abundance in the region. Sanibel Island, one of the world's premier shelling grounds, has numerous shops that sell shell products (including two named She Sells Seashells, at 1983 and 1157 Periwinkle Way). **The Shell Factory** in North Fort Myers claims to have the world's largest display of seashells and coral. *2787 N. Tamiami Trail (U.S. 41). Open daily 9–6.*

Fine Shopping Those who gravitate toward exclusive boutiques have a wealth of them to explore in southwest Florida. In Sarasota, St. Armand's Key (just west of downtown Sarasota) has Harding Circle, a circular string of shops and restaurants that cater to consumers seeking out-of-the-ordinary items and willing to pay high prices for them.

In Fort Myers, there are two such centers—**Bell Tower** (U.S. 41 and Daniels Rd., South Fort Myers) and **Royal Palm Square** (Colonial Blvd., between McGregor Blvd. and U.S. 41). Both have about 36 shops and restaurants. Both are worth visiting if just to look at the elegant tropical landscaping, which includes ponds full of huge oriental carp and parrots that stand sentry from perches among the palms. Neither center is enclosed, but both have covered sidewalks. In Naples, 3rd and 5th streets south are lined with fine boutiques and restaurants.

Flea Markets **Wagonwheel** is 100-plus acres containing some 2,000 vendors and a variety of food concessions. Parking costs $1. There is a tram from the parking lot to the vendor area. *7801 Park Blvd., Pinellas Park, tel. 813/544–5319. Open weekends 8–4.*

Red Barn has the requisite big red barn, in which vendors operate daily except Mondays. The number of vendors increases to about 1,000 on weekends. *1707 1st St. E, Bradenton. Open weekends 8–4.*

Dome has sheltered walkways under which can be found dozens of stalls selling new and recycled wares. *Rte. 775, west of U.S. 41, Venice. Open weekends 9–4; closed Aug.*

Ortiz also features covered walkways and hundreds of vendors selling new and used items. *Ortiz and Anderson avenues, east of Fort Myers. Open weekends 8–4.*

Beaches

You can't drive on them like you can in Daytona. And the scantily attired college-age revelers who pack Fort Lauderdale each spring are not found in abundance here. But there are myriad reasons why a growing number of Florida-bound beach goers are heading to the southwest coast. For sun worshipers, there are beaches on which to bask in relative solitude; for singles, there are sands on which to see and be seen; for shell collectors, there is treasure to unearth. And not one beach offers less than a spectacular sunset.

Charlotte County

Englewood Beach, near the Charlotte-Sarasota county line, is popular with teenagers, although beach goers of all ages frequent it. In addition to a wide and shell-littered beach, there are barbecue grills, picnic facilities, and a playground.

Collier County

Bonita Springs Public Beach is 10 minutes from the I–75 exit at Bonita Beach Road, on the southern end of Bonita Beach. There are picnic tables, free parking, and nearby refreshment stands and shopping.

Delnor–Wiggins Pass State Recreation Area is at the gulf end of Bluebill Avenue, off Vanderbilt Drive in North Naples. The well-maintained park offers miles of sandy beaches, lifeguards, barbecue grills, picnic tables, a boat ramp, observation tower, rest rooms with wheelchair access, lots of parking space, bathhouses, and showers. Fishing is best in Wiggins Pass at the north end of the park. Admission: $1 for the operator of a vehicle, plus 50 cents per passenger. Boat launching costs $1. No alcoholic beverages allowed.

Lowdermilk Park stretches along Gulf Shore Boulevard in Naples. There are 1,000 feet of beach plus parking, rest rooms, showers, a pavilion, vending machines, and picnic tables. No alcoholic beverages or fires permitted.

Tigertail Beach is on Hernando Drive at the south end of Marco Island. Singles and families congregate here. Facilities: parking, concession stand, picnic area, sailboat rentals, volleyball, rest rooms, and showers.

Lee County

Estero Island, otherwise known as **Fort Myers Beach,** is 18 miles from downtown Fort Myers. It has numerous public accesses to the beach, which is frequented by families and young singles. In most areas, you are never far from civilization, with houses, condominiums, and hotels nestled along the shore. The island's shores slope gradually into the usually tranquil and warm Gulf waters, affording a safe swimming area for children. From Fort Myers, it is reached via San Carlos Boulevard; from Naples and Bonita Springs, via Hickory Boulevard.

Lynn Hall Memorial Park is on Estero Boulevard, in the more commercial northern part of Fort Myers Beach. Singles can be found playing in the gentle surf or sunning and socializing on shore. A number of night spots and restaurants are within easy walking distance. A free fishing pier adjoins the public beach. Facilities: picnic tables, barbecue grills, playground equipment, and a bathhouse with rest rooms.

Carl E. Johnson Recreation Area is just south of Fort Myers Beach. The admission of $1 per adult, 50 cents per child includes a round-trip tram ride from the park entrance to Lovers Key, on which the park is situated. Shelling, bird-watching, fishing, canoeing, and nature walks in an unspoiled setting are the main attractions here. There are also rest rooms, picnic tables, a snack bar, and basic showers.

Sanibel and **Captiva** islands are about 23 miles from Fort Myers and are reached via a toll bridge on the Sanibel Causeway. Though the $3 round-trip toll may seem steep, avid shell collectors and nature enthusiasts are apt to get their money's worth. Sanibel beaches are rated among the best shelling grounds in the world. For the choicest pickings, get there as the tide is going out or just after a storm. Windsurfers need go only as far as the Sanibel causeway to find a suitable place to set sail.

Gulfside Park, off Casa Ybel Road, is a lesser-known and less-populated beach, ideal for those who seek solitude and do not require facilities.

Lighthouse Park, at Sanibel's southern end, attracts a mix of families, shellers, and singles. Rest rooms are available. One of the draws is a historic old lighthouse.

Bowman's Beach is mainly a family beach on Sanibel's northwest end, but naturists have been known to bathe unabashedly in more secluded areas of the beach.

Manatee County

Anna Maria Island, just west of the Sunshine Skyway Bridge, boasts three public beaches. **Anna Maria Bayfront Park,** at the north end of the municipal pier, is a secluded beach fronting both the Intracoastal Waterway and the Gulf of Mexico. Facilities include picnic grounds, a playground, rest rooms, showers, and lifeguards. At mid-island, in the town of Holmes Beach, is **Manatee County Beach,** popular with all ages. It has picnic facilities, a snack bar, showers, rest rooms, and lifeguards. At the island's southern end is **Coquina Beach,** popular with singles and families. Facilities: picnic area, boat ramp, playground, refreshment stand, rest rooms, showers, and lifeguards.

Egmont Key lies just off the northern tip of Anna Maria Island. On it is Fort Dade, a military fort built in 1900 during the Spanish-American War, and Florida's sixth brightest lighthouse. The primary inhabitant of the two-mile-long island is the threatened gopher tortoise. The only way to get to the island is by boat. Shellers will find the trip rewarding. An excursion boat makes trips on Tuesday and Thursday. The *Miss Cortez* departs from Cortez, just west of Bradenton (tel. 813/794–1223).

Cortez Beach, on the mainland, just north of Coquina, is on Gulf Boulevard in the town of Bradenton Beach. This one's popular with those who like their beaches without facilities—nothing but sand, water, and trees. The Palma Sola Causeway takes Manatee Avenue on the mainland to Anna Maria Island and also offers beach goers a long, sandy beach fronting Palma Sola Bay. There are boat ramps, a dock, and picnic tables.

Greer Island Beach is at the northern tip of the next barrier island south on Longboat Key. It's accessible by boat or via North Shore Boulevard. The secluded peninsula has a wide beach and excellent shelling, but no facilities.

Pinellas County

Tarpon Springs has two public beaches: **Howard Park Beach,** where a lifeguard is on duty daily 8:30–6 Easter through Labor Day, and **Sunset Beach,** where there is similar lifeguard duty as well as rest rooms, picnic tables, grills, and a boat ramp.

Caladesi Island State Park lies three miles off Dunedin's coast, across Hurricane Pass. The 600-acre park is one of the state's few remaining undeveloped barrier islands. It's accessible only by boat. There is a beach on the gulf side and mangroves on the bay side. This is a good spot for swimming, fishing, shelling, boating, and nature study. A self-guided nature trail winds through the island's interior. Park rangers are available to answer questions. Facilities: boardwalks, picnic shelters, bathhouses, a ranger station, and concession stand. A ferry runs regularly between Caladesi Island and Honeymoon Island to the north. Call for ferry information (tel. 813/734– 5263).

Clearwater Beach is another popular, more accessible island beach. It is south of Caladesi on a narrow island between Clearwater Harbor and the gulf. It is connected to downtown Clearwater by Memorial Causeway. Facilities: marina, concessions, showers, rest rooms, and lifeguards.

The St. Petersburg beaches are numerous and wide-ranging in character.

Bay Beach (North Shore Dr. and 13th Ave. NE, on Tampa Bay) charges 10 cents admission. It has showers and shelters.

North Shore Beach (901 North Shore Dr. NE) charges $1 admission. Facilities: pool, beach umbrellas, cabanas, windbreaks, and lounges.

Maximo Park Beach (34 St. and Pinellas Point Dr. S) is on Boca Ciega Bay. There is no lifeguard. There is a picnic area with grills, tables, shelters, and a boat ramp.

St. Petersburg Municipal Beach (11260 Gulf Blvd.) is a free beach on Treasure Island. There are dressing rooms, metered parking, and a snack bar.

Pass-a-Grille Beach, on the gulf, has parking meters, a snack bar, rest rooms, and showers.

Fort DeSoto Park consists of the southernmost beaches of St. Petersburg, on five islands totaling some 900 acres. Facilities: two fishing piers, picnic sites overlooking lagoons, a waterskiing and boating area, and miles of beaches for swimming. Open daily until dark. To get there, take the Pinellas Bayway through three toll gates (cost: 65 cents).

Sarasota County

The county contains 10 beaches, ranging from five to 113 acres. **South Lido,** at the southern tip of Lido Key, is among the largest and best beaches in the region. The sugar-sand beach offers little for shell collectors, but the interests of virtually all other beach lovers are served on its 100 acres, which probably accounts for the diverse mix of people it attracts. Facilities: fishing, nature trails, volleyball, playground, horseshoes, rest rooms, and picnic grounds.

Siesta Beach is on Beach Road on Siesta Key. The 40-acre park contains nature trails, a concession stand, soccer and softball fields, picnicking facilities, play equipment, rest rooms, and tennis and volleyball courts.

Turtle Beach is farther south on Siesta Key's Midnight Pass Road. Though only 14 acres, it includes boat ramps, horseshoe courts, picnic and play facilities, a recreation building, rest rooms, and a volleyball court.

North Jetty Park is at the south end of Casey Key, a slender barrier island. It's a favorite for family outings. Amenities include rest rooms, a concession stand, play and picnic equipment, fishing, horseshoes, and a volleyball court.

Nokomis Beach is just north of North Jetty on Albee Road. Its facilities are similar to those at North Jetty, except that it has two boat ramps and no horseshoe court.

Caspersen Beach, on Beach Drive in south Venice, is the county's largest park. It has a nature trail, fishing, picnicking, rest rooms, plus lots of beach for those who prefer space to a wealth of amenities. Along with a plentiful mix of shells, observant beachcombers are likely to find sharks' teeth on Venice beaches, washed up from the ancient shark burial grounds just offshore.

Manasota Key spans much of the county's southern coast, from south of Venice to Englewood. It has two choice beaches: *Manasota*, on Manasota Beach Road, with a boat ramp, picnic area and rest rooms; and *Blind Pass*, where you can fish and swim but will find no amenities.

Participant Sports

Biking Call the nearest chamber of commerce or bike store for the best bike paths. Two of the best are at Boca Grande and Sanibel Island.

Tampa Bay. There are many places to rent bikes, but not much in the way of bike paths. Rental stores include **Clearwater:** *Chainwheel Drive* (tel. 813/367–5001); **St. Petersburg:** *The Beach Cyclist* (7517 Blindpass Rd., tel. 813/367–5001) and *Village Bike Shops* (7326 Central Ave., tel. 813/381–6667 and 2236 62nd Ave., tel. 813/867–6667); **Largo:** *D & S Bicycle Shop* (2073 Seminole Blvd., tel. 813/393–0300); and **Tarpon Springs:** *Bi-Sick* (tel. 813/937–3030).

Sarasota/Bradenton. No bike paths. Rental shops include **Bradenton:** *Bicycle Center* (2610 Cortez Rd., tel. 813/756–5480); **Sarasota:** *Mr. CB's* (1249 Stickney Point Rd., tel. 813/349–4400), *Backyard Bike Shop* (5440 Gulf of Mexico Dr., tel. 813/383–6341); and *Pedal N Wheels* (Merchants Pointe Shopping Center, 2881 Clark Rd., tel. 813/922–0481); and **Venice:** *The Bike Doctor* (291 Trott Circle, tel. 813/426–4807); and *Bicycles International* (1744 Tamiami Trail S, [U.S. 41], tel. 813/497–1590).

Fort Myers/Naples. There are several bike paths in the area. **Boca Grande,** an hour's drive from Fort Myers or Sarasota, has good bike paths. Rentals are available at *Fun Rentals* (4th St., tel. 813/964–2070). **Fort Myers:** The best choice here is the path along Summerlin Road. For rental, try *Trikes & Bikes* (3234 Fowler St., tel. 813/936–4301). **Sanibel:** The island's extensive bike path is well used. It is in good condition and runs throughout the island, keeping bikers safely apart from the traffic and allowing them some time for reflection on the waterways and wildlife they will encounter. Rent bikes at *Finnimore's Cycle Shop* (1223 Periwinkle Way, Sanibel, tel. 813/472–5577) and *Jim's Bike & Scooter Rental* (11534 Andy Rossi La., Captiva, tel. 813/472–1296). **Naples:** *Pop's Bicycles* (4265 Bonita Beach Rd., Bonita Springs, tel. 813/947–4442) and *A to Z Rental Center* (990 3rd Ave. N, tel. 813/262–6551). **Mar-co Island:** *A to Z Rental Center* (Marco Town Center, tel. 813/394–4010).

Canoeing For those who like to travel slowly and under their own power, canoe rentals abound. Among them are **Art's Swap Shop** (Tampa, tel. 813/935–4011), canoe and car racks for rent; and **Myakka River State Park,** 15 miles south of Sarasota near Venice (tel. 813/924–1027), canoes, paddles, and life vests for rent. **Canoe Outpost** offers half-day, full-day, and overnight canoe-camping trips from a number of southwest Florida locations, including Little Manatee River (18001 U.S. 301 S, Wimauma, just north of Sarasota, tel. 813/634–2228) and Peace River (Rte. 7, Box 301, Arcadia, 25 miles east of Port Charlotte, tel. 813/494–1215). **Lakes Park** in Fort Myers (tel. 813/481–7946) rents canoes on waterways where you can see the carp swimming, and, if you are quiet enough, some herons and osprey flying overhead; **Canoe Safari** (Arcadia, tel. 813/494–7865) has half- and full-day trips, plus overnighters including camping equipment; **Parkland Ventures** (Fort Myers, tel. 813/482–1328) has guided nature treks in canoes or kayaks; and **Tarpon Bay Marina** (Sanibel, tel. 813/472–8900) has canoes and equipment for exploring the waters of the J. N. "Ding" Darling National Wildlife Refuge.

Fishing Anglers flock to southwest Florida. You need very little to get started—a rod and reel will suffice. Just wander out to a bridge and cast off. Tampa Bay and its inlets are known for yielding tarpon, kingfish, and speckled trout. Snapper, grouper, sea trout, snook, sheephead, and shark are among the species to be found throughout the region. You can also charter your own boat or join a group on a party boat for full- or half-day outings.

Party boats in the area include **Flying Fish** (Marina Jack's, U.S. 41 and bay front, Sarasota, tel. 813/366–3373), **L-C Marine** (215 Tamiami Trail S., [U.S. 41], Venice, tel. 813/484–9044), **Cecil Charter Service** (Burnt Store Marina, Punta Gorda, tel. 813/637–7758), **Gulf Star Marina** (708 Fisherman's Wharf, Fort Myers Beach, tel. 813/463–2219), **Lehman's Fishing Charters** (Bokeelia, tel. 813/283–2217), **Deep Sea Charter Fishing** (Old Marine Market Place, Naples, tel. 813/263–8171).

Golf Courses open to the public include **Apollo Beach Club** (Tampa, tel. 813/645–6212), **Babe Zaharias Golf Course** (Tampa, tel. 813/932–4401), **Rocky Point Golf Course** (Tampa, tel. 813/884–5141), **Clearwater Golf Park** (Clearwater, tel. 813/447–5272); **Dunedin Country Club** (Dunedin, tel. 813/733–7836), **Pasadena Golf Club** (St. Petersburg, tel. 813/345–9329), **Manatee County** (Bradenton, tel. 813/792–6773), **Bobby Jones** (Sarasota, tel. 813/955–8097), **Forest Lake** (Sarasota, tel. 813/922–1312), **Longboat Key** (Longboat Key, tel. 813/383–8821), **Bird Bay Executive** (Venice, tel. 813/485–9333), **North Port** (North Port, tel. 813/426–2804), **Deep Creek Golf Club** (Charlotte Harbor, tel. 813/625–6911), **Bay Beach Club Executive** (Fort Myers Beach, tel. 813/463–2064), **Cypress Pines Country Club** (Lehigh Acres, tel. 813/369–8216), **Fort Myers Country Club** (Fort Myers, tel. 813/936–2457), **Pelican's Nest** (Bonita Springs, tel. 813/947–4600), and **Hibiscus Country Club** (Naples, tel. 813/774–3559).

Motorboating Much of southwest Florida's charm lies beyond its shoreline. Fortunately, there are many concerns that rent boats of all sizes.

In Sarasota, **Don and Mike's Boat and Ski Rental** (tel. 813/366–6659) has water skis, jet skis, Windsurfers, wavejammers, and miniboats plus instruction in windsurfing and waterskiing. At Marina Jack and Island Park, downtown waterfront of Sarasota.

Siesta Key Marina (1265 Stickney Point Rd., Siesta Key, tel. 813/349–8880) has pontoon boats available for half- or full-day rentals.

Harbor Boat Rental (Albee and Circuit Rds., Nokomis, tel. 813/485–3076) has 15-foot boats for rent by the hour, day or week. Bait and tackle available.

Boat House of Sanibel (Sanibel Marina, tel. 813/472–2531) rents power- or sailboats.

Getaway Bait and Boat Rental (1091 San Carlos Blvd., Fort Myers Beach, tel. 813/466–3200) rents powerboats and fishing equipment and sells bait.

Brookside Marina (2023 Davis Blvd., Naples, tel. 813/263–7250) rents 15- to 24-foot powerboats.

Sailing Sailing schools and guided or bare-boat rentals are plentiful. Spend a week learning the ropes or a few hours luxuriating on a sunset cruise.

Gulfcoast Sailboat Charters (9600 W. Gulf Blvd., Treasure Island, tel. 813/367–4444); **O'Leary's Sarasota Sailing School** (near Marina Jack's, U.S. 41 and the bay front, Sarasota, tel. 813/953–7505) offers sailing charters and instruction at all levels; **Boat House of Sanibel** (Sanibel Marina, tel. 813/472–2531); **Wheel and Keel** (1668 I St., Fort Myers Beach, tel. 813/463–5363) rents catamarans, Sunfishes, and Windsurfers; **CSA Charters** (110 Gulf Shore Blvd. N, Naples, tel. 813/649–0091); and **Marco Island Sea Excursions** (1281 Jamaica Rd., Marco Island, tel. 813/642–6400).

Scuba Diving Dive shops are found all over the region. However, most make excursions to the Florida Keys or the east coast of Florida rather than dive in this area.

Tennis Many hotels and motels in Florida have outdoor tennis courts, some lighted for night use. For those who are motivated to find other courts, a list of public ones follows:

City of Tampa Courts (15 Columbia Dr, Davis Islands, Tampa, tel. 813/253–3782), **Arlington Park and Recreation Center** (Bath & Racquet Athletic Club, Sarasota, tel. 813/921–6675), **Cedar Tennis Club** (Longboat Key, tel. 813/383–6461), **Port Charlotte Tennis Club** (22400 Gleneagles Terrace, Port Charlotte tel. 813/625–7222), **Bay Beach Racquet Club** (120 Lenell St., Fort Myers Beach, tel. 813/463–4473), **The Dunes** (949 Sand Castle Rd., Sanibel, tel. 813/472–3522), and **Forest Hills Racquet Club** (100 Forest Hills Blvd., Naples, tel. 813/774–2442).

Spectator Sports

Baseball The season comes early to Florida with the annual convergence of the Grapefruit League—seventeen major league teams offer exhibitions in March and April. These teams hold their spring training in southwest Florida. For information on all the teams, tel. 904/488–0990. Home bases for area teams are Bradenton: **Pittsburgh Pirates** (McKechnie Field, 9th St. W and 16th Ave., tel. 813/748–4610); Clearwater: **Philadelphia Phillies** (Jack Russell Stadium, Seminole and Greenwood Ave., tel. 813/442–8496); Dunedin: **Toronto Blue Jays** (Grant Field, 311 Douglas Ave., North of Rte. 88, tel. 813/733–0429); Port Charlotte: **Texas Rangers** (Charlotte County Stadium, Rte. 776, tel. 813/625–9500); St. Petersburg: **St. Louis Cardinals** (Al Lang Stadium, 1st St. and 2nd Ave., tel. 813/893–7490); Sarasota: **Chicago White Sox** (Payne Park, U.S. 301 and Ringling Blvd., tel. 813/953–3388); and Tampa: **Cincinnati Reds** (Al Lopez Field, Dale Mabry Hwy. and Tampa Bay Blvd., tel. 813/873–8617).

Football NFL football comes in the form of the **Tampa Bay Buccaneers,** who play at Tampa Stadium (4201 N. Dale Mabry Hwy.). For information, tel. 800/282–0683 or 813/461–2700.

Soccer The lone competitor in the area is the **Tampa Bay Rowdies** (tel. 813/877–7800). The team plays indoors at the Bayfront Center (400 1st St., St. Petersburg) and outside at Tampa Stadium in Tampa.

Gambling Casino gambling has yet to find its way into the state, but the odds are that there are more than enough alternatives to suit bettors. There is **horse racing** at Tampa Bay Downs (Race Track Rd. off Rte. 580, Oldsmar, tel. 813/855–4401, with Thoroughbred races Dec.–Mar.) **Dog racing** occurs somewhere in the region all year: Jan.–May at Derby Lane (10490 Gandy Blvd., St. Peterburg, tel. 813/576–1361); Sept.–Jan. at Tampa Greyhound Track. (8300 N. Nebraska Ave., Tampa, tel. 813/932–4313); June–Sept. at the Sarasota Kennel Club (5400 Bradenton Rd., Sarasota, tel. 813/355– 7744); and Oct.–Aug. at the Naples–Fort Myers Kennel Club (10601 Bonita Beach Rd., Bonita Springs, tel. 813/334–6555). **Jai alai** is offered at the Tampa Jai-Alai Fronton (S. Dale Mabry Hwy. and Gandy Blvd., Tampa, tel. 813/831–1411) Jan.– mid-June. Big-time **bingo** can be found at the singular Seminole Bingo Hall (5221 Orient Rd., Tampa, tel. 800/282–7016), run by the Seminole Indians. Jackpots regularly exceed $60,000.

Dining and Lodging

Dining. As in most coastal regions, fresh seafood is plentiful. Raw bars, serving just-plucked-from-the-bay oysters, clams, and mussels, are everywhere. The region's ethnic diversity is also well represented. Tarpon Springs adds a hearty helping of classic Greek specialties such as moussaka, a ground meat and eggplant pie, and baklava, delicate layers of pastry and nuts soaked in honey. In Tampa, the cuisine is Cuban. Standard menu items include black beans and rice and paella, a seafood, chicken, and saffroned-rice casserole. In Sarasota, the accent is on the Continental, both in food and service. Heading toward Fort Myers and Naples, seafood reigns supreme, especially the succulent claw of the stone crab, in season October 15–May 15. It's usually served with drawn butter or a tangy mustard sauce. There are some people who proclaim its flavor superior to that of lobster.

The most highly recommended restaurants in each price category are indicated by a star ★.

Category	Cost*
Very Expensive	over $60
Expensive	$40–$60
Moderate	$20–$40
Inexpensive	under $20

**per person without tax (6% in Florida), service, or drinks*

The following credit card abbreviations are used: AE, American Express; CB, Carte Blanche; DC, Diners Club; MasterCard; V, Visa.

Lodging. There are old historic hotels and ultramodern chrome-and-glass high rises, sprawling resorts and cozy inns, luxurious waterfront lodges and just-off-the-highway budget motels. In general, inland rooms are considerably cheaper than those on the islands. The most expensive accommodations are those with waterfront views. Rates are highest mid-December–mid-April. The lowest prices are available May–November. Many apartment-motels are springing up in the area and can prove economical for families that wish to prepare some of their own meals or for groups who can share an apartment. Price categories listed below apply to winter rates. Many drop to a less expensive category at other times of the year.

Category	Cost*
Very Expensive	over $120
Expensive	$90–$120
Moderate	$50–$90
Inexpensive	under $50

**per person, double occupancy, without 6% state sales tax and nominal (1%–3%) tourist tax.*

Bradenton
Dining

High Seas. Choose the open deck or the wood-and-brass interior of this establishment that looks out on sparkling Palma Sola Bay. Continental cuisine is featured, with an emphasis on fresh seafood. *9915 Manatee Ave. W, tel. 813/792–4776. Dress: casual. Reservations suggested. AE, CB, DC, MC, V. Moderate.*

Charlie Brown's. Lots of antiques and collectibles here create a turn-of-the-century decor. A menu laden with steaks and fresh seafoods poses a difficult choice for diners. *7051 Manatee Ave. W, tel. 813/794–3138. Dress: casual. Reservations for parties of 10 or more. AE, CB, DC, MC, V. Moderate.*

Lodging

Holiday Inn Riverfront. A Spanish Mediterranean–style motor inn near the Manatee River. *100 Riverfront Dr. W 34205, tel. 813/747–3727. Facilities: restaurant, lounge, pool, whirlpool, marina. AE, CB, DC, MC, V. Moderate.*

Cape Coral
Dining

Cape Crab House. Crabs are served Maryland-style—with mallet and pliers and heaped on a tablecloth of newspaper. *Coralwood Mall, Del Prado Blvd., tel. 813/574–2722. Dress: casual. Reservations accepted. AE, MC, V. Moderate.*

★ **Chan's Hunan.** No egg *foo young* or chop suey here. The hot-and-sour soup is just that, and the *kao pao* chicken combines chicken, peanuts, and a zesty sauce with just a bit of bite. *4725 Del Prado Blvd., tel. 813/549–2119. Dress: casual. No reservations. AE, MC, V. Inexpensive.*

Siam Hut. Thai music pings and twangs in the background while the dishes do the same to your tastebuds. Get it fiery hot or extra mild. Specialties: *Pad Thai* (a mixture of noodles, crushed peanuts, chicken, shrimp, egg, bean sprouts, and scallions) and crispy Siam rolls (spring rolls stuffed with ground chicken, bean thread, and vegetables). *1873 Del Prado Blvd. (Coral Pointe Shopping Center), tel. 813/772–3131. Dress: casual. No reservations. AE, MC, V. Closed Mon. Inexpensive.*

Lodging **Cape Coral Inn & Country Club.** A resort for golf and tennis enthusiasts who also seek economy. Understated decor reflects the sporty atmosphere. *4003 Palm Tree Blvd. 33904, tel. 813/542-3191. Facilities: restaurant, lounge, golf, driving range, tennis, pool, baby-sitting. AE, CB, DC, MC, V. Moderate.*

Quality Inn. Conveniently located in downtown Cape Coral. *1538 Cape Coral Pkwy. 33904, tel. 813/542-2121. Facilities: restaurant, lounge, and pool; pets accepted. AE, CB, DC, MC, V. Moderate.*

Clearwater
Dining **The Kapok Tree.** A cluster of dining rooms serving steak and seafood overlook tropical gardens. A strolling minstrel performs. *923 McMullen Booth Rd., tel. 813/726-0504. Dress: casual. Reservations suggested. AE, CB, DC, MC, V. Moderate.*

Bob Heilman's Beachcomber. Southern-fried chicken and mashed potatoes with gravy have long been the Sunday staple at this 75-year-old restaurant. Also known for its seafood, homemade desserts, and hearty portions. *447 Mandalay Ave., Clearwater Beach, tel. 813/442-4144. Dress: casual. Reservations suggested. AE, DC, MC, V. Moderate.*

94th Aero Squadron. On the west side of the Clearwater–St. Petersburg Airport, this restaurant, set in a French farmhouse, has a classic World War I aviation theme. Steaks are the house specialty. *94 Fairchild Dr., tel. 813/536-0409. Dress: informal. Reservations suggested. AE, CB, DC, MC, V. Moderate.*

Lodging **Belleview Biltmore Hotel & Spa.** This large, historic resort on Clearwater Bay has extensive facilities and transportation to the beach. *25 Belleview Blvd. 34616, tel. 813/442-6171. Facilities: restaurant, lounge, pools, whirlpools, saunas, golf, tennis, bicycles, playground, fishing, sailboats. AE, CB, DC, MC, V. Very Expensive.*

Adam's Mark Caribbean Gulf Resort. Situated on the gulf shore, this modern resort offers comfort. A taste of the islands is provided by the steel-drum band that plays poolside. *430 S. Gulfview Blvd. 34630, tel. 813/443-5714. Facilities: restaurants, lounge, beach, pool, wading pool, whirlpool. AE, CB, DC, MC, V. Expensive.*

Sheraton Sand Key Resort. A resort for those who want lots of sun, sand, and surf. Balconies and patios overlook the gulf and well-manicured grounds. *1160 Gulf Blvd., Clearwater Beach 33515, tel. 813/595-1611. Facilities: restaurant, lounge, pool, wading pool, beach, whirlpool, playground, tennis courts, windsurfing, sailboats. AE, CB, DC, MC, V. Expensive.*

Comfort Inn–St. Petersburg/Clearwater Airport. This is a comfortable, unpretentious motor inn near the airport and Tampa Bay. *3580 Ulmerton Rd. (Rte. 688) 34622, tel. 813/577-1171. Facilities: restaurant, pool, whirlpool, fitness center. AE, CB, DC, MC, V. Moderate.*

Fort Myers
Dining **La Tiers.** Serious cuisine served with Continental flair and flavor. An extensive menu includes seviche (sea scallops marinated in lime juice and served with ground green chilies, tomatoes, and spices), conch chowder with hazelnuts, and broiled lobster and chicken breast in champagne sauce. *Sheraton Harbor Place Hotel, 2500 Edwards Dr., tel. 813/337-0300. Dress: Dressy. Reservations advised. AE, CB, DC, MC, V. Expensive.*

★ **The Prawnbroker.** Its ads urge you to scratch and sniff. There is no odor, says the ad, because fresh fish does not have one. What there is is an abundance of seafood seemingly just plucked from gulf waters, plus some selections for landlubbers. Almost always crowded. *6535 McGregor Blvd. tel. 813/489–2226. Dress: stylishly casual. Reservations accepted. AE, MC, V. Moderate.*

Smitty's Beef Room. An old and reliable local restaurant, offering an assortment of steaks, prime rib, and seafood. A great meat-and-potatoes place that is popular with locals and visitors. *2240 W. 1st St., tel. 813/334–4415. Dress: casual. AE, CB, DC, MC, V. Moderate.*

The Veranda. Within a sprawling turn-of-the-century home is served an imaginative assortment of American regional cuisine. This is a popular place for business and governmental bigwigs to rub elbows. *2122 2nd St., tel. 813/332–2065. Dress: stylishly casual. AE, CB, DC, MC, V. Moderate.*

Miami Connection. If you hunger for choice chopped liver, lean-but-tender corned beef, and a chewy bagel, this kosher-style deli can fill the bill. The sandwiches are huge. It is, as the local restaurant critic aptly said, "the real McCohen." *11506 Cleveland Ave. or 2112 2nd St., tel. 813/936–3811. Dress: casual. No reservations. No credit cards. Inexpensive.*

Woody's Bar-B-Q. A no-frills barbecue pit featuring chicken, ribs, and beef in copious amounts at bargain-basement prices. *6701 N. Tamiami Trail (U.S. 41), North Fort Myers, tel. 813/997–1424. Dress: casual. No reservations. MC, V. Inexpensive.*

Lodging

Sanibel Sonesta Harbour Resort. This high-rise apartment hotel sits on the east side of the Sanibel Causeway, not quite in Fort Myers, not quite on Sanibel. It overlooks San Carlos Bay and has a full complement of amenities. *7260 Harbor Point 33908, tel. 813/466–4000. Facilities: restaurant, lounge, pools, health club, tennis, whirlpool. AE, DC, MC, V. Very Expensive.*

Sheraton Harbor Place. Opened two years ago, this high-rise hotel commands a dominant spot on the downtown Fort Myers skyline, rising above the Caloosahatchee River and Fort Myers Yacht Basin. *2500 Edwards Dr. 33901, tel. 813/337–0300. Facilities: baby-sitting, a game room, whirlpool, dock, exercise room. AE, DC, MC, V. Expensive.*

Best Western Robert E. Lee Motor Inn. Rooms are spacious, with patios or balconies overlooking the Caloosahatchee River. *6611 U.S. 41N, North Fort Myers 33903, tel. 813/997–5511. Facilities: lounge, pool, dock. AE, CB, DC, MC, V. Moderate.*

Fort Myers Beach

Dining

★ **The Mucky Duck.** Slightly more formal than its waterfront sister restaurant on Captiva, this restaurant concentrates on fresh, well-prepared seafood. A popular dish is the bacon-wrapped barbecue shrimp. *2500 Estero Blvd., tel. 813/463–5519. Dress: casual. Reservations for large parties only. AE, MC, V. Moderate.*

Snug Harbor. Casual, rustic atmosphere is evident at this seafood restaurant on the harbor at Fort Myers Beach. *645 San Carlos Blvd., tel. 813/463–4343. Dress: casual. No reservations. AE, MC, V. Moderate.*

Lodging

Seawatch-on-the-Beach. A modern seven-story hotel with two-bedroom suites. Each has a whirlpool, kitchen, and a view of the gulf. *6550 Estero Blvd. 33931, tel. 813/481–3636. Facilities:*

beach, pool, tennis, baby-sitting. AE, MC, V. Very Expensive.

The Boathouse Beach Resort. A nautical theme pervades this all-suite hotel, with lots of teak and brass throughout. *7630 Estero Blvd. 33931, tel. 813/481–3636 or 800/237–8906 outside FL. Facilities: kitchens, beach, pool, whirlpool, shuffleboard. AE, MC, V. Expensive.*

Sandpiper Gulf Resort. Gulf-front apartment-motel. *5550 Estero Blvd. 33931, tel. 813/463–5721. Facilities: pools, beach, whirlpool, playground, shuffleboard. MC, V. Moderate.*

Marco Island
Dining

Marco Lodge Waterfront Restaurant & Lounge. Built in 1869, this is Marco's oldest landmark. Fresh local seafood and Cajun entrees are features, as is live Dixieland jazz Tuesday–Saturday. *1 Papaya St., Goodland, tel. 813/394–3302. Dress: casual. Reservations suggested. AE, DC, MC, V. Moderate.*

★ **European Cafe Restaurant.** A small and intimate European-style cafe specializing in seafood and Continental cuisine. Pompano is prepared in a multitude of ways. All fish comes from the family-owned fish market. Owned and operated by Kare DeMartino, a fifth-generation Marco Islander. *918 Collier Blvd., tel. 813/394–7578. Dress: casual. Reservations accepted. AE, MC, V. Inexpensive.*

Lodging

Eagle's Nest Beach Resort. This resort contains one- and two-bedroom villas (with French doors opening onto screened patios) clustered around a large tropical garden and a high rise with two-bedroom suites overlooking the gulf. *410 S. Collier Blvd. 33937, tel. 813/394–5167. Facilities: kitchens, beach, pool, whirlpool, sauna, exercise room, tennis, racquetball, sailing, windsurfing. AE, MC, V. Very Expensive.*

Marco Bay Resort. An all-suite motor inn on Marco Bay. *1001 N. Barfield Dr. 33937, tel. 813/394–8881. Facilities: restaurant, lounge, kitchens, pools, whirlpools, dock, fishing, putting green, transportation to beach, tennis. AE, CB, DC, MC, V. Very Expensive.*

Marriott's Marco Island Resort. Large rooms with balconies surrounded by lush, tropical grounds right next to the gulf. *400 S. Collier Blvd. 33937, tel. 813/394–2511. Facilities: restaurants, lounge, pools, beach, whirlpool, waterskiing, sailboats, windsurfing, tennis, bicycles, golf, exercise room. AE, CB, DC, MC, V. Very Expensive.*

Radisson Suite Resort on Marco Island. All 214 one- and two-bedroom suites in this medium high-rise resort contain kitchens fully equipped with utensils to give a home-away-from-home touch. The casual decor of the suites contrasts sharply with the marble floors and chandelier in the lobby. Built in 1986, the resort faces a large beachfront. *600 S. Collier Blvd., Marco Island 33937, tel. 813/394–4100 or 800/333–3333. Facilities: restaurant, lounge, pool, beach, whirlpool, exercise room, game room, water-sports equipment available. AE, CB, DC, MC, V. Very Expensive.*

Naples
Dining

★ **The Chef's Garden.** A mixture of Continental, traditional, and California cuisines has consistently won this restaurant awards over the past decade. Some daily specials include Scottish smoked salmon with avocado and caviar, roast rack of lamb, and spinach and fresh mango salad with toasted cashews and honey vinaigrette. *1300 3rd St. S, tel. 813/262–5500. Jackets during winter season. AE, CB, DC, MC, V. Expensive.*

Cafe La Playa. The soul is French, and from it comes classic offerings such as pâté de fois gras, veal in a Dijon mustard sauce, and vichyssoise. The view is of the gulf, either indoors or from the broad-screened patio. *9891 Gulfshore Dr., tel. 813/597-3123. Dress: semidressy. Reservations recommended. AE, MC, V. Moderate.*

★ **St. George and the Dragon.** A long-lived seafood-and-beef restaurant, with a decor reminiscent of an old-fashioned men's club—heavy on brass, dark woods, and deep-red tones. Among the specialties are conch chowder, various cuts of prime rib, and shrimp steamed in beer. *936 5th Ave. S, tel. 813/262-6546. Dress: dressy. No reservations. AE, CB, DC, MC, V. Closed Sun. and Christmas. Moderate.*

Truffles. The less-formal bistro upstairs from The Chef's Garden. A wealth of ethnic specialties appears on the frequently changing menu. Exceptional desserts such as chocolate-peanut butter pie, banana cream pie, and chocolate-mousse cake. *1300 3rd St. S, tel. 813/262-5500. Dress: casual. No reservations. AE, CB, DC, MC, V. Moderate.*

Lodging

Edgewater Beach Hotel. An all-suite gulf-front hotel on fashionable Gulf Shore Drive, long an elegant address in Naples. Close to downtown. *1901 Gulf Shore Blvd. N 33940, tel. 813/262-6511. Facilities: beach, pool, exercise room. AE, CB, DC, MC, V. Very Expensive.*

The Registry Resort. Built just three years ago, this luxurious high-rise resort is a half mile from the beach and offers a wealth of amenities, including a shuttle through the mangrove wetlands to the beach. *475 Seagate Dr. 33940, tel. 813/597-3232. Facilities: restaurants, lounge, pools, whirlpools, bicycles, tennis, health club. AE, CB, DC, MC, V. Very Expensive.*

Ritz-Carlton Hotel. Opulence reigns from its sweeping palm-lined driveway and through every inch of this Mediterranean-style resort on the gulf. *280 Vanderbilt Beach Rd. 33963, tel. 813/598-3300. Facilities: restaurants, lounge, beach, pool, saunas, whirlpool, tennis, bicycles, exercise room, golf, children's program, windsurfing. AE, CB, DC, MC, V. Very Expensive.*

Comfort Inn. Modern motel on the banks of the Gordon River. *1221 5th Ave. S 33940, tel. 813/649-5800. Facilities: pool. AE, CB, DC, MC, V. Moderate.*

Port Charlotte/ Punta Gorda

Dining

Salty's Harborside. Seafood served from a dining room that looks out on Burnt Store Marina and Charlotte Harbor. *Burnt Store Marina, Burnt Store Rd. Punta Gorda, tel. 813/639-3650. Dress: casual. Reservations suggested. AE, CB, DC, MC. V. Moderate.*

Mexican Hacienda. Tex-Mex of a high order in humble surroundings. The building matches its well-worn neighbors; inside are well-interpreted guacamole dip and tacos made with tender shredded beef. *123 E. Retta Esplanade, Punta Gorda, tel. 813/639-7161. Dress: casual. Reservations: parties of 6 or more. MC, V. Inexpensive.*

★ **Ria's Ristorante.** This small, hard-to-find establishment serves a range of pastas (lasagna, spaghetti, stuffed shells), seafoods, and meats on tables lined with red-and-white-checked oilcloth. *Olean Plaza, 21202 Olean Blvd., Port Charlotte, tel. 813/625-3145. Dress: casual. Reservations accepted. No credit cards. Inexpensive.*

Lodging **Burnt Store Marina Resort.** For golfing, boating, and getting away from it all, Burnt Store can fill the bill. One- and two-bedroom modern apartments are situated along a relatively undeveloped stretch of vast Charlotte Harbor. Two-bedroom units available only on a weekly or monthly basis. *3150 Matecumbe Key Rd., Punta Gorda 33955, tel. 813/639–4151. Facilities: restaurant, lounge, kitchens, pool, golf, marina, boats, tennis. Credit: AE, CB, DC, MC, V. Expensive.*

Days Inn of Port Charlotte. Recently built mid-rise motel on Charlotte County's major business route. *1941 Tamiami Trail (U.S. 41), Port Charlotte 33948, tel. 813/627–8900. Facilities: pool. AE, CB, DC, MC, V. Moderate.*

St. Petersburg
Dining **King Charles Room.** Quiet elegance, attentive service, and soothing harp music are to be found in this restaurant on the fifth floor of the Don CeSar Beach Resort. Continental specialties include beluga caviar on ice and smoked salmon stuffed with crab mousse. *3400 Gulf Blvd., tel. 813/360–1881. Dress: dressy. Reservations recommended. AE, CB, DC, MC, V. Very Expensive.*

★ **Peter's Place–Cafe International.** Small, elegant dining rooms with subdued lighting and fresh flowers atop crisp linen tablecloths offer Continental food that is seasoned and served with flair and imagination. Specials change daily. Favorites include breast of capon in a honey-lemon sauce and roast duckling with brandied peaches and just a suggestion of Amaretto. A five-course prix fixe dinner, $27.50. *208 Beach Dr. NE, tel. 813/822–8436. Dress: presentable. Reservations advised. CB, DC, MC, V. Closed Sun. and Mon. Expensive.*

The Wine Cellar Restaurant. The decor is Swiss chalet; the food, classic French. This popular spot is usually crowded, which sometimes makes for indifferent service. *17307 Gulf Blvd., North Redington Beach, tel. 813/393–3491. Dress: presentable. Reservations advised. AE, CB, DC, MC, V. Closed Mon. Expensive.*

★ **Ted Peters Famous Smoked Fish.** The menu is limited to mackerel and mullet, but both are smoked and seasoned to perfection and served with heaping helpings of German potato salad. All meals are served outdoors. *1350 Pasadena Ave. S, Pasadena, tel. 813/381–7931. Dress: casual. No reservations. No credit cards. Closed Tues. Inexpensive.*

Lodging **Tradewinds on St. Petersburg Beach.** Old Florida ambience is offered here, with white gazebos, gondolas gliding along canals, and hammocks swaying on 13 acres of beachfront property. *5500 Gulf Blvd., St. Petersburg Beach 33706, tel. 813/367–6461. Facilities: restaurant, lounge, kitchens, pools, wading pool, beach, sauna, whirlpools, boating, dock, fishing, tennis, racquetball, bicycles, playground, exercise room, scuba instruction, waterskiing, windsurfing. AE, CB, DC, MC, V. Very Expensive.*

Don CeSar Beach Resort. This palatial, pink-rococo resort sprawls across the gulf front. A favorite of author F. Scott Fitzgerald in the 1920s and '30s. *3400 Gulf Blvd., St. Petersburg Beach 33706, tel. 813/360–1881. Facilities: restaurants, lounge, pool, whirlpool, beach, saunas, tennis, children's program, exercise room, sailboats, parasails, jet skis. AE, CB, DC, MC, V. Expensive.*

Colonial Gateway Resort Inn. This gulf-front hotel is family-oriented, with half of its 200 rooms equipped with kitchenettes. The resort was remodeled in the past year to give it a contemporary look for young families. *6300 Gulf Blvd., St. Petersburg Beach 33706, tel. 800/237–8918 outside FL, 800/282–5245 in FL. Facilities: restaurants, lounge, beach bar, pool, water sports activities. AE, CB, DC, MC, V. Moderate.*

Sanibel/Captiva

Dining

The Bubble Room. It's hard to say which is more eclectic here, the atmosphere or the menu. Waiters and waitresses wearing Boy Scout uniforms race amid a dizzying array of Art Deco, ★ while music from the 1940s sets the mood. The aged prime rib is ample enough to satisfy two hearty eaters—at least. Chances are you'll be too full for dessert, but it can be wrapped to go. *Captiva Rd., Captiva, tel. 813/472–5558. No reservations. AE, CB, DC, MC, V. Expensive.*

The Greenhouse. Though the kitchen is in full view of the diminutive dining area, all is calm and quiet as you wend your way through the day's specials, which might include a salad with edible flowers or smoked Muscovy hen in raspberry and cassis sauce. One special almost certain to be offered is Maryland crab cakes in a Key-lime mayonnaise. *Captiva Rd., Captiva, tel. 813/472–6066. Dress: stylishly casual. Reservations advised. No credit cards. Expensive.*

Jean Paul's French Corner. French food, finely seasoned with everything but the highfalutin attitude often dished up in French establishments. Salmon in a creamy dill sauce, sautéed soft-shell crabs, and roast duckling in fruit sauce are among the few but well-prepared choices on the menu. *Tarpon Bay Rd., tel. 813/472–1493. Dress: informal. Reservations suggested. MC, V. Expensive.*

McT's Shrimphouse and Tavern. Somewhat of a departure from most Sanibel establishments, McT's is lively and informal, featuring a host of fresh seafood specialties, including all-you-can-eat shrimp and crab. *1523 Periwinkle Way, Sanibel, tel. 813/472–3161. Dress: casual. No reservations. AE, CB, DC, MC, V. Moderate.*

★ **Thistle Lodge.** A New Orleans–style mansion in the midst of the mangroves serving Cajun, Creole, and Continental fare, including fiery blackened grouper, a less spicy but zesty jambalaya, and creamy, rich Key-lime pie. Dining room looks out on the Gulf of Mexico. *Casa Ybel Resort, 2255 W. Gulf Dr., Sanibel, tel. 813/472–9200. Dress: stylishly casual. Reservations recommended. AE, MC, V. Moderate.*

Lodging

Casa Ybel Resort. One- and two-bedroom gulf-front condominium villas on 23 acres of tropical grounds, complete with palms, ponds, and a footbridge. *2255 W. Gulf Dr., Sanibel 33957, tel. 813/481–3636 or 800/472–3145 outside FL. Facilities: restaurant, lounge, kitchens, pool, whirlpool, biking, tennis, sailing, playground, shuffleboard, game room, baby-sitting. AE, CB, DC, MC, V. Very Expensive.*

South Seas Plantation Resort and Yacht Harbour. Virtually an island unto itself, South Seas lies on the northernmost 330 acres of Captiva Island. There are villas and cottages clustered at various secluded spots throughout the grounds. *South Sea Plantation Rd., Captiva 33924, tel. 813/472–5111. Facilities: restaurants, lounges, kitchens, boat docking, beauty parlor, baby-sitting, fishing, golf, game room, playground, pools, sailboats, sailing school, tennis, waterskiing, windsurfing, and a windsurfing school. AE, CB, DC, MC, V. Very Expensive.*

Sundial Beach & Tennis Resort. The largest all-suite resort on the island; many suites look out upon the Gulf of Mexico. *1246 Middle Gulf Dr., Sanibel 33957, tel. 813/472–4151 or 800/237–4184. Facilities: restaurants, lounge, kitchens, pools, beach, bicycles, tennis, sailboats, recreational program, children's program, baby-sitting, game room, shuffleboard. AE, CB, DC, MC, V. Very Expensive.*

Sarasota
Dining

★ **Cafe L'Europe.** Located on fashionable St. Armand's Key, this greenery- and art-filled cafe specializes in fresh veal and seafood. Menus change frequently, but might include fillet of sole Picasso, Dover sole served with a choice of fruits, Wiener schnitzel sautéed in butter and topped with anchovies, olives, and capers. *431 Harding Circle, tel. 813/388–4415. Dress: semidressy. Reservations suggested. AE, CB, DC, MC, V. Expensive.*

Marina Jack. Have a dinner cruise on the *Marina Jack II* or eat fresh seafood overlooking Sarasota Bay. *2 Marina Plaza, tel. 813/365–4232. Dress: semidressy. Reservations suggested. No credit cards. Expensive.*

★ **The Bijou Cafe.** Wood, brass, and sumptuous green carpeting surround diners in this gas station turned restaurant. Chef Jean Pierre Knaggs's Continental specialties include crispy roast duckling with tangerine brandy sauce or cassis and blackberry sauce, rack of lamb for two, and *crème brûlée*, a custard with a carmelized brown-sugar topping. *Corner of 1st and Pineapple Sts., tel. 813/366–8111. Dress: semidressy. Reservations suggested. AE, MC, V. Moderate.*

Cafe La Chaumiere. This French gem is easy to overlook, since it sits inconspicuously next to the K mart on U.S. 41 in south Sarasota. Inside is classic French cuisine and attentive service that are worth taking the time to find. *8197 S. Tamiami Trail (U.S. 41), tel. 813/922–6400. Dress: informal. Reservations suggested. AE, CB, DC, MC, V. Moderate.*

Lodging

Hyatt Sarasota. Recently renovated, the Hyatt is contemporary in design and conveniently located in the heart of the city. Some rooms overlook Sarasota Bay. *1000 Blvd. of the Arts 34236, tel. 813/366–9000. Facilities: restaurant, lounge, pool, sauna, sailing, health club, dock. AE, CB, DC, MC, V. Very Expensive.*

The Meadows Golf & Tennis Resort. This all-suite resort is a bit removed from downtown, but it is like a small city unto itself, including 54 holes of golf and 16 lighted tennis courts. *3101 Longmeadow Dr. 34234, tel. 813/378–6660. Facilities: restaurants, lounge, pool, sauna, golf, tennis, bicycles, children's program. AE, CB, DC, MC, V. Expensive.*

Days Inn Sarasota–Siesta Key. Modern, built in 1986, with earth-tone rooms, this inn is one mile from the beaches. *6600 S. Tamiami Trail (U.S. 41) 34231, tel. 813/924–4900. Facilities: pool, whirlpool. AE, CB, DC, MC, V. Moderate.*

Hampton Inn Sarasota Airport. On the main drag, convenient to beaches and downtown. Budget prices. *5000 N. Tamiami Trail (U.S. 41) 34234, tel. 813/351–7734. Facilities: pool, exercise room. AE, CB, DC, MC, V. Moderate.*

Tampa
Dining

★ **Bern's Steak House.** Specialties include aged prime beef and an extensive wine list—some 6,000 choices, with selections ranging in price from $10 to $10,000 a bottle. The vegetables are grown on owner-chef Bern Lexer's organic farm. Upstairs are the dessert rooms: small, glass-enclosed rooms where sumptuous desserts are served. Each room is equipped with a control panel for TV, radio, or listening in to the live entertainment in the lounge. *1208 S. Howard Ave., tel. 813/251–2421. Dress: somewhat dressy. Reservations advised. AE, CB, DC, MC, V. Expensive.*

Brothers Too. A gardenlike setting that blocks out bustling West Shore Boulevard complements the fine Continental cuisine served here. One recent specialty: baked shrimp stuffed with crabmeat, artichoke hearts, peppers, and Monterey Jack cheese. *1408 N. West Shore Blvd., tel. 813/879–1962. Dress: casual. Reservations suggested. AE, CB, DC, MC, V. Expensive.*

CK's. This revolving restaurant sits atop Tampa International Airport's Marriott Hotel. An eclectic Continental menu includes stir-fried shrimp and red snapper. Champagne brunch on Sunday. *Tel. 813/879–5151. Reservations accepted. AE, CB, DC, MC, V. Moderate.*

Colonnade. The wharfside location of this popular restaurant is reflected in its nautical decor. Seafood—particularly grouper, red snapper, and lobster—is a specialty, but steak and chicken dishes are also served. *3401 Bayshore Blvd., tel. 813/839–7558. No reservations. AE, CB, DC, MC, V. Moderate.*

★ **Columbia.** A Spanish fixture in Tampa's Ybor City for more than 80 years, this restaurant has several airy and spacious dining rooms and a sunny atrium with tile decor. Specialties include the Columbia 1905 salad—lettuce, ham, olives, cheese, and garlic; and paella—saffron rice with chicken, fish, and mussels. Flamenco dancing. *2117 E. 7th Ave., tel. 813/248–4961. Reservations accepted. AE, CB, DC, MC, V. Moderate.*

Selena's. New Orleans Creole food served here with some Sicilian dishes as well, in antique-filled dining rooms. Shrimp scampi and other fresh seafood featured. *1623 Snow Ave., tel. 813/251–2116. Dress: casual. Reservations suggested. AE, CB, DC, MC, V. Moderate.*

★ **Bella Trattoria.** Brightly lit, slightly noisy, and filled with the smells of such Italian fare as *capelli di l'Angelo*—smoked salmon and caviar tossed with spinach and angel-hair pasta in a vodka and cream sauce—and *Bella! Bella!*, a truffle torte of bittersweet, semisweet, and white chocolates. Crayons and paper tablecloths afford a public outlet for frustrated artists. *1413 S. Howard Ave., tel. 813/254–3355. Dress: casual. No reservations. AE, MC, V. Inexpensive.*

Lodging **Harbour Island Hotel.** Elegant ambience, with lots of dark wood paneling, substantial furniture, and attentive service. *725 S. Harbour Island Blvd. 33602, tel. 813/229–5000. Facilities: restaurant, lounge, pool, dock, sailboats, tennis, health club. AE, CB, DC, MC, V. Very Expensive.*

Saddlebrook. This modern tennis and golf resort on sprawling, heavily wooded grounds is 15 miles north of Tampa. A variety of accommodations and amenities. *100 Saddlebrook Way, Wesley Chapel 34249, tel. 813/973–1111. Facilities: restaurants, lounge, kitchenettes, pools, wading pools, whirlpools, saunas, fishing, golf, tennis, bicycles, health club. AE, CB, DC, MC, V. Very Expensive.*

Guest Quarters. Modern all-suite hotel midway between Tampa International Airport and downtown Tampa. *555 N. Westshore Blvd. 33609, tel. 813/875–1555. Facilities: restaurant, lounge,* *pool, whirlpool, sauna, exercise room, transportation to airport; accepts pets. AE, CB, DC, MC, V. Expensive.*

Hyatt Regency–Downtown. A large, elegant high-rise hotel with a modern, mirrored ambience. *2 Tampa City Center 33602, tel. 813/225–1234. Facilities: restaurant, lounge, pool, whirlpool, sauna, exercise room. AE, DC, MC, V. Expensive.*

Holiday Inn Busch Gardens. A family-oriented motor inn just one mile west of Busch Gardens. *2701 E. Fowler Ave. 33612, tel. 813/971–4710. Facilities: restaurant, lounge, pool, sauna, exercise room, transportation to Busch Gardens. AE, CB, DC, MC, V. Moderate.*

Tahitian Inn. This family-run motel offers comfortable rooms at budget prices. *601 S. Dale Mabry Hwy. 33609, tel. 813/877–6721. Facilities: pool. AE, CB, DC, MC, V. Inexpensive.*

Tarpon Springs
Dining

★ **Louis Pappas' Riverside Restaurant.** The decor consists mainly of wall-to-wall people who pour into this waterfront landmark for all manner of Greek fare, especially the Greek salad, made with lettuce, feta-cheese chunks, onions, and olive oil. *10 W. Dodecanese Blvd., tel. 813/937–5101. Dress: casual. Reservations advised. AE, CB, DC, MC, V. Moderate.*

Lodging

Innisbrook Resort. There are deluxe rooms and suites here, some with balconies or patios at this get-away-from-it-all resort on 1,000 wooded acres. *Box 1088, U.S. 19 34689, tel. 813/942–2000. Facilities: dining rooms, nightclub, golf, tennis, racquetball, pools, health club, children's program (May–Sept.), miniature golf, saunas. AE, CB, DC, MC, V. Very Expensive.*

Venice
Dining

★ **The Attic at Kissin' Cuzzins.** The ambience is barnlike and the helpings of Pennsylvania Dutch fare are enough to feed a large and hungry horse. *1775 S. Tamiami Trail (U.S. 41), tel. 813/493–3666. Dress: casual. Reservations accepted. AE, MC, V. Moderate.*

Schuett's Wharf. A large dining room overlooks the Intracoastal Waterway. Not surprisingly, the focus is on fresh local seafood. *449 N. Tamiami Trail (U.S. 41), tel. 813/485–4885. Dress: casual. Reservations accepted. AE, CB, DC, MC, V. Moderate.*

Lodging

Best Western Venice Resort Inn. Modern motor inn on the gulf. *455 N. Venice Bypass 34292, tel. 813/485–5411. Facilities: restaurant, lounge, pool, beach, whirlpool, playground. AE, CB, DC, MC, V. Moderate.*

Park Inn. Comfortable rooms in motor inn on the main business route through town. *1710 S. Tamiami Trail (U.S. 41) 34293, tel. 813/493–4558. Facilities: restaurant, lounge, pool; accepts pets. AE, DC, MC, V. Moderate.*

The Arts

Not too many years ago, southwest Florida was content to bask in the warmth of the sun and leave cultural matters to others. But as the population has boomed, a growing number of transplanted northerners have been unwilling to sacrifice the arts for nature. Hence, there are curtains going up at performing-arts centers throughout the region.

If you are interested in cultural events while staying in Florida, it's a good idea to purchase tickets before you arrive, especially during the busy winter tourist season. Most halls and theaters accept credit-card charges by phone. The area chambers of commerce (*see* Important Addresses and Numbers) can supply schedules of upcoming cultural events.

The **Tampa Performing Arts Center** (1010 W. C. MacInnes Pl., Box 2877, tel. 813/222–1010) occupies nine acres along the Hillsborough River and is said to be the largest such complex south of the Kennedy Center in Washington, DC. The festival hall, playhouse, and small theater accommodate opera, ballet, drama, and concerts.

Ruth Eckerd Hall (1111 McMullen Booth Rd., Clearwater, tel. 813/725–5573) also plays host to many national performers of pop, classical, and jazz music; ballet; and drama.

Sarasota's **Van Wezel Performing Arts Hall** (777 N. Tamiami Trail, tel. 813/953–3366) is easy to find. Just look for the purple shell rising along the bay front. It offers some 200 performances each year, including Broadway plays, ballet, jazz, rock concerts, symphonies, children's shows, and ice skating. For tickets and information, contact the box office.

Fort Myers's center for the arts is the **Barbara B. Mann Performing Arts Hall** (Edison Community College/University of South Florida campus, College Pkwy., tel. 813/489–3033), a 1,770-seat theater that opened in 1986. Plays, concerts, and ballets by local, national, and international companies perform here. For more information, contact the box office.

Theater

Tampa Bay

The **Tampa Theater** (711 N. Franklin St., tel. 813/223–8981) presents shows, musical performances, and films. Area dinner theaters include the **Country Dinner Playhouse** (Gateway Mall, 7951 9th St. N, tel. 813/577–5515), the **Encore Equity Dinner-Theatre** (1850 Central Ave., tel. 813/821–6676), and the **Showboat Dinner Theatre** (3405 Ulmerton Rd., tel. 813/223–2545). All offer dinner and a variety of Broadway and off-Broadway shows throughout the year.

Sarasota/Bradenton

The **Asolo State Theater** (Drawer E, tel. 813/355–5137) offers productions nearly year-round. Located at the Ringling Museum in Sarasota, it is known for its well-rounded rotating repertoire. Long housed in a small relocated 18th-century Italian court playhouse, it is scheduled to move soon into its new $10-million home in the Asolo Performing Arts Center, just northeast of its present spot. The theater's company of actors performs about 10 plays per season (Dec.–Aug.). For tickets or information, contact the theater.

Florida Studio Theatre (1241 N. Palm Ave., Sarasota, tel. 813/366–9796) is a small professional theater that presents contemporary dramas, comedies, and musicals.

Golden Apple Dinner Theatre (25 Pineapple Ave., Sarasota, tel. 813/366–5454) combines a buffet dinner with musicals and comedies.

The **Players of Sarasota** (U.S. 41 and 9th St., tel. 813/365–2494), a long-lived troupe, provided opportunities for then-unknowns Pee-Wee Herman, Montgomery Clift, and Polly Holiday. The community theater features volunteer actors and technicians and performs comedies, thrillers, and musicals.

Theatre Works (1247 1st St., Venice, tel. 813/952–9170) presents professional, non-Equity productions at the Palm Tree Playhouse.

Venice Little Theatre (140 W. Tampa Ave., Sarasota, tel. 813/488–1115) is a community theater offering comedies, musicals, and a few dramas during its October–May season.

Fort Myers/Naples **The Naples Dinner Theatre** (Immokalee Rd., halfway between U.S. 41 and the I–75 interchange, tel. 813/597–6031) is open October–August and features professional companies performing a variety of mostly musicals and comedies. Admission includes buffet.

The **Naples Playhouse** (Harbour Town Shopping Center, 399 Goodlette Rd., tel. 813/263–7990) has winter and summer seasons. The winter shows often sell out well in advance.

Concerts
Tampa Bay Area The **Florida Orchestra** (tel. 813/221–2365 in Tampa, 813/892–5010 in St. Petersburg) performs throughout Tampa Bay each fall, at Clearwater's Eckerd Hall, St. Petersburg's Bayfront Center, and the Tampa Performing Arts Center.

The **Tampa Bay Chamber Orchestra** (tel. 813/251–2388) offers concerts throughout the region, though only during the Florida Orchestra's off-season. Its 35 members performs works for chamber orchestras.

Sarasota/Bradenton The **Florida Symphonic Band** (Van Wezel Hall 709 N. Tamiami Trail [U.S. 41] Sarasota, tel. 813/955–6660) includes 50 players, many of whom are full-time musicians. The group performs monthly concerts.

Florida West Coast Music, Inc. (tel. 813/953–4252) consists of a number of area groups that perform in the city regularly. Included are the *Florida West Coast Symphony*, *The Florida String Quartet*, *Florida Brass Quintet*, *Florida Wind Quintet*, and *New Artists String Quintet*.

Opera
Tampa Bay Area **Florida Opera West** (tel. 813/381–2151) brings in guest soloists for its major operatic performances at Ruth Eckerd Hall in Clearwater and the Bayfront Center in St. Petersburg.

The **St. Petersburg Opera Co.** and the **Florida Lyric Opera Company** perform at the Bayfront Center.

Sarasota The **Sarasota Opera** (61 N. Pineapple Ave., tel. 813/953–7030) operates from its home in a historic theater downtown at the corner of 1st and Pineapple streets. The company's season runs from February to March. Internationally known singing artists perform the principal roles, supported by a professional apprentice chorus—24 young singers studying with the company.

Dance
Tampa Bay Area The **St. Petersburg Concert Ballet** performs periodically throughout the year, mostly at the Bayfront Center in St. Petersburg.

The Tampa Ballet performs at the Tampa Bay Performing Arts Center.

Film All areas have conveniently located commercial movie houses. Check the local newspapers for shows, times, and locations.

Sarasota The **Ringling Fine Arts Film Series** brings classic, foreign, and second-run films to the Asolo State Theater on Mondays (5401 Bayshore Rd., tel. 813/355–5101). The **Sarasota Film Society** operates year-round, showing foreign and nonmainstream films on weekends at the Plaza Theatre (Crossroads Shopping Center, tel. 813/388–2441).

Nightlife

Bars and Nightclubs **Harbour Island Hotel** (Harbour Island, Tampa, tel. 813/229–5000). Great view of the bay, large-screen television, and thickly padded, comfortable chairs.

Coliseum Ballroom (535 4th Ave. N, St. Petersburg, tel. 813/894–1812). Ballroom dancing Wednesday and Saturday night.
The Pier (Memorial Pier, Bradenton, tel. 813/748–8087). An incomparable view of the Bradenton waterfront.
The Patio (Columbia Restaurant, Harding Circle, St. Armand's Key, tel. 813/388–3987). A casual lounge with live music nightly.
The Beach Club (1915 Colonial Blvd., Fort Myers, tel. 813/939–2582). Live music, large-screen television, sand, and volleyball in a casual, open-air establishment.
'Tween Waters Inn (Captiva Rd., Captiva, tel. 813/472–5161). Live entertainment and large-screen TV catering to casual, over-30 crowd.

Jazz Clubs Most offer jazz several nights a week. Call for details.
Baxters (714 S. Dale Mabry Hwy. Tampa, tel. 813/879–1161).
Brothers Lounge (Lincoln Center, 5401 W. Kennedy Blvd., Tampa, tel. 813/879–9378).
Brothers Too (1408 N. Westshore Blvd., Tampa, tel. 813/879–1962).
Maestro's (14727 N. Florida Ave., Tampa, tel. 813/961–5090).
Don's Beach Bar (Bilmar Hotel, 10650 Gulf Blvd., St. Petersburg, tel. 813/360–5531).
Hurricane Lounge (807 Gulf Way, Pass-a-Grille Beach, tel. 813/360–9558).
Harp & Thistle (650 Corey Ave., St. Petersburg Beach, tel. 813/360–4104).
Victoria Pier (2230 Edwards Dr., Fort Myers, tel. 813/334–4881).

Rock Clubs **Volley Club** (1512 N. Nebraska Ave., Tampa, tel. 813/972–0176). Live rock-and-roll rings from the rafters Tuesday–Saturday.
Studebaker's (2516 Gulf-to-Bay Blvd., Clearwater, tel. 813/799–4147). The ambience and music are of the nifty fifties.
306th Bomb Group (6770 N. Tamiami Trail, Sarasota, tel. 813/355–8591). Amid World War II gear, a DJ spins top-40 tunes for a generally over-25 clientele.
Horsefeathers (1900 Main St., Sarasota, tel. 813/366–8088). A mainly professional crowd gathers at this lounge, where top-40 music spins nightly.
Club Yesterdays (2224 S. Tamiami Trail, tel. 813/493–2900). Top-40 is king every night at this club popular with the under-30 set.
Flashbacks at Mainstreet (4800 S. Cleveland Ave., Fort Myers, tel. 813/936–8545). Oldies from the '50s and '60s nightly, tea dances Sundays.
Edison's Electric Lounge (Holiday Inn, 13051 Bell Tower Dr., Fort Myers, tel. 813/482–2900). Top-40 tunes, usually live bands, rock nightly.

Country-Western **Joyland Country Night Club** (11225 U.S. 19, St. Petersburg, tel. 813/577–4324).
The Barn (13800 W. Hillsborough Ave., Tampa, tel. 813/855–9818).
Country Corner (22nd St. at 50th St., Tampa, tel. 813/242–2558).
Dallas Bull North (Hwy. 301, Tampa, tel. 813/985–6877).
Carlie's (5641 49th St., St. Petersburg, tel. 813/527–5214).
Marina 31 Restaurant and Lounge (Rte. 31, Fort Myers, tel. 813/694–1331).

Comedy Clubs

Comedy Corner (3447 W. Kennedy Blvd., Tampa, tel. 813/875–9129).

Coconuts Comedy Club at Barnacle Bill's (Howard Johnson's, 6110 Gulf Blvd., St. Petersburg, tel. 813/360–4575).

Ron Bennington's Comedy Line (Ramada Inn, 2560 U.S. 19, Clearwater, tel. 813/796–1234).

Laughs R Us (Reunion Bar, Holiday Inn, 3000 34th St. S, St. Petersburg, tel. 813/867–1111).

Friendly Tavern (13121 Gulf Blvd., Redington Shores, tel. 813/393–4470).

Bijou Comedy Club & Restaurant (McGregor Point Shopping Center, Fort Myers, tel. 813/481–6666).

Naples Comedy Club (Above Bogey's Restaurant and Lounge, 4110 Golden Gate Pkwy). Naples, tel. 813/353–1489).

Discos

The Ocean Club (4811 Cypress Ave., Tampa, tel. 813/875–6358). Fashionably dressed revelers dance and mingle at this two-level club with music videos and a light show.

Club Paradise (1927 Ringling Blvd., Sarasota, tel. 813/366–3830). A rock-and-roll palace, complete with extensive light show, music videos, a DJ, and several bars. Especially popular with the younger set.

Norma Jean's (4797 U.S. 41, Fort Myers, tel. 813/275–9997) packs in the singles (21 and up) with such events as hot legs and lip-sync contests, hot-tub night, live bands and disc jockeys.

11 North Florida

Introduction

by Joice Veselka and Honey Naylor

A freelance writer, Honey Naylor has contributed to Travel & Leisure, USA Today, New Orleans Magazine, *and* Travel Today, *as well as other Fodor's guides. Joice Veselka, a resident of Tallahassee, is the Sunbelt editor for* Chevrolet Magazine; *her travel articles have appeared in* Signature, *The* Miami Herald, *the* New Orleans Times-Picayune, *and the* Fort Lauderdale News.

If you think Florida is just one big beach, you're only partly right. And if, so thinking, you drive into the state from Alabama or Georgia, you'll probably figure you were totally wrong. In the northwestern part of Florida, called the Panhandle, there are gently undulating hills, natural swamplands, and thick forests of pine and oak trees. Tallahassee, the state capital, lies in the foothills of the Appalachians and, like Rome, rolls over seven hills. As you move east the terrain levels out, and the Atlantic coastal plains are as flat as the proverbial pancake. Sandbars and islands protect much of the mainland from the Atlantic Ocean, but the waters sneak through the marshlands north of Jacksonville, creating a maze of rivers, inlets, and islands.

But north Florida is not without beaches—not by a long shot. The waters of the Gulf of Mexico nudge the coast of the Panhandle, where the modestly named Miracle Strip is a 100-mile stretch of lush white carpet dotted with hotels, condominiums, shops, shacks, and restaurants. The northeast coast is also awash, so to speak, with sun-kissed beaches, and the ocean is a fit place for surfing, snorkeling, scuba diving, and sailing.

In the 400-mile stretch between the Atlantic Ocean on the east and Pensacola in the Panhandle, you'll find ancient forts, deep caverns, and archaeological sites to explore; wineries to see (and wine to sip); historic districts with narrow old-brick streets; and a plethora of antique shops to poke around in. There are football games, fishing piers, canoeing and tubing, greyhound races, jai alai, lush hiking and biking trails, and water sports of every sort. If you are not athletically inclined, you can while away a fair amount of time simply counting the number of tennis courts and golf courses in north Florida. And you'll never be far from a spot where you can just drop down and worship the sun for a spell.

Getting Around

By Plane The main airport for the region is **Jacksonville International.** It is served by American (tel. 800/433–7300), Continental (tel. 800/231–0855), Eastern (tel. 800/327–8376), Piedmont (tel. 800/251–5720), TWA (tel. 800/221–2000), United (tel. 800/241– 6522), and USAir (tel. 800/428–4322). Vans from the airport to area hotels cost $8 per person. Taxi fare is about $21 to the downtown area, $31 to the beaches, and $35 to Amelia Island. Among the limousine services, which must be booked in advance, is *AAA Limousine Service* (tel. 904/751–4800 for Jacksonville and beaches, tel. 904/277–2359 for Amelia Island). The charge is $30 for one or two persons to downtown, $35 for one or $40 for two to the beaches, and $15 per person to Amelia Island.

Tallahassee Regional Airport is served by Delta (tel. 800/221–1212), Eastern, Piedmont, and Piedmont Regional (tel. 800/368–5425). Taxis (among them, *Yellow Cab*, tel. 904/222–3070) cost about $11 to area hotels. Some of the hotels provide free van service.

Both **Panama City-Bay County Airport** and **Fort Walton Beach/Eglin AFB Airport** are served by Continental Express (tel.

800/525–0280), Delta Connection (tel. 800/282–3424), Eastern Express (tel. 800/327–8376), and Northwest (tel. 800/225–2526). At the Panama City airport, *Deluxe Coach Limo Service* (tel. 904/763–0211) offers van service for $7–$7.50 to downtown Panama City and $10–$18 to Panama City Beach. Taxis (*Yellow Cab*, tel. 904/763–4691) charge about $7 to town. The cost to hotels depends on location. At Fort Walton, taxis (*Yellow Cab*, tel. 904/244–3600) charge $8–$13 to Fort Walton Beach, $15 and up to Destin. *Airport Limousine* (tel. 904/244–5638) charges $8 to Fort Walton Beach, $12.50–$16 to Destin.

Pensacola Regional Airport is served by Continental, Delta, Eastern, Northwest Airlink, Piedmont, and Piedmont Regional. Other than free van service provided by hotels, the only transportation from the airport is by taxi (*Yellow Cab*, tel. 904/433–1143). The cost is about $7 to downtown, $15 to Pensacola Beach.

By Car Interstate 10 is the major east–west artery across the top of the state. U.S. 90 plays along with it for the most part, but cavorts off here and there to see the small towns that are bypassed by the interstate. North–south routes through central Florida are I–75, I–95, U.S. 301, U.S. 17, and U.S. 1, with U.S. 331 and U.S. 231 dipping into the Panhandle.

By Train Jacksonville is Florida's entry city for **Amtrak** service (tel. 800/USA–RAIL), with two southbound and two northbound trains daily. Other stations are at Waldo (in the Gainesville area) and Palatka. Schedules vary with the season.

By Bus **Greyhound/Trailways Bus Line** has extensive service throughout the region, with stations in Jacksonville (tel. 904/354–8543), St. Augustine (tel. 904/829–6401), Gainesville (tel. 376–5252), Tallahassee (tel. 904/222–4240), Panama City (tel. 904/785–7861), Fort Walton Beach (tel. 904/243–1940), and Pensacola (tel. 904/432–5196).

Scenic Drives

Rte. 399 from Pensacola Beach to Navarre Beach takes you along Santa Rosa Island, a long white ribbon rolled out on blue-green waters. **U.S. 98** offers about 100 miles of soul-stirring views as it sweeps along the Gulf of Mexico eastward from Destin. The **Buccaneer Trail (Rte. A1A)** on the Atlantic Coast goes from Fort George Island through marshlands laced with inlets and rivers, past unspoiled beaches, and on to Fernandina Island, a 300-year-old coastal village that was once a haven for freebooters. **Rte. 13** from Jacksonville to East Palatka winds along the banks of the north-flowing St. Johns River and drifts through sleepy hamlets, past citrus groves and the breathtaking Ravine Gardens, which is awash with azaleas in the early spring. **I–10** between Tallahassee and Milton rolls over the wooded foothills of the Appalachians, past deep ravines and lovely lakes.

Guided Tours

Right This Way, Pensacola (2875 W. Michigan Ave., tel. 904/944–1700) offers package tours personally tailored to your interests.

The ***Capt. Anderson*** and the ***Capt. Anderson II*** cast off for a variety of sightseeing and dinner/dance cruises. The *Capt. Anderson* (Capt. Anderson's Pier, Panama City Beach, tel. 904/234–5940) cruises to Ship Island (Mar.–Nov.) at a cost of $5.50 adults, $3 children. The *Capt. Anderson II* (Pensacola tel. 904/432–6999, Ft. Walton Beach tel. 904/243–3463) offers sightseeing and dinner/dance cruises for $15 and $18.95, respectively, during its June–September season.

Glass Bottom Boat (Panama City Beach, tel. 904/234–8944) offers a Bay & Bayou Cruise on Tuesday, Thursday, and weekends ($11), and a Sea School Cruise on Wednesday and weekends ($8). Both outings include dolphin feedings, demonstrations of shrimp nettings, and stops on Shell Island.

Riverwalk Cruise Line (St. Johns River, Jacksonville, tel. 904/398–0797) offers daily sightseeing cruises aboard the *First Lady of Jacksonville* ($8.50 adults, $4.25 children), as well as lunch, moonlight, and dinner/dance cruises.

The ***Annabelle Lee*** (tel. 904/396–2333), Jacksonville's newest stern-wheeler, does twice-monthly dinner cruises (more often in the summer). Cost: $25.

St. Augustine Historical Tours (tel. 904/829–3800) has a trolley you can take for a 7½-mile narrated city tour. The trolley operates daily 8:30–6, and tickets can be purchased at 167 San Marco Avenue and at ticket booths throughout the city. A one-time charge of $7 adults, $2 children is good for the duration of your visit, and you can get off the trolley at the major sights and reboard later.

St. Augustine Sightseeing Trains (170 San Marco Ave., tel. 904/829–6545) offers tours that combine highlights of the historic district with other points of interest. Tours range from a one-hour orientation tour ($7) to special packages of three to 10 hours ($12–$27). All have one-time fees that are good for the duration of your stay.

Colee Sightseeing Carriage Tours (St. Augustine, tel. 904/829–2818) offers horse-drawn carriage tours through the narrow streets of the historic district with drivers who entertain you with a mix of fact and fiction. Tours begin on Bayfront near the entrance to Fort Castillo de San Marcos, 8:30–5 daily. Cost: $7 adults, $3 children.

The ***Spirit of St. Augustine*** (tel. 904/824–3090), a new replica of a stern-wheeler that Henry Flagler operated in St. Augustine in the 1800s, offers sightseeing and dinner/dance cruises. Cost: $7 adults, $3 children.

Suwannee Country Tours (White Springs, tel. 904/397–2349) has a variety of specialty tours at various prices, including bicycle tours, canoe trips on the Suwannee River, and a history tour that combines biking and walking in St. Augustine with an overnight stay in a country inn.

Important Addresses and Numbers

Tourist Information

Amelia Island–Fernandina Beach Chamber of Commerce (102 Centre St., tel. 904/261–3248). Open weekdays 9–5.

Apalachicola Bay Chamber of Commerce (45 Market St., tel. 904/653–9419). Open weekdays 9–5.

Cedar Key Chamber of Commerce (2nd St., tel. 904/543–5600). Open Monday, Wednesday, and Friday 10–2.

Destin Chamber of Commerce (Holiday Inn, Suite D, 1021 U.S. 98E, tel. 904/837–6241). Open weekdays 9–5.

Fort Walton Beach Chamber of Commerce (34 Miracle Strip Pkwy., U.S. 98, tel. 904/244–8191). Open weekdays 8–5.

Convention & Visitors Bureau of Jacksonville and Its Beaches (33 S. Hogan St., tel. 904/353–9736). Open weekdays 8:30–5.
Jacksonville Beaches Chamber of Commerce (413 Pablo Ave., tel. 904/249–3868). Open weekdays 8–5.
Panama City Beach Visitors & Convention Bureau (12015 W. U.S. 98 Alt. tel. 904/234–6576). Open weekdays 8–5.
Pensacola Visitor Information Center (1401 E. Gregory St., tel. 800/343–4321). Open daily 8:30–5.
St. Augustine Visitor Information Center (10 Castillo Dr., tel. 904/824–3334). Open daily 8:30–5:30.
Tallahassee Visitor & Convention Bureau (100 N. Duval St., tel. 904/224–8116). Open weekdays 8:30–5.

Emergencies Dial 911 for **police** and **ambulance** in an emergency.

Hospitals Emergency rooms are open 24 hours at the following: **White-Wilson Medical Center** (1000 Airport Rd., Destin, tel. 904/837–3848), **Shands Hospital** (1600 S.W. Archer Rd., Gainesville, tel. 904/395–0111), **University Hospital** (655 W. 8th St., Jacksonville, tel. 904/350–6988), **Beaches Hospital** (1430 16th Ave. S, Jacksonville Beach, tel. 904/246–6731), **Bay Medical Center** (615 N. Bonita Ave., Panama City, tel. 904/769–1511), **Baptist Hospital** (1000 W. Marina St., Pensacola, tel. 904/434–4011), **Flagler Hospital** (Health Park Blvd., off U.S. 1, St. Augustine, tel. 904/824–8411), **Tallahassee Memorial Regional Medical Center** (1300 Miccosukee Rd., Tallahassee, tel. 904/681–1155).

Pharmacies The only 24-hour pharmacy in the region is **Eckerd Drug** (4397 Roosevelt Blvd., Jacksonville, tel. 904/389–0314).

Exploring North Florida

Interstate 10 is the fastest way to get from Pensacola to St. Augustine. However, after our tour of Pensacola we'll head east on U.S. 98 and dawdle in the coastal resorts of Fort Walton Beach, Destin, and Panama City. There are any number of sybaritic distractions, and at the very least you'll probably pull off the road, kick off your shoes, and wade on the beach. The beaches are almost irresistible; the pure white sands are 99% quartz, formed several thousand years ago by rivers flowing from the Piedmont of the Appalachians, and the blue-green waters are quite enticing. Having dried off, we'll visit Fort San Marcos de Apalache, whose history dates from 1528, and Wakulla Springs, where glass-bottom boats glide over the world's deepest freshwater spring. Next, we'll take in a bit of Tallahassee, the capital city, and continue eastward. Jacksonville, home of the Gator Bowl and site of the annual Georgia-Florida football game, sits on the banks of the north-flowing St. Johns River, while the Jacksonville Beaches bask on the Atlantic Coast. Our final destination is the nation's first city, St. Augustine, founded by the Spanish in 1565, where we'll wander ancient narrow streets and see the Oldest House, the Oldest Schoolhouse, and a whole raft of other "oldests."

1 Had it not been for a hurricane, **Pensacola** would be the nation's oldest city. In 1559, six years before the founding of St. Augustine, Don Tristan de Luna and 1,500 Spanish troops landed on Pensacola's shores. Shortly after their arrival the big wind blew through, taking with it not only de Luna's dreams of a Spanish settlement, but most of his fleet as well. It was not until the mid-18th century that a permanent Spanish settlement was established.

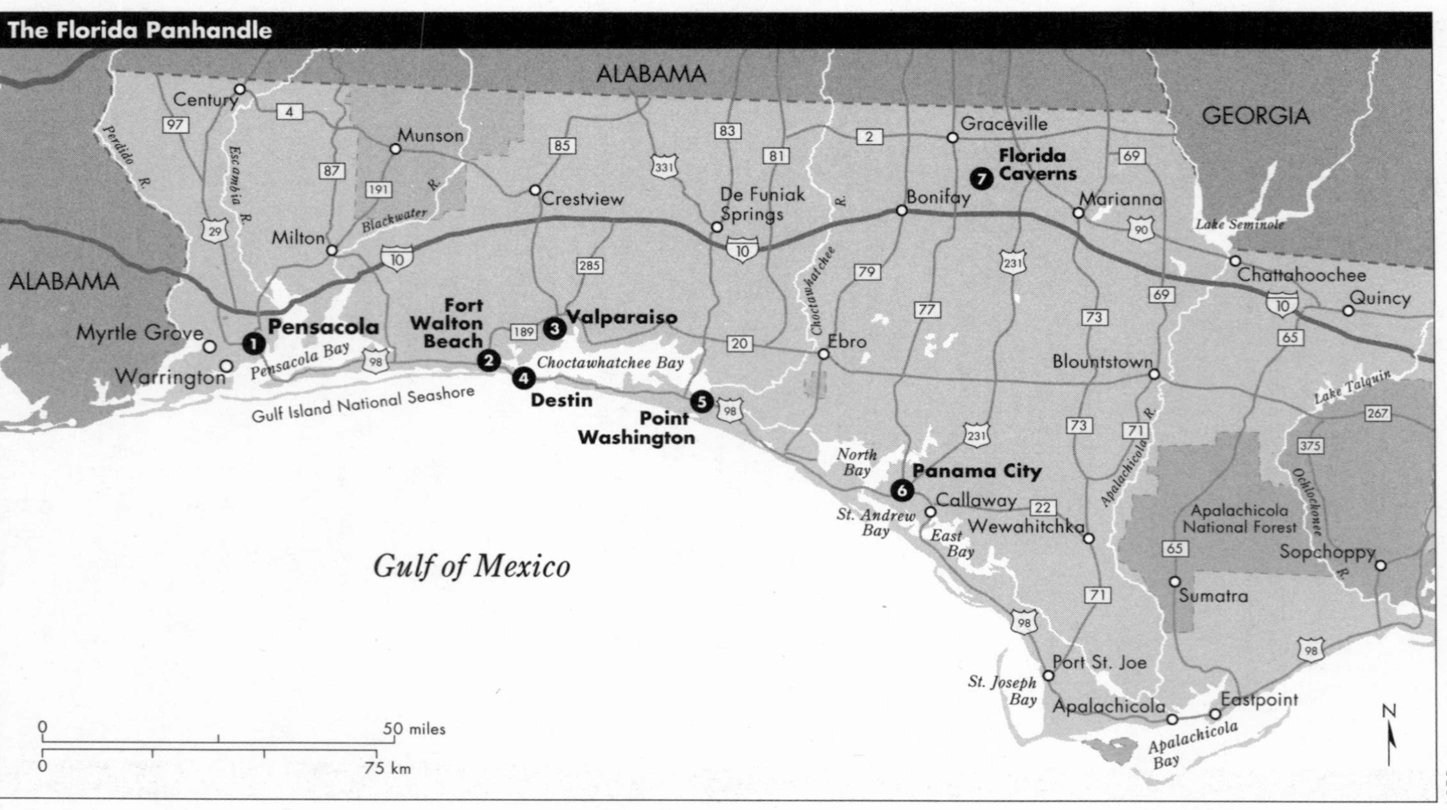

The Florida Panhandle
ALABAMA
GEORGIA
ALABAMA
Century
Munson
Crestview
De Funiak Springs
Graceville
Florida Caverns
Bonifay
Marianna
Lake Seminole
Chattahoochee
Quincy
Milton
Myrtle Grove
Warrington
Pensacola
Pensacola Bay
Fort Walton Beach
Valparaiso
Choctawhatchee Bay
Destin
Point Washington
Gulf Island National Seashore
Ebro
Blountstown
Lake Talquin
North Bay
Panama City
Callaway
St. Andrew Bay
East Bay
Wewahitchka
Apalachicola National Forest
Sopchoppy
Sumatra
Port St. Joe
St. Joseph Bay
Apalachicola
Eastpoint
Apalachicola Bay
Perdido R.
Escambia R.
Blackwater R.
Choctawhatchee R.
Apalachicola R.
Ochlockonee R.
Gulf of Mexico
0
50 miles
0
75 km
N

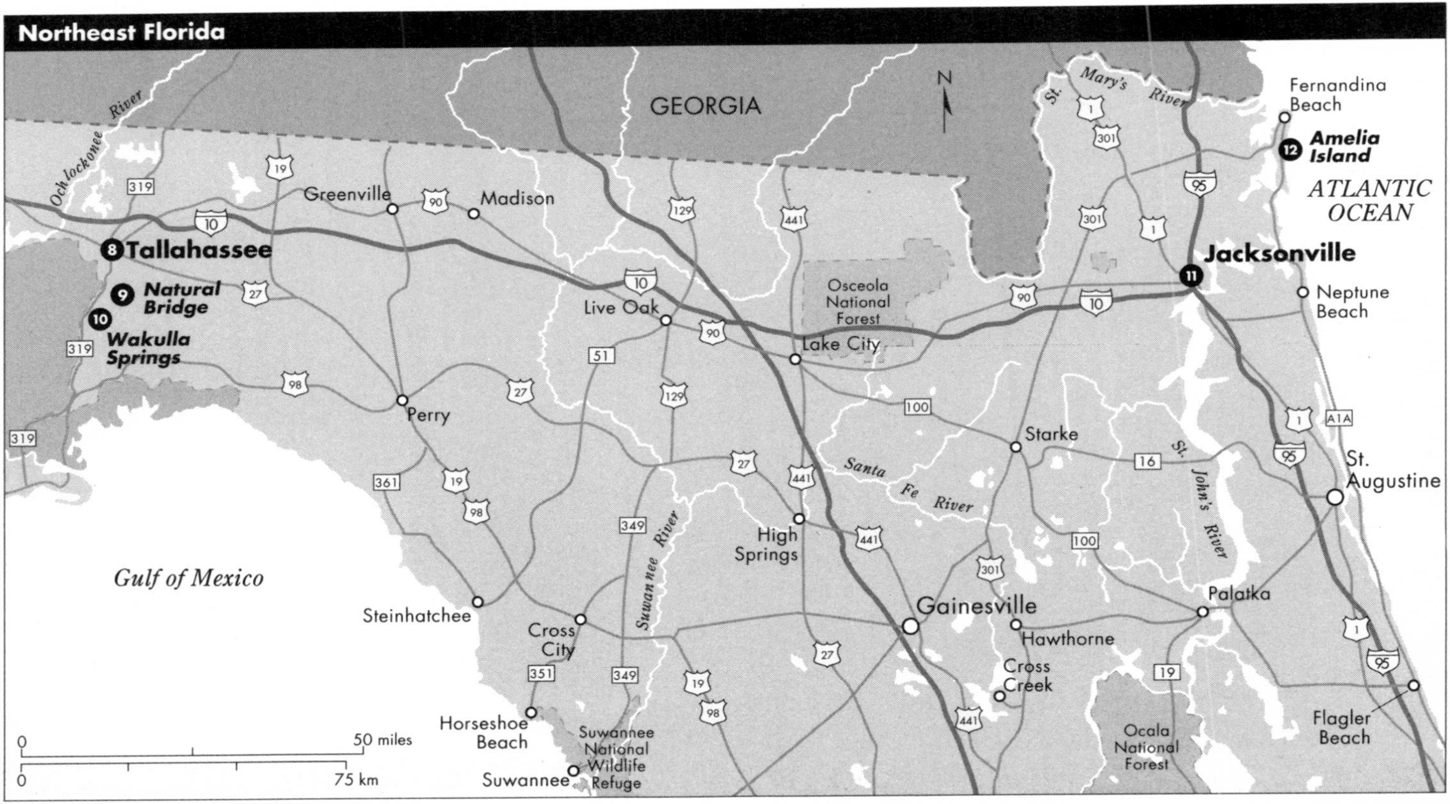
Northeast Florida
GEORGIA
N
Och lockonee River
St. Mary's River
Fernandina Beach
12 Amelia Island
ATLANTIC OCEAN
11 Jacksonville
Neptune Beach
8 Tallahassee
9 Natural Bridge
10 Wakulla Springs
Greenville
Madison
Live Oak
Osceola National Forest
Lake City
Perry
Starke
Santa Fe River
St. John's River
St. Augustine
High Springs
Suwannee River
Gulf of Mexico
Steinhatchee
Cross City
Gainesville
Hawthorne
Palatka
Cross Creek
Horseshoe Beach
Suwannee National Wildlife Refuge
Suwannee
Ocala National Forest
Flagler Beach
319
19
90
10
129
441
301
1
95
27
51
98
100
A1A
361
16
349
351
0
50 miles
0
75 km

Be sure to stop first at the **Visitor Information Center** at the foot of the Pensacola Bay Bridge. You can pick up loads of brochures and maps, including self-guided walking tours of the city's two historic districts.

Palafox Street is the main thoroughfare in downtown Pensacola, and it is lined with structures that reflect the city's Spanish origins. The two historic districts lie to the east and the west of Palafox Street.

The **North Hill Preservation District** is bordered by Palafox, Reus, LaRua, and Blount streets. Driving through the 60-block district, you'll see fine turn-of-the-century southern homes with broad verandas, cupolas, turrets, and ornate gingerbread trim. The homes are private residences, so you'll have to do your admiring from the street.

Continuing down Palafox Street toward the Bay, you'll pass **Palafox Place.** Buildings in the three-block area from Garden Street to Government Street are decorated with handsome wrought-iron balconies that preserve the flavor of Old Pensacola. At Palafox and Garden streets you'll see the San Carlos Hotel, which dates from 1910. It's closed now, but for more than 50 years it was the center of the city's business and social life. At the corner of Palafox and Intendencia streets, a plaque marks the spot where Andrew Jackson lived when he was Florida's first territorial governor.

The **Seville Square Historic District** is just to the west, tucked in between Palafox, Cedar, Cervallos, and Chase streets. This restoration is near the site of the permanent Spanish colony of 1752. Park your car and wander along the old brick streets. You'll find shops, restaurants, and museums, most of them in restored 18th- and 19th-century homes. In the heart of the district at Adams and Zaragoza streets, Seville Square is a tree-shaded park with a lacy gazebo.

Time Out **Dabo's,** a block off the park on Zaragoza Street, has a wonderfully decadent dessert called Hello Dollies, which is made of layers of chocolate, butterscotch, coconut, and pecans on a graham-cracker crust. *Tel. 904/433–1133. Open Sun.–Fri. 10–2:30, Sat. 10–4. MC, V.*

At the West Florida Museum (Alcaniz and Garden Sts.), pick up a free walking tour brochure of St. Michael's Cemetery. The cemetery, which dates back to the early 1800s, is on Chase Street at the northern border of the Historic District.

Follow Garden Street (U.S. 98) west to Navy Boulevard, which leads to the **Pensacola Naval Air Station,** the nation's first naval training station, established 1914. The NAS is home to the USS *Lexington,* a World War II veteran now used as a training vessel. When she's in port you can board the Lady Lex on weekends 9–3. Just inside the main gate of the NAS you'll find the **Naval Aviation Museum** (tel. 904/452–3604), which traces the history of aviation from 1911 to the space age. It's a huge structure, where you can see a Skylab Command Module, the NC–14 Flying Boat that made the first transatlantic air crossing, a replica of the Navy's first Curtiss biplane, and a variety of other exhibits. Just northeast of the Naval Museum, Sherman Field is home to the famed **Blue Angels** precision flying squadron. The Angels perform twice annually in the Pensacola area, in the summer and the fall. *Navy Blvd., tel. 904/452–2311. Admission free. Open daily 9–5.*

Retrace your route and follow U.S. 98 across the Pensacola Bay Bridge. The view of the bay is spectacular, with blue waters and bright-white ships. Continue through Gulf Breeze and cross the bridge (toll 35 cents) to **Santa Rosa Island.** At the western tip of the island, Fort Pickens is the site of a fort that once held Geronimo captive.

Rte. 399 takes you along a breathtaking section of the Gulf Islands National Seashore between Fort Pickens on the west and Navarre Beach on the east. You're right on the Gulf of Mexico, passing, if you can resist them, miles and miles of white-sand
2 beaches. To reach **Fort Walton Beach,** take the Navarre Bridge to U.S. 98 and head east.

Eglin Air Force Base covers acres and acres of land northeast of Fort Walton Beach. Tours of the mammoth facility are offered January–March and June–August. *Main Gate is off Rte. 85, tel. 904/882–3932. Admission free.*

Just outside the main gate of Eglin, you'll find the **Air Force Armament Museum.** The museum has a vast collection of military weaponry, and there is a park with a display of aircraft and bombs. *Off Rte. 85, tel. 904/882–4062. Admission free. Open daily 9:30–4:30.*

Hurlburt Field Air Park has a display of vintage aircraft, including a special exhibit of the first Special Operations Wing that evolved from the famed Air Commandos of World War II. *6 mi west of Eglin AFB, tel. 904/884–7464. Admission free. Open daily 9–4:30 in summer; hours vary at other times of the year.*

The **Indian Temple Mound Museum** preserves an ancient Indian temple mound right in the heart of town. A reconstructed temple site atop the mound, and a small museum displays artifacts recovered from this mound and from others long gone. *U.S. 98, downtown Fort Walton Beach, tel. 904/243–6531. Admission: 50 cents. Open Mon.–Sat. 9–4, Sun. 1–4 summer only.*

A short detour north of Fort Walton Beach on Rte. 85 will bring
3 you to the little town of **Valparaiso.** The **Valparaiso Historical Society** displays the complete official records of the Union and Confederate armies, as well as a steam-powered cotton gin. *115 Westview Ave., tel. 904/678–2615. Admission free. Open Tues. –Sat. 11–4, Sun. 2:30–4:30.*

4 As you approach **Destin** on U.S. 98 you'll see yet another splendid view of white boats bobbing on turquoise waters. The Fort Walton Beach–Destin area is one of the most popular attractions in the Panhandle. There are all sorts of water sports and places that cater to the beach crowd.

The **Village Art Gallery** is the Panhandle's oldest gallery, displaying the works of some 25 artists. *110 Melvin St., tel. 904/837–2228. Admission free. Open Mar.–Dec., Tues.–Sat. 11–4.*

The **Museum of the Sea and Indian** focuses on plant and animal life from the seven seas, and Indian artifacts from North and South America. *4801 Hwy. 98E (Old Hwy. 98). Admission: $3.25 adults, $1.75 children. Open daily 8–5.*

5 Twenty-five miles east of Destin, **Eden State Gardens** border a graceful antebellum mansion that perches on the brink of Choctawatchee Bay in **Point Washington**. The mansion, veiled in magnolias and moss-draped oaks, has a striking sleigh-bed

among its period furnishings. In the spring, the gardens are ablaze with color. *Off U.S. 395N in Point Washington, tel. 904/231–4214. Admission: $1. Park open 8–sunset; mansion tours conducted on the hour Thurs.–Mon. 9–4. The mansion is closed Tues. and Wed.*

Continuing on U.S. 98 you'll come to **Panama City Beach,** another hot ticket during the summer. U.S. 98 Alt. is the route to the beaches, and you should note that in the summer this alternate is jammed with traffic. This is the Miracle Strip, awash with hotels, motels, condominiums, amusement parks, bars, lounges. This is the place with the splendid beaches, and it is the launching point for sightseeing excursions, sailing, and boating—all of which adds up to bumper-to-bumper traffic.

Top of the Strip Tower, 203 feet above it all, goes in and out of business regularly, but it always manages to be in operation when summer rolls around to provide a gull's-eye view of the goings-on. *12001 W. Hwy. 98. No phone. Admission: 50 cents. Usually open Mar.–Labor Day only. Hours vary.*

Time Out The **Coffee Kettle** is a 24-hour eatery serving waffles, omelets, sandwiches, salads, soups, and steaks. There are several of them sprinkled through the beach area. One is at 16818 U.S. 98 Alt. *No credit cards.*

At the Treasure Island Marina, the **Treasure Ship** is a full-size replica of a schooner. It houses four levels of restaurants, snack bars, lounges and gift shops. The open-air observation decks offer a lovely view of Grand Lagoon and the beaches.

If you continue east on Thomas Drive, you'll come to **St. Andrews State Recreation Area,** at the eastern tip of the peninsula, one of the state park system's most scenic facilities. Within its 1,063 acres you can swim, wander amid the dunes, stroll a nature trail, and fish from either of two piers.

6 In **Panama City,** the **Junior Museum of Bay County** has science, art, and nature exhibits designed for children. There are concerts, puppet shows, and a pioneer village with a log cabin. Nature trails lead through a hardwood swamp, a pine island, and a hardwood hammock. *1731 Jenks Ave., tel. 904/769–6128. Admission free. Open Tues.–Sat. 9–4.*

Before heading east toward Tallahassee, we'll take a look at two other points of interest in the Panhandle.

Drive north on County Rte. 77A; in about an hour you'll reach **Falling Waters State Recreation Area.** There you'll find the awesome Falling Waters Sink. It's a cylindrical, smooth-wall pit, 100 feet deep and 15 feet in diameter, with a small stream flowing into it. *Rte. 77A, tel. 904/638–4030. Admission: $1 driver, 50 cents each passenger over age 6. Open daily 8 AM–sunset.*

7 From there, take I–10E and exit on Rte. 167 to reach the **Florida Caverns State Park.** The 1,217 acres of the park contain a network of caves with unusual rock formations. Tours of the caves are conducted hourly. The park also offers camping, fishing, hiking, picnicking, and swimming. *Rte. 167, tel. 904/482–3632. Admission to caverns: $2 adults, $1 children. Open daily 9–5.*

I-10 rolls over the foothills of the Appalachians through thick
8 pine forests. **Tallahassee,** the capital city, is noted for its lush canopies of trees.

Stop in the **Visitor and Convention Bureau** at Bronough Street and Park Avenue to pick up information about the capital and the surrounding area. The bureau is housed in The Columns, the city's oldest structure.

The **Museum of Florida History** houses hands-on exhibits that trace the state's history from prehistoric Indians to space shuttles. There is a skeleton of a mastodon, ancient gold doubloons, and a pre-Civil War dugout boat. *500 S. Bronough St., tel. 904/488-1484. Admission free. Open Mon.-Fri. 9-4, Sat. 9-4:30, Sun. and holidays noon-4:30.*

The **LeMoyne Art Gallery** is in an 1853 house with a small garden in the back. Works of Florida and Georgia artists are displayed, and there is a special children's section where paintings are hung lower. *125 N. Gadsden St., tel. 904/222-8800. Admission free. Open Tues.-Sat. 10-5, Sun. 2-5.*

St. John's Cemetery, at Call and Boulevard streets, holds the graves of Napoleon Bonaparte's nephew and his wife—the great-grandniece of George Washington.

The **Brokaw-McDougall House,** home to the Historic Tallahassee Preservation Board, is an antebellum mansion shaded with oaks and beautifully restored. *329 N. Meridian St., Tallahassee, tel. 904/488-3901. Admission free. Open weekdays, 8-5.*

North of town, the **Maclay State Ornamental Gardens** are ablaze in the spring with azaleas, dogwoods, and other showy plants and trees. There are reflecting pools, winding pathways, and a tiny walled garden. The 308-acre park also holds the Maclay residence, with period furnishings. *3450 Thomasville Rd. (U.S. 319), tel. 904/893-4455. Admission: $1 driver, 50 cents per passenger May 1-Jan. 1; free rest of the year. Open daily 8 AM-sunset.*

9 To the south, the **Natural Bridge State Historic Site** is where a Confederate force of schoolboys and old men staved off Union troops in 1865, making Tallahassee the only southern capital east of the Mississippi to elude capture. Each March a colorful reenactment is staged. *On Natural Bridge Rd., Rte. 354, off U.S. 363 in Woodville, tel. 904/925-6216. Admission free. Open daily 8 AM-sunset.*

10 About 25 miles south of Tallahassee, **Wakulla Springs State Park** contains the world's deepest spring, the bottom of which has yet to be found. Glass-bottom boats take you over the springhead, which flows at 600,000 gallons per minute. *Off Rte. 61, tel. 904/224-5950. Admission: $1 driver, 50 cents per passenger; cruises: $3.75 adults, $1.75 children. Open daily 9-5:30.*

San Marcos de Apalachee State Museum commemorates the site visited by Pánfilo de Narváez in 1527 and by Hernando de Soto in 1539. The crumbling ruins of a riverside fort attest to the presence of the Spanish in 1679, and there is a small interpretative museum. *Off Rte. 363, St. Marks, tel. 904/925-6216. Admission free. Open daily 9-5.*

Time Out **Posey's,** "Home of the Topless Oyster," is a down-home place where the house specialty is half-shall oysters in hot sauce. *Old*

Fort Dr., off Rte. 363, tel. 904/925–6172. No credit cards. Open only during oyster season (Sept.–Apr.).

11 From Tallahassee, I–10 is the direct route to **Jacksonville,** the hub of Florida's "First Coast."

Jacksonville is on the banks of the St. Johns River, one of the few rivers that flow from south to north. Most of the activity in the city takes place around the riverside developments. **Southbank Riverwalk** is a boardwalk that ties a string of hotels, restaurants, and kiosks to St. Johns River Park, whose Friendship Fountain, lighted at night, sprays as high as a ten-story building. On the opposite bank, both accessible by water taxi, you'll find **Jacksonville Landing,** a glitzy festival marketplace, and the 23-acre **Metropolitan Park,** with a canopied pavilion where special events are held.

The **Cummer Gallery of Art** occupies the gardens of a former lumber baron's riverside mansion. Artworks, including a noted collection of Old Masters and early Meissen porcelain, fill 10 galleries. *829 Riverside Ave., tel. 904/356–6857. Admission free. Open Tues.–Fri. 10–4, Sat. noon–5, Sun. 2–5.*

In Jessie Ball du Pont Park, adjacent to the IBM Building on S. Main Street, the **Treaty Oak** is an 800-year-old tree that stands 66 feet tall and has a limb span of 180 feet. It is said that beneath this tree Indians and white settlers negotiated a truce.

The **Jacksonville Art Museum** displays the works of local and national artists. Its permanent exhibits include oriental porcelain and pre-Columbian artifacts. *4106 Boulevard Center Dr., tel. 904/398–8336. Admission free. Open Tues., Wed., and Fri. 10–4; Thurs. 10–10; weekends 1–5.*

12 Before heading south from Jacksonville, make a stop at **Amelia Island,** the vacation community in the Atlantic. Besides the self-contained apartments and rental units on Amelia Island (some available for overnight), there is the salty little seaport of Fernandina Beach.

St. Augustine

To reach **St. Augustine,** take U.S. 1 south and head straight for the **Visitor Information Center** (10 Castillo Dr.). The center has loads of brochures, maps, and information about the nation's oldest city.

1 The massive **Castillo de San Marcos National Monument** hunkers over Matanzas Bay, looking every century of its 300 years. Park rangers provide an introductory narration, after which you're on your own. This is a wonderful fort to explore, complete with moat, turrets, and 16-foot-thick walls. The fort was constructed of coquina, a soft limestone made of broken shells and coral, and it took 25 years to build it. Garrison rooms depict the life of the era, and special artillery demonstrations are held periodically on the gun deck. *1 Castillo Dr., tel. 904/829–6506. Admission: $1 adults, children under 13 and senior citizens free. Open daily 8:30–5:15.*

2 The **City Gate,** at the top of St. George Street, is a relic from the days when the Castillo's moat ran westward to the river and the Cubo Defense Line (defensive wall) protected the settlement against approaches from the north. Today it is the entrance to the popular restored area.

Basilica Cathedral, **4**
Castillo de San Marcos, **1**
City Gate, **2**
Flagler College, **10**
Flagler Memorial Church, **11**
Fountain of Youth, **12**
Lightner Museum, **9**
Mission of Nombre de Dios, **13**
Museum Theatre, **3**
Oldest House, **8**
Oldest Store Museum, **7**
Plaza de la Constitution, **5**
Ximinez-Fatio House, **6**

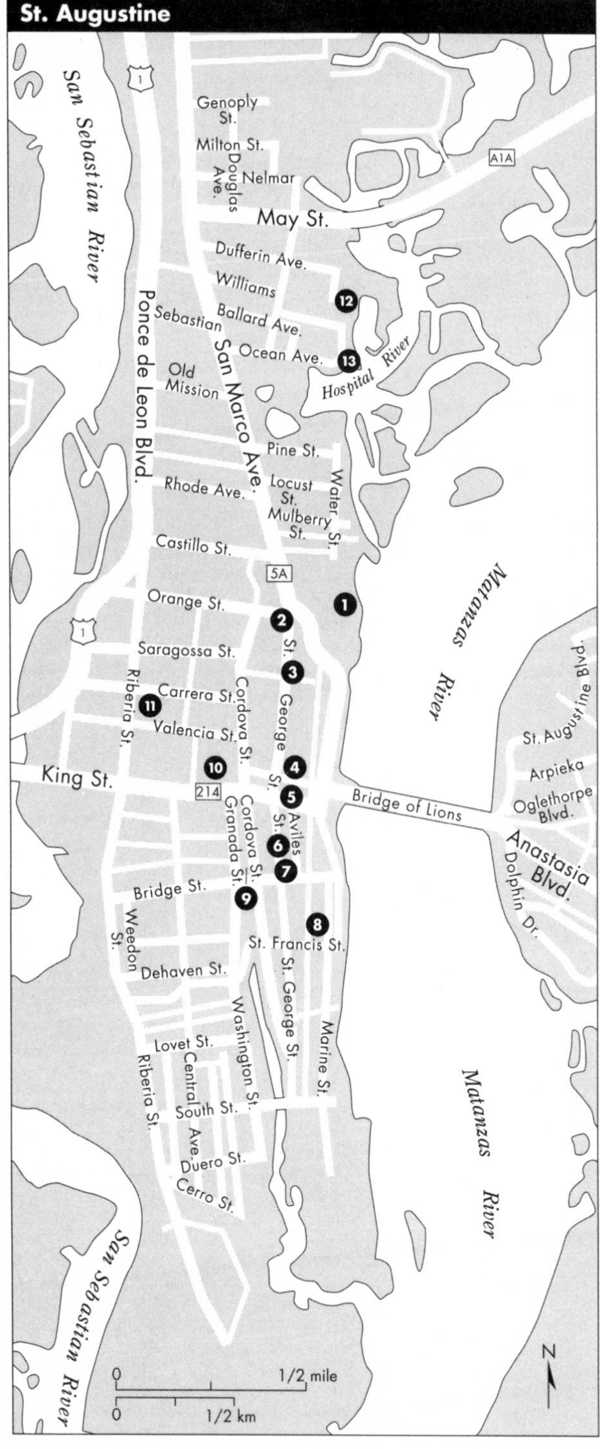

3 The **Museum Theatre** screens two 30-minute films several times daily. One tells the story of the founding of the city in 1565, and the other depicts life in St. Augustine in 1576. *5 Cordova St., tel. 904/824–0339. Admission: $2 adults, $1.50 children under 15; combination ticket for both films: $3 adults, $2.50 children. Open daily 9:30–5:30.*

The **Oldest Wooden Schoolhouse** (14 St. George St.) is a tiny 18th-century structure that, because it was the closest structure to the city gates, served as a guardhouse and sentry shelter during the Seminole Wars.

San Agustin Antiguo is a state-operated living-history village with eight sites. You can wander through the narrow streets at your own pace. Along your way you may see a Colonial soldier's wife cooking over an open fire; a blacksmith building his shop (a historic reconstruction); and craftsmen busy at candle-dipping, spinning, weaving, and cabinetmaking. They are all making reproductions that will be used within the restored area. *Entrance at Triay House, 29 St. George St., near the Old City Gate, tel. 904/824–6383. Admission: $2.50 adults, $1.50 students 6–18; $5 family ticket. Open daily 9–5.*

Time Out **Spanish Bakery,** behind Casa de Calcedo on St. George Street, has meat turnovers, cookies, and fresh-baked bread made from a Colonial recipe. *No credit cards.*

4 **Basilica Cathedral of St. Augustine** has parish records dating back to 1594, the oldest written records in the country. Following a fire in 1887, extensive changes were made to the impressive structure, which dates from 1797. It was remodeled in the mid-1960s. *40 Cathedral Pl., tel. 904/824–2806. Admission free, but donations requested. Open weekdays 5:30–5, weekends 5:30 AM–7 PM.*

5 **Plaza de la Constitution,** at St. George Street and Cathedral Place, is the central area of the original settlement. It was laid out in 1598 by decree of King Philip II, and little has changed since. At its center there is a monument to the Spanish constitution of 1812; at the east end there is a public market dating from early American days. Just beyond is a statue of Juan Ponce de León, who discovered Florida in 1513.

6 The **Ximenez-Fatio House** was built in 1797, and it became a boarding house for tourists in 1885. *20 Aviles St., tel. 904/829–3575. Admission free. Open Mar. 1–Aug. 31, Sun.–Thurs. 1–4.*

7 The **Oldest Store Museum** re-creates a turn-of-the-century general store. There are high-button shoes, lace-up corsets, patent drugs, and confectionery specialties. Had you been in the neighborhood in the 1800s, you'd have come here to have your teeth pulled, your spectacles fitted, and your hair cut. *4 Artillery La., tel. 904/829–9729. Admission: $2.50 adults, $1 children 6–12. Open Mon.–Sat. 9–5, Sun. noon–5.*

8 The **Oldest House,** operated by the Historical Society, reflects much of the city's history through its changes and additions, from the coquina walls built soon after the town was burned in 1702 to the house's enlargement during the British occupation. *14 St. Francis St., tel. 904/824–2872. Admission: $3 adults, $2.75 senior citizens, $1.50 children. Open daily 9–5.*

9 The **Lightner Museum** is housed in one of two posh hotels built in 1888 by railroad magnate Henry Flagler, who wanted to cre-

ate an American Riviera. The museum contains a collection of ornate antique music boxes (ask about demonstrations!), and the Lightner Antique Mall perches on three levels of what was the hotel's grandiose indoor swimming pool. *75 King St., tel. 904/824–2874. Admission to museum: $3 adults, $1 students, children under 12 free. Museum open daily 9–5; mall open Wed.–Sun. 10–5.*

10 Across from the Lightner Museum, **Flagler College** occupies the second of Flagler's hotels. It's a riveting structure replete with towers, turrets, and arcades and decorated by Louis Comfort Tiffany. The front courtyard is open to the public.

At Valencia and Sevilla streets, behind Flagler College, the
11 **Flagler Memorial Presbyterian Church,** which Flagler built in 1889, is a splendid Venetian Renaissance structure. The dome towers more than 100 feet, and it is topped by a 20-foot Greek cross. The church is *open Monday–Saturday 9–5.*

12 The **Fountain of Youth** salutes Ponce de León, who might be called the patron saint of Madison Avenue. In the complex there is a springhouse, an explorer's globe, a planetarium, and an Indian village. *155 Magnolia Ave., tel. 904/829–3168. Admission: $3 adults, $1.50 children 6–12, under 6 free. Open daily 9–5.*

13 The **Mission of Nombre de Dios** commemorates the site where America's first Christian mass was celebrated. A 208-foot stainless-steel cross marks the spot where the mission's first cross was planted. *San Marco Ave. and Old Mission Rd., tel. 904/824–2809. Admission free, but donations requested. Open daily 7 AM–8 PM summer; 8–6 winter.*

What to See and Do with Children

Wild Water Kingdom has water slides, miniature golf, go-carts, and an arcade with electronics games. *2 Via de Luna, Pensacola, tel. 904/934–3205. Admission: $9 per person. Open daily June–Labor Day; weekends only Apr.–May. Closed Sept.–Mar.; arcade open weekends in Mar.; hours vary; call for current schedule.*

Pirate Island Amusement Park has rides, games, and arcades. *On Okaloosa Island, at the foot of the U.S. 98 Bridge, tel. 904/244–3336. Amusements are priced individually. Operating dates and hours vary; call for current schedule.*

Hidden Lagoon Super Golf is a miniature-golf facility. *14414 W. Hwy. 98, Panama City Beach, tel. 904/234–9289. Prices, operating dates, and hours vary with the season; call for current schedule.*

Gulf World is a tropical garden with flamingos and peacocks, a talking parrot show, dancing dolphins, sea lions, penguins, and a shark channel. *15412 W. Hwy. 98A, Panama City Beach. Admission: $7.50 adults, $5.50 children. Open daily Mar.–Labor Day, 9–3 early in the season, 9–5 in the summer.*

Miracle Strip Amusement Park has among its rides a roller coaster with a 65-foot drop, a miniature train, and a hair-raising critter called the Sea Dragon. There are several snack bars, a game arcade, and a gift shop. *12000 W. Hwy. 98A, Panama City Beach, tel. 904/234–9873. Gate admission only: 75 cents adults, children under 4 free. Gate admission, including coupons for rides: $12 adults, $10 children under 10. Open Aug.–Sept., Mon.–Thurs. 6 PM–10 PM, Fri. 6 PM–11 PM, Sat. 1 PM–11:30 PM, Sun. 3 PM–11:30 PM.*

Shipwreck Island, adjoining the Miracle Strip Amusement Park, is a splashy place with a Zoom Flume, a wave pool, a Lazy River for old-folk tubing, a Tadpole Pond for the little tads, and a 300-foot racing slide. *12000 W. Hwy. 98A, Panama City Beach, tel. 904/234–9873. Admission: $12 adults, $10 children 5–10, free for children under 5 and senior citizens. Operating hours vary; call for current schedule.*

Snake-A-Torium features reptile shows and exhibits. *9008 W. Hwy. 98A, Panama City Beach, tel. 904/234–3311. Admission: $3.70 adults, $2.70 children. Open daily 10–4.*

Black Hole Waterslide is a 620-foot water slide full of twists and turns (a junior slide is also available). *W. Hwy. 98 amusement area, Panama City Beach, tel. 904/235–1025. Admission: $3.95. Open spring–Labor Day. Operating hours vary; call for current schedule.*

Fun Land Arcade has a wide variety of games and diversions. *14570 W. Hwy. 98, Panama City Beach, tel. 904/234–6557. Games priced individually. Open 24 hrs daily Mar.–Sept.; 7 AM to either 8, 9, or 10 PM Oct.–Apr. Call for current schedule.*

Tallahassee Junior Museum covers a vast outdoor area that contains a log cabin, exhibits of wagons and buggies, a snake house, picnic grounds, a turn-of-the-century farm, an array of Florida wildlife, nature trails, and a restored plantation home. *3945 Museum Dr., Tallahassee, tel. 904/576–1636. Admission: $3.50 adults, $1.50 children. Open Tues.–Sat. 9–5, Sun. 12:30–5.*

Jacksonville Zoo is home to 700 animals, including a herd of rare white rhinos and an outstanding collection of rare waterfowl. There are elevated walkways and observatories, elephant rides, and a miniature train for zoo touring. *On Heckscher Dr., a half mi east of I–95, Jacksonville, tel. 904/757–4462. Admission: $2.75 adults, $1.25 children, $1 senior citizens. Open daily 9–4:45.*

The Museum of Science/Alexander Brest Planetarium's exhibits range from antique dolls to live snakes and treasures of the Spanish fleet. The planetarium produces multimedia sky shows and light shows to classical or rock music. *1025 Gulf Life Dr., Jacksonville, tel. 904/396–7061. Admission: $2 adults, $1 children 5–18, children under 4 free. Open Mon.–Sat. 10–5, Sun. 1–5.*

Dolls in Wonderland displays 723 rare antique dolls, miniatures, and toys, all in a storybook setting. *9 King St., St. Augustine, tel. 904/824–6462. Admission: $2.50 adults, $1.50 children. Open daily 9–5.*

Ripley's Believe It or Not Museum displays oddities collected by Robert Ripley from 198 countries. *19 San Marco Ave., St. Augustine, tel. 904/824–1606. Admission: $4.95 adults, $2.75 children, free for children under 5. Open daily 9–9 (June–Labor Day), 9–6 (Labor Day–May).*

The Old Jail displays early weapons and methods of incarceration. *167 San Marco Ave., St. Augustine, tel. 904/829–3800. Admission: $3 adults, $2 children 6–12, children under 6 free. Open daily 8–5.*

St. Augustine Alligator Farm, in operation since 1893, features gators, gators, and more gators. There are hourly wildlife shows, plus alligator wrestling demonstrations and a petting zoo. *Rte. A1AS, tel. 904/824–3337. Admission: $5.95 adults, $5.45 senior citizens, $2.95 handicapped, $3.95 children 3–11, children under 3 free. Open daily 9–5.*

Marineland has more than 300 windows for observing sea creatures on their own turf, so to speak, plus a stadium for watching the acrobatic feats of dolphins. *Rte. A1AS, St. Augustine, tel. 904/471–1111. Admission: $9.95 adults, $4.95 children 3–11, children under 3 free. Open daily 9–5:30.*

Off the Beaten Track

The space is meager but the surprises are many in **De Funiak Springs'** tiny **public library**. The one-room library, measuring only 17 feet by 24 feet, was built in 1887 and is Florida's oldest continuously operating public library. It houses about 14,000 volumes, some of them rare books as old as the library itself. There is also an impressive collection of European armor, with some pieces dating back to the Crusades (1100–1300). The Crusades? In De Funiak Spring? Therein lies one of the pleasures of this little place: tracing the history of the collection and learning how it came here. *Walton-De Funiak Public Library, 100 Circle Dr., De Funiak Springs, about 30 mi north of Destin, tel. 904/892–3624. Open Mon. 9–7, Tues.–Fri. 9–6, Sat. 9–3.*

If you hanker for some fresh seafood—the kind you pull in yourself and cook right there on the beach—join the locals who gather at **Indian Pass**. (On road maps it's shown as McNeills, which is the name of the family who first settled here.) This is serious oystering/shrimping/fishing country, where the locally owned Indian Pass Seafood Co. has its commercial oyster farms. The oysters in Indian Lagoon's shallow waters are up for grabs, and the place is also popular for castnetters going after the plentiful mullet. On the gulf side of the narrow spit of land, blue crabs are so plentiful in late summer that most crabbers dispense with nets and lines and use a garden rake to drag them onto the sand. *Public access area on Rte. 30, about 10 mi south of Port St. Joe.*

Beaches

Pensacola Beach. Pensacola's liveliest beach is located on Santa Rosa Island, five miles south of Pensacola. You'll have to cross two bridges to reach it—one to Gulf Breeze and the other to Santa Rosa Island. This is the center of the action, with a concentration of beachfront hotels, a fishing pier, bars, and a new water park. Beach-seekers will find a central parking lot, changing facilities, and lifeguards during the season.

Gulf Islands National Seashore. This 150-mile stretch of islands and keys between Ocean Springs, Mississippi, and Fort Walton Beach is rich with beaches and recreational areas. The **Fort Pickens area,** nine miles west of Pensacola Beach at the tip of Santa Rosa Island, is popular with families for its swimming beach, the Dunes Nature Trail, picnic areas and campgrounds, a fishing pier, jetties, parking facilities, outdoor showers, and lifeguards during the season. Ten miles east of Pensacola Beach, the **Santa Rosa Day Use Area** has undeveloped and uncluttered beaches, where there are parking and picnic areas, restrooms, and lifeguards in season. This section of the national seashore draws an almost equal mix of young singles and families. About 20 miles northwest of downtown Pensacola, **Johnson's Beach** on Perdido Key has miles and miles of quiet, white-sand beaches; there are outdoor showers, restrooms, parking and picnic facilities, and lifeguards in the summer.

John C. Beasley County Park is Fort Walton's showplace. It's across the bridge from Fort Walton Beach on Okaloosa Island

and is especially popular with families. There is a boardwalk to the beach, covered picnic tables, a playground, changing rooms, freshwater showers, and lifeguards during the summer season.

Eglin Reservation Beach, about three miles west of the bridge from Fort Walton, is a five-mile stretch of undeveloped military land open to the public (restricted areas are clearly posted) and is popular with the younger crowd of beachcombers.

Crystal Beach Wayside Park, five miles east of Destin, commands the most beautiful sweep of beach, buffered for an additional five miles on each side by undeveloped state-owned property. It draws singles and families, the young and the old, and even passing motorists who stop to dig their toes into the sand. Its facilities include picnic tables, shelters, changing rooms, restrooms, and summer lifeguards.

Grayton Beach State Recreation Area, about 30 miles east of Destin, is tucked away on Rte. 30A near the little communities of Santa Rosa Beach and Grayton Beach. It's a quiet hideaway for dawdling and daydreaming amid the dunes, and there are changing rooms and restrooms, swimming, snorkeling, and a scuba-diving area. It's open daily 8–sunset, and because it's a state park, there is an admission charge: $1 driver, 50 cents per passenger.

St. Andrews State Park, at the eastern end of the Panama City Beach area, is the resort strip's most scenic and popular public facility, with swimming and snorkeling area on the gulf and in a protected area behind the jetty. There are bathhouses and picnic areas, as well as other park facilities.

Panama City Beach's public beach areas, near the county pier across from the amusement area, are aswarm with singles and families during the summer. There is a profusion of beachside shops, bars, eateries, arcades, and places to rent everything from floats to catamarans. You can also expect bumper-to-bumper traffic in the summer.

Wayside Park, opposite Panama City Beach in the western area near Laguna Beach, uses a flag warning system to notify swimmers of weather conditions. There's an even mix of young people and families; showers and changing facilities are available.

Jacksonville Beach is the liveliest of the long line of Jacksonville Beaches. Young people flock to the beach, where there are all sorts of games to play and also beach concessions, rental shops, and a fishing pier.

Neptune Beach, adjoining Jacksonville Beach to the north, is more residential and offers easy access to quieter beaches. Surfers take to the waves, and consider it one of the area's two best surfing sites.

Atlantic Beach, north of Neptune Beach, is the other favored surfing area. Around the popular Sea Turtle Inn, you'll find catamaran rentals and instruction. Five areas have lifeguards on duty in the summer 10-6.

Fort Clinch State Park, on Amelia Island's northern tip, may be the only state park that includes a municipal beach and pier. But that's where Fermandina Beach's city beaches are, meaning you pay a state-park entrance fee to reach them. But the beaches are broad and lovely, and there is parking right on the beach, bathhouses, picnic areas, and all the facilities of the park itself, including the fort.

Amelia Island's lower half is mostly covered by the Amelia Island Plantation resort. However, on the island's extreme southern tip you can go horseback riding along the wide, almost deserted beaches.

St. Augustine has 43 miles of wide, white, level beaches. The young gravitate toward the public beaches at St. Augustine Beach and Vilano Beach, while families prefer the Anastasia State Recreation Area. All three are accessible via Rte. A1A: Vilano Beach is to the north, across North River, and Anastasia State Park and St. Augustine Beach are both on Anastasia Island, across the Bridge of Lions.

Participant Sports

Boating North Florida's watery playgrounds range from small bays, sounds, and freshwater rivers to the Gulf of Mexico and an ocean of considerable note. Powerboats for fishing, snorkeling, and waterskiing can be rented at **Dolphin Marine Service** (600 Barracks St., Harbor Village at Pitt Slip, Pensacola, tel. 904/438–6637) and at **Merc Charter** (3024 Harbor Dr., Cove Yacht Harbor, Camachee Island, St. Augustine, tel. 904/825–0100). Paddle boats can be rented at **Blue Surf, Inc.** (Navarre Beach, tel. 904/939–2741).

Canoeing You don't have to be an experienced canoeist to enjoy north Florida's rivers, streams, creeks, and spring runoffs—though if you are, you can find some challenging waters with shoals and rapids. The Blackwater River, dotted with white sandbars, flows through the lush Blackwater River State Forest. You can rent canoes at **Blackwater River Canoe Rental** (Rte. 16, Box 72, Milton, tel. 904/623–0235) and at **Adventures Unlimited** (12 mi north of Milton off Hwy. 87, tel. 904/626–1669). The Adventures Unlimited outlet near Pensacola (River Annex Rd., Cantonment, tel. 904/968–5529) can set you up for a day or overnight trip on the Coldwater and Perdido rivers. For a trip on the Wakulla River, near Tallahassee, contact **TNT Hideaway** (Hwy. 98, St. Marks, tel. 904/925–6412). For a jaunt down Econfina Creek, contact **Econfina Creek Canoe Livery** (Hwy. 20, Strickland Rd., tel. 904/722–9032).

Diving A World War II British tanker and a jet airplane are among the sunken vessels in the Gulf of Mexico, and diving to the wrecks is a popular sport. In the Panama City area, wreck dives are offered by **Panama City Dive Center** (4823 Thomas Dr., by St. Andrews State Park, tel. 904/235–3390) and **Hydroplane Dive Shop** (3605 Thomas Dr., next to Treasure Ship, tel. 800/874–3483 or 904/243–3063). In the Destin–Fort Walton Beach area, divers favor the natural reefs about two miles offshore, where there is a wealth of sponges, coral, sea fans, and sea whips. Area firms offering outings are **Fantasea** (1 U.S. 98, Destin, tel. 904/837–6943) and **Scuba Shop** (230 N. Eglin Pkwy., Fort Walton Beach, tel. 904/863–1341).

Fishing Your options range from fishing piers to luxury charters. If you opt for the former, you can stroll out and drop a line on the **Old Pensacola Bay Bridge,** called the world's longest fishing pier, and at the 3,000-foot **Destin Catwalk** along the East Pass Bridge. The **Jacksonville Beach Fishing Pier** extends 1,200 feet into the Atlantic, and the cost for fishing is $3 for adults, $1.50 for children and senior citizens, or 50 cents for watching. **Okaloosa Island Pier,** 1,216 feet, is $3.50 to fish, 75 cents to observe. **Panama City Beach's** 1,642-foot city pier is $2 for fishing, $1 for watching. Fishing from the county pier is free. You can get bait and tackle at **Soundside Bait & Tackle** (¼ mi north of Navarre Beach on Hwy. 87, tel. 904/939–1804), **Penny's Sporting Goods** (1800 N. Pace Blvd., Pensacola, tel. 904/438–9633), and at **Hook, Line & Sinker** (Camachee Cove Yacht Harbor, St. Augustine, tel. 904/829–6073). Boat rentals, bait, and tackle are available at **North Beach Camp Resort** (2300 Coastal Hwy., 4 mi north of St. Augustine on Rte. A1A, tel. 904/824–1806) and **Riverside Fishing Camp** (1 mi north of St. Augustine on Rte. A1A, tel. 904/829–8314).

Among the charter options (at $350 for a half day, $550 for a full day), there are **Barbi-Anne Charter Boats** (off U.S. 98 in Destin, at the docks next to Bayou Bill's, tel. 904/837–6059), **The Moorings** (655 Pensacola Beach Blvd., Pensacola Beach, tel. 904/932–0305), **The Duchess** (Treasure Island Marina, Panama City Beach, tel. 800/874–3483), **Monty's Marina** (Mayport, tel. 904/246–7575), and **Camachee Cove Charters** (Camachee Island, tel. 904/824–3328).

Party boats are more economical, carrying up to 100 anglers at a cost of $35–$40 per person (including tackle and bait). Contact ***Capt. Anderson's*** (Capt. Anderson's Pier, Panama City Beach, tel. 800/874–2415 or 904/234–3435), ***Her Majesty II*** (Destin, tel. 904/837–6313), or ***Sea Love II*** (St. Augustine, tel. 904/824–3328).

Golf North Florida boasts acres and acres of fairways. There are 18-hole courses at the **Fort George Island Golf Club** (11241 E. Fort George Rd., Jacksonville, tel. 904/251–3132), **Hyde Park Golf & Country Club** (6439 Hyde Grove Ave., Jacksonville, tel. 904/786–5410), the **Jacksonville Beach Golf Club** (605 S. Penman Rd., tel. 904/249–8600), the **West Meadows Golf Club** (11400 W. Meadows Dr., Jacksonville, tel. 904/781–4834), and the **St. Augustine Shores Country Club** (295 Shores Blvd., tel. 904/794–0303). In the Pensacola area, there are two 18-hole courses at the **Tiger Point Golf & Country Club** (3455 Santa Rosa Dr., Gulf Breeze, tel. 904/932–1333) and one 18-hole course at the **Carriage Hills Golf Club** (2355 W. Michigan Ave., Pensacola, tel. 904/944–5497). The semipublic course at the **Sandestin Resort** has 36 holes with lots of water and bunkers (U.S. 98E, Destin, tel. 904/837–2121). Other 18-hole courses are the **Indian Hill Golf Club** (Airport Rd., Destin, tel. 904/837–6191), **Signal Hill Golf Course** (9615 N. Thomas Dr., Panama City Beach, tel. 904/234–3218), **Fort Walton Beach Municipal Golf Club** (Lewis Turner Blvd. and Mooney Rd., Fort Walton Beach, tel. 904/862–3314), and **Killearn Golf & Country Club** (100 Tyron Circle, Tallahassee, tel. 904/893–2186).

Sailing Hobie Cats can be rented at **The Hobie Shop** (12705 W. Hwy. 98, Panama City Beach, tel. 904/234–0023). Sailing instruction and bare-boat rentals are offered by **Friend Ship Charter Sailing** (500 Hwy. 98, Destin, tel. 904/837–2694). Sailing lessons, rentals, and charters are available at **The Boat** (housed in a 1922 concrete-hull troopship at 32 Miracle Strip Pkwy., Fort Walton Beach, tel. 904/243–BOAT). Sunfish, catamarans, and lessons are available from **Key Sailing** (289 Pensacola Beach Blvd., Gulf Breeze, tel. 904/932–2000).

Scuba Diving and Snorkeling The clear waters of the Destin–Fort Walton Beach area have an underwater visibility range of 40–100 feet. You can rent equipment at **The Scuba Shop** (230 N. Eglin Pkwy., Fort Walton Beach, tel. 904/863–1341), the **Fantasea Scuba Headquarters** (1

U.S. 98, Destin, tel. 904/837–6943), and the **Panama City Dive Center** (4823 Thomas Dr., Panama City, tel. 904/235–3390).

Tennis **Amelia Island Plantation** (Amelia Island, tel. 904/261–6161) has 19 clay courts and two hard courts in a world-class tennis center. **Sandestin Resort** (U.S. 98E, Destin, tel. 904/837–2121) boasts the area's only grass courts, and nearby **Seascape Resort** (Destin, tel. 904/837–9181) offers tennis clinics for the whole family. Courts are available in 30 locations in and around Pensacola, among them the **Pensacola Racquet Club** (3450 Wimbledon Dr., tel. 904/434–2434). There are 12 courts at the **Fort Walton Beach Tennis Center** and another 12 at various locations (contact Parks & Recreation Dept., 132 Jett Dr., Fort Walton Beach, tel. 904/243–3119). There are 10 courts at the **Destin Racquet Club** (Airport Rd., Destin, tel. 904/837–8548). In Jacksonville, there are eight courts at the **Whalen Tennis Center** (6009 Powers Ave., tel. 904/737–8800) and six at **Huguenot Park** at the beach (200 16th Ave. S, tel. 904/249–9407). There are 15 courts at the **Ponte Vedra Club** (Ponte Vedra Beach, tel. 904/285–6911), 10 at the **St. Augustine Beach & Tennis Resort** (3960 Rte. A1A, tel. 904/471–9111), and six at the **Ponce de León Lodge & Country Club** (U.S. 1N, tel. 904/824–2821).

Windsurfing Windsurfers can be rented from **The Surf Station** (1002 Anastasia Blvd., St. Augustine Beach, tel. 904/471–9463), **The Boat** (32 Miracle Strip Pkwy., Fort Walton Beach, tel. 904/243–BOAT), and **Pensacola Sailing Center** (Pensacola Beach Causeway, tel. 904/932–8585). Places offering parasailing include **Bonifay Water Sports** (460 Pensacola Beach Blvd., Pensacola Beach, tel. 904/932–0633) and **PBS Watersports** (1320 Hwy. 98E, Fort Walton Beach, tel. 904/244–2933). **The Surf Station** (St. Augustine Beach, tel. 904/471–9463) even rents "boogie boards," which you ride on your stomach.

Spectator Sports

Baseball The **Jacksonville Expos,** a Class A Southern League professional team, play home games in Wolfson Park, Gator Bowl complex (1400 E. Duval St., Jacksonville, tel. 904/358–2846).

Dog Racing Greyhounds race year-round in the Jacksonville area, with seasons split among three tracks: **Jacksonville Kennel Club,** March–May (1400 N. McDuff Ave., tel. 904/388–2623); **Orange Park Kennel Club,** November–March (U.S. 17 at I–295, tel. 904/264–9575); and **Bayard Raceway,** March and September (18 mi south on U.S. 1, tel. 904/268–5555). In the Panhandle, there is racing April–September at **Pensacola Greyhound Park** (U.S. 98W, tel. 904/455–8598) and May–September at **Jefferson County Kennel Club** (Monticello, tel. 904/997–2561).

Football The annual **Gator Bowl** (1400 E. Duval St., downtown, tel. 904/633–2900) and the annual grudge match between Florida and Georgia are played in Jacksonville.

Golf The Tournament Players Championship is a March event at the **Tournament Players Club** (near Sawgrass in Ponte Vedra Beach, tel. 904/285–7888), which is national headquarters of the PGA Tour. The annual Pensacola Open is held in October at the **Perdido Key Resort** (Perdido Key, tel. 904/456–8863).

Jai Alai This fast-paced Basque sport is presented November–May at **Big Bend Jai-Alai Fronton** (off I–10 south of Quincy, tel. 904/442–1111).

Tennis The top-rated Women's Tennis Association Championships is held in April at **Amelia Island Plantation** (Amelia Island, tel. 904/387–5497).

Dining and Lodging

Dining The state is embraced by the Atlantic Ocean and the Gulf of Mexico and is laced with waterways, which means that seafood is prominently featured. In coastal towns, the catches often come straight from the restaurant's own fleet. Shrimp, oysters, snapper, and grouper are especially popular.

Category	Cost*
Very Expensive	over $60
Expensive	$40–$60
Moderate	$20–$40
Inexpensive	under $20

**per person, exclusive of wine, service, or tax (6% in Florida)*

Lodging Accommodations range from splashy beachfront resorts and glitzy condominiums to cozy inns and bed-and-breakfasts nestled in historic districts. As a general rule, the closer you are to the center of activity in the coastal resorts, the more you'll pay. You'll save a few dollars if you stay across from the beach rather than on it, and you'll save even more if you select a place that's a bit removed from the action.

Category	Cost*
Very Expensive	over $120
Expensive	$90–$120
Moderate	$50–$9
Inexpensive	under $50

**per double room, exclusive of 6% state sales tax and nominal tourist tax*

The most highly recommended restaurants and lodgings are indicated by a star ★.

The following abbreviations are used for credit cards: AE, American Express; CB, Carte Blanche; DC, Diners Club; MC, MasterCard; and V, Visa.

Amelia Island
Dining
★ **Snug Harbor.** The New Orleans roots of the restaurant owner show in the Mardi Gras masks and beads that decorate this cozy place. The Cajun-inspired menu includes a blackened sampler of fish, chicken, and prime rib. Appetizers include fried zucchini and boiled shrimp, and among the entrees are crabmeat Norfolk (crabmeat sautéed in butter and spices), trout meunière, and a seafood platter that comes in three sizes: petit, regular, and pig-out. *N. 2nd and Alachua Sts., tel. 904/261–8031. Dress: casual. No reservations. MC, V. Inexpensive.*

Lodging
★ **Amelia Island Plantation.** This 1,250-acre luxury sports resort sprawls over about a third of the island and is so much a part of

the natural setting that you may be surprised when you round a curve and encounter a building. There are rental villas with one to four bedrooms (some with private indoor pools) and, in the main building, rooms with balconies or terraces overlooking the Atlantic. *800 Amelia Pkwy, Amelia Island 32034, tel. 800/874–6878 outside FL or 800/342–6841 in FL. 340 apts. 24 rooms with bath. Facilities: 17 pools, 5 restaurants and lounges, tennis center with stadium, golf, beach club, health club, and numerous water sports and recreational activities. AE, CB, DC, MC, V. Expensive–Very Expensive.*

Shoney's Inn. The island's first chain facility, this modern motel is spic-and-span and has a helpful staff that sees to things. *2707 Sadler Rd., 32034, tel. 904/277–2300. 110 rooms with bath. Facilities: pool, Jacuzzi, tennis courts, restaurant, lounge. AE, CB, DC, MC, V., Moderate.*

Cedar Key
Dining

The Captain's Table. This dockside seafood restaurant sits on stilts and has a fine view of the anglers on the pier and the artists on the sea wall. Broiled seafood is the specialty, but there are fried dishes, and some chicken and steak offerings as well. The captain's platter includes lobster tail, deviled crab, shrimp, crab fingers, and scallops. The restaurant is particularly proud of its soft-shell crabs. You can get a side order of swamp-cabbage salad, which is lettuce and cabbage palm, sprinkled with dates and tropical fruit and topped with a house dressing. *On Dock St., tel. 904/543–5441. Dress: casual. Reservations recommended for Sat. dinner. MC, V. Inexpensive.*

Lodging

Island Place. One- and two-bedroom suites that sleep four are available in this two-story condominium complex right on the gulf. The roof is tin, and the balconies and terraces offer a splendid view. *Box 687, Cedar Key 32625, tel. 904/543–5307. 25 suites with bath. Facilities: pool, Jacuzzi, sauna, laundry room. MC, V. Moderate–Expensive.*

Destin
Dining

Capt. Dave's. This branch on the beach is a newer, quieter version of Capt. Dave's on the harbor. The changing menu might include such specialties as grouper spectacular (grouper layered with celery, onions, bell peppers, tomatoes, and ripe olives, topped with mozzarella). *U.S. 98E, 5 mi east of Destin, tel. 904/837–1271. Dress: casual. No reservations. AE, MC, V. Inexpensive–Moderate.*

★ **Harbor Docks.** You can dine inside or on the deck of this dockside seafood eatery, and if you arrive as the sun sets you can watch the shrimp fleet come in. Sautéed red snapper with artichoke hearts is a specialty, and there is a taste of Thai in the stir-fried shrimp and chicken dishes. Live music nightly ranges from rock or reggae to jazz. *538 U.S. 98, tel. 904/837–2506. Dress:casual. No reservations. AE, MC, V. Inexpensive–Moderate.*

Lodging

★ **Sandestin Beach Resort.** A sprawling (2,800-acre) luxury resort that impresses without intimidating. Lodging sites include rooms in a bay-side inn, cottages and villas amid lagoons or fairways, condominium units in a high rise, and waterside patio homes with large decks and tiny gazebo docks. *Emerald Coast Pkwy., Destin 32541, tel. 800/874–3950 outside FL or 904/267–8000 in FL. 88 rooms, 120 villas with bath. Facilities: numerous pools and restaurants, 2 golf courses, tennis courts, shopping mall, private beach, marina, water sports. AE, DC, MC, V. Expensive–Very Expensive.*

Summer Breeze. This small Victorian-style condominium has a white picket fence, overhanging tin roof, and gingerbread trim. Each one-bedroom suite has queen-size bed, sleeper sofa, and bunk beds, and each can accommodate six people. The traditional decor is done in mauve and aqua. It's located about halfway between Destin and Sandestin. *3885 U.S. 98E, Destin 32541, tel. 904/837–4853. 35 1-bedroom condominiums. Facilities: pool, Jacuzzi, laundry room. MC, V. Moderate.*

Village Inn. This two-story, family-oriented Best Western facility was built in 1983. Rooms are "modern motel," with either king-size beds or two queens. *215 U.S. 98E, Destin 32541, tel. 904/837–7413. Facilities: pool, cable TV, restaurant, lounge. AE, DC, MC, V. Inexpensive–Moderate.*

Fort Walton Beach

Dining

Liollio's. Relax quietly here and enjoy some Greek-spiced seafood or a steak, the specialties of the local restaurateur, who also owned the earlier restaurant on this site overlooking the sound. *14 Miracle Mile Strip Pkwy., tel. 904/243–5011. Dress: informal. Reservations accepted. AE, DC, MC, V. Inexpensive–Moderate.*

★ **Seagull Restaurant.** At this restaurant on the sound, you'll find crisp white napery, broiled and sautéed seafood specialties, and, if you come early enough, a splendid sunset. Gourmet offerings include scallops St. Jacques (poached in white wine with Mornay sauce, scallions, and green onions, and topped with grated Parmesan cheese). Snapper *amandine* is a small tender fillet topped with a sour cream–based sauce with Dijon mustard and almonds. The menu also lists lobster tails and several steak offerings. This is a family-oriented place that caters to its local clientele. *1201 E. U.S. 98, tel. 904/243–3413. Dress: informal. Reservations recommended. AE, CB, DC, MC, V. Inexpensive–Moderate.*

Lodging

Bluewater Bay Resort. This major resort property, 18 miles north of Fort Walton Beach, is a bit out of the way, but the setting is lovely. It spreads over 1,800 acres and is surrounded by thick forests, freshwater lakes, and the blue waters of the Choctawatchee Bay. Accommodations are in motel-type rooms that overlook the 120-slip marina, or in three-room villas, some of which have fireplaces and fully equipped kitchens. *Rte. 20E, Box 247, Niceville 32578, tel. 904/897–3613 or 800/874–2128 outside FL. Facilities: several pools, 2 18-hole golf courses, tennis stadium, private beach, marina, water sports, exercise rooms, bicycles, playground. AE, MC, V. Moderate–Very Expensive.*

Ramada Beach Resort. This property has changed hands a few times, but it is once more a Ramada after a short stint as the Regency Beach Resort. Its design and decor are less imaginative than the more recent of the chain's facilities, but its location and 800-foot beach more than offset its boxy exterior. It's located on Okaloosa Island, just beyond the bridge. *U.S. 98E, Fort Walton Beach 32548, tel. 800/874–8962 or 904/837–4853. 454 rooms with bath. Facilities: numerous pools, outdoor Jacuzzi, complete spa facilities, exercise room, tennis courts, several restaurants and lounges, 5-story waterfall with grotto bar. AE, DC, MC, V. Moderate–Expensive.*

Jacksonville/ Jacksonville Beach

Dining

★ **Homestead.** A down-home place with several dining rooms, a huge fireplace, and country cooking, this restaurant specializes in skillet-fried chicken, which comes with rice and gravy. Chicken and dumplings, deep-fried chicken gizzards, buttermilk biscuits, and strawberry shortcake also draw in the locals.

1712 Beach Blvd., Jacksonville Beach, tel. 904/249–5240. Dress: informal. AE, DC, MC, V. Inexpensive.

The Tree Steakhouse. You select your steak and watch the staff cook it over a charcoal fire. Charbroiled chicken is also on the list, and there are several seafood dishes, too. The atmosphere is low-key and casual. *942 Arlington Rd., in Arlington Plaza, Jacksonville, tel. 904/725–0066. Jacket required. AE, CB, DC, MC, V. Inexpensive.*

Lodging

★ **Jacksonville Omni Hotel.** The city's newest hotel is a 16-story, ultramodern facility with a splashy lobby atrium and large, stylish guest rooms. All rooms have either a king-size or two double beds. You'll feel pampered anywhere in the hotel, but the extra frills are to be found in the two floors of the concierge level. *245 Water St., Jacksonville 32202, tel. 904/355–6664. 354 rooms with bath. Facilities: heated pool, restaurant, lounge, exercise room, nonsmokers rooms, cable TV. AE, DC, MC, V. Expensive–Very Expensive.*

Sheraton at St. Johns Place. This five-story luxury hotel, connected to the Riverwalk complex, has modern rooms with either a king-size or two double beds. It's located right in the center of things, and the hotel bustles with activity inside and out. Be sure to ask for a room that overlooks the St. Johns River. *1515 Prudential Dr., Jacksonville 32207, tel. 904/396–5100. 350 rooms, 18 suites. Facilities: concierge, pool, 2 lighted tennis courts, 2 restaurants, lounge, shopping arcade, privileges at Downtown Athletic Club, nonsmokers rooms, facilities for handicapped persons. AE, CB, DC, MC, V. Expensive.*

Holiday Inn Oceanfront. A $2.5-million refurbishment in 1988 brought a bright new look to this perennial favorite on the beachfront. The atmosphere remains light and friendly; beds come in king, queen, or double sizes. *1617 N. First St., Jacksonville Beach 32250, tel. 800/331–6151 outside FL or 800/331–2817 in FL. 149 rooms with bath. Facilities: pool, sauna, exercise room, tennis courts. AE, DC, MC, V. Expensive.*

Sea Turtle Inn. A long-time area favorite, this high-rise property fronts on a wide beach. It's a family-oriented hotel with a pleasant atmosphere. *1 Ocean Blvd., Atlantic Beach 32233, tel. 800/874–6000 outside FL or 800/831–6600 in FL. Facilities: pool, restaurant, lounge. AE, CB, DC, MC, V. Moderate–Expensive.*

Panama City Beach

Dining

★ **Boar's Head.** This is a casually elegant eatery that features live Maine lobster, gulf sea critters, steaks, prime rib, duckling, veal, and baby back pork ribs. Starters include fried blue-crab fingers and oysters baked with artichoke hearts. One of the casserole dishes is lightly spiced shrimp baked with fresh tomatoes and studded with capers and chunks of feta cheese. *17290 W. Hwy. 98, tel. 904/234–6628. Tie and jacket required. Reservations recommended. AE, CB, DC, MC, V. Open daily for dinner. Inexpensive–Moderate.*

★ **Capt. Anderson's.** This is a landmark seafood restaurant, where a long wait is the name of the game. The 600-seat restaurant overlooks the Grand Lagoon and has tables made of hatch covers. Some of the recipes originated on the Greek island of Patmos, whence came the father of the present owners. Fried crab fingers open things up; entrees include stuffed gulf flounder, crab cakes, and "the world's finest seafood platter." *5551 N. Lagoon Dr., tel. 904/234–2225. Dress: casual. No reservations. AE, MC, V. Closed Sun. Inexpensive–Moderate.*

Mai Lin. This is the only place in Panama City where you can satisfy your taste for *moo goo gai pan*, sweet and sour pork, cashew chicken, and lemon chicken. There are a few hot and spicy Szechuan dishes and four combination dinners. Several American seafood dishes and a children's menu round things out. *14662 W. Hwy. 98 in Open Sands Shopping Center, tel. 904/233–1311. Dress: casual. AE, DC, MC, V. Inexpensive.*

Lodging **Edgewater Beach Resort.** Luxurious condominium resort with modern one- to three-bedroom units in beachside towers or golf villas. Its sprawling, 11,500- square-foot lagoon pool is replete with *palapas*, islands, waterfalls, whirlpools, and a veritable forest of vegetation. *11212 Hwy. 98 Alt., Panama City Beach 32407, tel. 800/874–8686 outside FL or 904/235–4044 in FL. Facilities: golf, miniature golf, 12 lighted tennis courts, pool, private beach, lawn games, health club, game rooms. AE, MC, V. Very Expensive.*

Marriott's Bay Point Resort. A glamorous and gracious Bermuda-style, pastel-colored resort on Grand Lagoon, this $40-million complex was originally a residential yacht and country club. There are vaulted ceilings, solid oak accents, and balconied guest rooms and suites with gulf or golf-course views. *100 Delwood Beach Rd., Panama City Beach 32407, tel. 800/874–7105 outside FL or 904/234–3307 in FL. Facilities: 2 golf courses, 5 swimming pools, indoor heated pool and Jacuzzi, 12 lighted tennis courts, numerous restaurants and lounges, a 145-slip marina, sailing school, and water sports. AE, MC, V. Very Expensive.*

Silver Sands. One of the smaller properties with a gulf-front location, this hotel is family-oriented and offers efficiencies, suites, and one- and two-bedroom apartments. *8601 Surf Dr., Panama City Beach 32407, tel. 904/234–2201. 24 units. Facilities: pool, shuffleboard. AE, MC, V. Moderate.*

Pensacola

Dining

★ **Jamie's.** An intimate French setting is evident in this Victorian house with soft candlelight and fireplaces in each of its four rooms. For lunch you might start with escargots Bourguignonne and move on to tournedos with mushroom sauce or marinated chicken breasts served with steamed vegetables. The dinner menu features smoked salmon; sweetbreads layered with prosciutto in a mushroom with port-wine sauce; and shrimp sautéed in a cream sauce flavored with Pernod. There are more than 200 labels on the wine list. *424 E. Zaragoza St., tel. 904/434–2911. Jacket and tie required for dinner. Reservations recommended for dinner. AE, MC, V. Moderate.*

Scotto's. Pat and Richard Scotto's eatery is in a pink gothic-style house in Seville Square. Recipes are those of Richard's grandfather, who came here from Capri. Among the appetizers are oysters Florentine and fried calamari. Fettuccine Scotto is crabmeat and shrimp sautéed in butter and covered with a light cream sauce. Chicken *bianco* is breast of chicken stuffed with prosciutto and provolone, simmered in a white cream sauce, and served with fresh mushrooms over fettuccine. For the *dolci*, cheesecake is the specialty, but the chocolate amaretto mousse is also memorable. *300 S. Alcaniz St., tel. 904/434–1932. Jacket and tie required for dinner. Reservations recommended for dinner. AE, DC, MC, V. Closed Sun. Moderate.*

★ **The Hopkins House.** Dining in this North Hill Preservation District house is done family-style at long tables. The fare is southern, and bowl after bowl is passed around: fried chicken,

chicken and dumplings, roast beef, green beans, creamed corn, biscuits, and cornbread. *900 N. Spring St., tel. 904/438–3979. Dress: casual. No reservations. No credit cards. Inexpensive.*

Perry's Seafood House & Gazebo Oyster Bar. This big red house in Seville Square dates from 1858, and in the 1950s it was a fraternity house. There is an extensive menu of fried, boiled, broiled, and baked sea creatures. Perry's baked fish comes with a topping of Greek garlic sauce and lemon juice. "Tips and Tails" is lobster and broiled filet mignon. There are homemade pastries for dessert. *2140 S. Barrancas Ave., tel. 904/434–2995. Dress: casual. No reservations. AE, MC, V. Closed Tues. Inexpensive.*

Lodging

Holiday Inn/Pensacola Beach. This is a landmark facility with 1,500 feet of beachfront, rooms with either king-size or two double beds, and an informal, friendly atmosphere. *165 Ft. Pickens Rd., Pensacola 32561, tel. 904/932–5361 or 800/HOLIDAY. 150 rooms and suites. Facilities: heated pool, tennis, golf, restaurant, lounge, courtesy airport transportation. AE, CB, DC, MC, V. Moderate–Very Expensive.*

Pensacola Hilton. A renovated railway depot dating from 1912 serves as the lobby for this glitzy hotel. Fresh flowers and turn-of-the-century accent pieces decorate the lobby, which connects with the high-rise hotel via a two-story glass-canopied galleria. Standard rooms are spacious and modern; bilevel penthouse suites have wet bars, whirlpool baths, and a spectacular view. The hotel is right in the center of things, near the Seville Square Historic District. *Box 12148, Pensacola 32590, tel. 904/433–3336. 212 rooms. Facilities: courtesy airport limo, heated pool, tennis, health club, restaurants, lounges, shopping arcade. AE, CB, DC, MC, V. Moderate–Expensive.*

Perdido Bay Resort. This is a luxury sports resort that sprawls over 2,800 acres. The championship golf course is the site of the PGA Pensacola Open. *1 Doug Ford Dr., Pensacola 32507, tel. 904/492–1212. 150 units. Facilities: pool, lighted tennis courts, 18-hole golf course, private beach with cabanas, 2 restaurants and lounges. AE, MC, V. Moderate–Very Expensive.*

New World Landing. You'd never know that this was once a waterfront warehouse. Public areas have wood paneling, parquet floors, and oriental rugs. Furnishings in the individually decorated guest rooms are Chippendale, Queen Anne, and Louis XV, with accent pieces collected from around the world. There are four-poster or canopied beds in king or queen sizes, ceiling fans, and baths with handsome brass fixtures. *600 S. Palafox St., Pensacola 32501, tel. 904/432–4111 or 800/258–1103 outside FL. 14 rooms, 2 suites. Facilities: complimentary Continental breakfast on weekends, cable TV, 3 restaurants, lounge. AE, CB, DC, MC, V. Moderate.*

Hospitality Inn. A new all-suites budget inn with modern furnishings, kitchenettes, and kings- or queen-size beds. There is a giant-screen TV in the lobby where you can watch movies and eat popcorn. *6900 Pensacola Blvd., Pensacola 32503, tel. 800/321–0052 outside FL, 800/821–2073 in FL. 126 units. Facilities: pool, kennels, laundry, in-room movies. AE, DC, MC, V. Inexpensive.*

Ponte Vedra Beach

Lodging

★

Marriott at Sawgrass. This luxury seven-story hotel is the center for resort operations of the popular Sawgrass complex. The attention to detail shows everywhere, from the impressive public areas to the spacious, well-appointed hotel and villa rooms.

Box 600, Ponte Vedra Beach 32982, tel. 800/874–7547 outside FL or 800/432–1270 in FL. 350 units. Facilities: 5 golf courses, 13-court tennis center, several pools, private beach, cabana club, marina, water sports, fishing, horseback riding, exercise rooms, bicycles, several restaurants and lounges, shopping village. AE, CB, DC, MC, V. Expensive–Very Expensive.

St. Augustine
Dining

Columbia. This is a huge Spanish structure with courtyards, verandas, and 28 dining rooms where Latin fare is featured. Specialties are paella, snapper *alicante* served with shrimp and almonds, and *arroz con pollo*. There are old family recipes from 1905, such as the salad of yellow rice with herbs. *98 St. George St., tel. 904/824–3341 or 800/227–1905. Dress: casual. Reservations advised. AE, CB, DC, MC, V. Inexpensive–Moderate.*

Fiddler's Green. A half mile east of the Vilano Beach Bridge, this cozy Continental eatery has a huge stone fireplace, wicker furniture, and big windows overlooking the beach. Begin with snails baked in butter with herbs and garlic or oysters Rockefeller, then you can contemplate the variety of seafood specialties. Offerings include fish Vilano, a fillet stuffed with Parmesan and ricotta, then layered with eggplant and mozzarella, topped with marinara sauce, and served over pasta. *50 Anahma Dr., Vilano Beach, tel. 904/824–8897. Dress: casual. No reservations. AE, MC, V. Inexpensive.*

★ **Raintree.** You may enjoy tarrying over a mint julep on the front porch of this restored Victorian house. The menu includes Maine lobster, filet mignon béarnaise, and rainbow trout *amandine*. A specialty is the grouper fillets, which are stuffed with crab mousse and baked in puff pastry. Tender veal medallions are filled with ricotta and prosciutto and served with a mustard sauce. *102 San Marco Ave., tel. 904/829–5953. Jacket and tie required. Reservations advised. AE, DC, MC, V. Inexpensive.*

Lodging

★ **Ponce de León Resort & Convention Center.** This is the city's most famous hotel, and it occupies a good-size piece of land north of town. Public rooms are spacious and airy, with massive wrought-iron chandeliers and Spanish/Moorish flourishes. Accommodations range from rooms to two-bedroom villas with kitchenettes. *Box 98, St. Augustine 32085, tel. 800/228–2821 in FL or 800/824–2821 in USA. 200 units. Facilities: pool, restaurants, lounge, 18-hole championship golf course, putting green, tennis courts, playground, shuttle to historic district. Expensive–Very Expensive.*

Casa de Solana. The "house of the sun" is a renovated Colonial home that dates from 1763. There are four suites filled with antiques; some have fireplaces and some have balconies overlooking the lush garden or the bay. There is a formal guest dining room where breakfast is served. Amenitities include Cable TV, chocolates and a decanter of sherry in every room, and bicycles for touring the city. *21 Aviles St., St. Augustine 32084, tel. 904/824–3555. 4 suites with private bath. Expensive.*

★ **Westcott House.** This is another frilly Victorian house, dating from the late 1880s. The eight guest rooms are furnished with American and European antiques, oriental rugs, and queen- and king-size beds. Continental breakfast is served to you either in the courtyard or in your room. Amenities: complimentary bottle of wine upon arrival, turndown service with chocolates and snifter of brandy, terry-cloth robes, cable

TV, central air-conditioning and heat, private phones, non-smokers rooms. *146 Avenida Menendez, St. Augustine 32084, tel. 904/824–4301. 8 rooms with private bath. MC, V. Moderate–Expensive.*

Casa de la Paz. A three-story Mediterranean Revival house overlooking Matanzas Bay, the "house of peace" is a mere youngster by St. Augustinian standards. It was built between 1910 and 1917. The antique-filled rooms and suites have hardwood floors, ceiling fans, and tiled baths. Amenities include central air-conditioning and heat, cable TV, complimentary sherry or wine, non-smokers rooms, room service, Continental breakfast. *22 Avenida Menendez, St. Augustine 32084, tel. 904/829–2915, 5 units, including 2 suites. AE, MC, V. Moderate*

★ **Victorian House.** This gingerbread house is one of several bed-and-breakfasts in the heart of the Historic District. Here, you'll find pine floors with hand-hooked rugs, canopy beds with handwoven coverlets and quilts, stenciled walls, and 19th-century antiques. In the morning a full breakfast is served in the dining room. *11 Cadiz St., St. Augustine 32084, tel. 904/824–5214. 5 rooms and 1 suite, all with private bath. AE, MC, V. Moderate.*

St. Francis Inn. Señor Gaspar Garcia built this house in 1791, and it has been used as a boarding house or inn since 1845. Accommodations come in a variety of sizes and shapes, from rooms to apartments to a five-room, two-story cottage. Amenities: central air-conditioning and heat, cable TV, private parking lot, complimentary admission to the nearby Oldest House, Continental breakfast, pool. *279 St. George St., St. Augustine 32084, tel. 904/824–6068. 6 units, 3 suites, and cottages, all with private bath. MC, V. Inexpensive.*

Seaside
Lodging

★ **Seaside.** Victorian cottages, graceful beach pavilions, gazebos, broad brick roads and every imaginable amenity make up this planned community. The cottages are individually owned and individually decorated, but all fit into the grand Victorian plan, with white picket fences, gingerbread trim, and porches with rocking chairs. The cottages have from two to five bedrooms, and they are furnished right down to vacuum cleaners. The community is right on the gulf; each street leads to a private beach pavilion and miles of unspoiled beaches. More private and quiet than this there isn't. *County Rte. 30A, off U.S. 98 west of Panama City, Seaside 32454, tel. 904/231–4224. 38 fully equipped cottages, and development continues. Facilities: pool, tennis court, croquet and badminton, bicycles rentals, Hobie Cats, beach chairs and umbrellas, nearby restaurants and lounges. AE, MC, V. Very Expensive.*

Tallahassee
Dining

Andrew's Second Act. Below the street you'll find a small Continental eatery that's reminiscent of a European cafe. It's a casual place for noontime soups and salads, but things turn more formal after dark. The dinner menu includes tournedos St. Laurent (beef broiled with garlic, scallions, and parsley butter) and rack of lamb Dijonnaise. **Andrew's Upstairs** is a salad bar/hot bar with mesquite grill, and **Andrew's Adams St. Cafe** is a deli. *102 W. Jefferson St., tel. 904/222–2759. Jacket and tie required. Reservations advised. MC, V. Inexpensive–Moderate.*

Silver Slipper. This is the city's landmark steak house, with numerous small private rooms surrounding the main dining room.

531 Scotty La., tel. 904/386–9366. Jacket and tie required. Reservations advised. AE, CB, DC, MC, V. Inexpensive–Moderate.

Lodging ★ **Governor's Inn.** There is a country ambience in this chic hotel that sits in the shadow of the capitol. There are skylit hallways, brick floors, and warm wood paneling throughout. The suites, in a 100-year-old carriage house, have private entrances and are furnished with antique four-poster beds, rock maple armoires, and black-oak writing desks. Some have loft bedrooms, whirlpools, and wood-burning fireplaces. Amenities include Continental breakfast, newspapers, turndown, terry-cloth robe, laundry/valet, room service, and cable TV with HBO and ESPN. *209 S. Adams St., Tallahassee 32301, tel. 904/681–6855. 41 units. Facilities: restaurant, lounge. AE, DC, MC, V. Moderate to Expensive.*

Ramada Inn North. Newest of the city's three Ramadas, this one has striking modern lines and above average facilities. It's at the intersection of I–10 and U.S. 27. Amenities include valet service, remote-control TVs, and baby-sitting service. *2900 N. Monroe St., Tallahassee 32303, tel. 904/386–1027. Facilities: pool, restaurant, lounge, spa privileges. AE, DC, MC, V. Moderate.*

Wakulla Springs
Lodging **Wakulla Springs Lodge.** This Spanish-style lodge is surrounded by 800,000 acres of national forests and wildlife refuges. In the lobby and public rooms there are Moorish arched doorways, and ceiling paintings trace the area's history from the Aztecs to the Spanish. There is a huge walk-in fireplace in the lobby, and walk-in closets are in the spacious rooms. Rooms are functional, but they do have private baths and phones. *Rte. 61 and Rte. 267, Wakulla Springs 32305, tel. 904/224–5950. Facilities: restaurant, gift shop, boat rides, spring-fed swimming area. MC, V. Inexpensive–Moderate.*

The Arts and Nightlife

The Arts Broadway touring shows, top-name entertainers, and other major events are booked into the **Florida Theatre Performing Arts Center** (128 E. Forsyth St., Jacksonville, tel. 904/355–ARTS), the **Jacksonville Civic Auditorium** (300 Water St., tel. 904/633–2900), the **Saenger Theater** (118 S. Palafox St., Pensacola, tel. 904/438–2827), the **Tallahassee–Leon County Civic Center** (Box 10604, Tallahassee 32302, tel. 904/487–1691), and the **Marina Civic Center** (8 Harrison Ave., Panama City Beach, tel. 904/769–1217).

Concerts **Jacksonville Symphony Orchestra** (tel. 904/630–0701) presents classical, pops, and youth concerts at the Civic Auditorium (300 Water St.).

St. Johns River City Band (tel. 904/396–0200) is a professional brass band that performs free concerts during the fall, spring, and summer at Jacksonville's Metropolitan Park and at Jacksonville Landing.

Pensacola Symphony Orchestra performs a season of five concerts at the Saenger Theatre (114 S. Palafox St., tel. 904/435–2533).

Tallahassee Symphony Orchestra presents five performances annually during the winter and spring at Florida State University's Ruby Diamond Auditorium (203 N. Gadsden St., tel. 904/224–0461).

Dance **The Florida Ballet** (123 E. Monroe St., tel. 904/353–7518) performs classic and modern dance in the fall and winter and at Christmas.

Film **The Film Institute of Jacksonville** (tel. 904/743–5531) presents a series of films twice weekly at the Jacksonville Museum and Florida College Kent Campus.

Opera **The Lyric Opera Company** (tel. 904/264–5796) presents three operas each year in the Jacksonville Civic Auditorium.

Theater ***Cross and Sword*** (Box 1965, St. Augustine 32085, tel. 904/471–1965), Florida's official state play, is performed annually mid-June–mid-August at St. Augustine's Amphitheater.

The Pensacola Little Theatre (186 N. Palafox St., tel. 904/432–8621) performs plays and musicals during its season, fall–spring.

The River City Playhouse (128 Park St., Jacksonville, tel. 904/355–6137) is a local professional group that stages musicals, dramas, comedies, and children's theater. Local playwrights are often showcased.

Theatre Jacksonville (2032 San Marco Blvd., Jacksonville, tel. 904/396–4425) is one of the nation's oldest community theaters.

Alhambra Dinner Theatre (12000 Beach Blvd., Jacksonville, tel. 904/641–1212) presents six major musicals each year. Performances are in a 388-seat Spanish-style castle.

Nightlife North Florida nightlife ranges from free-wheeling beachfront bars to mellow piano bars. In the major cities, pick up a copy of the free *See* magazine to see what's doing in town. The *Panama City Beach Times*, also free, has a rundown of what to do when the sun goes down.

Bars and Nightclubs **Spinnakers** (28 Thomas Dr., Panama City, tel. 904/234–7822) has 19 bars on the beach and draws a very lively young crowd. **Pineapple Willie's** (in Pier 99 Motor Inn, 9900 W. Beach Blvd., Panama City Beach, tel. 904/235–0928) features live music of the 1960s, '70s, and '80s; it caters to an over-25 crowd. **McGuire's Irish Pub** (600 E. Gregory St., Pensacola, tel. 904/433–6789) attracts local politicos, aviators, and tourists who like live traditional Irish music. The Pensacola Hilton's **L&N Lobby Bar** (200 E. Gregory St., Pensacola, tel. 904/433–3336) is a favorite yuppie meeting place. An over-30 crowd dances nightly at the **Boar's Head** (17290 W. Hwy. 98A, Panama City Beach, tel. 904/234–6628) to live '60s–'80s music. A classy crowd dances to live hits at **Tickets** (Pensacola Hilton, tel. 904/433–3336). A crowd that remembers the '50s and '60s gathers at **Happy Days Again** (5061 Mobile Hwy., Pensacola, tel. 904/456–6819). **Jamaica Joe's** (790 Santa Rosa Blvd., Fort Walton Beach, tel. 904/244–4137) is a popular hangout for the young set.

Comedy Clubs **The Punch Line** (8535 Bay Meadows Rd., Jacksonville, tel. 904/737–9399) is on the coast-to-coast circuit of comic performers. Performances are Tuesday–Sunday evenings.

Discos There's a hip crowd and a hip DJ at **Victor Hugo's** (101 S. Jefferson St., Pensacola, tel. 904/433–0010). Young people dance to discs and live bands at **La Vela Beach Club** (8813 Thomas Dr., Panama City Beach, tel. 904/234–3866). You can expect a young crowd also at **Copa Cabana** (2901 N. Hayne St., Pensacola, tel. 904/438–6267) and at **Mac's Disco** (623 Osceola St., Tallahassee, tel. 904/575–7365).

Index

Personal Itinerary

Departure *Date*

Time

Transportation

Arrival *Date* *Time*

Departure *Date* *Time*

Transportation

Accommodations

Arrival *Date* *Time*

Departure *Date* *Time*

Transportation

Accommodations

Arrival *Date* *Time*

Departure *Date* *Time*

Transportation

Accommodations

Personal Itinerary

Arrival *Date* *Time*

Departure *Date* *Time*

Transportation

Accommodations

Arrival *Date* *Time*

Departure *Date* *Time*

Transportation

Accommodations

Arrival *Date* *Time*

Departure *Date* *Time*

Transportation

Accommodations

Arrival *Date* *Time*

Departure *Date* *Time*

Transportation

Accommodations

Addresses

Name

Address

Telephone

Name

Address

Telephone

Name

Address

Telephone

Name

Address

Telephone

Name

Address

Telephone

Name

Address

Telephone

Name

Address

Telephone

Name

Address

Telephone

Name

Address

Telephone

Name

Address

Telephone

Name

Address

Telephone

Name

Address

Telephone

Name

Address

Telephone

Name

Address

Telephone

Name

Address

Telephone

Name

Address

Telephone

Fodor's Travel Guides

U.S. Guides

Alaska
American Cities
The American South
Arizona
Atlantic City & the New Jersey Shore
Boston
California
Cape Cod
Carolinas & the Georgia Coast
Chesapeake
Chicago
Colorado
Dallas & Fort Worth
Disney World & the Orlando Area
The Far West
Florida
Greater Miami, Fort Lauderdale, Palm Beach
Hawaii
Hawaii *(Great Travel Values)*
Houston & Galveston
I-10: California to Florida
I-55: Chicago to New Orleans
I-75: Michigan to Florida
I-80: San Francisco to New York
I-95: Maine to Miami
Las Vegas
Los Angeles, Orange County, Palm Springs
Maui
New England
New Mexico
New Orleans
New Orleans *(Pocket Guide)*
New York City
New York City *(Pocket Guide)*
New York State
Pacific North Coast
Philadelphia
Puerto Rico *(Fun in)*
Rockies
San Diego
San Francisco
San Francisco *(Pocket Guide)*
Texas
United States of America
Virgin Islands *(U.S. & British)*
Virginia
Waikiki
Washington, DC
Williamsburg, Jamestown & Yorktown

Foreign Guides

Acapulco
Amsterdam
Australia, New Zealand & the South Pacific
Austria
The Bahamas
The Bahamas *(Pocket Guide)*
Barbados *(Fun in)*
Beijing, Guangzhou & Shanghai
Belgium & Luxembourg
Bermuda
Brazil
Britain *(Great Travel Values)*
Canada
Canada *(Great Travel Values)*
Canada's Maritime Provinces
Cancún, Cozumel, Mérida, The Yucatán
Caribbean
Caribbean *(Great Travel Values)*
Central America
Copenhagen, Stockholm, Oslo, Helsinki, Reykjavik
Eastern Europe
Egypt
Europe
Europe *(Budget)*
Florence & Venice
France
France *(Great Travel Values)*
Germany
Germany *(Great Travel Values)*
Great Britain
Greece
Holland
Hong Kong & Macau
Hungary
India
Ireland
Israel
Italy
Italy *(Great Travel Values)*
Jamaica *(Fun in)*
Japan
Japan *(Great Travel Values)*
Jordan & the Holy Land
Kenya
Korea
Lisbon
Loire Valley
London
London *(Pocket Guide)*
London *(Great Travel Values)*
Madrid
Mexico
Mexico *(Great Travel Values)*
Mexico City & Acapulco
Mexico's Baja & Puerto Vallarta, Mazatlán, Manzanillo, Copper Canyon
Montreal
Munich
New Zealand
North Africa
Paris
Paris *(Pocket Guide)*
People's Republic of China
Portugal
Province of Quebec
Rio de Janeiro
The Riviera *(Fun on)*
Rome
St. Martin/St. Maarten
Scandinavia
Scotland
Singapore
South America
South Pacific
Southeast Asia
Soviet Union
Spain
Spain *(Great Travel Values)*
Sweden
Switzerland
Sydney
Tokyo
Toronto
Turkey
Vienna
Yugoslavia

Special-Interest Guides

Bed & Breakfast Guide: North America
1936...On the Continent
Royalty Watching
Selected Hotels of Europe
Selected Resorts and Hotels of the U.S.
Ski Resorts of North America
Views to Dine by around the World

Join us in updating the next edition of your Fodor's guide

Title of Guide:

1 Hotel ☐ Restaurant ☐ *(check one)*

Name

Number/Street

City/State/Country

Comments

2 Hotel ☐ Restaurant ☐ *(check one)*

Name

Number/Street

City/State/Country

Comments

3 Hotel ☐ Restaurant ☐ *(check one)*

Name

Number/Street

City/State/Country

Comments

Your Name *(optional)*

Address

General Comments

Business Reply Mail

First Class *Permit N⁰ 7775* *New York, NY*

Postage will be paid by addressee

Fodor's Travel Publications
201 East 50th Street
New York, NY 10022